THERE'S A RIOT

*Also by Peter Doggett*

Are You Ready for the Country?

The Art and Music of John Lennon

Growing Up in Public

# THERE'S A RIOT GOING ON

Revolutionaries, Rock Stars,
and the Rise and Fall of the '60s

by
Peter Doggett

CANONGATE

Edinburgh · New York · Melbourne

First published in Great Britain in 2007 by
Canongate Books Ltd., Edinburgh, Scotland

Printed in the United States of America

ISBN-13: 978-1-84767-193-6

Canongate
841 Broadway
New York, NY 10003
Distributed by Publishers Group West
www.groveatlantic.com

09 10 11 12    10 9 8 7 6 5 4 3 2 1

# CONTENTS

**For Rachel, with all my love**

And also for Becca & Catrin Mascall, Anna & Alick Doggett, and Georgia & Tom Ansell, in the hope that their generation finds the will to question authority and the vision to change the world

# FOREWORD

## THE THRILL OF PROPAGANDA

In June 1972, John Lennon and Yoko Ono released a record entitled *Some Time in New York City*. It was a collection of protest songs and political anthems, tackling subjects that ranged from America's prison system to the British 'occupation' of Northern Ireland. Packaged like a street newspaper, it amounted to nothing less than a trumpet-call for revolution, from the world's most prominent rock musician. Thirty-five years later, the audacity of Lennon's project is still breathtaking.

Despite Lennon's hopes that he might become the standard-bearer for youthful radicalism, his 'political' album was widely derided. 'What can one say when confronted with incipient artistic suicide?' asked *Rolling Stone* magazine, which had previously supported Lennon's career. The same review dismissed the record as 'embarrassingly puerile', 'awful', 'shallow', 'derivative', 'sloppy', 'witless' and 'egotistical' – critical judgements that have been reinforced ever since.

Less analytical listeners responded more openly to Lennon's message. Raised in an atmosphere of polite English conservatism, I was ripe for the illicit thrill of rebellion in 1972. *Some Time in New York City* appealed to my emerging sense – I was just 15 years old – that there might be life beyond conformity. It fulfilled my adolescent desire for idealism, without any unsettling ambiguity. Already an undiscriminating admirer of Lennon's work and public persona, I inhaled the record's revolutionary spirit, and was radicalised by my initial exposure to its slogans and propaganda. 'Woman is the Nigger of the World' introduced me to the concept of feminism, a principle that suddenly seemed shockingly, blindingly obvious (and, for too many years, impossible to connect to my own life). 'Luck of the Irish' and 'Sunday

Bloody Sunday' provided a guide to the history of English colonialism. The police and politicians were corrupt and barbaric. The people were ready to rise against their oppressors. The album was full of such unthinking certainties; and so was I.

The naivety was not mine alone. It was clear that Lennon's mutation from pop icon into agitprop minstrel had been fuelled by borrowed rhetoric and second-hand emotions. His artistic judgement appeared to have been distorted by his infatuation with his recent acquaintances, Abbie Hoffman and Jerry Rubin of the anarchic leftist group the Yippies, and black power activist Bobby Seale of the Black Panther Party. By the time *Some Time in New York City* was released, two of its songs – pleas for the release of radical heroes John Sinclair and Angela Davis – were out of date, as their subjects had already been freed. Others were built upon a crassly simplistic view of political reality, and were tinged with paranoia, a childish pleasure in rabble-rousing, and Lennon's willingness to believe everything that he had been told by his comrades. Nowhere in the album was there a moment's awareness that this radical energy might be about to expire, and that the revolution might prove to have been a chimera, which had bewitched and then betrayed a generation.

Yet for all its faults, lyrical and analytical, *Some Time in New York City* blazed with an intensity rarely equalled in Lennon's work, testifying to the zeal of his conversion to ultra-left radicalism. From its artwork to the epic grandeur of its production, the record declares his glorious faith in the inevitability of revolution. It was a message that might have been designed to appeal to a teenager searching for a horizon beyond the mundane predictability of English bourgeois life.

John Lennon and I weren't alone in the assumption that revolution was both inescapable and desirable. What's apparent as one scours the back pages of history, and speaks to those who participated in the tumultuous events that occurred between 1965 and 1972, is that the hope, or fear, of a violent assault on the established order linked young and old, socialist and conservative, rich and poor. Visions of how this revolution might arrive, and what it might achieve, varied from person to person, and continent to continent. Some envisaged a peaceful reorientation of social and economic power; others imagined a bloody war between classes, races or genders. What was common to all these dreams and nightmares was the belief that Western society, and its global power structure, could not survive unchanged; that there could be no hope of world (or local) peace until some degree of liberation was offered to the oppressed people of the planet.

The exact identity of those oppressed souls was a matter of subjective opinion. Feminists sought the liberation of women from male dominance and aggression. African-Americans wanted an end to racism and, in many cases, the establishment of their own exclusive homeland. Students in Paris and New York fantasised about the overthrow of the restrictive educational system that, in their view, smothered free thought and expression. Committed Marxists required nothing less than the toppling of global capitalism, and thereafter an end to imperialism. Africans dreamed of the day when their colonial masters were banished from the continent. And across the world, all these forces were united in the campaign to end the Vietnam War, and exile America's soldiers and 'advisers' from South-East Asia.

Through the 1960s and into the early 1970s, a bewildering array of radical organisations (and acronyms, from SDS to the IRA) began to dominate the news. Perhaps inevitably, these groups often had wildly different goals, and when their agendas coincided, they tended to set upon each other, rather than their agreed enemy. Equally inevitably, the forces of authority around the world witnessed this threatening activity, and assumed that a global conspiracy was at work. Their response was to unleash waves of oppression that stretched from mild persecution (arrests, water cannons, eavesdropping, infiltration) to appalling violence (torture, massacre, attempted genocide).

As communications around the world improved, and young people began to form their own information networks, via underground newspapers and the shared language of rock music, these disparate struggles and battles began to coalesce. It was therefore now possible for a student in England to be suffering nothing worse than mild dissatisfaction with his or her teachers, but to feel acute solidarity with guerrillas in Vietnam, student rioters in Mexico City, anti-government rebels in Czechoslovakia, the Black Panther Party in California, and liberation forces in South Africa or Rhodesia. (It was sadly much less likely, at least until the early 1970s, that this fictitious student would have expressed much solidarity with the feminist movement, especially if he were male.) Bulletins from these far-flung frontlines filled the pages of the *International Times* and the *Berkeley Barb*, the *East Village Other* and *Oz*, and no doubt hundreds of equivalent periodicals in the non-English-speaking countries of the world. Even a 15-year-old schoolboy with the most limited grasp of world events could easily determine which side he was on.

This incendiary climate was heightened by the feverish commentary provided by the era's most potent youth icons, the rock stars. The youth movement now shared its own culture – or rather counter-culture, running in opposition to the prevailing orthodoxy of capitalism, imperialism, sexism, racism and emotional repression. Under this spotlight, there was a price to be paid by any counter-culture hero (or, more rarely in these pre-feminist times, heroine) who failed to offer the correct response on any issue from Vietnam to the Chicago Conspiracy Trial. And so 'revolution' entered the rock lexicon – rarely defined or explained, but a catch-all refrain that symbolised a generation's quest to overturn the old order and replace it with a new climate of liberation, that would free body, mind and soul.

Anyone – a 15-year-old teenager in England, perhaps – who was attracted by the seductive power of rock, and the flamboyance of its emotional and political rhetoric, found themselves swept into what appeared to be a life-or-death struggle for survival and freedom. The songs told the story: not just Lennon's parade of revolutionary anthems, but Jefferson Airplane's 'Volunteers' ('got a revolution') and 'We Could Be Together' ('up against the wall motherfuckers'), the Rolling Stones' 'Street Fighting Man' ('the time is right for fighting in the streets'), the Who's 'Won't Get Fooled Again' ('I'll tip my hat to the new revolution') and dozens more besides, berating the war, racial hatred, rabid commercialism, sexual restrictions, and the lavish crimes of that evil entity known as 'the man'. Carried on this tide of radical fervour, one didn't need expert knowledge of ghetto America or the Cambodian jungle to imagine that revolution was imminent, thrilling and inevitable. Small wonder that governments and authority figures around the world took this awe-inspiring rhetoric at face value, and prepared to repel a global assault on the establishment and all its orthodoxies.

And then, during 1972, just as John Lennon declared that the revolution was nigh, the radical impulse withered and died. Its demise seemed mysterious and ominous, not least for the future of radicalism. Minor advances had been achieved, presaging more meaningful developments to come: feminism was admitted to the debating table, sexual barriers were lifted, America's government slowly eased the plight of its ghetto children, and most crucially, US troops left Vietnam. None of these apparently progressive developments was remotely secure, however; all of them could, and many of them would, be clawed back at a moment's notice.

The withdrawal of American soldiers from South-East Asia should, one might have imagined in 1970 or 1971, have marked a massive shift of power away from the establishment and towards the forces of dissent. Instead, for a complex variety of reasons, dissent simply disappeared. Student riots ceased, the black power movement imploded, revolutionary organisations turned on their own members, and the revolution ran out of energy, passion and joy. Predictably slow to receive the message, rock's radical superstars continued to spout incendiary rhetoric for a few more months, and then turned about-face. Suddenly there was no more talk about revolution; no more anthems designed for the barricades. A collective embarrassment seized the most visible icons of the revolutionary left. Those who had survived (and many had perished along the way) plunged into rampant egotism, self-enlightenment, drug abuse, religious cults, Hollywood celebrity status, anything that would protect their fame and leave them free of political responsibility. For the audience that had obtained its political information from rock star radicals and their activist buddies, the reversal was both bewildering and deeply disillusioning.

Almost immediately, history began to be rewritten. John Lennon was merely the most prominent of the former radicals who recanted their beliefs, bemoaned their own naivety, and derided those who maintained the principles that they had once espoused. This rejection of the past could take many forms, from Black Panther leader Eldridge Cleaver's multiple religious conversions, to Yippie activist Jerry Rubin's transformation from a dangerous radical into a stockbroker. Yet some of the counter-culture's political tenets were confirmed by the passage of time. There was general agreement, for example, even among those who had been 'running' the war, that America's involvement in Vietnam had been a flawed enterprise from the start; a consensus, too, that African-Americans and women had been discriminated against, and that a more liberal approach to racism and sexism might bear fruit. But the apocalyptic imagery of revolution, which had provided an unsettled landscape for half a decade or more, was abandoned and left to rot by the roadside.

Such disturbance could not be forgotten forever. The fault-lines beneath Western society remained. At moments of crisis – during the 1992 Los Angeles riots, perhaps, or the invasion of Iraq in 2003 – the distant rumblings of the past were heard once again, as a fresh generation of the angry and oppressed began to expose the cracks. Western governments and power structures responded with an unprecedented level of paranoia, callously using the potential threat of terrorist outrage as a blunt device to shape public opinion and quell dissent. Most insidious of all was the malignant manipulation of the media that forms one of the cornerstones of power in the 21st century. Under these circumstances, there was a grim symmetry – not to mention an inevitability – to the fact that images of the revolutionary fervour of the 1960s and early 1970s began to resurface, not as a threat to the status quo, but as chic artefacts from a more innocent age.

## THE CURSE OF LEADERSHIP

No one symbolised the ambiguous relationship between music and revolution more accurately than Bob Dylan. Despite repeatedly denying that he was motivated by political impulses, Dylan's heritage of early 1960s protest material ensured that he was widely regarded as a beacon of radicalism by the counter-culture. During the late 1960s and early 1970s, his sympathies came under intense scrutiny, as supporters of the revolution tried to locate gestures of support amidst his increasingly detached songs.

In 2003, shortly after the invasion of Iraq, Dylan completed work on a critically maligned movie entitled *Masked & Anonymous*. In keeping with its title, the singer – who had finally shed the curse of political leadership that had burdened him for decades – co-wrote the screenplay under a pseudonym. Unnoticed by the critics, Dylan used the film as an opportunity to revisit his troubled relationship with the late 1960s revolutionary movement, which had borrowed his name and his work without permission, and then hounded him for a declaration of solidarity until he finally (and briefly) gave way.

*Masked & Anonymous* is set in an unnamed land, aflame with chaos. The location is deliberately vague: perhaps a banana republic enduring its latest coup; perhaps a post-Orwellian America. Dylan plays 'Jack Fate', a once-iconic rock star freed from a subterranean dungeon so that he can headline a 'benefit concert' designed, in ambiguous fashion, to aid the victims of the country's unending civil strife. No one's motives are clear, least of all Fate's, who might stand as a hero, were he not so clearly running on self-interest and apathy.

Dylan shambles through the scenario as a cypher, muttering enigmatic, cynical dialogue. His screen nemesis is Tom Friend, played by actor Jeff Bridges. Characterised by Fate's sidekick as 'a leech, a bleeder, some kind of two-faced monster, a spy', Friend is merely a journalist, portrayed as Dylan had experienced them during his prime – inquisitive, exploitative, deluded, egomaniacal, relentless in his pursuit. In a series of delicious encounters, Fate and Friend are thrust into verbal combat. 'You're supposed to have all the answers,' Friend snaps at the recalcitrant rock star. 'What makes you tick, man?' The scenes are reminiscent of Dylan's own encounters with the media, in which the singer deftly eluded intrusive enquiries with a mixture of silence and contempt.

Friend's aggressive but futile attempts to provoke Fate into passing judgement on his generation echo the insistent pressure that was placed upon Dylan during the late 1960s and early 1970s. The questioning seems ridiculous, because Fate has already been portrayed as a man with no answers. Dylan, we assume, found his unwanted role as spokesman for the counter-culture, or whatever amorphous entity he was believed to represent, equally laughable. Yet in a time of extreme turmoil, Dylan's words were regarded as having something approaching scriptural authority, as if they could be unravelled to reveal the secrets of the universe, or at least the state of contemporary America.

Like Dylan, Jack Fate finds it impossible to shed his political significance. The TV network has specified a list of songs that Fate must perform in order to fulfil his contract, and ensure his freedom. The promoter (portrayed by John Goodman) reads them out – the Beatles' 'Revolution', the Rolling Stones' 'Street Fighting Man', the Who's 'Won't Get Fooled Again', the Robins' 'Riot in Cell Block # 9', Neil Young's 'Ohio', Barry McGuire's 'Eve of Destruction' and the MC5's 'Kick Out the Jams'. With the exception of the Robins' mid-1950s hit (which has a weird significance of its own), they were the most potent anthems of the Vietnam War era, which collectively formed the soundtrack for the revolutionary stirring that ended the 1960s.

From 1965 ('Eve of Destruction') to 1971 ('Won't Get Fooled Again'), these songs were greeted as direct interventions in the social ferment surrounding the counter-culture. They commented on student riots and racial conflict, the Vietnam War, and the vague longing for liberation shared by millions from different backgrounds and perspectives, all of whom were ready to sign up for the prospect of revolutionary deliverance. Yet the songs shared a more perverse quality. Each of them stood, on the surface, for rebellion, but actually represented something altogether more ambiguous. In every case, their creators stopped short of providing the handbook for revolution that their listeners desired – though in some cases this was achieved so subtly that the audience did not notice. By singling out those songs, Dylan the scriptwriter provided his filmic character with a repertoire steeped in the rhetoric of counter-revolution – betrayal, reticence, role-playing and ultimately incoherence.

Jack Fate's compromised freedom dissolves symbolically into blood and treachery. The journalist Tom Friend – who seems in *Masked & Anonymous* to represent not just journalistic cynicism, but also the spirit of the 1960s rock establishment, as maintained by the 21 st-century nostalgia industry – is first knocked to the ground by a well-concealed kidney punch from Fate, and then beaten to death by his roadie. The instrument of murder is a guitar. With that scene, Dylan takes his revenge on every disciple who had ever wanted to load the salvation of a generation onto his fragile shoulders. It scarcely matters that Fate is arrested for the killing, and shipped back to prison, with the words of the film's female Judas ringing in his ears: 'You can put his whole life on trial'.

What's more telling than Jack's fate is the fact that, decades after he was freed from the roles of prophet and saviour, Bob Dylan felt compelled to revisit the troubled battleground of the late 1960s, in the strangely familiar context of the Iraq War. As another misbegotten adventure on foreign soil mutated into tragedy, so other snapshots of the past flashed into the global consciousness, acting as unreliable evidence of the farcical circularity of history.

## BLURRING THE PAST

In 2006, playwright Tom Stoppard replayed the collision between political revolt and musical rebellion in his acute and poignant play, *Rock and Roll.* Set in Czechoslovakia and Cambridge, Stoppard's text captured both the boundless optimism of the late 1960s, and the ways in which rebellion and self-expression could be dampened and smothered by the state. Simultaneously, Czechoslovakia's most celebrated political rock band, the Plastic People of the Universe, arrived in London, to rekindle memories of their prolonged battle against Communist bureaucrats in the late 1960s and beyond. Veterans of another struggle for freedom, against the Brazilian military dictatorship, were also greeted in London as heroes of the resistance. Caetano Veloso, Gilberto Gil and Os Mutantes performed ecstatically received concerts, apparently proving that culture will always outlive repression. Gil exemplified this belief: in 2003, he was appointed the Brazilian Minister of Culture.

Yet none of these nostalgic recreations of a half-forgotten struggle for revolution was exactly what it seemed. Radical icons may have survived, but their meaning had changed. The image of guerrilla leader and Cuban rebel Che Guevara is inescapable in the 21st century: his face decorates T-shirts, posters, CD artwork and countless other commercial artefacts. The Victoria and Albert Museum in London devoted an exhibition to the many reincarnations of the long-dead revolutionary hero. But none of the objects that bore his picture represented anything more than rebellion by association. Whether he was the subject of a Hollywood movie (*The Motorcycle Diaries*) or parodied by Madonna (on her *American Life* CD), Guevara was nothing more potent or threatening than an outlaw symbol, removed from the class-warfare milieu that he had inhabited.

In this curious second level of existence, even self-consciously 'political' rebirths offered less than they promised. To celebrate her husband's status as an enemy of the repressive government of President Nixon in the early 1970s, Yoko Ono supervised the making of a documentary entitled *The US vs John Lennon*. It portrayed the ex-Beatle as a political dissident, whose activities had so alarmed the Nixon administration that they schemed to have him deported from America. Yet the film shied away from any suggestion that Lennon had linked himself with revolutionaries whose quest was the overthrow of the US government. Instead, it emphasised the standard posthumous view of Lennon as an inveterate peacenik, who abhorred violence and those who were prepared to use it. The real Lennon – who dabbled naively with the IRA, the Black Panthers, the Yippies and Zippies, all of whom wanted revolution rather than reform – was mysteriously ushered off screen.

There are specific individual reasons for these compromises. Che Guevara's appeal to Western youth was always rooted as much in his rock star appearance as in the minutiae of his formulae for guerrilla warfare. Few of those who had chanted his name at rallies and demonstrations in the late 1960s could have explained his precise significance to the Cuban revolution. In the case of John Lennon, Yoko Ono has long since refashioned her late husband as a symbol of the peace movement, judging correctly that this particular aspect of his multifaceted personality is most likely to appeal to those born after his death in 1980. Peace, in the vaguest sense, was the cause with which Lennon and Ono had first announced themselves to the public in 1969, and which they again proselytised in Lennon's final interviews, so Ono is not so much revising history as allowing it to run more smoothly.

But there are political consequences to this gentle blurring of the past. In times that offer forms of repression that would have seemed strangely familiar to the activists of the 1960s; in an era in which the Western powers are once again transporting their troubling revision of democracy into distant lands; in a climate that threatens dramatic curbs on freedom of speech and expression; against that landscape, the disarming of political heroes cannot help but seem like an act of conservatism, of submission to all that is banal and oppressive in the modern world. Robbed of their context and the uncomfortable reality of their sometimes violent quest for global liberation, Lennon and Guevara – and their fellow activists, from the Black Panthers and the Weather Underground to the freedom fighters in Africa and South America – are blunted and neutered, stripped of their humanity and power. In this censored form, they are merely the pale shadows of heroes, alienated from the causes that inspired their chaotic and sometimes misguided crusades.

They are thus the perfect companions to the rock stars who apparently stood alongside them on the barricades in the late 1960s and early 1970s. The lesson of revolutionary rock is that the music, and its idealistic ideology, was compromised and sold in the very instant that it was made. Over and over again, musicians believed that they were striking blows for liberation (sexual, political, conceptual) and the revolution. Over and over again, their every move had already been softened and contained by the contaminating presence of the same industry that they were using to announce their dissent – the music business.

That, on one level, is the sorry story told in this book: of faith in utopia, betrayed by commercialism and naivety. But that is only one facet of the tale. The other concerns a generation who fixed their sights on nothing less than a transformation of the way in which global society was organised, and who staked their energy, and often their lives, on the success of their quest. Their ultimate failure does not detract from the courage of their struggle. If their revolution was doomed to fail, at least they dared to dream. Their lesson should act as a salutary reminder to the apathetic and the cynical that change can only come from collective action, not from a retreat into the shadow world of technology and consumerism.

Across the epic canvas of this book, a dozen revolts against the established order are played out simultaneously, sometimes colliding in the least expected of circumstances. The chaotic and sometimes surreal journey of 'the revolution' is traced from its stirrings in the civil rights crusades and bohemian imagination of the 1950s and early 1960s, through its ecstatic heyday in the final years of that decade, to its shambolic demise a few short years later. All along the route, the soundtrack of popular music reflects and sometimes propels the action. Musicians and revolutionaries intertwine, to the point where it is difficult to tell them apart. Rock stars pose as radicals, and radicals as rock stars, compromising their idealism but feeding off each other's cultural power. Through it all, governments are forced to react to this unexpected coalition of forces, and become inexorably drawn into a landscape that is often beyond their understanding. It's a long, dangerous and, yes, sometimes ridiculous trip, touched by disillusionment but fired by the spirits of optimism and anger.

Those emotions neatly capture the transformation of the counter-culture between the psychedelic hedonism of 1966–67, and the radical rebellion of 1968 and beyond. It took just five short years for John Lennon to move from proclaiming 'All You Need Is Love' to, consciously or otherwise, providing funds for the IRA. Such an abrupt shift of direction and ideology seems especially shocking today, when cynicism, apathy and despair are the most common responses to injustice and repression. In an era when Bono, the hand-in-glove darling of the global political establishment, and Bruce Springsteen, the personification of cosy liberalism, are revered as rock's most potent protest icons, it's timely to be reminded of an era when artists were prepared to court unpopularity (and worse) for their ideals.

During the years covered by this book, as its title suggests, there was almost always a riot going on. That phrase was originally heard in the chorus of Jerry Leiber and Mike Stoller's song 'Riot in Cell Block #9', recorded by the black vocal group the Robins in 1954. That record was a three-minute movie in sound, untouched by politics or reality. In 1970, the song was rewritten by the Beach Boys, never previously known as political animals, under the title of 'Student Demonstration Time'. This version, which was widely interpreted as a radical protest against the American police and government, retained the riotous chorus-line of the original. In reality, as we shall see, the Beach Boys' song was fatally compromised, undermining the forces it pretended to be supporting.

A year later, *There's A Riot Going On* became the title of an album by the rock-funk group Sly & The Family Stone. The record responded to the grim reality of street life for African-Americans by offering an enticingly delicious escape into solitude, shaped by drugs and hedonism. Tellingly, the title track

of the record was entirely silent. A year before the rest of the world, Sly
Stone had realised that the riot was already over. But the aftershock continues
to this day – if we are not afraid to listen.

*Peter Doggett*
*February 2007*

# PROLOGUE: 1965

Q: 'What are your opinions of Vietnam?'
JOHN LENNON: 'I think it's lousy. It should be stopped.'
Q: 'Do you have any plans or ideas on how you'd stop war?'
JOHN LENNON: 'No, I don't think you can stop war.'

(Beatles press conference, New York, 15 August 1965)

## DOMINO THEORY

Vietnam – a country that few Americans could locate on a map – soured the American Dream around the world in the 1960s. More than forty years after the start of the Vietnam War, and sixty since America's first confused intervention in Indo-China, the origins of this troubled episode in US foreign policy are still being debated by historians.

Like most superpower adventures on alien soil, the Vietnam conflict (war was never officially declared by the USA) was born from an unhappy coupling of arrogance and ignorance. Irony was never far from the scene of the crime, either. In a scenario that ought to have provided a salutary lesson, the USA once funded and supported the very forces that became its sworn enemy. Few American leaders had a clearly defined objective in Vietnam, or even a logical battle plan. As a result, the USA became embroiled in a military morass that had already exhausted France, its colonial predecessor in South-East Asia.

In 1947, President Harry Truman chose to back Ho Chi Minh and his tiny band of guerrilla fighters against the French. Less than twenty years later, President Lyndon Johnson committed America's first combat forces against the army attempting to deliver South Vietnam into the hands of Ho Chi Minh's North Vietnamese government. Between those two events,

Vietnam experienced forced partition into communist North and capitalist South states; the birth of a national liberation movement amongst the people of the South; the retreat of the French after their failed attempt to return Vietnam to its pre-World War Two status as a colony; and the collapse of a succession of puppet regimes in the South, each increasingly dependent on American financial and (ultimately) military backing.

Lyndon Johnson's generals convinced him that Vietnam represented the frontline of the global struggle against communism. Their 'domino theory' warned that if Vietnam fell under communist control, the rest of South-East Asia would follow, leaving Australia and New Zealand under imminent threat. American military 'advisers' had been aiding the South Vietnamese government since the 1950s. President Kennedy increased their numbers dramatically, but died before he was able to deliver on his pledge to withdraw the US presence if the South's political regime stabilised. Johnson assumed office in November 1963 determined to maintain Kennedy's policy, but was swiftly overwhelmed by events. No sooner had he won re-election in late 1964 than he approved a drastic increase of military action in Vietnam. By March 1965, US combat troops had arrived in the country, and US planes had launched Rolling Thunder, a concerted bombing campaign designed, so Johnson promised, to deliver 'peace through pressure'.

America was now enmeshed in the jungle forests of Vietnam. For the rest of the decade, the USA concocted a series of 'decisive' actions against the National Liberation Front in the South, and eventually against Ho Chi Minh's forces in the North. Each time, it became more deeply entangled in the region's hostile terrain and complex allegiances. The Vietnam conflict claimed hundreds of thousands of American lives, drained the nation's resources, and sapped its self-belief. Beyond its shores, 'Vietnam' was shorthand for every crime, real and imaginary, committed by the world's most powerful capitalist state.

And so it was that 'Vietnam' united a diverse set of adversaries and dissidents, within America's borders and across the globe. They shared no common ideology or manifesto; from Berlin to Berkeley, Mexico City to Madison Square Garden, they were linked only by their opposition to American policy in South-East Asia, and by their determination to change it. That change, it was universally assumed, would not stop at foreign policy; from a thousand different perspectives, the anti-war protestors looked forward to a revolution that would sweep the old order, and its culture, from power.

Many coincidences and historical forces combined to lay the ground for a global campaign against the Vietnam War. Throughout the so-called Third World, the vast colonial empires of the pre-1939 era were disintegrating under the pressure for every sovereign state to determine its own future. Liberation movements in Africa, South America and Asia acted as beacons of defiance for disaffected young people in North America and Europe. So too did the communist regimes of the Soviet Union and China, whose revolutionary, egalitarian rhetoric had not yet been exposed as hollow – or, at least, not clearly enough to dispel the romantic haze that still surrounded them in the eyes of Western students.

Within the West, an economic boom during the late 1950s and early 1960s prompted a surge of consumerism that engulfed the adult population, but left the idealistic young feeling hollow and unfulfilled. Higher education was now open to a wider section of society than ever before, and a generation of students was being educated by the state to question the principles by which it operated. Meanwhile, hallucinogenic chemicals and herbs were enabling those same students to explore the limits of their own consciousness, and to conclude that consumerism offered poor nourishment for the human psyche. Yet consumer society offered young people a web of media via which they could communicate and share their own culture – underground newspapers, films, books, and most important of all in the 1960s, rock music.

In the course of a decade, popular music had mutated from a form of entertainment into the exclusive language of a generation and a (counter-) culture. In the mid-1950s, the savage spirit of rock'n'roll had already divided youths from their parents. When that imprecise sense of rebellion reached the newly disaffected students of the 1960s, rock was there to carry a more focused message of revolt – and eventually revolution – around the world.

No rock act was followed more fanatically than the Beatles. After initial parental disquiet at the unruly length of their hair, the group seemed likely to take their place in the mainstream of popular entertainment, alongside former rebels such as Elvis Presley and Marlon Brando. Yet the group were unwilling to be assimilated so easily. Keeping barely ahead of their increasingly experienced admirers, the Beatles steered a generation into the heady worlds of surrealism, self-analysis, and spiritual enlightenment. Inevitably, they were also drawn into the most urgent political debate of the decade.

'Vietnam was not a burning issue in Britain in 1965,' explains the Beatles' friend, counter-culture luminary Barry Miles. 'There was no underground press to spread the word, and anything which could be interpreted as counter-culture was centred around the arts, especially experimental films and avant-garde music.' For Miles, and the Beatles, the situation in Vietnam was brought into sharp perspective by beat poet Allen Ginsberg, who first met the group that summer. 'Allen had been to Vietnam a couple of years earlier and been horrified by the stories he'd heard there,' Miles says. 'He had a knack for assembling enormous numbers of press clippings on a subject that he felt passionately about, and then extracting what was really happening by reading between the lines. He was the one who first told me what was going on in Vietnam. And he probably did the same thing for the Beatles.'

'For years, on the Beatles' tours,' John Lennon recalled shortly before his death, '[Beatles manager] Brian Epstein had stopped us from saying anything about Vietnam or the war. He wouldn't allow questions about it. But on one of the last tours, I said, "I am going to answer about the war. We can't ignore it." I *absolutely* wanted the Beatles to say something about the war.' As the group's press officer Tony Barrow recalls, Vietnam was not their only prohibition: 'Brian asked the Beatles not to discuss their love lives, their sexual preferences, politics or religion with the media. His ban on political topics included Vietnam. But it was quite rare for such things to be brought up in pop interviews.'

So central had Vietnam become to America's consciousness by 1965, however, that the question was eventually posed. 'Behind the scenes,' Barrow explains, 'the Beatles, particularly John and George [Harrison], talked current affairs in general and topics such as Vietnam in particular. They were very much against war, having seen the results of bombing in Liverpool as kids. Talking about Vietnam was also a way of demonstrating to Epstein that they were beginning to resent being told what to do.'

Eager to find out more about the conflict, Paul McCartney contacted veteran peace campaigner Bertrand Russell. 'Paul would do that a lot,' Miles recalls. 'He'd call people up, and say, "This is Paul McCartney, would you like to have dinner?" Most people said yes. He saw Russell because he realised that he wouldn't get the truth about Vietnam from the London press. So the thing to do was go to the top, and as far as Paul was concerned, that was Russell. He probably also talked to the writer William Burroughs, whom he met around the same time. William had done an enormous number of cut-ups and weird prose pieces about Vietnam, so he could well have discussed those with Paul.' As yet, McCartney's analysis remained unsophisticated: he and the other Beatles were against the war as a gut instinct, rather than as a critique of US imperialism. Besides, as he noted in 1967, 'What happens if you identify with the other side? You lose the power to sway people.'

McCartney's comment was made when hundreds of American activists were burning their draft cards in public, brazenly risking imprisonment for their refusal to go to war. They clearly didn't share his concern about upsetting public opinion. Even in August 1965, when Lennon ventured his first opinion about the war, he was scarcely leading a crusade. On 3 July 1964, pacifist David Dellinger had organised an anti-war demonstration, promoting a Declaration of Conscience expressing opposition to American military involvement in South-East Asia. Folk-singer Joan Baez, a veteran of marches and rallies in support of black civil rights, lent her name to this protest. President Lyndon Johnson responded by authorising the departure of a further 50,000 'advisers' to South Vietnam. After a mysterious 'attack' on US ships in the Gulf of Tonkin, Congress gave the President carte blanche to extend military operations as he saw fit.

Three months away from the presidential election, Lyndon Johnson was careful to obscure his nation's deepening involvement in Vietnam. He was selling himself as 'the peace candidate'; his TV commercials portrayed his opponent, Senator Barry Goldwater, as a trigger-happy maniac eager to provoke a nuclear showdown with the Soviet Union. The Gulf of Tonkin provided Johnson with a perfect opportunity to heighten the role of the US military, whilst still appearing moderate in his use of force. He duly secured re-election in November, and immediately widened the scope of US engagement. In February 1965, squadrons of bombers raided North Vietnam as the physical manifestation of Operation Rolling Thunder. A week after they hit their targets, the first US Marines landed on the Da Nang coast in South Vietnam. All pretence that they might be acting in an advisory role was now abandoned, as America took military control of South Vietnam's battle against the guerrillas of the National Liberation Front.

Students for a Democratic Society (SDS), a national organisation formed in 1960 to campaign for civil rights, took full-page ads in the fledgling underground press to denounce 'a civil war . . . a losing war . . . a self-defeating war . . . a dangerous war . . . a hideously immoral war'. During March 1965, US campuses played host to 'teach-ins', at which sceptical faculty and students debated the morality of the conflict. The first was held in Ann Arbor,

Michigan, a near neighbour of Detroit that became a hotbed of radical politics, and music, for the rest of the decade. On 17 April, SDS staged an anti-
war rally at the Washington Monument, where Joan Baez, Judy Collins and
the Freedom Singers performed the now-familiar anthems of the protest
movement for 20,000 demonstrators. Many protestors pushed for a spontaneous move towards the Capitol Building, the home of the US Congress
and Senate. But the SDS sponsors shouted it down, and only a few hundred
disheartened activists headed towards the seat of government.

In mid-June, SDS staged its national conference – and effectively deflated
this youthful radicalism by refusing to organise a national campaign against
the war. This abdication of responsibility profoundly affected the course
of the anti-Vietnam movement over the next few years. It removed the most
visible source of opposition at a moment when the American public as not
yet fully aware of the nature of the war, and was therefore still susceptible
to argument. But SDS's withdrawal also cleared the path for someone else
to take centre stage. The vacuum was filled by the first superstar of the
revolutionary movement: Jerry Rubin.

## POEMS OF THESE STATES

'Being a celebrity is a powerful weapon,' Rubin wrote from jail in 1970,
'people listen to you and tell other people about you. You are myth. You
are media.' It was a lesson he learned in 1964, when this former sports
reporter and university dropout migrated to the University of California
campus at Berkeley, and witnessed the birth of the Free Speech Movement.
The episode was provoked by a petty UC rule outlawing unauthorised distribution of political literature on campus, and spiralled into a crusade that
effectively created a counter-culture amongst students and radicals. The irre-
pressibly exuberant Rubin, who exploited his passing physical similarity to
legendary Cuban guerrilla Che Guevara, made a playful contribution to the
Free Speech Movement. Liberated, as a non-student, from any academic
burden, he was ideally placed to channel his anarchic spontaneity into the
anti-war movement.

Rubin was a prime mover behind the Berkeley teach-in on 15–16 May
1965, which attracted speakers such as novelist Norman Mailer, child psychologist Benjamin Spock, and comedian Dick Gregory. It stretched for almost
36 hours, and attracted some 50,000 people – 'the biggest teach-in in the
history of the world,' Rubin declared. 'That experience taught us to believe

in the Apocalyptic Action. History could be changed in a day. An hour. A second. By the right action at the right time.'

Though the war dragged on, the excitable Rubin believed that the teach-in signalled the beginning of the end. He dubbed the occasion Vietnam Day, and proclaimed himself the head of the Vietnam Day Committee. In this role, he was responsible for recruiting musical entertainment for the teach-in, in the form of folk-singer Phil Ochs. Though he had yet to register on America's youth consciousness, Ochs was renowned in folk circles as the movement's most flexible and prolific balladeer. As early as 1963, he had lampooned US involvement in South-East Asia in a song entitled 'Talking Vietnam'. His repertoire also contained laments for the victims of racist violence, reportage on the class struggle, and clarion calls for freedom and justice. The title song of his recently released album, *I Ain't Marching Anymore*, was acclaimed as the anthem of the anti-war campaign. In Berkeley, Rubin asked Ochs to perform whenever the audience's attention began to wander. Instinctively political but used to acting alone, the singer was swayed by the realisation that he could combine his music with a mass movement. He also fell under the spell of Rubin's charisma. 'If I'd been Phil Ochs' father,' his manager Arthur Gorson reflects, 'I might have suggested that Jerry wasn't a good influence. But I wasn't his father, I was an activist, like Phil. So I can't say the influence was negative. But Jerry certainly made Phil feel like a conservative.'

For Rubin, Ochs' involvement was welcome but hardly constituted the Apocalyptic Action he was searching for. Rubin traced the beginning of his generation's revolt to the emergence of rock'n'roll in the mid-1950s: 'Hard animal rock energy beat/surged hot through us, the driving rhythm arousing repressed passions. Music to free the spirit. Music to bring us together.' He believed that, 'Rock'n'roll marked the beginning of the revolution'. He must have been heartened by the folk-rock protest tunes that now littered the charts.

Despite its reputation as a golden year for pop, 1965 saw such banal ditties as 'Mrs Brown You've Got a Lovely Daughter' and 'I'm Henry VIII, I Am' topping the US best-sellers list. But the summer of America's first overt military action in Vietnam also witnessed a flurry of opportunistic records that reflected a growing cultural unease. The tone was set by Bob Dylan's 'Subterranean Homesick Blues', a rewriting of Chuck Berry's rock'n'roll hit 'Too Much Monkey Business' for the beat generation. Its quickfire hipster imagery was vague enough to throw out a hostage to fortune – a phrase in the song would later inspire the formation of a revolutionary terrorist group (the Weather Underground). But many of Dylan's lines acted as instant slogans: 'Look out, kid, it's something you did'; 'twenty years of schooling and they put you on the day shift'; and, most enduring of all, 'don't follow leaders, watch the parking meters'.

Protest had been a prominent tone of the topical folk song movement for many years. The addition of electric rock rhythms transported this dissidence from the small ads to the front page. Many of 1965's protest singles came from folkies who were imitating Dylan's flirtation with rock'n'roll. Indeed, Phil Ochs experienced his own electric baptism, souping up 'I Ain't Marching Anymore' into an unconvincing rock opus.

Professional tunesmiths soon recognised the commercial potential of leaping aboard this bohemian bandwagon. The result was a flurry of earnest complaints, including 'The Universal Soldier' (Donovan and Glen Campbell), 'It's Good News Week' (Hedgehoppers Anonymous) and that perfect encapsulation of teenage angst, 'Let Me Be' (the Turtles). But the unchallenged bard of incoherent dissatisfaction was Sonny Bono. With his teenage bride Cher, this journeyman songwriter and defiant non-singer became the hottest pop act in America. They dressed in proto-hippie garb: beads, bells, hipsters and furs, topped by Bono's Samson-styled hair. Their outlandish appearance caused them to be barred from a plush Hollywood restaurant, provoking Bono to pen the gloriously self-pitying 'Laugh at Me'. When this single hit the Top 10 – despite Bob Dylan declaring it 'a drag' – Bono was inspired to compose a follow-up, in which he provided pop's first direct commentary on radical politics: 'A man has the right to talk about what's on his mind/But that doesn't necessarily mean he's The Revolution Kind'.

Sonny's single – which failed to match the popularity of its predecessor – made passing reference to a hit single that, for good or ill, epitomised the summer's protest theatrics. The songwriting team of Phil (P.F.) Sloan and Steve Barri had served their apprenticeship as the creators of surfing anthems before penning the Turtles' 'Let Me Be'. But their biggest success came with 'Eve of Destruction', a catch-all assault on establishment values which folkie Barry McGuire growled like a weary prophet. The record sounded like a collage of the prime musical motifs of the era, from Byrds-style electric guitar to flagrantly Dylan-flavoured snorts of harmonica. Within its three and a half minutes, Sloan and Barri exposed a parade of social ills: religious hypocrisy, the menace of Red China, American racism, environmental doom, and above everything the shadow of nuclear apocalypse that provided the song with its title. The song was spectacularly crass – one verse rhymed 'coagulating' with 'contemplating' – and its success outraged the purists of the folk protest movement.

In September 1965, when 'Eve of Destruction' was the most popular song on American radio, beat poet Allen Ginsberg was composing his epic 'Beginning of a Poem of These States'. Like a latter-day Whitman, Ginsberg set out to take the temperature of the land and compare it with the burning passion of his own blood. As he crossed America by car, he ingested the 'mass machine-made folk song' that had defined the summer. 'Speeding thru space,' he wrote, 'Radio the soul of the nation. The "Eve of Destruction" and "The Universal Soldier".' With each passing month, President Johnson ordered more American troops into action, and the soldiering became more universal.

So did the protests. Two of Ginsberg's fellow poets, Ed Sanders and Tuli Kupferberg, had formed a musical ensemble named the Fugs in late 1964. They took the name from the euphemism that Norman Mailer invented for a common four-letter word in his novel *The Naked and the Dead.* The choice was satirical: Sanders published an occasional journal entitled *Fuck You: A Magazine of the Arts,* while the slogan of Kupferberg's magazine *Yeah* was 'Fuck for peace'.

Both publications were wound up in the summer of 1965 so their creators could concentrate on the Fugs' anarchic brand of folk-rock, which (they boasted) 'utilised the literary and artistic heritage of the Lower East Side combined with the energy of the civil rights and peace movements'. Ed Sanders recalled that the group's ethos reflected 'our concept that there was oodles of freedom guaranteed by the US constitution that was not being used'. Like comedian Lenny Bruce, they set out to explore the limits of censorship. At the heart of their work was their crusade against the Vietnam War. They composed several potent anti-anthems for the movement, including 'Kill for Peace' ('If you don't kill them, then the Chinese will') and 'Strafe them Creeps in the Rice Paddy, Daddy'. Their satirical reach extended to government agents: 'Who can train guerrillas by the dozen?', they asked rhetorically on the rollicking 'CIA Man'.

In early October 1965, as 'Eve of Destruction' gave way to the less bombastic 'Hang On Sloopy' at the top of the US charts, Sanders announced the imminent departure of 'The Fugs' Cross Country Vietnam Protest Caravan'. They intended to drive their Volkswagen camper across the nation to California, breaking their journey for performances and demonstrations at universities 'and wherever spontaneous concerts may be held'. Not forgetting their beat heritage, the Fugs also scheduled ten-minute silences at venues such as the grave of actor James Dean, and the birthplace of novelist William Burroughs.

'People are ready to die for freedom or the flag, but rarely think about what these things are,' Kupferberg complained. 'Americans like to kill and be killed – aggression is a reaction to frustration. If we can put some joy, some real sexy warmth into the revolution, we'll really have achieved something.' Their revolution imagined a society in which poetry could be fired in place of bullets, and a 'group grope' would be a normal means of sexual expression. For the Fugs, 'horny cunt-hunger blues' was central to what Sanders declared as 'Total Assault on the Culture (anti-war/anti-creep/anti-repression)'. Plus, as bandmate Ed Weaver noted, in an uncanny prophecy of the Yippie rhetoric of 1968, 'a man who's laughing can't shoot a gun worth a damn'.

It was no coincidence that the Fugs were heading for California, as the state was now the focal point of anti-war activity. In August 1965, Jerry Rubin had flown to the Assembly of Unrepresented People in Washington, DC, as the leader of the Vietnam Day Committee. The conference voted to create the NCC (National Coordinating Committee to End the War in Vietnam). This organisation proved to have the briefest of lifespans: delegates from the Trotskyist Socialist Worker Party and the Moscow-backed Communist Party soon allowed their perennial battle over the precise timetable for a Marxist revolution to sabotage the NCC. But it cohered long enough to accept Rubin's plan for two International Days of Protest against the Vietnam conflict, on 15/16 October 1965. In New York City, a young Catholic pacifist named David Miller became the first American to burn his draft card as a statement of defiance. He was rewarded with a two-year jail term. Back in Berkeley, Rubin masterminded a typically extravagant demonstration, which featured a performance from a local folk-singer, Country Joe McDonald.

As his father had been investigated by the House Un-American Activities Committee in the mid-1950s, McDonald imbibed political awareness from a young age. 'I heard protest songs at home,' he recalls, 'and I saw in left-wing newspapers stories about lynchings and union strikers being shot. So I knew about this stuff when I was ten years old.' Yet he noticed an immediate gulf between himself and Rubin. 'Jerry and the others in Berkeley were of a different socio-economic class from myself,' he explains. 'They were university students, who had encountered left-wing politics for the first time after they left home, rather than at home like myself.' It was an early recognition of a divide between the old left and the new left that would underpin events for the rest of the decade.

Not that Berkeley students were immune from harsh political realities. Bruce Barthol, who would soon play alongside McDonald in Country Joe & the Fish, recalls that the University of California campus was far from a radical haven. 'The right-wing was always very vivid in my consciousness,' he recalls. 'The John Birch Society were very big back then. After I'd become involved in the Berkeley Free Speech movement, I discovered later that a fellow student, a friend of mine, was reporting on us to the John Birchers. They backed a magazine that printed pictures of student radicals, so that the right-wingers would know who the enemy were. Plus there were stories about another right-wing group, the Minutemen, training in the Santa Barbara mountains with artillery, getting ready for a race war or a fascist takeover. So I certainly didn't get into politics thinking that there was a utopian revolution around the corner. My idea of success was if we managed to avoid being put in concentration camps.'

The same mood of dread was beginning to seep through the country. Psychologically drained by his despair at America's policies in Vietnam, a Quaker named Norman Morrison followed the example of Buddhist monks in South Vietnam who had immolated themselves as a desperate gesture of selflessness and peace. He poured paraffin over himself and, placing his baby daughter on the pavement just out of harm's way, set fire to himself outside the Pentagon, home of the US war machine. He died several hours later in hospital. A week later, his example was copied by another pacifist, Roger LaPorte, who chose the equally emblematic United Nations building in Manhattan as the venue for his protest. He lingered in hospital for more than a day, long enough to murmur his lack of regret for his action.

Morrison and LaPorte's suicides jolted Americans who had chosen to remain ignorant of what their government was doing in their name. Yet the extreme nature of their protests also hinted that the peace movement had reached the limits of conventional activism. Even in Berkeley, rifts were

appearing in the Vietnam Day Committee. Protestors planned on several occasions to march on the Oakland Army Terminal, where new recruits were
inducted into the service. Like the Pentagon, the Terminal symbolised the
relentless machinery of war. But an initial protest foundered when the authorities refused to grant permission. Rubin and his fellow activists wanted to defy
them, but the majority chose to draw back. A second attempt was halted by
the intervention of several hundred members of the Hells Angels motorcycle
club, who believed that they were making a patriotic stand for America against
the forces of communism.

Allen Ginsberg and fellow beat poet Gary Snyder attended these VDC
protests, Ginsberg making his characteristic contribution to the jollity of the
proceedings by chanting a Buddhist mantra. Faced with the threat of assault
by the Angels, he prepared a handbill entitled 'Demonstration or Spectacle
as Example, as Communication or How to Make a March/Spectacle'. If his
advice was followed, he declared, the marchers could 'embody an example
of peaceable health, which is the reverse of fighting back blindly'. The
chosen battleground should be 'our imagination', he continued, neatly separ-
ating himself from more conventionally militant protestors. His tactics
included lining up 'psychologically less vulnerable groups' such as mothers,
poets and professors in the vanguard of the demonstration. 'Marchers should
bring harmonicas, flutes, recorders, guitars, banjos and violins', he asked. If
they were confronted with 'heavy anxiety, confusion or struggle in isolated
spots', they should be ready to respond with music – the Lord's Prayer,
perhaps, or 'Three Blind Mice' ('sung', he specified), or even, four years
before Jimi Hendrix subverted the tune at Woodstock, 'The Star Spangled
Banner'.

Should these measures prove insufficient, then a PA system on a truck
should be introduced, to broadcast the Beatles' hit 'I Want to Hold Your
Hand' at deafening volume. The procession should also, he said, be supported
by sound stages along the route, where San Francisco's newest folk-rock
bands, such as the Charlatans and Jefferson Airplane, could perform. This
scheme would 'pick up on the universal youth rockroll protest of Dylan,
"Eve of Destruction", "Universal Soldier", etc.,' he wrote, 'and concretise
all that consciousness in the parade.' If all else failed, the demonstrators
should threaten to march with a team of women who could pull down the
trousers of anyone opposing them. 'This is a sort of press release joke to
lighten the atmosphere', he explained carefully. The manifesto was printed

in the underground newspaper the *Berkeley Barb* before the march, but not put into operation. As Jerry Rubin recalled, 'The Hells Angels called a press conference. They announced they were going to spend the day getting drunk.'

Almost two weeks later, Ginsberg shared a Japanese meal in San Francisco with two contemporaries from the beat movement, Peter Orlovsky and Lawrence Ferlinghetti. Joining them was Bob Dylan, in town for two shows at the Berkeley Community Theater. One of Ginsberg's biographers describes the poet as 'now obsessed with the Vietnam War', and he spent the evening attempting to cajole Dylan into making a public statement against the conflict.

It was an ironic reversal of the circumstances under which the two men had first met, in 1963. 'Dylan was coming that night from his meeting with the Emergency Civil Liberties Committee's annual banquet, who had given him an award,' Ginsberg recalled later. 'Dylan had declared a sort of independence of any specific political allegiance and that upset them a bit. So we talked about poetry and politics, how poetry was just a reflection of the mind, independent of politics.' Two years later, in Ginsberg's mind, poetry and politics could no longer be separated.

That banquet in 1963 marked Dylan's first visible step away from the role of leading protest singer in the topical folk song movement. Like his hero, Woody Guthrie, Dylan was perceived as a political commentator first and an artist second. Like Guthrie, he slipped in and out of political garb as it suited him. 'Every artist's first responsibility is to himself,' said fellow radical folkie Tom Paxton. Dylan increasingly adopted this credo as his own.

His early repertoire spoke against him, however. His albums, *The Freewheelin' Bob Dylan* and *The Times They Are A-Changin'*, included several of the most potent 'protest' songs of the early 1960s: 'Masters of War', 'Oxford Town', 'Only a Pawn in their Game' and 'The Lonesome Death of Hattie Carroll'. Other tunes, such as 'Blowin' in the Wind' and 'A Hard Rain's A-Gonna Fall', avoided overt political comment, but spoke directly to those who were troubled by racism or impending nuclear apocalypse. More explicit tunes littered Dylan's vast catalogue of unreleased songs: 'The Ballad of Donald White', 'Let Me Die in My Footsteps', 'John Brown' and 'The Death of Emmett Till'. And then there was 'Talkin' John Birch Paranoid Blues', which achieved notoriety when Dylan walked off TV's *Ed Sullivan Show* after the producers refused to allow him to perform his satirical assault on the right-wing John Birch Society.

There were hints within the '11 Outlined Epitaphs' that acted as liner notes for *The Times They Are A-Changin'* that Dylan was rejecting conventional political discourse. Again, this chimed with the mix of cynicism and idealism that fired his youthful audience. Few doubted that if lines were drawn, Dylan would be on their side of the barricade. So there was disquiet amongst the topical folk song community when he released *Another Side of Bob Dylan* in 1964. 'A love song can be political too', he noted many years later, but that was too subtle for those who rated folk songs by their radical content. The opaque verbosity of one song, 'My Back Pages', glazed the song's meaning, but its intention seemed clear. Stripped of the role of campaign leader, Dylan felt 'younger than that now'.

'Dylan told me one time, "I could never figure out why people thought I was a political songwriter",' says singer John Mellencamp. 'But we were all convinced that he was political.' From the vantage point of 1978, Dylan reflected that 'I don't really understand what politics are . . . I'm concerned with injustice . . . I'm not attuned to politics, I'm just attuned to people.' He distanced himself from Phil Ochs, who 'used to write songs with a point of view that was his own, and I guess a lot of other people's point of view . . . But somebody who wasn't really interested wasn't gonna believe him.'

Tapping into the vein of electricity in 1965, Dylan stepped further away from the 'lies that life is black and white'. His new songs, aired on *Bringing It All Back Home* and *Highway 61 Revisited*, were animated in vivid technicolour. But their verbal landscape had shifted from realism to symbolism. The heroes and villains of his 'protest' songs were replaced with shapes from a surreal nightmare; the prophet shifted his gaze from the society he shared with his listeners, to the world that existed in his own head.

Ironically, withdrawing from the role of political commentator merely inflated Dylan's mystique. The more oblique and fantastic his lyrics, the more they intrigued his followers. In 1963, Dylan was popularly believed to be leading a nationwide crusade for justice and equality. In 1965, he was seen as a visionary whose songs carefully disguised the secret of life. Accurately deciphered, lyrics such as 'Desolation Row' and 'Tombstone Blues' would surely liberate the soul, body and mind.

Meanwhile, the media in late 1965 had noticed the plethora of social commentary in the pop charts, and decided that something must be happening. Their cuttings files told them that Dylan was the leader of the protest movement, and so they came to him for assistance. 'How many protest singers are there?' he was asked that December. Dylan first pretended not to have understood the question, and then drawled sarcastically: 'I think there's about a hundred and thirty-six.'

A press conference was staged in San Francisco on 3 December 1965, the morning after Dylan's Japanese meal with Ginsberg. That evening he was due to perform at the Berkeley Community Theater. It was also the night of the latest Vietnam Day Committee demonstration in the town. A reporter asked Dylan whether, as someone who symbolised the protest movement, he would be standing alongside the VDC outside the Fairmont Hotel. 'No, I'll be busy tonight,' Dylan quipped.

It was the same question that Jerry Rubin had asked Dylan before his trip to Berkeley. 'Jerry had sent a message to him, would he join the march, lead the march?' Ginsberg recalled. 'So Dylan said, OK – paraphrase – "Except we ought to have it in San Francisco right on Nob Hill where I have my concert, and I'll get a whole bunch of trucks and picket signs – some of the signs will be bland and some of them have lemons painted on them and some of them are watermelon pictures, bananas, others will have the word Orange or Automobile or the words Venetian Blind. I'll pay for the trucks and I'll get it all together and I'll be there, and we'll have a little march for the peace demonstration."' Dylan repeated the same riff at the press conference, though he rambled into a rap about how he'd formed his own party, not of the left or right but of the centre, though it was 'kind of on the uppity scale', and on and on until the joke ran dry.

In the Japanese restaurant, Dylan had complained to Ginsberg that Rubin's demonstration was 'too obvious, it's a bad show, chickenshit poetry, they don't know what the kids want, who's their public?' Ginsberg conveyed Dylan's Dadaist suggestion to Rubin and the VDC but, he recounted, 'They didn't act on it, they didn't realise what was being offered them on a silver platter. I think Dylan offered it somewhat ironically, but I think he would have gone through with it. I think he was interested, he wanted to do something, but the terms of the march were too negative, not good enough theater, not even good theater, not even effective as propaganda, it never would have penetrated through to the young kids who didn't want to get involved in a crazed anger march. I think that was the beginning of our realisation that national politics was theater on a vast scale, with scripts, timing, sound systems. Whose theater would attract the most customers, whose was a theater of ideas that could be gotten across?' Though Dylan would probably have baulked at the idea, the seeds of the Yippie movement were sown that night in Berkeley.

The songwriter's Californian encounter group widened on 4 December 1965, when Ginsberg took Dylan to the City Lights bookstore in San Francisco, the spiritual home of the beat poetry movement. They posed for photographs with poet and dramatist Michael McClure, who gave Dylan one of the 600 privately printed copies of his long howl of outrage against the Vietnam War, *Poisoned Wheat*. Almost exclusively printed in capital letters, *Poisoned Wheat* found poetry collapsing into rage, as McClure struggled to contain his emotions on the page: 'I AM A LIVING CREATURE/I AM NOT RESPONSIBLE FOR THE TRAITOROUS FASCISM AND TOTALITARIANISM THAT SURROUND ME'.

Later, watching his third concert in consecutive nights at the Masonic Auditorium in San Francisco, McClure turned to Ginsberg after Dylan had performed 'Gates of Eden', and whispered that the revolution had begun. Backstage, the two poets talked to Joan Baez and Dylan's manager, Albert Grossman. Baez suggested that McClure and Ginsberg should act as Dylan's conscience, a constant reminder of the world beyond his imagination. It would be an increasingly barren task, as the war congealed, and Dylan edged further into the shadows.

## FRAGILE COALITION

Before Vietnam, activists marched in the name of civil rights. For the best part of a century, from the abolition of slavery until 1957, black citizens had theoretically enjoyed equal rights to their white compatriots, but rarely in practice. Traditional barriers to the employment of African-Americans had been lowered during World War Two. Many whites assumed that the old order would be resumed once Japan surrendered in 1945; likewise, blacks hoped that the racial climate might change for good. Both sides were to be disappointed.

Beginning with Harry Truman, who took office as the war finished, a succession of US Presidents pledged their support to ending America's endemic, almost instinctive racial discrimination. Progress was painfully slow. Eventually, in August 1957, the Senate passed a Civil Rights Act that made it marginally easier for blacks to register to vote – although there were sufficient loopholes to allow the more repressive states to manipulate the law against their African-American minorities.

Even if they could vote, blacks were still treated like the victims of an apartheid system. It took a lengthy boycott of the bus system in Montgomery,

Alabama – a protest initiated by Rosa Parks and spearheaded by the Revd Martin Luther King Jr – for the Supreme Court to rule it illegal for public facilities to be divided between 'blacks only' and 'whites only'. King formed the Southern Christian Leadership Conference (SCLC) as a vehicle for blacks to seek further civil rights. In 1960, this organisation spawned the Student Nonviolent Coordinating Committee (SNCC), whose manifesto ran: 'We affirm the philosophical or religious ideal of nonviolence as the foundation of our purpose, the presupposition of our belief, and the manner of our action.'

SCLC and SNCC (pronounced 'snick' by its adherents) both entered the battle for voter rights during the early 1960s. But it was a third organisation, James Farmer's Congress of Racial Equality (CORE), which launched the most confrontational and effective campaign of the period. On 4 May 1961, two buses filled with black and white activists left Washington, DC, on the first Freedom Ride. Their destination was New Orleans; their purpose to challenge segregation in bus terminals across the Southern states. The buses were savagely attacked by racists in Alabama, forcing the uninjured protestors to fly to New Orleans. At this point, SCLC and SNCC entered the campaign, and over the next few months a dozen busloads of activists rode the gauntlet of racist hatred in the name of liberty.

For the next few years, civil rights activists quietly continued their work across the South, while public attention focused on a series of flashpoints. In Birmingham, Alabama, Revd King led yet another protest against segregation. The action hovered beneath the nation's radar until TV cameras showed police attacking black children with dogs, clubs and water cannons. President Kennedy intervened to calm the dispute. During his 1960 election campaign, he had repeatedly promised that segregation could be ended 'with the stroke of a pen'. Yet it was only in June 1963 that he submitted the relevant legislation to Congress.

Unconvinced that Kennedy would fulfil his pledge unless he was put under duress, SNCC, SCLC and CORE staged a march on Washington on 28 August 1963. The cream of the folk protest singers – Baez, Dylan, Odetta, Harry Belafonte, and Peter, Paul & Mary – performed in front of 250,000 demonstrators. Martin Luther King captured the imagination of the assembly and the world with his remarkable 'I have a dream' speech.[1] Three weeks later, the gulf between King's dream and reality was spotlighted when racists detonated a bomb in a Birmingham church, killing four black teenage girls.

The assassination of John F. Kennedy in November threatened to halt the hesitant legal battle against segregation. But his successor, Lyndon B. Johnson, steered the most effective anti-racism legislation to date through Congress and onto the statute books by 2 July 1964. A month later, America's fragile racial coalition appeared to be in tatters. All summer, SNCC had sent black and white activists (among them an idealistic 28-year-old from Massachusetts named Abbie Hoffman) deep into Mississippi to ensure that black citizens were registered to vote. On 20 June, three volunteers disappeared from the jail into which they had been thrown. Their bodies were discovered on 4 August, and the murderers escaped justice.

During the futile search for the missing men, the focal point of racial tension had switched to New York City. A 15-year-old black youth called James Powell was shot dead outside a Harlem summer school on 16 June by a policeman who claimed that Powell had confronted him with a knife. 'This is worse than Mississippi,' one girl shouted as 300 teenagers congregated at the scene. Anger intensified over the next two days. A hitherto unknown organisation, the Harlem Freedom Fighters, prepared a flyer containing instructions on how to make a Molotov cocktail.

On 18 June, civil rights organisations and local clergymen staged a protest rally. Activist Jesse Gray called for '100 skilled revolutionaries who are ready to die', as protestors began to stone and firebomb the police house. Violence spread throughout Harlem, flared through the night, and smouldered for another week. The disturbances paled alongside those in the same community in 1935 and again in 1943, when several people were killed. But commentators were shocked by the degree of hatred between the races in an area where, as *Time* magazine reported in affronted terms, African-Americans habitually referred to whites as 'the man', 'Mr Charlie' or 'whitey'.

That same article referred to Harlem romantically as 'the noise of Congo drums from a dark window and a throbbing twist beat on a transistor radio'. *Time*'s musicology may have been suspect, but the district was home to the legendary Apollo Theater and had been the heart of New York City's R&B scene for two decades. Yet it also suffered from a murder rate six times higher than that of New York as a whole, with twelve times as many drug addicts. Small wonder, then, that (as Eldridge Cleaver later wrote) 'It was time for the blacks . . . to riot, to sweep through the Harlem night like a wave of locusts, breaking, screaming, bleeding, laughing, crying, rejoicing, celebrating, in a jubilee of destruction, to regurgitate the white man's bullshit they'd been eating for four hundred years'. Within weeks, the jubilee spread down the coast into New Jersey, and across into Brooklyn.

Its soundtrack, *Time*'s 'throbbing twist beat', did not come, contrary to popular myth, from Martha & the Vandellas' 'Dancing in the Street': that anthem only reached the radio as the riots cooled. The hottest soul song in New York the week of the Harlem riots was Curtis Mayfield's 'Keep On Pushing', performed by his trio, the Impressions. Widely interpreted since as a call for civil rights, it lent itself to being translated in more militant terms. 'I've got my strength', Mayfield cried in his aching falsetto voice, 'and it don't make sense, not to keep on pushing'. Its popularity was timely but coincidental: no soul song, no matter how affecting, could raise a riot, or indeed quell one. Yet there was a strain of black music in the air, across Harlem and beyond, that reflected the political atmosphere. Years before rock allied itself with the cause of revolution, jazz had declared independence from the entertainment business, from white America, and even from the accepted laws of music itself.

It is the jazz issuing from the friction and harmony of the American Negro with his environment that captured the beat and tempo of our times.

(Eldridge Cleaver, *Soul On Ice*)

## BLACK ARTS

The revolutionary potential of the civil rights campaign was spotlighted by the August 1963 call of Chinese Communist leader Mao Tse-tung for 'the people of the world to unite to oppose racial discrimination by US imperialism and support the American Negroes in their struggle against racial discrimination'. Duly alarmed, the white establishment was suspicious of any gesture that appeared to confirm Mao's manifesto. Hence the disquiet aroused by that least incendiary of objects, a poem. It was, warned the *New York Times*, 'a call for black revolutionaries to rape and murder in the service of liberation'. The offending text was 'Black Dada Nihilismus', published in the Harlem summer of 1964, and recited against the exploratory jazz music of the New York Art Quartet that November. The author was LeRoi Jones, a rare black voice in the beat poetry movement of the 1950s. Gradually he had edged away from his fellow beats, his imagination captured and then shaped by the rhetoric of black nationalism. It

was a path that would lead him to full-scale confrontation with the white
American establishment during the Newark riots of 1967, and to his rein-
carnation as Imanu Amiri Baraka, a fearsome and outspoken proponent
of African-American pride and power.

Since 1959, Jones had also moonlighted as a jazz critic, one of only a
handful of black men to command such a post. 'Most jazz critics have been
white Americans but most important jazz musicians have not been,' he noted
pointedly in the (white-run) magazine *Down Beat*. By 1964, his artistic purpose
was to sound the dawn of a black revolution, and to propel that revolution
into existence by undermining the power structure of white America, in
jazz, poetry and beyond.

Never a man to shy away from confrontation, Jones used 'Black Dada
Nihilismus' as a weapon to goad his oppressors. Part surreal wordplay, part
wilful acceptance of the white man's darkest view of black America, part
wish fulfilment, the poem shifted suddenly from oblique, self-consciously
'poetic' imagery into the lines that disturbed the *New York Times*:

> Come up, black dada
> nihilismus. Rape the white girls. Rape
> their fathers. Cut the mothers' throats.

Yet the lines that the *New York Times* ought to have remarked most closely
were sweeping in their condemnation of the American empire:

> money, God, power,
> a moral code, so cruel
> it destroyed Byzantium

Read – indeed, almost purred – against the unsettling music of Roswell
Rudd and the New York Art Quartet, 'Black Dada Nihilismus' marked the
confluence of free jazz, free poetry, and the quest for free black America.
Little more than a year later, Jones issued his famous proclamation of war:
'The Black Artist's role in America is to aid in the destruction of America
as he knows it.' By then, he had written the poem 'Black Art', a notorious
collage of revolutionary manifesto, nightmare imagery, and shameless
misogyny and anti-Semitism. It called for:

dagger poems in the slimy bellies
of the owner-jews. Black poems to
smear on girdlemamma mulatto bitches
whose brains are red jelly stuck
between 'lizabeth taylor's toes. Stinking
whores!

But Jones illustrated the potential diversity of 'Black Art' in his optimistic coda:

Let Black people understand
that they are the lovers and the sons
of warriors and sons
of warriors Are poems & poets &
all the loveliness here in the world
We want a black poem. And a
Black World.
let the world be a Black Poem
And Let All Black People Speak This Poem
Silently
or LOUD.

Like 'Black Dada Nihilismus', 'Black Art' became a jazz poem when Jones recorded it with Sonny Murray, for the evocatively named Black Arts record label. The quest for Black Art, and a structure within which it could exist, preoccupied Jones during the middle 1960s. 'I think that perhaps the most creative work a black man can do at this point,' he commented in 1966, 'is to try to free himself and his people.'

Jones' statement echoed the message of the album that first tied contemporary jazz to the crusade for civil rights. In August and September 1960, musicians from several diverse strands of black music gathered to record *We Insist! Max Roach's Freedom Now Suite*. A veteran of landmark sessions with Coleman Hawkins, Charlie Parker and Miles Davis, drummer Roach composed a cycle of pieces that traced the sorry history of slavery and racism. The record reflected the elevation of the civil rights struggle to the forefront of America's national life, and signalled themes that would recur across the next decade – black America's identification with Africa, its awareness that civil rights were part of a global struggle for freedom, and the mixture of agony and incandescent rage that made up the stifling atmosphere of African-American life.

Roach's future wife, singer and actress Abbey Lincoln, gave these emotions voice. On 'Triptych: Prayer, Protest, Peace', she howled her despair and defiance against a tempestuous percussion backdrop. Roach and Lincoln were married in 1962, and their partnership was undoubtedly strained by the pressure exerted on them as their involvement in the civil rights campaign intensified. Invitations for them to record began to disappear. After cutting *Straight Ahead* with Roach, Lincoln endured almost a decade of invisibility as a singer until she re-emerged on safer ground with gospel material in 1971. Roach, too, found studio time difficult to obtain: there was a similar hiatus in his career that spanned the harshest years of militant black politics.[2] It was the price he paid for gestures such as his unscheduled appearance during a performance by Miles Davis and Gil Evans at New York's Carnegie Hall. The concert was a fundraiser for the Africa Relief Foundation, and Roach marched across the stage carrying a 'Freedom Now' banner – a protest fired by the Foundation's tacit support for the colonial system.

Introducing a new tune at New York Town Hall, Charles Mingus compared the treatment of civil rights protestors to that of German Jews during World War Two. There were concentration camps, he declared, across the Southern states: 'The only difference is that they don't have gas chambers and hot stoves to cook us in yet. So I wrote a piece called "Meditations As To How To Get Some Wirecutters Before Someone Else Gets Some Guns To Us".' The composition aroused a standing ovation at the 1964 Monterey Jazz Festival – a fact dutifully reported in *Time* magazine, which carefully omitted any mention of the political message.

LeRoi Jones understandably welcomed the defiance of such statements. But even this avowed activist concluded that 'The music is finally most musicians' strongest statement . . . and the new music . . . is "radical" within the context of mainstream America. Just as the new music begins by being free. That is, freed of the popular song . . . It wants to be freed of that temper, that scale. That life. It screams. It yearns. It pleads. It breaks out (the best of it). But its practitioners do not.'

Was jazz inherently political, radical, revolutionary? The debate simmered for the rest of the decade. Looking back, Max Roach differentiated between two artistic traditions: 'Politically, I see jazz as very democratic music, whereas European classical music expresses imperialism. In jazz, we debate a topic, the musicians are free to discuss it. It's like a meeting.' But Jones was no longer interested in mimicking democracy: for him, the point of art was to change the world, not open a debate about it. If jazz in its conversational, co-operative mode was a form of democracy, then desperate times required the creation of a style of music, and politics, that would cut through the stale conventions of liberalism. The politics was revolution; the music was free jazz.

In the 1940s, the emergence of be-bop had destroyed and rebuilt the traditional structure of the jazz tune, and extended the limits of instrumental improvisation. Ornette Coleman's groundbreaking 1959 LP, prophetically and arrogantly titled *The Shape of Jazz to Come*, moved a crucial step further. In Coleman's quartet, there was no hierarchical distinction between the front-line horns, and the traditionally supportive rhythm section. A year later, the 37-minute piece that filled the *Free Jazz* album provided boundless space for each player to express his liberation.

Even at its most expansive, Coleman's music was *composed*, rather than improvised. But its sense of adventure and epic landscape inspired his contemporaries to think beyond the confines of the jazz heritage. Another telling influence was the tenor saxophone of John Coltrane, whose modal improvisations on the album *My Favorite Things* (1960) wiped away another set of self-imposed boundaries, in the way that the twelve-tone scale had rewritten the vocabulary of classical music. Other musicians, such as Eric Dolphy (on 1960's *Far Cry*) and Cecil Taylor (1962's *Nefertiti the Beautiful One Has Come*), used Coleman and Coltrane's innovations as a jumping-off point. This school reached its apogee in 1964, when both Dolphy's *Out To Lunch* and Coltrane's *A Love Supreme* achieved a mesmerising blend of spontaneity and design.

Although LeRoi Jones was one of several black critics of the 1960s who lauded John Coltrane as a revolutionary artist, he reserved his most fervent praise for another saxophonist: Albert Ayler. After nursing his be-bop ambitions through several years in R&B bands, Ayler combined with Don Cherry, and then his own brother Don, in 1964–65 for an explosive series of albums. From *Spirits/Witches & Devils* (cut in February 1964) to *Spirits Rejoice* (September 1965), Ayler channelled his own artistic frustration and his generation's rage into playing that accepted no boundaries. Confronted by his landmark 1964 album *Spiritual Unity*, Jones briefly considered that he might have found a substitute for political action: 'It might cool you out from hurting somebody!'

Rewriting musical laws was not the only revolutionary gesture open to jazz musicians in the mid-1960s. Max Roach had already pinpointed another crucial battleground, when he called for the black nationalism he had expressed in *Freedom Now* to be translated into an assault on the white capitalist system that held it back. Jazz, he declared, needed to be 'nationalised': 'When I say "nationalise", I'm speaking of just in the area of our controlling what we create. Within the context of the society we live in, if we're the ones everybody feeds on, if we're the ones who are creating this great music . . . we should be the ones who control it.' LeRoi Jones focused on specific forms of musical distribution that needed to be overturned: 'Even though Radio is "black", to the extent that we hear our own sounds, &c., still, make no mistake the [white] boy is most always in control and shooting his stuff through . . . For this reason stores, communications centers, are worth a great deal to us . . . the revolutionaries must come to own them somehow.'

Across America, there were record companies (Motown being the most prominent), venues, record stores, even radio stations, in black hands. But they existed within, or outside, a white-run corporate structure that controlled distribution to the (white-run) major stores and (white-run) concert halls, and restricted access to the (white-run) radio and TV networks. Independence and near-bankruptcy could still provide the perfect breeding-ground for pioneering music. Jazz eccentric Sun Ra (whom Jones described as wanting 'a music that will reflect a life-sense lost in the West, a music full of Africa') formed his Saturn record company in the mid-1950s. It existed so far beneath the commercial radar that it might as well have been buried underground. But it provided a vehicle for Sun Ra's stunningly prolific output with his Arkestra, allowing him to release dozens of albums at a pace that would have been impossible via a major label.

More public were the efforts of Charlie Mingus and Max Roach to escape the formal structures of the jazz industry, whether they were setting up a rival to the Newport Jazz Festival, or making shortlived attempts to found their own record labels. Both musicians soon succumbed to the power of the mainstream, Roach by being exiled from the recording industry, Mingus by resuming his tempestuous career within corporate

America. It was coincidental, perhaps; or inevitable, if you take a deter-minist view of the relationship between culture and economics; but, in either event, fitting, that the most determined efforts to evade the power structures of jazz were made by musicians who also championed freedom from musical traditions.

Several of the leading players of free jazz collaborated in the New York Contemporary Five, or under the leadership of Archie Shepp. Among them was trumpeter Bill Dixon, a woefully under-recorded musician who as early as 1964 decided that he could exert more influence as an educator and impre-sario than as a performer. That October, he promoted a series of free music events at the Cellar Café in New York (also the venue that summer for several Albert Ayler recordings). These were not concerts, in the traditional sense, nor likewise jam sessions of the old school, but some hypnotic level of existence in between, where the most experimental free-thinkers in contem-porary jazz could explore the possibilities of their music. In a sly (and, in 1964, courageous) reference to the Russian Bolshevik uprising of 1917, Dixon named the season 'The October Revolution in Jazz'.

Dixon enticed the likes of Sun Ra, Ornette Coleman and Archie Shepp to participate, alongside younger musicians such as Carla Bley and Mike Mantler, who would remain bastions of the avant-garde for decades to come. Their collective zeal was channelled into a utopian organisation named the Jazz Composers' Guild, backed by Dixon, Shepp, Mantler, Cecil Taylor, Roswell Rudd and saxophonist John Tchicai. During its butterfly existence, the JCG staged concerts in New York, and founded its own orchestra (the JCGO), under the leadership of Mantler and Bley. Within weeks, however, the Guild dissolved into competing factions. The JCGO shortened its name to the Jazz Composers' Orchestra, acting as a beacon for experimental souls in the USA and Europe.

Yet even in this restricted form, the JCO operated as a force for social and artistic change. Like several other groupings that emerged around this time, it did its best (in the words of academic Frank Baskerville) 'to present free concerts and open music academies within black inner-city communi-ties to provide musical training for young people'. That last aim was what fired the AACM (Association for the Advancement of Creative Musicians), established on 8 May 1965 by Chicago-based pianist Muhal Richard Abrams. Its ethos involved developing original (black) material, promoting gigs, and teaching both jazz and self-reliance to ghetto kids. Gradually, Abrams attracted a cabal of like-minded musicians, including Henry Threadgill, Anthony Braxton, and the future members of the Art Ensemble of Chicago.

Over the next decade, more than a dozen such co-operatives came into existence. During the mid-1960s, the most significant – certainly the most publicised – was founded, almost inevitably, by LeRoi Jones. In February 1965, he made a symbolic journey from Greenwich Village, home of the beats, to Harlem. There he assembled a coterie of activists and artists who shared his vision. It was time, he believed, for the creation of a Black Arts, that would reflect the turbulent mood of the times – the battle for civil rights in the South and self-respect on every street, the emergence of independent black Africa, the discovery that theatre, music and literature could flourish outside white America. Jones summed up his quest: 'An art that would reach the people, that would take them higher, ready them for war and victory, as popular as the Impressions or the Miracles or Marvin Gaye. That was our vision, and its image kept us stepping, heads high and backs straight, no matter some of the wacky bullshit we got into on occasion.'

Jones rented a building on 130th Street, high up in Harlem, as the home of the Black Arts Repertory Theater/School (BARTS). 'Sun Ra became our resident philosopher,' he recalled, 'having regular midweek performances in which he introduced the light-show concept that white rock groups later found out about and got rich from.' BARTS went overground on 28 March 1965, with a benefit concert at the Village Gate that allowed Impulse! Records producer Bob Thiele to record a sampler album of the avant-garde scene entitled *The New Wave in Jazz*. Alongside Sun Ra, whose music was considered too bizarre for the LP, the concert featured an almost unfeasible array of talent: John Coltrane, Albert Ayler, Archie Shepp, McCoy Tyner, Cecil Taylor, Sonny Murray and more besides. According to Taylor, Impulse! Records' engineers treated the mighty Coltrane as a hired hand, three times interrupting him as he began to play because they weren't satisfied with the sound. 'Would any record company have dreamed of treating a "legitimate" – that is, white – artist in such a contemptuous manner?' asked jazz critic Frank Kofsky. 'Can you imagine the reaction of Glenn Gould or Isaac Stern under these circumstances? But then, Gould and Stern are not black jazz musicians.' Other BARTS events saw the likes of Pharoah Sanders, Shepp, Taylor and Coltrane performing from specially converted trucks on the streets of Harlem. 'The only bad incident', Jones later recounted, 'was when a white-media-famous tenor man came up with an integrated group and someone threw an egg at him. We told the musicians we wanted black groups and boycotted them if they refused to make their groups all black.'

Racial separatism was a recurrent theme. That winter of 1964–65, Jones held court in the Village, challenging the white intellectuals and bohemians who regarded him as a comrade. For several months, he had been preaching that communication between blacks and whites was pointless in a society that continued to institutionalise racism. In a contemporary essay entitled 'The Last Days of the American Empire', he wrote: 'The hope is that young blacks will remember all of their lives what they are seeing, what they are witness to just by being alive and black in America, and that eventually they will use this knowledge scientifically, and erupt like Mt Vesuvius to crush in hot lava these willful maniacs who call themselves white Americans.'

Jones lived out his own manifesto. At the Village Vanguard, he and Archie Shepp clashed with his old friend, Jewish artist Larry Rivers, during a symposium on 'Life vs Art'. Several accounts of what happened have been published, each subtly different, but Rivers' version is typical: 'Soon things began to get wild. LeRoi told me I was making art for a bunch of uptown fags. Archie brought up the twelve million blacks in the Congo annihilated by slavery and the Belgians. I began to make an allusion to the Holocaust, trying to see just exactly what I felt about Germans. Before I had finished half a paragraph, Archie pointed his finger at me and shouted, "There you go again, always bring up the fucking Jews". He couldn't talk about his pain without Jews bringing up theirs! The intimidated moderator threw the ball to the audience. LeRoi's and Archie's responses to the questions amounted to: There's only one kind of white – Whitey who hates Negroes.' Author Harold Cruse added that when Shepp was asked about white (often Jewish) civil rights workers who endangered their lives by campaigning for blacks to be able to vote in Mississippi, he replied: 'I give [them] no civil service charity for going to Mississippi to assuage their consciences.' Jones' biographer, Jerry Watts noted: 'While these whites were in Mississippi assuaging their consciences, Shepp remained in New York City, away from the fray.'

Despite being lauded (and not just by LeRoi Jones) as one of the most exciting new talents on the jazz scene, Shepp found it difficult to score regular work, and had to rely on a menial day job at the department store Abraham & Straus. When he quit on the promise of West Coast gigs that fell through, he was forced to pawn his saxophone. He claimed that he was then tricked by Impulse! Records into signing away his publishing rights.

Few black men in Harlem had saxophones to pawn, or journalists to chronicle their complaints. But Shepp's experience reflected the struggle for survival that was the daily landscape of African-American lives. The sullen resentment of centuries had hardened since World War Two into simmering rage; and nobody was better able to express that revulsion at the callousness of white America than the preacher Malcolm X.

Lazily described by many commentators as an apostle of violence, in sharp contrast to the pacifist Martin Luther King, Malcolm X undertook one of the longest and most courageous spiritual journeys of the 20th century. Born Malcolm Little in Omaha, he drifted into a life of petty crime and casual aggression. While serving an eight-to-ten-year sentence in Massachusetts for burglary, he was introduced to the black separatist ideas of Elijah Muhammad and the brothers of the Nation of Islam. 'Despite my many experiences with whites,' he wrote shortly before his death, 'when my brother told me that God had taught Mr Elijah Muhammad that the white race was a race of Devils, my eyes came open on the spot.' Out of jail, Malcolm became the Nation's most powerful speaker and incendiary presence. A generation of African-Americans were drawn to the Nation's Manichean rhetoric and complex mythology, which hinged around the conviction that black men had been cheated out of their eternal birthright by the devil, incarnate in the inferior form of the white man.

Elijah named his disciple Malcolm X, but it was the younger man who transformed the fortunes of the Nation and propelled its Islamic philosophy into the startled faces of white America. With his close-cropped hair, sober suit, white shirt and tie, he looked anything but a firebrand. But when he spoke, he could electrify an audience – and a nation. For black power activist Eldridge Cleaver, then resident in Folsom Prison, Malcolm was a Messiah, a political leader, a hero on every level: 'His style, fearlessness and mental prowess gave us a hero to worship and follow. Like me, he had been a gangster, ruthless and gun-toting. He also encouraged the technique of analysis and brought this to play in pulling off the layers of white racism and oppression. He was well read, travelled a lot, and always seemed to have whitey on the defensive.'

Malcolm's notorious comment after President Kennedy's assassination on 22 November 1963 that 'the chickens have come home to roost' demonised him in the minds of whites; it also sparked a scolding from Elijah Muhammad that, according to Cleaver, effectively 'destroyed' the Black Muslim movement. There was a strange hiatus, from December 1963 to February 1964, when Malcolm dutifully obeyed the instruction that he should make no public statement for ninety days. But Elijah Muhammad also told Malcolm that he should not be seen in public with heavyweight boxer Cassius Clay, who was due to fight Sonny Liston for the world title on 26 February. The two men were friends, and Malcolm had been instrumental in secretly persuading Clay to join the Nation of Islam. Malcolm appeared ringside as Clay shocked the boxing world by defeating the apparently impregnable Liston; and was there again the following day, when Clay sent shockwaves through America by announcing that he was a Muslim, who should henceforth be addressed as Cassius X (later, Elijah renamed him Muhammad Ali). Also present at the fight was R&B star Sam Cooke, whose conversations with Malcolm and Cassius were monitored by an FBI informer. Cooke's personal respect for Malcolm did not extend to joining the Nation; his most militant action during the civil rights campaign was composing 'A Change Is Gonna Come', an artistically brilliant but politically benign statement of cautious optimism that justice would eventually triumph over despair.

By the time of that post-fight summit, the relationship between Elijah and Malcolm was soured beyond repair. On 8 March 1964, Malcolm X announced that he had left the Nation of Islam. Four days later, he revealed that he was forming a new organisation, the Muslim Mosque Inc. It was intended as a vehicle for a more political brand of black nationalism than that practised by the Nation. At its heart was an intensification of the struggle for civil rights. He predicted that 1964 would prove to be bloodier on this battleground than any year to date.

Stripped of the spiritual, financial and numerical support of the Nation, Malcolm X could have disappeared into sectarian anonymity. Instead, via his canny use of the media, he resurfaced as a figure of global stature. In April 1964, he made a pilgrimage to Mecca, during a lengthy tour of Africa and the Middle East in which he was treated as an ambassador for black Americans. In the Islamic holy city, he experienced a revelation, an awareness of the oneness of mankind. It was an epiphany that forced him to rethink the entire basis of his faith, and his political agenda. No longer could he espouse a philosophy of hating whites, regardless of their character or deeds. In future, he declared, he would be prepared to work alongside white activists who were sincere in their quest to free African-Americans from the trappings of slavery. This shift of perspective encouraged him to forge ever-

deeper links with Africa, and the revolutionary movements that were liberating the continent from colonialism. Both themes would echo through the
black power movement for the next decade.

Returning from his self-imposed exile in November 1964, however,
Malcolm X was an increasingly threatened and isolated figure. Almost imme-
diately, he was denounced as a traitor in the Nation of Islam's newspaper,
*Muhammad Speaks*. His detractor was Louis X, now better known as Louis
Farrakhan, who in the early 1950s had worked as a calypso performer under
the name of The Charmer.[3]

The relentless criticism from his former brothers, and the haphazard
nature of his political base, sapped Malcolm's energy in the final weeks of
1964. Earlier that year, he had seemed to edge closer to a rapprochement
with the more peaceful philosophy of Martin Luther King. Now, it was as
if he had lost patience, with himself as much as his enemies, white and
black. In a series of interviews and speeches, he riffed on a single, compelling
theme: 'I'm for the freedom of the 22 million Afro-Americans by any means
necessary. BY ANY MEANS NECESSARY. I'm for a society in which our
people are recognised and respected as human beings, and I believe that we
have the right to resort to any means necessary to bring that about.' By any
means necessary: that phrase soon legitimised many different methods of
revolt against the state, by groups whose philosophy sometimes bore no
other resemblance to Malcolm's than their shared despair and defiance.

In the early hours of 14 February 1965, Malcolm awoke at his New Jersey
home to the smell of burning. The house had been firebombed: the Nation
alleged that he'd staged the arson attack himself, to win public sympathy,
but his supporters believed that his former comrades were the most likely
culprits. Malcolm remained enigmatically silent. Four days later, on the same
day Archie Shepp recorded – and finished, so he believed – his *Fire Music*
album, Malcolm spoke in public for the last time, at Columbia University.

On the afternoon of 21 February, Malcolm walked onto the stage of the
Audubon Ballroom in Detroit, the city where he had first hinted at his
quarrel with the Nation fifteen months earlier. After the firebombing, he'd
talked grimly about his impending doom, speculating: 'I'll probably be shot
to death in the street one day. Or maybe while I'm speaking.' At the Audubon,
he was introduced as 'a man who is willing to put himself on the line for
you . . . a man who would give his life for you'. It was a promise worthy of
a saviour.

Malcolm acknowledged the applause, waited for the crowd to settle, and murmured a traditional Arabic greeting. The audience responded in kind, and then swivelled their heads as two men among them rose to their feet and began to shout. Security guards rushed to quell the disturbance, while Malcolm pleaded for calm. With attention distracted, another man left his seat, and strode towards the stage. He was carrying a shotgun, from which a dozen large pellets tore a gaping hole in Malcolm's chest. Two other gunmen rushed towards his body and emptied revolvers into his trunk and legs. By then, Malcolm was already dead in all but name.

Like other assassinations in modern American history, the killing of Malcolm X has become the hub of competing conspiracy theories. Evidence pointed towards members of the Nation as the culprits, with or without the knowledge of Elijah Muhammad. But the Nation blamed the US government, as proof of the white man's perfidious devilishness. Either way, the murder jolted black America into a state of hyper-awareness, just as it propelled Malcolm from rebel hero to eternal martyr.

The shockwaves ran deep and carried far; in a way, they are still travelling today. Everything that happened in the collective life of black America over the next decade, every manifestation of violence and the rejection of violence, took place in Malcolm's shadow, and shuddered with his own dying breath.

'We are murdered, in amphitheaters, on podia . . . Malcolm! My people. Dear God . . . Malcolm!' Just over two weeks after the killing, tenor saxophonist Archie Shepp returned to the studio, to recite a poem over a jumbled, disjointed, eerily placid backdrop. He titled it 'Malcolm, Malcolm – Semper Malcolm'; and with it, his album of *Fire Music* was completed. 'I call it "Malcolm Forever" because of my belief in his immortality,' Shepp told Nat Hentoff after the session. 'I mean, he was killed, but the significance of what he was will continue and will grow. He was, among other things, the first cat to give actual expression – though he didn't act it out – to much of the hostility most American Negroes feel. Malcolm knew what it is to be faceless in America and to be sick and tired of that feeling. And he knew the pride of black, that negritude which was bigger than Malcolm himself. There'll be other Malcolms.' That pledge gave the title of *Fire Music* a currency that stretched beyond the frantic squealing of Shepp's saxophone.

For LeRoi Jones, Malcolm's murder provided the impetus to abandon Greenwich Village and ride north to Harlem, 'seeking revolution!' He and countless others read the editorial in the *New York Times*, which dismissed Malcolm as 'an extraordinary and twisted man' with a 'strangely and pitifully twisted' life based around a 'ruthless and fanatical belief in violence'. They recognised neither Malcolm X, nor themselves, in the newspaper's disdain. But that recognition could be found in the events that shook black America over the next decade, and in the increasingly aggressive music that came from those who followed Archie Shepp's path into *Fire Music*.

'Do I really want to be integrated into a burning house?' novelist James Baldwin had asked in his pioneering essay 'The Fire Next Time' two years before Malcolm's death. Through 1965, the conflagration spread. In March, while Archie Shepp taped his paean to Malcolm, freedom marchers gathered in Selma, where white racists had confronted the crusade for black equality. The summer of protest had begun early. Then, in August, as Barry McGuire's 'Eve of Destruction' ('Take a look around at Selma, Alabama') rose up the charts, the Los Angeles ghetto of Watts erupted into riots that made Harlem 1964 seem like a church picnic. Upstate in Oakland, Donald Warden, the founder of the Afro-American Association, an organisation that included future black power leaders Bobby Seale, Huey Newton and Ron Everett, believed that 'the masses were at breaking point'. He channelled his outrage and their fury into an album entitled *Burn, Baby, Burn*, which pitched his sermonising calls for civil rights against a rhythmic backdrop churning with angry voices. The record's distribution was limited, but it captured the mood of the ghettos perfectly. And through it all, the cloud of Vietnam cast an ever-darker shadow across black America, whose native sons were, strangely, always at the top of the draft board's list.

No wonder, then, that at year's end, Archie Shepp, declaring his independence from the jazz establishment in an article entitled 'An Artist Speaks Bluntly', should declare: 'I am about 28 years in these United States which, in my estimation, is one of the most vicious, racist social systems in the world – with the possible exceptions of Northern Rhodesia, South Africa and South Vietnam.' He laid out the charge sheet, the musicians such as Billie Holiday and Charlie Parker, 'murdered out of a systematic and unloving disregard'; the 'nigger shooting heroin at 15 and dead at 35'; the 'perennially starving families'. But as a musician, a black man, a human being, Shepp refused to live out that destiny: 'I am the persistent insistence of the human heart to be free . . . My aesthetic answer to your lies about me' – he was talking to the editors of *Down Beat* magazine, and over their heads to America at large – 'is a simple one: you can no longer defer my dream. I'm gonna sing it. Dance it. Scream it. And if need be, I'll steal it from this very earth.'

As he announced a few weeks earlier in a *Down Beat* symposium, Shepp saw no distinction between political engagement and playing jazz. By its existence, he announced, jazz was inherently 'anti-war; it is opposed to Vietnam; it is for Cuba; it is for the liberation of all people.' In 'An Artist Speaks Bluntly', he spelled out the revolutionary nature of his music: 'I am an anti-fascist artist. My music is functional. I play about the death of me by you.' He was staring his interrogator, and his country, straight in the eyes. 'I exult in the life of me in spite of you. I give some of that life to you whenever you listen to me, which right now is never. My music is for my people.' Seven years later, Shepp still felt that he had to devote an album to what he called *The Cry of My People*.

In 1965, that cry was clamouring to be heard. 'Don't you wonder just what my collective rage will be like,' Shepp declared, 'when it is – as it inevitably must be – unleashed? Our vindication will be black as the colour of suffering is black, as Fidel is black, as Ho Chi Minh is black.' *Down Beat* tried unsuccessfully to persuade Shepp to withdraw these comments. 'You know what people will say about you,' editor Don DeMichael told him. Shepp recalled his response: 'I said, "All right, man, let them say that, because the FBI has already been to my house." And they have.'

The FBI also noted the provocative live sets offered by Charles Mingus during the weeks after the Watts riots. His performance at the Monterey Jazz Festival in mid-September 1965 was cut short, so a week later, on the UCLA campus in Los Angeles, he delivered the entire repertoire he'd intended for the festival-goers. It was a surreal, chaotic night; Mingus seemed distracted, ill at ease with himself and his musicians. At one point, he halted the concert, and ordered half of his band to leave the stage because they weren't playing well enough. Amidst the confusion, however, he laid bare his outrage at the savagery of his country. His set included 'Once Upon a Time there was a Holding Corporation Called America'; 'They Trespass the Land of the Sweet Sioux'; and, most pertinently, 'Don't Let It Happen Here'. This tune echoed the title of Sinclair Lewis's 1934 novel, *It Can't Happen Here*, which had warned about the danger of America slipping towards fascism. During the piece, Mingus recited Pastor Martin Niemoller's compelling short poem about the creeping advance of Nazism in Germany: 'First they came for the Communists . . .' The analogy was unmistakable. Racked by personal crises and political disillusionment, Mingus effectively retired from the jazz scene for the rest of the decade.

From his vantage point inside Folsom Prison, convict Eldridge Cleaver watched impatiently as black America shuddered on the edge of revolt. Removed from the fray, he found it easy to issue proclamations of apocalypse: 'We shall have our manhood. We shall have it or the earth will be leveled by our attempts to gain it.'[4] Writing to his lawyer, Beverly Axelrod, on 5 September 1965, Cleaver unleashed his frustration and rage: 'I am angry at the insurgents of Watts. They have pulled all the covers off me and revealed to all what potential may lie behind my Tom Smile.' A month later, he hoped that black America might find a leader worthy of the revolt to come: 'How I'd just love to be in Berkeley right now, to roll in that mud, frolic in that sty of funky revolution, to breathe in its heady fumes, and look with roving eyes for a new John Brown, Eugene Debs, a blacker-meaner-keener Malcolm X, a Robert Franklin Williams with less rabbit in his hot blood, an American Lenin, Fidel, Mao-Mao . . .'

'Rabbit' was a cheap shot at Robert F. Williams, the Chairman-in-Exile of the first black nationalist group in modern America to propose the revolutionary overthrow of the white American government. In the late 1950s, he had been the president of a North Carolina branch of the civil rights organisation, the NAACP. He was also one of eight African-Americans seconded onto the founding committee of the organisation Fair Play For Cuba, which achieved notoriety in 1963 when one of its members, Lee Harvey Oswald, was accused of assassinating President Kennedy.

When the black community of Monroe, North Carolina, was faced with repeated violence from the local Ku Klux Klan, Williams took the profound step of urging his comrades to take up arms. 'All those who dare to attack are going to learn the hard way that the Afro-American is not a pacifist, that he cannot forever be counted on not to defend himself', he declared in his influential book, *Negroes With Guns* (1962). 'Those who attack him brutally and ruthlessly can no longer expect to attack him with impunity.' Williams' rhetoric inevitably attracted the attention of law enforcement officers. They were quick to seize upon an ambiguous incident in 1961, when Williams and his wife Mabel went to the aid of Freedom Riders who were marching through Monroe. They claimed that they had given shelter to a young white couple who, it transpired, were associated with the Klan; the authorities alleged that they were guilty of kidnapping. Fearing that they had been set up, and would inevitably be railroaded into lengthy prison sentences, the Williams family fled to New York, and then to Canada. They finally found sanctuary in Castro's Cuba, where Williams founded a militant newspaper entitled *The Crusader*. The Cubans also provided Robert and Mabel with the facilities to broadcast a nightly programme called *Radio Free Dixie*. The CIA did its best to block the signal, just as the FBI intercepted copies of *The Crusader* as it reached American shores, but tapes of the shows were often aired by maverick radio stations such as WBAI in New York, and KPFA in Berkeley.

After the initial, ironic blast of the traditional tune 'Dixie' that introduced each broadcast, the Williamses launched into a collage of political rhetoric and cutting-edge African-American music. John Coltrane, Archie Shepp and Albert Ayler were among the jazz musicians who received more airplay from *Radio Free Dixie* than they ever did in their homeland. The station also acknowledged the increasing contribution of radical white musicians to the black struggle. 'The rock cats can no longer be written off and indiscriminately stereotyped as screaming, stomping alley cats without a message,' Mabel Williams declared on 21 January 1966. 'Many of the most socially conscious rock'n'roll musicians are becoming the epic poets of the Afro-American revolt.' But the main focus of *Radio Free Dixie* was the incipient black revolution, a fight to escape from what Robert Williams called 'the horrible jungle of death . . . the racist social jungle'.

On 30 July 1965, Williams told his scattered audience in his lazily calm voice: 'We are now in the Year of Fire. This is going to be a long hot summer . . . Let our people take to the streets in fierce numbers and meet violence with violence. Let our battle cry be heard around the world: freedom, freedom, freedom now – or death.' Two weeks later, the people of Watts heard his cry, through the airwaves or the ether, and the Year of Fire burned with fresh intensity.

*Radio Free Dixie*'s broadcasts, and the explosive testimony of *Negroes With Guns*, were cited by black activist Max Stanford as prime motivations for the formation of the Revolutionary Action Movement (RAM) – the group that claimed Williams as its Chairman-in-Exile. Stanford drew his inspiration from every current of revolutionary thinking, Mao Tse-tung's interpretation of Marxism, black nationalism and Malcolm X's pan-global unity among them. Indeed, Malcolm was 'elected' RAM's International Spokesman in the summer of 1964. Stanford recruited students as the

vanguard of what was planned as a national underground network of guerrilla fighters, confronting the racist state in individual acts of retaliation.
RAM's quarterly periodical *Black America* issued 'Greetings to our Militant
Vietnamese Brothers' in 1964, one of the earliest attempts to unite the
anti-Vietnam and black nationalist causes. Ultimately, however, the organisation was better at claiming responsibility for social upheaval (such as
the Watts uprising) than at fermenting it. 'I got frustrated with those cats,'
recalled jazz drummer and Oakland RAM member Bobby Seale. 'I didn't
think they were going to do anything and I became very discouraged about
being able to work with them.'

One of Seale's beefs with RAM was that they refused to allow his light-
skinned friend Huey Newton to join. At Merritt College in Oakland, the
two men assumed leadership of the Soul Students Advisory Council, whose
manifesto, according to Seale, was 'to go to the black community and serve
the black community in a revolutionary fashion'. High on their agenda was
the draft: Vietnam was no longer a distant foreign policy issue, but a very
real threat hanging over young African-American men.

On 17 March, Seale, Newton and a 'brother' called Weasel drove to the
University of California in search of a record store that would sell blues
records by T-Bone Walker, Lightnin' Hopkins and Howlin' Wolf – 'those
downhome brothers', Seale called them, whose music now appealed more
to the roots-music aficionados of the folk protest movement than it did to
urban blacks. For Newton, these blues records signified 'the inner soul of
the brother off the block'. After checking out the stores, the trio began
walking down Telegraph Avenue. Seale (who had worked as a comedian
since the early 60s) began to rap out some radical street poetry. A white
policeman walked over towards Seale, so he repeated the most inflammatory lines, staring out a challenge. The policeman told Bobby Seale he was
under arrest. A scuffle broke out, and it was Huey Newton who ended up
in cuffs. 'It took us three days to get Huey bailed,' Seale remembered.

The tension between Newton and Seale, and the 'cultural nationalists' of
RAM, gradually increased. 'They claimed to function as an underground
movement,' Newton wrote later, 'but instead of revolutionary action, they
indulged in a lot of revolutionary talk, none of it underground. They were
all college students, with bourgeois skills, who wrote a lot. Eventually, they
became so infiltrated with agents that when an arrest was made, the police
spent all their time showing each other their badges.'

'Bourgeois': this was exactly the epithet that had been used by RAM to denounce Newton. Like RAM, Newton talked black revolution. But in his apartment, he sat back and smoked dope, and played the same record, over and over again, to the point where it became a part of his soul. It wasn't by Howlin' Wolf or T-Bone Walker; not by John Coltrane or Archie Shepp; not even black at all. Instead, it was an album by a white folk-singer who'd stepped away from the protest movement at the moment when civil rights, Vietnam and revolution were about to collide; a record decried by politically active members of the folk community as a betrayal of its principles, a craven seduction by the plastic jewels of commercialism. As Huey Newton inhaled his dream of a new revolutionary movement that could unite the entire black community in open revolt, his hi-fi blared out Bob Dylan's *Highway 61 Revisited*. From LeRoi Jones' apprenticeship amidst the Greenwich Village beatniks, to the Ginsberg-inspired surrealism of Dylan's electric fantasies: a revolution in words fuelled a revolution in deeds, for a young black generation ready to erupt.

# SECTION I

# CHAPTER 1: 1966

We have paraded, we have picketed, we have petitioned our government, we have fasted, we have 'sat-in' – yet for over two years American
military involvement in Vietnam has escalated relentlessly. Many of us
are filled with a growing sense of weariness and despair.

(New York anti-Vietnam War activists, July 1966)

When the anti-war movement realised that conventional protest
was being ignored by the White House, pressure grew for a more
radical solution to the Vietnam crisis. From 1966 onwards, the
campaign against the war began to merge with the crusade against racism,
the first stirrings of feminism and the quest for liberation from the morals
and methods of capitalist society. This crush of causes squeezed protestors
out of their comfortable liberalism, into a state of consciousness where
revolution – of the mind, body and spirit – became not only a dream, but
a necessity. Over the next two years, this impulse would grow to the point
where it seemed that only a cataclysmic attempt to overthrow the state would
ease the pressure.

## A GREAT SOCIETY

In the seven-second flurry of bullets that ended his life, President John F.
Kennedy was translated into the realm of sainthood. In its shock and horror,
America preferred to remember their lost leader as a symbol, not a flawed
human being who had failed to deliver on his promises about civil rights,
and steered his nation closer to its fatal entanglement in Vietnam. Older,
uglier, a dirty-nailed squabbler in the political mire, his successor struggled
to escape Kennedy's shadow. In the months after the assassination, Lyndon

B. Johnson searched for a magical phrase, a statement of purpose, which could sprinkle the glitter from Kennedy's Camelot over his own presidency.

JFK had informed the American public that they stood 'on the edge of a new frontier – the frontier of the 1960s, a frontier of unknown opportunities and paths, a frontier of unfulfilled hopes and threats'. By 1964, with Kennedy in Arlington Cemetery and tidings darkening on every horizon, Americans were fearful that the 'threats' were no longer 'unfulfilled'. That March, a TV interviewer enquired whether LBJ could offer Americans a replacement for JFK's New Frontier. He scratched around for a moment, and said: 'Well, I suppose all of us want a better deal, don't we?'

That wasn't the poetry that history demanded. In April 1964, Johnson tried again during a speech in Chicago. 'We have been called upon . . . are you listening?' he interjected, to highlight the significance of what he was about to say – '. . . to build a great society of the highest order, a society not just for today or tomorrow, but for three or four generations to come.' It was enough – a Great Society[1], a purpose that could be bent to every vision of the future, a beacon bright enough to call out to the doubtful, but yet so vague that it could be reshaped as circumstances required. It was enough to win Johnson the election in November 1964: that, and the threat, reinforced by Johnson's slick TV advertising campaign, that his Republican challenger might lead America blithely into World War Three.

Yet even the most loyal Johnsonite must have struggled to recognise the President's dream at the dawn of 1966. In the aftermath of Selma and Watts, the civil rights issue simmered just below the surface, waiting for the first spark of spring to renew the inferno. Meanwhile, it was increasingly difficult to boast that the war in Vietnam was going to plan. More than 800 Americans had perished there between August and December. As the year began, 120,000 US fighting troops were installed in South-East Asia, plus more than 60,000 euphemistic 'advisors'. Generals had already informed LBJ that the war was unwinnable unless he committed at least 400,000 soldiers to it, and even then it would take years, not months. The financial burden was decimating Johnson's welfare campaign; Vietnam was now costing the USA more than $35,000,000 per day. Johnson now realised that 'If I left the woman I really loved – the Great Society – in order to get involved in that bitch of a war on the other side of the world, then I would lose everything at home.' With each passing month, the bitch sank her nails deeper into Johnson's back.

The president's exhaustion was slowly suffocating his land. Anti-war protestors had naively expected the moral force of their argument to bring the conflict to an immediate end. Meanwhile, civil rights activists sighed at the prospect of another year of begging for an end to segregation and prejudice, while all across the Southern states African-Americans were still denied the opportunity to vote. 'Negroes are defined by two forces, their blackness and their powerlessness,' noted the charismatic SNCC activist Stokely Carmichael. In Folsom Prison, Eldridge Cleaver drew the connections: 'The link between America's undercover support of colonialism abroad and the bondage of the Negro at home becomes increasingly clear.'

All this smacked of Marxism, declared David Noebel of the Christian Anti-Communist Crusade. It was not Vietnam or civil rights that had sapped young people's optimism, he alleged, but the entertainment they were fed by the Communist conspiracy. 'Throw your Beatle and rock'n'roll records in the city dump,' he begged. 'Let's make sure four mop-headed anti-Christ beatniks don't destroy our children's emotional and mental stability.' Listen to Barry McGuire's 'Eve of Destruction', he added, as it was 'obviously aimed at instilling fear in our teenagers as well as a sense of hopelessness. "Thermonuclear holocaust", "the button", "the end of the world" and similar expressions are constantly being used to induce the American public to surrender to atheistic international Communism.' Meanwhile, the draft loomed over 'our teenagers', who from February 1966 would for the first time be eligible for military service even if they were college students.

America was a nation edgy with impatience and frustration, and increasingly riven on generational and racial grounds. Within the civil rights movement, anger at the slow pace of change was hardening attitudes and identities. Some African-American protestors were beginning to resent the presence of young white supporters in their midst. The influx of white liberals into Mississippi in 1964 had brought national attention to the racism inherent in Southern society. Two years later, however, as activist Andrew Young recalled, 'There was a decision on the part of some of the blacks in SNCC that we don't just want to get people free, we want to develop indigenous black leadership.'

'The disagreement over whites was not on having whites,' explained Stokely Carmichael, who took over the leadership of the most confrontational civil rights organisation, SNCC, in April 1966. 'The disagreement was on having white leadership. White liberals could work with SNCC but they could not tell SNCC what to do or what to say.' Carmichael was also responsible for

SNCC's decision in January 1966 to highlight the direct link between America's homegrown racism and its imperialist foreign policy. Other civil rights groups, who had not given up hope of exerting peaceful persuasion on the Johnson government, moved swiftly to distance themselves from SNCC's more militant line.

## GENERAL MOTORS FASCISM

Peter Coyote of the San Francisco Mime Troupe, a radical theatre group that had grown out of California's burgeoning hippie scene, looked blearily at the chaos around him. He predicted: 'We're passing now into a time of death, and we have to confront death with the vision of life.' He saw an 'ideology of failure' that was gripping the nation: 'There are internal contradictions in the society that have become heightened to such a degree that the country has become the equivalent of fascist. It's General Motors fascism. That's out front. Our lives are in fact revolutionary within the context of General Motors fascism. We expect to live our lives and to defend them. We have been cultural outsiders in this civilisation. We will become the political dynamic of the new society because we are living a new civilisation.' Asked what he saw ahead, he replied starkly: 'Civil war, with some attendant trips.' But which way would the country crack first?

Faced with the prospect of open warfare between black and white, of annihilation in the jungles of Vietnam, of losing one's soul in 'General Motors fascism', many young people reached for an alternative. Peter Coyote's 'attendant trips' exerted more pull than his 'civil war'. Instead of risking death on the battlefield or at the hands of the Ku Klux Klan, millions chose to consider a different adventure – a journey into the void of their own souls. There was, according to *Time* magazine in March 1966, an epidemic of drug use among the young, who were choosing to lose their identity and (so *Time* suggested) risk their sanity by swallowing a chemical compound called lysergic acid diethylamide (LSD), or 'acid'. The patron saint of acid experimentation was a former Harvard psychologist called Timothy Leary. He declared that political involvement was meaningless: 'Any external or social action, unless it's based on expanded consciousness, is robot behaviour.' LSD was the common currency of mind expansion through the mid-1960s. Along with rock music, it became the most important ingredient of the development of the counter-culture known variously as flower power, the hippie movement or, simply, as a historical cliché, 'The Sixties'. Dr Leary formed an organisation called the League of Spiritual Discovery, to normalise the use of LSD. In California, hippies organised 'acid tests', at which an LSD 'trip' would be accompanied by suitably psychedelic music from the Grateful Dead, one of the many rock bands who set out to reproduce the acid experience in sound.

Fame and wealth provided no refuge for 'cultural outsiders'. In February 1966, John Lennon invited journalist Maureen Cleave into his plush home in the stockbroker belt. She admired his playthings, but couldn't help but notice the spiritual emptiness that they represented. This was the other extreme of 'General Motors fascism' – the endless consumerism available to the rich, objectified in Lennon's life by his cars, his tape recorders, his television sets, 'the telephones of which he knows not a single number'. It was alienation personified, and Lennon knew it: 'There's something else I'm going to do, something I must do – only I don't know what it is. That's why I go round painting and taping and drawing and writing and that, because it may be one of them. All I know is, this isn't *it* for me.' Cleave reported that Lennon was 'reading extensively about religion'. Lennon's studies and his relaxed relationship with Cleave led him to make one of the most notorious public statements of the century: 'Christianity will go. It will vanish and shrink. I needn't argue about that; I'm right, and I will be proved right. We're more popular than Jesus now. I don't know which will go first – rock'n'roll or Christianity.' His comments passed without notice in Britain, where a certain amount of bohemian eccentricity was expected from its celebrities. But when the interview was reprinted in the US teen magazine *Datebook*, it prompted an outbreak of antipathy that made David Noebel's criticisms sound mild by comparison.

Lennon's ennui chimed with his bandmate George Harrison, who chose the year commonly regarded as the pinnacle of 1960s pop to lament that only Indian music turned him on these days: 'It makes Western three-or-four-beat type stuff seem somehow dead.' As Lennon noted in another 1966 interview, 'We are all old men.' The Beatles' escape routes – the recording studio, hallucinogenic drugs, the trancelike music of India, and soon Eastern spirituality as well – took them inward, at the moment when Vietnam and racism defaced the external, physical, political world.

Academic Nick Bromell has argued that the acid generation's excursions had a subtle political effect. 'After getting high or tripping,' he wrote, '60s users realised that their belief in a core self was naive, their faith in stability was foolish, and so they were fully prepared to see through *everything*, including truth, justice, and the American way.' All astute watchers of America's travails in Vietnam shared that lack of 'faith in stability', but there were other ways of coming to mistrust 'truth, justice, and the American way' – avoiding ambush by Vietnamese guerrillas, for one, or facing down crazed racists in Mississippi.

## PRETENTIOUS FOLK FRONT

In 1966 America trudged deeper into the swamp of South-East Asia, convinced that with every step it was reaching higher ground. Meanwhile, the American nation looked on, bewildered. Anti-war protestors were equally mystified and jaded. Individual events drew massive crowds: International Days of Protest in March brought 50,000 people onto the streets of New York, and as many again in other US cities. Yet with Students for a Democratic Society having abdicated responsibility for the peace movement the previous year, there was no organisation strong or courageous enough to direct a prolonged campaign of disobedience and dissent.

In Berkeley, the Vietnam Day Committee kept the faith, working towards Jerry Rubin's high-profile but electorally unsuccessful bid to become the city's mayor. The VDC continued to stage low-key benefit concerts throughout this period, calling on the services of Country Joe McDonald and guitarist Barry Melton, who was now performing with Joe as 'the Fish'. In September 1965, McDonald had contributed to a record called *Songs For Opposition*, which featured the original versions of two of the most memorable protest songs of the era. 'Superbird' (its title borrowed from Mac Gerson's satirical play) lampooned the president as a low-budget superhero, devoid of special powers. 'I-Feel-Like-I'm-Fixin'-To-Die Rag' combined the title of one vintage blues tune with the melody of another, as a backdrop to savagely comic commentary on the war. The result was an unforgettable 1960s anthem, still potent enough four years later to enliven 500,000 stoned hippies at the Woodstock festival. For the moment, though, both songs were scarcely heard beyond the San Francisco bay.

Country Joe & the Fish mutated from a duo into a folk-rock band by early 1966. The extended line-up included Berkeley activist and bassist Bruce Barthol, and Paul Armstrong, whose penance for evading military service was to work in a center where the bodies of dead American soldiers were shipped from Vietnam. Thinking politically was second nature to the band. 'At a rally for a radical candidate for Congress,' explained the duo's manager

Ed Denson, 'we saw the Fugs put on what was then a really mind-blowing show. The audience was stunned, and we were overjoyed. Contacting them, we arranged for a concert on the Berkeley campus presented by the Pretentious Folk Front.' McDonald reeled off his new protest gems, while the band sported T-shirts bearing peace symbols, and Melton proudly displayed a sweatshirt featuring the face of Beethoven, and the simple caption: 'Marx'. 'We thought we might be arrested for singing our songs,' Denson recalled. But as Barthol explains, 'There was no fantasy of rock stardom on the early San Francisco rock scene. The "air guitar" scenario hadn't been invented yet. The band was never intended to be anything more than a minor underground happening. Everything that happened after that took us by surprise.'

Down the coast in Los Angeles, the avant-garde elite gathered for a Concert Happening at Aerospace Hall in February 1966. Alongside a programme of experimental pieces by John Cage and Schonberg, Joseph Byrd performed a 'composition' entitled 'The Defense of the American Continent from the Viet Cong Invasion'. After several years working along-side artists such as George Maciunas and Yoko Ono in the Fluxus group, Byrd had formed the New Music Workshop with Don Ellis. His composi-tion was inspired, Byrd recalls, by 'the absurdity of the US Defense Department (no longer the "War Department") entering into a longer and more protracted war in South-East Asia'. Within the skeletal 'score' of Cage's *Notations*, Byrd arranged for eight musicians, 'representing ROTC [Reserve Officers' Training Corps] units, to improvise airplane sounds on their instru-ments, i.e. drones. They should start softly, and build until they intercepted the Viet Cong bomber threatening California. At whatever time each player reached the target, he would stop improvising, and begin playing a chorale arrangement I'd written of "America the Beautiful", which repeated until everyone had completed the mission. So there was a gradual transition from drone to hymn.'

Byrd remembers that 'the piece went by virtually unnoticed'. But another performance that night provoked a fiercer reaction. 'I'd scheduled one of Nam June Paik's "Playable Pieces",' he explains, 'which are mostly concept art, not playable at all. There was just one that could be performed: "Cut your left forearm a distance of 10 centimeters". It was performed very much like any solo concert piece. I walked onstage, removed and hung up my jacket, rolled up my sleeve, and cut. I'd expected it to be painful, but it wasn't. The problem was, the initial cut wasn't deep enough for blood to flow, so I had to repeat it. The blood slowly trickled into a stainless steel bowl, and the entire procedure took less than a minute. And that should have been that.

'Only it wasn't. The audience became increasingly disturbed. By the time I was finished, people had walked out, others were booing, and some cheering, but no one was unaffected. And it became a cause célèbre. It was a revelation for me as well. Here, at a time when my country was bombing and napalming villages, with only a fringe domestic opposition, people could be revolted and horrified by a small, self-inflicted wound and a little blood! It definitely made me re-embrace the Fluxus approach that art could be a factor in revolution.' But, as Byrd admits, 'Fluxus – which was about the synthesis of radical art and radical politics – was in real life performed by, and for, a sophisticated elite.' Aware of the paradox of attempting to effect political change via an elitist medium, Byrd began to consider the subversive potential of experimental music rooted in the rock tradition.

Another attempt to cross-pollinate artistic genres in the name of protest was marked by the unveiling in New York of the first ever rock musical, Megan Terry's *Viet Rock*, at the Open Theater in Café La MaMa. The production was staged in several New York locations during 1966, to the bafflement of the city's drama critics. 'Not one cogent thing is said about our involvement in Vietnam,' moaned Walter Kerr in the *New York Times*, while Harold Clurman in *The Nation* dismissed the play as 'an irregular chain of improvisation, in feeble rock'n'roll style'. Terry's script certainly encouraged the free expression of ideas and actions, combined with the kind of scything satire previously heard from the Fugs and shortly to enter the commercial mainstream via Frank Zappa and the Mothers Of Invention.

These were isolated events, though, in a year when Vietnam seemed to merge into the American landscape. The only concerted artistic attacks on US foreign policy during 1966 came from poet Allen Ginsberg and singer Phil Ochs. In a leap into the fantastic that would have impressed his poetic mentor, Walt Whitman, Ginsberg celebrated St Valentine's Day 1966 by composing 'Wichita Vortex Sutra'. He tore into the empty rhetoric of America's military leaders, page after impassioned page, lamenting that, 'almost all our language has been taxed by war'. Then, 'in this Vortex named Wichita', Ginsberg experienced his revelation, a conceptual declaration of peace:

> I lift my voice aloud,
> make Mantra of American language now,
> I here declare the end of the War!

To reinforce his one-man cessation of hostilities, Ginsberg issued a press release: 'As US language chief I hereby use language to make a unilateral declaration of the end of the Vietnam War. The poet says the whole war's nothing but black magic caused by the wrong language & authoritatively cancels all previous magic formulas & wipes out the whole war scene without further delay.' As his friend and biographer Barry Miles notes, 'That was a typical gesture for Allen to make. It supported Shelley's notion that poets are the real legislators, not politicians. So if he proclaimed that the war was over, it counted as a prophecy, because he was a poet. Poetically, he had ended the war.'

Ginsberg's *coup de théâtre* left little mark on the American public, but it resonated with Phil Ochs, who would soon borrow the concept. Meanwhile, Ochs mounted his own 'unilateral declaration' of opposition to America's overseas adventures. The latest target was merely 'South-East Asian Birmingham', as he had noted astutely in his late 1963 song 'Talking Vietnam', written in the wake of the shambolic coup that claimed the life of South Vietnamese president Diem. In a sardonic and strangely prophetic couplet, Ochs sniped at the US Army's claim to be acting as advisors: 'Well, "training" is the word we use/Nice word to have in case we lose'. A later verse provided the inflammatory punchline: 'Friends, the very next day we trained some more/We burned some villages down to the floor'.

By the time Ochs recorded *I Ain't Marching Anymore* in 1965, he was grappling with a more personal struggle: maintaining his integrity in the face of his own minor celebrity. His public wanted to imagine him as an unimpeachable symbol of political virtue and righteous outrage. But Ochs was already showing signs of the cynicism and despair that would torture him later in the decade. He enjoyed a relationship with fame that was, at best, ambiguous. Paul Rothchild, who produced both his early folk albums, described Ochs as 'a fucking heavy duty capitalist'. In an unguarded moment, the singer told *New York Times* reporter Robert Shelton: 'I want to be the first left-wing star.' In a prose poem he posed himself the question: 'Do you really believe in what your songs are saying?' His protest anthems, ringing with fire and anger, made any answer superfluous. But the compulsively truth-telling Ochs was also capable of informing the *Village Voice*: 'There's nothing noble about what I'm doing. I'm writing to make money. I write about Cuba and Mississippi out of an inner need for expression, not to change the world. The roots of my songs are psychological, not political.' His manager, Arthur Gorson, is adamant that he was simply being provocative: 'Phil wasn't motivated by money. He was very pure in his politics – his attitude was, "We are right, so we will win." That was his real motivation.'

His songs certainly spoke in his defence. 'His potency was the confrontational nature of his material,' Gorson believes. 'He used to stand at the edge of the stage for a quick getaway, because he was always convinced that someone would kill him because of the power of his words. If he didn't believe that he had danger and impact, then it wasn't worth his carrying on.' *I Ain't Marching Anymore* included another cutting piece of black comedy, 'Draft Dodger Rag'. Ochs described the scenario: 'In Vietnam, a 19-year-old Viet Cong soldier screams that Americans should leave his country as he is shot by a government firing squad. His American counterpart meanwhile is staying up nights thinking of ways to deceptively destroy his health, mind, or virility to escape two years in a relatively comfortable camp. Free enterprise strikes again.' The album nailed a dozen other targets with the same stiletto wit – Mississippi's racism, arms dealing, unemployment lines, the Harlem riots, capital punishment, right-wing union bosses, Governor George Wallace of Alabama, rural poverty, and more besides.

Ochs was convinced that the perils of contemporary world politics would become too urgent for any entertainer to ignore; war would replace love as the common currency of the popular song. In the future, he wrote in his programme notes for the Newport Folk Festival, 'I wouldn't be surprised to see an album called "Elvis Presley Sings Songs of the Spanish Civil War", or the Beatles with "The Best of the Chinese-Indian Border Dispute Songs".'[2]

Burdened by his country's sins, Ochs increasingly lost faith in its ability to mend itself and purge the world of its crimes. In the same interview in which he envisaged political superstardom, he stepped over the line between revolt and what could legally be classed as treason. 'The Vietcong are right', he declared, 'because they provide an extreme answer to the extreme problems of poverty, famine, disease.' Then, in case any of his readers thought he had become one of 'Them Commies', he added: 'We should support Ho Chi Minh as the last workable bulwark against Communist China in Asia' – this at a time when official US policy was that South Vietnam, not the North, was the final defence against Asia and Australia toppling domino-fashion into Communist hands.

Ochs was now writing protest material faster than he could record it. In the final months of 1965, Vietnam inspired two new songs. 'Cops of the World' took a satirical swipe at America's role as global policeman, while 'White Boots Marching in a Yellow Land' chimed with Stokely Carmichael's much-quoted remark that the war was 'white people sending black people to make war on yellow people in order to defend the land they stole from red people'. As he had in 'Talking Vietnam', Ochs provocatively envisaged his nation suffering defeat: 'We're fighting in a war we lost before the war began.'

Both songs were in Ochs' repertoire when he lined up alongside a galaxy of folk stars at the Sing-In For Peace at Carnegie Hall, in September 1965. The one absentee from the protest pantheon was Bob Dylan, who allowed his name to be quoted as a member of the organising committee, but made sure he was elsewhere on the night. That month, Ochs and Dylan clashed ideologies in a meeting that has been mythologised beyond the reach of accurate recall. The essentials are these: Ochs lectured Dylan about his social responsibilities; Dylan demurred, and played Ochs a new song (either 'Can You Please Crawl Out Your Window' or 'One of Us Should Know', accounts differ). Ochs replied that it wasn't one of Dylan's best songs; Dylan dismissed Ochs' own songwriting with a damning phrase that haunted him into the grave: 'You're nothing [or perhaps "You're not a songwriter"] but a journalist.' At some point, there was a car journey, from which Ochs was expelled after goading Dylan once too often. Dylan biographer, Anthony Scaduto, got the story first-hand from Ochs, who also remembered Dylan telling him: 'The stuff you're writing is bullshit, because politics is bullshit. It's all unreal. The only thing that's real is inside you. Your feelings. Just look at the world you're writing about, and you'll see you're wasting your time. The world is, well . . . it's just absurd.'

Absurdity was the dominant tone of Dylan's songwriting during this period: even when he employed a cast of real people, from T.S. Eliot to William Shakespeare, he manipulated them like plasticine puppets into surreal poses. You could listen to 'Tombstone Blues' or 'Desolation Row', both from Dylan's mid-1965 album *Highway 61 Revisited*, and conclude that a society capable of creating the Vietnam War and the Ku Klux Klan was indeed as comic and mutant as Dylan's verse suggested. But nowhere did Dylan offer a solution to either problem, or even acknowledge their existence as anything more than another level of black comedy. With that incisive wit and emotional distance, Dylan maintained a healthy – for him – gulf between social commentary and social responsibility. In private and in public, he disclaimed all connection with politics, protest, socialism, liberalism, anything but his own skewed vision of the universe. Joan Baez remembered him prowling around his dressing-room in December 1965, goading anyone who attempted to drag him back into the political cockpit: 'Hey, man, if ya gonna bomb Hanoi, whyn't the fuck, man, they bomb Hanoi? I mean, I don't give a fuck if they bomb Hanoi.' Even at his most cynical, Phil Ochs would have been incapable of maintaining such a pose.

But neither was Ochs willing to follow folk-singer Joan Baez's route from outrage to civil disobedience. It was one thing for Ochs to spout pro-Vietcong slogans in interviews; another for Baez actively to defy the American government. In 1965, she informed the Internal Revenue Service that 'I am not going to volunteer the 60% of my year's income tax that goes to armaments'. Her rationale was simple and incontrovertible: 'I do not believe in war. I do not believe in the weapons of war . . . I am no longer supporting my portion of the arms race.' She established a foundation in her adopted hometown of Carmel, California, called the Institute for the Study of Nonviolence. In retrospect, this was worth a lifetime of revolutionary posturing; in the mid-1960s, as she recalled, she 'bashed on regardless, slipping Gandhi in between songs and winning a few hearts and minds and annoying the "radical" left with my "moderate" ideas'.

Between Dylan's withdrawal of support from the radical left, and Baez's equally stark abdication of responsibility for the American war machine, Ochs attempted to fashion a revolution of his own – artistic, political, or some strange hybrid of the two. In November 1965, he toured Britain for the first time, haunted from town to town by questions about his relationship with Bob Dylan. Ochs had already suggested that the hysteria surrounding Dylan had become so intense that Bob might soon find it impossible to perform. It was ironic, to say the least, that when Ochs turned off his conscious mind during a long drive between UK shows, and allowed a remarkably visionary set of lyrics to come through, he should title the finished song 'Crucifixion'. He believed it was about JFK, and interpreted it that way until he died, but many lines could just as easily have been written about Dylan.

On his *In Concert* album, the singer juxtaposed his playful new protest tunes, and his more visionary compositions, although he reserved 'Crucifixion' until he felt more confident that there was an audience for something so richly metaphorical. 'It was a thing of beauty, which didn't rely on a specific political message,' remembers Arthur Gorson, 'so he was slightly wary of what the audience reaction would be.' Instead of penning his own liner notes, Ochs chose to reprint seven poems by the Chinese Communist leader, Mao Tse-tung. Underneath he posed the question: 'Is this the enemy?' One critic wondered pertinently whether Chairman Mao would have allowed a similar gesture to go unpunished in China. There was retribution in America as well, as Arthur Gorson explains: 'It definitely caused us problems. Record stores didn't like it, and some refused to stock the album. But Phil had a point to make which had nothing to do with whether you agreed with Mao or not, which was: Is it art? How does it affect the common man? Phil was touched by the beauty of the poems, and he wanted to share them with his audience.' The episode was an effective piece of what Tom Wolfe would later call 'radical chic'.

## THE OPENING SHOTS

Revolutionary role-playing was in the air. Jerry Rubin, Ochs' comrade from the Vietnam Day Committee demonstrations of 1965, was simultaneously running for the office of Mayor in Berkeley, and facing investigation by the House Un-American Activities Committee (HUAC) for his anti-Vietnam demonstrations. 'I began thinking about HUAC as theater,' he wrote. 'I knew that I could not play on their stage, because they hold power in their gavel. I had to create my own theater to mindfuck HUAC and capture the nation's attention.' So he attended the hearing dressed in full costume from the Revolutionary War, just like the US pop band Paul Revere & the Raiders. 'We went back to Berkeley,' he remembered, 'where we were greeted by cheering mobs.' It was a lesson not lost on Rubin or his associates.

In the carnival of California 1966, Rubin's theatrics blended in with the pioneering lights shows at dance halls such as the Fillmore and the Avalon, the face-painting and body decoration, the beads, the feather boas, the tie-dye shirts, the mind-expanding music, the chemicals that introduced their users to colours not found in the spectrum. The ethos of free jazz, if not its musicianly discipline, was being introduced into rock, as performances extended to match the receding horizons of the acid trip. It was a time of fearless experimentation, when the effortlessly hip folk-rock band the Byrds could share a bill at Bill Graham's Fillmore Auditorium with *Dutchman*, LeRoi Jones' provocative drama about murderous racial confrontation, and nobody would find the juxtaposition absurd. In the midst of this hedonism, there was little space for the cold realism of conventional political protest. The National Mobilization Committee to End the War in Vietnam (alias Mobe) was formed in autumn 1966, with its energy focused on a long weekend of dissent in early November. But its initial demonstrations suffered the same depletion of numbers and enthusiasm that had sapped recent events by the Vietnam Day Committee.

To persuade young white kids to take to the streets, you needed an issue that hit them where they lived. On Sunset Strip in Hollywood, police continually harassed the middle-class youths who spilled onto the streets out of clubs such as the Whisky and Gazzari's. When the cops abruptly closed down a meeting-place called Pandora's Box in December 1966, hundreds of kids battled them on the Strip, launching several nights of sporadic but furious fighting. In response, Buffalo Springfield leader Stephen Stills, a Southern-born blues freak with minuscule patience for prejudice or pettiness of any kind, penned the first rock protest anthem of the psychedelic era: 'For What It's Worth'. 'I wanted to write something that had to do with the guys in the field in Vietnam,' Stills explained years later, 'and how they had very little to do with the policy that put them in harm's way in the first place. And then I ran into this ridiculous situation on Sunset Boulevard and the two things just came together, and I wrote the song in about 15 minutes.' As an anthem, it was anything but revolutionary: the song's protagonists carried signs saying 'Hooray for our side', while the 'young people speaking their minds' were facing merely 'resistance from behind'. But Stills did successfully conjure up an air of suspicion, a fear that people were being manipulated by mysterious forces beyond their understanding – a mood that translated the song into an all-purpose commentary on strange times.

At least one observer watched the *Riot on Sunset Strip* (as it was celebrated in a hastily shot movie) and imagined he was witnessing the beginnings of a revolution. John Wilcox, never far from the counter-cultural frontline as the publisher of the peripatetic newspaper *Other Scenes*, reported: 'The opening shots were fired in California last month in a war that is going to engage America's attention increasingly in the next few years. It is going to be a civil war that may or may not be bloodless, but that will certainly revolutionise the lives and habits of everybody in America and, eventually, the world. That's assuming, of course, that the world doesn't blow up first.' What was this civil war – the struggle between communism and capitalism, or between black and white? Not according to Wilcox: 'It's the war between what Tim Leary calls the middle-aged whisky drinkers and the young people. And the young people, with plenty of time on their side, will inevitably win.' Wilcox displayed a faith in the inherent radicalism of youth that would be severely tested by the end of the decade.

## TO A MAN

Almost to a man – the noun is deliberate – the underground press in 1966 would have accepted Wilcox's view of America as their own. Drawing on the pioneering example of the *Village Voice* in New York, founded in 1955 as a vehicle for bohemian, leftist and experimental opinions in the arts and politics, the likes of the *Los Angeles Free Press*, the *Berkeley Barb*, the *Chicago Seed* and, in London, the *International Times* (for whom Wilcox had been reporting on Sunset Strip) acted as community newspapers. They effectively created their own readership by reporting on student demonstrations, draft protests, drugs busts, rock'n'roll shows and radical theatre. The melange was topped with listings of forthcoming events, and often seasoned with provocative ads for girlie bars, sexual encounter groups, and dope paraphernalia. Most of these papers declared at least some form of allegiance to the objectivity espoused (at least in theory) by the *Times* in London and New York. But no matter how serious their intentions, they consistently ignored the birth of one genuine revolution in Western society.

In fact, the underground press played its own shameful part in the process of repression. The vast majority of their reporters were men; women were allowed to type, make coffee, manage the office, the usual functions of the underclass. As historian David Bouchier wrote, 'In the memoirs of the period one finds, over and over again, the growing realisation that women in the radical sub-culture were being used by the men as secretaries, tea-makers and sexual partners, and their status in the supposedly egalitarian organisation was as low as it would be outside.' In many places, this discrimination was formalised when the papers listed their contributors: men would be credited in full, women by their Christian names alone, and usually in some cosy, diminutive form ('Jacki', 'Suzi', 'Toni') that emphasised their decorative value. If they were particularly attractive, they would be invited to pose,

nude or near enough, in adverts designed to boost subscriptions or advertising sales; if nobody in the office could be persuaded to shed their clothes
for the counter-culture, then the art editors would steal photos from men's
magazines instead. Barry Miles was an early contributor to the *East Village
Other*, and edited the *International Times* for several years. 'IT started out being
interested in personal politics, not traditional party politics,' he explains. 'In
fact, it was very much a reaction against politics. Unfortunately it was in the
spirit of the times that the underground papers should be edited and
controlled by men. Feminism was a foreign concept in Britain during the
1960s. It literally didn't exist.'

Under these conditions, it is scarcely surprising that the first flowerings
of the women's liberation movement – a revolution that solicited the involvement of more than half the world's population, with the aim of altering the
mindset of the male minority – should have passed beneath the radar of
the underground press. In October 1966, Betty Friedan, the middle-aged,
middle-class author of *The Feminine Mystique*, was elected the inaugural president of the alliance she had instituted four months earlier: the National
Organisation of Women (NOW). Its manifesto was, in retrospect, modest
enough, yet at the same time a radical assault upon the status quo. It was
founded, NOW insisted, on 'a fully equal partnership of the sexes', in which
men would no longer be expected to be the sole breadwinners, nor women
to bear the solitary brunt of housework and childcare. In return,
women could no longer be assured of being maintained financially by their
husbands: work was not only an opportunity, but their responsibility. Beyond
the home, there should be an end to sexual discrimination, just as the civil
rights groups had called for a halt to racial prejudice. 'You have to start a
national organisation to fight for women, like the civil rights movement for
blacks,' Friedan had been advised.

Sexual equality didn't figure in popular culture as anything but a joke.
Samantha, the witchy wife in the TV sitcom *Bewitched*, might have wielded
all the power in her typical suburban household, but her husband was a
brow-beaten wimp, not any kind of role model. On TV and in the movies,
women achieved their goals by a combination of 'feminine wiles', sexual
favours, and good old-fashioned nagging. On the radio, women (especially
white women) were either sultry nightclub singers or eager adolescents; and
in either case they were massively outnumbered by men. The entire pop
industry was controlled by men, for the profit of men, at the expense of

young women. Either they paid by buying records, posters and concert tickets, or else they joined the queues of hopefuls who waited outside the hotel bedrooms of (for example) the Beatles, in the hope of meeting 'one of the boys'.

Long before anyone coined the word 'groupie', pop stars claimed the right for consequence-free sex with any teenage girl in the vicinity. As this perk was usually extended to their entourage and visiting journalists, few detailed accounts have emerged. Pressmen on the Beatles' 1964 tour of Australia were indiscreet, however. 'John [Lennon] and Paul [McCartney], especially, rooted themselves silly,' reporter Jim Oram recalled. 'A seemingly endless and inexhaustible stream of Australian girls passed through their beds . . . John once told me, "We've got the best cover in the world. If a girl comes home after being out all night and breaks down under the old man's questioning and admits that she had spent the night with one of the Beatles, he tells her not to lie and goes up the road to kick the bum of the boy next door."' By the time any of the girls discovered they were pregnant, the Beatles were long gone. Not that the stars of the show appear to have gained any great pleasure from their privileges: 'They had become supremely indifferent to it all,' recalled DJ Bob Rogers, 'as women and girls continually prostrated themselves in their presence . . . I was convinced that they would all end up homosexuals, out of sheer boredom with conventional sex.'

Within a morally and mentally constrained capitalist society, sexual liberation represented a goal that was as urgent – for those who weren't facing any more immediate threat to life and limb – as any other form of political relief. Yet it would be a long time before sexual liberation and what was soon being called 'women's lib' coincided. The popular songs of 1966 may have suggested a daring moral revolution (witness the furore created when the Rolling Stones attempted to sing 'Let's Spend the Night Together' on US TV). But they contained no hint that freedom would benefit the female of the species. As John Lennon sang on the Beatles' *Rubber Soul* album, 'I'd rather see you dead little girl than to be with another man . . . You better run for your life if you can, little girl'. The diminutive didn't add to the level of respect.

This tone wasn't confined to the Beatles (for whom, to be fair, it alternated with starry-eyed romance, except in the altogether more cynical work of George Harrison). Misogyny was the stock-in-trade of Mick Jagger, as mouthpiece for the Rolling Stones. Their 1966 album *Aftermath* included the aggressively intolerant 'Out of Time', aimed at cutting down any woman who dared to think for herself, and the even more contemptuous 'Stupid Girl'. Jagger and his co-writer Keith Richards made it clear how they regarded any woman who didn't toe their line: 'She purrs like a pussycat/Then she turns round and hisses back/She's the sickest thing in this world/Look at that stupid girl'. Yet this paled alongside 'Under My Thumb', a song so rotten with male chauvinism that one would like to think it was a parody. While 'her eyes are just kept to herself', Jagger crowed that 'I can still look at someone else'. The inference was that the young woman in question had once owned an independent personality, but that Jagger had beaten it out of her: 'It's down to me . . . The way she talks when she's spoken to/Down to me, the change has come/She's under my thumb'. Jagger closed with an instruction to his audience: 'Say it's alright'. In 1966, no one, boy or girl, thought to question his logic. These were just the most blatant examples: pop was erected (I choose the verb carefully) on exactly the same (im)balance of power as society itself. Nor was pop the only contemporary forum in which casual sexism was a way of life. In 1964, SNCC spokesman Stokely Carmichael had been asked at a conference to make room for discussion of the position of women in the movement. He replied: 'The only position for women in SNCC is prone.' It was a cheap shot, delivered as playfully as John Lennon's line that 'women should be obscene but not heard'; and it's unjust that Carmichael's long history of 1960s activism should be erased by one sexist joke. But the fact that the line was still being repeated years later – and goading leftist women into standing up for their rights – reveals just how wounding and familiar it was.

## BLACK POWER

If the anti-Vietnam movement stalled during 1966, and feminism remained virtually invisible, the battle for civil rights intensified. The struggle moved forward on several fronts, sometimes harmonious, but just as often divided by suspicion or disagreement. The Revd Martin Luther King was the figurehead of the traditional wing of the crusade – dignified, defiant, peaceful under any provocation. Rivalling him for media leadership was Stokely Carmichael, charismatic, quick to anger and equally quick to inspire, thinking on his feet, creating principles as circumstances required. When Carmichael was elected chairman of SNCC in April 1966, the gulf between their position and King's widened. King still accepted – indeed, expected – help from sympathetic whites. Carmichael was prepared to accept their support, but not their orders. 'SNCC proposes', he announced, 'that it is now time for the black freedom movement to stop pandering to the fears and anxieties of the white middle class in the attempt to earn its "goodwill", and to return to the ghetto to organise these communities to control themselves.'

Before reaching the ghetto, SNCC still had to battle for survival in the South, with any assistance it could muster. In September 1962, James Meredith had been at the centre of a key symbolic battle, when as a black man he was refused admission by the University of Mississippi. Bob Dylan immortalised the moment in his song 'Oxford Town'. Four years on, Meredith courageously – some said suicidally – announced his intention to stage a march through the same state, to prove that the black man was now free to walk wherever he liked. He was answered on the second day by a volley of shots from the Ku Klux Klan. Eager to seize the moment, King, Carmichael and other leading campaigners agreed to join forces and continue Meredith's march; he recovered sufficiently by the end of the month to join them.

Every step of the way, Carmichael rallied the troops, and every day his rhetoric hardened. More conservative activists withdrew their support, but Carmichael was in his element. 'I'm not going to beg the white man for anything I deserve,' he told a crowd in Memphis. 'I'm gonna take it.' A week later, the march reached Greenwood, Mississippi, where almost exactly three years earlier Bob Dylan had performed at a voter-registration rally. This time the cameras were trained on Carmichael. He repeated a trick that he'd heard one of his aides pull earlier that day. 'What do we want?' he called out, and answered his own question: 'Black power.' When he asked again, the crowd took up the chant, and that was what white America heard on the evening news.

Black power: it was a slogan open to endless interpretation. Martin Luther King begged Carmichael to amend it to 'black equality', but he refused. Other groupings fled the impromptu coalition. Just as Malcolm X had polarised opinion between King's peaceful tactics and his own call for freedom 'by any means necessary', so Carmichael had dragged the movement to a crossroads from which there was no road home. The call for black power, according to historian Lawrence Lader, 'would destroy the unity of the civil rights era, terrify many whites, and lead to an increasing backlash of repression'. It would also inspire a generation of young urban blacks to break out of the ghettos and attempt their own American revolution.

In those ghettos, the temperature had barely cooled since the Watts riots of August 1965. That community erupted again in March 1966. 'These rebellions were violent uprisings in which African-Americans exchanged gunfire with police and army troops,' explained Stokely Carmichael, 'burned down stores and took from the stores those commodities that are rightfully ours – food and clothing that we never had. These rebellions are increasing in intensity and frequency every year. Now practically every major city has seen us rise to say: "We will seize the day or be killed in the attempt."'

The flames that signified America's racial divide were blowing inexorably towards Chicago. The city had been the traditional refuge for blacks escaping the South, straight up Highway 61 from Mississippi. It had emerged as the cauldron of electric rhythm and blues music, when the sounds of the Delta and the stale memory of slavery reached the Great Lakes of the North. Yet it was also widely regarded as the most segregated city in the nation. Moreover, it was controlled by one man: the omnipotent Mayor, Richard Daley. Via a vast network of bought and scared officials, Daley ruled Chicago like an emperor. The web of corruption ran deep: every neighbourhood owed its privileges to Daley's party machine, and nobody, black or white, dared to contradict him. It was as if Chicago existed as a separate city state deep in the American heartland, pledging only token allegiance to the government in Washington.

Free access to the vote was as restricted for African-Americans as it was in the South. Revd Martin Luther King intended to highlight this injustice when he chose Chicago as the location for his latest crusade in July 1966. But King's arrival stirred up other issues, notably the housing restrictions that kept the black community caged in one section of the city. Over a long weekend in mid-July, riots scarred the Chicago ghetto. The flames from Chicago soon caught the wind, and within days there were similar upheavals across the nation, in Brooklyn, Jacksonville and Cleveland. In September, the street battles switched to Atlanta. In the eyes of Stokely Carmichael, this was the terrain where the shape of the future would be determined. 'The inner city in most major urban areas is already predominantly Negro,' he noted in September, 'and with the white rush to suburbia, Negroes will in the next three decades control the heart of our great cities. These areas can either become concentration camps with a bitter and volatile population, whose only power is the power to destroy, or organised and powerful communities able to make constructive contributions to the total society.'

For many African-Americans, Chicago's inner city already felt like a concentration camp. Through July 1966, civil rights marchers staged demonstrations in the city, many of which were broken up by police. In August, Martin Luther King and Mayor Daley signed an agreement to end segregation in Chicago's housing department. But supporters of both sides greeted the deal as a sell-out. Even amongst the marchers, opinions were divided. On the streets of America's major cities, this was the season when civil rights gave way to black nationalism. Inevitably, Carmichael set the mood: 'We are not going to wait for white people to sanction black power,' he told a crowd in Berkeley that September. 'We're tired of waiting . . . This country knows what power is. It knows what black power is because it deprived black people of it for over 400 years.'

Just as California was the breeding ground of the white hippie counter-culture in 1966/67, so it also spawned the most concentrated array of black nationalist groups. More than thirty sprang up in the San Francisco area alone. Their exact political aims differed from group to group, but they shared the conviction that liberation was impossible in a white-controlled society. Working within the current electoral system was a pointless compromise. African-Americans had to build their own political structure – which is the point where schisms began. The spectrum of possibilities ran from reversing the slave trade and shipping America's black population back to Africa; through claiming 'colony' status from the United Nations, or demanding that America cede the Southern states as an entirely black independent nation; to concentrating on reclaiming communities from the white man, block by block, street by street, bullet by bullet.

The most potent symbol in black America in 1966 was the black panther. 'The nature of the panther is that he never attacks,' wrote Huey Newton, who that summer was still searching for an outlet for his frustrated radicalism in Oakland. 'But if anyone attacks him or backs him into a corner, the panther comes up to wipe the aggressor or that attacker out.' By the end of 1967, Newton would become synonymous with the latent menace of the panther. But the beast was uncaged two thousand miles away, in Lowndes County, Alabama. In August 1965, the struggle for voter registration had stumbled into a community where access to the ballot was locked tight. 'George Wallace was then head of the Alabama Democratic party,' recalled Stokely Carmichael. 'The Alabama Democratic party was racist. Its symbol at that time had a white rooster, a white cock, and the words, "White

Supremacy". So here it would be easy for us to tell our people, "Hey, look, this party is not for us. We need our own party."' After months of violence from white racists and state troopers, Carmichael's team of SNCC activists formed a party called the Lowndes County Freedom Organisation (LCFO). 'But the law stipulated that you had to have a symbol,' Carmichael explained. Enter the panther, supported by a jingle to remind Lowndes County's black voters of where their interests lay: 'Vote for the panther, then go home'. The results were dramatic: hundreds of black citizens braved the white back-lash to register, and by the end of the decade one of the LCFO's prime movers had become the county sheriff.

'A man needs a black panther on his side when he must endure . . . loss of job, eviction, starvation and sometimes death for political activity,' Carmichael wrote in August 1966. 'One of the tragedies of the struggle against racism is that up to now there has been no national organisation that could speak to the growing militancy of young black people in the urban ghetto.' He noted that 'in some places, such as Alabama, Los Angeles, New York, Philadelphia, and New Jersey, independent organising under the black panther symbol is in progress. The creation of a national "black panther party" must come about.' The question was who would own the symbol, and control the party.

For Max Stanford and the leadership of the Revolutionary Action Movement, ownership was already decided. In Harlem, where RAM had already supported the birth of Black Women Enraged, Stanford formed a Black Panther Party just a few days before Carmichael wrote his article. RAM also gave its blessing to Panther groupings in Los Angeles, San Francisco, Chicago and Detroit; the San Francisco group, led by Ken Freeman, was effectively the local RAM chapter under another name. Stanford envisaged the Panthers as a coalition of RAM and SNCC, which would lead the most militant wing of the civil rights movement into a new era of confrontation with the authorities. But, at the same time, the new organisations would remain inside the law: 'The purpose of the Black Panther Party', Stanford declared, 'was to exhaust the legal avenues of struggle within the system.'

In San Francisco, where Freeman's Black Panther Party of Northern California were recruiting members, a rival grouping reared its head. Having lost patience with the talk-don't-shoot philosophy of RAM, Huey Newton and Bobby Seale had been studying alternative ways to confront the authorities. Seale was working for the North Oakland Service Center community project, and Newton spent weeks in its law library familiarising himself with the citizen's rights. He had discovered that under California state law, it was legal to carry a firearm in public as long as it was in open view, and was not loaded. 'We were at the stage of testing ideas that would capture the imagination of the community,' he recalled. 'We began, as always, by checking around with the street brothers.' Through Oakland, Berkeley, Richmond and into San Francisco itself, Newton and Seale preached the gospel of armed resistance against the police. 'Wherever brothers gathered, we talked with them about their right to arm,' Newton explained. 'In general, they were interested but sceptical about the weapons idea. They could not see anyone walking around with a gun in full view. To recruit any sizeable number of street brothers, we would obviously have to do more than talk. We needed to give practical applications of our theory, show them that we were not afraid of weapons and not afraid of death.'

In August 1966, black activists equipped with walkie-talkies had been driving around the Los Angeles suburb of Watts, shadowing police cars, under the guise of the Negro Citizen Alert Patrol. Newton resolved to follow their example, with one crucial difference: their patrols would be armed. The name of their organisation would be the Black Panther Party For Self Defense.

In their respective autobiographies, *Revolutionary Suicide* (Newton), *Seize the Time* and *A Lonely Rage* (both Seale), neither man acknowledged that there were Black Panther groups in operation before their own was officially founded on 15 October 1966. Their existence – especially the rival unit led by Freeman – is left as an inexplicable mystery. Neither the name, nor the initial concept, of Newton and Seale's organisation was original. But the two men, especially Newton, shared one advantage that ensured their version of history would supplant all others: their masterful command of publicity, from the street to the global media stage.

Their first coup was to compose a blueprint for their revolution: a 10-Point Program that laid out What We Want and What We Believe. While some of their demands – for decent housing, employment, 'education that teaches us our true history' – could have been shared with any vaguely liberal group, others were more extreme. All black prisoners should be freed from jail; no black men should be forced to serve in the US Army; white America should pay reparations to the black community for the sin of slavery; finally, there should be a 'United Nations-sponsored plebiscite . . . held throughout the black colony', so that African-Americans could decide their own destiny, including presumably the right to secede from the rest of the nation.

Having listed their demands, Newton and Seale appointed themselves Minister of Defense and Chairman, respectively, of their two-man party. In the early weeks, every recruit – Richard Aoki, who donated their first guns; 15-year-old L'il Bobby Hutton – automatically joined the Panthers' cabinet. By November they were mounting their first police patrols; on 1 January 1967, they opened a headquarters office on what is now Martin Luther King Jr. Way in Oakland. They raised funds by buying copies of Chairman Mao's *Little Red Book* wholesale, and selling them on the University of California campus in Berkeley to students eager for some revolutionary credentials. Most importantly, in terms of their national impact, they imposed a strict uniform code: an impossibly hip combination of black beret, worn at a cocky angle, blue shirt, black leather jacket, black trousers and black shoes. With that single gesture, the Black Panther Party For Self Defense guaranteed its immortality as a symbol of rebellion.

One final element was required to cement the Black Panthers' place in history: a writer, chronicler, rabble-rouser, and provocateur who would become the most quoted and quotable figure in the black power struggle after the death of Malcolm X. His name was Eldridge Cleaver, and he had been sending regular articles from his jail cell to *Ramparts* magazine. His prose was flamboyant, strident, sometimes fantastic, always charismatic. Echoing novelist Norman Mailer, who had declared his intention to achieve 'nothing less than a revolution in the consciousness of our time', Cleaver declared that the African-American community was 'engaged in the deepest, the most fundamental revolution and reconstruction which men have ever been called upon to make in their lives, and which they absolutely cannot escape or avoid except at the peril of the very continued existence of human life on this planet'. He added an apocalyptic warning: 'The embryonic spirit of kamikaze, real and alive, grows every day in the black man's heart.' On 12 December 1966, Cleaver was paroled from prison into a journalist's post at *Ramparts*. Over the next year, he would lead the Panthers, and the counter-culture, into the heart of revolutionary suicide.

## LUXURIOUS EGO DEMONSTRATION

As Martin Luther King left Chicago, the best-selling black record in America was 'Blowin' in the Wind' by Stevie Wonder – the first Motown hit written by a white artist. Wonder's associate Lee Garrett recalled the reaction of many of the singer's friends: 'It was as if singing black music wasn't good enough for that bastard anymore; as if he would rather be white than one of them niggers; as if money could obviously buy everything and Stevie would betray the black people with what he was doing.' To LeRoi Jones, however, Wonder had translated Dylan's protest tune – emblematic of early 1960s civil rights rallies – from something 'abstract and luxury' into 'something that is actual in the world and is substantiated by the life of the man singing it'.

The Beatles evoked equally contradictory reactions. Jones dismissed them as a 'group of Myddle-class white boys who need a haircut and male hormones', who had been 'stealing music . . . stealing lives (energy)'. It was a common suspicion: white boys getting rich on the black man's music. Eldridge Cleaver added a lick to the riff: the Beatles 'were playing homosexual', which in Cleaver's psychological spectrum was little short of a synonym for white, anyway. But he had a more sophisticated theory to impart. 'The Beatles', he argued, were responsible for 'injecting Negritude by the ton into the whites'. They were 'soul by proxy, middlemen between the Mind and the Body'.

Black men, he suggested, personified 'the Body', and were thereby in closer communication with their biological roots than other Americans. Their music was 'Body-based', and 'the basic ingredient, the core, of the gaudy, cacophonous hymns with which the Beatles of Liverpool drive their hordes of Ultrafeminine [in other words, white upper-class] fans into catatonia and hysteria. For Beatle fans, having been alienated from their own Bodies so long and so deeply, the effect of these potent, erotic rhythms is electric'. It was a tangled logic, which at times (see Cleaver's essays in *Soul On Ice*) seemed to have no deeper function than justifying the writer's sexual desire for classy white women. But it also represented a sharp deviation from the customary rhetoric found in militant black writing of the 1960s: black music good; white music debased and inauthentic, and therefore bad.

Just as white radicals explored the limits of their political sensitivity through the lyrics of Bob Dylan, many of their black counterparts also recognised that the songwriter had tapped into a method of interpreting reality that ran deeper, if more obscurely, than the skeletal truths of the protest singers. LeRoi Jones was suspicious of the easy rebelliousness of rock's response to the Vietnam War, calling it 'a generalising in passionate luxurious ego demonstration'. He dubbed the Fugs, the Mothers of Invention and Bob Dylan as 'Freaks'. Their political stance was, he admitted, a 'superficial advance. The liberal cool protest. Viet. Oh Viet-Rock. Yeh. LBJ ain't no good. Yeh. But what, what? will happen . . .', and his sarcastic rant tailed off into a run of dollar signs. Their music was 'stealin' all from the niggers'; while 'white crooks is good and hates war, for dough. (Wins either way!)'

Yet Jones was a lone voice, amongst the most prominent black radicals, in not singling Dylan out from the pack. 'Hey, Bobby Dylan has the perfect line for you cats,' Stokely Carmichael told a white TV audience in Chicago; 'something is happening but you don't know what it is, do you, Mr Jones?' It was the hookline from 'Ballad of a Thin Man', the song at the heart of Dylan's August 1965 album, *Highway 61 Revisited*. Another song on that record, 'Like a Rolling Stone', has widely been heralded as signalling the moment when pop (ephemeral, trivial) mutated into rock (enduring, significant). But it was 'Ballad of a Thin Man' that captured the imagination of the men who were promising Black Power.

Songwriter and journalist Julius Lester, author of the deliciously titled *Look Out Whitey! Black Power's Gon' Get Your Mama!*, borrowed Dylan's lyrics to nail half-hearted white sympathisers: 'There is a class of whites who call themselves liberals, who will agree with anything a revolutionary may say up to the point of agreeing to what must be done to solve the problem. At that point he "puts his eyes in his pocket and his nose to the ground", as Bob Dylan so graphically described the phenomenon of consciously refusing to see. The white liberal is the Mr Jones who knows that something is happening and knows what it is and all he can do is become filled with despair.' Having neatly erased the negative from Dylan's original line, Lester concluded by borrowing from another of his songs: 'Everybody's saying they ain't gon' work on Maggie's farm no more'.

By far the most vivid interpretation of 'Ballad of a Thin Man' – a song which Dylan has steadfastly refused to explain, beyond oblique hints as to the identity of 'Mr Jones' – came from the Minister of Defense of the Black Panther Party. When Huey Newton and Bobby Seale were assembling the first issues of the party newspaper, Newton kept the first side of *Highway 61 Revisited* on permanent repeat, each replay climaxing in another rendition of Dylan's 'Ballad'.

'I could hear the melody to this record,' Seale recalled, 'I could hear the sound and the beat to it. But I really didn't hear the words.' So Newton explained the song to him, 'what the lyrics meant in the history of racism that has perpetuated itself in this world . . . Huey would say, "Listen, listen – man, do you hear what he is saying?" Huey had such insight into how racism existed, how racism had perpetuated itself.'

Each of Dylan's verses set up a scenario of dreamlike incomprehension, which he rammed home with the chorus line Carmichael had addressed to the great American public. One verse grabbed Newton's imagination – the one about 'the geek' who 'hands you a bone'. Seale complained again that it made no sense, so Newton interpreted the song for him, in a description so vivid that it is impossible to paraphrase; Seale's book *Seize the Time* carries the full text. After several pages, Seale attempted to summarise what he'd learned: 'Huey says that whites looked at blacks as geeks, as freaks. But what is so symbolic about it is that when the revolution starts, they'll call us geeks because we eat raw meat. But the geek turns around and hands Mr Jones a naked bone and says, "How do you like being a freak?" And Mr Jones says, "Oh my God, what the hell's goin' on?" And Bobby Dylan says, you don't know what's happening, do you, Mr Jones? And to hand him the naked bone was too much – was really too much.' As this account suggests, Newton hadn't so much explained the song as buried it. But the fact that he thought it was worthy of such concentrated effort was notable in itself.

Huey wasn't the only radical thinker paying close attention to what 'Bobby' Dylan was really saying. In New York City, radical student Alan 'A.J.' Weberman and his girlfriend Dana (no surname; it was the 1960s) were dropping acid, and discovering that Dylan was singing in code. 'Dylan was trying to get a political message onto AM radio,' Weberman explained later. 'The only way he could do this was to make his ideas as cryptic as possible. His language had to be something that straights wouldn't respond to – but that kids would find. I knew that Dylan had put the meanings there for people like me to find. So I decided to devote myself to explaining the Secret Language of Rock to the world.' Among Weberman's discoveries were that 'morning' and 'nightfall' were both translations of 'dope'; 'rain' equalled 'violence' (hence the Hard Rain that's a-gonna fall); and Maggie's Farm denoted the capitalist system. Stokely Carmichael wouldn't have argued with this interpretation; Dylan certainly would.

Back to Bobby Seale in Oakland: 'This song Bobby Dylan was singing became a very big part of that whole publishing operation of the Black Panther paper. And in the background, while we were putting this paper out, this record came up and I guess a number of papers were published, and many times we would play that record. Brother Stokely Carmichael also liked that record. This record became so related to us, even to the brothers who had held down most of the security for the set.

'These brothers would get halfway high, loaded on something, and they would sit down and play this record over and over and over, especially after they began to hear Huey P. Newton interpret that record. They'd be trying to relate an understanding about what was going on, because old Bobby did society a big favor when he made *that* particular sound. If there's any more he made that I don't understand, I'll just ask Huey P. Newton to interpret them for us and maybe we can get a hell of a lot more out of brother Bobby Dylan, because old Bobby, he did a good job on that set.'

Throughout the mid-to-late 1960s, radicals looked in vain to 'brother Bobby Dylan' for a conclusive statement against the Vietnam War. As Huey P. Newton and A.J. Weberman illustrated, Dylan spoke far more eloquently in his absence than he could ever have done as a political sloganeer.

## LATENT ANGER

Another coincidence of music and the black power struggle: new on the charts when Huey Newton and Bobby Seale formed the Black Panther Party was a James Brown record, 'Don't Be a Drop-Out'. In James Brown, LeRoi Jones heard 'a people and an energy, harnessed and not harnessed by America'. That energy came out in Brown's rhythms, which carved up the beat into ever more propulsive fragments, as if all the latent anger of his people had uncoiled like a tightly wound spring across the dancefloor. On stage, Brown acted out that same compulsive frenzy, his feet chattering as his throat let rip a succession of fearsome yelps. 'James Brown's screams, etc., are more "radical" than most jazz musicians sound,' Jones concluded.

'Don't Be a Drop-Out' was different, a throwback to the sound of Sam Cooke in the early 1960s, smoothed to appeal to the widest possible audience. Brown wanted nothing to impede the message: 'without an education, you might as well be dead'. Vice-President Hubert Humphrey, second in line in America's war machine, had established a commission to determine the causes for the unrest in the nation's black communities. The answer, it seemed, was education, or the lack of it: the rioters were skipping school, and the results were obvious. So Humphrey approached many of the highest profile black entertainers in America, and asked them to lend their support to his 'stay in school' campaign. James Brown rode up to Washington in his private Lear jet to discuss the problem with the Vice-President, then flew home and recorded 'Don't Be a Drop-Out'. Neither the song, nor the gesture, needed interpretation from Huey Newton. But Brown's sound was so black, his rhythms so righteous, that none of the black power activists criticised him for consorting with the enemy.

Nor did Otis Redding suffer criticism when he started recording Beatles and Rolling Stones songs, or revealed that he was tempted to cut Bob Dylan's 'Just Like a Woman'. Nobody gave him the same treatment as Stevie Wonder, maybe because they knew that the anodyne quotes he gave the white press were cancelled out by the altogether more confrontational interviews he was starting to give to black journals such as the Nation of Islam's *Muhammad Speaks*. They were, noted LeRoi Jones approvingly, 'more "radical", Blacker, than many of the new [jazz] musicians'.

Like James Brown, Otis Redding would catch hold of a verbal riff and run it down, play with it, scream it out over and over until the words were lost in the moment. Painting 'SOUL' loud and proud on his door, Stokely Carmichael employed the same technique in the speeches with which he launched black power: 'Only thing gonna stop us today is a bullet, and we spittin' 'em back, and we spittin' 'em back.' And again: 'The next thing comes the marines, comes the marines. And if we're talking seriously, we get prepared for the marines. Now if some black people do not think that the white man is gonna wipe us out completely, then it won't be no harm being prepared just in case he decides to do it, just in case he decides to do it. So there'll be no harm in preparing ourselves for the marines.'

Carmichael was there in late 1966 when two traditions of American improvisation lent their services to SNCC at the Fillmore West in San Francisco. In November, the blues-flavoured soul of James Cotton and Johnny Talbot lined up with the Quicksilver Messenger Service and the Grateful Dead, two bands whose speciality was working up R&B hits – 'Dancing in the Street', 'Turn On Your Love Light' – and launching off them into extended space. Two weeks later, it was the turn of jazz musicians Archie Shepp, Jackie McLean and Marion Brown. Brown and Shepp were veterans of the black liberation struggle (and of John Coltrane's epic 1965 album, *Ascension*), but it was McLean's first venture into the fire. Noticeably absent from the SNCC benefits, however, were soul artists, such as James Brown, Otis Redding, or the Impressions.

Across the city in Berkeley, student protests were rekindling the anger of the Free Speech Movement two years earlier. Mary Hughes participated in the demonstrations, which combined anger at the university authorities with opposition to the Vietnam War: 'The polarisation is much more acute. The students are much more radical, in feeling if not in political point of view . . . for the most part we are flipping the bird to the surrealistic construct in which we live. You know you're going to get the ice-pick and soon: so you retaliate first with a strike, and when that loses (because it's old stuff, it can scare, but not for long, it's old stuff and they understand it), you retaliate with something they don't understand, you exit en masse singing "Yellow Submarine".' She described how the strike ended with the students roaring out chorus after chorus of the Beatles' recent hit single, a nonsense song intended for children. It signified, she explained, 'that we will continue to blow their minds'.

Culturally empty, 'Yellow Submarine' became a kind of Rorschach test for radical minds. Kids and sports fans had already borrowed its tune for their own chants. Now students at the London School of Economics happily rewrote its chorus into a boast: 'We all live in a red LSE'. On picket lines in Britain, striking workers sang: 'We all live on bread and margarine'. The folk magazine *Sing Out!* printed an anti-Vietnam War interpretation, with the refrain: 'We're all dropping jellied gasoline [napalm]'. At a Mobe protest in San Francisco, reported *Time* magazine, 'a yellow papier-mâché submarine cruised through the crowd, symbol of the psychedelic set's desire for escape'. This was an interpretation with which LeRoi Jones might have agreed. He viewed the song as an arrogant cultural boast of whitey's distance from the real world: 'The Beatles can sing "We all live in a yellow submarine" because that is literally where they, and all their people (would like to) live. In the solipsistic pink and white nightmare of "the special life", the artifactbeings worshiping their smells frozen in glass and gaudy jewellery.' In another, less flamboyant but equally outraged moment, Jones gave the Beatles' ditty a strictly political reading: '"We all live in a yellow submarine", with all their fiends [sic], etc., the exclusive white . . . exclusive meaning isolated from the rest of humanity . . . in the yellow submarine, which shoots nuclear weapons. In the yellow submarine. Chances are it will never come up.' But in the shortlived California paper *P.O. Frisco*, an anonymous reviewer flipped the craft over, 180 degrees: 'The Yellow Submarine may suggest, in the context of the Beatles' anti-Vietnam War statement in Tokyo this year, that the society over which Old Glory floats is as isolated and morally irresponsible as a nuclear submarine.'

When Jones and *P.O. Frisco* highlighted the isolation of the Beatles' submarine, it was an uncanny coincidence. The group chose the month in which that song was released to withdraw from public performances. In future, their only engagement with their audience would be refracted through the media. In June, when they voiced their opposition to the war as they had done a year earlier in America, they were threatened with death by right-wing Japanese religious fundamentalists, upset that they were performing in a 'sacred' hall, the Budo Kan in Tokyo. They flew on to the Philippines, where they inadvertently snubbed the dictator Marcos, and narrowly escaped a beating by his riot police. Then John Lennon's 'we're bigger than Jesus' interview was published in the US, and the group were subjected to a campaign of record-burning and more threats to their lives, this time by fundamentalists of the Christian faith – from the same Southern states that had been killing voter registration activists since the start of the decade. The Beatles flew in to Chicago on 12 August, to find a city tense between riots, anxiously awaiting the results of the stand-off between Mayor Daley and Martin Luther King. Fortunately, perhaps, the American press was too preoccupied with Lennon's 'blasphemy' to ask him where he stood on the issue of segregated housing.

So the Beatles retreated into their own lives, and when hedonism began to pall, they searched for solace in spirituality. Meanwhile, Bob Dylan was ensconced in his home in upstate New York, recovering from the after-effects of a motorbike crash. The two most potent musical icons of the decade had withdrawn from the fray; and as 1967 began, their audience followed them into the diversions of drugs, dressing up and discovering God in a blade of grass. While they played, the temperature outside the yellow submarine inexorably rose, and the fuse that held back a global uprising grew shorter, month after month. The summer of love was nigh; so too was the summer of the fire next time.

# CHAPTER 2: 1967

## SPIRITUAL REVOLUTION

Down Haight Street they came, past the Free Medical Clinic and the Straight Theater, the I-Thou coffee shop and the studio where poster artist Stanley Mouse was silk-screening the new shape of San Francisco. Then across the park to the crest which marked the edge of the running track; and there, below, banners waving like the standards of a medieval army comprised of a hundred families united in the cause of justice, were their sisters and brothers – 'thousands of them', so Tom Wolfe recounted, 'in high costume, ringing bells, chanting, dancing ecstatically, blowing their minds one way and another'.

It was the Polo Field in San Francisco's Golden Gate Park, the wafer-shaped playground that leads from Haight Ashbury to the Pacific Ocean, which played host to the event variously described as the Gathering of the Tribes or the Human Be-In, on 14 January 1967. On the posters that covered the Haight like bulletins from the Chinese cultural revolution, people were asked to 'bring food to share, bring flowers, bears, costumes, feathers, bells, cymbals, and flags'. Entertainment was promised in the shape of 'all SF rock groups': the Grateful Dead, Jefferson Airplane, Quicksilver Messenger Service, and Big Brother & the Holding Company. There would be appearances from beat poets Allen Ginsberg and Gary Snyder, acid guru Timothy Leary – and Vietnam Day Committee activist Jerry Rubin.

An announcement in the *Berkeley Barb* sounded the call in apocalyptic tones. 'Materialism and empire have thwarted and veiled the spiritual foundations of man and woman and their relations in America,' it began with a prophet's voice. 'Profit and Desire are one-tenth of the divinity of man. We declare the necessity of spiritual exercise, experience and celebration for the proper education of man.' Spirituality, extending the bounds of experience: it was the ideal of the hippie movement. But then came a sharp left turn into the demands of the (every)day: 'We declare and prophesy the end of wars, police states, economic oppression and racism.' And then the vision: 'When the Berkeley political activists and the love generation of the Haight Ashbury and thousands of young men and women from every state in the nation embrace at the Gathering of the Tribes for a Human Be-In at the Polo Field in Golden Gate Park the spiritual revolution will be manifest and proven. In unity we shall shower the country with waves of ecstasy and purification. Fear will be washed away; ignorance will be exposed to sunlight; profits and empire will lie drying on deserted beaches; violence will be submerged and transmuted in rhythm and dancing; racism will be purified by the salt of forgiveness.'

The tribes were eager to gather: there were '20,000 blown minds together', according to counter-culture scribe John Wilcock, assembled 'for nothing more than love and joy, to celebrate our oneness'. Yet there was a more ominous scattering of tribal opinion, between those who dreamed of a 'spiritual revolution' that could cloak their hedonistic identity in oneness, and those for whom the concept of spirituality represented an evasion of reality. 'Racism will be purified by the salt of forgiveness': a latter-day Jesus could have asked for nothing more. But could this salt heal the wound of Vietnam?

Rock Scully, the manager of the Grateful Dead, was involved with planning the Gathering. He resented the fact that Berkeley radicals 'kept busting into our meetings'. In contrast with the 'rabble-rousing' of Jerry Rubin and his associates, Scully and the Dead preferred a more passive approach to the repressive society: 'Let's make it fun, not misery. We've won already, we don't have to confront them. Why go on their trip? Why battle? Dissolve. Disappear. Let them be the ones looking for a fight.'

But the fight continued, round the bay in Oakland, and across the ocean in Vietnam. 'Why battle?' echoed Allen Ginsberg's hopeful declaration the previous year that the war was already over. In the Polo Field, however, Ginsberg and Gary Snyder chanted a mantra of political optimism: 'Peace in America, Peace in Vietnam, Peace in Mississippi, Peace in Saigon'. As John Wilcock noted, 'The crowd reacted mildly to the political haranguing and it was difficult to detect their mood on this.' The most blatant statement of physical reality came from Berkeley activist Jerry Rubin, who launched into his standard assault on the war. 'The words didn't matter,' Grateful

Dead guitarist Jerry Garcia complained. 'It was that angry tone. It scared me, it made me sick to my stomach.' His distaste was shared by much of the crowd, who didn't welcome Rubin interrupting their acid dream. They were more responsive to Timothy Leary, who provided a slogan for an era with a brief speech: 'Turn on to the scene. Tune in to what is happening. And drop out – of high school, college, grad school, junior executive, senior executive – and follow me, the hard way.' This allusion to Christ was conscious and deliberate. But the inference was that Leary's disciples should not only drop out of high school: they should abandon the hassle of political involvement as well.

'There was a difference between Berkeley and us,' says Paul Kantner of Jefferson Airplane, who alongside the Dead were the most prominent San Francisco band of the era. 'We didn't give a shit about politics. We created our own special space and we figured out a way to do things differently. We felt that we didn't have any responsibilities, except maybe to provide a good example on a personal level, and get along with everyone we met. So people in Berkeley were disdainful of us in San Francisco. We would support them, but we didn't want to live the way they did. We weren't prepared to put up with any bullshit, or accept that there was only one way to live your life. We wanted the freedom to make our own choices.'

This gulf was epitomised by the Gathering of the Tribes. 'It was badly organised,' said *Berkeley Barb* publisher Max Scherr. 'There was great potential here for protest. If I could have got to a microphone, I would have said what was in my heart. The organisers implied that they were against the war but that they didn't want to bother people about it on this occasion.' As John Wilcock concluded, 'The dichotomy over political action and dropping out seems to have been the major issue raised by the first Human Be-In. Who controls this new, genuine grassroots movement? Nobody yet. And yet what a potent force sits there waiting for direction. Who will get hold of it?'

It was a question that remained unanswered throughout 1967. Mythology has immortalised the year as the 12-month-long Summer of Love, a halcyon era of *Sgt. Pepper*, flower power, love, peace, beads, tuning in, dropping out, and especially turning on. If you invite acid into your brain, George Harrison reminisced happily, 'You suddenly experience the soul as free and unbound . . . LSD gave me the experience of "I am not this body. I am pure energy soaring about everywhere."' Yet the energy was poised precariously on the edge of an inferno. Approached in a negative frame of mind, the acid trip could rapidly descend into a nightmare. No wonder that psychedelic explorers were so unwilling to confront the evils of the planet, when the wonders of the universe were easier to reach, and infinitely preferable to experience.

Contemplating the war, Paul McCartney tortured himself about his duty to the world: 'What could we do? Well, I suppose that, at a Royal Command Performance, we could announce a number and then tell people exactly what we thought about Vietnam. But then we'd be thought to be lunatics.' It was a risk that British intellectuals and authors, such as Iris Murdoch, Alan Sillitoe and J.B. Priestley, had already taken. As McCartney agonised, these establishment figures sent a telegram to the Prime Minister, Harold Wilson, asking his government to 'dissociate itself publicly from American bombing of the civilian population of Hanoi and communicate its condemnation to the American government'. No figures from the rock'n'roll community signed the telegram.

## CULTURAL REVOLUTION

It was left to the *New York Times*, rarely a harbinger of rebellion, to reveal to the outside world the 'collateral damage' from US bombing raids. Defence officials replied that 'it is impossible to avoid all damage to civilian areas', especially when the enemy insisted on housing its citizens within range of legitimate military targets. Meanwhile, the Pentagon promised that the North Vietnamese were about to receive a 'knockout blow'. US troop numbers continued to rise: there were now 400,000 young Americans stationed in Vietnam, with a further 75,000 readied for departure. In the time-honoured tradition of military propaganda, the defence department primed the media with anecdotes designed to paint American actions in a rosy light. This tale from *Time* magazine was typical: 'When they are not patrolling, the Marines help the villagers and try to get to know them better. In Phuoc Trach, the Marines have even taught their Vietnamese friends how to dance to rock'n'roll. Says Lance Corporal Leroy Lomax, a 20-year-old Negro from California: "They go, man, they go".'

Had Leroy Lomax not gone, man, gone, he could have participated in another conflict, for the militant black soul of the San Francisco bay. In the early weeks of 1967, the Revolutionary Action Movement urged the African-American community to prepare for a 90-day war of liberation. Slogans thundered from their West Coast headquarters, where the Black Panther

Party of Northern California carried RAM's manifesto onto the streets: 'America is the Black Man's Battleground'; 'Black Power' (concise, if not original); 'Unite or Perish'. The last of these was ironic, given the mutual distrust that crackled between RAM's Panthers and the Black Panther Party For Self Defense in Oakland. The two camps staged an uneasy summit meeting near the Fillmore ballroom in February 1967, watched by *Ramparts* journalist Eldridge Cleaver. 'I spun around in my seat,' the besotted Cleaver recalled of his first exposure to Huey Newton's troops, 'and saw the most beautiful sight I had ever seen: four Black men wearing black berets, powder blue shirts, black leather jackets, black trousers, shiny black shoes – and each with a gun!' Weapons clearly counted for more than words: when the two Panther parties collaborated later that month, escorting Malcolm X's widow from San Francisco airport, both carried guns, but only Newton's posse had bothered to pack ammunition. This detracted heavily from the Northern Californians' macho stance, at least in the eyes of Newton and Cleaver, who pledged his allegiance to the Oakland Panthers thereafter. 'I see now that Eldridge was not dedicated to helping Black people,' Newton commented perceptively later, 'but was in search of a strong manhood symbol.' Not that Newton's men were averse to demonstrating their hormonal power over RAM's troops, who had been dubbed 'Paper Panthers' by Huey's right-hand-man, David Hilliard. 'A few weeks after this we went to San Francisco,' Newton recalled, 'where the Paper Panthers were having a fish fry, and issued an ultimatum: they could merge with us or be annihilated. When they said they would do none of these things, we waded in. I took on one of them and hooked him in the jaw. It was a short battle, ending a few moments later when somebody fired a shot in the air and people scattered. After that, the Paper Panthers changed their name.'

On the streets of Oakland, the apparently fearless Newton had already stared down armed policemen with an arsenal of cocked weapons, instinctive bravado and instantaneous recall of the California penal code. The Panthers dubbed his surprise tactics 'shock-a-buku' – 'keeping the enemy off balance through sudden and unexpected maneuvers that push him towards his opponent's position'. Perhaps RAM had been subjected to the same slick moves, as their revolutionary programme that spring comprised armed self-defence in local communities (Newton's innovation), coupled with a policy of fermenting uprisings in ghettoes and colleges. Newton complained that RAM was 'good for nothing but running a mimeograph machine and fat-mouthing'. One of the RAM position papers that infuriated him laid out the thinking behind the organisation's plan for toppling white American culture: 'The purpose of a Black Cultural Revolution would be to destroy the conditional white oppressive mores, attitudes, ways, customs, philosophies, habits, etc., which the oppressor has taught and trained us to have. This means, on a mass scale, a new revolutionary culture.'

This chimed with the prevailing mood among the black revolutionary left. In Newark, New Jersey, LeRoi Jones was still pondering a formula for the relationship between art and revolution. 'The fact of music was the black poet's basis for creation,' he explained later. 'And those of us in the Black Arts movement were drenched in black music and wanted our poetry to *be* black music. Not only that, we wanted that poetry to be armed with the spirit of black revolution. An art that could not commit itself to black revolution was not relevant to us.' Jones drew a clear line between black art and its creator: John Coltrane remained his musical touchstone throughout the decade, despite the fact that the saxophonist rarely expressed any definite opinions on political matters.

Jones would never have joined Newton, Cleaver and Stokely Carmichael in greeting Bob Dylan as a guide to the ills of white America. 'A lot of black people are schizophrenic,' Jones complained in 1967. 'They'll be talking about black politics, getting a nation, even nationalists – straight-out nationalists – and really all the time they will be connected up with white culture. They will still be digging Mozart more than James Brown. If all of that shit – Mozart, Beethoven, all of it – if it has to be burned now for the liberation of our people, it should be burned up the next minute. Frankly, I wouldn't feel I was losing anything.' Instead, Jones declared, 'You have to be for the resurrection of new black forms and the resurrection of old forms, traditional forms, that will instruct you in what you're doing and give you a connection with your past.'

It was a conundrum, 'the resurrection of new black forms' – how could you revive what had never existed? But that paradox was flourishing in 1967, via one of the most enigmatic figures in the history of African-American culture. He was born Ron McKinley Everett in 1941, and had stood alongside future adversary Huey Newton in the Afro-American Association. After a spell in Watts, which overlapped with the 1965 riots, he returned to San Francisco as the head of a nationalist group called US – not short for United States, of course, or for United Slaves, as was popularly believed, but a proud declaration that it was US against THEM. He was no longer Ron Everett, but Ron Karenga – Maulana Ron Karenga, to be precise, the title awarding him the status of 'master teacher' in the Swahili language, while his new surname translated as 'the original nationalist'. 'Swahili is a pan-African language,' he explained. 'We don't know what tribe we came from, so we chose an African language that is non-tribal.' On this basis Karenga formulated US's entire philosophy in the Swahili tongue.

Karenga's most enduring contribution to American life was the invention of an exclusively black holiday season: Kwanzaa. It ran from Boxing Day to New Year in the Christian calendar, but was, so Karenga insisted, a revival of a traditional African harvest festival. Unknown outside the US, Kwanzaa is now celebrated by around 20 million people every year, including President George W. Bush, who has regularly sent out Kwanzaa greetings to his fellow citizens.

Not content with leading a militant nationalist party, and creating his own version of Christmas, Karenga intended to establish himself as an African-American philosopher. 'There must be a cultural revolution before the violent revolution,' he announced. 'The cultural revolution gives identity, purpose and direction.' He declared that all existing judgements of the arts, based on Western tradition, were invalid when it came to the work of black men, who would create their own revolutionary methods of judging the beauty of black art. 'All art must reflect the Black Revolution,' he added, 'and any art that does not discuss and contribute to the revolution is invalid, no matter how many lines and spaces are produced in proportion and symmetry, and no matter how many sounds are boxed in or blown out and called music.' Black art 'must commit us to a future that is ours . . . It must not teach us resignation.'

The prime casualty of Karenga's philosophy was the central pillar of black popular music: the blues. 'We say the blues are invalid,' he pronounced, 'for they teach resignation, in a word acceptance of reality – and we have come to change reality.' In the late spring of 1967, Karenga had the opportunity to debate this point with LeRoi Jones – author of the pioneering musical critique *Blues People*. For Jones, blues represented 'black reality' – a quality that had been stolen and besmirched by white R&B groups who understood the structure but not the cultural meaning of the music. 'The Rolling Stones come on like English crooks,' he had complained in 1965. In his eyes, jazz lost its purity and purpose when it ignored the tradition of the blues:

'Jazz, no matter the intellectual basis, [if it is] moved too far away from its most meaningful sources and resources, is weakened and becomes, little by little, just the music of another emerging middle class.'

Karenga visited Jones' cultural home, the Spirit House in Newark, accompanied by two bodyguards. He was, Jones recalled, 'short, stocky, bald . . . this dynamic little fat man', with 'little cheap nondescript shoes' and 'bargain basement overcoat and sale socks'. Then he pulled himself up short and realised that 'I was some kind of elitist, trained that way by my long-term residence in and worship of the white elitist culture and aesthetic'. After that, Jones was a pushover: '[Karenga] was quick-witted, sharp-tongued, with a kind of amusing irony to his putdowns'. Jones was impressed by the military efficiency and discipline with which Karenga ran his US organisation; by the karate training given to all its members; by the African dashikis they sported, and the Swahili greetings they swapped; by Karenga's control over the African names which his disciples adopted, their living arrangements, even the names of their children.

The Africanisation of black America in the late 1960s coincided with the increasing influence of the Nation of Islam, the so-called 'Black Muslims'. Claiming or reclaiming an ethnic heritage became one simple way of enacting a cultural revolution. In 1967, LeRoi Jones was given the Muslim name of Ameer Barakat (or 'blessed prince'). Within a few weeks, Karenga 'Swahilised' Jones' name to Amiri Baraka, as he has been known ever since.

In his new guise, Jones/Baraka began to search for Africanism as a vital constituent of African-American music. He found a primal source in Sun Ra who, he claimed, 'wants a music that will reflect a life-sense lost in the West, a music full of Africa'. Convinced he was witnessing the authentic voice of African tradition, Jones concluded: 'a totally different epoch is conjured'. Sun Ra might not have agreed: he was more concerned with other and outer worlds, as titles such as 'Atlantis', 'Mu' and 'Next Stop Mars' suggested.

The black nationalist jazzman Horace Tapscott acknowledged Africa more overtly with the formation of his Pan-Afrikan Peoples Arkestra. Chicago saxophonist Roscoe Mitchell launched his solo career in 1966 with the album *Sound*, on which he layered instruments in patterns that approximated the tuning of drums in traditional West African music. But the most powerful influence of Africa in the mid-1960s was displayed by John Coltrane. Running alongside his fascination with Eastern spirituality, it coloured everything from 1961's *Africa/Brass*, through *Ole Coltrane* the same year (the album that included

'Dahomey Dance'), to 1965's *Kulu Se Mama*, built around an Afro-Creole chant by percussionist Juno Lewis. Quizzed in August 1966 about whether he and his peers were looking to Africa and Asia for their inspiration, Coltrane responded carefully: 'I think so, I think they look all over. And inside.' Pushed further, he revealed: 'I intend to make a trip to Africa to gather whatever I can find, particularly the musical sources.' Asked why, he resumed his naturally vague tone: 'It's a thing of the times.'

Coltrane never made it to Africa; he died of cancer in July 1967, his passing almost unnoticed by the mainstream American media. LeRoi Jones was driven to inevitable fury: 'In the halls of his government when John Coltrane died there was no memorial. They have never even heard of him. How can they judge us? They do not even understand HOW we feel!' Coltrane preferred to let his music voice his anger or pain. As saxophonist and SNCC sympathiser Marion Brown noted early in 1967, 'great revolutionaries don't raise their voices'. But as the year progressed, the black community found it impossible to restrain the volume of its anger.

## VIOLENCE AND RHETORIC

The promise, or threat, of cultural revolution hung over much of the world in spring 1967. Beyond the coincidence of time, there were perhaps few links between the post-revolutionary upheavals in Communist China, the challenges of post-independent Africa, the influx of Western influences into totalitarian Eastern Europe, the battle for the overthrow of the South Vietnamese government and its America patrons, and black America's search for liberation. Yet as global communications improved, each of these revolutionary struggles began to inform and alter the course of its contemporaries. Collectively, they congealed into an all-purpose, ideologically confused thrust of violence and rhetoric, from which passionate observers – such as Ron Karenga – could cherry-pick slogans and tactics at will.

The idealised Africa from which Karenga had borrowed the language of his cultural revolution – Swahili, never spoken by the millions of West African slaves kidnapped to North America – scarcely matched the political reality. From 1957 onwards, the colonial continent had slowly and painfully been liberating itself from its European masters, as Belgium, France and Great Britain realised that they could no longer contain the urge for self-determination. In the British colony of the Gold Coast, Kwame Nkrumah became the first hero of the African revolution by emerging from prison to become the inaugural president of an independent Ghana. A year later, in 1958, Sekou Toure called the bluff of French leader Charles de Gaulle, declared that he would rather see 'independence in poverty than riches in slavery', and led Guinea into a financially precarious state of independence.

In good faith and bad, Toure became a worldwide symbol of African liberation. He was at the forefront of the crusade for an end to colonialism and for African unity. But he controlled Guinea with an increasingly heavy hand and paranoid spirit, continually claiming to recognise the first stirrings of French-inspired counter-revolutionary plots, which inevitably led to show trials and executions. These flaws were readily overlooked by anyone desperate to see Guinea as an emblem of Pan-African pride. Toure declared that Guinea should throw off the decadent trappings of Western art, with all its imperialist connotations. The nation of Mali, joined with Ghana and Guinea in a loose West African federation after its own independence in 1960, followed Toure's example. The 'authentic' African culture that resulted from these politically inspired policies came to represent the ultimate goal of the black cultural nationalists in the US.

Africa was not their only source of inspiration; they also borrowed heavily from a starry-eyed interpretation of the Marxist philosophy that, theoreti- cally at least, governed half of Europe, and much of Asia. Yet Communism was hardly the global monolith that Americans feared. During 1967, rela- tions between China and the Soviet Union were broken off, as China reeled under the internal assault of its own cultural revolution. Mao's Red Guard, a fanatical, mostly teenage elite, interpreted his teachings to mean that all the nation's reactionary forces should be overthrown and scattered. This included not just anyone who was suspected of trying to engineer the toppling of Mao, but also such running dogs of imperialism as industrial workers in China's cities, bureaucrats, professionals such as teachers and doctors, and indeed the country's president, Liu Shao-chi. A battle that was originally enacted via giant wall posters in Peking disintegrated into open warfare in the streets. The army's loyalty was divided, and for several weeks it appeared as if Mao himself was in danger of being ousted. 'We don't know what they mean,' admitted US Secretary of State Dean Rusk when he was asked about the latest reports from Peking, 'but that doesn't embarrass us, because Mao Tse-tung obviously doesn't know what they mean either.' Rusk greeted turmoil in China favourably, as it appeared to lessen the chances that Mao's army would lend active support to the forces of North Vietnam.

Across the Communist world, in Eastern Europe, cultural revolution was more subtle, though equally confusing. Unable to prevent the imperialist strains of the West from infiltrating the Iron Curtain, the Soviet-backed regimes of Czechoslovakia, the German Democratic Republic (East Germany) and Hungary attempted to pull off the precarious trick of offering freedom to their citizens while controlling the extent to which that freedom was exercised. The treatment of popular music epitomised their dilemma. In Poland, visits from British bands such as the Animals and the Hollies were permitted in 1966, until the authorities decided that they encouraged concert-goers to vent their newly liberated emotions in scuffles with police. Preconceptions were rife on both sides. Hollies vocalist Graham Nash was amazed to turn on the radio in his Warsaw hotel room and hear his group's latest record, just as he might have done in London. But a few minutes later, Nash heard a more disturbing sound. 'I looked out the window, and there was all this shooting going on,' he remembers. 'It was a battle, happening outside the hotel. I thought, "Holy shit, what the fuck is going on here?" I thought war had broken out between the East and the West.' He rushed off to find out if they were in immediate danger – and discovered that a Hollywood film crew was shooting location footage for the World War Two drama *The Night of the Generals*, starring Peter O'Toole.

No further tours by UK bands were permitted for several months, but the order was relaxed by spring 1967 – just in time for the Rolling Stones to schedule a performance in Warsaw on 13 April. This was not, perhaps, one of the more enlightened political decisions of the era. In non-Communist Switzerland, the Stones' appearance provoked a riot by more than 12,000 Zurich fans, who ripped up seats until police armed with clubs fought them back. A day earlier, in Warsaw, similar scenes had ensued when teenagers without tickets stormed the police barriers erected outside the Palace of Culture. The cops replied with tear gas, dogs and water cannons. Meanwhile, those fans with a legitimate pass to enter the Palace apparently witnessed an example of democracy in action, courtesy of guitarist Keith Richards. He realised early in the show that the front few rows were filled by members of the ruling Communist Party and their families: 'They're sitting there with their diamonds and their pearls and their fingers in their ears. About three numbers [in], I say, "Fucking stop playing, Charlie. You fucking lot, get out and let those bastards in the back down front."' It was to be the Stones' last invitation to play behind the Iron Curtain.

No Communist bloc country endured a more ambiguous relationship with Western culture than Czechoslovakia. Visits by Western pop bands were encouraged in 1965, and when British R&B group Manfred Mann played two shows in Prague that October, they inspired the formation of dozens of soundalike outfits. The authorities did little to halt the import of records from the West, allowing Czech musicians to remain abreast of contemporary developments in a way not possible elsewhere in the Soviet bloc. By 1967, bands such as Olympic and the Primitives were experimenting with psychedelia, tackling songs by the likes of Pink Floyd, the Fugs, Frank Zappa and Jimi Hendrix. Yet at the same time the broadcasting output of the national radio station was strictly controlled, and Western pop hits could only be heard if they were translated into the Czech or Slovak languages. 'The main problem with American lyrics is that they are too gushy for our listeners,' one of the state-sanctioned lyricists complained. 'Under our system we are conditioned to be less sentimental.' So it was that Nancy Sinatra's 1966 hit 'These Boots are Made for Walking', a playful song about sexual revenge, was rendered into Czech as a cry of despair: 'These boots trample on everything beautiful . . . with these boots I stamp out our love . . . I am stamping on my own happiness'.

In Greece, the spring of 1967 ushered in its own despair; 28 May was the date set for democratic elections in this troubled monarchy, which was poised precariously on the margins of Europe and the Communist bloc. The most likely victors were the Centre Union party led by former prime minister George Papandreou. He had been removed from power almost two years earlier by King Constantine, who objected to his liberal policies. Both the King and his army now feared that Papandreou might regain power in a coalition with the Greek Communist Party. Under the guise of saving the nation from a Marxist takeover, 300 junior army officers seized power in a military coup on 28 April. The junta's leader, Colonel George Papadopoulos, ordered the arrest of thousands of alleged Communists, who were herded into detention centres and sports arenas. Many were tortured; some were executed without trial.

The military's immediate target was the degenerate state of Greek culture, which had, they claimed, fallen prey to the worst excesses of Western materialism. Under the new regime, Greek citizens were ordered to dress soberly: miniskirts were banned; any males caught with indecently long hair were forcibly shorn. All young Greeks were required to attend church. All criticism of the regime was forbidden. All newspapers and radio reports were subject to fierce censorship. Papadopoulos applied a medical metaphor: 'If the patient is not strapped to the table, the surgeon cannot perform a successful operation.'

The new Puritanism required radio stations to broadcast traditional Greek music, not provocative Western rock. Also banned, the junta proclaimed, were any live performances that 'disturb public order, promote subversive theories, discredit the Greek nation or tourism, offend the Christian faith, the King or the government, undermine the people's social traditions, or harm the aesthetic advance of the people – particularly youth'. Sadly for the Greek economy, tourism had already been 'discredited' by the coup, and by warnings that any visitor to the country who behaved or dressed indecently was liable to arrest and deportation.

Into the midst of this political ferment, in July 1967, flew the Beatles. John Lennon had recently become close to a Greek electronics expert named Alexis Mardas. Aware that the Beatles wished to purchase an uninhabited island that they could customise into a communal home and artistic base, Mardas suggested that they should investigate the possibilities of Greece. One of the group's aides was deputed to discover a suitable site. He returned with photographs of the island of Leslo, which was situated alongside four ancillary islands that might have been designed for habitation by millionaire pop stars. Mardas and the Beatles immediately flew out to Greece on a tour of inspection, and agreed on an asking price of £90,000.

'The idea was [to] get an island where you can just do what you want,' Paul McCartney explained in his authorised biography, 'a sort of hippie commune where nobody'd interfere with your lifestyle. I suppose the main motivation for that would probably be no one could stop you smoking. Drugs was probably the main reason for getting some island.' In another authorised tome, the 1968 biography *The Beatles*, author Hunter Davies wrote: 'They didn't care about the military regime which had just taken over in Greece'. Others did care, however, including the Co-ordinating Committee for the Campaign against Tourism to Greece. They issued leaflets in the British underground press, headed: 'Danger! Dictatorship!' The text explained that 'The Greek people ask us to stay away! Every pound we take to Greece finances their oppressors. The country is now ruled by a handful of army officers who seized power at gunpoint and now maintain it through tanks, concentration camps and torture.' The conclusion was simple: don't travel to Greece, as 'THE DICTATORS DESPERATELY NEED YOUR MONEY TO SURVIVE'. It was a message lost on the Beatles in July 1967. 'I'm not worried about the political situation in Greece, as long as it doesn't affect us,' John Lennon told Davies. 'I don't care if the government is all fascist or Communist. I don't care.' 'I was horrified by their stance,' the Beatles' friend Barry Miles recalls. 'As I remember it, Paul was faintly embarrassed by it all, but John wasn't concerned. As far as I can gather, the entire trip to Greece was just a haze of LSD, though. None of them really knew where the hell they were.'

Ultimately, the plan of purchasing an idyllic island hideaway in a land ruled by a military dictatorship came to nothing. Despite their efforts to exile rock music from Greece, the junta recognised the commercial potential of being seen to welcome the Beatles to their shores, and agreed to let the sale proceed. British currency regulations insisted, however, that the departure of such a large sum from UK had to be authorised by the Chancellor of the Exchequer's office. By the time this approval was given – despite its opposition to the coup, Britain's Labour government didn't want to stand in the way of the Beatles, for fear of losing the youth vote – the Beatles' attention had wandered elsewhere. But the episode signalled their remoteness from the real world.[1]

## BLIND ACCEPTANCE

Other British musicians did not share the Beatles' political isolation. The Move won media attention for their violent stage act, during which they attacked television sets and effigies of politicians with an axe. 'We're kind of hitting out at anti-social things,' explained singer Carl Wayne. 'TV is anti-social, that's why we attack it. We also attack other evil things, like apartheid.' It was the Chinese cultural revolution that captured the attention of the blues-rock trio Cream, rapidly emerging as one of the most influential British bands of 1967. Bass guitarist Jack Bruce had been raised in a militant trade union household, and had sung in the Young Communist League choir as a child. He retained an idealistic belief in the progressive intentions of Mao's regime. 'I rather admire the Chinese for what they are trying to do with their ideas of social equality,' he told a rather baffled pop interviewer that January. 'I hope they don't get loused up in this revolution.' His bandmate, drummer Ginger Baker, reflected the suspicion of the non-Marxist British public: 'I hope there is a civil war [in China] – it's the only sure way to stop them dropping bombs on everyone. Those Red Guards are the Hitler Youth movement all over again.'

Such direct political comment was still unusual in a pop scene dominated by an obsession with style, not context. Music and fashion acted as dual lightning rods for London's youth aristocracy, sparking each other to fresh heights of invention through 1966 and into 1967. Developments from America were noted and incorporated but not necessarily followed; it would take several months before the casual anarchy of Haight Ashbury's hippies entered the British mainstream. In an era when transatlantic travel was still exceptional, only the financial and artistic elite could bring back first-hand reports on what was happening in the USA.

Rolling Stones guitarist Brian Jones was more elite than most, and retained a political conscience even while he was under pressure from the British police. When the *News of the World* newspaper interviewed Jones about his drug use in late January 1967, they misidentified him as Mick Jagger, which in turn provoked police to raid a private party being held by Jagger and Keith Richards at the latter's Sussex home in February. The *News of the World* were on hand to gain an exclusive account of the arrests, thanks to a tip-off from a mysterious guest named David Schneiderman. He brought drugs to the house, and then vanished as the police arrived, shrouding himself in suspicion. The underground press investigated his background, and fingered him as the source of another rumour, that Britain was harbouring a Black Muslim sect bent on urban terrorism. That story was soon forgotten, and Schneiderman never resurfaced, but the Stones' drug charges rumbled on for several more months.

Despite being arrested himself in a separate bust, Brian Jones continued to talk in public about the ways in which his drug use had affected his thinking, as he discussed the varying merits of 'an almost blind acceptance of religion' and 'unidentified flying objects, which seem more real to me'. Between these flashes of acid revelation, however, Jones didn't forget the physical world. He aligned himself with the hippies of New York, noting that 'nearly all of them think like us and are questioning some of the basic immoralities which are tolerated in present day society – the war in Vietnam, persecution of homosexuals, illegality of abortion, drug taking. All these things are immoral.' Considering the relative merits of art and politics, he added: 'We are making our own statement – others are making more intellectual ones.' His list of evils was slightly self-serving; besides his own indulgence in illegal drugs, he had a roomful of illegitimate children to his name, and must sometimes have wished that abortion had been legally available. In keeping with the Stones' image, and the Neanderthal sexual politics of the age, he made no mention of feminism. But his championing of homosexuality was enlightened at a time when same-sex activities were still illegal in the UK (as they remained until 28 July 1967).

Consciously or not, Jones was lining up alongside the Black Panthers and the Maoists when he stated: 'We believe there can be no evolution without revolution.' Three months later, Mick Jagger added some flesh to this theoretical bone: 'Teenagers the world over are weary of being pushed around by half-witted politicians who attempt to dominate their way of thinking and set a code for their living. They want to be free and have the right of expression; of thinking and living aloud without any petty restrictions.' His call could have been echoed in Birmingham, Alabama; in Prague; in Salisbury, Rhodesia; in Athens; and certainly in California, from Oakland to the Sunset Strip. 'This is a protest against the system,' Jagger concluded, before warning: 'I see a lot of trouble coming in the dawn.'

His own situation must have coloured his words. On 27 June 1967, Jagger, Richards and gallery owner Robert Fraser went on trial at Chichester Assizes on charges relating to the February party. All three were found guilty on 29 June of drugs offences, and sent to prison. There was an immediate demonstration outside the offices of the *News of the World*, while 30 June brought a sizeable protest in Piccadilly. When the disturbances moved into a third day, the Stones' management quickly distanced themselves from the protests. By then, Jagger and Richards had been released awaiting an appeal, which saw their sentences quashed. But the furore aroused by their trial, which spilled into the editorial columns of *The Times*, sparked a series of rallies in July calling for the legalisation of 'pot' (cannabis). When the Beatles and other public figures signed an advertisement in *The Times* in support of the same cause, drug culture briefly entered the realms of mainstream politics.

Several months earlier, Tom McGrath, the editor of the underground London paper the *International Times*, had underscored the political significance of the drugs issue: 'No matter how many raids and arrests the police make on whatever pretence – there can be no final bust because the revolution has taken place WITHIN THE MINDS of the young.' Some of the leading advocates of that revolution were now beginning to suspect that their victory might be hollow, however. In August 1967, George Harrison visited the Haight Ashbury district, spiritual (and now commercial) home of the Californian counter-culture, and was repelled by the emptiness and greed he saw. 'It wasn't what I thought, spiritual awakening and being artistic,' he recalled 25 years later, 'it was like alcoholism, like any addiction . . . That was the turning-point for me, that's when I went off the whole drug cult.'

Later that month, Harrison invited the other Beatles to a London lecture by an Indian guru, 50-year-old Maharishi Mahesh Yogi. He was the leader of a worldwide movement of Spiritual Regeneration, via the practice of Transcendental Meditation (TM) – an enhanced form of mental application through which one could understand the teachings of the Lord Krishna, in the sacred text of the Bhagavad-Gita. Devotees could escape the cares of the everyday by achieving a state of bliss and total spiritual awareness. The Bhagavad-Gita, the Maharishi assured his followers, 'brings fulfilment to the life of the individual. When society accepts it, social well-being and security will result, and when the world hears it, world peace will be permanent.'

Transcendental Meditation seemed to promise eternal respite from the traps and traumas of the everyday world; unlimited access to the higher and deeper realms that had been haphazardly available through psychedelic drugs; peace and harmony in a world sadly lacking in both. It valued inner growth over outward action; individual contact with the godhead, rather than a collective crusade for justice; peace of the spirit, not peace on the battle-field. TM had already attracted a cult following in the West, but when the Beatles attended a weekend conference organised by the Maharishi in late August – and their manager Brian Epstein died while they were there – the attention of the world's press was focused on their new guru. For much of the next year, the Beatles – especially Harrison and John Lennon – pros-elytised for the Maharishi in the press and on television. They composed songs inspired by his teachings; spread the message to their rock star friends, such as the Beach Boys and Donovan; and acted as an efficient recruitment aid for the TM organisation.

The mainstream media treated the so-called 'giggling guru' as little more than a joke, the latest eccentricity from a group of self-indulgent millionaires who had already claimed to find enlightenment via a variety of drugs, herbal and chemical. For the underground press, and the counter-culture in general, the impact of the Maharishi was more profound. Few were willing to dismiss outright anyone who wished to increase the global level of spiritual aware-ness, especially as he heralded from the Eastern religious tradition that had already won much support among the hippie community. But especially in America, there was some disquiet that the political consciousness of a generation might now be distracted from the war and racism into an entirely individual form of salvation.

These qualms were not lessened when the Maharishi submitted himself to the PR process. 'I am concerned with the suffering of the world,' he told one London journalist, 'but I don't become angry with those who are suffering, because I know through love I could make them happy.' It was a novel approach to human misery, compounded when the Maharishi turned to the subject of global violence. 'I am not bothered with one war in Vietnam or one war in China or one war here or there,' he pronounced. 'I want to eradicate the very cause of war for all times, and for that I am working to purify the atmosphere of the world . . . It is the stress and strain of every individual that contaminates this atmosphere.' Dictators and warmongers the world over breathed a sigh of belief. Nor was the Maharishi any more militant on the subject of collective action. 'I have a very poor opinion of Communism,' he declared. 'I am no authority on any politicalisms but just on the surface of the word, I would say Communism means weak-ism. Communism – someone who can't stand on his own leg . . . If someone hangs on to community, then he is a weak individual.'

The Maharishi was finally confronted about his beliefs when he flew into New York, ahead of a disastrous shared concert tour with the Beach Boys. Quizzed about whether young men should refuse to accept the draft into the US military, he looked puzzled. 'His Holiness doesn't understand draft,' an aide said. The concept was explained to him, and the Maharishi duly informed the press that it was a man's duty to serve his country. The poet and anti-war activist Allen Ginsberg edged forward in the room, sat at the Maharishi's feet and, in his own words, 'literally started yelling at him'. 'Allen knew a lot of people in India,' his friend Barry Miles explains, 'and he had discovered that the Maharishi had a lot of connections to right-wing politicians. Also, the Maharishi was breaking one of the fundamental rules of Hinduism, which was that teaching should always be available for free, whereas he charged his followers a week's income as a tithe.'

Fired with this knowledge, Ginsberg challenged the guru. He explained to him why the Vietnam War was such a potent issue for American youth, and pointed out that 'he, the Maharishi, hadn't covered the problem satisfactorily. He [replied that] Johnson and his secret police had more information and knew what they were doing. I said they were a bunch of dumbbells and they don't know, and his implicit support of authoritarianism made lots of people wonder if he weren't some kind of CIA agent. He giggled, "CIA?" His devotees began screaming, so I said it was a common question, it should be posed. Then I asked, what about draft resistant kids, going to war and murder? He said, either way, meditate.' Ginsberg concluded: 'I thought his political statements not so much evil as dim and thoughtless, somewhat sucking up to the establishment so as not to cause opposition and trouble . . . In a sense, his position is not far from [fellow guru] Krishnamurti or [Timothy] Leary: stay out of politics, avoid the authorities, get into meditation and inner peace.' It was a recipe not for pacifism, but for passive-ism; another invitation to maintain a crucial distance from political commitment; another excuse not to confront the men behind the war.

## ANGRY ARTS

There was a teasing hint of peace in Vietnam during the early months of 1967, as Ho Chi Minh's government and the Americans tentatively considered the idea of peace talks. The Pentagon's press spokesmen maintained a steady flow of good news stories; each bombing raid brought the inevitable collapse of Communism closer; each wave of fresh US troops merely increased their numerical and firepower superiority. By March, however, less reassuring whispers began to emanate from Washington, as it became clear that Secretary of Defense Robert McNamara was beginning to doubt the US policy of regular bombing of North Vietnamese targets. McNamara's qualms were silenced by a crescendo of artillery targeted at North Vietnamese army camps, the coastline and strategically important rivers. President Johnson denied that this formed a policy of 'escalation', but did concede that 'this is action over and above what has been taking place . . . Certainly, it is more far-reaching.'

New draft measures introduced that spring meant that 19-year-old men were now first in line for the call-up; and that graduate students (apart from those set on a career in medicine) could no longer claim automatic deferment. The US Court of Appeals ruled that it was not legal for the government to use the call-up as a punishment for anyone who campaigned against its policies. But anyone facing imprisonment for refusing the draft now had only one other alternative: accepting military service after all.

These devil's choices had little impact on the protest movement. Besides regular demonstrations, anti-war activists were now concentrating on burning or turning in draft cards. In California, Berkeley peacenik David Harris formed an organisation called Resistance, whose energies were centred on a week of draft refusal planned for October 1967. Meanwhile, the National Mobilization Committee had scheduled a week of actions in April. 'We have argued and demonstrated to stop this destruction,' their broadside declared. 'We have not succeeded. Powerful resistance is now demanded: radical, illegal, unpleasant, sustained.' It was a threat worthy of the militant wing of the black power movement, yet during Vietnam Week it translated into a massive but entirely peaceful march through the streets of New York from Central Park to the United Nations building, where 170 activists brought forward their draft cards to be burned. The Secretary of State, Dean Rusk, responded: 'I have no doubt that the Communist apparatus is very busy indeed in these operations.' His pronouncement sounded strangely at odds with a protest where marchers held placards proclaiming 'PEACE WITH BEATLE-POWER, TO FUNLOVE FOR LIFE!'

15 April 1967 found 25,000 protestors gathered in San Francisco's Kezar Stadium, across the park from the site of the Gathering of the Tribes three months earlier. The march to Kezar tapped into some of the Be-In's anar-chic, joyful spirit, but any spontaneity was smothered when Berkeley's seasoned politicos took control. Vietnam Day Committee leader Jerry Rubin marked this as the occasion when he began to shift allegiance: 'On the speaker's platform stood lifeless professors, ministers, Reform Democrats, union leaders, intoning speech after lifeless speech,' he complained. 'Why were we standing around watching them?' The schedule for the rally prom-ised speeches from Eldridge Cleaver and actor Robert Vaughn, plus music from folkies Jon Hendricks and Judy Collins[2] (who were allowed one song apiece), and local acid-rock bands Big Brother and Country Joe & the Fish.

Country Joe had shared the stage with Rubin at a dozen benefits over the previous 18 months, most recently the Mobe's Angry Arts festival at Longshoreman's Hall, alongside the Grateful Dead and Quicksilver Messenger Service. But at Kezar, his band was unceremoniously pulled off stage during their second song, to make room for more speakers. 'We were pissed off,' Rubin recalled. 'The Peace Movement was trying to put on a respectable front to convince straight people that you don't have to have long hair to be against the war.' Country Joe McDonald restricted himself to a single barbed comment as he left the stadium: 'Man, I learned one thing this afternoon. There's more than one revolution.' A month later, he and the Fish graphically illustrated the point when they released their debut album, *Electric Music for the Mind and Body*. A masterpiece of acid-inspired California rock, it mixed Dylanesque lyrical imagery with psychedelic improvisation. Aside from a revival of McDonald's 1965 satire of LBJ, 'Superbird', it contained not a hint of political comment – not least because their record label, Vanguard, barred the Fish from including the already semi-legendary 'I-Feel-Like-I'm-Fixin'-To-Die Rag'. But even in this censored form, the album symbolised a counter-culture deeply at odds with the clean-cut conservatism of many Berkeley radicals.

That sense of community was never displayed in more flamboyant finery than at the Monterey International Pop Festival in June 1967. The ethos of the event was simple: 'Be happy, be free, wear flowers, bring bells – have a festival'. There was no mention of Vietnam, the draft or black power. But the organisers were no strangers to the wider struggle: John Phillips, leader of the Mamas & Papas, had begun to pepper his group's live performances with sarcastic comments about the war, while press officer Derek Taylor vividly recalled a recent acid trip with several of the Beatles, during which his psychedelic nirvana was interrupted by visions of refugees trudging through the jungles of Vietnam. For midsummer 1967, however, a sunnier aura was considered more appropriate, with the proceeds earmarked for charity, black and white acts sharing the bill (though one local pop newspaper cancelled out that gesture by issuing two racially segregated souvenir programmes), hippies and straights working in unity, eyes and ears open to the sounds of the future, from Jimi Hendrix and Ravi Shankar alike. Stalls offered jewellery, hash brownies, silks and denims, though nowhere to turn in your draft card.

But politics did enter the festival fairgrounds, anyway, when Country Joe reprised his showstopping 'I-Feel-Like-I'm-Fixin'-To-Die Rag' (censored no longer, it became the title track of the Fish's second album, later in the year); when Lou Rawls rekindled memories of the civil rights campaign with his version of 'Tobacco Road'; and when David Crosby of the Byrds ushered some chic controversy onto the stage by questioning the US government's official explanation of the assassination of JFK. 'This is your country,' he challenged the audience; but in a sea of lavish colours and perfumed air, nationality seemed irrelevant. It was an occasion, proclaimed the apolitical, marijuana-scented pages of the *Oracle* newspaper, when 'the mutants of the psychedelic evolution–revolution gathered to talk to each other in their own form of musical sounds', with no Jerry Rubin to endanger the good vibrations. Looking back at the festival, veteran San Francisco jazz critic Ralph J. Gleason – one of the sponsors of the new rock-based fortnightly paper *Rolling Stone* – explained that Monterey's hippies 'are not just dropping out into Limbo or Nirvana. They are building a new set of values, a new structure, a new society . . . attacking the very principle on which this society is built: it is more sacred to make money than to be a good man.' Somehow the war had vanished from Gleason's equation as well.

Three days after the Monterey festival closed with a validating set from the Mamas & the Papas, another Californian happening offered an alternative slant on the temper of the times. On 23 June 1967, Lyndon Johnson arrived in Los Angeles for a lunchtime speech to the President's Club at the Century Plaza Hotel, where businessmen had paid $500 for the privilege. That morning, the *LA Times* had run a paid advertisement, proclaiming: 'As of this date, we 8,000 Democrats of Southern California are dissociating ourselves from you because of your conduct of the war in Vietnam.' More than 5,000 spectators, Democrats and hippies alike, congregated in front of the hotel, to be greeted by 1,000 California police, who rushed at the demonstrators, and beat many of them to the ground.

It was a suitably violent opening to the 11-day-long Angry Arts Festival, staged around the Los Angeles area. Opposite the Century Plaza, folk-singer Phil Ochs and the Guerrilla Theater accompanied the pitched battle. Ochs had been musing over Allen Ginsberg's proclamation, more than a year earlier, that he had unilaterally declared the end of the Vietnam War. He chose this moment to debut a song on the same theme. 'The War is Over' made pointed reference to 'The mad director [who] knows that freedom will not make you free', while inside the hotel LBJ reprised his promise to the Vietnamese people that the war would liberate them from the Communist menace. Yet Ochs also satirised the very event in which he was participating: 'Angry artists painting angry signs/use their vision just to blind the blind/Poisoned players of a grizzly game . . . Pardon me if I refrain'. A week later, Ochs played a benefit for Angry Arts at the Ash Grove, while Canned Heat, Hourglass, Kaleidoscope, Taj Mahal and bluesmen Sonny Terry & Brownie McGhee also offered their services to the festival. Clearly the ambiguity between conviction and commerciality that Phil had exhibited two years earlier still itched at his conscience, twisting his idealism into cynicism.

The Angry Arts cause reverberated all the way to London, where an anti-war benefit was staged under the same banner at the Roundhouse on 1 July 1967. Topping the bill were Procol Harum, psychedelic pop stars of the moment thanks to their Bach-meets-Dylan pastiche, 'A Whiter Shade of Pale'. The Yardbirds and the Crazy World of Arthur Brown also performed, but the only hint of anger was displayed by the Social Deviants, a rowdy ensemble from the heart of West London's bohemia, Ladbroke Grove. Their leader was Mick Farren, whose most enduring contribution to the British rock scene was as an agent provocateur. Always more comfortable in biker boots and jacket than bells and beads, Farren occupied the lonely role of Old Testament prophet in London's 'flower power' scene. In the week that the Beatles' *Sgt. Pepper* album was released – the epochal moment of 1967, according to many historians – Mick Farren's article 'Pop in the Police State' was published in the *International Times*.

His thesis was that pop's rebelliousness was nothing more than street theatre, incapable of resisting the physical power of the state. He listed the hallowed symbols of 'the revolution that began with James Dean and Presley' – '[The Who's Pete] Townshend smashed £200 guitars almost nightly, Jagger's body spelt "Fuck you if you don't know" in semaphore, the Beatles refused to remain lovable mop-tops, and Dylan wrote songs of violent anarchy'. None of these had done more than to antagonise the authorities, Farren wrote. Then he sounded the alarm: 'Let's make no mistake, we are living in something of a police state. The police are playing a game, the government is playing its game. There is no "Bring the People into Line Act", and so the drugs and obscenity laws and being used as a stock prod. The leaders of the herd are being bust – Jagger, [American pop artist] Jim Dine, Brian Jones, Donovan, etc. With the hope that if the rest of the flock are harassed a bit, they will fall into panic and confusion, and eventually return to the straight and narrow. If this action doesn't succeed, and it doesn't seem to, except insofar as it makes life uncomfortable, then the police state has two alternatives. It can either give up and withdraw, or else really force the pressure, put curfews on under-25s, draft the non-straight into a labour corps. If this happens, the only answer is street fighting.'

Although the occasional arrests of pop and rock performers continued, building towards the moment in 1968 when the police felt brave enough to seize one of the Beatles, Farren's more paranoid predictions proved to be unfounded. The summer and autumn of 1967 were a time of lavish hedonism, at least within London's hip community. Elsewhere in the capital city, however, other currents were beginning to stir. In July, the Roundhouse – a prime venue for psychedelic rock performances – played host to a conference grandly titled The International Congress of the Dialectics of Liberation. Besides – almost inevitably – an anarchic live set from the Social Deviants, the event delivered an array of the era's most radical Western thinkers: social philosopher Herbert Marcuse, radical psychiatrist R.D. Laing, poet Allen Ginsberg and Emmett Grogan from the Californian anti-materialism collective, the Diggers.

Media coverage of the event was centred almost entirely on another speaker: SNCC leader Stokely Carmichael. Within the conference, he staged a militant rally that cracked a whip through the decorous air of intellectualism. His analysis of the racism inherent in the capitalist system broke no new ground, but it had rarely been aired in Britain with such fervour. The media reported that every mention of violence in his speech was cheered; every suggestion of non-violence booed. 'The real revolutionary proletariat', he declared, comprised 'the young bloods who clearly understood the savagery of white America, and who were ready to meet it with armed resistance.' He reserved sarcasm for white hippies: 'Come inside the ghetto, if you believe in all that flower power and so on. And when the cops are shooting at us, stand in between us and throw your flowers at them!' His final message to Britain's black population was stark: 'The death and damage concomitant with the rebellion are a price to be paid in the revolutionary struggle. My solution is – an eye for an eye, and a tooth for a tooth.'

Carmichael was scheduled to follow this appearance with a lecture tour around Britain, but his 'inflammatory' comments led to his being hurriedly deported from the country. His engagements were fulfilled by a man who had also spoken at the Roundhouse, where his comments about 'white monkeys' prompted an investigation by Scotland Yard. Michael de Freitas had been born in Trinidad, and arrived in Britain in the mid-1950s as a sailor. In Cardiff's Tiger Bay community, he scuffled for money as a pimp and drug dealer; he once claimed to have killed a white man, and 'felt nothing'. By the late 1950s, he had moved to Notting Hill in West London, where he won a local reputation as an activist during the race riots of 1958, telling a meeting of threatened West Indians: 'What you need is to get a few pieces of iron and a bit of organisation, so that tonight when they come in here we can defend ourselves.'

Besides working as an enforcer for a notoriously corrupt property baron, de Freitas began to mingle amongst London's more adventurous young bohemians, mixing with beat poets, painters and designers. When Malcolm X visited London a few days before his death, in February 1965, de Freitas ensured that he was photographed by the preacher's side. He claimed to Malcolm that he was the leader of a militant black group of his own, the Racial Adjustment Action Society (RAAS). After the American had flown home, he put his boast into practice. Claiming that he was now a Black Muslim, he forged a new identity as Michael X – conferred upon him, he said, by Malcolm himself. Over the next 18 months, RAAS was a prominent presence during strikes by black workers, and Michael X crowed that his organisation now operated nationwide and had several thousand members. The truth was that RAAS could never count on the support of more than about 200 young black men, almost all of them in London.

Using skills he'd picked up during the 1958 riots, Michael X was recruited by the Rolling Stones' organisation to stage the loudest of the public demonstrations against the *News of the World* after the conviction of Mick Jagger. He became the homegrown black radical of choice whenever the UK media required some inflammatory comments on race relations. When he took Carmichael's place in July 1967, the occasion demanded words of fire. At a meeting in Reading, Michael X duly obliged. 'If ever you see a white man laying hands on a black woman,' he instructed the small gathering, 'kill him immediately . . . The most savage human being in the world is the white man.' Arrested on the evidence of a police informer in the crowd, he was found guilty of contravening the Race Relations Act in October 1967, and sentenced to a year in prison. In his final interview before his conviction, he reopened the gulf between black power and white sympathisers: 'The party that calls itself "radical white" is no such thing – it will be just a pack of other vicious white men.'

## THE MOBILE BUTCHER SHOP

It was not 'vicious white men' who scared America in the summer of 1967. The time had passed for integration between black and white, LeRoi Jones announced, because integration was simply 'the mobile butcher shop of the devil's mind'. Jones continued: 'To be an american one must be a murderer. A white murderer of coloured people.'

As Stokely Carmichael toured the nation's campuses and black communities, white America reacted in fear to his knife-edge rhetoric. Like Jones, he high-lighted the black man's distance from his nation: 'I do not want to be part of the American pie. The American pie means raping South Africa, beating Vietnam, beating South America, raping the Philippines, raping every country you've been in.' The alternative was to seize power, whatever that might entail. Stopping just short of risking immediate arrest by threatening murder, Carmichael said calmly during a speech in Baltimore: 'When I decide to kill, since it is the greatest crime that man can commit, I alone will make that decision, and I will decide whom to kill.' It would not be a citizen of Vietnam – 'no Viet Cong ever called me nigger', as Muhammad Ali declared when he refused the draft and lost his championship belt as a result – but, so he inferred, it might be a white American.

Increasingly, the currents of anti-war protest and black power were begin-ning to blur into one. During the march to Kezar Stadium in April, white students had been accompanied by SNCC members holding placards that carried Muhammad Ali's slogan. Meanwhile, Martin Luther King lent his symbolic weight to the crusade against the Vietnam War, with a speech in which he drew comparisons between America's use of chemical weapons and Nazi medical experiments in World War Two. Liberals who were prepared to accept King's civil rights actions baulked at seeing him on a platform along-side Carmichael, as he was at Kezar. For all Jerry Rubin's misgivings about the pointlessness of speeches, King's rhetoric set the stadium ablaze: 'Let us save our national honour – stop the bombing. Let us save American lives and Vietnamese lives – stop the bombing. Let us take a single instantaneous step to the peace table – stop the bombing. Let our voices ring out across the land to say the American people are not vainglorious conquerors – stop the bombing.' America, he concluded, was now 'an arch counterrevolutionary nation'. In the ferment of 1967, there were few more grievous insults.

That ferment reached the streets in the amorphous shape of a summer of riots in black ghettos. The season began in Nashville in April, where Stokely Carmichael was blamed for provoking racial conflict. The same charge followed a meeting outside Montgomery in early June, when Carmichael was arrested for allegedly threatening a police chief who had shot dead a black man wrongly arrested on a murder charge. In Tampa, the spark was the shooting – in the back – of a black youth running away from the scene of a robbery. The patrolman claimed that the kid was in danger of getting away, though he was only a few yards in front of the cop when he was killed.

The fire continued to spread. In mid-June, Cincinnati erupted when police killed a man demonstrating against the death sentence passed against his cousin, a convicted murderer. After several days of clashes, arson attacks on shops and residences, and casual violence from both sides, the city itself fell calm, but its near neighbour Dayton, Ohio, picked up the torch. In the absence of Carmichael, who had recently resigned his post with SNCC in order to join the Black Panthers, suspicion passed to his replacement as SNCC chairman, H. Rap Brown. The police alleged that he had deliberately incited rioting in the city by proclaiming: 'The honky is your enemy. How can you be non-violent in America, the most violent country in the world? You better shoot that man to death.'

'Negroes with Guns', to borrow a book title from Robert Williams, became the US media's No. 1 obsession during 1967. The leader of the Black Panther Party in Oakland, Huey Newton, achieved national prominence when he launched a campaign to stop the California state legislature from passing the Mulford Act, designed to prevent all display of loaded weapons in public areas. On 2 May, a group of thirty Panther members, led by Chairman Bobby Seale, entered the State Capitol building in Sacramento, carrying rifles. This brazen gesture of defiance misfired when Seale took a wrong turning, and led his troops onto the floor of the Assembly Hall, where weapons were illegal under existing legislation. All twenty-four men (but none of the six women with them) were subsequently arrested on conspiracy and concealed weapon charges, although ultimately only two were convicted, Bobby Seale and Warren Tucker, both of whom received six-month sentences for 'disturbing the State Assembly'. Newton responded by telling the *New York Times* that black people were entitled to kill any policemen who 'brutalised' their community, as they were members of 'an occupying army'.

His fearless stance inspired Stokely Carmichael to join Newton, who told Panther members: 'Black people must now move to seize by any means necessary a proportionate share of the power vested and collected in the structure of America.' He appointed Carmichael the Field Marshal of the party, and offered the honorary post of Minister of Justice to H. Rap Brown, in the hope of encouraging a merger between SNCC and the BPP. Brown preferred to maintain SNCC's independence, so the Panthers looked elsewhere for partners in an attempt to take centre stage in the country's radical hierarchy. 'During this period we were having hot conversations with two groups interested in our defence,' Eldridge Cleaver recalled, 'the Communist

Party and the Socialist Worker's Party. Each group had a team of lawyers, but there was no way that we could get them together to figure out our best strategy. They were still arguing pro and con between Stalin and Trotsky, rehashing nitpicking points thirty years ago.' Eventually, Cleaver pulled the Panthers out of the negotiations with 'those two windbags'. But the prospect of a union between age-old bugbears of the establishment and the new black kids on the block aroused fury and terror in the Federal Bureau of Investigation. On 1 August 1967, FBI chief J. Edgar Hoover plunged more funds into an existing intelligence programme codenamed COINTELPRO. Its aim was the subversion of militant organisations that were, in the eyes of the FBI, threatening the stability of the state. Its methods involved a prolonged campaign of misinformation, designed to provoke splits within the radical groups, spark mutual suspicion amongst them, and sabotage any attempt to build a unified front against the US government. In a memorandum on the same day, Hoover instructed his officials to 'neutralise' and 'destroy any attempts of a Messiah rising' in the black power movement. The inference was that the threat of Martin Luther King could be managed and controlled (by phone-tapping and rumour-mongering, it later transpired) but that the likes of Stokely Carmichael, Rap Brown or Huey Newton might prove more difficult to contain.

This threat to the status quo paled alongside the next eruption from ghetto America. For two weeks in mid-July, two major city centres exploded into an ecstatic orgy of violence and destruction. With the summer heat bringing African-Americans' impatience to boiling point, it took the slightest of sparks to ignite an inferno. In predominantly black Newark, New Jersey, the home of LeRoi Jones, a taxi driver named John Smith was arrested late one night and escorted to police headquarters. Rumours spread that he had been shot dead, bricks and bottles were thrown, and for the next four days, Newark played host to a bacchanalian *pas de deux* of torched buildings and indiscriminate police retaliation. More than twenty people died, almost all black. *Time* magazine interrupted its accusations about the criminality of black citizens to note that life in Newark lived down to the message of a recent Lou Rawls soul hit: 'I'm living on a dead end street/a city without a heart'.

While the white media decried 'senseless violence', Jones believed that this was the revolution in action. 'The Black Liberation movement was raising up full out,' he wrote later. 'It was a war for us, a war of liberation. One had to organise, one had to arm, one had to mobilise and educate the people.'

Driving home through eerily quiet streets in the dark hours of the morning, Jones was pulled over by police, accused of attempting to kill them, and savagely beaten. 'I felt the clubs, the guns,' he recalled. 'They had even bashed one of my teeth out and loosened some more with fists and clubs. I would be scarred for life.' And he recognised the sound of Newark, of incoherent anger pulsing into 'hot music's beat'. It was the sound of free jazz, of unfettered horns screaming the pain of a nation: 'Why do you think [Col]Trane and Albert [Ayler] sounded like that?' he asked rhetorically. 'They wanted the essence of what flailed alive on all sides of us now.' In an eerie coincidence, John Coltrane died of cancer on the same day that Newark subsided into uneasy calm.

There were three days of grace, and then, to the horror of Newark's politicians, the city played host to the National Conference on Black Power. No fewer than 286 African-American organisations were represented at the event. Ron Karenga and Rap Brown were among the leaders who joined LeRoi Jones for a press conference at his headquarters, the Spirit House. They called for the United Nations to send in peacekeeping troops, to save the black community from police brutality. Rap Brown provoked more headlines when he urged delegates to 'wage war on the honky white man'. Meanwhile, the House of Representatives prepared to pass a new bill making it an offence to cross state lines with the intention of provoking a riot. Among legislators, it was known, unofficially, as the 'Rap Brown amendment'.

Neither Brown nor his fellow provocateur, Stokely Carmichael, was anywhere near the city of Detroit on the final day of the conference. It was there that the worst riots in recent American history occurred, between 22 and 27 July 1967. When the smoke began to clear, at least forty-three people lay dead, most of them black; there were probably more bodies that were never recovered from the wreckage of burnt-out stores and housing projects. The touchpaper was lit by an incident that was both insignificant and maddening in its relentless predictability. A squadron of police cars raided an after-hours drinking den – a 'blind pig', in local parlance – arresting more than seventy customers. The rest was inevitable: rocks, broken bottles, then flames, looting, and police bullets, some targeted, some striking cruelly at children and people locked in their homes for safety.

To the outside world, Detroit meant two things: automobiles and Motown. Workers on the Dodge car assembly line were inspired by the riots to form DRUM, the Dodge Revolutionary Union Movement. Berry Gordy's Motown

Records, however, was never subject to such militancy. It was one of the largest black-operated businesses in America. Yet even this institution feared the wrath of the crowd. There had been anonymous death threats earlier in the year when two Motown acts, the Four Tops and the Supremes, performed at a concert in New York sponsored by a white-owned beer company. Gordy had often raised his voice in support of Dr Martin Luther King's non-violent civil rights crusade, to the extent of issuing records of his speeches. But the chasm between King and the rioters had grown too wide to be breached by a businessman, no matter the colour of his skin.

Three years after it had hit the charts, Martha Reeves & the Vandellas' single 'Dancing in the Street' became the unofficial anthem of the riots, much to the chagrin of Reeves and Gordy. The previous week, Reeves had been in New Jersey during the Newark disturbances, and had joined James Brown in broadcasting pleas for 'people to go home and take care of their families – to stop shooting, stop looting the stores, and protect themselves, because it's not a time to steal, shoot and kill one another'. Now she found herself at the heart of a second riot, having to abandon her week-long residency at the Fox Theater downtown. Many of Motown's biggest stars were in the city that week. 'I watched it happen,' recalls Smokey Robinson. 'It was impossible to believe that this could be taking place in our hometown.' Marvin Gaye stayed home and followed the violence on TV. His singing partner Tammi Terrell, who days later was struck down by a brain haemorrhage, was the Motown employee deputed to phone Berry Gordy, who was supervising a residency by Diana Ross & the Supremes in Las Vegas. 'Berry told us to shut the studio down until it was safe to work again,' Robinson says. Within weeks, Gordy had entered nego-tiations to buy a home in Hollywood, the first step in the slow transfer of power that saw the label shift its headquarters to California at the start of the next decade.

Almost all of Detroit's brightest vocal talent during the 1960s eventually signed with Motown, which slowly gobbled up the rest of the city's in-dependent labels (though not Joe Von Battle's Von label, all of whose mas-ter tapes were destroyed by fire during the riots). But one group who es-caped Gordy's grasp were the Dramatics. The quintet, then just beginning their illustrious career as a harmony soul outfit, had been on the abandoned bill at the Fox. When their shows were cancelled, two of the group sheltered with friends at a low-class flophouse called the Algiers Motel. There they watched as the city burned, and police and rioters battled outside their window. On the first day of the riot, officers burst into their room and questioned them aggressively before letting them go. Two days later, the residents of the Algiers Motel were less lucky. What provoked the invasion isn't clear: there were rumours of a sniper in the vicinity, while young men in the next room were reportedly fooling with a starting pistol. Whatever the cause, police once again raided the motel. One black youth was shot dead immediately; the others, plus two young white females who were with them, were ordered into the lobby. The two women were stripped by police, and then all the 'suspects', men and women alike, was callously beaten. In turn, each of the men was taken out of sight of the others, and subjected to a mock execution – except that one group of policemen misunderstood their instructions, and actually murdered their prisoners. Only then were the two Dramatics singers, Roderick Davis and Larry Reed, freed and told to run for their lives.

On local radio playlists during the rioting was a record called 'Detroit is Happening' – rapidly pulled from the air in case it was interpreted as an incitement to fresh disturbances. It featured baseball star Willie Horton rapping about the attractions that the city offered to kids that summer, while two members of the Supremes reworked their recent hit, 'The Happening', behind him. Berry Gordy regularly encouraged his artists to take part in such positive social gestures. Once the riots had died down, Smokey Robinson & the Miracles raced into the Motown studio to record a song entitled 'I Care About Detroit'. It was written by Jimmy Clark and Jack Cook, whose most notable composition to date had been the anthem of the Boy Scouts of America. Their new song was equally anodyne, as Robinson crooned, 'I'm proud to call this city my hometown . . . Let's learn to live and work in harmony.'

Another Detroit native, veteran bluesman John Lee Hooker, maintained a more realistic perspective. Two months after the riots, he recorded the grim 'The Motor City is Burning', which chronicled the progress of the fires before concluding, 'My hometown is burning down to the ground, worster than Vietnam'. He cut a second protest tune with a similar message: 'I Don't Wanna Go to Vietnam'. 'You men in the street have so much trouble of your own,' he lectured, 'why they wanna fight in Vietnam?' Quizzed later about the riots, he replied: 'It was racial, but they kinda tried to smother it, you know what I mean? It finally got too hot, people got so fed up, that the riot broke out.'

It was coincidence, not politics, which brought a rock song by the Doors to the top of the national sales charts the week of Detroit. Not that commentator John Sinclair, penning his column 'The Coatpuller' in the city's underground paper, the *Fifth Estate*, saw it that way: "'Light My Fire" rises through the radio ranks for weeks and when it hits number one on the stations, the people respond and burn the city down. Or play Archie Shepp's *Fire Music* album as background music for the Detroit purification: the scope and feeling of the people's mood is there; an elegy for Malcolm.' It was as if the temperature of the nation was only now echoing the inferno that had raged from Archie Shepp in 1965 – or indeed from his long-time booster, LeRoi Jones. In one of his final acts before adopting his new identity of Amiri Baraka, Jones formed a record label – provocatively named Jihad, or holy war against the infidels – as a vehicle for several recordings he had made since 1965. Among them was *Sonny's Time Now*, a wild free jazz session (credited to drummer Sonny Murray) which included Jones reciting his incendiary poem 'Black Art'. Sun Ra provided incidental music for an audio performance of Jones' drama *A Black Mass*, an interpretation of the Yaqub creation myth favoured by the Nation of Islam. But the most intriguing of Jihad's three albums was credited to Jones alone. *Black & Beautiful, Soul & Madness* mixed Jones' verse with R&B rhythms and textures, reaching a poetic pinnacle when he recited 'Beautiful Black Woman' while a doo-wop-inspired vocal group repeated the chorus line from the Motown hit 'Oooh Baby Baby' by Smokey Robinson & the Miracles. It was as if Jones was presenting his own reading of 'I Care About Detroit', with the message of the riots, not the sanctity of the city, uppermost in his mind.

Not that Jones was averse to the cleansing sound of sweet soul delivered by the Miracles and their contemporaries. After the summer riots, Curtis Mayfield, leader and songwriter of the Chicago vocal trio the Impressions, added his voice to the national debate about the place of the black man in American society. Issued at Christmas 1967, 'We're a Winner' was a typically gentle piece of case-pleading, couched vaguely enough to pass as a romantic ballad. Even when it was more explicitly political – there was a repeated refrain of 'We'll just keep on pushing, like your leaders tell you to' – the specifics were left unspoken. As a result, the tune could be claimed by everyone from Martin Luther King to LeRoi Jones, who riffed around those lines in an essay as the song raced to No. 1 on the R&B charts: 'Do what your leaders tell you to – all of us gonna get ready. Ready to tear down what needs to be tore down. But ready readier to build what needs to be builded. BE YOUR SELF. BLACK MAN. FOR GOD'S SAKE.' Speaking in a contemporary interview, Jones added: '"We're a Winner" is more revolutionary than most jazz you hear.' Within the field of commercial soul music, however, 'revolutionary' was a tag that few artists were yet willing to accept. As Jones noted acidly when James Brown recorded the patriotic 'America Is My Home' a couple of months later, 'To sing lies about America is not beneficial to the Black Nation.' Exactly what constituted the Black Nation would become an increasingly contentious issue over the next two years.

## GUERRILLA LOVEFARE

On the first evening of the riot, MC5 guitarist Wayne Kramer and singer-songwriter Tim Buckley were driving towards Detroit along Grand River Boulevard. 'As we headed into the city just after sunset,' Kramer recalled, 'we could see huge flames rising up on either side of the street ahead. My first reaction was just like any red-blooded American kid: "Oh boy, a fire!" But then I remembered what time it was in America.' It was apocalypse time in the inner city, and Detroit scenemaker John Sinclair had already tagged the MC5 as the perfect soundtrack for the age – 'the band that will prepare us for the bomb when it comes'. Now it had arrived.

If Detroit scarred the memory of everyone who experienced the riots, it also heightened the MC5's self-image as outlaws. Their publicity machine boasted later that they were clad in clothes liberated from vandalised stores on Trumbull Avenue. They incorporated John Lee Hooker's lament, 'The Motor City is Burning', into their repertoire, refining it into a paint-stripping blast of high-octane rock'n'roll. 'We felt that we could be the vanguard and the voice for our community,' Kramer said.

In July 1967, that sprawling underground arts community was led by John Sinclair. A tireless champion of black music, marijuana and revolutionary rhetoric, Sinclair had formed idealistic co-ops like the Detroit Artists' Workshop and the Wayne Street University Artists' Society as early as 1964. His passion for avant-garde jazz inspired him to write several poetry collections during the mid-1960s, including *This Is Our Music* (named for an Ornette Coleman album), *Fire Music* (for Archie Shepp) and *Meditations: A Suite for John Coltrane*. He also edited underground arts papers including *Work, Change, Whe're* and *Guerrilla*, filling their pages with his fervid prose-poems; was one of the founders of the Underground Press Syndicate, the counter-culture's news agency; and wrote regular columns for the *Fifth Estate*.

He was also forced to waste unwarranted energy on fighting drugs charges. After an initial bust in 1963 won him a lengthy period of probation, he was arrested for possession of marijuana in October 1965. The following February, he was sentenced to six months in prison, during which he wrote 'Poem for Warner Stringfellow', a diatribe aimed at the narcotics agent who had already targeted him twice. During his imprisonment, financial problems entailed the collapse of the Detroit Artists' Workshop. While planning its successor, he was arrested again – alongside more than fifty associates – on 24 January 1967 after being tricked by undercover drugs officers into giving them two marijuana cigarettes. There ensued a legal battle that would stretch for more than two years, and affect the entire American counter-culture.

His spirit undiminished, Sinclair launched a new venture in February 1967 – 'a total cooperative tribal living and working commune' entitled Trans Love Energies Unlimited. It was a utopian attempt to bypass the mainstream, with Sinclair and his colleagues taking on the roles of concert promotion, artist management, publishing and related spiritual support. 'During the Detroit Uprising,' Sinclair concluded, 'we distributed free food and clothes to poor black and white people who didn't have anything to eat after all the neighbourhood stores had been looted and burned down.'

Wayne Kramer, singer Rob Tyner, guitarist Fred Smith, Dennis Thompson and Michael Davis came together as the Motor City 5 (soon abridged to MC5) in 1965. 'We moved to the beatnik neighbourhood,' Kramer recalled. 'That's where we met John Sinclair – the archetypal beatnik poet.' The band appeared at an August 1966 festival organised by the Detroit Artists' Workshop during Sinclair's imprisonment. Six months later, they were on the bill of the 'Guerrilla Lovefare' poetry/music event at Wayne State University, which doubled as a fundraiser for the *Guerrilla* paper and a launching pad for Trans Love Energies.

On 30 April 1967, the MC5 and Sinclair were involved in the Detroit Love-In, a self-policed underground happening on Belle Isle. Six thousand hippies wallowed in the afternoon sunshine, before excess alcohol cancelled out the marijuana vibrations and packs of bikers beat up random members of the crowd. A local band, Seventh Seal, ignored police orders to quit the stage, and so the cops herded the crowd off the island, and back onto the city streets, where two hours of sporadic violence ensued. Sinclair subsequently blamed 'straights' and 'weekend hippies' for the counter-revolutionary fracas.

Interviewed by Sinclair several days later, Rob Tyner spouted generic hippie clichés, along the lines of 'everyone's a magician, man'. Gradually, however, the MC5 began to ingest Sinclair's radical optimism. They already shared his enthusiasm for free jazz, and when a June 1967 Trans Love Energies promotion teamed them with Sun Ra, their most experimental yearnings were awakened. Their regular Detroit live shows, billed as 'avant rock', rapidly developed into terrifyingly intense fusions of incendiary rock'n'roll and atonal jazz, typified by their epic improvisation vehicle, 'Black to Comm'. By the end of the year, Sinclair, who was already managing another Detroit band, the Up, had assumed a similar role in the career of the MC5. Commercial recognition was slow to come, however: when the band supported avant-garde protesters the Fugs at a benefit gig for Sinclair's legal defence fund on 26 November 1967, only 88 people were prepared to pay the $3.50 entrance fee.

'We will force you to support us', wrote Fug and beat poet Tuli Kupferberg earlier that year, 'to support the artists who are digging your dark grave . . . Mass your media – you are helpless before our skills. You don't know if we are parodying you or you are parodying us anymore . . . This is our magic. With this we break open heads & new worlds emerge. Wd you believe?' As he discovered in Detroit, the new worlds emerging were not always ready to confront the 'dark grave'. Ambiguous signals flashed from the counter-culture throughout 1967, and mutated as they were picked up by the mainstream. Few bands personified the psychedelic ethos more completely than Jefferson Airplane from San Francisco, with their communal lifestyle and proclamation of acid as the key to an ultimate layer of reality. Yet the Airplane became bona fide pop stars that spring, and celebrated by taping a series of advertisements for Levi's jeans – unorthodox, to be sure, but brazenly commercial in their impact. While the Airplane prided themselves on their subversion of Madison Avenue, former SNCC activist Abbie Hoffman penned a typically moralistic letter to the *Village Voice*: 'It summarised for me all the doubts I have about the hippie philosophy. I realise they are just doing their "thing", but while the Jefferson Airplane grooves with its thing, over 100 workers in the Levi Strauss plant on the Tennessee–Georgia border are doing their thing, which consists of being on strike to protest deplorable working conditions.'

Hoffman's pained idealism epitomised a traditional socialist approach that was struggling to deal with a revolution of the mind, not the streets. As Frank Zappa explained to Marxist critic Frank Kofsky: 'Today, a revolution can be accomplished by means of mass media, with technical advances that Madison Avenue is using to sell you washing machines and a loaf of bread and everything else. This can be used to change the whole country around, painlessly.' When the unconvinced Kofsky retorted that he would be unlikely to trigger a shift in the power structure, Zappa replied: 'It will never look to them like I'm going to take everything away from them, because I'm not taking it all away from them . . . [But] I have one basic human drive on my side that they can't defeat – greed . . . A lot of the industries now are aware of the fact that they're in a vicious cycle: in order to sell their goods to the youth market, which accounts for the major market of most American products, that same market that buys most of the records, you have a weird situation where in effect record companies especially are helping to disseminate the information which will cause the kids to wake up and move and eventually destroy what they stand for, and they can't help it.'

It was as if Karl Marx's theory about the inherent contradictions of capitalism had been transported to Sunset Strip. But it begged a shot of pessimism: what happened if the youth market, rather than destroying the system, became trapped in its embrace – if, to borrow a phrase from George Melly, revolt mutated into style? Another of 1967's hip icons, the Doors, unconsciously illustrated precisely this fear. In Jim Morrison, they boasted a genuinely charismatic entertainer whose every breath exuded illicit sexuality. 'Light My Fire', their accidental soundtrack to the summer's riots, suggested that his claim to be 'an erotic politician' might carry genuine substance. Quizzed about his relationship to the revolution, however, Morrison was more circumspect: 'I've always been attracted to ideas that were about revolt against authority . . . I like ideas about the breaking away or overthrowing of established order. I am interested in anything about revolt, disorder and chaos, especially activity that seems to have no meaning. It seems to me to be the road towards freedom.' Jean-Paul Sartre might have warmed to this exemplary demonstration of existentialism, but 'ideas' with 'no meaning' posed little threat to America's war machine. Neither, it seemed, did Country Joe & the Fish's second album, or else Vanguard Records might not have marketed it with adverts suggesting: 'Nothing Else Has Been Able To Stop The War . . . Maybe The Fish Can!'[3] Subversion was being marketed like soap, and reported like a ball game, so how could it still be subversive? 'There can be no revolution', concluded John Wolfe in the first issue of a new radical paper entitled *Distant Drummer*, 'when *Life* [magazine] turns its camera on the newest underground five minutes after it has been formed.'

The confusion was everywhere. From the radical right came David Noebel of the Christian Anti-Communist Crusade (CACC), veteran of tirades against the Beatles and 'Eve of Destruction', who was now convinced that Columbia Records was 'the home of Marxist minstrels', and that Bob Dylan and Joan Baez were leading the folk movement into the hands of the Soviet Union. The CACC put forward its own folk Madonna, Janet Greene, a mid-30s housewife whose repertoire included 'Be Careful of the Commie Lies'. Conservative cartoonist Al Capp maintained the pressure on Baez with his creation of 'Joanie Phoanie', a Commie sympathiser who spouted revolution for $10,000 a night, and whose records included 'If it Sounds Phoanie, it's Joanie'. Baez was not amused: 'Either out of ignorance or malice,' she complained, 'he has made being for peace equal to being for Communism, the Viet Cong and narcotics.' Capp hit back: 'She should remember that protest singers don't own protest. When she protests about others' rights to protest, she is killing the whole racket.' Today, Baez laughs at the confrontation: 'I was considered a hippie, no-account pinko! Joanie Phoanie was pretty funny, in retrospect, but obviously I didn't see the joke at the time.' Meanwhile, the left in Berkeley and across Europe scolded Baez for her refusal to align herself with the Viet Cong. 'Peace was always controversial,' she concludes. Dylan, likewise, was criticised for withdrawing from the fray, although not unanimously. The release of the enigmatic album *John Wesley Harding* at the end of 1967 tempted some supporters, such as A.J. Weberman, to search for contemporary political resonances. He found it in 'I Pity the Poor Immigrant', 'who wishes he would have stayed home' – a clear reference, Weberman claimed, to the disillusionment of American forces in Vietnam.

That summer, Dylan and the musicians who became The Band committed dozens of roughshod recordings to tape, documenting new compositions and playful retreads of folk, country and pop standards. This material, known collectively as *The Basement Tapes*, appears in retrospect to occupy a place outside time, and certainly outside the milieu of 1967's contemporary music. But, argues critic Greil Marcus, 'In many ways those performances do reflect the war in Vietnam, the riots that are sweeping the country, and the mindless utopianism of the so-called "Summer of Love", in the way that they reject all these things. The best pop music doesn't affect events, it absorbs them, and that's what *The Basement Tapes* do. The creators of those songs are aware that the world around them is exploding into pieces. That's one of the things that, for example, "This Wheel's on Fire" is about. It doesn't broadcast that association, or reflect that influence directly. It all comes out translated into another kind of language.' Yet it is tempting to read a more overt message to the left in the title of one Dylan song from the Basement sessions: 'I'm Not There (I'm Gone)'.

Left unreleased for another eight years, *The Basement Tapes* had no impact on the public at large. For US troops in South-East Asia, the ambiguity of these songs would, in any case, have provided scant comfort. As their morale slowly decayed, they escaped into the same alternative reality as those who had burned their draft cards and stayed home. From 1967 onwards, marijuana (or its local equivalent) mixed with the smell of napalm in the air, while soldiers soaked up the same acid rock soundtrack that filled the airwaves in San Francisco and New York. Alongside Jefferson Airplane and the Doors, they were listening to a former member of the US paratroops corps, a black American who had travelled to England to become an icon of swinging London. Jimi Hendrix dressed in Carnaby Street chic, floated through interviews on a high of hippie slogans, and offered enough comic-book stage theatrics to convince critic Robert Christgau that he was nothing more than 'a psychedelic Uncle Tom'. He was ignored by black radio in the States, despite the R&B base of his music, and treated like a member of an exotic species by the white rock audience. His music, pitched on the borderline between anguish and ecstasy, captured the absurdity and violence of America's misadventure in Vietnam. But in 1967, Hendrix refused to line up cosily alongside the peaceniks: 'The Americans are fighting in Vietnam for the complete free world. As soon as they move out, [Vietnam]'ll be at the mercy of the communists. For that matter, the yellow danger [China] should not be underestimated. Of course war is terrible, but at the present it's still the only guarantee to maintain peace.'

That was not a view widely shared in the counter-culture in October 1967. After months of scattered action, the shards of the American anti-war movement were aimed at a single statement of purpose: Stop The Draft Week. There would be Vietnam Peace Parades on Sunday 15 October; protests outside draft centres; and then, on 21 October, a march on the seat of American power in Washington, DC. From the outset, however, it was apparent that the coalition of protest groups was fragile, and fissile. Trotskyist members of the students' movement, SDS, dismissed the peaceniks as 'bourgeois moralists' for their refusal to use the protest as a trigger for a socialist uprising. Even within the Resistance group planning the blockade of the army induction centre in Berkeley, there were extreme differences of opinion about tactics. Resistance founder David Harris, who was now romantically involved with Joan Baez, was insistent that the protest should be non-violent. Others disagreed. 'You'd get a lot of people needlessly beaten up,' Harris remembered thinking. 'I thought these guys were off the wall. I didn't want to be associated with them.'

It didn't help that the one person tireless and fearless enough to marshal these divided forces was the increasingly volatile and unorthodox Jerry Rubin. His success as the spokesperson for the Vietnam Day Committee persuaded the National Mobilization Committee in New York to recruit him as co-ordinator for the week's activities. Veteran peace campaigners were alarmed when Rubin arrived in militant hippie garb, chain-smoking dope and spouting provocative rhetoric. By his side was the equally mercurial Abbie Hoffman. Since his days with SNCC, Hoffman had also moved to New York, where he'd opened a free store in the style of San Francisco's Diggers commune. In August 1967, he and several associates stood on the viewing platform above the New York Stock Exchange, and threw dollar bills down onto the heads of the stockbrokers, who abandoned their trading and scrabbled like children for the cash. It was the first display of Hoffman's zany, Marx Brothers style of politics, which undermined the system by mocking it. His theatrics relied on the infallibly gullible nature of the national media, who swallowed his increasingly playful stunts and reproduced them to the outside world as deadly serious protest. No wonder that Hoffman concluded: 'There's no source out there for checking reality. The only reality is in your head.'

Rubin and Hoffman met like firecrackers and matches. Rubin supplied the radical ambition; Hoffman the surreal spark that turned a campaign into a media event. Mobe's march on Washington provided a perfect example of the pair in tandem. Peace activists had originally suggested a lobby of Capitol Hill. Rubin upped the ante by suggesting the more provocative target of the Pentagon. And then Hoffman declared that the demonstrators would not only march on the Pentagon, they would levitate it, three hundred feet off the ground. At this point, it would turn orange, and then start to shake, until all the evil had exited the building.

Together, Rubin and Hoffman were unstoppable, and sometimes insuffer-
able. When Phil Ochs played Carnegie Hall on 1 October 1967, he invited
the devilish duo to join him during his encore, to inform the audience of
their plans to protest at next summer's Democratic National Convention in
Chicago. As Rubin began to read his announcement, Hoffman grabbed the
microphone and began to shout: 'Fuck Lyndon Johnson! Fuck Robert
Kennedy! And fuck you if you don't like it!' As some of the audience started
to howl their discontent, Hoffman leaped off the stage and prowled among
them, shouting four-letter words in their faces. Ochs' triumphant evening
dissolved into chaos, while backstage Hoffman and Rubin congratulated themselves on upsetting the cosy liberalism of his fans. 'The audience was caught
off guard,' recalls Ochs' brother Michael. 'Some people liked it, some didn't,
but the bulk went along with it, because it was an event. Phil wasn't overjoyed by what happened; he made some disparaging comment about them
from the stage. But he and Jerry were good friends, and they always disagreed
a lot. This was just another one of those occasions as far as he was concerned.'

Rubin and Hoffman's plans for the Pentagon were equally anarchic. While
Mobe assembled an array of leading writers to head the march, including
Norman Mailer (who immortalised the event in *The Armies of the Night*) and
Robert Lowell, Hoffman and Rubin teased the media and the authorities.
First, Hoffman led a deputation to 'measure' the Pentagon, so they could
calculate how to perform the levitation. Then they made an official application to raise the building from the ground. In a rare show of official
humour, the authorities elicited a promise from Hoffman that the Pentagon
would rise no more than ten feet. Meanwhile, the duo convinced the media
that, to counter the cops' supply of Mace, they had created a substance
called Lace. Anyone who was sprayed with this concoction would automatically tear off their clothes and make love with the person nearest to them.
They demonstrated its effects with the aid of three hippie couples in front
of the New York press corps.

On 15 October, Phil Ochs, fellow folk-singer Richie Havens, jazz musicians Archie Shepp and Charles Mingus, plus the Fugs, appeared at New
York's Vietnam Peace Parade. The following morning, attention switched to
the Oakland induction centre. At 5 a.m., more than 200 protestors blocked
the doors through which new recruits were supposed to pass. 'I am going
to try and talk with the young men going in, talk with them against all wars,'
Joan Baez told a reporter. The recruits were handed leaflets, but none of

them stopped to engage with the demonstrators. Within minutes, almost all of the peaceniks had been arrested. Baez, her sister Mimi Farina and their mother were all seized by the police. Her arrest was greeted with gentle applause by her supporters, as she walked towards the police vans with her arms raised in symbolic triumph. She was subsequently sentenced to 120 days in prison. Her family's place was taken by 2,000 more campaigners. Similar scenes took place at army centres around the country, as draft cards were burned or handed in to the authorities. Baez served just ten days of her sentence, and was arrested again within weeks for another induction centre protest. Second time around, she spent forty-five days in the Santa Rita Rehabilitation Center. 'Something is disastrously wrong when our nation pursues an unjust war,' she told the press.

The same spirit of betrayal fuelled the spectacular assault on the Pentagon. The demonstrators were variously numbered at 35,000 (*Time* magazine) and 350,000 (Mobe). *Time*'s account captured the contempt of the establishment: the dissenters comprised 'hard-eyed revolutionaries and skylarking hippies', who were 'ranting and chanting' and 'aroused by acrimony and acid-rock'; 'speakers caterwauled in competition with blues and rock bands'; alas, 'the lighthearted surrealism of the hippie approach was soon short-circuited by the hard-line elements'. This devious subversion haunted *Time*'s copy: 'Unsophisticated pacifist or anti-draft outfits and digger do-gooders from the hippie subculture are frequently suckered into the hard-line camp,' the magazine declared, 'and end up unwittingly propagandising as activists'.

*Time*'s reporters were alarmed by such escapades as the 'exorcism' of the Pentagon, staged by members of the Fugs. The band had been edging along the borderline between the counter-culture and the mainstream for more than two years, arousing an increasingly stellar following for their lengthy residency at the Players Theater in New York. Placing morals before money, they had sabotaged their opportunity of exposure to the mass audience. They were invited onto Johnny Carson's top-rated TV talk show early in 1967, but the Fugs replied that they would only appear if they sang their anti-war ditty, 'Kill for Peace'. The invitation was hastily withdrawn. At the Pentagon, poet Ed Sanders prepared a magical ceremony, a pagan expulsion of the demons behind America's war machine, which was answered by a repeated chant of 'Out demons out!' by the multitude.

Phil Ochs was anxious to soak up the chaos. 'When the tear gas was let off,' his brother Michael recalls, 'Phil went out of his way to walk into the cloud, so he could find out exactly what it felt like.' Not every protestor found so much to celebrate. Cass Elliott, visual and vocal icon of the Mamas & the Papas, was 'right in the front, taking pictures, just being there to find out what was happening'. In the mêlée, she complained, 'I was knocked down and stomped on. I don't want to do that again. It didn't accomplish anything.' In an increasingly polarised America, observers were likely to be swept under foot by both sides.

Revolution ancient and modern collided again in early December 1967, when a debate was held between Jerry Rubin and the Socialist Worker Party presidential candidate, Fred Halstead, under the highly relevant banner: 'What Policy Next for the Anti-War Movement?' Halstead spoke with his usual passion for thirty minutes. Then Rubin was called to the rostrum. He carried with him a portable gramophone and a handful of records. He cued up a disc, sat back in his chair, and watched the audience as Bob Dylan's 'Ballad of a Thin Man' boomed out. When the song ended, there was an expectant silence as people waited for Rubin to interpret Dylan's words, like Huey Newton or A.J. Weberman. Instead, he reached for another record, and the Dadaist wordplay of the Beatles' 'I Am the Walrus' filled the hall. And so he continued for his full thirty minutes, letting Dylan and the Beatles speak for the future. 'It was the first time in the history of the Socialist movement', Rubin boasted, 'that someone didn't say a word during the time allotted for political argument.'

The same combination of avant-garde advertising and absurdist theatre inspired Phil Ochs to revive his declaration of peace. He might also have wanted to preserve the political copyright on his idea, after the Straight Theater company in Berkeley staged an event entitled 'The End Of The War' on 5 November. 'It's not that we can't do anything ABOUT the war,' their spokesman explained. 'It's that we can't do anything BECAUSE of the war. The war is a media prison.'

Ochs set out to prove them wrong. He may also have been anxious to demonstrate his commitment to the anti-war cause: his latest album, *Pleasures of the Harbor*, a work of some sophistication, had lacked the overt protest material of old. Having learned the value of publicity from Rubin and Hoffman, he 'sold' his New York version of 'The War Is Over' via an ironic ad in the *Village Voice*: 'Does protesting the war leave you tired and upset? Does civil disobedience leave you nervous and irritable? . . . Is everybody sick of this stinking war? In that case, friends, do what I and thousands of other Americans have done – declare the war over. . . . If you are surprised the war is over, imagine the incredulity of this administration when they hear about it.'

Ochs scheduled a rally for lunchtime on Saturday 25 November, in Washington Square Park. 'Suppose one day 5,000 trucks travelled through a city announcing "The war in Vietnam is over! The war is over!",' wrote his friend Jerry Rubin exuberantly. '[The President] would have to go on TV to reassure the Amerikan people that the war was still on.' The demonstration didn't quite match that fantasy, but Ochs still succeeded in assembling around 2,000 people. He sang 'The War Is Over', and then he, Allen Ginsberg and Gregory Corso led the crowd through the streets of lower Manhattan, carrying signs, cheering and whooping as if peace really had been declared. 'He needed a companion for this quixotic event,' recalls singer Judy Henske, 'so I went along. Most people were hostile, shouting out things like, "This is no time for a joke". Phil just smiled at them and waved. It was a happening, not a demonstration. But people didn't want it to be a joke.' As Michael Ochs remembered the event, 'Lots of people believed it was real, and street people started waving and shouting with excitement. There were some vicious attacks when people realised it was a parody.' Like Orson Welles staging his alien invasion on radio, Ochs had briefly conjured up an alternative reality that disrupted the real world. A week later, a reprise of October's Stop The Draft protests evoked a disappointing response. It was easier, it seemed, to raise the collective pulse with anarchic imagination than winter-cold orthodoxy.

It was an ill omen for those hoping to alter the shape of America via democratic means. A year before the November 1968 presidential election, candidates lined up on both sides of the narrow political divide. While Republicans weighed millionaire Nelson Rockefeller against the loser of 1960, Richard Nixon, Democrats began to consider the unthinkable – overthrowing their incumbent president. On 2 December 1967, Senator Eugene McCarthy of Minnesota broke ranks against Lyndon Johnson by declaring his own candidacy on an anti-war ticket. He gathered young and radical Democrats behind him, but few imagined that he had a realistic chance of toppling the president.

With neither of America's main parties able to galvanise public opinion, and McCarthy viewed by many on the anti-war left as an opportunist, some attention was focused on the potential of third-party candidates. A loose confederation of left-wing groups gathered under the banner of the

Peace & Freedom Party (PFP) in late 1967. Their first goal was to be allowed to place their candidate – as yet unselected – on the ballot. Flatbed trucks travelled through the streets of San Francisco that December pleading for support; to make sure that they were noticed, activists recruited a young Latin-rock outfit, the Santana Blues Band, to perform in the parade and at fundraisers. In Los Angeles, meanwhile, the PFP staged a Rally For The Ballot on New Year's Eve, at which country-rockers the Nitty Gritty Dirt Band joined an all-star jazz ensemble and the R&B vocal group the Chambers Brothers. Appealing though they were to the PFP's likely audience, however, these events had little impact on the party's fortunes. What pushed the PFP onto the ballot was the support – silent at first, and then increasingly strident – of the militant black community.

## DUDES ON THE BLOCK

SNCC was the first organisation to pledge its energies to creating a viable radical presence in the election campaign. But SNCC was a fading force by December 1967. Far more crucial was the decision of the Black Panther Party For Self Defense to lend its weight to the PFP. Overnight – literally – the Panthers had been transformed from an Oakland sect to a national phenomenon. On 15 October, Panthers leaders Huey Newton and David Hilliard had attended the demonstration at the Oakland induction centre, and were ignored by the underground press. Yet within two weeks, Newton and his party were known across America.

The catalyst was an incident that was instantly mythologised and has never been satisfactorily explained. For all his intellectual pretensions and mastery of the legal system, Huey Newton was a volatile and often violent man. 'The dudes on the block thought I was "out of sight" and sometimes just plain crazy,' he wrote in his autobiography. Eldridge Cleaver, now firmly established as the Panthers' media spokesman, recognised the charismatic benefits of Newton's temperament: 'Huey showed that you also have to have . . . what I called "the courage to kill": the courage not only to risk your life, but to take the initiative in the pursuit of your liberation and your freedom and be willing to take the life of your oppressor when he's moving to take your life.'

Newton's violence was not always so precisely targeted. At a social gathering in 1964, he argued with an older black man. Twice he turned away from the discussion in disgust; twice his opponent grabbed his arm and held him back. When it happened again, Newton pulled out a knife and stabbed the man several times. It was, he alleged, an act of self-defence. Charged with assault with a deadly weapon, he was 'found guilty, but only because I lacked a jury of my peers' – street-wise young blacks, in other words, who might have empathised with his actions.

He served a six-month prison sentence, and was then paroled for a further two and a half years. On 27 October 1967, he celebrated the end of his parole at late-night parties in Oakland. Some time after 4 a.m., he and a friend, Gene McKinney, were driving along Seventh Street, when they were pulled over by a police cruiser. Patrolman John Frey examined Newton's driver's licence, and radioed for assistance once he realised that he had stopped the leader of the Panthers. When a second car arrived, Frey and Officer Herbert Heanes searched the two men. Newton reached for his lawbook, and said something like 'You have no reason to arrest me.' Frey apparently replied: 'You can take that book and shove it up your ass, nigger.' Within twenty seconds, Frey lay dead on the ground, Heanes had been hit by several bullets, and Newton had been shot four times in the stomach and once in the thigh.

The exact circumstances of the shooting remain cloudy to this day. Newton claimed that he remembered being shot in the stomach by Frey, after which: 'There were some shots, a rapid volley, but I have no idea where they came from. They seemed to be all around me. I vaguely remember being on my hands and knees on the ground, disoriented, with everything spinning. I also had the sensation of being moved or propelled.' At no point did he admit having held or fired a gun, or even having one in his possession. There were several theories: that a third Panther, passing on the street, had gunned down the policemen; that the two officers had fired on each other in their haste to gun down Newton; or that Newton himself had drawn a gun, provoking a flurry of shooting from both sides. In public, Newton steadfastly maintained his innocence; yet several associates have claimed that shortly before his death, he finally confessed to Frey's murder.

Nobody on the radical left raised that possibility in the years that followed. From the moment that pictures were released of Newton strapped to a hospital gurney like a medieval torture victim, the Panthers' leader became a Movement martyr, and myth. As he recovered from his injuries, he was charged with first-degree murder, assault with a deadly weapon, and the kidnapping of a passer-by whose car he and McKinney had commandeered to take him to hospital. If convicted of murder, he faced the gas chamber. From across black America and the counter-culture came the cry: Free Huey! And it was on that unifying issue that the Peace & Freedom Party and the Panthers found common cause, alongside the Young Lords (the 'Latin Panthers'), Honkies For Huey, and a hundred other organisations who recognised in Newton's imprisonment – or 'persecution' – the spark for a revolutionary uprising.

Yet half of radical America was automatically excluded from this coalition. At the 1967 SDS conference, two activists from Chicago attempted to propose a motion calling for the liberation of women from their 'colonial status'. The male organising committee ensured that the proposal was sidelined, while (male) delegates chortled at the suggestion that their revolutionary time should be wasted on such fripperies. In the aftermath of the conference, which respected every radical cause except feminism, a small group of female SDS members began to meet once a week to discuss their status and future tactics. Two months later, they issued a manifesto, addressed broadly 'To the Women of the Left'. 'Our political awareness of our oppression', they wrote, 'has developed through the last couple of years as we sought to apply the principles of justice, equality, mutual respect and dignity which we learned from the Movement to the lives we lived as part of the Movement; only to come up against the solid wall of male chauvinism.' That wall extended from the Black Panther Party, where women were initially denied the right to bear arms, to the upper echelons of the rock community, and into the Peace & Freedom Party, where numerous names were considered as electoral candidates, none of them female. As 1968 dawned, change was visible in Vietnam, in the struggle for black power, in Africa's anguished attempts at independence, amongst the Greek colonels and the Czech secret police, the Red Guard in China and the Democratic Party in Alabama – everywhere but the home, and the workplace, and any other sphere of life where men shared their space with women, but not their power. Women's time would come. First, the boys had games to play.

# SECTION II

# CHAPTER 3: 1968

L ike Swinging London's summer of love and Huey Newton's living martyrdom, 1968 passed into mythology before it had ended. 'There has never been a year like 1968, and it is unlikely that there will ever be one again,' wrote chronicler Mark Kurlansky. It has been immortalised as the year of the barricades, the year when student power nearly toppled governments, the year of anger and of hope, the year of assassinations and of anarchy, 'the year that rocked the world', as Kurlansky put it. Yet, when the smoke subsided and the myth solidified, there was still war in Vietnam, still capitalism and communism poised at each other's throats around the world, still black power to be won, still feminism to be pursued, still a revolution on the horizon. There were events in 1968 that stamped their brand on the Western consciousness: two political assassinations in America, student protests in France, Russian tanks in Prague. But in the history of the planet, decades or centuries hence, none of these may match the global significance of 1967's cultural revolution in the most populous nation on earth. If 1968 signified anything, it was a sense of revolutionary potential, which crackled through the West like electronic static, and ensured that this year was not the climax of the struggle, but merely the prelude. The prospect of revolution obsessed the American counter-culture, and overshadowed the event that seemed to haunt all the year's phantasms and alarms: the Democratic National Convention in Chicago.

## THE CREEPING MEATBALL

People today have a genuine fear of stepping out and thinking on their own. 'Creeping Meatballism' is this rejection of individuality. It's conformity. The American brags about being a great individualist, when actually he's the world's least individual person . . . The guy who has been taken in by the 'Meatball' philosophy is the guy who really believes that contemporary people are slim, and clean-limbed, and they're so much fun to be with . . . because they drink Pepsi-Cola. As long as he believes this, he's in the clutches of 'Creeping Meatballism'.

> (Jean Shepherd, 'The Night People Vs Creeping Meatballism', *Mad Magazine*, 1957)

Rise up and abandon the creeping meatball!

> (Yippie manifesto, 1968)

What more appropriate place in 1968 to find a symbol for America – and American dissent – than the pages of *Mad Magazine*? The nation seemed to sink into a swamp of madness, floundering like a drowning man, kicking up ferocious sprays of mud but moving precisely nowhere. Meanwhile, hundreds of lives were sacrificed on the battlefield every month, staining America with their blood.

All this mayhem coalesced in Chicago in August 1968, when the counter-culture staged its assault on the establishment. It was an event without meaning, which reverberated through the year, echoing the laughter of fools and the weeping of saints. Chicago was a joke, a crime, a charade and a hall of mirrors in which the state and its rebels could gaze at each other's reflections in bafflement and fear. It signified what the left had already feared from its experiences in Paris and Prague: that revolution would inevitably fail. But it also hardened the divide between generations, classes and creeds, to the point where the threat of revolution would cause American power to shudder, at home and abroad.

As dexterous manipulators of the media, Abbie Hoffman and Jerry Rubin claimed the farce of Chicago as their own invention. They became the public face of the Yippies, alias the Youth International Party, an assembly of anarchists, idealists and misfits whose antics seized global attention. Yet the initial impetus for the Yippies – or, at least, for a protest movement that would tackle the establishment with the sarcasm it so richly deserved – came from a long-forgotten source, publisher Bob Ockene.[1] Having slipped into the Pentagon during the October 'levitation' on borrowed press credentials, he observed the ensuing fracas from behind police lines. He was angered by the gulf between the fiery rhetoric of the demonstration's leaders, and their less courageous behaviour in the face of the National Guard. He decided that the counter-culture required a non-authoritarian leadership that reflected its own sprawling chaos.

Through November and December 1967, Hoffman, Rubin, Ockene, satirist Paul Krassner and other like-minded oppositionists traded ideas and fantasies. During a conference in Manhattan, poet and Fugs member Ed Sanders reminded Rubin of the totemic power of that summer's Monterey Pop Festival. 'Rubin said that it was inspirational that some of the major rock bands in America were willing to play for free at a large tribal-type gathering of people,' Sanders recalled, 'and I said that we should consider convening something for the following year – a free rock festival comprised of all the major rock bands in America.'

Abbie Hoffman recalled a December 1967 meeting with Rubin and Krassner, at which they discussed the need to stage an emblematic demonstration against the Johnson administration's policies in Vietnam. The ideal location, they decided, would be the Democratic Party's National Convention, at which it was assumed that Johnson would be confirmed as his party's candidate for the 1968 election. The Convention was scheduled for Chicago in late August. According to Hoffman, Rubin 'said that it would be a good idea to call it the Festival of Life, in contrast to the Convention of Death, and to have it in some kind of public arena, like a park or something'. The gathering would be announced as an international festival of youth, Rubin concluded. Krassner then made his historic intervention: 'I said we should have a better name for it, something that would be more catchy, and the words Youth International Party came out as a switch on International Youth Party. Then suddenly I shouted out, "YIP – Yippie!".' What really mattered, Hoffman concluded, was to demonstrate an alternative lifestyle to that on display from the police and the National Guard: 'That is the only sane thing to do.'

Later that month, Rubin visited novelist Norman Mailer, whom he'd met during the march on the Pentagon. By Mailer's account, Rubin's vision had already expanded beyond a rock festival into a direct confrontation with Chicago's authorities: 'It was his idea that the presence of 100,000 young people in Chicago at a festival with rock bands would so intimidate and terrify the establishment that Lyndon Johnson would have to be nominated under armed guard. I said, "Wow". I was overtaken with the audacity of the idea and I said, "It's beautiful and frightening". Rubin said, "I think that the beauty of it is that the establishment is going to do it all themselves. We won't do a thing. We are just going to be there and they won't be able to take it. They will smash the city themselves. They will provoke all the violence.'" Rubin, Mailer concluded, was a brave – perhaps perilously brave – young man.

On 4 January 1968, Rubin invited Sanders to his apartment. The pair meditated in front of a portrait of Cuban guerrilla leader Che Guevara, already the poster child of the counter-culture just two months after his death at the hands of the Bolivian army. Their sensory adjustment continued with a thirty-minute session designed to toughen their feet, presumably in preparation for a long march towards justice. Rubin and Sanders strapped plastic bags filled with ice-cubes to their feet, and marched relentlessly around the room until their bodies were as numbed as their minds. Finally, they were ready to talk. Rubin laid out his festival scenario, which Sanders recalled as 'a convening of all people interested in the new politics, guerrilla theatre, rock and roll, the convening of the hemp horde from all over the various tribes in the United States'. Rubin asked him to act as talent co-ordinator for the event, 'since [he] knew the major rock groups in the United States'. Sanders agreed to make the appropriate calls.

The response was supportive but mostly vague. Only a handful of artists were prepared to nail their colours to the Yippie mast, among them Judy Collins, Country Joe McDonald and, almost inevitably, Phil Ochs. 'I helped design the party,' Ochs testified at the 1969 trial of the Chicago 'conspirators'. 'Yippie was to be a form of theatre politics, theatrically dealing with what seemed to be an increasingly absurd world and trying to deal with it in other than just on a straight moral level.' Ochs was adamant that Rubin and Hoffman were anxious to avoid violence, even pledging to fly to Chicago so they could discuss their festival with the city's notoriously intransigent mayor, Richard Daley.

'Phil loved the idea of the Yippies,' Michael Ochs recalls. 'He always loved the Theatre of the Absurd. He was a social democrat, basically, but he liked to play both sides. He wanted to work inside the system and outside it at the same time. Ultimately, though, he always believed that democracy could be made to work.' Hence his desire to see the Yippies operate within the law. From the outset, Phil made sure that Rubin and Hoffman pursued official permission to stage whatever Chicago might turn into. The same concern worried virtually all of the musicians who were approached to take part.

Arlo Guthrie met with the Yippies at an underground radio station, and immediately told them: 'It would be rather difficult for me to get involved in that kind of thing, as we had a lot of trouble before with festivals and gatherings because of police violence.' At the Chelsea Hotel in Greenwich Village, Rubin and Hoffman arranged a summit meeting with Country Joe McDonald, Fish bassist Bruce Barthol, their manager, 'Banana' Ed Denson, Irwin Silber from the folk magazine *Sing Out!*, and singer/activist Barbara Dane. McDonald said that 'it was a good idea to do something positive to counterbalance all the negative political vibrations'. That way, he explained, they could broadcast the fact 'that there are people in America who are not tripped out on ways of thinking which result only in oppression and fear, paranoia and death'. Denson soon raised the question of legality: 'If there were no permits, the bands involved would probably get arrested.' They were assured by Rubin and Hoffman that the Yippies were already negotiating with city authorities. On this basis, McDonald promised to seek support from other West Coast musicians.

As a veteran of numerous anti-war protests, and a key figure at the Pentagon the previous October, Allen Ginsberg was a natural recruit to Hoffman's cause. Both capable of blazing streams of rhetoric, the poet and the activist enjoyed an inspirational meeting in February, each easing the other towards his own vision of the world until the two seemed to have become one. 'He said that politics had become theatre and magic,' Ginsberg recounted, 'that it was the manipulation of imagery through mass media that was confusing and hypnotising the people in the United States and making them accept a war which they did not really believe in.' Hoffman envisaged an anarchic teach-in, wherein he and Ginsberg could 'present different ideas of what is wrong with the planet, what we can do to solve the pollution crisis, what we can do to solve the Vietnam war, to present different ideas for making the society more sacred and less commercial, less materialistic.' It was a long way from Monterey Pop; a long way also from what Chicago became.

Much of Ginsberg's idealistic fervour survived when Rubin and Hoffman announced their plans to the media. 'YIPPIES MEET NATIONAL DEATH PARTY', screamed the headline. 'Join us in Chicago in August,' the two pranksters continued, 'for an international festival of youth, music and theatre. Rise up and abandon the creeping meatball! Come all you rebels, youth spirits, rock minstrels, truth-seekers, peacock-freaks, poets, barricade-jumpers, lovers and artists.' Having called the entire counter-culture to arms, they laid out their beatific vision: 'It is summer. It is the last week of August, and the National Death Party meets to bless Johnson. We are there! There are 500,000 of us dancing in the streets, throbbing with amplifiers and harmony. We are making love in the parks. We are reading, singing, laughing, printing news-papers, groping and making a mock convention, and celebrating the birth of Free America in our own time.' It was the Human Be-In extended over a summer of love, as Monterey's soundtrack blended with the ecstatic cries of orgasm. And after climax would come rebirth: 'A new spirit explodes in the land. Things are bursting in music, poetry, dancing, newspapers, movies, cele-bration, magic, politics, theatre and lifestyles. All these new tribes will gather in Chicago. We will be completely open. Everything will be completely free.' Then an abrupt change of tone, into the apocalyptic: 'The life of the American spirit is being torn asunder by the forces of violence, decay and the napalm-cancer fiend. We demand the Politics of Ecstasy [a phrase coined by acid guru Timothy Leary]! We are the delicate spores of the new fierceness that will change America. We will create our own reality, we are Free America! And we will not accept the false theatre of the Death Convention.' With their final words, Rubin and Hoffman turned the festival over to the people: 'We will be in Chicago. Begin preparations now! Chicago is yours! Do it!'

The announcement rapidly reached the pages of the *New York Post*, and mutated from there. While the overground press traded paranoid fantasies about the atrocities that the Yippies might be ready to perpetrate, the tradi-tional anti-war movement became equally alarmed. Michael Rossman, the self-proclaimed 'moral philosopher' of the Free Speech Movement in Berkeley, had been sparring with Rubin for years. 'Chicago in August will harbor the nation's richest pool of uptight bad vibes, set to flash,' he warned. 'Pack 200,000 kids in there, with where we are in America these days when not even our inner millennium has come, and it's sure to blow.' The problem, he explained, was that 'black Chicago and white alike throb with anti-hippie hatred'. His somewhat naive suggestion was that the Yippies should abandon the concept of a festival, and allow the people to create their own demon-stration without leadership.

The students' socialist organisation, SDS, was equally dismissive of the Yippie plan. It was 'manipulative at best', claimed a spokesperson, for Rubin and Hoffman to lure people to Chicago 'to groove on rock bands and smoke grass and then to put them up against bayonets' in the expectation that it would be 'a radicalising experience'. 'The idea would not be bad,' SDS conceded, 'were it not for the Illinois National Guards and the Chicago police.'

Rossman and SDS were concerned that the Yippies' Festival of Life would dampen or damage the anti-Johnson demonstrations that other left groupings were preparing for Chicago. In December 1967, veteran peace campaigner Dave Dellinger, and Tom Hayden and Rennie Davis of SDS, had voiced their intention to mark the Democratic National Convention with a protest march. 'Dellinger was older than the other guys,' Judy Collins recalls. 'He had been a conscientious objector during the Second World War, and he was a wonderful, bright, thoughtful, very deep man.' Hayden and Davis had recently returned from a fact-finding mission to North Vietnam, during which their hosts had released several American prisoners of war into their care. Their experiences heightened their conviction that the war must be stopped. The pair established a Chicago office in February to co-ordinate the left's activities.

This conventional, albeit radical, politicking did nothing to dissuade the Yippies from pursuing their own version of militancy. On 17 March 1968, Rubin and Hoffman staged a press conference in New York, to announce that the Festival of Life was a reality. Poets and musicians – among them Allen Ginsberg, Phil Ochs, Arlo Guthrie and Judy Collins – were on hand to prove that the crusade had support beyond the Yippies' narrow ranks. Ginsberg chanted a mantra; Collins sang Malvina Reynolds' anti-war ballad, 'Where Have All the Flowers Gone'. Their presence also underlined that the Festival was intended foremost as a cultural protest, not a violent assault on the establishment. Collins emphasised that she wanted 'to see a celebration of life, not of destruction'; that 'life is the force that I wish to make my songs and my life known for'.

'My background made me completely ready to participate in the revolution,' Collins says today. 'My father had a radio show in which he castigated the McCarthy witch-hunts in the 1950s. We were raised to speak our minds. So it was natural for me to sing about peace, war and injustice, as well as love. When people started to do that in a singer-songwriter kind of way, it was so new and fresh that it probably gave us the idea that we could make a difference politically as well. We began to believe that we really could stop the war in Vietnam.' She had no aspirations towards becoming a politician:

'I hated having to play at all those rallies and demonstrations,' she says. 'Who wanted to go on marches? But we had no choice.'

When she was approached by the Yippies, her initial reaction was reluctance: 'I was always very leery of movement things. I didn't mind leading people in song, but I was not a joiner. I think a lot of us artists were like that. Our role was to give other people a certain amount of courage through our music. So that's why I insisted that I sing at the press conference – *that* was what I did.'

Aware that culture was their most direct route to their audience, the Yippies sold the Festival as primarily an artistic gathering. 'The music will be free,' Rubin promised. 'The performers will be playing for their community. Definite already are Country Joe & the Fish, the Fugs, Arlo Guthrie, Phil Ochs, the United States of America band, Pageant Players, Bread & Puppet Theatre, Allen Ginsberg, Timothy Leary, Paul Krassner [and the] Steve Miller Blues Band.' It was a roll-call of familiar names from the counter-culture – poets, visionaries, self-publicists, folkies, psychedelic anarchists, theatrical iconoclasts. 'The technique is very crude, very personal, very political,' promised the publicity blurb for the drama group the Pageant Players. 'They are against war and other aspects of modern life.' So too were the United States of America, an eclectic rock ensemble formed by a veteran of the earliest musical protest against Vietnam, Joseph Byrd (who, incidentally, has no memory of ever meeting Hoffman or Rubin, or being asked to appear at their festival).

It was fare fit for a Manhattan benefit show, not a rally designed to shake the walls of the military-industrial complex. Hence Rubin's promise of more impressive names to follow: 'Invitations are now going out to Dylan, Eric Burdon & the Animals, the Monkees, the Jefferson Airplane, Richie Havens, Simon & Garfunkel, the Doors, the Who, the Blues Project, the Beatles, Mothers of Invention, the Mamas & Papas, Janis Ian, the Cream, and the Smothers Brothers, to name but a few.' This wish list comprised everyone with whom any of the organisers could claim some acquaintance. 'Hoffman asked me if I could contact the Beatles or Bob Dylan and tell them what was afoot and ask them if they could join us,' Ginsberg testified at the conspiracy trial. Neither the Beatles nor Dylan was willing to commit themselves. Nor were Jefferson Airplane any more enthusiastic: 'We talked about it to Abbie,' Paul Kantner recalls, 'and we told him that we thought the idea was fucked up from the start. I appreciate the fact that some people did bother to go there and get their heads kicked in on our behalf, but I couldn't see any reason for us to go and get beaten up.'

As Rubin admitted, dropping the most potent names in rock culture triggered an exponential increase in the event's notoriety: 'Kids asked each other, "Going to Chicago?" Plans spread by the greatest conspiracy of all – word-of-mouth. Was Dylan coming? Sure! The Beatles? Sure! Rolling Stones? Yippie! The Viet Kong sending a delegation? Sure! The Pope coming? Why not? Dr Spock importing the suburbs? Outasight! Martin Luther King marching? Sure! Che? Right on! Eldridge? Yippie? Jesus Christ? Sure! Absolutely! We denied nothing. We embellished every rumour and passed it on to ten more people. What a monster we had unleashed! We were creating a bigger myth for Chicago than the Democrats were.'

Everyone from the upper echelons of the Democratic Party to the Yippie leaders envisaged the Chicago Convention as a crowning of the incumbent president. In late March, Jerry Rubin and Ed Sanders of the Fugs conceived the idea of running a rival candidate to Lyndon Johnson – a pig. Sanders made Rubin promise that the Yippies' figurehead would not become bacon after its symbolic bid for the presidency. Then the President himself intervened. On 31 March, Johnson made a rambling 40-minute TV broadcast from the White House. His speech was nearly over when he uttered the words that stunned the nation, friends and foes alike: 'I shall not seek, and will not accept, the nomination of my party for another term as your President.' Chicago had been intended to lampoon and harass Johnson; maybe even force him to change his mind. Now he had removed himself from the fray before the Yippies had even recruited their troops.

Across the anti-war movement, activists regarded Johnson's imminent resignation as a triumph. The Democratic Party field was now left open for either of the candidates who had aligned themselves against his Vietnam policies: Eugene McCarthy and Robert Kennedy. But with serious politicians ready to fight for the nomination at the Chicago conference, why would the movement wish to become entangled with the Yippies' theatrics?

It was a question that bothered Jann Wenner, editor and publisher of the recently launched rock magazine *Rolling Stone*. Its in-depth interviews and *New York Times*-style coverage of the counter-culture had already attracted a readership beyond the dreams of the underground press. But Wenner remained distrustful of any attempts to steer rock, his paper or indeed the counter-culture into political activism.

His misgivings were allowed full vent in a cover story in May 1968, published under a headline worthy of the mainstream tabloid press: 'Musicians Reject New Political Exploiters. Groups Drop Out From Chicago Yip-In.' There was little evidence in his lengthy article to support his second assertion, or indeed his first, except on the grounds that he was the ethical guardian of the musical community. His prejudice was evident from the very first line: 'A self-appointed coterie of political "radicals" without a legitimate constituency has formed itself into a "Youth International Party", opened up offices in New York City, and begun a blitzkrieg campaign to organise a "hip" protest.' The Nazi connotations of 'blitzkrieg' weren't accidental. Wenner proceeded to ridicule Rubin and Hoffman's command of the publicity machine, as being 'as up to date as the cleverest Madison Avenue "media buyer" and as brassy as any showbiz promotion man', before pronouncing: 'It looks like a shuck.' Most damning, in Wenner's eyes, was the YIP's 'grasping to itself the potent charm of the music of the young'.

And this, surely, was the underlying motive of Wenner's attack: the desire to keep rock music and its 'potent charm' free from the taint of 'radical politicos'. He admitted as much when he claimed: 'Rock'n'roll is the ONLY way in which the vast but formless power of youth is structured, the only way in which it can be defined or inspected.' Ironically, his equation of the youth movement with rock'n'roll was exactly what had motivated the Yippies to make music the focus of their Festival of Life: they imagined that rock'n'roll had more power than politics to attract a vast youth audience. Where they differed was that Rubin and Hoffman imagined that rock was inherently revolutionary, and would therefore prepare the young masses for political action; Wenner seemed equally convinced that the rock revolution signified nothing beyond the fact of its own existence.

## CHE CHIC

By coincidence or fate, this was the moment when one of the most successful entertainment organisations in America, Columbia Records, launched an advertising campaign 'as brassy as any showbiz promotion man'. Its first fruits were included in many of the same papers that contained news of the Yippies' plans, including *Rolling Stone*. The company was marketing a sampler album featuring its most prestigious underground rock acts, under the faintly ridiculous title *Rock Machine I Love You*. To sell the album, Columbia boasted: 'The Revolutionaries are on the Rock Machine'. It was a theme the company would pursue for the next year.

Almost overnight, the iconographies of rock and revolutionary politics began to intertwine. Poster companies advertised heavily in the underground press, offering portraits of rock stars such as Frank Zappa, Jimi Hendrix, Bob Dylan and even bluesman John Mayall, alongside political items such as 'Smash Capital Now!' and an image entitled Vietnam Papercut ('proceeds from this poster donated to the People's War in Vietnam'). Not to be outdone, the *Black Panther* newspaper in Oakland responded with posters and badges proclaiming 'Free Huey!' Ubiquitous (except in the *Black Panther*) was the face of Che Guevara. Once Fidel Castro's deputy in the Cuban revolution, Guevara had lent his mystique to Bolivian rebels, only to perish at the hands of government troops in October 1967. Within weeks, he had become a revolutionary poster child all over the world, from Brazil (where he was proclaimed 'A Saint of Our Time') to London, where self-consciously rebellious students took to greeting each other with a touch of the fists and the single word, 'Che'. 'I can't think of a revolutionary in the last century who had his romantic appeal,' noted Tariq Ali, one of the leaders of the anti-war movement in Britain.

Like Jim Morrison of the Doors, whose image was mass-marketed around the same time, Guevara's portraits boasted matinee idol looks, fashionably dishevelled hair, and a faraway zeal in his eyes. He was an altogether more attractive figure than the heavily bearded Fidel Castro, or the wizened Ho Chi Minh. But while Hollywood directors competed to rush the first Guevara biopic onto the screen, and students lapped up copies of his handbook, *Guerrilla Warfare*, any sense of the rebel leader as a political being, complex and sometimes deluded, was forgotten.

The first musical celebration of Che Guevara was composed by Joseph Byrd for the United States of America. A gorgeous, yearning ballad, 'Love Song for the Dead Che' appeared on the group's solitary album in 1968, sung by Byrd's one-time partner, Dorothy Moskowitz. 'That song is my personal favourite of everything we did,' Byrd says today. 'It was written not with art and deliberation, but spontaneously on learning of Che's death. Che was a mysterious figure to me. Why didn't he stay and rebuild Cuba after the 1959 revolution? The answer was that revolution was an end, for him, not a means. When the Cuban revolution was over, he had to find another one. In any case, I was writing about Che the romantic hero. The reality was surely very different.'

Powerfully meditative beneath its apparently romantic surface, 'Love Song for the Dead Che' was the most overtly political song on an album rich with cultural and social resonances. The United States of America had originally teamed Byrd and Moskowitz with Michael Agnello, who had collaborated with Byrd on several earlier projects. 'We both saw rock as an opportunity for social radicalism,' Byrd recalls, 'or at least for stirring up the coals. But Michael was a Trotskyist-anarchist hippie, and I was a Communist, so that didn't work out too well.' He characterises the gulf between himself and Agnello in practical and political terms: 'From the start, my long-term goal was to create revolution through our music, but also to have fun and be outrageous in the process. I wanted to use the principles of the Fluxus group – concept art, performance art, provocation. Michael's ambitions were no less lofty, but 90 degrees removed from mine. His idea was that we would be the musical wing of the Diggers, and a commune would be set up to support us and keep us performing – all of this happening, of course, without the use of money. Somehow these two opposing directions co-existed until we made our demo, and I sent it off to Columbia. Even then, there was no conflagration, because no one but me really thought we would be offered a contract. It was only when word came that Columbia wanted to sign us, that Mike exploded.' For Byrd, it was inevitable that a member of the Communist Party and a Trotskyist would come to blows: 'You need to recall the bitter internecine divisions that plagued the left in the 20th century. Hitler, for example, came to power because neither the Socialists nor the Communists would co-operate with each other.'

Dorothy Moskowitz offers a contrasting view of the divide within the United States of America. 'I joined the band with a couple of preconceived notions, some of them admittedly naive,' she explains. 'Having a group name that openly mocked our country was, to me, a patriotic expression of opposition to the war in Vietnam. Therefore, we would all act like left-leaning counter-cultural radicals. I also believed that alongside Joseph's skill with musical experimentalism, the band would also maintain some of the absurdist theatrics that Michael practised. He was very influenced by the Provos and the Diggers, who respectively gave away bicycles in the Netherlands and food and clothing in San Francisco, as expressions of political street theatre. Mike recognised at the outset that signing with a major "establishment" label like Columbia would compromise our vision, so to speak, and so he quit the band.'

Moskowitz remembers the band's first gig at the Ash Grove in Los Angeles: 'Michael bewildered the crowd before we performed "Love Song for the Dead Che" by drawling "Che Guevara . . . Che Guevara" into the mike, like some inscrutable gnome. If the band were to be rebellious, Mike took it upon himself to rebel in turn against the band. I was pretty amused by the ambiguity, but Joe Byrd wasn't. Our producer, David Rubinson, confessed to me later that part of his attraction to the band was because of the agit-prop tone Agnello lent to it. Michael never knew. Without him we went on, under Byrd's leadership, to become an electronic progressive rock group, recognised for being musically innovative in its day. But I think we could have been much more.'

Instead, racked by internal disagreements, the band fell apart within a year. Byrd dismisses any idea that the United States of America might have compromised its principles by working with a major corporation such as Columbia. 'I take issue with the thought that my work was less revolutionary because it used the tools of capitalism,' he says. 'On the contrary, it sought to wield those tools to educate, satirise and polemicise. The album's first and last pieces, "The American Metaphysical Circus" and "The American Way of Love", were comments on the media as a means of thought-control, and the bourgeois sentimentality of the hippies' "Summer of Love" compared to the realities of love under capitalism. Of course, if I was trying to ferment something, I failed. But that was the idea. And the fact that Columbia was paying for it all? Delicious!'

The ambiguous relationship between capitalism and revolutionary zeal was illustrated by another 1968 album issued by the same record company. *Underground* by jazz pianist Thelonious Monk portrayed him as a guerrilla hero, carbine strapped over his shoulder as he fingered his keyboard, grenades and sidearms scattered around the room, a Nazi officer roped to a chair behind him. A helpful liner note explained that the artwork was a celebration of 'Monk's forays as a member of the French Resistance movement in World War II. He was part of the underground then – for years in post-war America his piano was part of the underground of jazz . . .', and so it ran, neatly making its point and laughing at it simultaneously.

That elusive combination – political purpose and humour – echoed the Yippies' activities during early 1968. If their antics also solidified the cult reputation of Jerry Rubin and Abbie Hoffman, lining them up for immortality on posters, so much the better. As they shifted from fantasising about the future to intervening in the concrete world, they discovered that clowns were not immune from consequences. But the two men were ready to face down violence; indeed, Hoffman seemed eager to provoke attack, as if he was curious to find out how far both he and his opponents were prepared to go.

The Yippie couple were not universally popular in the underground. 'They always struck me as massive egomaniacs,' says Barry Miles, who encountered them many times during his own counter-culture adventures. 'Maybe I was being old-fashioned, as I was looking for a political party with an elected leadership, rather than these mad people who just assumed leadership and thought they were representing everybody. I didn't think they represented anyone. They didn't have a bunch of followers who wanted them to be spokesmen. It was just that the press was looking for somebody, and the more interviews they gave, the more they started to believe that they did represent people. But I thought they were just pains in the arse.'

Two Yippie events in New York were intended to recruit converts for Chicago – a Yip-In at Grand Central Station, followed by a Yip-Out in Central Park at Easter. The Yip-In promised a celebration of grooviness at the railway terminus on 22 March. While revellers assembled, hip DJs assembled playlists of train songs to encourage others to join them. Ultimately 3,000 kids filled Grand Central, impeding commuters and inciting the police to break out their riot shields, while the anarchist group Up Against The Wall Motherfuckers ripped the hands off the giant station clock and shouted 'time is meaningless'. Several people were injured, and many more assaulted by the police. 'That was the beginning of the death of Yippie,' remembered Ed Sanders. The Yip-Out a couple of weeks later was bucolic and peaceful by comparison.

As planning for Chicago continued, a cloud of foreboding gathered over the Festival of Life. Selfless gestures somehow backfired. Al Kooper, the leader of Blood, Sweat & Tears, assembled a band for a Yippie fundraiser at the Electric Circus. He left his guitar – 'an amazing Fender Telecaster' – in the dressing-room for a few minutes, and came back to find it gone. He stormed off to confront Abbie Hoffman: 'Hey, my fucking guitar got ripped off. What are you going to do about it?' Hoffman looked at Kooper and said, 'Nothing. Fuck you. So what, if your guitar was ripped off?' 'That was the sum total of my political career,' Kooper recalls. 'There might have been a song or two after that which commented on politics, but I never did another benefit like that.'

Yippie rhetoric in the months before Chicago suggested that the city might be under siege, with acid dropped into the water supply, convention delegates poisoned in their hotel rooms, and female activists deputed to seduce and blackmail politicians. As propaganda, it was more playful than menacing, but like an exercise in karma it provoked a reaction. In April 1968, Country Joe McDonald reported back to Jerry Rubin after trying to persuade other San Francisco bands to join the Festival. 'They were constantly relating to me stories that at least 2,000 civilian vigilantes were being authorised as deputies to arrest all troublemakers around the Convention,' he told Rubin. 'The National Guard was being assembled to prevent people from getting close to the Convention Hall; the sewers of Chicago were being prepared as dungeons to put demonstrators in; generally the vibrations around Chicago were very, very uptight and getting worse, and there was a possibility of incredible brutality, maliciousness, and fascistic-type tactics on the part of the police force.' As a result, McDonald explained, 'I was having a hard time getting people to be responsive to the possibility of anything positive happening in Chicago.' In the culture clash between the Festival of Life and the National Death Party, both sides were losing ground.

## TET ON TELEVISION

The same dichotomy between hope and despair, fantasy and reality, life and death, was obvious in Vietnam. The previous year had seen a steady decline in support for the war among the American population, and a corresponding increase in disquiet overseas. On 31 January, the night of Tet, the Vietnamese New Year, Viet Cong guerrillas and North Vietnamese troops combined to launch a shocking assault on towns and US army bases across South Vietnam. Any military advantage gained by the so-called Tet Offensive was swiftly cancelled out. Losses amongst North Vietnamese regulars and guerrillas were appallingly heavy. But the effect on morale in the South, and among the American military and public, was devastating. Veteran American newscaster Walter Cronkite watched the first reports of the Offensive, and muttered: 'What the hell is going on? I thought we were winning this war.'

President Johnson responded by increasing the number of American soldiers sent to Vietnam. To make up the numbers, fresh blood was required. University students had once been immune from the draft; now they were subject to exactly the same threat of call-up as their less privileged brothers, with only those studying medicine and dentistry – and the priesthood – retaining their deferment status. Country Joe & the Fish bassist Bruce Barthol was among those who received the call. 'I turned up for a draft physical in 1968,' he remembers, 'and to be honest, I was pretty fucked up. They took one look at me and isolated me from the rest of the men. It was enlistment day for the Marine Corps. I had long hair, and there were guys calling me "faggot". I was too stoned to answer any questions, but they passed me fit for combat. So I started planning my escape. A lot of American kids went to Canada to avoid the draft. Others went to Europe. A real community of deserters was in Sweden, of all places. These were guys who ran away from Vietnam, found their way to Russia, and then travelled across to Scandinavia, where they were safe from being sent back.'

Opposition to the war was hardened by the images seen nightly on the TV news. Vietnam was the first freely reported conflict of the television age. Seven hundred US reporters were on the frontline with their troops, facing few restrictions on their coverage. Casualties – and there were several hundred deaths every month amongst the American forces – were no longer statistics, but recognisable young men, their bodies shown bleeding in every home. By the end of March, opinion polls suggested that most Americans believed they were losing the war. That week, Johnson announced his decision to step down from the Presidency at the end of his term. Cabinet insiders have since suggested that the threat of health problems forced his hand; in the event, he died only a few months after the end of what could have been his second term. But his 'resignation' was widely viewed as an admission of failure, both personal and military, and even by some as a display of cowardice. With Eugene McCarthy and Robert Kennedy emerging as credible candidates for president, America seemed to have taken a decisive step towards ending the war.

Scepticism about the conflict was now rife. The summer of 1967 had seen the formation of a peace movement among returning American soldiers, under the banner of Vietnam Veterans Against the War (VVAW). On 15 January 1968, around 5,000 women marched to Congress, representing the Jeanette Rankin Brigade (named after and led by an 87-year-old feminist pioneer). Among the marchers were Coretta Scott King, wife of Martin Luther King, and folk-singer Judy Collins. 'I was born a feminist,' Collins explains. 'My family instilled in me the idea that I could do anything, that there was nothing that was prohibited to me because I was a woman. So I was an easy recruit for the cause.'

The march reflected the tactical divisions growing within the anti-war movement. In a Yippie-style stroke of street theatre, the newly formed New York Radical Women conducted 'The Burial Of Weeping Womanhood', designed to highlight traditional gender roles and release women from a passive role in political debate. A large 'ultra-feminine' dummy was pushed through the streets of Washington towards Arlington National Cemetery. 'Traditional Womanhood Is Dead', declared one banner; another proudly proclaimed, 'Sisterhood Is Powerful!' The Radical Women performed feminist songs, before delivering a rallying-cry at the graveside: 'We must learn to fight the warmongers on their own terms, though they believe us capable only of rolling bandages.' This vision of the future went unreported by the mainstream press, who preferred to imagine American women as simple souls, grieving for their lost sons and fathers.

## ASSASSINATION AND AFTERMATH

Another significant gathering also hovered beneath the media radar. On 16 March 1968, the Peace & Freedom Party held its founding convention in Richmond, California. The event opened with a perfect display of West Coast street theatre, as the San Francisco Mime Troupe Gorilla Band performed the 'Star Spangled Banner'. As they reached the line about the 'rockets' red glare, the bombs bursting in air', the Troupe howled and screamed like Vietnamese civilians undergoing martyrdom by napalm. At the conference, the PFP announced its electoral merger with the Black Panther Party – who were drawn to their peacenik partners by the fact that the PFP owned a sound-truck and were prepared to lend it to the BPP. Their union came under immediate strain, however, when Panthers leader Bobby Seale insisted on haranguing the delegates immediately rather than awaiting his democratic turn.

The BPP and PFP had already made a public show of solidarity at two 'Free Huey!' rallies. The Panthers audaciously booked the Oakland Auditorium for the 18 February event, and succeeded in selling 5,000 tickets to hear Seale, Cleaver, Rap Brown, Stokely Carmichael and other luminaries. Numbers were boosted by the Chicago vocal trio the Impressions, riding high in the R&B Top 10 with 'We're a Winner'. The group posed for photographs with Carmichael, before performing their hit song. Carmichael stole the headlines, however, with his outspoken rhetoric. 'Many of us feel – many of our generation feel – that they're getting ready to commit genocide against us,' he declared. 'We have to recognise who our major enemy is. The major enemy is the honky . . . If they become a threat, we off them.' Rap Brown clicked the tension higher with a typically incendiary speech, calling for the Panthers to unite with other 'dispossessed' citizens of America, such as Mexicans and Puerto Ricans.

The next day, a second rally at the equally capacious Los Angeles Sports Arena spotlighted the schisms within the black power movement. Once again, Stokely Carmichael's speech, heavily rhythmic and repetitive like a funk anthem, ignited the crowd. Behind the scenes, however, there was a stand-off between the Southern California Panthers, and Ron Karenga's US group, the co-sponsors of the event. US had invited the LA police to act as security, which angered the Panthers; but as one of the BPP organisers was Earl Anthony, secretly working undercover for the FBI, the argument between Karenga and the Panthers may have been carefully orchestrated. Attendance was much lower than in Oakland, and few of the receipts ever made their way into Huey Newton's defence fund.

Beyond the media spotlight, other fault-lines were cracking the Panthers' coalition. The BPP leadership had appointed Carmichael honorary prime minister of the Black Nation, and in this guise he had recently visited North Vietnam, West Africa and Cuba, to secure a global alliance of revolutionary forces. Amongst his new friends was Sekou Toure, the president of Guinea – and leader of an oppressive one-party regime. Newton learned that anti-Toure forces within Guinea were angry that Carmichael, and therefore the liberation warriors of the BPP, should have joined forces with the man who was restricting their own freedom. 'When he aligned himself with reactionary African governments, he lost his credibility,' Newton complained.

Meanwhile, Carmichael was equally perturbed by the links that had been forged between the BPP and PFP. 'Stokely warned that whites would destroy the movement, alienate Black people and lessen our effectiveness in the community,' Newton recalled. The BPP leader claimed that Carmichael's analysis was wrong but, purely by chance, his conclusions were correct. The union with the PFP, Newton admitted, meant that the Panthers 'were brought into the free speech movement, the psychedelic fad, and the advocacy of drugs, which we were and are dead set against'. That must have been news to Eldridge Cleaver, who had maintained channels of communication with the more progressive elements in the white hippie movement in San Francisco, and appeared to have a much more lenient attitude towards mind-expanding drugs. Cleaver's response to the Carmichael situation sounded like a line from a hippie exploitation movie: 'I dig Stokely, you know? But I'm pissed off at him.'

The students' organisation SDS announced in March that the struggle for black liberation would now be its central campaigning issue. Vital though the crusade for black power was, SDS's decision was another blow to the anti-war movement. A more enlightened policy would have been to combine the two issues, relating them as evidence of white imperialist tendencies at home and abroad. Isolating foreign and domestic issues merely encouraged fragmentation amongst a movement that was already groaning under its own internal pressure.

Vietnam and the black struggle couldn't help but collide during the first week of April 1968. On the 4th, while Americans were still adjusting to Lyndon Johnson's abdication of power, Dr Martin Luther King was shot dead outside his motel room in Memphis. In international eyes, he was the very incarnation of the civil rights campaign, a principled, self-sacrificing champion of freedom. Outside America's black community, few noticed the chasm that had emerged not just between King and the Nation of Islam, as evidenced by his earlier rivalry with Malcolm X, but also between his policy of non-violent protest and the 'by any means necessary' philosophy that groups such as the BPP, US and even SNCC had inherited from Malcolm.

King's assassination coincided with a widening of his political activism. He had been in Memphis to support striking garbage workers. Indeed, a week earlier, he had been widely accused of inspiring a riot that erupted on Beale Street during a protest march. In an issue published just before his death, *Time* magazine declared that King's 'non-violent mantle was in tatters'.

Militant black organisations had long regarded him as an 'Uncle Tom', unwilling to confront his white oppressors with the gun. Eldridge Cleaver had been among his prime detractors, convinced that non-violence would never benefit the liberation struggle. But in the wake of King's death, while BPP supporters flocked to the party's Oakland HQ to ask for guns, Cleaver borrowed King's tactics for one evening: 'I went to a junior high school in Oakland and talked the kids, who were in a mindless fury, out of burning the place to the ground. I told them there were responsible ways that a caring, determined black youngster could more fully honour the ideals of that martyred preacher.'

It was a small gesture of non-violence in a theatre of anger. More than 150 cities suffered rioting after King's murder, though the total deaths were no more than during the 1967 Detroit riots. Six casualties followed an R&B concert at a Kansas City church, during which police threw tear gas into the basement, and then shot many of the black kids who retaliated with missiles.

Another R&B performance has become legendary for cooling down America's ghettos after King's assassination. One of the earliest rock encyclopaedias states that James Brown 'was personally thanked by the US President for his part in calming down racial tensions during riots of the late 1960s, by putting on a marathon TV show to help keep people off the streets'. Variations on that theme have been repeated ever since, with the site claimed as being Washington, DC, New York, Brown's adopted hometown of Atlanta, Georgia, or Los Angeles.

The actual location was Boston, and the circumstances shed some light on the ambiguous relationship between music, money and racial politics in the late 1960s. There were three key players in the drama: Boston's white mayor, Kevin White, tipped as a possible Vice-Presidential contender in that year's election; black councilman Tom Atkins, a thorn in White's side; and Brown, an ambiguous symbol of black pride and champion of black capitalism. Legend has it that Brown stepped into the fray in the hours after King's death, seizing the airwaves and calming the ghettos with hour after hour of solid, riot-quelling funk. But the gig at the centre of this myth took place some 26 hours after the murder, on the evening of 5 April 1968, at the 15,000-seater Boston Garden. Following a night of sporadic rioting in the Roxbury and North Dorchester sections of the city, Mayor White wanted to declare downtown a no-go area the next evening, to prevent looting and further destruction. He ordered that all public events should be cancelled, and the word went out on local radio stations. Lines formed outside the Garden as ticket-holders applied for refunds. Atkins, however, queried the wisdom of assembling several thousand disgruntled James Brown fans in the city centre after nightfall. 'I tried to convince the mayor that the city's interests dictated that he reversed himself,' he recalled. He also noted that any violence sparked by the cancellation would rebound unfavourably on White's political ambitions.

Enter James Brown, who arrived in Boston to hear that the show, far from being sold out, had now been cancelled. Under those circumstances, he could have reclaimed his prospective earnings from the city's insurers. But then White came round to Atkins' view that 'if the show was cancelled, it might light the fire to the fuse' and agreed that the performance should go ahead. Brown was suddenly faced with a concert in front of a half-full arena, and a substantially lower take from his share of the box-office.

Now it was the singer who threatened to pull out, unless the city covered his loss of income. Mayor White was faced with a dilemma: give in to Brown's demand for a $60,000 cash payment, or subject his city to the potential of violence that might cost millions of dollars, plus untold lives. It was no choice at all, and White took the only decision he could, promising Brown the money out of his mayoral budget. At this point, the mayor showed a stroke of the political genius that had carried him to power. He flexed his muscle with a local TV station, who agreed to broadcast Brown's show live that evening, with an immediate repeat to follow. The singer was now back on the defensive, forced to approve the broadcast, or risk being condemned for his refusal to heal racial tensions. White cleverly capitalised on his coup by declaring that the event would not only be a James Brown concert, but a memorial to Dr King. Radio announced that the show was back on, and everyone came out a hero.

Within the Boston Garden, however, there were political points to be scored. As the city's first black councilman for sixteen years, Tom Atkins was allowed to make the introductions. Tumultuous cheering greeted Brown and his band, but the singer remained out of the spotlight while Atkins fumbled his way through the rest of his speech. In mid-sentence, his microphone was seized by Brown, who proceeded to introduce 'a swinging cat', and out stepped Mayor White. It was a potentially incendiary moment: a predominantly black crowd facing a white city boss. The police who lined the stage tightened their grip on their weapons. Mayor White hadn't achieved high office for nothing, however, and he proceeded to toast both Brown and Dr King in glowing terms. 'Twenty-four hours ago,' he announced, his voice ominous and deep, 'Dr King died for all of us, black and white.' There were a few murmurs of dissent, but they were masked by applause. King's prayer, the mayor continued, was that 'we may live together in harmony, without violence, and in peace'. He had the crowd now, and even though some voices echoed from the darkness of the hall, complaining that harmony was easier to find in a mayor's mansion than in a ghetto, White soared above the criticism. 'I'm here to ask for your help,' he cried, 'to make Dr King's dreams a reality in Boston. This is our city, and the future is in our hands. Martin Luther King loved this city . . .', and now he was in his element, on the stump, with the assurance that at any moment he could hand the stage over to one of the greatest showmen on the planet.

Brown matched his reputation with a blend of old-school theatrics and cutting-edge funk, spiralling and sliding around the stage like a marionette on ice. As he careered into his recent hit single, 'I Can't Stand It', a black youth leapt to his side from the front row. A dozen policemen raced to throw him back into the stalls – perhaps fearful of another assassination, perhaps primed to regard every young black man as a target. Brown ushered them back: 'It's all right, I'll be fine.' Then there were a dozen more fans beside him, and as many again clambering in their wake. For a minute, the show teetered on the brink of anarchy, as Brown insisted on handling the interlopers himself, while the police battled their instinctive desire to drive them off with force. 'Let me finish the show,' Brown chanted like a mantra, 'everybody wants to see the show.' As stewards, police and musicians combined to clear the stage, the atmosphere crackling with tension, Brown addressed the whole crowd: 'We are black . . . we are black.' It was the ultimate statement of unification, and it left its mark. Brown was able to scold the invaders like a teacher: 'You're not being fair to yourself, or me either, or your race.' As the show closed a few minutes later, he stared contemptuously at the police who once again gathered on the stage, his eyes declaring: these are my people, and we don't need you to control them. Over the next few days, the Boston press congratulated Brown, and their mayor, for ensuring that there was less trouble on the streets that night than in any other major city in America. '[He] is a credit to his race,' declared *Billboard* magazine.

That same night, 200 miles up the East Coast, another black man faced the challenge of responding to Martin Luther King's murder. At Newark Town Hall, Jimi Hendrix performed with two white musicians in front of a predominantly white audience, in a city that boasted as high a proportion of black inhabitants as any metropolis in the country. 'We got down to Newark, to the venue,' recalled his bassist, Noel Redding, 'and there were tanks in the street.' More than 200 buildings around the city were already ablaze, although unlike the disturbances of 1967 there was no loss of life. Redding's diary set the scene in the barest of terms: 'All riots. Only did one show instead of two' – this at the request of the police. Hendrix made no political pronouncements about Dr King's death, though friends remember his being stunned by the news. He let his music speak for itself, closing the show with the pertinently titled 'I Don't Live Today'. The song was customarily a vehicle for Hendrix's stage theatrics, but this night it took on a profoundly melancholy air. Later that year, the guitarist recorded a suitably incendiary commentary on black America's urban devastation, 'House Burning Down'. Its vivid imagery and ambiguous mix of ecstasy and despair were doubtless informed by what he'd seen in Newark.

Hendrix endured several further lessons in changing political realities over the next year. In interviews, he continued to describe himself as 'apolitical'. But with the fierce waves of sound that emerged from his guitar, at least one critic in the underground press was able to imagine that Hendrix 'ruthlessly attacks not only imperialism but the entire foundation of oppressive Western civilisation . . . the music of revolt has found its poet.' Hendrix was beginning to feel pressure from the Black Panthers, whose representatives regularly visited his dressing room at West Coast shows, quizzing him about his political and racial loyalty. In late June, meanwhile, he donated $5,000 to the Martin Luther King memorial fund, and attended a tribute concert at Madison Square Garden in New York. He specifically asked not to be identified from the stage, but promoter Sid Bernstein couldn't resist, and ordered the spotlights to pick him out, much to Hendrix's embarrassment.

The King benefit was a strange, deliberately bland affair. In his review in *Rolling Stone*, critic Jon Landau noted that 'the audience had no racial identity'; that was probably supposed to be a compliment. Atlantic Records provided the music: the label, which had made its name and money from R&B music, had already donated $5,000 to King's family and to his civil rights organisation, the SCLC, as an advance on the royalties of two non-hit singles, by Solomon Burke and the Hudson Chorale. At Madison Square, they contributed a multi-racial bill featuring the queen of soul, Aretha Franklin, alongside Sam & Dave, the Rascals, Joe Tex and, bizarrely, Sonny & Cher. All these acts made pronouncements of racial harmony from the stage.

Atlantic's chief rival as a source of mid-1960s R&B, Stax Records, was based in Memphis, the city where King died. Although its artist roster was almost entirely black, its musicians, producers and owners came from both sides of the American divide. King's murder undermined Stax's racial equilibrium. 'It had a tremendous impact,' co-owner Jim Stewart recalled. 'It kind of put a wedge, or at least opened up that suspicious element, in the company.

Everybody started withdrawing, pulling back from that openness and close relationship that we felt we had.' Songwriter/producer Isaac Hayes, creator of Sam & Dave's hits, registered the assassination as a personal blow: 'It affected me for a whole year. I could not create properly. I was so bitter and angry. I was rebellious. I was militant.' Hayes would re-emerge in 1969 with a pioneering form of orchestral soul that he used as the vehicle for powerful statements of black pride.

His anger was echoed by Nina Simone, once dubbed 'the true singer of the civil rights movement' by Stokely Carmichael. While James Brown confronted his black identity in Boston, and Jimi Hendrix dodged his in Newark, Simone marked the loss of the civil rights leader in Westbury, Long Island. That evening, she debuted a song written by her bassist, Gene Taylor: 'Why (the King of Love is Dead)'. Yet love was no longer uppermost in her heart: shortly before her death, she recalled that King's murder had signalled to her that non-violence was no longer a viable form of protest. 'My husband persuaded me to go on singing rather than go charging in with a gun,' she explained. Over the next few months, Simone edged closer towards the Black Panther Party.

Despite his conciliatory words in Oakland, the Panthers' eloquent Minister of Information, Eldridge Cleaver, could foresee only apocalypse ahead. 'That there is a holocaust coming, I have no doubt at all,' he wrote two days later. 'The violent phase of the black liberation struggle is here, and it will spread. From that spot, from that blood, America will be painted red. Dead bodies will litter the street.' It was an eerie prophecy. That night, Cleaver led a convoy of cars across Oakland. As ever with the Panthers, reality and myth are difficult to untangle. Cleaver claimed that he stopped his car to urinate in the street, and was confronted by armed cops. 'We were walking on eggshells and knew it,' he wrote later of this period. 'We expected to be killed at every moment.'

Seconds later, there was gunfire. Only in the final months of his life did Cleaver admit that the shoot-out had been instigated by the Panthers. 'I pled not guilty,' he revealed, 'but we did it, we attacked the police because we were mad.' In search of cover, Cleaver and 18-year-old Lil' Bobby Hutton, the Party's first ever recruit, headed for a nearby basement. For thirty minutes, the two sides traded shots, until the police fired a tear-gas grenade into their hideout. The canister struck Cleaver in the chest, knocking him over, and within seconds the house was on fire. As the smoke spread, the two men stripped off their clothes, but eventually could stand the heat no longer. They shouted that they were surrendering and stumbled into the street unarmed and with their hands held high. Cleaver was reportedly stark naked (though he later denied this, for reasons of male pride); Hutton dressed only in boxer shorts. Both men lay down on the floor, and then, according to Cleaver, were told they must run to a nearby squad car. Cleaver had been struck in the leg by a ricocheting bullet, and could hardly walk, but Hutton obeyed the police order. 'It was a sickening sight,' Cleaver recalled, 'Little Bobby, coughing and choking on the night air that was burning his lungs as my own were burning from the tear gas, stumbled forward as best he could, and after he travelled about ten yards the pigs cut loose on him with their guns.' The police claimed that Hutton had been trying to escape. Either way, the teenager lay dead.

Bobby Hutton was the Black Panthers' first martyr, his face emblazoned on the next issue of the party newspaper. Reportedly a black policeman left the local force in disgust at Hutton's shooting, but a grand jury investigation found that the police had no case to answer. Like Martin Luther King, Hutton registered with the liberal white community as a victim of America's racial agony. Mama Cass Elliott summed up their reaction: 'I didn't even know him, but I didn't have to know him to know it was wrong. He may even have been a bad person, or a rapist, or a walking hallucinogenic drug. But he didn't have to die.' Country Joe & the Fish dedicated their forthcoming album, *Together*, to 'Bobby Hutton: Black Revolutionary'. Actor Marlon Brando spoke at Hutton's funeral: 'That could have been my son lying there. It's up to each individual to do something. I've got a lot to learn. I haven't suffered the way you have suffered.' The Panthers responded by allowing Brando honorary membership of the party.

Meanwhile Cleaver, who had attracted national attention for his collection of prison essays, *Soul On Ice*, was charged with attempted murder and assault with a deadly weapon. His parole was immediately revoked, though he was freed on appeal in June, when he took the Panthers' case to the United Nations' headquarters on Riverside Drive in Manhattan. Then he concentrated on orchestrating the media campaign before the opening of Huey Newton's murder trial in mid-July.

Each stage in this drama, from King's death to Newton's trial, comprised a panorama that became the shared landscape of the militant black community. Against this backdrop, the conduct of America's black icons came under strict scrutiny. No black man in America was under more pressure to align himself with the Panthers and SNCC than James Brown. 'Is this the most important black man in America?' asked a cover story in the magazine *Look*. That reputation was enhanced by the Boston concert after King's murder, and by Brown's subsequent visit to Washington, DC. The US capital had suffered continued violence since the assassination, and Brown volunteered to stage another televised concert in the hope of clearing the streets. He also taped a message for the city's black youth: 'Get off the streets, go home. Nothing could be gained by the looting and burning, only sorrow and misery.' Then he turned his attention to the nation's politicians, begging them: 'Give the kids a chance to learn.' An invitation to the White House followed, where Brown briefly met President Johnson, and renewed his acquaintance with Vice-President Humphrey. The singer agreed to campaign for Humphrey in the forthcoming Democratic primaries.

No other entertainer with the faintest claim to street credibility shared Brown's conviction that Humphrey was the best candidate to replace Johnson. The Vice-President's staff had made a token attempt to corral the youth vote by approaching Jefferson Airplane for a campaign anthem. 'We were the hip new thing,' Paul Kantner says sardonically, 'so they figured we might do them some good. Unfortunately, I sent them back a song called "You are the Crown of Creation", the next line of which is, "and you've got no place to go". Then they decided we weren't so suitable after all.' Humphrey's rivals had a wider following amongst the music community. Robert Kennedy's supporters staged a massive fundraising concert at the Los Angeles Sports Arena, where musicians who made up one of the more eclectic bills in show business history lent their names to his campaign. The evening featured crooner Andy Williams, the Byrds, gospel singer Mahalia Jackson, Sonny & Cher, and composer/bandleader Henry Mancini. 'That was the only polit-ical benefit we ever played,' says Byrds leader Roger McGuinn. 'I really believed in Bobby Kennedy.' The other avowed anti-war candidate, Eugene McCarthy, attracted a less flamboyant but equally surreal mix of performers, including Phil Ochs, jazz drummer Shelly Manne, and the easy-listening instrumental group Trombones Unlimited.

In early June 1968, as the crucial California primary approached, Humphrey appeared on stage with James Brown at a concert in Los Angeles. 'You can do the boogaloo, man,' Brown told him, 'if you got soul' – whereupon the hapless Vice-President shook his hips and wanly tried to appear funky. 'The footage of this was incredible,' recalled academic Robert Farris Thompson. 'James was preaching to his people: "Here is my man, you NEED to have him, he's my friend, he's a righteous man, he's THERE!" Then the camera swivels to Humphrey and up turns this bland countenance, with NO sense of resynchronising his body language to this volcano next to him. If ever there was a moment to tell you Humphrey was a loser, that was it!' Humphrey duly flopped in the California primary, which was won by Robert Kennedy – a crucial stride, it seemed, towards the White House. At the Ambassador Hotel in Los Angeles, Kennedy made his victory speech, then stepped back-stage into a crowded kitchen. Seconds later he lay mortally wounded, gunned down at close range by a mysteriously catatonic American Arab named Sirhan Sirhan. Kennedy died the following day, and with him perished a realistic hope that an anti-war candidate might inherit the White House. Humphrey quietly eased himself into the succession, and the liberal fervour that had spurred McCarthy and Kennedy to enter the race soured into despair and anger.

James Brown's espousal of the Vice-President provoked similar reactions among America's young blacks. It didn't help that Brown then flew to Vietnam to entertain US troops. As an unjustly high proportion of the soldiers was black, called up against their will, Brown was perhaps showing his support for their predicament. But his trip was widely interpreted as support for the war. His conservative image was consolidated by his latest record, 'America Is My Home'. Set to a typically funky rhythm track, the performance was less political than its title suggested, as Brown extolled any land in which a man like him could travel from a country shack in Georgia to the White House, and declared that America was the greatest nation on the planet, for sure. But it received short shrift from those who expected him to act as a champion of his people.

As criticism surrounded him, James Brown made a rare trip out of the country. He had been invited to the former French colony of the Ivory Coast in West Africa, to attend the celebrations for the eighth anniversary of the state's independence. He appeared in public alongside President Felix Houphouet-Boigny, performed two concerts in the capital, Abidjan, and filmed a one-hour TV special. It was his first trip to the continent, and it appears to have heightened his awareness of his black heritage. On his return, he recorded his toughest funk side to date, a record that provided militant black America with its national anthem: 'Say It Loud, I'm Black and I'm Proud'.

'Proud' wasn't just a rhyme: it reflected Brown's interpretation of the black man's goals in America. 'I was never into black power,' he explained years later. 'I was black pride. It's different. What influence I had over people is not power. Power's what ruins people.' Parts of the song read like a testament for black capitalism. But one line signalled a more rebellious stance: 'We'd rather die on our feet than keep living on our knees'. Huey Newton couldn't have put it better. 'Say It Loud' was exquisitely timed to reflect the defiance of young black America in August 1968. Brown's sincerity could not be doubted; but would he have written the song if he hadn't aroused antipathy on the streets with his recent political actions?

Many white journalists regarded 'Say It Loud' as a call to black revolution. Veteran British reviewer Derek Johnson expressed his sympathy for the cause of civil rights, but then complained: 'When the militant Black Power offshoot gains a foothold in pop music, that's when it's time to draw the line. I dislike this record intensely – it's double-sided, and consists only of James Brown shouting out the aims of the Black Power movement, while the group chants the title phrase and over and over . . . Don't get me wrong – I think he has a very valid case. But pop music is not the place in which to argue his cause.' *New Musical Express*, Britain's leading pop paper, later argued that Brown had been relatively unsuccessful in the UK because he was seen as 'a Black Power artist'. That was precisely why 'Say It Loud, I'm Black and I'm Proud' made such an impact in the United States, where it topped the R&B charts for six weeks and became the year's biggest-selling black record. His record company cunningly promoted Brown's image of black pride: 'We know the Negro deejay won't play this record. We know the colored deejay won't play this record, but every BLACK deejay will play this record!' On stage, however, Brown distanced himself from any suggestion that he was a militant: during a Dallas show a few days after the song was released, he insisted that both blacks and whites should join in the refrain. 'No communication can ever come between two people if they can't talk to each other in a conversation,' he lectured. 'Remember that. A little love won't hurt.' The predominantly black audience greeted his remarks with murmurs of discontent.

Ironically, Brown's apparent militancy spurred the US government to begin monitoring his activities more closely. Over the next few years, he was targeted by the Internal Revenue Service with intensive tax audits, and was put under surveillance by the Federal Bureau of Investigation. Whether it was black power or black pride, any gesture of racial identity aroused suspicion in the fevered atmosphere of 1968.

## IMPULSE FOR LIBERATION

Around the world, governments of various hues struggled to make sense of the global impulse for liberation. America's trauma in Vietnam and the compelling political drama of its black power crusade aroused confused stirrings of discontent that matched each nation's own problems. In several countries, the situation spiralled into violent confrontation during the year, each disturbance casting a distorted shadow on its counterparts. There was nothing inherently revolutionary about 1968, no global recipe for student violence and the undermining of authority. But the turmoil in Vietnam, Memphis and Los Angeles echoed through Mexico City, Rio De Janeiro, Prague, Paris and London, with unpredictable results.

It was probably inevitable that the tremors of the US counter-culture began to be felt across the Mexican border. The country had a proud heritage of independence: Mexico's 20th-century leaders considered themselves a Revolutionary Family. The existence of Castro's Cuba, in the Gulf between Mexico and the USA, reminded the Central American republic of the fruits of liberation. Nineteen sixty-eight was the year of the Mexico City Olympiad: the focus of the world would be on the Mexican capital that October. As early as January, African-American athletes were being urged to boycott the games as a protest against Vietnam and oppression in the ghettos. This protest attracted little support among the Mexican people, who were anxious not to endanger their moment in their global spotlight. But more primal forces in Mexican society were starting to test their own strength.

The country's attitude towards America, its vast rival towards the north, was clouded by the past. After the secession of Texas and the Spanish–American War, the relationship between the two nations was always destined to be ambiguous. The Mexican response to American rock'n'roll illustrated their uneasy friendship. The Mexican press were outraged when Elvis Presley reportedly said: 'I'd rather kiss three black girls than a Mexican.'[2] Subsequent investigation showed that the remark had been invented as anti-American propaganda.

Keen to preserve their youth from diseased foreign influences, Mexican officials regularly censored films featuring the likes of Elvis or the Beatles. When local bands covered American songs, they excised any risqué elements, toning down the lyrics and the accompanying dance moves. By 1967, however, the haze of the counter-culture had drifted down from California. What united the first psychedelic generation of Mexican teenagers was not, at first, politics (on a local or global scale) but the inescapable gulf between tradition and modernity. Mexico's equivalent of the Movement was La Onda (literally, 'the wave'). Cultural critic Carlos Monsivais may have pronounced that La Onda was a combination of Che Guevara, Malcolm X, Allen Ginsberg, Fidel Castro and Mick Jagger; but until 1968, it held none of the political implications that those names would have carried elsewhere. Then the student organisation Comite Nacional de Huelga began to recognise its potential power, and to issue statements criticising not only American policy in Vietnam, but – more worryingly – social restraints at home.

The situation in Brazil was more polarised than in Mexico. The republic's recent history was scarred with coups, assassinations and repression. In 1964, President Goulart's attempt to impose universal suffrage and nationalise Brazil's oil industry provoked an intervention from the armed forces. Power was now impossible to wield without military support. When presidential elections were cancelled in 1965, it was the generals who selected the country's leader. Marshal Costa e Silva took over the reins in March 1967, and imposed draconian 'national security' laws, designed to outlaw 'opinions, sentiments, attitudes or behaviour counter to the achievement of national objectives'. Journalists now faced two-year prison sentences for printing any criticism of the military or the government. Only one opposition party was allowed to operate, and even that was banned in December 1967. There were now two options for anyone who didn't support the army: conform, or break the law. In March 1968, guerrilla warfare broke out in São Paulo, the start of a protracted bout of self-consciously revolutionary struggle by armed groups who saw themselves as successors to Che Guevara. Meanwhile, students and workers began to organise against the dictatorship. When a young student was shot dead by police, a giant rally was staged in Rio de Janeiro.

Two of Brazil's most prominent young musicians, Gilberto Gil and Caetano Veloso, travelled to take part in this demonstration. 'Politics was never my forte,' Veloso confessed later. But he was living in a country where what he called 'the cultural movement' was displaying 'markedly leftist overtones, bringing together writers, actors, singers, directors, plays, films and the public in a kind of spiritual resistance to the dictatorship'. The irony was that Veloso and Gil were themselves provoking a very similar kind of 'spiritual resistance' – not because of their opposition to the ruling regime, but because they were daring to bring 'foreign' (i.e. American) influences into the music.

Veloso's first solo album, recorded in 1967, stepped outside Brazil's rich tradition of samba and bossa nova music. Blatantly inspired by the psychedelic pop of the Beatles, it appalled many who imagined that Veloso might follow in the footsteps of Joao Gilberto and Antonio Carlos Jobim. One of its songs, 'Tropicalia', lent its name to a 1968 album that combined the talents of Veloso, Gil, Gal Costa and the rock band Os Mutantes. Thereafter, these artists were disparagingly grouped under the heading of 'tropicalismo'. Veloso welcomed his new outsider status: 'I was a tropicalista, free of ties to traditional politics, and therefore I could react against oppression and narrowness according to my creativity.' His songs continued to offer social satire, but fell short of providing anthems for the thousands of student protestors who were now massing in city centres. Through the summer of 1968, government, opposition and psychedelic mavericks all maintained their positions, heading on an inevitable collision course.

The same fate awaited Czechoslovakia – with the stark difference that there, the rebellion came not from the people, but from within the government. On 5 January 1968, the First Secretary of the ruling Communist Party, Antonin Novotny, was voted out of power (though he retained the titular post of president until April). His place was taken by the relatively young (46) Alexander Dubček, who promised to loosen the Communist Party's iron grip on Czech culture. His initial reforms were startling, as he pledged to introduce elements of democracy into the one-party state, making the rulers partially accountable to their subjects for the first time since the Soviet Union had seized political control after World War Two. Overnight, he abolished layers of censorship, allowing the making of several potentially subversive feature films and freeing press comment. The man with the sinister title of Minister of Ideology was dismissed, and replaced by a Dubček protégé who declared that the Communist Party should have no role in trying to control the arts.

There were immediate rumours of a military coup in preparation. But Dubček's government insisted that this liberalisation of Czech society could proceed without endangering either the dominant Marxist philosophy or the unity of the Soviet Bloc. As one minister noted, it was now time for two great forces to merge: freedom, and socialism. Russian troops staged training manoeuvres just across the border with East Germany, poised as a warning of what might happen if Dubček went too far. Moscow called the other Soviet Bloc leaders to a conference, to discuss the implications of events in Czechoslovakia.

For artists and students entranced by tales of what was happening in the West, the so-called 'Prague Spring' was a magical moment of liberation, when rival schools of thought were encouraged to flourish. Writers and musicians were also allowed a rare opportunity to visit the West. Playwright Václav Havel travelled to New York: 'I took part in demos and rallies and student protests,' he told Lou Reed in 1990. 'We wandered around Greenwich Village and East Village, and I bought a lot of posters which I still keep, psychedelic posters which I have hanging in my cottage.' Havel returned to Prague with Czechoslovakia's first copy of an album by Reed's band, the Velvet Underground, which was widely copied amongst his friends, and inspired a generation of underground rock bands. Amongst them were the Plastic People of the Universe, whose name was inspired by a Frank Zappa song. 'The whole spirit of the 60s [in the USA], the rebellion against the establishment, affected significantly the spiritual life of my generation and of the younger people,' Havel recalled, 'and in a very strange way, transcended into the present.'

'The rebellion against the establishment': nothing illustrated that 60s spirit more chaotically or profoundly than the events in France during May 1968. There was no shortage of causes for unrest in Charles de Gaulle's Fifth Republic; the President was in his tenth year of autocratic rule, unemployment was high, wages were being slashed, students were enduring archaic conditions and facing stunted futures, and the democratic system offered constant change but no progress. Yet similar problems existed elsewhere in the Western world, without sparking the same combination of protests from students and workers that led Prime Minister Georges Pompidou to warn that France was in a 'pre-revolutionary state'. There was rioting in the streets, a brutal police response, and a general strike that briefly threatened to bring the capitalist system to its knees. For a few magical days, revolutionary idealists around the world watched in awe as one of the world's most prosperous nations teetered on the brink of a classic working-class revolution. Then, just as quickly as it had arisen, the 'pre-revolution' subsided, the Communist-backed trade unions refused to use their power to topple the government, and France returned uneasily to its previous shape. May 1968 was left behind as a fantasy, a myth, and a source of recriminations and regrets on the political left.

Marxist analysis – and all the world's revolutionary forces in 1968 paid at least lip service to one interpretation or another of Marxism – insisted that revolt could only come from the working-class, seizing the means of production from the owners and operators of capitalism. In the late 1960s, complex theoretical study was devoted to the class status of university students. They were, by virtue of their privileged position in society, institutionally bourgeois. But some of their philosophers claimed that they occupied a previously undocumented position at the vanguard of the working class, as they could use their education to guide the workers into revolutionary situations. May 1968 appeared to offer the perfect justification of this theory. In Paris and beyond, protests began in university buildings, and swept without pause into the factories and the streets.

The May 1968 rebellion was enacted on many different frontiers, from the surreal sloganeering of the anarchist Situationist International to the split between Communists and Trotskyist splinter groups over the correct preparation for revolution. One aspect of French culture remained perversely isolated from the struggle, however: popular music. Elsewhere in the world, musicians played with politics and politicians played with music, both invading the others' territory to seize the imagination of their audience. In France, there was virtually no musical counterpoint to the 'pre-revolution'; or indeed any musical consequence. Any collisions between the sound and the fury were tangential, such as the use of May 1968 'found sound' on *Monster Movie*, the first album by the experimental German rock band Can; or the debut performance, during the Sorbonne occupation, by the French group Red Noise.[3] This was indeed, as one commentator put it, 'une revolution sans musique'.

French popular music has an honourable tradition of social comment, however, and several *chansons* did reflect the May 1968 experience, such as Evariste's jaunty 'La Revolution', and Francois Beranger's 'Les Nouveaux Partisans'. There were no equivalents from rock performers, however. Compared with Britain and the United States, France lacked a recognisable counter-culture. Perhaps because surrealism and the avant-garde had always found a place within the French artistic mainstream, there was a less pressing need for the formation of a distinctive 'underground' culture than in other

Western nations. France had also prided itself on maintaining a unique artistic heritage of its own, making it less likely than Mexico and Brazil to translate the American notion of a counter-culture into its own artistic life.

May 1968 may not have triggered a working-class revolution. But it did lay the seeds for a distinctive French musical underground, which emerged in two linked but separate traditions: free jazz, and experimental hard rock. By 1969, Paris had become the home of a generation of American free jazz players, who were attracted by the city's sense of artistic liberation and its supposed freedom from racial discrimination. When Paris wanted rock music that reflected the ideals of the counter-culture, however, it looked to America and Britain, and in particular to the glamorised rebellion represented by such artists as the Doors, Jimi Hendrix and the Rolling Stones.

## STREET FIGHTING MEN

There was all this violence going on. I mean, they nearly toppled the government in France. De Gaulle went into this complete funk, as he had in the past, and he went and sort of locked himself in his house in the country. And so the government was almost inactive. And the French riot police were amazing. Yeah, it was a direct inspiration, because by comparison, London was very quiet.

(Mick Jagger, on the genesis of 'Street Fighting Man')

While Paris trembled at the suggestion of revolution, London waited to see if the spirit of rebellion would cross the channel. The city watched the Prague spring, the killings of King and Kennedy, civil strife in Brazil and Nigeria, the student protests firing like beacons across America and the European continent. But aside from some half-hearted imitations of US campus disorders, and a couple of mysterious incidents – a machine-gun attack and a bomb at two embassies, both claimed by the 'First of May Group' – London was the vacuum of late 1960s rebellion. It was the perfect place for an observer who wanted to see and be seen, to experience but not to become involved. It was the perfect place for Mick Jagger.

Ever since a sub-editor had penned the headline 'Would You Let Your Daughter Marry a Rolling Stone?', the Rolling Stones had trailed clouds of notoriety, carefully shaped by their original manager, PR marvel Andrew Loog Oldham. But after the furore aroused by their 1967 imprisonment, the

Stones appeared to lose their sureness of touch. While guitarist Brian Jones stumbled from one drugs bust to the next, barely conscious of his own existence, songwriters Mick Jagger and Keith Richards grasped after vanishing trends like embarrassing uncles at a hippie ball. *Their Satanic Majesties Request*, the Stones' belated response to the Beatles' *Sgt. Pepper*, was widely greeted as an embarrassment. The band entered 1968 in disarray, searching for a route back to cultural relevance.

Unlike the Beatles, the Stones had rarely commented on political issues. Yet even the slowest of minds, and Jagger's was far from that, could not help but notice that the psychedelic frippery of 1967 had been replaced by a grimmer, more determined mood. What London lacked was the sense of urgency supplied by imminent danger. Without the shadow of the draft or the crackle of rifle fire, British youth had little incentive to crawl out of its winter cocoon. As Jagger noted in May 1968, 'This country's so weird, you know ... it always does things slightly differently, always more moderately and always very boringly, most of it, the changes are so suppressed. The people suppress them.'

Among Britain's psychological blockages was its reaction to the war in Vietnam. Prime Minister Harold Wilson had refused the US request that Britain should send troops to the conflict. But in every other way, the UK supported the US position. There was a collective sense on the left and among the young that the war was unethical and unjustifiable. But it was only in October 1967 that the first major demonstration was staged, when approximately 10,000 people marched through London to coincide with the Stop The Draft Week events in the United States. The protest was organised by the Vietnam Solidarity Committee (VSC), headed by former student radical Tariq Ali. The comparative success of that event encouraged planning for a second march, this time set to convene at the American Embassy in London's leafy Grosvenor Square. The precise objectives of the protest were unclear: would demonstrators break through the embassy gates, or would they settle for shouting at the US from the streets outside? Equally uncertain was how the government and police would react, particularly if the event deteriorated into violence.

On 17 March 1968, 20,000 campaigners crowded into Trafalgar Square, to hear Ali, Vanessa Redgrave and other activists denounce American policy in Vietnam. Then the human crocodile began to trudge through London's West End towards the embassy, where they were met by a heavy detachment of police officers, many of them on horseback. There ensued two hours of violent skirmishes, which both sides denied starting, but which seem to have been triggered by poorly trained policemen overstepping their official instructions. At times, the scene in the square resembled a 19th-century cavalry battle, with horses rearing up and demonstrators attempting to unseat their riders with fenceposts and tree branches, while trying to avoid the thud of a police baton. 'It was nothing like as violent as Paris,' recalls underground chronicler Barry Miles. 'Mostly people were throwing clods of earth. There were no stones around for them to throw, but there were other kinds of debris. People were throwing back tear-gas canisters that the police had fired at them.'

When the march entered Grosvenor Square, an electric tingle ran through the crowd, as word spread that Mick Jagger had been spotted among the demonstrators. He was actually maintaining a careful presence on the periphery of the march, chatting amiably to students and clutching a camera to document the day's excitement. Photographer Michael Cooper captured Jagger's image – surrounded by demonstrators, but clearly not one of them, a wry distance written across his face. He was obviously relishing the smell of battle, but had no intention of taking part; and his celebrity sent out strange waves of distraction, inexorably pulling the attention of those around him away from the focus of the demonstration. As the fighting began, Jagger prowled around the edge of the square, searching for a better vantage point, and then vanished into one of the houses that faced the embassy when the violence came too close for comfort.

'He definitely felt that he ought to be there,' remembers Miles, who spent some time with Jagger that afternoon. 'He did have a genuine revulsion against the Vietnam War. But I think much more that it was also the thing to do. That's what everybody in Chelsea was doing that week, going to that demonstration. It was rare for the Kings Road people, because that end of the underground was very much a hedonistic scene of wealthy aristocrats taking drugs. But there was a political awareness on the Kings Road, even if it was transformed into fashion. Michael Rainey, who owned the Hung On You boutique, had a whole season of Maoist fashions. When you went in, one whole wall was filled with an enlarged photograph of Mao Tse-tung swimming across the Yangtse River, one of the most famous Chinese propaganda pictures of that era. So Jagger wasn't the only one of that crowd to have noticed that there was a war on.'

But his infatuation seems to have been shortlived. 'Demonstration in

Grosvenor Square – for what?' the singer said disdainfully a few weeks later, before realising he might be blowing his radical cool. 'I mean, I don't really put it down. I think it's a gas.' Quizzed further about his attitude to 'the revolution', he conducted a strange conversation with himself, as if trying to feel his way towards an opinion: 'What are you aiming for? To have a proper revolution. To have a change. There is no alternative society. There is none. There are lots, but they're not alternatives, not really. You can have a left-wing revolution, I mean, there's all those, but they're just the same. I can't see it as an alternative society. The only thing I can see, looking at it a lot, is that you're in a fantastic change period.' It was hardly a manifesto to chalk on the walls of an embassy. As Jagger continued to ramble, he talked himself into believing that police and protestors were interchange-able: 'They're looking at each other, and they're the same fucking thing! And they'll degenerate to the same thing, they'll degenerate to putting helmets on and fighting each other, and when they come out, they won't know who the fuck they are!'

Only one aspect of the Grosvenor Square experience captured Jagger's imagination: the cathartic violence: 'That's our way out, cause we love it! And it's our excuse, see? We can't be guerrillas. We're so violent, [that] we're violently frustrated. We haven't got enough violence, we've no opportunity.' Hence his excitement at seeing the Rolling Stones' audiences lose control: 'The energy's great. I mean, they give you SO much energy, I just don't know what to do with it, man ... I never went on stage with the idea of keeping everything cool. I never wanted it to be peaceful.' For Jagger, Grosvenor Square was the concert hall writ large, with greater capacity for violence and for retaliation. The one subject left unmentioned in his analysis was the original purpose of the march: the war in Vietnam.

As the Rolling Stones began work on a new record, Jagger assembled songs that would reflect his atavistic relish of violent confrontation, and his sense that Western society was nearing some kind of apocalyptic crisis. 'I can imagine America becoming just a blaze,' he noted in May 1968, 'just being ruined.' That possibility found its way into a song he wrote that month, with the provisional title 'The Devil Is My Name'. Eventually released as 'Sympathy for the Devil', it sidestepped the uneasy terrain of politics by fingering Beelzebub as the author of global turmoil, from the Russian Revolution to the assassination of President Kennedy.[4] For Jagger, 'Sympathy for the Devil' performed the useful task of establishing comparisons between himself and Satan, which would serve him well as a media image for the next few years, before he called a halt to the game with the sarcastic 'Dancing with Mr D' in 1973. But it had nothing to say about the complexity of a world in transition, beyond the fact that it was too strange to explain. Another song, 'Salt of the Earth', initially registered as a message of solidarity with the working people of the world – patronising, perhaps, from a soon-to-be-millionaire rock star, though heartfelt nonetheless. But one verse revealed an altogether more ambivalent attitude towards the masses, as Jagger observed 'the faceless crowd, a swirling mass of greys and black and white'. This was the class who would lead Tariq Ali's revolution, but Jagger could only confess: 'They don't look real to me, in fact, they look so strange.' Isolated from the proletariat and activists alike, happy to lean on an imaginary source of evil as the explanation for political unrest, Jagger remained as uncommitted an artist as he had been a demonstrator in March.

The week after the VSC's assault on Grosvenor Square, Jagger and the Rolling Stones began work on a song that was interpreted as their revolutionary anthem for 1968. After watching TV news coverage of the disturbances on the streets of Paris, Jagger abandoned his original set of lyrics and started anew. The result was 'Street Fighting Man' – its title another masterful stroke of media manipulation, which effectively masked the message of the song. Over a chopping guitar rhythm that mimicked the bewildering choreography of a riot, Jagger spat out images of confusion, filled with 'marching charging feet'. It was time for 'fighting in the street', for 'a palace revolution', he sang. But the chorus pulled him away from the fray: 'What can a poor boy do, 'cept to sing in a rock'n'roll band? Cos this sleepy London town just ain't no place for a Street Fighting Man'. Jagger was the poor boy, of course, lusting after the glory of the Street Fighting Man. But the music – tense, hustling, gloriously defiant – erased the chasm between the revolutionary in Grosvenor Square and the singer until the two became one.

'Street Fighting Man' and 'Sympathy for the Devil' were taped at Olympic Studios in London during late May and early June 1968. The recording of the latter was filmed by the French director Jean-Luc Godard. In less than a decade, Godard had progressed from creating technically brilliant portraits of modern Parisian life, edited with enormous daring, to devoting his films to an outspokenly political agenda. From the mid-1960s onwards, his movies were part manifesto, part savage critique of the banality and emptiness of French capitalist society. In a world where Vietnam could be tolerated, conventional narrative and discourse were absurd, Godard suggested. With each new project he stepped further away from the familiar language of the cinema and into the maelstrom of revolutionary politics.

In the spring of 1968, the director wanted to pursue the relationship between political power and the potency of the rock performer; and its antithesis, the emptiness of fame as a vehicle for image creation. He initially wanted John Lennon to portray Leon Trotsky, the doomed anti-hero of the Russian Revolution, who represented both the most brutal and the most idealistic aspects of the Bolshevik cause. Godard visited Lennon at the Beatles' office, but his enigmatic description of his project made the singer suspicious. Afterwards, Godard publicly criticised the Beatles for their lack of political commitment. 'Right, he said we should do something,' Lennon snapped back. 'That's sour grapes from a man who couldn't get us to be in the film. Dear Mr Godard, just because we didn't want to be in the film with you, it doesn't mean to say that we aren't doing any more than you.'

An approach to the Rolling Stones proved more acceptable. 'I've seen all his pictures,' Mick Jagger explained that summer, 'and I think they're groovy.' Godard's crew captured the development of 'Sympathy for the Devil' from rough sketch to finished record. That concluded the Stones' involvement in the film, leaving the band faintly mystified. 'I have no idea, really,' Jagger admitted the week after Godard's departure, when quizzed about the nature of the project. 'I mean, he's completely freaky.' The singer then attempted to relate what little Godard had told him about the narrative: 'Well, it's his wife who plays the lead chick. She comes to London and gets totally destroyed with some spade cat. Gets involved with drugs or something. Anyway, while she is getting destroyed, we find the Rolling Stones freaking out at the recording studio . . . I think the idea for the movie is great, but I don't think it will be the same when it's finished.' It was the only aspect of Godard's film that Jagger showed any sign of understanding.

## EXPOSING THE UNDERGROUND

There can only be a short time left before we reach a point beyond which we are truly doomed. Perhaps we have already passed it . . . A new morality must be developed but where will it come from? . . . Some people seem to have found an answer and others must be very close to it but they cannot tell us where it is – we must find it ourselves, and soon. There are fingers pointing in many different directions and perhaps they all point to the same ultimate thing. Is it meditation? Or UFOs? Or what?

(Disc jockey John Peel, January 1968)

After the perfumed garden of the Summer of Love, many leaders of the British counter-culture were slow to confront political reality as 1968 dawned. Hippies were understandably reluctant to leave behind the mental playground they had discovered through pot or acid, especially when the world outside was clouded in foreboding. Far more attractive were the roads to spiritual enlightenment signposted by the Maharishi, Gurdjieff, Buddha and many other gurus, ancient and modern. The spirit of the age was epitomised by the Beatles' chaotic 'home movie', *Magical Mystery Tour*, a surreal journey through a landscape that was part provincial England, part psychedelic dream. 'The Magical Mystery Tour is coming to take you away,' the group promised, and escape offered better vibes than Vietnam.

BBC disc jockey John Peel was regarded as the voice of the underground, a role he occupied by virtue of his regular column in the *International Times*, and his late-night radio show, which provided a rare showcase for commercially marginal rock. His bewilderment in the early months of 1968 summed up the predicament of those trying to ignore the existence of conflict and discrimination. The universal-love ethos that comprised his radio persona was continued on the page, where he was prone to end his prose ramblings by telling his readers, 'I love you', or 'I must not lose you now that I have found you', like an adolescent penning a Valentine's Day card. He quoted from the poems of J.R.R. Tolkien; offered regular news bulletins on the health of his pet hamster, Biscuit; and confronted the outside world with the pained bafflement of a toddler awoken from an entrancing dream.

The disturbances in Grosvenor Square clearly caused him much pain. America, he recognised, was 'in the grip of a total and manic delusion that the rest of the world should want the dubious benefits of the American way'. But violent political demonstrations, he felt, were not the way to declare independence from America's cultural domination. Instead, he wrote, 'We could have said, "We are here, not to hurt or destroy, but so that you can see the sadness and fear in our faces. Count our heads, read our eyes, and try, really try to understand." Sadly, they would almost certainly have been unmoved, but there would have been a chance.' Nothing was to be gained by attacking police horses with knitting needles, as he alleged some demonstrators had done; anyway, 'politics carry the stench of death'. Indeed, death might even cause a bad trip.

The choice was to belong to the world, or to disappear into the mansions of the imagination. But the Beatles pretended that they were exempt from this dilemma. In 1967, the group's accountants warned them that they needed to divert their corporate profits into a new business venture, in order to avoid a crushing tax bill. They were advised to form a series of companies, into which they could invest the enormous royalties pouring into their coffers from sales of their *Sgt. Pepper* album. It was a standard business manoeuvre, and the group's advisers imagined that they might open a chain of boutiques or sponsor a guitar factory – anything to keep the taxman at bay.

Instead, the Beatles devised Apple – not so much a method of tax evasion as a way of life. Paul McCartney became the corporation's prime mover, and it was he who coined the utopian description of its philosophy: 'a kind of Western communism'. Under the umbrella of their holding company, Apple Corps Ltd, the Beatles launched an array of divisions, targeted at areas such as Films, Electronics, Clothing, Records, Music and Books. The retail operations were designed, as John Lennon explained, 'to see if we can create things and sell them without charging three times our cost'. It was a direct attack on the profit ethos of capitalism. Equally revolutionary was the group's insistence that artists should control the methods by which their art reached the public. The Beatles hoped to expose new talent, and to allow it to flourish without jumping through the corporate and financial barriers they had encountered. At the same time, they hoped to seize complete command over the distribution, marketing and sale of their own work, individual and collective. Taken together, these aims did indeed add up to as close an approximation of 'Western communism' as it was possible to imagine within the capitalist system.

'The concept as outlined by Paul', revealed his friend Barry Miles in summer 1968, 'is to establish an "Underground" company above ground, as big as Shell/BP or ICI, but there is no profit motive, as the Beatles' profits go first to the combined staff and then are given away to "the needy".' The only problem was time. 'Apple is in a disorganised state and very chaotic,' Miles admitted. 'However, it is hoped that it will be functioning as outlined above in about a year.' In effect, he concluded, the Beatles were an example of communism in action, as 'they represent the workers seizing control of the means of production'.[5]

One aspect of 'the means of production' that was beyond the Beatles' reach was their own recording contract with the EMI corporation. The previous year, they had signed an exclusive nine-year deal with EMI, whose Parlophone label released the group's records. No matter how utopian the Beatles' ideals, it was naive of them to imagine that EMI might release them from the deal without vast financial compensation. The group were allowed to use their Apple logo on all their subsequent records, but their ties with EMI remained as tight as ever. It was an early indication for the Beatles that their concept for Apple might prove to be commercially unworkable.

While Mick Jagger had been patrolling the Grosvenor Square demonstration in March, three of the Beatles were in Rishikesh, India, with the Maharishi Mahesh Yogi. They returned home soon afterwards with their spiritual trust in their guru dented by his interest in the physical world, as personified by film star Mia Farrow. As John Lennon revealed later, their trek to the meditation centre had not erased all thoughts of the political world they had left behind. 'I wanted to say what I thought about revolution,' he recalled. 'I'd been thinking about it up in the hills in India. And I still had this "God will save us" feeling about it.' Back in London in early May, he watched entranced as French students took to the streets of Paris, pulling the workers in their wake. 'I didn't really know much about the Maoists,' he admitted. 'I just knew that they seemed to be so few and yet they . . . stood in front of the police waiting to get picked off.' Suspicious of the motives of the French student groups, he began to question their tactics: 'I thought, if they wanted revolution, if they really want to be subtle, what's the point of saying, Well, I'm a Maoist and why don't you shoot me down? I thought that was not a very clever way of getting what they wanted.'

Lennon's confused desire to be involved, to comment and to criticise was channelled into a song entitled, appropriately enough, 'Revolution'. It was completed days after the French protests of May 1968 dissolved into compromise. Consciously or not, his lyrics reflected the divide at the heart of the revolutionary left: between the 'permanent revolution' envisaged by Trotskyist parties, and the gradual, socialism-by-stealth approach favoured by the official, Soviet-backed Communists. French Trotskyists complained that the Communist Party had betrayed socialism by its refusal to help overthrow the government. They believed that revolution could be achieved by instigating violent demonstrations against the establishment. Lennon responded to this fantasy: 'If you talk about destruction, don't you know that you can count me out'. Before revolution could be considered, 'We'd all love to see the plan'.

Elsewhere, Lennon's song became more politically confused. He declared his refusal to support 'people with minds that hate', as if, in the tradition of a Beatles single from the summer of love, all you needed was love. 'Free your mind instead', he retorted to those who wanted a change of political rule. By the end, he was falling back on mockery: 'You say you'll change the constitution . . . we all want to change your head'. In a final snide couplet, he condemned the extremists to eternal rejection, sexual as well as political: 'If you go carrying pictures of Chairman Mao, you ain't gonna make it with anyone anyhow'. Every verse ended with the same repeated refrain: 'Don't you know it's gonna be all right?' He may have disowned the Maharishi, but his blind faith in the future owed much to his experience of Transcendental Meditation.

On 18 May 1968, as millions of workers in Paris raised the red flag of rebellion, Lennon and the other Beatles gathered at George Harrison's home in the Surrey stockbroker belt, to record demos of their new songs. Clearly under the influence of some exotic smoke, the Beatles romped through Lennon's 'Revolution' like a campfire singalong. Over the next ten days, Lennon watched *les evenements* in Paris move towards a crescendo, and then slide into anti-climax. While the prospect for revolution waned, he began a sexual and romantic relationship with Yoko Ono, a Japanese artist from the Fluxus group, who began to loosen his ties to orthodoxy in every area of his life.

At the end of the month, the Beatles began the laborious five-month creation of their crowning artistic achievement, the so-called *White Album*. At Lennon's insistence, the first song they attempted was 'Revolution'. Abandoning the carefree hi-jinks of their blueprint, they fashioned a strange, lumbering pastiche of 1950s American rock'n'roll, overlaid with acerbic electric guitar. There was one crucial difference in the song: when he reached the lines about violent dissent, Lennon whispered, 'Don't you know that you can count me out', paused for a second, and then added: 'in'. 'I wasn't sure,' he explained later. 'I don't fancy a violent revolution happening all over. I don't want to die. But I'm beginning to think, what else can happen? It seems inevitable.'

The master take of 'Revolution' stretched for almost ten minutes, as the song dissolved into a barrage of instrumental noise that was as chaotic as Lennon's political philosophy. To extend the sonic metaphor, Lennon, Ono and George Harrison began to collate sound effects and dislocated dialogue. These were layered over the final six minutes of the recording, creating a cacophonous collage that was much closer to the spirit of May 1968 than Lennon's words. The song was then separated from the sound effects to create two 'Revolution' tracks, numbered 1 and 9. 'I thought I was painting in sound a picture of revolution,' Lennon confessed later. 'But I made a mistake. The mistake was that it was anti-revolution.' The Beatles subsequently recorded 'Revolution' again, this time in a hard rock arrangement, as Lennon attempted to persuade his colleagues that the song should be released as a single. Destruction was now conclusively 'out', not 'out, in'. Almost simultaneously, and without being aware of each other's actions, the two most influential groups in British rock had each documented their reaction to the events in France. Political reaction to the two songs would be markedly different.

## VIETNAM VOYEURS

Lennon and Jagger responded to May 1968 as individuals, not representatives of a generation. But the notion of revolution was now so central to youth culture's conception of itself that both men were almost required to speak out, by the urgency of the times if not (yet) by their audience. Student protests were on the front page in Europe and the USA. German college kids followed their French counterparts onto the streets in May, as their native SDS (unrelated to the US organisation, but fulfilling a similar purpose) called unsuccessfully for an insurrection that would shake the government as the Paris uprising had done. In New York, meanwhile, Columbia University was occupied by students appalled by issues both international and local, from the faculty's backing of the Vietnam War to the decision to exile residents of Harlem from facilities and land owned by the university. Columbia's president, Grayson Kirk, grew so impatient with the sit-in that he called in the New York police, who evicted the protestors with extreme force. Officers attacked journalists and photographers as they entered the building, and their brutal assault on the unarmed students was captured on film, further polarising public opinion. The fracas inspired similar unrest in campuses across the USA.

Columbia, Martin Luther King, Bobby Hutton, Bobby Kennedy, Paris, Vietnam: the turbulence of 1968 was inescapable. Even middle-of-the-road entertainers were now routinely quizzed about their attitude to the war and racial tension, while any artist with pretensions to representing youth was expected to share a political 'line' on the radical issues of the day. Hence the slight bafflement that greeted Bob Dylan's *John Wesley Harding* album in the first days of 1968. The singer had been silent since suffering a motor-cycle crash in June 1966, and his return was widely anticipated. Many hoped – indeed, insisted – that Dylan would provide the key to the heightened drama of America's collective life, or at least offer sardonic commentary on the war, the Johnson presidency and the other scars on the culture. Instead, *John Wesley Harding* offered a collective of short but enigmatic ballads, haunted by imagery borrowed from the Old West or the Bible, and entirely lacking in anything that resembled an overt comment on America's national traumas.

That didn't prevent keen Dylan student A.J. Weberman from extending his study of the bard's work. 'To really understand Dylan,' he declared soon after the release of *John Wesley Harding*, 'you really have to be a revolutionary. You have to have an extreme dislike for our present society and a strong desire to overthrow it.' Weberman was convinced that 'many of his singles are against the war', but Dylan refused to draw any such conclusions. Had he issued any explanatory statement about his most recent album, he might have noted that art could serve other masters than politics; or that political opinions could be inferred just as easily by an absence of speech as by a worthy torrent of slogans. But his only statement came in his liner notes, a teasing parable about exactly the same enigma that his audience required him to unlock.

Many of Dylan's followers were outraged by his political passivity. 'Dylan's new album is the biggest piece of tripe,' exploded Country Joe McDonald. 'We're napalming kids in Vietnam, the cops are smashing people's heads all over the fucking country, the fascists are taking over the world, and he wants to hold his breath. He's got *responsibilities*.'[6] Fish guitarist Barry Melton joined the fray: 'How can he be apathetic with all the stuff that's going on? Riots in the streets, bombs, hatred . . .' Bassist Bruce Barthol pinpointed a specific cause that Dylan had refused to support: 'What if Dylan said he was going to come to Chicago this summer, how many people would come? Ten thousand? Twenty? Thirty? A hundred thousand?' 'They couldn't kill that many people,' McDonald exclaimed gleefully. 'They'd have to napalm the entire city!'

It was an overstatement worthy of Abbie Hoffman and Jerry Rubin, whose campaign to stoke up excitement about the Chicago convention had dragged in the names of the world's top rock acts as potential guests of their Festival of Life. 'Abbie was a clown, a showman, constantly outrageous,' Judy Collins recalls fondly. Through the late spring of 1968, he and Rubin took the politics of the absurd to new heights, parodying and terrifying the forces of law and order in the same breath. August, they promised, would see a full-scale Yippification of the city of Chicago, with LSD in the water mains, police officers forced to make love to the nearest bystander, and days of riots that would reduce the city centre to ruins. Chicago's police and the FBI were arming themselves for nothing short of a Paris-style insurrection.

It was now that the FBI's COINTELPRO operation moved into full swing. An internal memorandum explained the scheme by noting that New Left activists 'urge revolution in America and call for the defeat of the United States in Vietnam. They continually call and falsely allege police brutality and do not hesitate to utilise unlawful acts to further their so-called causes.' In reply, the FBI proposed 'to neutralise the New Left and the Key Activists . . . The purpose of this program is to expose, disrupt and otherwise neutralise the activities of this group and persons connected with it. It is hoped that with this new program their violent and illegal activities may be reduced if not curtailed.' COINTELPRO involved not just the FBI's customary surveillance of suspicious individuals – a category that stretched from urban terrorists to peacenik folk-singers – but also a campaign of disinformation and infiltration. The FBI had already begun to place operatives within black groups such as US and the Black Panthers, to incite mutual distrust and enmity. Now it intended to widen this policy to the entire New Left, even attempting to bribe or blackmail some of the movement's leaders into acting as double agents. The COINTELPRO philosophy worked skilfully on two levels. While its activities remained secret, it could provoke splits and disagreements between and within some of the New Left's most powerful groups. Once its cover was blown, and the existence of COINTELPRO was confirmed, then the 'Program' was even more effective, as it planted seeds of paranoia that any New Left member, no matter how senior, might be working for the other side.

Uncertainty already shadowed the planning for Chicago. Rubin and Hoffman came close to abandoning the entire enterprise when it appeared that Robert Kennedy was likely to win the Democratic nomination for the presidency. Both men greeted his assassination with ill-disguised glee, which upset and alienated many of their comrades. Jerry Rubin even crowed that the assassin, Sirhan Sirhan, must be a Yippie. Kennedy's death cleared the path for Vice-President Hubert Humphrey to relaunch his stalled campaign. Under these circumstances, Chicago was not just revitalised; Hoffman and Rubin believed that it was now a moral and political necessity, a last attempt to shake the Democratic Party free from its death's-head embrace with geno-cide.

Unfortunately for the Yippies, their theatrical scare tactics affected more people than they had intended. The potential stars of the Festival of Life read the stories that Hoffman and Rubin had planted in the press, and began to wonder what they'd got themselves into. Of the names promised as festival attractions, only Phil Ochs was now fully committed to the project.

The jewel in the Yippies' crown, if his friend Ginsberg could have reached him, would have been Bob Dylan. But his participation remained a distant dream. Dylan had returned to seclusion in upstate New York, learning to paint, studying the Bible, and mourning the death of his father. In summer 1968, he agreed to a rare interview with the folk magazine *Sing Out!*, conducted by two of his old friends from Greenwich Village, John Cohen and Happy Traum. Perhaps Dylan hadn't realised the extent to which the war had perme-ated daily life in America. The magazine had, after all, recently printed the lyrics to the 'Hymn of the National Liberation Front of South Vietnam', alongside such homegrown anti-war songs as 'Hell, No! I Ain't Gonna Go' and 'The Ballad of Ho Chi Minh'. Cohen and Traum made a concerted attempt to elicit political opinions from Dylan, with little success. He denied any contact with student activists or black militants; and claimed not to follow the news any more closely than 'the lady across the street does'. Traum, the more sensitive of his two inquisitors, asked Dylan: 'Do you foresee a time when you're going to have to take some kind of a position?' 'No,' Dylan answered curtly. Pushed harder, he explained: 'The decisions I would have to make are my own decisions, just like anyone else has to make his own. It doesn't necessarily mean that any position must be taken.' In effect, Dylan's stance had not changed since 1964, the year when he first abdicated responsibility for anyone but himself.

Traum constantly returned to politics during the interview. He attempted to explain to Dylan why the world situation required every thinking person to take sides, while Dylan evaded his jabs like a prizefighter, stonewalling defensively: 'How so? . . . Where's the nearest ghetto? . . . What events?' Traum wasn't helped by Cohen's tendency to declaim political speeches, often just at the moment when Dylan appeared to be cornered. Eventually, Dylan conceded, 'Well, I'm for the students, of course, they're going to be taking over the world. The people who they're fighting are old people, old ideas.' But conflict wasn't the way forward: 'They don't have to fight. They can sit back and wait.' A Zen master couldn't have put it better.

A few days later, the three men assembled again, and this time Traum confronted Dylan: surely, as an artist and a public figure, he was morally bound to declare his views about the war? Dylan refused the bait, teasing Traum: 'I know some very good artists who are for the war.' Anyway, 'for' or 'against' was an illusion: 'That really doesn't exist.' And he mentioned a painter friend – probably his Woodstock neighbour, Bruce Dorfman – who was 'all for the war. He's just about ready to go over there himself. And I can comprehend him.' Traum was outraged: 'Why can't you argue with him?' 'I can see what goes into his paintings,' Dylan replied, 'and why should I?'

Traum tried one more time. How could Dylan bear to be friends with someone who supported the war? 'I don't think it would be possible for you and him to share the same basic values,' he added. From his side, Dylan was equally uncomprehending: 'I've known him for a long time, he's a gentleman, and I admire him, he's a friend of mine. People just have their views.' Then, as if that wasn't heresy enough, he slipped a stiletto blade into the heart of the counter-culture: 'Anyway, how do you know I'm not, as you say, *for* the war?' Shocked and/or disbelieving, neither Traum nor Cohen followed up this inflammatory comment; it was like Jesus arriving for the Second Coming and announcing that he didn't believe in God.

After the political sparring, Dylan proved more forthcoming, letting slip some comments that explained eloquently the relationship between his song-writing, his audience and the outside world. The discussion had turned to 'Masters of War', his incisive and timelessly topical attack on the cynical barons of the arms trade. The song had been written in 1963, when Dylan was widely accepted as the prince of the folk protest movement. 'That was an easy thing to do,' Dylan recalled of the song's genesis. 'There were thousands and thousands of people just wanting that song, so I wrote it up.

What I'm doing now isn't more difficult, but I no longer have the capacity to feed this force which is needing all these songs. I know the force exists, but my insight has turned into something else.' It was a recognition that there were still 'thousands and thousands of people' waiting for Dylan to lacerate the warmongers of the Vietnam conflict. What was missing was Dylan's 'capacity to feed this force' – drained, perhaps, by his personal indifference to responsibility; or by the changes in his lifestyle since he'd crashed his motorbike and abandoned touring; or perhaps by some deep-rooted psychological block which left him unable to speak for anyone but himself. Either way, the *Sing Out!* interview demonstrated that anyone searching for political leadership from Bob Dylan was destined to be disappointed.

## RADICAL NOISE

Dylan would not travel to Chicago in August, but his longtime rival, Phil Ochs, had promised to be there. In spring 1968, he'd left New York and moved to California, where he became a regular companion of Jerry Rubin. The two men staged a public debate, during which Rubin indulged in his standard rant about the oncoming revolution, and Ochs – who described himself at this point as 'a semi-Yippie' – added a touch of realism. The Yippies, he complained, were simply 'lashing out at the approaching armed tractor with yo-yo's'. The military-industrial complex could not be toppled by theatrical gestures; besides, it was hot-wired for survival. Rubin lashed out at his friend: 'I do not want the system to survive. You do. I want to help destroy America's military domination of the world, and her cultural imperialism.' 'I thought either McCarthy or Kennedy was going to save the country,' Ochs admitted the following year.

Ochs was naturally attracted to Rubin's flamboyant rhetoric, but couldn't escape the stinging intuition that neither flamboyance nor fiery words would stop the war. He was recording a new album, *Tape From California*, which emerged just before the Chicago convention. Its cover showed a postcard, on which Ochs scrawled a slightly despairing prose poem. 'I left my life in LA', he wrote, alluding to Kennedy's assassination. He quoted a Viet Cong battle cry ('tonight American pigs you die!') as if it came from his own lips, and noted the gulf between the fearless Viet Cong soldiers and his American public: 'You are afraid you are alone'. With his final lines, he revealed how Vietnam had become a psychological battle, both for himself and for America: 'Can it be the War of Liberation has finally come home?'

*Tape From California* was 'a pretty confused album', he admitted the following year, because it was inspired by the war. Indeed, it included his 1967 anthem, 'The War Is Over'. Even with a new military band arrangement, the song sounded powerless, as the war continued unabated. Elsewhere Ochs spotlighted 'the spiritual decline of America', tracing what he called its 'mystical, artistic and social decay'. The album sold poorly: Ochs was carving complex metaphors when his audience, sitting-in at their colleges or burning their draft cards, required a barrage of slogans. Like Dylan, he no longer had 'the capacity to feed [the] force'.

Yet Ochs' name still resonated in the counter-culture, which is why it was central in the Yippies' publicity for their Chicago escapade. One heavily circulated poster listed 500 attractions on offer at the Festival of Life, from 'Heart Transplant For LBJ' to 'Dancing', 'Revolution' to 'Slapstick'. Then there were the names, with Jimi Hendrix, Pete Seeger and countless others joining the cast list. Even without Dylan or the Beatles, it was shaping up to be the event of the season.

Many of those already checking out their airline schedules for late August did not appreciate the Yippies' playfully cavalier attitude towards fact. Just as Jerry Rubin and Abbie Hoffman used exaggeration as a political weapon against the Chicago authorities, they also wildly overstated the co-operation they were expecting from the rock'n'roll community. Several artists on their list, including Hendrix, Seeger and Blood Sweat & Tears, had either not been approached to appear at the Festival of Life, or had already turned the invitation down. Even some of those who had allowed their names to accompany the Yippies' original announcement were now wavering. Arlo Guthrie, the son of folk legend Woody Guthrie, had achieved a degree of fame as the composer of a musical shaggy dog story entitled 'Alice's Restaurant'. In January 1968, he played the song to Rubin and Hoffman, and offered it as the anthem for their festival. Six months later, at the Newport Pop Festival on Rhode Island, Guthrie ran into the Yippies again. 'They asked me if I would come to Chicago to sing that song,' he recalled. 'I said to both of them that I was still concerned about the fact that the permits had not been granted yet, and that I would not attend.' Furthermore, he said he would advise other musicians not to answer the call, 'because of the fear of police violence'.

Judy Collins left her decision closer to the wire, but came to the same conclusion as Guthrie. Nearly forty years on, she concedes: 'I would never have gone to Chicago, because I was not interested in putting myself into a situation that was going to be chaotic and possibly dangerous. I felt very uncomfortable about that. Plus I was working all the time, trying to make a living. I liked and supported what Abbie was doing, but I was also a very personal singer and writer.'

No front-line rock performers had made more radical noise in the months leading up to the festival than Country Joe & the Fish – so much so, in fact, that the staid music-business magazine *Billboard* complained that 'they veil their talent with a slew of insults hurled at President Johnson, seeking to draw attention to themselves'. Besides slating 'that bastard LBJ' on stage, Country Joe McDonald launched his own facetious 'Joe for President' campaign, with the platform: 'Show contempt and don't vote'. It was a slogan the Yippies might easily have coined, although McDonald did sully the purity of his non-involvement by pledging to play benefit shows for the Peace & Freedom Party. Like the two main parties, the PFP were undertaking a lengthy process to determine their presidential candidate. Dr Benjamin Spock, comedian Dick Gregory and, remarkably, Eugene McCarthy were under consideration, although McCarthy himself had made no meaningful gestures of support for PFP. But in keeping with the radical mood of the times, and the symbolism of the PFP's union with the Black Panther Party, Eldridge Cleaver was the eventual choice of party members. His candidacy too was symbolic: approaching his 33rd birthday, he was more than two years too young to be elected president under US law.

The PFP's aim was not votes – even their most idealistic supporters never imagined they might win – but exposure. The party was using the system to undercut the system. Country Joe & the Fish were among the first rock artists to confront the similar paradox that they were using the profit-oriented record industry as a vehicle for subversion. 'Right now,' declared Barry Melton, 'we are selling peace to the people for $3.98, and in a consumer society that's the way to do it, right?' In a business where major record companies could boast of their roster of 'revolutionaries', it was only natural that the artists should respond in kind. But, as Melton admitted, 'we're not going to try to fuck up the record industry. We are *using* the record industry to make money.' Their summer 1968 album *Together* maintained their careful balance of the playful, the psychedelic and the political. It contained one of the most powerful musical statements yet recorded about Vietnam. McDonald gave this vivid account of a bombing raid on innocent civilians the name

'An Untitled Protest'. Words failed him when confronted by America's national war crime, as 'Delegates from the western land' came 'to join the death machine'.

As the Chicago convention neared, McDonald maintained his radical stance. 'We're in a revolution right now,' he announced. But there were limits, and the threat of violence from Mayor Daley's police concentrated his mind. Asked by Abbie Hoffman to make a pledge of support, he pulled out of the event. 'A lot of people are going to get hurt,' he told the underground press. 'If you want to have a bunch of people get together, have them get together where they won't get their heads clubbed in by anybody – the Grand Canyon, maybe.'

Not all of McDonald's bandmates shared his pessimism. 'Success is a motherfucker,' Fish bassist Bruce Barthol laughs. 'As soon as you start to gain some kind of position in the world, whether it's in business or rock'n'roll, then all of a sudden you have something to lose. I felt that Joe and the other guys in the band were worrying too much about their own safety and image, and not enough about what the movement was trying to achieve.' Alone in the Fish camp, Barthol remained adamant that the band should continue to support the Yippies' festival. 'I really went over the line,' he recalls of the arguments that followed. 'I felt it was vital that we should play. Joe was concerned that we might get hurt, or have our equipment smashed. But I felt that we owed it to our audience to put ourselves in the front line. I was a lone voice. In fact, at one point Joe was saying he wanted to take out an ad in the New York and Chicago papers, accusing the Yippies of irresponsible revolutionary leadership. Fortunately, everyone was too stoned to get it together.'

By democratic decision, though, the Fish were now out of the reckoning. 'If we had gone to the Yippies' festival,' Barthol believes, 'we could have made a difference, even if it was only to our enlightened self-interest. So we might have got hurt, but so what? There were two hundred American kids a week dying in Vietnam, plus god knows how many Vietnam.' Soon after the convention, disillusioned by the Chicago fiasco and anxious to avoid the draft, Barthol announced that he was leaving the Fish. 'He was probably the conscience we should have listened to,' Barry Melton conceded. 'There was a push from the business side of things not to shake the boat too much. I think Bruce had a distinct aversion to fame and money, but I also think he sensed the mission was being lost.'

These desertions did little to dampen the Yippies' zeal. In the final days before the Democratic Convention, Rubin and Hoffman distributed flyers headed (after the Impressions' gospel-based civil rights anthem) 'People Get Ready'. Even without Arlo Guthrie, Judy Collins or the Fish, the Festival's art would outshine the establishment's. 'Johnson and his delegates will make ugly speeches and play ugly campaign music,' they proclaimed, 'while we, the living, breathing youth of the world, will make the city a theatre, and every restaurant Alice's.' It was the moment for a 'whole new culture' to rise from 'the ashes of America'. There would be rock groups in the park, while Democrats and dopers frolicked in hotel corridors. The Yippies' irrepressible surrealism provided the final vision of ecstasy: 'Long boats filled with Vikings will land on the shores of Lake Michigan, and discover America! Chicago will become a river of wild onions!' And if the onions were peeled, then the river might run with tears.

## DREAM MUTATIONS

While the Yippies sketched paradise on the map of Chicago, another utopian dream mutated into nightmare. The 'communist democracy' of Alexander Dubček's reforms in Czechoslovakia provided a beacon of hope for socialists and revolutionaries around the Western world. Left-wing activists always had to confront the argument that every communist regime acted as a dictatorship, favouring censorship over openness and autocracy over plutocracy. Now Dubček had raised the possibility of a humanitarian, culturally aware form of socialism, in which public debate was encouraged and the people were allowed the responsibility to govern themselves. In Prague, it was possible for the first time in decades for people to take part in discussions about the future of their society without fear of intimidation or arrest. Citizens could watch theatre groups performing works by authors previously denounced as counter-revolutionary, or even attend a 'rock musical' cabaret that satirised the government.

From its headquarters in Moscow, the Soviet Bloc issued warnings that Dubček was leading his country into corruption and capitalism; worse still, that the leader himself was a counter-revolutionary (the worst insult in the communist dictionary). He was summoned to a meeting of communist leaders, and warned to control his regime's liberalisation, or else Soviet troops would do the job for him. In particular, he was asked to cancel a meeting of Czechoslovakia's ruling committee, at which it was expected that hard-line supporters of Novotny and Moscow would be expelled from power. After several days of negotiations, Dubček returned to Prague insisting that he would not back down. The country had recently been the site of Soviet Bloc military manoeuvres; now Russia ordered the tanks and soldiers to be withdrawn. For a precious week, Czechoslovakia basked in the illusion that the danger was over.

Then, late on the evening of Tuesday 20 August 1968, the dream was violently disrupted. In a carefully co-ordinated operation, Soviet Bloc tanks rumbled across the Czech border in a dozen different locations. Meanwhile, scores of Russian transport planes landed at Prague airport a minute apart, each disgorging more troops and supplies. Major towns were seized in minutes, while in Prague the invading soldiers headed for strategically important sites, such as radio stations and government buildings. The incursion had been timed to coincide with a government meeting, making it the easiest of tasks for Dubček's committee to be placed under arrest. Moscow claimed that its troops were responding to a plea from the Czech people, to save them from tumbling into a counter-revolutionary abyss.

Over the next two weeks, events followed a predictable course. Dubček and his closest colleagues were flown to Moscow, roughed up by their captors, and given a stark choice: dismantle eight months' worth of reforms, or watch their homeland disappear, carved into pieces and annexed by the surrounding states. A tearful Dubček returned home, with bruises visible on his face, to plead with his people that they should accept the reversal of everything they had come to recognise as liberation. Overnight, the sounds of freedom vanished from the streets of Prague, as the satirical cabaret closed, the radio stations abandoned their programmes of Western acid-rock, and newspapers and TV bulletins reflected the closed mind of Moscow's communist dictatorship. It was a stark reminder to would-be revolutionaries around the world that no superpower would give up its power lightly.[7]

The Russian invasion of Czechoslovakia cast a final ill omen, as the American left prepared to launch a decisive thrust against the ruling Democratic Party in Chicago. Almost every radical element in the nation was ready to demonstrate against the Johnson administration's policy in Vietnam. Meanwhile, Mayor Daley's office issued a series of statements promising that any illegality would be met with the maximum force allowed by the law. The National Guard were set to intervene as soon as demonstrations or marches began, while several thousand army troops were stationed outside the city, in case of insurrection.

Despite the conspiracy charges that were brought later against some of the most prominent figures in the New Left, plans for the Chicago protests were anything but co-ordinated. The two major forces in the movement, Mobe and SDS, each had its own agenda. The Mobe proposed a programme of picket lines, rallies and workshops, climaxing in a march to the International Amphitheater, where the convention was being staged. SDS dismissed Mobe's plans as a bourgeois acceptance of the status quo. It saw Chicago as an opportunity to recruit activists for the revolution: 'This will be an organising job and not a picnic,' members were told. 'Chicago is pig city and they are uptight.' The assumption was that the events planned by the Yippies and Mobe would inevitably result in street fighting, in which SDS should be prepared to exercise a controlling hand.

Countless other groups – some pacifist, some much more warlike – were scheduling their own rallies. New Left leaders imagined that at least half a million demonstrators would travel to the city. But they had not reckoned on the effect of months of hyperbole about the possible effects of the Yippies' antics. Tales of delegates being poisoned, on the one hand, and protestors being gunned down in cold blood, on the other, helped to dampen the revolutionary ardour of all but the most committed protestors. Those who attended did so in the knowledge – perhaps even the expectation – that they would be risking their skins, and possibly their lives.

As if the splits and potential schisms among the New Left weren't enough, the two guiding forces of the Yippie movement were not speaking to each other by late August. Virtually inseparable in their YIP playpen all year, Jerry Rubin and Abbie Hoffman argued violently over what their own role in the week's events should be. It 'almost resulted in a fist fight', one of the police informers who were tailing Hoffman reported. 'I felt Abbie was trying to exclude me,' Rubin recalled, 'trying to dominate the media. I was saying, you're not the story here, Abbie. The story is the war, the story is the confrontation of cultures.' It was an ironic point of disagreement: the two superstars of the New Left, who created lasting careers out of their involvement in the Chicago protests, were squabbling about who should be the focus of the demonstrations.

The omens were still against them. On the night of Wednesday 21 August, 24 hours after the invasion of Czechoslovakia, Chicago police confronted two teenagers who were violating the city's curfew. Seventeen-year-old Dean Johnson pulled out a pistol, and was immediately shot dead. He had only just arrived in the city to attend the Yippies' festival. On Thursday, the Yippies, Mobe and SDS planned a memorial for the teenager, which the Yippies wanted to combine with a ceremony in honour of the departed soul of Czech freedom. But SDS, unable to decide upon a single revolutionary position on the Russian invasion, insisted that the two issues should not be confused.

On Friday 23 August, the Yippies' irrepressible sense of the theatrical took over. Months earlier, Jerry Rubin had suggested that the YIP should run its own presidential candidate – a pig, named Pigasus. Abbie Hoffman located a prime porker, but Rubin rejected it on aesthetic grounds, claiming that it wasn't ugly enough to be president. So Rubin and Phil Ochs set off to find an alternative candidate. They eventually found a suitable animal, and transported it back to the city, where Rubin had scheduled a press briefing outside the Civic Center. He had already taken the liberty of drafting a speech for Pigasus, which he proceeded to read while the candidate urinated on the sidewalk. 'The opening sentence was something like, "I, Pigasus, hereby announce my candidacy for the Presidency of the United States",' Ochs remembered. 'He was interrupted by the police, who arrested us.' Seven Yippies, including the singer, were seized by the police, as was the pig. While Pigasus was passed into the hands of the American Humane Society, the Yippies spent the day in jail. On their journey to police HQ, they discussed whether they were likely to be beaten up when they were out of public view. The tension was relieved when a policeman entered their cell and said: 'I've got bad news for you, boys. The pig squealed.' Not to be outdone, Abbie Hoffman arrived at Lincoln Park with a pig purporting to be Mrs Pigasus. She, too, was taken into protective custody.

For nearly six months, the Yippies had sounded a clarion call through the counter-culture – a promise that they would stage a Festival of Life, a gathering of the dissenting tribes, which would shake the foundations of the ruling Democratic Party, and present an alternative vision of America. They had offered a wish-fulfilled fantasy of Convention City in August: 'There are 500,000 of us dancing in the streets, throbbing with amplifiers and harmony . . . celebrating the birth of Free America in our own time.' They awoke on Sunday to the realisation that their half-a-million dancers of liberation numbered no more than a few thousand; and to the inevitability that the throbbing sound on the Chicago streets would not be harmony but conflict. Months of negotiations with Mayor Daley's staff about music permits and legal use of the park had dissolved into nothing. Few of the musicians whose names had been used to publicise the festival were now prepared to appear.

Country Joe & the Fish, whose album *Together* was high in the US charts during the week of the festival, were the ace in the Yippies' pack – a potent symbol of the underground, with proven commercial appeal. For months, Abbie Hoffman had pleaded with Country Joe McDonald to ignore the legal issues and think about the revolution. How could the composer of the anti-war movement's anthem care about the approval of Mayor Daley's bureaucrats? In an ironic twist of fate, the Fish's touring schedule brought them to the Electric Theater in Chicago the night before the Festival of Life began. Both Jerry Rubin and Abbie Hoffman attended the show, but surprisingly they made no attempt to change the band's minds. Indeed, neither McDonald nor Bruce Barthol can remember talking to either of the Yippie leaders that night. 'They were not even speaking to each other,' McDonald notes drily.

Ironically, McDonald found confrontation in Chicago impossible to avoid. The Fish duly played at the Electric Theater, then walked towards their car. A group of men described by McDonald as 'drunk motorcyclists' shouted insults at them, but 'We tried to be polite and avoided a violent conflict'. They arrived at the Lake Shore Hotel and met with more trouble. 'We were followed by three men about my age with crew cuts – straight-looking with slacks and shirts – who were drunk,' McDonald recalled. 'One of them began yelling about having served in Vietnam and wanted to know how I could walk around the streets looking like that.' Bruce Barthol and Chicken Hirsch were slightly in front of McDonald: they collected their room keys from the lobby, and then watched from the elevator as the man with the crew cut ran towards the rest of the band, shouting 'Don't you like America, hippies?' Then the door closed. As McDonald and keyboardist David Cohen moved towards a second elevator, the man threw himself at the Fish's leader. 'I was struck in the face,' McDonald said. 'My nose was fractured. My organist attempted to get out of the elevator to get to a phone to call the police. He was then struck in the face. They scuffled about in the lobby. Then all three of the men ran out the back door.' Police officers escorted the anti-war icon to hospital.

At 4 p.m. on Sunday, as scheduled, Ed Sanders stood before the paltry crowd in Lincoln Park, and declared the Festival of Life open. With no stage to lift him above the crowd – it had been barred by police – he was effectively invisible to anyone standing more than a few feet away. Sanders read some of his anti-war poetry, while behind him on the grass, a sound crew set up an amplification system. Then radical disc jockey Bob Fass came to the microphone to introduce John Sinclair's protégés from Detroit: the MC5. As the band launched into a typically incendiary set, the crowd edged forward, further increasing the tension. 'To the experienced few, there were obviously *agents provocateurs* in the crowd,' remembered MC5 guitarist Wayne Kramer. 'They were probably undercover cops or FBI. They walked around pushing people. They harassed and provoked fights. The MC5 played right down on the ground in front of the people and we were being watched, even filmed. We played our set, and we could feel the tension building.'

Phil Ochs, who was scheduled to play later in the proceedings, detected the same malevolent atmosphere: 'The amphetamine was in the air. It was incredibly intense.' Kramer described the feeling as 'tangible fear. It was an unsettling in the stomach; a gnawing, creepy feeling, like an inescapable cloak of dread. We felt it coming and there was absolutely nothing we could do about it.'

Events soon spiralled out of everyone's control. Around 5 p.m., the precarious sound system crackled loudly and then fell silent. 'I could see a number of people moving from the back of the crowd,' Abbie Hoffman said. 'Stew Albert came up to me and said that the police had come through the zoo and down into the park, about 200 police, and had started clubbing people and pushing them, and there had been some arrests. He was bleeding all over his head and face, there was blood pouring profusely.' In the confusion, cause and effect were difficult to distinguish. From the limited vantage point of Wayne Kramer, 'the first phalanx of motorcycle cops muscled through the crowd as soon as we stopped playing'. The education they'd received in riot situations in Detroit served the MC5 well: 'We weren't dummies. We knew from experience to get our amps and drums packed double-quick for our escape.'

When the police came through the crowd, Abbie Hoffman knew that the festival was over. The audience milled about in confusion, many of them hurling insults at the police officers. 'Pigs eat shit' was one constant refrain; others offered political satire by simply chanting 'Prague, Prague, Prague' at the invaders. After their initial foray, the police lined up before the crowd. Many of the festival-goers, determined to enjoy the celebration of a new era that they'd been promised, settled down in groups, sang protest songs, smoked dope, or lit small fires on the grass. Others continued to taunt the police, flinging missiles in their direction, then retreating when the officers retaliated.

Slowly, dusk fell on Lincoln Park, and only the flickering of flames distinguished police from protestor. Both sides drew daring and anger from the darkness: the missiles and invective grew more frequent, while the police removed their identification badges and prepared to mount serious battle. Around 9 p.m., fighting began in earnest, with riot-sticks cracking on protestors' heads, while members of the crowd responded with stones, tree branches or bottles. This time, there was no peaceful exodus from the park when the curfew was announced. While the crowd chanted, 'The park is ours', police herded them towards the exits. After prolonged violence, the crowd spilled out onto the streets, where photographers and pressmen were targeted indiscriminately alongside those who were intent on attacking the police.

And so the scene was set for a week of agony and agonising. On Monday night, as the Democratic National Convention was officially opened, there was open fighting in Lincoln Park and Grant Park. Tuesday saw the tension increasing, as Bobby Seale of the Black Panther Party flew in from California to deliver a short, typically inflammatory speech. His flamboyant rhetoric was familiar to audiences in Oakland, but many on both sides of the barricades in Chicago interpreted his tirades against 'the pigs' as literal incitement to kill any policeman who was lined up against the demonstrators. A few blocks away, several thousand people had gathered for President Johnson's Anti-Birthday Party. 'There were moments with Yippie that were pure ecstasy in terms of feeling fulfilled,' Phil Ochs recalled. 'That was the greatest moment [of Chicago] for me. I sang "The War Is Over", and when I came to the verse, "Even treason may be worth a try, this country is too young to die", the place exploded with people cheering for five minutes and the burning of draft cards. I couldn't finish the song, and had to leave the stage.' Protestors once again clashed with Chicago police into the early hours, their skirmishes chronicled by the ever-present cameras of TV news crews.

If one day symbolised the quandary of America in 1968 – the morass of Vietnam, the incoherent anger of the young, the gulf between politicians and those they governed – it was Wednesday 28 August. It began in farce, as Abbie Hoffman was arrested at breakfast for obscenity: he had scrawled the word 'FUCK' on his forehead. As an act of subversive leadership, it spelled out a more ambiguous message. Was it an abdication of responsibility? A desire to be removed from the action? A signal that he believed himself invulnerable to the forces of the law? Or, as his wife claimed, was he hoping to make himself invisible to the press, who would not dare to print a photograph displaying the offending word? Whatever his motive, Hoffman was kept in custody until the day's tumultuous events – which he had helped to shape – were almost over.

Phil Ochs also discovered the limitations of fame, or notoriety, that Wednesday. Outside the Conrad Hilton Hotel, he joined a small demonstration before a line of soldiers who were guarding the delegates. 'The thing I'm proudest of', he recalled when the Convention was over, 'is singing through a bull horn trying to get the soldiers to desert. I pointed the horn toward them and sang "I Ain't Marching Anymore", and asked them in the name of Robert Kennedy to leave the line.' What he didn't mention was their response. None of the soldiers budged an inch, except for one, who walked towards him and told him that he used to admire his music, but that he would never listen to a Phil Ochs album again. 'Phil was genuinely hurt by that,' recalled Stew Albert. 'He really seemed to expect that the troops would refuse to do what they were ordered to do. That he could not get them to throw down their arms when he asked them directly to do it, both in a speech and then actually going one-on-one, was really crushing for him.'

The focus of the day was the International Amphitheater, where the Democratic Party would choose its presidential candidate that evening. Before then, the movement had to decide how to handle its most public protest against the war. After a rally in Grant Park, they could disperse quietly; march in an organised parade towards the convention centre; or confront the delegates as they left their hotels. Veteran peace campaigner Dave Dellinger opened the ceremony and explained the options. Then Jerry Rubin took the microphone, telling activists: 'See you on the streets tonight.' After he spoke, a teenage protestor climbed the flagpole and pulled down the Stars and Stripes. It was a cue for police to surge into the crowd, assaulting people at random and without mercy. Incensed by the brutality of the police action, Tom Hayden urged his listeners to match the officers' venom with their own passion: 'We must move out of this park in groups throughout the city and turn this excited, overheated military machine against itself. Let us make sure that if blood is going to flow, let it flow all over this city.'

Many demonstrators took him at his word; others followed Dellinger on his peace march towards the convention hall. In the end, the distinction was purely theoretical. All the righteous anger and energy of the anti-war movement was funnelled towards the Conrad Hilton Hotel, and the waiting TV cameras, on South Michigan Avenue. Now every blow from a baton felt like martyrdom, and as the violence escalated, the media captured the brutality of the police response and carried it live, across America and into the convention hall. 'The whole world is watching,' demonstrators chanted, and in that instant the Democratic Party probably lost the 1968 election. Late night, Vice-President Hubert Humphrey was duly selected as the Democrats' candidate, but only after hundreds of delegates had expressed their horror at the scenes they had witnessed on the giant TV screens. Senator Abraham Ribicoff spoke for many when he used the convention platform to denounce Mayor Daley's 'Gestapo tactics on the streets of Chicago'. The cameras cut to the furious face of the mayor, mouthing the words, 'Fuck you, you Jew son of a bitch, you lousy motherfucker, go home'.

The response from the New Left was predictable. Thursday brought protest rallies across the city, marches, and more tear gas. Defeated candidate Eugene McCarthy gave the protestors his backing in an off-the-cuff speech outside the Hilton. From Tom Hayden came the call to 'Create 200 or 300 Chicagos everywhere'. Yet for Phil Ochs, the crushing of the Chicago demonstrations triggered only despair. 'It was like the soul of the country had been killed,' he explained later, 'and I felt myself partially murdered.' 'He was very depressed after Chicago,' his brother Michael confirms. 'He finally had to give up on the idea of changing the system from within, which was a real blow to his vision of America. He just moped around the house for months.'

Jann Wenner of *Rolling Stone* magazine, who had decried the Yippies as 'political exploiters . . . without a legitimate constituency' in May, responded to the events of August with predictable contempt. In an unsigned lead article entitled 'Everybody's Chicago Blues', Wenner distanced himself from both sides of the barricades. The problem, he contended, was 'the ugliness of power and the appalling hopelessness of those who fight against it'. As the champion of rock'n'roll culture, triumphantly isolated from the outside world, Wenner could find nothing to celebrate in the protests: 'The left wing of politics is a completely frustrating and pointless exercise of campus politics in a grown-up world. Everyone seems so ready to fault and scorn their fellow self-proclaimed "revolutionaries" for ideological infidelity and deviationism.' The fact that the Chicago police had united the New Left by treating them all with equal savagery escaped him. More typical of the reaction of the music community was a line from Mama Cass Elliott: 'Chicago was the truth, and all America saw it.'

In Grant Park, which many of the demonstrators had made their home during the convention, the week ended in surreal style, with a Back-To-School art festival for young kids. It was a microcosm of the national desire to pretend that nothing had happened, that Chicago, like the assassinations of Kennedy and King, and the ghetto riots of the summer before, and the deepening morass of Vietnam, was simply another glitch in the democratic system that could be lived through and then forgotten. The aftershocks rattled every section of American society, however, from the office of the President to the communes of those who sought to overthrow him. Chicago ripped the heart out of Humphrey's campaign, leaving him twenty points or more behind the Republican candidate, Nixon, in the opinion polls. He would rally over the weeks to come, but what could have been a certain coronation was now a desperate bid for survival. As the weeks passed, and the Humphrey bandwagon crawled too slowly back to life, the New Left had to consider the possibility that its protests – and the authorities' response to them – might have handed the forthcoming election to Nixon. Most activists didn't care, finding little to choose between two parties of big business and military-industrial power. Some welcomed the tide of repression that they assumed would be triggered by a Nixon presidency, in the belief that it would hasten the onset of the revolution. Why did it matter who won the election?

## CHAOTIC ELECTRICITY

The week that began with the deathly Festival of Life in Chicago ended with the release of two records that seemed to feed off the chaotic electricity of the moment. On Friday, the Beatles officially launched their utopian Apple Records company with 'Hey Jude', an anthemic Paul McCartney song. It was accompanied by John Lennon's commentary on 'Revolution'. On Saturday, the Rolling Stones responded with the equally confrontational 'Street Fighting Man'. It was both an uncanny coincidence, and a demonstration that leading rock musicians were more closely aligned to the temperature of the counter-culture than some of the radical journalists who made a living out of interpreting their work. The fact that the two leading rock groups in the world had chosen precisely this moment to comment on the burning issue of the hour seemed to offer more hope to the New Left than the ambiguous events of Chicago had done.

Not that ambiguity was altogether absent from either the Beatles' or the Stones' contributions. Of the two, the Stones' record provoked more opposition from the music industry, reinforcing the popular belief that 'Street Fighting Man' was a more dangerous proposition than the Beatles' counterpart. Decca Records, who released the Rolling Stones' records in the United Kingdom, informed Mick Jagger that they were unwilling to distribute 'Street Fighting Man' as a single, because it was 'subversive'. 'Of course it's subversive,' Jagger retorted sarcastically. But he was acutely aware of the limitations of his political power. 'It's stupid to think that you can start a revolution with a record,' he noted drily. 'I wish you could.' Guitarist Keith Richards added pertinently: 'We're more subversive when we go on stage, yet they still want us to make live appearances.'

In the context of the Chicago disturbances, some repercussions were probably inevitable. 'The fact that a couple of radio stations in Chicago banned the record just goes to show how paranoid they are,' remarked Richards. They weren't the only ones. London Records, Decca's US subsidiary, rushed 'Street Fighting Man' into the marketplace a week earlier than originally planned, to cash in on the furore. Then they were concerned that the record's artwork, depicting police and demonstrators in conflict, would be seen as glorifying street violence, and the sleeve was hastily withdrawn – halting the record's sales at the moment of peak demand. The artwork actually depicted the Sunset Strip riots of late 1966, but counter-culture legend suggested that the photographs had been taken on the streets of Chicago at the Stones' insistence, and were withdrawn by 'the man'. It all added lustre to the band's rebellious reputation.

The song was greeted with absurd idealism. 'Che Guevara's band were all poets,' one review began, 'Buckminster Fuller writes his architectural papers in poetry, the Rolling Stones sing Revolution! The pre-Socratic fusion of faith and reason is upon us.' Or, as another critic purred: 'Maybe you were not in San Francisco or Chicago or Paris or Prague and maybe you think the students were just a coincidence anyway. What do you mean you can't hear the words? Can't you feel it in the air?'

As the 'poor boy' in 'sleepy London town', Mick Jagger was greeted either as the street fighting man his song declared him to be, or as a sympathiser condemned to observer status by circumstances beyond his control. By contrast, John Lennon – sole author of the Beatles' study of 'Revolution' – was treated with much more suspicion by the counter-culture. It certainly didn't help his cause that the 'straight' press regarded the Beatles' song as a definitive dismissal of the New Left. As interviewer Jonathan Cott said accusingly to Lennon that September, '*Time* magazine came out and said, look, the Beatles say "no" to destruction.' Lennon's response did nothing to stem the criticism. 'There's no point in dropping out,' he floundered, 'because it's the same there and it's got to change. But I think it all comes down to changing your head, and yeah, I know that's a cliché.' Cott responded with an obvious question: 'What would you tell a black power guy who's changed his head and then finds a wall there all the time?' Lennon could only fall back on honest confusion: 'Well, I can't tell him anything, because he's got to do it himself. If destruction's the only way he can do it, there's nothing I can say that could influence him, because that's where he's at, really. We've all got that in us too, and that's why I did the "out and in" bit in a few takes. I prefer "out". But we've got the other bit in us. I don't know what I'd be doing if I was in his position. I don't think I'd be so meek and mild. I just don't know.'

Under pressure from the left, Lennon probably could have done without the support of Jann Wenner, who thought he recognised a kindred spirit. 'To say the Beatles are guilty of some kind of revolutionary heresy is absurd,' he wrote. 'They are being absolutely true to their identity as it has evolved through the last six years.' And that, many on the New Left noted, was exactly the problem. *Village Voice* reviewer Robert Christgau, usually a perceptive interpreter of the social significance (or otherwise) of rock'n'roll, felt only betrayal: 'It is puritanical to expect musicians, or anyone else, to hew to the proper line. But it is reasonable to request that they not go out of their way to oppose it. Lennon has, and it takes much of the pleasure out of their music for me.' The demand that musicians should be guided by their awareness of 'the proper line' seemed to veer perilously close to the artistic culture of Stalin's Russia.

There was now an obvious gulf between rock's most prominent voices and a portion, at least, of their potential audience. Anyone searching for leadership from Bob Dylan had to deal with his suggestion that he might actually support the Vietnam War. The Beatles wanted revolution, but not if it might intrude upon their personal comfort. The Rolling Stones were excited by the prospect of violence, but unable to connect it with the movement for change. Meanwhile, their counter-culture peers assumed their heroes would share their idealism and commitment. If they didn't, then they could expect to endure the wrath of the *Berkeley Barb* paper, who railed against the 'clear unmistakeable call for counter-revolution' that had come from the Beatles, 'who brought us the flower power fascist Maharishi last year'.

The criticism of the Beatles was expressed most cogently by a surprising source: the official Russian government journal of the arts, *Sovietskaya Kultura*. Ignoring the irony that only a handful of Western rock records were available to purchasers behind the Iron Curtain, the paper chided the Beatles for their 'indifference to politics'. Though the Beatles undoubtedly paid little mind to opinions in Moscow, they were more affected by voices from closer to home. Poet Adrian Mitchell, an acquaintance of Paul McCartney, examined the furore over the Beatles' statements about 'Revolution', and concluded: 'Many people hope that their courage increases.' Mitchell suggested that the group should tackle the problem of racism in Britain, which had been highlighted by the provocative statements made in recent months by the Conservative politician Enoch Powell. 'I'm not suggesting that Powellism could be stopped if the Beatles applied their considerable wits to a record called "Enoch",' Mitchell wrote. 'But they would be heard. They would also lose votes. They would be subject to a great deal of hatred. They have taken risks in the past but this would be a higher risk, one that might mean imprisonment (in a bad future) or might, by amplifying the small chorus of brave voices, mean that the future might be less bad.' A few weeks after Mitchell's article was published, Paul McCartney arrived at a Beatles recording session with a song satirising Powell's racist views, which had the working title of 'No Pakistanis'. Uncomfortable with the clumsiness of his lyrics, he soon reworked them into something less controversial: the 1969 hit single 'Get Back'.[8]

Meanwhile, John Lennon became embroiled in a political debate with the radical left. In May 1968, Tariq Ali (leader of the Vietnam Solidarity Campaign) and several associates published the first issue of a non-aligned socialist newspaper named *Black Dwarf* (after a 19th-century anarchist journal). In the wake of 'Street Fighting Man' and 'Revolution', the paper weighed the relative value of the Beatles and the Rolling Stones to the revolutionary cause. The Stones, argued Roland Muldoon, represented 'the seed of the new cultural revolution', while the Beatles were more concerned with 'safeguarding their capitalist investment'. In an adolescent flourish, Muldoon concluded: 'I hope [the Beatles] get so fucked up with their money-making that they become as obscure as Cliff Richard.'

The theme was maintained in the next issue of the paper, which juxtaposed the thoughts of communist pioneer Friedrich Engels on the importance of street fighting with a set of lyrics for 'Street Fighting Man' in Mick Jagger's hand. Reading the words, *Black Dwarf*'s editors noted, 'we [can] understand why it wasn't released' as a single. To highlight his radical ferocity, Jagger had written out one key line of the song – 'I'll kill the king' – in block capitals. 'We took "Street Fighting Man" very seriously,' *Black Dwarf* contributor John Hoyland recalls. 'It seemed to prove that the Rolling Stones were a genuinely progressive band, in political terms. In retrospect, it's ridiculous, because we were so wrong. Jagger was merely dabbling with the image of being a revolutionary. He was actually a home counties Tory, and he has been ever since. I should have known better, I realise now. I ought to have learned something from what had happened earlier that summer.'

In July 1968, Hoyland and fellow members of the Agitprop commune/arts project had staged a revolutionary festival in London's Trafalgar Square. 'It was called "Thang Loi!", which was Vietnamese for victory,' he explains. 'Several thousand people attended. We had poetry, radical theatre and rock music, with contributions from many different factions, including the Situationists. One thing I remember clearly is that someone had made a giant hamburger out of polystyrene, but where the meat should have been, there was the corpse of an American soldier.' Hoyland compered the event. 'As it neared its climax,' he remembers, 'I felt someone tugging on the leg of my trousers from in front of the stage. I looked down, and this guy shouted up to me, "We need a ladder". I established that he was the manager of Mick Farren and the Deviants, who were topping the bill. "You're on in fifteen minutes", I told him. "I know," he said, "that's why we need a ladder." "Why do you need a ladder?" "Mick's trousers are so tight, that they'll split if he has to climb onto the stage." I couldn't believe it. Here was this guy who was supposed to be a revolutionary, and he was worried about his velvet trousers splitting! Eventually several people lifted Farren onto the stage, so he didn't have to bend his legs and ruin his precious trousers.'

After his disillusioning encounter with Britain's leading proponents of revolutionary rock, Hoyland was perhaps extra-sensitive to the flaws in

Lennon's statement of 'Revolution'. 'I adored the Beatles,' he explains, 'but I was so disappointed by that song. I saw it as an attack on everything we were fighting for. It fell on the other side of the divide, as far as I was concerned, and I was self-righteously convinced that I had to speak out.' So the same issue of *Black Dwarf* that included Jagger's lyrics also contained Hoyland's 'Open Letter to John Lennon'. He repeated the familiar argument that Lennon's 'free your mind instead' was not an adequate response to 'a repressive, vicious, authoritarian system'. Revolution – the concept, not the song – was 'one of the most passionate forms of love'. In a line that must have wounded the composer of 'All You Need Is Love', Hoyland added: 'Love which does not pit itself against suffering, oppression and humiliation is sloppy and irrelevant.' Yet Hoyland was not entirely dismissive of the Beatle; Lennon, he recognised, had been the subject of oppression himself, both as a member of the working class and 'above all [because] you've been going out with a foreigner'. The Open Letter ended on a note of conciliation: 'Come and join us.' Hoyland admits today that 'I squirm when I read some of that letter. I was being very patronising, and naive. But I believed everything I said. Then, when Lennon was busted, I really thought it might shock him back into the revolutionary camp.'

A week before that issue of *Black Dwarf* was published, London police had raided the flat where Lennon and his partner, Yoko Ono, were living. They discovered a quantity of marijuana – to his dying day, Lennon insisted that the drugs had been planted – and arrested the singer. While the police ransacked their belongings in search of more evidence, Lennon rang the Beatles' office. 'Imagine your worst paranoia,' he told the group's aide, Neil Aspinall, 'cos it's here.' A month later, Ono miscarried the couple's baby, and the pair slipped into the shadow of heroin abuse. Under those circumstances, it is not surprising that Lennon reacted aggressively to *Black Dwarf*'s comments. It was one thing to be the subject of pressure from the establishment; quite another to be under attack from the radical left. Lennon phoned *Black Dwarf* editor Tariq Ali to demand an explanation. There was no concerted campaign against him, he was told; if Lennon wanted to use his right of reply, he should respond in writing.

Lennon's 'A Very Open Letter to John Hoyland' duly appeared more than two months later. At turns defensive and aggressive, it attempted to justify his political stance, and force Hoyland and *Black Dwarf* to examine their own philosophical limitations. 'I don't worry about what you, the left, the middle, the right or any fucking boys club think,' he began, rather begging the question of why he was bothering to write at all. '[But] I'm not only up against the establishment but you too.' Then he defended the Beatles' recent political commentary: 'I don't remember saying "Revolution" was revolutionary.' It was obvious, though, that Lennon didn't wish to be seen as anti-revolutionary, so he proceeded to explain the thinking behind the song: 'I'll tell you what's wrong with the world: people – so do you want to destroy them? Until you/we change our heads – there's no chance.'

The Beatles' Apple organisation, he continued, 'was never intended to be as big as Marks & Spencer . . . We set up Apple with the money we as workers earned, so that we could control what we did production-wise, as much as we could. If it ever gets taken over by other workers, as far as I'm concerned, they could have it.' It was a utopian vision of the group's corporation, which ignored its origins as a method of avoiding tax; utopian, too, in the suggestion that Lennon might stand idly by as 'other workers' seized control of the Beatles' cash-cow.

Lennon's letter ended with a simple manifesto: 'You smash it – and I'll build around it.' It was a defiant statement of purpose that resonated beyond politics. As a member of the experimental art group Fluxus, Yoko Ono had led the Beatle into areas that had previously been barred to him in his role as a commercial entertainer. Among the avant-garde, he had found a gulf between those who believed that it was sufficient to destroy the structures of the past in the name of modernism; and those who believed that destruction was meaningless unless more liberated structures were constructed in their place. As with art, so with society, Lennon insisted: as he'd sung in 'Revolution', 'we all want to see the plan'. And that was where he parted company with *Black Dwarf*, whose idealism (he believed) stopped short of imagining a practical substitute for the capitalist order it sought to overthrow.

The paper exercised its own right of reply, again written by Hoyland, beneath Lennon's Open Letter. Second time around, the criticism of the Beatle's political position asked questions he would have found difficult to answer. 'In "Revolution",' the paper noted, 'you say that people who want to change institutions should free their minds instead. Why *instead*? What makes you so sure that a lot of us haven't changed our heads in something like the way you recommend – and then found *it wasn't enough*, because you simply cannot be completely turned on and happy when you know that kids are being roasted to death in Vietnam, when all around you, you see people's individuality being stunted by the system. Why couldn't you say "as well", which is what I would say?'

Hoyland stressed that despite his complaints, he regarded Lennon as an important influence on his own thinking: 'The feeling I've got from songs like "Strawberry Fields Forever" and "A Day in the Life" is part of what has made me into the kind of socialist I am. But then you suddenly went and kicked all that in the face with "Revolution". That was why I wrote to you – to answer an attack you made on us. Now you say you're not against us after all. Well, that's nice, because I'm certainly not against you. I just wish you were a bit more on our side. (We could do with a few good songs.)' By the time this response was published, Lennon was awash in fresh troubles: the Beatles were attempting to create a new album under the unrelenting eye of a film crew, while the group's finances were on the verge of collapse. So the correspondence ended there, leaving Lennon to question how he could use his privileged position as a medium for positive protest.

The same dilemma troubled American soul artist Nina Simone. 'I was a woman on fire,' she reflected later, 'as I watched my people struggling for their rightful place in America.' Enraged by the murders of Martin Luther King and Bobby Hutton, plus many more black Americans whose names did not reach the headlines, she had found it difficult to equate her emotions with her musical persona. Her releases were increasingly dominated by contemporary material from white songwriters. In the summer of 1968, she recorded a song from the so-called 'tribal rock musical', *Hair* – a theatrical piece that cannibalised the rhetoric of hippies and radical youth in the interests of mildly scandalising the Broadway audience. As one underground press reviewer put it, 'The generation being canonised in *Hair* is the very generation which finds the work false and hypocritical.' The *Hair* score, with its orchestrated frenzy and psychedelic pastiches, never sounded more sincere than when Simone tackled 'Ain't Got No – I Got Life', translating the song into a declaration of racial pride. But neither that performance, nor borrowing vintage Bob Dylan protest songs such as 'The Times They Are A-Changin'', conveyed the full ambiguity of Simone's attitude towards America and the entertainment business.

Like the *Black Dwarf* collective, Nina Simone listened with interest to John Lennon's account of 'Revolution'. Reviewers of Simone's live shows were soon noting that she had incorporated the song into her repertoire.

That was not strictly accurate: Simone had actually written her own response to Lennon's song, loosely reworking the chord structure into a driving R&B tune. Her 'Revolution' climaxed in a cacophony that mirrored Lennon's attempts, on the Beatles' 'Revolution 9', to paint a sonic picture of a society in turmoil. Lyrically, the song commented on Lennon's argument, using the same verbal tags – evolution, destruction – to subtly different ends. Simone's 'destruction' was aimed at 'all the evil that will have to end'; where Lennon advised his listeners to 'free your mind instead', Simone instructed them: 'you know you got to clean your brain'. Her most acerbic couplet harked back to the anger of her classic civil rights protest song, 'Mississippi Goddamn': 'The only way that we can stand in fact/is when you get your foot off my back'. Clumsy but defiant, these lines were typical of an ambiguous performance that neither debunked Lennon's message nor defended it. When Simone was quizzed about the song, she shied away from subversion: 'Revolution means what is going on all over the world. If you listen to the lyric, you will see that although it does include the racial problem, it does also include all the revolts and rebellions going on all over the world – black against white, poor against rich, young against old, new breed against the establishment.'

Simone was talking to a white British journalist. Addressing her black comrades, she was more prepared to align herself with the militant forces of African-American opposition: 'The Black Panthers made these kids realise that there are black heroes who will fight and die if necessary to get what they want. That's what I find wonderful – they scare the hell out of white folks too, and we certainly need that.' For general public consumption, however, she preferred a less confrontational message. Towards the end of 1968, she asked her friend Weldon Irvine to write her a set of lyrics around a phrase coined by her late friend, playwright Lorraine Hansberry: 'Young, gifted and black'. Simone set his idealistic verses to music, and the result was an anthem of African-American pride that ignored political realities. 'We must begin to tell our young, there's a world waiting for you,' Irvine wrote, promising that the future would be 'a lovely precious dream'. Although the song became a Top 10 hit on the US R&B chart, Simone complained in later years that 'Black America promptly refused it'. She took this 'rejection' as a cue to abandon the struggle for liberation at home, and migrated to Africa.

Migration was a luxury unavailable to most black Americans. Eldridge

Cleaver may have claimed, in a writ of habeas corpus, that he had been 'consistently persecuted, hounded and harassed by the Department of Correction and the Adult Authority of California because he is black, and an active, vocal and militant defender of the oppressed black people of the nation'. But the oppression directed against the Black Panther Party – much of it covert, under the direction of the FBI's COINTELPRO programme – merely hardened their resistance against the American government.

## ESCAPING JUSTICE

The focal point of the black power struggle in the summer of 1968 was the trial of Huey Newton on a charge of murder. It stretched across two months, through the tumult of Chicago and beyond, winning the Panthers global publicity. The legal confrontation between The People Of The State Of California and Huey P. Newton began with a striking piece of street theatre, as 450 Panther members appeared outside the Alameda County Courthouse in full BPP uniform, chanting 'Off the Pigs' as a disdainful rejection of the justice system. 'The whole power structure wanted to hang Huey,' observed his Panther colleague Bobby Seale. 'They would do anything to get a conviction and send Huey to the gas chamber.'

The policeman who survived the encounter with Newton in October 1967 testified that the Panthers' leader had produced a gun whilst under arrest, and killed Officer John Frey. A bus driver claimed that he had seen Newton shooting the policemen; another witness said that Newton had told him, 'I just shot two dudes. I'd have kept shooting if my gun hadn't jammed.' Newton, meanwhile, insisted upon his innocence, but could offer no explanation for the shooting of the officers except that they might have fired upon each other.

As the trial progressed, some Panther members began to fear that only a violent assault on the white power structure could halt the 'racist' trial. While the Yippies plotted the dawn of the revolution in Chicago, the maverick Panthers planned to focus their energies on the West Coast. 'Some of the leadership wanted a private plane assault on all the prisons of California,' Eldridge Cleaver recalled later, 'with our people landing inside the walls and freeing everyone inside. Thousands of Panther-oriented prisoners would be released, and our grand strategy for guerrilla warfare against Washington could commence.' Yet this was clearly no more than fantasy. Meanwhile the party was unable to maintain its shaky alliance with SNCC, which had decided to follow the electoral path towards reform rather than the Panthers' more militant approach. It was the same tactical division that had already fractured the left coalition in France. Now the Panthers were isolated from their most obvious allies, just at the moment when they had attracted a global audience of sympathisers.

After several weeks of sporadic gun battles in California between Panthers and police, the Newton jury returned their verdict on 8 September 1968. They found him guilty of voluntary manslaughter, but not murder or assault with a deadly weapon. He was sentenced to the wonderfully vague term of two-to-fifteen years on 27 September – a far cry from the death sentence that had seemed his most likely fate. Righteously convinced of his innocence, however, Newton still regarded the verdict as a racist outrage. 'His own paranoia was functioning at fever pitch,' Cleaver observed. 'He kept telling people . . . that he wanted a "red light finale", the ultimate fulfilment for a revolutionary's death wish.' Newton envisaged the Panthers breaching the fortress of San Quentin in a massive frontal assault, and carrying him to freedom. 'I finally got to Huey and told him to forget that motion picture scenario,' Cleaver said. 'There was no way that a mass assault would work. He would be shot instantly inside, and a lot of dead Panthers would be stretched out on the parkways of California.'

Within weeks of Newton's verdict, Cleaver himself was the focus of Hollywood-style escape strategies. He was still awaiting trial for his role in the shoot-out in which Bobby Hutton had been killed. With his parole due to expire on 26 November, Cleaver feared that any prison term 'would be the equivalent to the death sentence'. He had hardly smoothed his path to justice since Newton's trial. The Governor of California, Ronald Reagan, had opposed the University of California's decision to allow Cleaver to lecture to students. In retaliation, Cleaver ended his first speech on the Berkeley campus by encouraging 5,000 students to chant, 'Fuck Ronald Reagan'. He then skipped a routine court appearance in San Francisco, claiming a prior speaking engagement at Harvard. By mid-November, it was apparent to the Panther hierarchy that he was not going to allow himself to fall into the hands of the legal system.

'I was surrounded with escape plans,' he explained. 'One group had me riding into the Rockies on horseback and then escaping to Canada. A couple of white sympathisers offered to hijack a jet (with hand grenades) and whisk me off to the islands. That was vetoed by everybody. Somebody else had a private launch to make the dash to Cuba.' Cleaver's own preferred option was altogether more apocalyptic: 'My plan was to take over Merritt College in Oakland and turn it into a fortress. It was an old two-storey, concrete building, complete with towers and a commanding view of the surrounding terrain. I wanted to hole up there with some fellow Panthers and tell the white power-police pig structure to come and get me.' Now it was Huey Newton who sent instructions that this plan was insane, and that Cleaver should make every effort to be smuggled out of the country.

The denouement was worthy of a Richard Pryor comedy. Two days before Cleaver was scheduled to turn himself in, the Panthers arranged a demonstration of support outside his San Francisco home. The police watched as Cleaver spoke to the crowd. Then he ducked inside for a moment, and a near lookalike, Ralph Smith, took his place on the front step. While Smith launched into a tirade of Eldridgean eloquence, the genuine Cleaver slipped out the back door, over a fence and into a waiting car, which raced him to San Francisco airport. En route, members of the San Francisco Mime Troupe disguised Cleaver as an old man. Clutching fake ID, he boarded a plane for New York, where he caught a connecting flight to Montreal, and then a freighter bound for Cuba. 'I had won,' he recalled. 'Here I was out of the clutches of the California courts, my wallet stuffed with $15,000 cash – a royalty check had just come from *Soul On Ice* – and I soon would be in sunny Cuba, setting up the big training camp while preparing to deal with Nixon's American Dream.' Cleaver reached Havana on Christmas Day 1968, by which time writers and public figures ranging from Bertrand Russell to Huey Newton, and Jean-Paul Sartre to Stokely Carmichael, had formed an International Committee to defend him. Ironically, by May 1969 Cleaver would be forced to leave the socialist paradise of Cuba, accused of raping a young American woman in his entourage.

Back in California, meanwhile, Bobby Seale was attempting to lead the Panthers towards a more socially responsible role in the black colony. After Christmas, he promised, they would inaugurate a Free Breakfast Program in Oakland, which would guarantee all local black children a healthy meal before they set off for school. The Panthers also planned to set up free health clinics in the ghetto, concentrating on the menace of sickle-cell anaemia. Both schemes would begin locally, and then spread out slowly across the nation. Ahead lay equally ambitious sketches for a series of 'black liberation schools'. It was both an exhibition of the Panthers' increasingly prominent place in African-American life; and an admission that the revolution might be farther away than the party's leaders liked to imagine.

## FLESHY SLICES OF FEMINISM

The inherent sexism of Cleaver's attitude to women was far from isolated in the revolutionary left. One of the Panthers' leading British supporters, Obi Egbuna, echoed his macho rhetoric: 'When a Black man is in bed with a white woman, he is not looking for pleasure. He is seeking revenge. As a symbol of European motherhood, she deserves to be raped. That is why the Black man in bed with a white woman behaves like a destroyer. Consciously or unconsciously, he is out to blast the hell out of what he considers two fleshy slices of ever greedy colonialism.' The possibility that these 'fleshy slices' of humanity might have rights of their own had never crossed his mind.

*Black Dwarf*, home to John Lennon's public debate about revolution, was little more in tune with the ethos of women's liberation, despite dedicating an issue to the cause early in 1969. 'DWARF DESIGNER SEEKS GIRL', ran a typical personal ad: 'Head girl typer to make tea, organise paper, me. Free food, smoke, space. Suit American negress.' The unconscious layers of sexual and racial discrimination betrayed by this advertisement did little to suggest that the far left was anything other than a boys' playground.

Sheila Rowbotham pioneered *Black Dwarf*'s coverage of feminism, though she recalled 'one left man coming up to me and with a pitying air saying he supposed it had helped me to express my personal problems, but it was nothing to do with socialism'. *Black Dwarf*'s editors briefly toyed with the idea of printing photographs of nude women to boost the circulation, but unlike most of their peers they decided against it – not on feminist grounds, but because sexual attraction had nothing to do with socialism.

Women's liberation was more organised and forceful in the USA. A series of events in the final months of 1968 and beyond established feminism as a potentially revolutionary force, with the power to attract media attention. The movement chose the Miss America beauty pageant in September 1968 as the focus of its first stunning demonstration. Around 100 activists gathered in Atlantic City, diverting NBC-TV's coverage by unfurling a banner proclaiming 'WOMEN'S LIBERATION' in front of the stage. Outside the hall, members of the New York Radical Women crowned their own Miss America in the form of a sheep, enacted feminist skits, revamped popular songs ('ain't she sweet, making profit off her meat'), and gathered symbols of female oppression into a 'Freedom Trash Can'. Among the offending objects were cosmetics, mainstream women's magazines, and brassieres. One press report suggested erroneously that the Trash Can had been set on fire, and so the myth of feminists burning their bras was born.

Like the anti-war left, the women's movement was made up of dozens of different groups, few of whose activities were co-ordinated. From New York came the Women's International Conspiracy From Hell, otherwise known – in a dual reference to the McCarthy era and the Salem trials of 1692 – as WITCH. This grouping set itself up as a continuation of the Yippie tradition of political theatre, consciously echoing the antics of Hoffman and Rubin in a series of 'zap actions'. They celebrated Hallowe'en by putting a hex on the stockbrokers in Wall Street (an event called Up Against The Wall Street); and mimicked the Yippies again by attempting to levitate the Pentagon, with no more success than their male predecessors. They broke new ground by invading a bridal fair at Madison Square Garden, chanting 'Here come the slaves, off to their graves', to the tune of 'Here Comes The Bride'. 'WITCH is an all-woman Everything,' their manifesto declared. 'WITCH lives and laughs in every woman . . . If you are a woman and you dare to look inside yourself, you are a witch. . . you are a witch by being female, untamed, angry, joyous and immortal.'

Few women in 1968's rock culture could claim more than two of those adjectives. Cultural stereotypes might have been shattered by the free-love philosophy of the summer of love, but even in the counter-culture, women were still judged as objects of sexual or romantic obsession, or else menial slaves. Outside the folk-/singer-songwriter tradition, which allowed females to act out the roles of poetic visionary (Joni Mitchell, Laura Nyro) or preacher (Joan Baez, Janis Ian), there was little room for a woman to develop a distinctive creative personality.

There were exceptions, each offering a lesson in the limitations of women's liberation in a world shaped by men. Soul queen Aretha Franklin had been raised as the prodigy of her father, a Baptist preacher; struggled through a teen pregnancy and an early divorce; and then been constrained as a standards singer. Only in 1967, when she signed to Atlantic Records, was she able to produce music that reflected her gospel roots, her earthy sensuality, and her affinity with the blues tradition. Atlantic unleashed not only her voice, and her uncannily soulful piano-playing, but also her unheralded talents as a composer. Unrestrained in her music, her songs exhibited a sense of pride that was both sexual and racial, culminating in the release in 1968 of a stunning reworking of Otis Redding's hit, 'Respect'. Her own composition, 'Think', with its incessant call for 'freedom', doubled as a demand for equality and a wake-up call to her man. In reality, however, Franklin was suffering abuse from her husband, battling depression, and experiencing little of the exhilaration that her music aroused in her listeners.

The public image of Janis Joplin, the sandpaper-voiced frontwoman of San Francisco band Big Brother & the Holding Company, was equally ambiguous. She was presented as the living embodiment of that media cliché, the 'rock chick' – glugging down Southern Comfort, rasping through a haze of cigarette smoke, her rapacious sexual appetite satisfied by a succession of young studs. It was a role she rarely rejected, although she confided to friends that she felt trapped by the responsibility of matching the world's fantasies. By late 1968, she was caught in a cycle of alcoholism and drug abuse, proving herself anything but 'joyous and immortal'. With no female, let alone feminist, support structure, Joplin was left to hang in the breeze of male approval, contorting herself in search of a stance that would satisfy her audience.

The only prominent woman who was able to demonstrate independent thought and action in the rock world of 1968 was Grace Slick. As co-lead vocalist with Jefferson Airplane, Slick benefited from a high media profile, without ever being regarded as the leader of the group. The Airplane's grasp of politics was often naive, but they operated as a genuine collective without sexual discrimination – despite, or perhaps because of, Slick's serial relationships with her colleagues. Slick was a late convert to feminism, and hardly an uncritical one, but every move she made in public demonstrated exactly the liberation that the feminists desired. She wrote her own material, with and without her fellow musicians, sharing vocals and songwriting duties without any sign of creative jealousy. Her stage presence was cool, even lofty, betraying her privileged upbringing, but hinting at a dark sensuality beneath. Never overly anxious in public, she seemed to occupy a space where the sexual revolution had already occurred and was now taken for granted.

Her songwriting was equally confident, whether she was examining mind expansion in 'White Rabbit' or the ironies of hippies ageing in 'Lather', about fellow band member Spencer Dryden reaching 30. The latter was one of the songs she performed on TV's *Smothers Brothers Comedy Show*, a blend of humour (much of it satirical) and music hosted by radical sympathisers Tommy and Dick Smothers.[9] For this October 1968 appearance, Slick raided the make-up trolley, covering her face and upper torso in black cosmetics. Though her appearance has passed into rock myth as 'blackface', it actually resembled a street urchin who had recently rolled through mud. According to Airplane manager Bill Thompson, Slick was offering a 'gesture of solidarity' with the black American athletes who had offered black power salutes during a medal ceremony at the recent Olympic Games. Backstage, Tommy Smothers asked Slick about the significance of her disguise, and the singer replied, 'I don't know.' Years later, Slick explained: 'It wasn't political. Women wear make-up, and it's very standardised. I thought, well, why not wear black?' The myth also insists that she ended the performance of 'Crown of Creation' with her own black power salute. But it was hidden beneath the flamboyant sleeves of her dazzlingly white dress.

## THE THEATRE OF REBELLION

'I think we're more conservative than most of the San Francisco groups,' admitted Spencer Dryden at the end of a post-Chicago political debate with the other Airplane musicians. The band had missed the Democratic Convention and were divided about the effectiveness of the Yippies' tactics. 'Even now, the people whose heads got busted still have busted heads,' reasoned Dryden. 'Who wants to be a martyr, man?' Slick retorted that 'there's no revolution that has been fought through, without there having been masses of bodies obstructing things.' Dryden argued the case for patience: 'When the older generation dies out, and the younger generation grows up, things will change.' 'But the older generation is hip to that,' Slick replied. 'They've got indoctrination programs for the young – but not me, as long as I'm free to do what I want.' After a while, Dryden completely reversed his position, and opted for the apocalypse: 'You're not going to have a peaceful revolution, man, it doesn't work. You get together, and you start with the police department and shoot them all.'

It was radical chic at its finest, confrontational and yet empty at the same moment. Nobody, least of all Spencer Dryden, imagined that he might man a machine-gun and mow down the city's finest. 'That, you see, is where it's at for the Airplane,' complained underground critic Ed Leimbacker. 'Theatricality. Harmless words and grand gestures rather than truly radical action.' *Ramparts* magazine reporter Michael Lydon noticed that the band's shared mansion on Fulton Street in San Francisco boasted: 'Eldridge Cleaver Welcome Here'. Were they serious? Would they risk arrest to harbour the fugitive Panther leader? 'I don't know, man,' Paul Kantner replied. 'I'd have to wait until that happened.' Lydon concluded: 'Cleaver would be well advised not to choose the Airplane's mansion for his refuge. For Kantner's mushy politics – sort of a turned-on liberalism that thinks the Panthers are "groovy" but doesn't like to come to terms with the nasty American reality – are the politics of the much touted "rock revolution".'

Film director Jean-Luc Godard was certainly convinced by the band's radicalism, however. In broken English, he declared that 'The Jefferson Airplane is the only rock group in the world that is me'. The final weeks of 1968 found Godard shooting his first film in the United States, a study of revolution in the making, under the working title of *1AM* (*One American Movie*). He hired the *cinéma-vérité* documentary crew headed by D.A. Pennebaker, best known for his portrait of Bob Dylan in *Dont Look Back* (*sic*), to assist him. While Godard waved frantic directions from across the street, Pennebaker filmed the Airplane that November, as they performed atop the lofty Schuyler Hotel on 45th Street in midtown New York. Their short set ended with singer Marty Balin being led away, smirking, by police.[10] The scene was intended as the finale of Godard's film, which also included an interview with Eldridge Cleaver. But the Frenchman soon abandoned the footage, leaving Pennebaker to assemble his own *1PM* (*One Parallel Movie*) from the rushes.

Godard recalled that Cleaver had told him: 'The Yippie people like toy guns. We black power people like real guns.' The film-maker clearly hoped to align himself with the 'real' revolutionaries. But the fate of his earlier foray into radical rock culture, with the Rolling Stones, signified the difficulties of creating art that was revolutionary in both spirit and form. Having documented the creation of a Stones record, Godard shot a series of provocative and self-consciously radical scenes across London. A character playing the part of black power leader Frankie Dymon recited extracts from Cleaver's *Soul On Ice*, while three white women in long white gowns were led blindfolded across a car breaker's yard in South London. They were machine-gunned to death while Cleaver's boast was heard on the soundtrack: 'We are going to get our freedom or no one, but no one, is going to get any peace on this earth.' Elsewhere, actors read from Hitler's autobiography, *Mein Kampf*, in a porn bookstore; and an actress playing the symbolic role of Eve Democracy uttered suitably enigmatic statements about art and society. Tantalising extracts from the Stones' recording session were edited between these disparate elements, as the band edged towards the perfect performance.

Godard intended the film, which he'd titled *One Plus One*, to be premiered at the London Film Festival on 29 November 1968. He hadn't bargained for the intervention of his producer, Iain Quarrier. Godard intended *One Plus One* to end with the Stones' record incomplete; the audience should solve the equation in the title, and rely on its own awareness of how the finished track sounded. Quarrier was anxious to recoup his investment, and so he prepared his own edit, under the more commercial title of *Sympathy for the Devil*. This version of the film ended with a complete performance of the title song. And it was this edit that was delivered for the premiere.

When Godard discovered what had happened, he said he would be boycotting the screening. He demanded that the audience should do the same, and send their ticket money directly to the Eldridge Cleaver defence fund. Then he announced that he would be showing his own cut of the film outside the cinema. A vote was taken among the Festival audience, and the majority chose to stay. 'You're fascists!' Godard exclaimed as he headed for the exit, taking a swing at his producer as he did so. 'I was very disappointed in the Rolling Stones,' he admitted later. 'It was very unfair for them to accept their being emphasised over all the others in the film . . . unfair to the black people.' Mick Jagger claimed never to have seen the film, and added: 'I don't think Godard understands anything about black people . . . He's such a fucking twat.'

It had become a familiar theme during the year: rock musicians failing to match the radical expectations of their admirers. A similar gulf of understanding separated Frank Zappa, leader of the anarchic rock satirists the Mothers of Invention, from his audience. Zappa had filled his early albums with sarcastic jibes at 'the insincere assholes who run almost everybody's country'. For every thrust at the authorities, however, Zappa aimed another straight at his listeners. Such subtleties were lost on the student activists who visited Zappa before an October 1968 performance at the Sports Palast in West Berlin. As Zappa recalled, 'They said, "There will be 8,000 people here tonight, and they have never demonstrated before. We want you to tell them to come with us."' The students intended Zappa to signal a youth assault on NATO's headquarters in the city. 'They wanted me to tell the audience to go with them to start a fire,' he continued. 'I told the guy, "You have bad mental health". And he didn't like it.'

The evening show turned into a struggle for power. In Zappa's account, 200 'student rebels' attended the performance: 'they had jars of paint, cherry bombs, banners, they made a mess out of the fucking show'. During the interval, the students cut some of the wires powering the band's equipment, leaving roadies to patch together some replacements. 'Toward the end of the show,' Zappa said, 'they figured this is their last chance to get the audience to go with them, so the student leader leaps onto the stage and grabs the microphone and starts babbling away in German. I gave Don Preston instructions to put our electric organ through a fuzztone and put both arms on the keyboard. That's an ugly fucking sound. And meanwhile our road crew was carrying instruments off the stage one at a time. I made my guitar feedback . . . and at the end we both unplugged our stuff and walked off, and just left him there babbling.'

Before he left the microphone, Zappa scolded the intruder: 'We came here as musicians, not to hear your drunken slogans.' It was the theme of the year, as rock's most prominent figures struggled to come to terms with their social responsibilities. That was the dilemma facing John Lennon a week before Christmas 1968, as he and Yoko Ono appeared at the 'Alchemical Wedding' in London's Royal Albert Hall. The event was designed to revive the magical spirit of 1967, but simply illustrated how irrelevant that spirit had become. Beat novelist Ken Kesey, members of the California Hell's Angels and the London Krishna Consciousness Society participated in the event, which had no focus, and for most of its duration, no real activity. Hence the excitement caused when a female member of the audience took off her clothes, a spectacle quickly halted by the Metropolitan Police.

The Lennons chose to debut their concept of 'bagism' – clothing themselves in a white bag to enable 'total communication' with their audience, without prejudice. On this occasion, though, they had nothing to communicate. They disappeared from view beneath white sacking and, as underground journalist David Mairowitz reported, 'Nothing happened'. Later the couple reappeared on stage, and the house lights went up: 'Again, WE were the event,' Mairowitz concluded.

The audience's attention was seized from the Lennons by a solitary protestor – 'a spectre of fury and wrath', according to Mairowitz, 'the bloated conscience of England'. He walked towards the stage, bearing a placard on which was written: 'The End of the World is at Hand for 7,000,000 People in Biafra'. Like an Old Testament prophet, he proclaimed his message of doom, shouting out: 'Do you care, John Lennon? Do you care?' But Lennon had already slipped into the wings, apparently unwilling to risk a public confrontation. 'Was this the end to an evening of Silence?' wrote Mairowitz. 'No one knew. No one had an idea. There were no ideas.'

## TRAILING CARNAGE

Against its will, Britain was being forced to confront the horrors of Biafra, the oil-rich eastern province of Nigeria, which had declared its independence in 1967, and precipitated a corrosive civil war. While America was lambasted by the left for intervening in Vietnam, so Britain was accused of genocide for refusing to intervenc in Biafra. After Nigeria gained independence and shed its colonial status in 1960, a frail coalition of interests held together a nation that had been artificially created by Britain from the homelands of a plethora of rival tribes. In 1966, the federal government was overthrown by two military coups, unleashing tribal unrest that resulted in the killing of tens of thousands of Igbos resident in the north of Nigeria. Approximately one million survivors left their homes to return to the apparent safety of their native eastern province. In May 1967, Colonel Ojukwu, the region's governor, formally seceded from the republic, establishing the independent state of Biafra with, he boasted, 'the biggest army in Africa'. Oil supplies to Britain and Europe were immediately affected; so in July 1967, the federal government's army 'invaded' the rebel territory of Biafra.

The new country was immediately recognised by many other African states – including the racist governments of South Africa and Rhodesia. As historian Guy Arnold has noted, 'it was in the interests of the white regimes in Southern Africa to prolong the war in Nigeria since chaos and breakdown in Africa's largest, most promising black state boosted their claims to maintain white minority control'. Tacit support for Biafra came from France, Spain and Portugal, again for reasons of self-interest. Many non-Igbo Nigerians sympathised with the plight of the oppressed tribe – until Biafra launched its own invasion of Nigeria in August. The Biafran troops were swiftly beaten back, and by the end of the year, the nation was effectively under siege.

Initially, Biafra hoped to survive indefinitely thanks to its rich stocks of food, and potential oil revenue. This judgement proved to be recklessly optimistic.

While Nigerian forces tightened their grip around the margins of Biafra, its people began to starve to death, in full view of the world. Millions now became refugees; hundreds of thousands died of hunger. British Prime Minister Harold Wilson tried in vain to broker a peace deal, but there was little that Wilson's government, let alone John Lennon, could have done in December 1968 to relieve the crisis or end the fighting.

Yet the question raised by the protestor at the Royal Albert Hall still hung in the air. Did John Lennon – or any of his superstar contemporaries – care? And if they did, what power could they wield, to alleviate hunger or overthrow a capitalist regime? Was their star status meaningless, or did it carry both the potential and the responsibility to alter society for the better? It was a debate dominated, through 1968, by apathy, caution and self-interest. As George Melly noted the following year, 'This was surely the moment when you might have expected pop to provide the anthems, the marches, the songs for the barricades. In fact it did nothing of the sort.' Melly might have noted that on 27 October 1968, there had been a second mass demonstration against the US policy in Vietnam, again organised by Tariq Ali's Vietnam Solidarity Committee. Several thousand marchers broke away from the planned route to mount an assault on the American Embassy in Grosvenor Square, resulting in a pitched battle with police. Many of the marchers were answering the call of a poster campaign issued to coincide with the Vietnam march. This called for participants to 'follow the lead of the revolutionary workers and students of France: SMASH CAPITALISM'. Lennon, Jagger and their fellow rock radicals were nowhere to be seen. The season for street fighting men was clearly over. Melly concluded that: 'Pop [music] acts out revolt, rather than provokes it. It's almost a substitute for revolution in the social sense, and is anyway geared, even these days, to the capitalist system. At all events the political upheaval of 1968 proved that pop music, in the revolutionary sense, was a non-starter, a fake revolt.'

But were the other revolutionary movements of 1968 any more successful? Did the impotence of rock's leading performers undercut the efforts of the Yippies, the Black Panthers and their ilk, or simply mirror their own lack of progress? What had the push towards international revolutionary consciousness achieved? In France, President Charles de Gaulle had banished memories of the May uprising by winning a crushing majority in a referendum. In Vietnam, the war dragged on, trailing carnage in its wake. In Czechoslovakia, the glimmer of freedom inspired by the Prague

Spring had been extinguished by the resumption of totalitarian control. And in America, the pro-war Republican candidate, Richard Nixon, narrowly defeated the pro-war Democrat, Hubert Humphrey, in the race for president. Far from triggering a revolution, the August events in Chicago had simply guaranteed the defeat of the marginally more liberal candidate. The white supremacist Governor of Georgia, George Wallace, polled more than ten million votes, or 14% of the turn-out; left-wing candidates, such as Eldridge Cleaver, attracted the support of no more than 200,000 of the 200 million US population.

On election day in November 1968, former Country Joe & the Fish bassist Bruce Barthol was at JFK Airport in New York, awaiting a flight for London with the intention of evading his draft call-up. 'It seemed like the end of everything,' he recalls. 'Richard Nixon was the one man who my parents had raised me to hate.' A few days later, Barthol found himself on the Left Bank in Paris, where militant students were still demonstrating at the Sorbonne. 'I wanted a cheese omelette,' he recalls, 'but I didn't know how to order it, so I was walking around looking for someone who might be able to help me. I ran into this French guy who'd been in Berkeley, and we hooked up. I went to get my passport from my room, and when I came back, there were five French *flics* surrounding my new friend. They were shouting at him, saying he was a disgrace to France because he looked like a hippie, and they were kicking at his ankles. I'd flown 3,000 miles to get away from that kind of harassment, but Paris was just as hostile as Chicago.'

Repression of dissidents in the West paled alongside the treatment of protestors elsewhere in the world – in the Soviet Bloc, where they were routinely imprisoned or exiled; in China, where they would be executed or sentenced to a lifetime of hard labour; or in Brazil, where the fragile stalemate between the military dictatorship and student dissidents had collapsed. In October 1968, 800 students were arrested at their union congress, a clear sign that the ruling generals were no longer prepared to accept outright signs of opposition. Yet the playful musicians of the tropicalismo crowd – Caetano Veloso, Gilberto Gil, Os Mutantes – continued to poke fun at the symbols of Brazilian tradition, from the church to the samba, as if they were living in a different world.

Early in December 1968, the tropicalistas launched a television music series, entitled *Divine, Marvellous*. As they frolicked before the cameras, parodying the rituals of Catholicism, they seemed unaware of the precarious situation outside. 'What we were doing was certainly giving offence to some people,' Veloso remembered, 'but we, proud and confident, remained unintimidated.' That changed on 13 December, when troops and police collaborated to impose a new orthodoxy on the Brazilian people. Peacetime legislation was abandoned, and the army was given the power to round up anyone it regarded as a potential dissident. Hundreds of new prisons were established, and just as soon filled with students, university professors, union leaders, journalists, anyone who might speak out against the military. Torture became institutionalised, less to obtain information than to impose a climate of fear.

Still the tropicalistas played on. The last of their weekly shows was broadcast at Christmas. Two days later, Veloso and Gil were seized by troops, and transported to a prison camp. 'Neither Gil nor I had imagined we would be arrested,' Veloso recalled. It took imprisonment to make him realise that he had more to fear than criticism from musical traditionalists.

The largest country in South America was now ruled by terror. The same spirit was loose in Mexico, a loyal ally of the USA in the global struggle for ideological and military supremacy. It was there that the polarisation between youth and age, and militancy and conformity, was played out in a brutal piece of street theatre.

Like the May demonstrations in Paris, the disturbances that rocked Mexico in the late summer of 1968 mutated from minor student unrest into the threat of revolution. The main students' organisation focused its protests on educational reform, as in France. Yet disquiet at the conservatism of the state school system chimed with wider discontent about Mexico's repressive moral and social structure. They were now calling for the release of political prisoners, the scrapping of the elite riot police, the censuring of Mexico City's senior police officers, and an amnesty for anyone arrested during earlier disturbances. With the Olympic Games in Mexico City set to command global attention in October, the authorities were intent on dampening down the unrest as ruthlessly as possible. The youth magazine *POP*, which had documented the shy growth of the Mexican counter-culture, supported the government. 'The days of being a "rebel" are past,' it warned its readership in late September. 'Now you're a MAN . . . And men are responsible for their acts . . . Don't listen to demagogic agitators because YOU ARE NOT SHEEP, BUT MEN. Don't take to the streets and commit crimes against your country; that will be left to the half-wit "rebels".' It was the authentic voice of compromise, as heard around the world in 1968. Once again, it was ignored.

On 2 October 1968, thousands of students marched through Mexico City to protest against the army's occupation of the city's largest student campus. The daytime protest passed without serious incident, and in the evening, more than 5,000 students and activists gathered in the Tlatelolco area, in the Plaza de las Tres Culturas, to hear more speeches. Hundreds of riot police and soldiers sealed off the square, trapping the protestors. Then gunfire rang out, and the army and police began to shoot indiscriminately into the crowd. There was a brief lull, filled with panic as students tried to help those who had been injured; and then the shooting resumed. By the time that medical staff were allowed into the square, the area was littered with bodies.

The government claimed that snipers had opened fire on the soldiers from buildings overlooking the square, and that the army and police had responded in self-defence. The official account estimated that around 25 people had been killed. Protestors alleged that they had been slaughtered like animals in an abattoir, and that the death toll ran into hundreds, or maybe even thousands. The actual number is still unknown, though most researchers guess that between 250 and 350 died. The massacre was reported elsewhere in the world, but not in Mexico, and the Olympics began on schedule later that week. 'I was at the International Youth Camp at Oaxtepec,' recalls Louise Cripps, a student helper at the Games. 'I discovered what had happened from a Mexican friend, who had known some of the kids who had attended the demonstration and not come back. But most people hadn't heard about it.' The repression in Brazil passed equally unnoticed. 'We knew almost nothing about it in Britain,' remembers Barry Miles. 'It's pathetic, and amazing, that something so awful could be happening and yet we didn't know. It just illustrates the way in which different struggles were cut off from each other.'

And so went 1968, the year of carnival and carnage, of false hopes and punctured dreams. Poised between suicidal courage and apathy, the counter-culture waited to see which way the balance would tip. Around the globe, isolated pockets of radicals dreamed of a revolutionary wave that would surge unstoppably from continent to continent, fuelled by the combined energy of students, workers, oppressed minorities, empowered women, and rock icons, whose music would signal the battle cry. It was a dream in which

Che Guevara and Mick Jagger would stand hand in hand, rebel leader and rocker, twin symbols of a future that could not be restrained. On students' walls, from San Francisco to Prague, their two portraits promised a revolution that was surely on the horizon. It scarcely seemed to matter that Guevara was dead, and Jagger was already edging away from his brief moment of political allegiance. The time was right for street fighting men – and maybe even women – to stand and be counted.

# CHAPTER 4: 1969

We're just not strong enough leaders. You need someone who's gonna make people jump. You just need a Hitler figure, internationally, for kids.

(Roger Daltrey, July 1969)

Fuck off! Fuck off my stage!
(Pete Townshend to Abbie Hoffman, Woodstock, August 1969)

During the Who's set at the Woodstock festival, Abbie Hoffman tried to commandeer the microphone to deliver a political speech. Guitarist Pete Townshend threw him abruptly off the stage. It was a symbolic confrontation, in a year that saw activists preparing for an imminent revolution, musicians expected to obey political instructions, and the record industry discovering that radicalism could be a potent marketing tool. That momentary collision of counter-culture superstars – preserved as a context-free soundbite on the Who's 1995 CD box set – was, in retrospect, perhaps the most significant moment of this legendary rock festival. It suggested that the coalition between hippies, rock stars and revolutionaries was in danger of collapsing, as the battle lines were redrawn, and the stakes grew more perilous.

## CORPORATE REVOLUTION

Who owns the music? This question burned through the global rock community in the year between Chicago and Woodstock. In the wake of 'Revolution' and 'Street Fighting Man', dissidence seemed to have replaced the acid trip as the defining motif of the counter-culture. Yet both of these apparently subversive statements were the products of multi-national corporations, whose activities ranged from broadcasting to the manufacture of weapons.

Advertising agencies and entertainment conglomerates joined forces in October 1968 to stage a conference about Selling the American Youth Market. For their $300 admission fee, delegates learned how to capitalise on the bewilderingly rapid changes witnessed over the previous year. Two months later, Columbia Records launched a campaign that perfectly illustrated the conference's theme. Columbia had already borrowed the magic word 'revolutionaries' for a March 1968 rock compilation. Now they proposed to extend the conceit. All of the company's rock, or 'underground', releases during January–March 1969 were branded under the slogan: 'The Revolutionaries are on Columbia'. In April, the company issued a triumphant press release: 'Victory in sight for Columbia's "Revolutionaries"'. The advertising scheme had proved so successful that, 'by field demand', it was being extended into the spring. Record stores would now be serviced with Revolutionaries posters and display racks to consolidate the public's awareness of Columbia's leading status in the music industry.

The promotion was launched in early December 1968, when Columbia took full-page space in America's best-selling underground newspapers to plug a range of new records. Under the headline, 'But The Man Can't Bust Our Music', were pictured a motley crowd of long-haired demonstrators, a token African-American among them. They were shown in a holding cell, obviously fresh from a student demonstration. Scattered at their feet were their banners, conveying strangely vague, apolitical messages: 'Grab Hold', 'Music Is Love', 'Wake Up'. The copywriter provided the context: 'The Establishment's against adventure. And the arousing experience that comes with listening to today's music. So what? Let them slam doors. And keep it out of the concert halls.' A list of the musicians followed. 'They're ear stretching,' the copy continued. 'And sometimes transfixing. And The Man can't stop you from listening. Especially if you're armed with these.' Below were pictures of the records that The Man wanted to bust.

It was a remarkably crass piece of work, guaranteed to alienate a larger audience than it enticed. In retrospect, Columbia president Clive Davis agreed: 'The ad had really missed the mark. *Rolling Stone* [magazine] had a marvellous time ridiculing the company with it, talking about Columbia's "identity crisis", how we were trying to be hip, etc. They were right. I may have resented them singling us out for ridicule, but they were right.'

'The Man Can't Bust Our Music' has passed into marketing legend as an example of ill-conceived advertising. What's rarely noted is the music that it was attempting to sell. The records were not rock releases at all, but (with the exception of an album demonstrating the range of the newly invented Moog synthesiser) left-field classical recordings, stretching from contemporary music by Terry Riley back to the pioneering early 20th-century compositions of Charles Ives. It was difficult to know which was more far-fetched: the belief that these records might be 'busted' by 'The Man', or the expectation that they would find a sympathetic audience amongst the readers of *Rolling Stone*.

Meanwhile, a more sinister marketing campaign was at work. In September 1968, a CIA analyst employed to monitor the anti-war movement reported back to headquarters. He was becoming increasingly alarmed by the 'filth, slanderous and libellous statements' and 'almost treasonous anti-establishment propaganda' published in the underground press. He had a simple suggestion: 'Eight out of ten would fail if a few phonograph record companies stopped advertising in them.' The proposal found its way to the offices of the FBI. The Bureau's office in San Francisco informed J. Edgar Hoover in Washington that one record company in particular 'appears to be giving active aid and comfort to enemies of the United States', by supporting the anti-establishment press with advertising. The culprit? Columbia Records, of course. The San Francisco office asked that headquarters should do its best to persuade Columbia to abandon this policy.

According to investigative journalist Angus Mackenzie, 'One of the first publications to feel the effect of this strategy was the *Free Press*, an alternative paper in Washington, DC. Its February 1 [1969] issue was the last to carry Columbia record ads, a vital source of revenue. By the end of the year the paper was dead.' The pattern was repeated across the country. 'Deprived of most of its record ads,' Mackenzie reported, 'the *Berkeley Barb* survived on lewd sex ads. At the *Barb*, as elsewhere, editors and staff had no clear indication of why a major source of revenue had suddenly evaporated.'

If the independence of the underground press, and their heroes, was compromised by their mutual indebtedness to 'The Man', then live performance seemed a safer arena. The epitome of independent rock promoters in the late 1960s was Bill Graham, a Polish immigrant to the USA. His mid-decade connections with the San Francisco Mime Troupe – the people who disguised Eldridge Cleaver in 1968 – brought him into the world of

Californian acid-rock just as that genre was about to emerge into the mainstream. His tireless enthusiasm, affinity with his artists and confrontational persona enabled him to run an increasingly influential stable of venues, such as the Winterland ballroom in San Francisco, and the Fillmore auditoriums there and in New York.

At the Fillmore East, this champion of underground rock was confronted by a truly subversive organisation: a bunch of Lower East Side anarchists who abandoned their original name of Black Mask for the more aggressive title of Up Against The Wall Motherfuckers. In their original guise, they had championed a direct link between art and revolution; one of their associates was Valerie Solanas, the founder of SCUM (Society for Cutting Up Men), notorious for attempting to murder Andy Warhol in June 1968. 'DESTROY THE MUSEUMS' was the group's cry as they announced a demonstration against New York's Museum of Modern Art in October 1966. 'Goddamn your culture, your science, your art. What purpose do they serve? Your mass-murder cannot be concealed.'

By the summer of 1968, Black Mask had adopted their new identity, borrowed from a poem by Amiri Baraka. They opened a 'free store' on the Lower East Side, like a tougher, New York version of the Diggers; and distributed a free newspaper. They had already heralded Chicago's Festival of Life by claiming that 'in America, to truly live is revolutionary. Not the sold, packaged media-freaked "revolution" but our real, bloody, dope-crazed, sex-mad, desire to exist.' Aligning themselves with the Black Panther Party and the Yippies, the Motherfuckers warned that they were 'under constant threat of arrest and of being wiped out'. Alongside such long-forgotten groupings as the Boston Freemen, the Flower Cong and the Church of the New Reality (Southwest), they dubbed themselves the 'International Werewolf Conspiracy', boasting: 'The worst fear is the fear of the unknown – and we are the unknown.'

The Motherfuckers regarded themselves as the embodiment of the 'Hip Community' on the Lower East Side. 'What's real to us is music we can dance to,' they declared. 'We cannot allow the man to define us or our space.' The adoption of the so-called 'underground' by mainstream media and corporations aroused their frustration and anger. 'Everywhere we turn,' they complained, 'Bullshit Amerika has been defining what we do and who we are. We have allowed the media, the record companies, the psychedelic merchandisers and the suburban imitators to tell us what the "Hip Revolution" is all about – NO

MORE.' In retaliation, they promised to 'launch a total assault on every form of oppression that seeks to limit our existence and our possibilities'.

High on their hit list was Bill Graham. The promoter had regularly provided radical political groups with free access to the Fillmore East for benefits and rallies. The Black Panthers had experienced his generosity on several occasions, as had the radical newspaper *The Guardian*, and the Mobe's anti-war efforts. Graham also allowed Lower East Side community organisations to use the hall. According to the Motherfuckers, Graham made them the same promise, allotting them exclusive use of the Fillmore every Monday night; and then changed his mind. So the Motherfuckers set out to 'liberate' one of the underground's favourite venues from its owner. Graham claimed never to have promised the Motherfuckers anything. The collective's leader, Ben Morea, decided to speak on behalf of the entire Lower East Side: 'The Fillmore's interests are not our interests, and that's the conflict. They're a business. We're not a business – we're a people who feel we have a culture which we want access to, that's been taken from us, and that's being used to make money for other people.'

On 22 October 1968, the Fillmore East was staging a benefit for the Living Theater, with whom Morea had a longtime connection. The Theater offered the Motherfuckers time to state their case, but when they began to harangue the crowd in the name of community action, Bill Graham strode onto the stage to protest. 'Nobody wanted to liberate this place a year ago when it was a rat-infested dump,' he argued. 'You can go liberate the Opera House.'

The Motherfuckers responded with a broadside aimed at the Hip Community. 'Tonight the people return this theater to themselves,' announced a leaflet circulated through the Lower East Side. 'Once we asked, now we take.' The declaration ended with a righteous manifesto: 'FREE THE THEATER. FREE BILL GRAHAM. FREE EVERYTHING. ONE NIGHT A WEEK OR THE SKY'S THE LIMIT.' The final phrase echoed the threats issued by the Black Panthers if Huey Newton was imprisoned. The campaign achieved its initial aim: Graham agreed to donate the hall to the community every Wednesday night. Predictably, the Motherfuckers' events at the Fillmore became gatherings of the Lower East Side tribes, replete with dope-smoking and petty vandalism. Under pressure from local police and his insurers, Graham announced that he would be withdrawing the Motherfuckers' privileges with immediate effect.

The day after Christmas 1968, the Fillmore East staged a concert by new

Elektra recording artists the MC5. Most of the tickets had been given away by New York radio stations, but several hundred were held back – and reserved for the Motherfuckers, so they claimed. Instead, they ended up in Bill Graham's hands. Elektra executive Bill Harvey received an anonymous phone call, warning that the Fillmore would be burned to the ground if the tickets were not donated to the community. Once again, the activists had their way, but as the concert began with a set by David Peel, several hundred people were still struggling to gain admission. When Bill Graham considered that the hall's capacity had been reached, he barred the door – and was lashed with a motorcycle chain by another anonymous figure, apparently a member of a motorcycle gang called the Pagans, who had (so Graham alleged) been hired to 'liberate' the hall by the Motherfuckers. Shocked by the sight of blood on his face, the crowd outside the Fillmore moved back, and the MC5's performance continued as planned.

As the band left the stage, hundreds of people climbed out of the audience and began to trash their equipment. Things were no calmer outside: when the people who had been refused admission saw the MC5 stepping into a plush limousine, they reacted like starving men walking into a banquet. One of Graham's employees, Kip Cohen, recounted how the band were pulled out of their car. The protestors 'messed them up a bit, threw their records at them, came back in, and announced to the crowd that they had been betrayed by phonies'.

'They projected themselves as a "revolutionary" rock group,' complained Ben Morea. 'They knew that there was something going on that was much deeper than politics, that had to do with exactly what they talk about: cultural revolution. They knew they could play a certain role. Nobody asked *them* to seize the theater, but there was no question that they could have done *something*. In fact, they did the opposite. They stood up there and said, "We're here to play music and we don't give a damn about politics". Then they ran out, symbolically getting into a limousine going to a restaurant which *nobody* in our community has *ever* been in. The whole image of that was rather obnoxious.'

The dispute eventually settled into an uneasy stalemate; Graham continued to operate the Fillmore East until May 1971. The problem this time was not local peer pressure, but Graham's disillusionment with the ethos of the rock business: 'In 1965 when we began the original Fillmore Auditorium, I associated with and employed "musicians". Now, more often than not, it's with "officers and stockholders" in large corporations – only they happen to have long hair and play guitars. I acknowledge their success, but condemn what that success has done to some of them.' The Motherfuckers blamed Graham and the record companies for perverting the music that belonged to 'the people', and milking it for cash; Graham twisted that argument on its head, complaining that it was the musicians themselves who had sold out their principles. Either way, many of the musicians grew richer; while 'the people' tried to distinguish exactly which sections of the Hip Community meant them well or harm.

> Before I left in 1968, we were playing these big venues, and we'd automatically get standing ovations, no matter how well or badly we played. You end up in this terrible state of alienation from your audience, where you think that the people who like you are idiots, and the people who hate you are assholes.
>
> (Bruce Barthol, bassist of Country Joe & the Fish, 2006)

> The idea was to make the music totally real and human – a music that destroyed all separation between the 'pop-star' musicians and the audience which sat at their feet. No opportunity to play for the people was overlooked – every free concert, every benefit, every place where people wanted to hear the music and it was possible to set up the amps and plug it in, was a place we had to go to kick out the jams as best we could.
>
> (Frank Bach, lead singer of the Up, 1971)

## ASSAULT ON THE CULTURE

The 26 December debacle at the Fillmore East was not the MC5's first encounter with the Motherfuckers. Twelve days earlier, at the Boston Tea Party, the band and their mentor/manager John Sinclair had been lobbied by a supporter of the Motherfuckers, one of whom had been imprisoned for stabbing a sailor. MC5 frontman Rob Tyner duly made a plea on stage for cash to help finance his appeal. But this show was more memorable for Tyner's off-the-cuff suggestion that the audience should trash the venue, after the management cut short the show. The MC5 were now banned from both the Tea Party and the Fillmore, and had fallen out with New York's self-appointed guardians of hip morality. The quarrel with the Motherfuckers was mended when the band played a free show for them in March 1969. But the MC5's relationship with both the music business and the underground grew more fractious as 1969 progressed.

As Ben Morea had noted, the MC5 had taken an avowedly 'revolutionary' stance. Just as the Motherfuckers had declared 'a total assault on every form of oppression', so John Sinclair mounted 'Total Assault on the Culture!' in a March 1968 broadside. Sinclair announced the three key elements of his manifesto: 'rock and roll, dope, and fucking in the streets!' Rock and roll, he explained, was 'the great liberating force of our time and place here in the West'. It represented emotional, sexual and political freedom. Translated into the rhetoric of the age, Sinclair's philosophy was 'Wave your freek flag high! HIGH! YAAAAA! *Stone free* – do what you wanna!'

As a long-time disciple of free jazz and blues, who had hymned the revolutionary potential of John Coltrane and Archie Shepp in his own poetry, Sinclair inevitably chose the widest possible definition of rock and roll. 'We mean John Coltrane and Pharoah Sanders and Archie Shepp and Albert Ayler and Sun Ra and all those people as much as the Beatles and Jimi and the MC5 and Canned Heat and the Cream and the Grateful Dead and Big Brother & the Holding Company and the Up,' he explained.

Slotting two Detroit bands, the MC5 and the Up, into his pantheon wasn't just a canny piece of Michigan boosterism; as their manager and political philosopher, Sinclair had an unshakeable belief in the transcendent power of their music. Both the Up, led by his fellow journalist Frank Bach, and the MC5 were part of his Trans-Love Energies Unlimited collective, which shifted from Detroit to two period houses in Ann Arbor after an arson assault on Sinclair's home in April 1968. Both bands offered a visceral form of riff-based garage rock, fused in the case of the MC5 with the expansive jazz landscapes of Sun Ra. Sinclair himself added Coltrane-inspired saxophone when the MC5 embarked on one of their lengthy explorations of rebellious noise, such as 'Black to Comm' or the righteously radical improvisation released several decades later as 'I'm Mad Like Eldridge Cleaver'.

As Detroit's core of white revolutionary energy, Trans-Love was the target of regular police raids. In July 1968, John Sinclair and MC5 guitarist Fred Smith were charged with assault and resisting arrest, and then the entire band were held after disturbances at an outdoor concert. Sinclair's history of dope busts exposed him as an easy target for harassment, which in turn hardened his revolutionary invective. He issued a series of 'Rock & Roll

Dope' bulletins chronicling the collective's latest collisions with the law. One minute Wayne Kramer was accidentally exposing himself to a teenage audience in Tecumseh while changing his trousers on stage; the next Sinclair was being presented with a summons 'for having a noisy band!'

During an August 1968 visit to his friends at the *East Village Other* in New York, Sinclair was introduced to Danny Fields, A&R executive for Elektra Records. He arrived at Trans-Love in mid-September to find 'the men pounding on the table for food like cavemen, and all the women running in and out of the kitchen with long Mother Earth skirts on and no bras . . . The men did everything but drag them by the hair.' Trans-Love might not have been a bastion of sexual equality, but Fields was impressed by its leader: 'I'd never met anyone like Sinclair. He would sit on the can, taking a shit with the door open, barking out orders, like a Lyndon Johnson smoking dope.' Fields left a phone message for his friend, *Rolling Stone* critic Jon Landau: 'I have found it. Call me.' Intrigued, Landau travelled the next day to see the MC5 perform in Ann Arbor. He was overwhelmed by their sonic thrust and uncompromising radicalism, and began to spread the word. Meanwhile, Fields had convinced Elektra boss Jac Holzman to sign the band. 'I was intrigued by how the MC5 manoeuvred their music to drive their politics,' Holzman admitted, 'like a loudspeaker assault on the established order . . . I wanted to record them in the heat of the moment, which meant right away.'

The Elektra contract was sealed on 26 September 1968. Just over a month later, Holzman installed recording equipment at the Grande Ballroom in Detroit. For two nights, the MC5 powered through their concert repertoire in front of a rabidly wild audience, stoked to fever-pitch by the hellfire preaching of Trans-Love compere 'Brother' J.C. Crawford. 'I wanna hear a little revolution,' he cried. 'Brothers and sisters, the time has come, for each and every one of you to decide whether you are gonna be the problem, or whether you are gonna be the solution.' It was a verbal riff lifted from Eldridge Cleaver, when the lives of the militant black community were at stake. In Detroit, however, it was no more than revolutionary chic, as meaningless as Crawford's gospel call to the audience: 'I want to know, are you ready to testify?'

As captured on their Elektra album, *Kick Out The Jams*, the MC5's set continued in similarly frenetic vein. The music was fearsome in its intensity, but its overt political content was nil. Beyond the confrontational call to

'Kick out the jams, motherfuckers' and John Lee Hooker's post-riot commentary, 'The Motor City is Burning', the MC5's radicalism was expressed in the fury of their performance, not their words. It was not furious enough for the band, however, who lobbied Elektra for the chance to re-record the album. The label refused, and insisted that Rob Tyner revise his introduction to the title track so that it could be issued as a single. When the album was released in February 1969, Elektra prepared both censored and uncensored editions. By mistake, the retail chain Hudson's were sent the uncut version, and were so outraged that they refused to sell the record in either form. The MC5 reacted with an underground press advertisement that read: 'Kick Out The Jams, Motherfucker! And kick in the door if the store won't sell you the album on Elektra. FUCK HUDSON'S!' When Hudson's saw the ad, which had been prepared without Elektra's knowledge, they pulled all the label's product from their stores. 'I said to the MC5, "Hey, guys, you can't do that",' Jac Holzman recalled. 'They said, "Jac, we thought you were part of the revolution". I said, "I'm only interested in your music".'

Relations between band and record company soured from that point. Elektra received word that the band had taken to defecating on stage, 'as a cultural protest'. The reports were exaggerated, though Tyner did regularly play out a routine whereby an unwilling female member of the audience would be dragged on stage and 'seduced'. The victim was actually a member of the MC5's entourage, who went through the same ritual every night. But this did nothing to endear Elektra to their troublesome clients. 'Elektra is not the tool of anyone's revolution,' pronounced Holzman. 'We feel that the revolution will be won by poetics and not by politics.' The FBI were not convinced: they were sufficiently disconcerted by the MC5 to send out fake letters of complaint from 'concerned citizens' to university authorities which had staged the band's shows.

In San Francisco, the MC5 began to record their second album. Allegedly, they stole an expensive suite of sound equipment that had been hired by Elektra. 'I suggested they find another label,' Holzman explained. 'Sinclair was very cool; he thought I handled it in a righteous manner. They went across the street to Atlantic and straight away got a $50,000 release.' The new recording deal was signed in May 1969, the same month in which the band spouted their radical views in *Newsweek* magazine. Fred Smith announced that they were carrying out 'a revolution against cultural repression'. Bass guitarist Michael Davis denounced those who wanted to censor the MC5:

'What's obscene are city streets, dead fish, pollution of air and water. And war. Honky culture is death culture.'

That last line could have been pulled from a Black Panther Party manifesto. The similarity was no coincidence. On 1 November 1968, the day after *Kick Out The Jams* was recorded, John Sinclair and his Trans-Love comrade Pun Plamondon had announced the formation of the White Panther Party. Its primary purpose, Sinclair explained later, was to 'put the "cultural revolution" into an explicitly political context by merging the "total assault on the culture" programme of rock and roll, dope, and fucking in the streets with armed self-defence and what Eldridge Cleaver and Huey P. Newton called the "mother-country radical movement". We still considered our main function to be mass propagandists for the "revolution".' Central to the White Panthers' political thrust was the musical and ideological potency of the MC5.

Like Cleaver, Sinclair appointed himself Minister of Information. Like Newton, he drafted a ten-point manifesto, the first tenet of which was total acceptance of the Black Panthers' agenda. The second principle restated the dope and fucking rhetoric of old, before Sinclair issued demands that would satisfy hippies (free dope, music, bodies) and hardcore radicals (free prisoners, soldiers, people). 'We *breathe* revolution,' he boasted. The bragging didn't end there. Having name-checked 'brothers' with whom the White Panthers were proud to be united – Newton, Cleaver, Coltrane, James Brown – Sinclair added: 'These are *men* in America. And we're as crazy as they are, and as pure. We're *bad*.' No other white radical group in America had dared to align itself with the Panthers as an equal in the revolutionary struggle. But so deep was Sinclair's psychological identification with African-American culture that he never imagined that the Black Panthers might reject their White brethren. And he was right. The Black Panthers may not have considered Sinclair's organisation as a serious aid to their fight for liberation; but neither did they distance themselves from the White Panthers.

Sinclair continued to bombard radical Michigan with position papers, revolutionary statements and manifestos. 'Rock and Roll is a Weapon of Cultural Revolution,' he declared in December 1968, tracing the roots of the equation 'Music Is Revolution' back beyond capitalist society to the Stone Age. There was only one flaw in Sinclair's logic: the MC5's commitment to the revolution was waning. While the White Panthers envisioned themselves as a vanguard force of Marxist revolt, the MC5 defined revolution as a rock'n'roll stance – a defiantly raised middle finger to Top 40 radio, a declaration of outlaw independence. Sinclair's ultimate aim was the overthrow of the American cultural, legal and political systems. The MC5 dreamed of being uncompromising rock'n'roll stars. As Sinclair would later tell Wayne Kramer, 'You wanted to be bigger than the Beatles, while I wanted you to be as big as Chairman Mao.'

The band informed Sinclair that they were leaving the Trans-Love commune, and setting up headquarters in nearby Hamburg, Michigan. 'I could dig John living in the commune,' Wayne Kramer noted. 'But he couldn't dig me not living in one.' Perhaps inevitably, in an atmosphere where men made revolution and women made coffee, the dispute hinged around problems between the MC5's 'chicks' and those supporting the White Panthers. Sinclair remained their manager, but his influence began to be usurped by their new producer – rock critic Jon Landau, who believed that 'rock and roll in a lot of ways is bigger than politics'. In spring 1969, the MC5 began work on their second album, *Back in the USA*, a retro-styled album that carried little of the musical weight or revolutionary baggage of *Kick Out The Jams*. It ensured that the band would never rival the Beatles, let alone Chairman Mao.

Meanwhile, *Kick Out The Jams* failed to ignite the revolutionary fervour that Sinclair and the band had envisaged. Sales were discouraging, partly because of dismay at the album's censorship. Several underground reviewers ranked the MC5 alongside the Doors as exemplars of fake radicalism. The Doors' chart-topping *Waiting for the Sun* had included 'Five to One', a slice of political theatre rooted in self-parody. 'The old get old and the young get stronger,' Jim Morrison had sung like a 1950s juvenile delinquent, 'may take a week and it may take longer, they got the guns but we got the numbers. Gonna win, yeah, we're taking over.' The image of Morrison as an insurgent was pure illusion. Doors keyboardist Ray Manzarek recalled: 'On "Tell All The People" – "Tell all the people, get your guns, follow me down" – Jim said, "Wait a minute, man, I ain't gonna say that". Robbie [Krieger] said, "Well, those were the lyrics", and Jim said, "Well, I don't want people getting their guns and following me. I'm not leading a violent revolution or anything. I'm not putting my name on that song."'

On 2 March 1969, Morrison exposed himself, accidentally or otherwise, on stage in Miami, prompting one of the era's more enduring furores. He was arrested on charges of indecency and inciting the audience to riot. 'He was obscene, no question about it,' claimed the promoter's wife. 'You could say he was trying to incite a riot and not get much argument from me. He was saying, "Let's have a good time, let's have a revolution", everybody come up on stage.' As Doors manager Bill Siddons explained, Morrison was simply acting out another role: 'We had seen the Living Theater the night before, and Jim copped a few lines. He said some things like "Why don't we have a revolution here?", and things like that. But that's not inciting to riot.'

If revolutionary rock was merely play-acting, then perhaps the only effective method of preaching subversion in song was via comedy. Although Elektra Records were relieved to see the MC5 depart from the label, they had no qualms about releasing another dissident statement, *Have a Marijuana* by David Peel and the Lower East Side. Shambolic, endearing and permanently stoned, Peel's singalong ditties had none of the pretentious connotations of the MC5 or the Doors. His Elektra records – *American Revolution* was issued a year later – were like a musical enaction of Gilbert Shelton's underground comic strip, 'The Fabulous Furry Freak Brothers'. They portrayed a world shrouded in marijuana, in which smoking a joint, annoying a cop and overthrowing the government were equally subversive and fun. Not that Peel shied away from the radicalism of the counter-culture. 'I sang about American Revolution because that was what it felt like,' he recalls, 'the disobedience, the demonstrations, it was more like a civil war. America was at war with itself, that's what it was: the counter-culture was fighting the culture.'

Peel made his name via free performances in New York's Washington Square Park, fired by a philosophy that returned political idealism to the street. 'We always believed in doing it for free,' Peel explained. 'Enough of the rip-off. No rock musician ever paid to see an audience, so why should an audience pay to see them?' That ethos survived until Peel was tempted by fame. 'One day this guy came up to me between songs,' he recalls, 'and said, "I'm Danny Fields from Elektra Records". He bought me a steak dinner at Max's Kansas City, which really impressed me. He said he wanted to sign me. Now, the Doors were on Elektra, which meant that there was an immediate credibility of reference. I was into the streets and revolution, but I had no problem about signing the deal. I just wanted to get my music out to the people, and I thought that Elektra could do it.' Rather than removing Peel from the streets, Elektra decided to record the album in the park: 'I think that was the first time that had been done. And while we were doing it, a riot broke out!'

Peel was no stranger to disturbances on the streets: shortly after signing the Elektra deal, he had participated in one of the Yippies' most prominent Vietnam protests.

'I'd met Abbie Hoffman in Washington Square Park,' he recalls, 'and he invited me down to the anti-war rally at Grand Central Station. It was a state of siege down there. There were thousands of people and police, all this havoc, and in the middle of it all I was playing my music. In fact, this cop said to me, "Keep playing, boy, it'll keep the people calm". So I was singing "I like marijuana", and because my diction was so bad at that time, when *Time* magazine wrote about me, they said that I was singing "Have a marijuana". Danny and I liked that, so it became the title of the album.' *Have a Marijuana* duly became one of the era's cult records, finding an appreciative audience among the Beatles, among others. It also catapulted David Peel into the forefront of the Lower East Side counter-culture. Around 1969, he ran into the equally unconventional A.J. Weberman.

## BEYOND INTERPRETATION

Encouraged by his first published ventures into 'interpreting' Bob Dylan's lyrics the previous year, A.J. Weberman had extended his realm, offering the underground press his translations of songs by artists including the Beatles and Creedence Clearwater Revival. 'I only interpret the best,' he boasted. Having located hidden messages of support for the anti-war movement in Dylan's 1968 album *John Wesley Harding*, Weberman was prepared to scour the songwriter's next record with the same intensity. He wasn't prepared for *Nashville Skyline*, a mellifluous but slight album of country-pop tunes issued by Dylan in May 1969. 'I felt betrayed by that *"lay lady lay"*,' he sneers, still outraged by what he saw as the inanity of Dylan's response to the aftermath of Chicago. Enlisting the support of friends such as David Peel, Weberman announced the formation of the Dylan Liberation Front, whose manifesto was simply 'to help save Bob Dylan from himself'.

The cover photograph for *Nashville Skyline* was taken by Elliott Landy. He became an intimate friend of Dylan and the Band in Woodstock, an artistic enclave in upstate New York. Landy regarded himself as a radical, and shared the bafflement of Weberman – and the *Sing Out!* interviewers – that Dylan did not share their instinctive rejection of American foreign policy. 'I started talking about politics with Bob because I was involved in the anti-war movement,' Landy remembered. 'But he didn't want to talk about it; he didn't seem to be concerned with it. I asked him, "You mean you're not into politics? How can you write songs like 'Masters of War' without being political?'"

Yet *Nashville Skyline* was a statement, of sorts. Dylan was not the first rock artist to experiment with country and western music – the Byrds, Lovin' Spoonful, the Monkees and Buffalo Springfield had entered this field before him – but his guru-like status ensured that his efforts were the subject of intensive scrutiny. While Weberman could see only conservatism in his choice of white Southern music, others endeavoured to find evidence of socialist intent in his work. In this interpretation, Dylan was showing solidarity with the oppressed American working-class, throwing in his lot with his friend, Johnny Cash, who had long demonstrated his support for Native Americans, prisoners and other victims of discrimination and violence.

As Elliott Landy discovered, Dylan preferred not to reinforce such a cosy reading of his motives. 'It was sometimes hard to tell if he really meant the things he said,' Landy noted. 'I remember one time when he said he might even consider voting for George Wallace for President of the United States.' Wallace was the *bête noire* of the counter-culture, so right-wing that his celebrity support was restricted to a handful of ultra-conservative country singers. Landy continued: 'I could not believe I was hearing this from the "leader" of progressive popular political thought. He said it in the midst of a conversation we were having about politics, and I think he was just trying to point out that there were some positive aspects of conservative thought. I am certain he was not personally supporting the actions Wallace had taken against blacks. But he may have been putting me on completely.' Relying on Dylan as a comrade was clearly a rather dubious form of political insurance.

Dylan's folk contemporary, Phil Ochs, was enduring his own moment of ambiguity. His Yippie friends bounced back from the debacle of Chicago with their energy and self-belief undimmed. 'I can only relate to Chicago as a personal anarchist, a revolutionary artist,' declared Abbie Hoffman. 'I am my own leader. I make my own rules. The revolution is wherever my boots hit the ground.' Hoffman's defence of the Yippies' failure to trigger a revolution in Chicago was simple and convenient: 'There were never any Yippies and there never will be . . . It was the biggest put-on of all time. If you believed Yippies existed, you are nothing but a sheep . . . Everyone's Chicago came true.'

But not Phil Ochs': his Chicago was a nightmare, from which he found it hard to waken. It had been, he revealed, 'my trip to hell and back. A lot of despair, thoughts about suicide and trips into total fantasy and revolution.' As the man charged with guiding Phil's virtually static career, Michael Ochs had an unparalleled view of the confusion surrounding his brother in early 1969: 'I had an office in the Ed Sullivan building, and every day this weird procession of people would stop by – Yippies, radicals, revolutionaries, folk-singers.' All of them looked to Phil for enthusiasm, but for once this tireless radical was drained of optimism.

Michael Ochs is convinced that there was an additional stimulus for his brother's dark mood: 'Phil was definitely under surveillance by the FBI at this point. It was none too subtle, almost as if they wanted Phil to be aware of it. It helped to add to Phil's paranoia, which was bad enough without the FBI being added to the pile. I had a brief taste of what it was like after Chicago, when I was staying in this little shack in Topanga Canyon, which was still registered in Phil's name. These FBI guys arrived at the door: they didn't seem to have much idea what was happening, but they knew that they wanted Phil, and they assumed I had to be him. I couldn't really take the situation seriously, so I was being really cutesy with them. They asked me my name, and I said, "Steve McQueen" – anything to upset them. I actually got the giggles, because it was like something out of a bad B-movie: they really did have the whole good cop, bad cop thing going on. It was such a cliché. But I could afford not to take it seriously, as it wasn't me they were after. For Phil, it was different. He knew that wherever he was, there was likely to be someone watching him, and I think it all added to his sense of insecurity and pain.'

As Ochs slowly emerged from his emotional and political vacuum, he began to assemble an album. In recent years, his music had already shifted from political activism to dense allegorical commentary. His 1969 record *Rehearsals for Retirement* – even its title oozed desolation – stripped away the mask of language, exposing a mind at the end of its tether. 'It's like the soul of the country has been killed,' Ochs let slip during one of the painful interviews ostensibly intended to promote the album, 'and I feel myself partially murdered . . . So the album ends not with the revolutionary call, but as though I've been killed.' In his conversation, personal and political decomposed into one: 'It's like you don't have the heart left to try and stop it, it's like it doesn't matter, the mental state, the final point of everything.' To reinforce this bleak message, the front cover of *Rehearsals for Retirement* displayed a tombstone that Ochs had commissioned. 'PHIL OCHS (AMERICAN)', it read. 'BORN: EL PASO, TEXAS 1940. DIED: CHICAGO, ILLINOIS 1968.' Soon afterwards, Ochs composed his own epitaph, in 'No More Songs', a grim prophecy of his declining creative powers: 'Once I knew a sage who sang upon the stage, he told about the world . . . And it seems that there are no more songs'.

When Ochs' comrade, Jerry Rubin, chronicled this period in his autobiographical manifesto, *Do It!*, there was no hint that his enthusiasm for the struggle might ever have wavered. Yet as Richard Nixon was inaugurated early in 1969, one observer overheard Rubin's comment on the Mobe's counter-inaugural parade: 'Awful. The whole thing is depressing. No life, no direction. This may be the last demonstration.' He had just watched two groups of protestors fighting over whether they should deface a Stars-and-Stripes flag. 'The anti-war parade had turned savagely on itself,' noted the onlooker.

## FREE HUEY

The fragmentation extended beyond the Vietnam protest movement. Black liberation groups across America were united by the symbol of jailed martyr Huey Newton. A birthday party was staged in his absence in Hollywood, featuring speeches from James Baldwin and Kathleen Cleaver, and music from white rock bands such as Country Joe & the Fish, and Pacific Gas & Electric. Yet beneath the easy solidarity of the 'Free Huey!' campaign, the disinformation programme of the FBI's COINTELPRO campaign was leaving its mark. One of the first victims was Stokely Carmichael. In late January 1969, the man who had coined the 'Black Power' slogan and ignited the fire beneath the Panthers abandoned the American struggle and re-located to Africa. He'd been hounded out of the SNCC leadership the previous summer; now the Panthers too had lost faith in their ally. In particular, Eldridge Cleaver, himself in exile, had spread the word that Stokely was a coward and possibly a CIA agent. Carmichael replied sarcastically: 'Many of those now calling me afraid overlook the fact that when I was in Mississippi, as a young man of nineteen, facing guns and bullets, some of them were raping black women and writing love letters to white girls – very revolutionary acts, no doubt.' And he described his flight to Africa as a return to his homeland; in future he would insist the continent was the shared home of the black liberation movement, and its only feasible hope of freedom. Ironically, Cleaver would follow him to Africa a few months later, having endured in Cuban exile what he described as 'six months in a wretched and restless existence – sort of a San Quentin with palm trees'.

Conditions for the black activists still fighting in America were even less attractive. Infiltrators and informers were fracturing the Black Panthers' unity, sapping its self-confidence. By the early weeks of 1969, the Panthers' newspaper was printing regular denunciations of the 'provocateur agents, kooks and avaricious fools' in their midst. There was purge after purge of the Panther membership: individuals could be saluted as heroes in one issue, then declared traitors in the next. The atmosphere began to resemble the aftermath of the Chinese Cultural Revolution of 1967, as small cabals jockeyed for power, each claiming to represent the wishes of the Panthers' imprisoned leader.

In this climate of suspicion, even blatantly subversive activity could be viewed as counter-revolutionary. In early April 1969, the seeds of a cause célèbre were sown when the so-called 'New York 21', all local Panther members, were arrested on conspiracy charges. The police alleged that they had planned to detonate bombs across New York during Easter weekend, at targets including police stations, railroad lines, department stores and even the Bronx Botanical Gardens, not an obvious symbol of racist imperialism. The case took two years to come to trial, by which time suspicion about the 21's motives had spread like a malignant tumour through the New York office of the party. It subsequently transpired that at least six FBI informers were working there, none of them aware of the others' identities. 'There is certainly the possibility that undercover officers were reporting on undercover officers,' one of the six noted drily.

Even more draining was the violence visited upon the Panthers on an almost daily basis. Gun battles with the police robbed the party of many of its most active members, sometimes because the victims had used robbery as a means of fundraising. The Panthers were forced to stage a press conference to decry the 'bandits robbing service stations and taverns'. When the Panthers weren't being targeted by the police, they were being attacked by members of Ron Karenga's US group. The most notorious confrontation between the two radical African-American liberation forces took place on the campus of UCLA. US and the Southern California branch of the Panthers had agreed to meet there – unarmed – to dampen their recent tension. Instead, Alprentice 'Bunchy' Carter and John Huggins of the Panthers were gunned down by three US members who were later claimed to be in the pay of the FBI, who had allegedly supplied them with cash, drugs and pistols. The Panthers accused Karenga of having masterminded the shootings. The US leader received news of the clash when he was about to speak at the Rockland Palace in Harlem, where he was attending a rally of the Committee for a Unified Newark. Onlookers reported that Karenga had quailed when he heard about the shooting. But his adversaries remained suspicious, and the treatment of the assailants merely heightened their paranoia. The three gunmen were convicted of murder, but to separate them from imprisoned members of the Panthers, they were kept in a minimum security jail, from which they mysteriously vanished after a few months. The FBI were certainly intervening in the Panthers' activities, trying to fuel dissension between the Party and the powerful Chicago street gang the Blackstone Rangers.

It seemed as if all roads led back to Chicago. The city, and its misman-aged convention, supplied the spark that refocused both the New Left and the counter-culture. In late March, the Justice Department handed down indictments to eight key activists at the Democratic Convention, on charges of conspiracy to cause a riot. The eight were carefully selected to represent the widest possible range of dissident opinion, from Abbie Hoffman and Jerry Rubin of the Yippies, through Tom Hayden of SDS, to the previously low-profile Jerry Froines and Lee Weiner. The most surprising name was that of Black Panther chairman Bobby Seale, whose only contribution to Chicago had been to make a speech (albeit an inflammatory one) and then leave the city without contacting any of his other 'co-conspirators'. Hoffman and Rubin regarded the indictment as a badge of pride; perhaps they had already realised that the trial, set for that autumn, would inevitably descend into a political farce that could have been scripted by the Yippies themselves.

After the indictments were announced, Chicago again became a potent brand. So it was the ideal moment for Columbia Records – still bragging about their roster of 'Revolutionaries' – to launch a new band called Chicago Transit Authority.[1] To establish their radical credentials, the band fleshed out their first album with a suite inspired by the disturbances at the convention. One track, 'Prologue, August 29, 1968', comprised *audio vérité* recordings of the demon-strators outside the Convention Center (actually recorded on August 28). 'Someday (August 29, 1968)' attempted to capture the mêlée in apocalyptic (if clumsy) words: 'Would you look around you now and tell me what you see, faces full of hate and fear, faces full of me'. The suite was hardly the musical highlight of the *Chicago Transit Authority* album; the group's penchant for brassy commercial rock would prove much more enduring than their supposed radicalism. But its inclusion showed that the events of August 1968 had become part of the shared landscape of the counter-culture – a landscape that would take on a global perspective when the trial began in late 1969.

## THIS YEAR'S FLOWER POWER

> When you're twenty, you make assumptions about what's possible that turn out to be way overblown, in terms of how much you can change the world – you and your generation.
>
> (James Taylor, 2003)

Regardless of the political reality, all elements of the US youth movement maintained their faith in the inevitability of revolution during 1969. 'Everybody knows the revolution's coming,' commented the previously apolitical singer-songwriter Neil Young as he promoted his debut album that January. 'Can you imagine us going on without this coming to a head?' The same message came from every underground magazine, in Britain and America, besides the bulletins issued by revolutionary organisations from SDS to the Black Liberation Army. It was a new theory of historical process: youthful impatience as an irresistible political force. With President Nixon showing little sign of scaling back American involvement in Vietnam, African-American liberation no closer, and student dissatisfaction mounting across the Western world, surely the dam holding back the movement's impetuosity had to break? Even 56-year-old film director Michelangelo Antonioni, then shooting a study of youthful rebellion, *Zabriskie Point*, felt able to lecture the young about the dangers of their revolution being corrupted, without for a second questioning the fact that it would succeed. But his comments offered an overdue note of realism: 'The establishment, especially in America, has an ability to absorb the revolution. Rock music is big business. The presidents of the record company are part of the power structure; they're friends of the police. Revolution – as a word, not an act – has become very fashionable . . . You have to be careful. Revolution is commercial.'

Frank Zappa extended that theme during a much-anticipated lecture in London. In May 1969, the Mothers of Invention leader was invited to speak at the London School of Economics, whose students had a reputation for militancy. Not having read Zappa's cynical comments about radical chic in the US underground press, the British students were expecting a display of counter-cultural zealotry. But, as *International Times* correspondent Mitch Howard reported, 'Zappa didn't speak in terms of the heroic struggle of the Vietnamese patriots against the jackbooted Achilles heel of imperialism. He didn't tell them to take to the streets or fuck their mothers.' Refusing to call for immediate revolution, he was accused of being 'yet another bourgeois liberal camouflaging his innate reactionary tendencies'. He replied that there were more effective ways of challenging the establishment than taking to the streets with slogans and rocks. 'People should go into communications and the military and change them from the inside,' he said. 'I'm afraid that everyone will have a revolution and make a mess of it. They will wave their banners on the streets and brandish sticks and go home and brag about their bruises.' The students' political demonstrations had no connection with reality: 'It's this year's flower power,' he told them.

Zappa's denunciation of student naivety helped to undermine the unsteady alliance of the New Left and the hippie underground. The only concrete proposals for a post-revolutionary culture were coming from the traditional socialist and communist parties, whose theories, based on 19th-century ideology, presupposed the emergence of a post-capitalist economy; or from the Trotskyist revolutionary parties, whose vision of a Marxist society was more apocalyptic but much less precise. Only a tiny minority of young people were willing to commit themselves to either of these recipes for utopia. The remainder – the masses who made up the indefinite body that was the counter-culture – were united less by what they dreamed than by what they feared: Vietnam, racism, sexual repression, prohibitions on drug use, and a society organised around profit rather than play. In its inability to think beyond symbols, revolutionary rock was perhaps the perfect vehicle for this incoherent sense of dissatisfaction.

Yet as many of rock's more intelligent observers had already realised, a revolution without a goal was a revolution without purpose. And if it was impossible to imagine a revolution that could work, then maybe the concept of revolution itself was flawed. The conundrum frustrated John Lennon and his new wife, Yoko Ono, in the early months of 1969.

The Beatles, and in particular Lennon, had taken a beating in the underground for their apparent conservatism on the subject of revolution the previous year. Even their friend Jimi Hendrix had noted: 'The Beatles are part of the establishment ... We must watch out. It's like a young cat protesting in school, he goes out and everybody says, yeah, man, that's what it's about, man, we're with you. Soon as he reaches about 25 years old and starts getting into the establishment scene, he forgets it because he's comfortable now, he's nice and fat and got his little gig together, so then he just forgets about the younger people, all his friends, what they used to say when they were in school, and he melts into part of the establishment.'

That must have evoked a wry smile from Lennon. Since his relationship with Yoko Ono had become public knowledge, the couple had endured a barrage of racist criticism, not just from the media but from Beatles fans, and even among the group's entourage. If this was how it felt to be part of the establishment, Lennon must have wondered, what would life be like as an outcast?

The limits of their freedom were starkly exposed when they proposed the release of *Two Virgins*, a piece of avant-garde tomfoolery that featured nude photographs of the couple on the sleeve. The record carried the logo of the Beatles' Apple Records organisation, but it was still dependent on the approval of the EMI corporation, who held the sole rights to distribute Apple product. As Lennon explained, 'EMI (who have the *real* control) wrote warning letters to all their puppets around the world, telling them *not* to handle it in *any* way (this after Sir Joe [Joseph Lockwood, EMI chairman] had told us face to face that he would do "everything he could" to help us with it – and asked us for autographed copies!).'

When EMI refused to handle the album on grounds of moral decency, Apple was forced to seek alternative arrangements. 'Retailers everywhere were too scared to handle it and it sold very few,' Lennon added. 'It's very well *known*, but not many people could actually *get it*. In most other major markets, e.g. Japan, it has never been released.' There was little sign of a revolution in progress here.[2]

To coincide with their honeymoon, which was chronicled on a hastily recorded Beatles single ('The Ballad of John & Yoko'), the Lennons announced that henceforth their lives and work would be devoted to one cause: world peace. The decision was triggered by a letter from radical film-maker Peter Watkins, about 'how the media is controlled, how it's all run . . . it ended up, "What are you going to do about it?".' For a while, Lennon rested on his laurels as the composer of songs such as 'All You Need Is Love'. Eventually his conscience pricked him to use his fame as a weapon of peace. They began their crusade by opening their honeymoon to the press, who arrived expecting to find the couple consummating their marriage, and were instead treated to a seven-day orgy of peace campaigning. The 'bed-in' at the Amsterdam Hilton provoked global media coverage, equally divided between bewilderment and derision. 'It's a funny world when two people going to bed on their honeymoon can make the front pages in all the papers for a week,' Lennon commented. 'In Paris, the Vietnam peace talks have got about as far as sorting out the shape of the table they are going to sit around. Those talks have been going on for months. In one week in bed, we achieved a lot more.'

On their return to London, the Lennons threw themselves headlong into an exhausting schedule of peace propaganda, alongside which John's musical career took second place. It soon became apparent that their activities were not only intended as an alternative to the ineffectual efforts to end the conflict in Vietnam. The couple were also opposing the same people who had criticised Lennon's 'Revolution' song: the revolutionary left. While conceding that 'I'm as violent as the next man', he declared that their campaign was aimed 'mainly at people with violent inclinations for change. We believe violent change doesn't really accomplish anything in the long term, because in the over 2,000 years we've been going, all the violent revolutions have come to an end, even if they've lasted 50 or 100 years. The few people who have tried to do it our way, unfortunately, have been killed, i.e. Jesus, Gandhi, Kennedy and Martin Luther King. The way we might escape being killed is that we have a sense of humour and that the worst, or the least, we can do is make people laugh.' Yoko Ono added: 'We don't believe in revolution, we believe in evolution.'

Anxious to take their message to the people of America, the Lennons attempted to stage another bed-in there, only for John to be barred because of his recent drug conviction. Canada was more welcoming, and so in late May 1969 the bed-in circus resumed in a Montreal hotel room. There Lennon composed and recorded his first 'solo' single, 'Give Peace a Chance', released under the name of the Plastic Ono Band.[3] Bored by the regularity with which every protest demonstration ended with a rendition of the folk song 'We Shall Overcome', Lennon was offering an alternative. 'Our job is to write for the people now,' he claimed, 'so the songs they go and sing on their buses are not just love songs.'

The Montreal bed-in coincided with a symbolic confrontation in California. In June 1968, the officers of the University of California had demolished three acres of housing, close to the Berkeley campus, in order to prepare a soccer field. The following April, activist Mike Delacour launched a campaign to reclaim the land for the community. His team began to transform the waste ground into a garden and playground, under the idealistic name of People's Park. As 1960s radical historian Todd Gitlin explained, 'People's Park amounted to the spirits of the New Left and the counter-culture in harmonious combination: it was a trace of anarchist heaven on earth.' A blow had been struck against the establishment, but with nature and creativity, not a raised fist. The more confrontational elements of the left regarded the issue as a benign distraction; most participants believed that the university would concede that they had lost the propaganda issue, and yield the land to the people of Berkeley.

Instead, the university, the local police and the governor of California, Ronald Reagan, combined to turn People's Park into a battleground. On 15 May 1969, police blockaded the area from the public gaze, while bull-dozers reclaimed the land for chaos. The response was a riot, which began with smashed windows, and ended in shotgun fire from the police. One demonstrator was blinded; another received serious stomach wounds, and died four days later. Suddenly, radical Berkeley had become the frontline of the generational struggle between conformity and revolution. Imitation parks sprang up all over the community, only to be torn down by the police. A massive protest march was scheduled for 30 May, and many on both sides of the argument feared that it might provoke bloodshed.

On 28 May, many of the West Coast's leading rock bands – the Grateful Dead, Jefferson Airplane, Santana and Creedence Clearwater Revival among them – performed at Bill Graham's Winterland ballroom in San Francisco as a fundraiser for the Park. The following day, John Lennon placed a phone call from his Montreal hotel to the campus headquarters of the People's Park protestors, like a prophet issuing instructions from the mountaintop. He placed his iconic power squarely behind those who wished the demonstration to remain peaceful. Indeed, he went further, suggesting that abandoning the cause and avoiding violence was preferable to confrontation. 'Listen, there's no cause worth losing your life for, brother,' he told the campaigners. 'I don't believe there is any cause worth getting shot for. You can do better by moving on to another city or moving to Canada. Go anywhere – then they've got nothing to attack and nobody to point their finger at. Sing Hare Krishna or something, but don't move about if it aggravates the pigs. Don't get hassled by the cops and don't play their games.' Yoko Ono added: 'The only way you can get them to understand you is to extend your hand and really try to open their minds and give your love.' Lennon lapsed into passionate clichés: 'Entice them and con them. You've got the brains, you can do it. You can make it, man, we can make it, together. We can get it together. We can get it together – now, that's all!' The march passed off without violence, the issue subsided, but People's Park remained in the hands of the university. This unsatisfactory denouement widened the division between pacifists and militants in the American youth movement. To coincide with the march, activists issued a Berkeley Liberation Program, the principles of which ranged from 'create a soulful socialism' to 'unite with other movements throughout the world to destroy this motherfucking racistcapitalistimperialist system'.

That was too combative for John Lennon in May 1969. His intervention in the People's Park stand-off aroused further criticism across the underground. 'Singing Beatles' songs won't get rid of the Blue Meanies,' one of the People's Park protestors complained, referring to the cartoon villains of the group's latest film, *Yellow Submarine*. 'There's too much blue meanness in our hearts, and the Blue Meanies want to kill us. And now we are learning to want to kill them.' *Village Voice* columnist Robert Christgau considered that Lennon was merely 'firming up his newfound status as a pompous shit', with pretensions towards becoming a guru: 'After shrugging off the Maharishi, John is bidding to take his place.'

Lennon was learning that every action, or inaction, provokes unforeseen consequences. A fine example was provided by his brief encounter in Montreal with the LSD guru, Timothy Leary. Besides relishing the opportunity to be photographed alongside popular culture's leading celebrity, Leary had travelled to Montreal to commission a song from Lennon. He was about to announce his candidacy for the post of Governor of California, with the support, so he claimed, of 'major rock artists and other prominent young people'. He was convinced that a Lennon/McCartney anthem might swing the ballot in his favour. Leary supplied his campaign slogan, 'Come Together', and left the rest to Lennon. Distracted by his responsibilities as a global peace spokesman, Lennon could only muster a banal couplet ('come together/join the party'), set to an equally lacklustre melody. He left Leary with the promise of something more substantial to follow, and then used the slogan as the hook-line of a song that mixed self-mythology and sexual compulsion to stunning effect. When Leary heard the Beatles' recording of 'Come Together', he threatened Lennon with legal action. By then, however, Leary had more pressing concerns. He had been arrested and charged with illegal possession of drugs – not his trademark LSD, ironically, but mari-juana – and was also facing accusations from ultra-left political groups that his proselytising of psychedelic drugs proved that he was an agent of the CIA, working to distract global youth from revolutionary responsibility. Leary was linked with the Brotherhood of Eternal Love, a quasi-spiritual group based in California, which was responsible for distributing huge quantities of a revised form of LSD known as 'orange sunshine' – blamed by some historians of chemical stimulants for the Manson and Altamont fiascos later in the year, and by others for 'the demise of the New Left', no less, because it 'heightened the metabolism of the body politic and accelerated all the changes going on'.

'The Progressive Labor Party (PLP), a Maoist "old left" group, goes so far as to claim that Leary is a CIA agent,' recorded another sceptic, Mark Riebling. 'But', he added, 'the PLP is accusing everyone it disagrees with of being CIA.' With peace activists on the opposite side of the barricades to anti-war protestors, the underground's favourite scientist accused of treason, the very nature of revolution up for grabs, it was perhaps not surprising that the New Left was on the verge of fatal collapse, in which the PLP would play the assassin's role.

## WEATHER REPORTS

The Yippies may have dominated the theatre of radical politics in the late 1960s, but their exaggerated gestures and celebrity liaisons were largely a spent force after Chicago. For everyday campaigning, the movement depended on the less glamorous but much more substantial support of Students for a Democratic Society. It was SDS that had united the single-issue campaigns dominating counter-culture politics, from the Freedom Marches and voter registration drives to the draft card burnings and Moratoriums of the anti-Vietnam War crusade. But SDS had always defined itself by what it was against rather than what it stood for. There were so many possible interpre-tations of what might constitute a 'Democratic Society', so many pitfalls to negotiate, that SDS was in constant danger of disintegration, if it ever allowed internal policy differences to overshadow its shared disgust for American racism, imperialism, warmongering and capitalism.

As the 1960s progressed, and the dream (or fantasy) of revolution seemed more tangible, so the temptation arose for factions within SDS to carve out prime slices of post-revolutionary territory. That a revolution was now within reach, few doubted; but its nature, purpose and meaning were open to dispute. Within a year, this crippling debate would (literally) decimate SDS. Despite its active membership of around 100,000, and the tacit support of several million young people, SDS imploded during the final months of the 1960s. By the time the decade was over, it had diminished from a mass movement into a tiny splinter group that would eventually outpace the Yippies in both notoriety and theatricality. The psychology of political idealism entails that the more fervent an organisation is, the more quickly it will split into two even more fanatical factions. The death of SDS, and of the American counter-culture as a unified political force, illustrated this principle with grim perfection.

While most of its rank-and-file members supported SDS on grounds of conscience and revolutionary optimism, the PLP – or Progressive Labor (PL), as the group preferred to be known by 1969 – saw this decision as a recruiting ground for its own divisive Maoist philosophy. PL's position was that no revolution was possible unless it was led, in classic Marxian fashion, by the industrial working-class of America. Any attempt to found a revolutionary movement around the subversive potential of either militant students, or black liberation groups, was anti-Marxist, and therefore doomed to failure. PL might have been able to quote scripture from the gospels of Marx, Engels, Lenin and Mao to support their position, but their rejection of any leadership role for either students or African-Americans threatened to rob SDS of two of its major power bases.

Over a succession of bewildering conferences, different factions within SDS briefly seized control of the agenda, only to be defeated a few months later. While the war raged and the revolution stalled, the students kept debating, and disagreeing. Typically, they employed the vocabulary of rock'n'roll as their shared language; for example, one key position paper borrowed its title from two emblematic hits of the mid-60s, the Lovin' Spoonful's urban romance 'Summer in the City', and Bob Dylan's dystopian fable, 'Maggie's Farm'. (The full title was: 'Hot Town: Summer in the City or I Ain't Gonna Work on Maggie's Farm No More'.) The two lyrics went unexplained in the position paper, but offered a clearer philosophical statement than any finely argued political manifesto.

And so SDS lurched towards its June 1969 national conference, staged –
almost inevitably – in Chicago. On 18 June, the day the conference opened,
the journal *New Left Notes*, home of many an obscure discussion about tactics
and beliefs, published a 16,000-word statement by Bill Ayers, Jim Mellen
and a dozen comrades. One of the most significant, though least-read, political diatribes of the decade, it was titled 'You Don't Need a Weatherman to
Know Which Way the Wind Blows'. It was another borrowed line, of course,
one of many eminently quotable lines from Bob Dylan's 1965 recording,
'Subterranean Homesick Blues'. Translated into English, it means, quite obviously, that some things are so obvious that they don't need to be said. The
activists might just as easily have called their statement 'The Pumps Don't
Work Cos the Vandals Took the Handles', or 'Twenty Years of Schooling
and They Put You on the Dayshift', or any of a dozen equally memorable
slices of Dylan wisdom. It was just another affirmation of shared culture,
and proof that even after *Nashville Skyline*, Dylan's primacy as a movement
icon remained unchallenged.

Passionately written though it was, 'You Don't Need a Weatherman' was
also flawed by muddled thinking and over-reaching ambition. Its rhetoric
was hardly likely to spark a stampede to the barricades: 'We must be a revolutionary movement of people understanding the necessity to reach more
people, all working people, as we make the revolution.' You can rearrange
the words in that sentence in any order, and its sense would be effectively
unchanged. But the paper did contain some crucial imagery. To overthrow
the establishment would require revolutionaries to fight, as Huey Newton
would say, by any means necessary: 'A revolution is a war; when the Movement
in this country can defend itself militarily against total repression it will be
part of the revolutionary war.' The key word in that sentence is 'militarily'.
The promoters of the Weatherman paper were insisting that white students
must now be prepared to engage in the revolutionary violence that militant
African-American organisations had already assumed was inevitable.

The 2,000 delegates who assembled at the Chicago Coliseum – home of
the previous year's Yippie Anti-Birthday Party for President Lyndon Johnson
– were allowed little opportunity to dwell on the ramifications of Weatherman.
Their attention was stolen, and many of their stomachs turned, by the
internecine squabbling that dominated the conference. No subject, it seemed,
could provoke a show of unity: whether it was women's liberation, the plight
of Vietnamese civilians under American bombardment, or the imminent

arrival of the workers' state, every topic became a jousting field. Black Panther delegates were booed when they denigrated women; PL members were accused of racism for denying the Panthers' vanguard role in the struggle.

As the conference dissolved into chaos, a motion was proposed demanding that PL members should be expelled from SDS. Before the vote could be taken, two of the most vociferous and charismatic signatories to the Weatherman statement, Bernardine Dohrn and Mark Rudd, suggested that all of those who disagreed with PL's position should follow them into an adjoining hall. Around half the delegates followed, to hear Dohrn deliver a mesmerising speech, at the end of which she declared that the people in that room were now the SDS, and that the PL supporters they had left behind had voted themselves out of the organisation by default.

SDS was now under the control of the Weatherman cabal. Their aim was to strike a high-profile blow against the American government: a demonstration of defiance that would provoke the people to rise up against their masters. Prompted by the looming anniversary of the Chicago convention, and the impending trial of the so-called 'Chicago 8' conspirators, Weatherman proposed that the city should play host to another disturbance. Leaflets were soon circulating around the counter-culture: 'It has been almost a year since the Democratic Convention, when thousands of young people came together in Chicago and tore up pig city for five days. The action was a response to the crisis this system is facing as a result of the war, the demand by black people for liberation, and the ever-growing reality that this system just can't make it. This fall, people are coming back to Chicago: more powerful, better organised, and more together than we were last August. SDS is calling for a National Action in Chicago October 8–11. We are coming back to Chicago, and we are going to bring those we left behind last year.' It was a stirring call, but it didn't reflect another 'ever-growing reality': the movement, as a unified voice of dissent, was in the process of fragmentation.

## DISUNITED FRONT

Four weeks after the SDS split in Chicago, the Black Panthers sponsored a conference on their home turf of Oakland. Their aim was to form a United Front Against Fascism. Chairman Bobby Seale defined it as 'an American Liberation Front composed of all the people of this nation, to combat the avaricious businessman, the demagogic politician and the fascist pig cops who murder, brutalise and terrorise the people'. He envisaged black and white activists working together to scrutinise illegal police actions and free revolutionary prisoners. Huey Newton supported the project from prison; Tom Hayden, the most prominent of the decade's SDS leaders, also lent his support.

Delegates came to Oakland from a variety of groups across the nation, reflecting the increasingly multi-cultural nature of modern American society. From the Bible Belt of the Deep South came the Young Patriots, a revolutionary force of white kids. New York sent the Young Lords, a Puerto Rican street gang who had been politicised by Eldridge Cleaver's book *Soul On Ice*. They had shifted from petty crime and street battles with their rivals to emulating the Panthers with free clinics, a breakfast programme, and protests against police harassment. The Young Lords were part of a phenomenon that had been dubbed 'Brown Power': an upsurge of militant nationalist consciousness among the nation's Hispanic youth. The Brown Berets and the Mission Rebels had emerged from San Francisco; the Mexican American Youth Organisation from South Texas; and Los Lobos, a militant street gang, from San Jose.[4] Almost every poverty-stricken community in America, from the Appalachians to the Mexican border, now boasted its own liberation force, with goals ranging from equal pay to violent revolution.

Sadly, Oakland saw a replay in miniature of the divisions that had surfaced in Chicago. There were fistfights between rival leftists; Panther members refused to take orders or direction from white activists; and violent disputes arose between current Black Panthers and ex-members who had been purged for offences against the party line. By the end of July, Panthers leaders Bobby Seale and David Hilliard were openly referring to their white revolutionary comrades as 'pigs' and 'sissies'. And with that, the United Front Against Fascism collapsed.

Solidarity was hard to find that summer, even within the black liberation movement. There was positive news from Chicago, where former gang member turned black power activist Fred Hampton announced a truce between the city's two most feared street gangs, the Blackstone Rangers and the Black Disciples. 'Now we are all one army,' Hampton declared, and proved the point by joining the Black Panther Party. But the BPP itself was struggling to retain its focus. The FBI's campaign of harassment was now disrupting the distribution of the Black Panther newspaper; copies were mysteriously vanishing on cargo flights, or being destroyed as soon as they were unloaded. FBI Director J. Edgar Hoover declared that the BPP 'without question represents the greatest threat to the internal security of the country'. Under his encouragement, FBI members persistently raided local Panther offices on spurious charges, accusing activists of harbouring non-existent criminals, distributing drugs, or possessing explosives. The vast majority of these cases were subsequently dropped without publicity, leaving the public with the impression that the Black Panther Party and illegality went hand in hand.

Not that violence was ever far from the Panthers' door. In May 1969, Connecticut BPP member Alex Rackley was savagely tortured and then murdered by several fellow Panthers, who believed he was an FBI informer. Among those charged with the crime was Bobby Seale, whose successful struggle to defend himself monopolised his attention over the next two years. The feud between the BPP and US broke out again in California, with a series of killings over the summer. One of the Panthers' local officers in Detroit was shot dead during a protracted battle for local power. Prominent figures from California had to intervene to close the Detroit chapter down. There were regular shoot-outs between police and Panthers in Chicago, and a fatal confrontation in Santa Ana, California.

With Seale under suspicion of murder, Newton in prison, and Eldridge Cleaver in exile, the BPP leadership was now in disarray. Cleaver's stay in Cuba having been cut short, he moved to Algeria, where the socialist government offered him asylum. There he planned the formation of the North American Liberation Front, 'which will include the revolutionary forces in every country'. Its aims were certainly far-reaching: Cleaver declared that 'we have to fight a revolutionary struggle for the violent overthrow of the United States government, and the total destruction of the racist, capitalist, imperialist, neo-colonialist power structure'. At the same time, Cleaver mused that 'the more I think about my future plans, the more I consider the possibility that my life will not be very long . . . I plan to shed my blood and to put my life on the line and to seek to take the lives of the pigs of the power structure in Babylon.' By 1972, he dreamed, the USA would be engulfed in civil war, the military would take control, and the next presidential election would be cancelled. If he survived that long, Cleaver would be leading a liberation army down from the hills. But how much of this was a stoned fantasy? 'I'm a fat mouth and a fool, you know?' Cleaver confessed to a visiting journalist. 'I talk too much . . . I like to get high.'

In late July 1969, black power came to Cleaver, as Algiers hosted the twelve-day Pan-African Cultural Festival. Cleaver and other Panthers leaders spoke during the conference, but were criticised by delegates from other nations for encouraging a cult of personality to build up around them. Though Cleaver clearly imagined himself the most important figure there, the festival attracted delegations from no fewer than thirty-one independent African states, plus allies such as the Palestine Liberation Organisation (PLO). Artists, musicians and writers from the global black community also attended. There was Nina Simone, searching for a home after losing faith in the black liberation struggle in the US; the exiled South African singer Miriam Makeba; and her husband, Stokely Carmichael. From their new home in Guinea, he had recently resigned his membership of the BPP, alleging that he and his family had been the subject of death threats from party activists. He warned the Panthers against putting their trust in white radicals, as they had (briefly) done in Oakland; in particular, he said it was a 'fundamental error' to allow whites to categorise the Panthers as 'the revolutionary vanguard'. He was now convinced that the worldwide African 'nation' had to unite to overthrow the slave-traders of America and Europe. There was no such co-operation between Cleaver and Carmichael, however: the two men, rival superstars in exile, traded jibes throughout the conference.

## CONTINENTAL DRIFT

For visiting Americans who felt restrained by the close attentions of the FBI at home, independent Africa glistened welcomingly like paradise. Walking down streets where dashikis were everyday garb, US black nationalists felt as if they had finally returned to their native land. But the so-called 'dark continent' hid injustice and oppression of its own. Few of the newly independent nations could boast a flourishing democracy; indeed, many struggled under totalitarian rule. In Algeria, for example, President Boumedienne had dissolved parliament in 1965, and tolerated no 'indiscipline' or criticism of his single-party rule. In Stokely Carmichael and Miriam Makeba's adopted home of Guinea, leader Sekou Toure faced a succession of coup attempts, some imaginary, some all too real; again, open political debate was illegal. In Tanzania, where President Nyerere (the self-styled Mwalimu, or teacher of the nation) had imposed one-party rule in 1964, all American soul music was banned from the airwaves in 1969, on the grounds that it was both subversive and anti-African. And in the Congo, soon to become Zaire after President Mobutu visited communist China and returned home enamoured of the concept of cultural revolution, leading musician Tabu Ley faced government sanctions after recording songs interpreted as lending support to the illegal opposition.

These repressive measures paled alongside the protracted agony now afflicting Nigeria. The civil war had decayed into a military stalemate, with Federal forces blockading the rebel Biafrans into a shrinking homeland. General Gowan, leader of Nigeria since the last military coup, now had one simple battle plan: wait for the Biafrans to succumb to famine. To the increasing horror of the watching world, tens of thousands were suffering this fate every month.

Alongside this virtual genocide of the Ibo people, Nigeria's musical culture was both powerless and irrelevant. Most of the nation's leading bands broke up during the tribal dispersion that followed the outbreak of the civil war; the highlife scene never recovered from the loss of so many Ibo musicians. Record company offices, such as the local branch of EMI Records, were ransacked, and their employees were killed if they happened to represent a different tribe to the invading army.

In 1969, bandleader Fela Kuti – a member of the dominant Yoruba tribe – followed the Federal government's ideology by recording a single entitled 'Viva Nigeria', the message of which was 'Keep Nigeria one'. Despite his tribe's opposition to the Ibos, however, Kuti felt sympathetic to the Biafran rebels. 'I was not political at the time we had the Biafran war,' he explained later, 'but I believed [Biafran leader] Ojukwu was right ... Ibos were being slaughtered all over Nigeria.' Saddened by the plight of his country, Kuti led his band, Koola Lobitos, to the USA in June 1969. On the flight, he met Miriam Makeba, who gave Kuti the name of her booking agent. Kuti's bass guitarist, Felix Jones, skipped the band's opening showcase in New York, as he was an Ibo and feared deportation and the certain death it would bring. But Kuti soon discovered a more basic problem: despite Koola Lobitos's reputation as one of Nigeria's most popular bands, delivering a rousing mix of American-style R&B, highlife and vibrant jazz, bookings were almost impossible to obtain.

Kuti was no stranger to struggle: he had survived several years in London in the late 1950s and early 1960s, and had been singled out for government harassment in Nigeria from the mid-1960s, for his unconventional political views and espousal of 'igbo', the local equivalent of grass. He was anything but a conformist: when the Nigerian highlife scene became dominated by the proto-funk innovations of James Brown, Kuti was one of the last band-leaders to insist on maintaining purely African rhythms. Now, however, he followed the trail of America's white settlers, and moved west in search of work. When the band arrived in Los Angeles, they secured a booking at an NAACP civil rights benefit at the Ambassador Hotel. It didn't earn them a cent, but Kuti hoped that the publicity might win them other work. Instead, he met someone who would change his life.

After Koola Lobitos had performed, Kuti began speaking to a black American woman, Sandra Smith. 'Fela was singing in Yoruba,' she recalled. 'You couldn't understand anything he was saying, but the music was getting better and better. He was getting deeper into his African roots. But when I asked him what he was saying [in his songs], he said he was talking about what he likes in his soup! And I was saying, "No, you need to sing some conscious lyrics. You can pass a message in the music."'

Smith was not only a perceptive student of anthropology, and a budding singer, but a member of the Black Panther Party. 'Sandra gave me the education I wanted to know,' Kuti remembered. 'She talked to me about politics, history, about Africa.' Smith forced Kuti to read black nationalist histories of his continent, the jazz-inspired poems of Nikki Giovanni, Eldridge Cleaver's *Soul On Ice*, Malcolm X's autobiography – total immersion in the culture and ideology of black power. She also widened his musical horizons, playing him Miles Davis, Nina Simone, the latest funk releases, anything that would harden his pride in his race and his potential.

'It was incredible how my head was turned,' Kuti admitted more than a decade later. 'Everything fell into place. For the first time, I saw the essence of blackism. It's crazy: in the States, people think the black power movement drew inspiration from Africa. All these Americans came [to Africa] looking for awareness, but they don't realise they're the ones who've got it over there. We were even ashamed to go around in national dress until we saw pictures of blacks wearing dashikis on 125th Street.' Kuti was embarrassed by his lack of awareness of nationalist philosophy. 'I remember him telling me how Africans are so stupid,' Smith said.

The effect on Kuti's music was immediate. Soon after meeting Smith, he led his band into a residency at the Citadel D'Haiti in Hollywood. He renamed his ensemble Nigeria 70 (this became Africa 70 when he returned home) and began to compose material that was self-consciously African. Songs such as 'My Lady's Frustration' and 'Black Man's Pride' signalled another change.

Rather than Yoruba or the correct English favoured by most sophisticated Nigerian performers, Kuti began to write in a form of 'broken English'. As his compatriots spoke several hundred different African languages and dialects, this enabled the whole country to catch the gist of his message, and allowed him to widen his appeal beyond West Africa. By the time he returned to Nigeria, two months after the civil war ended in surrender by the Biafrans, he was able to channel his growing political resentment into exuberant, defiantly African dance music.

Among the poems that Kuti read in Nikki Giovanni's first verse collection, *Black Feeling Black Talk/Black Judgement*, was 'Revolutionary Music'. It sang the praises of America's most potent soul talent of 1969 – the multi-racial, funk-rock ensemble Sly & the Family Stone, whose music preached a colour-blind world, via songs such as the hit single 'Everyday People', and the more provocative 'Don't Call Me Nigger, Whitey (Don't Call Me Whitey, Nigger)'. As Giovanni wrote, 'you've just got to dig sly and the family stone damn the words'. Similarly, she excused the liberal leanings of James Brown and the Impressions – never mind the message, *feel* the message – and concluded 'we be digging all revolutionary music consciously or un, cause sam cooke said "a change is gonna come"'. In another piece, 'For Saundra', Giovanni admitted: 'i wanted to write a poem that rhymes but revolution doesn't lend itself to be be-bopping (...) so i thought again and it occurred to me maybe i shouldn't write at all but clean my gun and check my kerosene supply'. Then there was a pause, before she concluded: 'perhaps these are not poetic times at all'.

## SEIZE THE TIME

That wasn't a sentiment with which Elaine Brown would have agreed. Her journey from Los Angeles coffeehouses to the leadership of the unashamedly macho Black Panther Party was one of the more remarkable transformations of this quicksilver age. Raised in North Philadelphia, she moved to California in the mid-1960s, waited table for film stars and casino owners in Hollywood, and was introduced to the concept of socialism. By 1967, she had joined the Black Congress community organisation, and was writing 'poetry and freedom songs', which she performed at the House of Respect, formerly known as the Watts Writers Workshop. She flirted with Ron Karenga's US, before opting to join the Black Panthers after meeting Bunchy Carter – one of the BPP members murdered by US in 1969 – and Eldridge

Cleaver. At Bunchy's funeral, she delivered a powerful rendition of the spiritual tune 'Precious Lord Lead Me Home'.

When the Panthers' Chief of Staff, David Hilliard, heard her sing, he decided that her talent was a useful asset for the party. Brown performed several of her newly written freedom anthems for a roomful of activists: 'Assassination', 'The Panther', and 'The Meeting', which had been inspired by her first encounter with Cleaver. 'David cried,' she recalled, 'and ordained that the one for Eldridge became the Black Panther National Anthem. He had cassettes of it duplicated and distributed, and ordered all party members to learn it.' As Brown conceded, 'it was a strange song for an anthem'. Poignant rather than rousing, it described how Cleaver's words had fired her imagination. Her lyrics conjured up a spirit of romance, rather than political indoctrination: 'And we sat and talked about freedom and things, and he told me about what he dreamed, but I knew of that dream, long before he had spoken, and a feeling familiarly came through.'

Her first public performance of the National Anthem was in early April 1969, when Panthers members gathered in the newly renamed Bobby Hutton Park in Oakland, to commemorate the anniversary of the BPP martyr's death. A week later, Brown's name appeared way down the bill of a benefit concert for the John Huggins/Bunchy Carter Hot Breakfast Free Clinic Fund – a Panthers' fundraiser, in other words – at the Trade-Tech Auditorium. Phil Ochs was the prime musical attraction, alongside a rare appearance by Bobby Seale as a jazz drummer with the First Quintette of Uglam. The event received scanty coverage in the mainstream press, and then only because Panthers activist Masai Hewitt promised that the party intended 'to do something about this fucked-up, chickenshit, one-sided capitalist system'. Hewitt and Brown became lovers a few weeks later.

Her profile was raised in late April, when the Black Panther newspaper printed the words of her National Anthem. On 1 May 1969, Brown – now the Communications Secretary of the Panthers' Southern California chapter – performed the song again outside the Los Angeles Federal Building, at a rally to protest against the continued imprisonment of Huey Newton. She cut a slightly incongruous figure, singing into a megaphone, clad in the leather jacket that had become unofficial Panthers uniform, but with her handbag draped over her elbow like a housewife at the store.

Equally unsettling were the juxtapositions in her own life: police harassment and shoot-outs on the streets of Los Angeles, alternating with recording sessions for her first album. Hilliard envisaged the record as a means of furthering the Panthers' cause; San Francisco-based Vault Records grasped the commercial potential of music that was becoming compulsory listening for party members.

Vault arranged for Brown to work with jazz pianist, arranger and band-leader Horace Tapscott. A local legend in Los Angeles, Tapscott worked with a co-operative orchestra – the Union of God's Musicians and Artists Ascension – instead of a more conventional touring unit. By 1969, the Union had been revamped as the Pan-Afrikan People's Arkestra, to reflect his cultural nationalist philosophy. That April, he recorded an album, *The Giant is Awakened*, which channelled his political beliefs into music that extended the rhythmic and harmonic experiments of Thelonious Monk.

The encounter between his nationalism and Brown's socialism resulted in a perversely mellow set of arrangements, closer to supper-club jazz than the avant-garde. When the mainstream, and determinedly apolitical, jazz maga-zine *Down Beat* reviewed Brown's album, they noted that despite its Panther associations, it 'is far less controversial than much of what has appeared on establishment labels in recent times. Miss Brown possesses a pleasant, Edith Piafish voice, and her songs (she wrote them all) are proudly delivered hymns to the black man. If there is a message here, it is not one of hate.'

The mellifluous nature of *Seize the Time* – a title subsequently borrowed by Bobby Seale for his chronicle of Newton and the Panthers – did not dissuade the party from hyping Brown's record as a 'Revolutionary Record'. The Black Panther newspaper claimed that they 'are the first songs of the American Revolution', and that Brown – now promoted to become the BPP's Deputy Minister of Information, behind the exiled Cleaver – was 'first and foremost a revolutionary'. Emory Douglas, the party's chief artist, sketched the cover, on which the central image was not Brown but a gun. To ensure that nobody missed the point, the singer was billed as 'Elaine Brown, Black Panther Party'. 'She has tapped the feelings of the Black Panther Party,' the newspaper declared, 'and is inviting the people to enjoy and learn.' All proceeds from the record were directed to the Party's free breakfast programme. But *Seize the Time* sold poorly: its tame production alienated those in search of radical jazz or funk, while the spectre of the Black Panther Party ensured that it received little media exposure.

*Seize the Time* displayed no musical evidence of its origins as Panther propa-ganda, and Brown's lyrics didn't reflect the anger that fuelled the party.

Ironically, the Panthers' deadly rivals in the black liberation movement, Ron Karenga's US organisation, outflanked them with the almost simultaneous release of a record boasting some of the most fêted young talents on the jazz scene. The catalyst was James Mtume, a US member since 1966, who was the son of saxophonist Jimmy Heath and the nephew of drummer Albert Heath. During 1968, Mtume became the philosophical mentor of the sextet run by renowned keyboardist Herbie Hancock, who had recently left Miles Davis' band. Mtume preached the virtues of Karenga and his Afrocentric philosophy so vividly that Hancock and his cohorts agreed to record an album to promote US.

In the spirit of the US leader's metamorphosis from Ron Everett to Maulana Karenga, the musicians adopted Swahili names for the project, chosen for them by Mtume. This enabled Hancock to sidestep his exclusive recording deals with Blue Note and then Warner Brothers. His last Blue Note project, *The Prisoner*, was a tribute to Martin Luther King, recorded just after the first anniversary of his death. Hancock then launched his Warners contract with a soundtrack album for a Bill Cosby TV show – an entirely frivolous exercise alongside the record that Mtume was planning.

The US album, entitled *Kawaida*, opened with the gospel-jazz fusion of 'Baraka', clearly inspired by Karenga's ally, Amiri Baraka. Another piece paid tribute to Maulana himself; a third to Mtume's wife, Kamili. But the centre-piece was the title track, an ambitious and schematic work dedicated to explaining the principles of Karenga's teaching. Each of the musicians in turn recited extracts from the leader's writings, while the entire ensemble added Swahili chanting and eerie instrumental support on wooden flutes. The record eventually appeared on the US-run O'be label, credited to Kuumba (Albert Heath's pseudonym). The other musicians were listed as Mwandishi (Hancock), Tayari (Jimmy Heath), Fundi (Billy Bonner), Mganga (Eddie Henderson) and Mchezaji (Buster Williams). The result was more successful as propaganda than as contemporary jazz music, but the project clearly left its mark on the participants. Having completed his work for Bill Cosby, Hancock recorded an album called *Mwandishi* for Warner Brothers, and he and his bandmates retained their Swahili names for three further albums of experimental electronic jazz, featuring some of the most adventurous music of Hancock's career.

Whether or not they were tied to a specific revolutionary party, Afrocentrism and nationalism were key motifs on the contemporary jazz scene in 1969. That was the year when Archie Shepp's (white) bassist, Charlie Haden, formed his Liberation Music Orchestra, which would bear ecstatic fruit in 1970; Cal Massey penned his 'Huey Newton Suite' and 'Black Liberation Suite', which he performed with his Romos Orchestra but sadly never recorded; and pianist McCoy Tyner prepared the music for his African-inspired Blue Note album, *Extensions*. Yet none of this music came close to matching the cultural and musical impact of Miles Davis' pioneering fusion of jazz and rock, signalled by the recording of *In a Silent Way* in February 1969 and *Bitches Brew* that August. This churning, propulsive, unforgiving music, which evolved almost organically from the interaction of the players, was delivered by Davis with no overt political message, beyond the fact that his interviews were full of accusations about racism in the music business. Perhaps Davis was evading his responsibilities by refusing to comment on the need for revolution; perhaps he had already imagined that his contribution to the struggle might prove to be more enduring than those of Karenga or the Black Panthers.

## ACROSS THE BORDERLINE

In 1969, countless American hippies drifted across the border into Mexico, in search of cheap drugs and freedom from responsibility. Apparently unaware of the Mexican government's dislike of social dissidence, let alone the previous year's massacre of students, they were arrested in droves, either for drug possession or offences under the vague heading of 'immorality', and sent home. Their careless adventures did nothing to encourage a more liberal policy towards Mexico's own dissidents. Not only was political opposition repressed, but hippies (known locally as jipis or jipitecas) were condemned for their 'feminine' appearance. Many media commentators noted that they would prefer to see a respectable outbreak of rebellious machismo, which would at least have been in the great Mexican tradition of revolution, instead of the 'homosexual' antics of the long-haired, flower-wearing hippies.

Into this unsettled climate, in June 1969, came those icons of American hippie culture: the Doors. In keeping with their status as gurus of the youth revolution, the band were originally scheduled to perform in front of a mass audience, at the Plaza de Mexico bullring. Instead, they found themselves performing at the Forum. 'It was a small supper-club for rich kids,' recalls Louise Cripps, a teenage student who attended one of the shows. 'It was a totally incongruous place to find the Doors.' There was apparently some disquiet on the opening night, when the audience failed to recognise the portly and bearded Jim Morrison, who introduced himself on stage as 'Fidel Castro'. It was a weak attempt at subversion, no more convincing than Morrison's political rhetoric.

At almost exactly the same moment, another California rock band, the Beach Boys, were on tour in Czechoslovakia. The Beach Boys had flirted with political activism in recent times, in the person of youngest member Carl Wilson, who had refused to accept being drafted into the US Army on the grounds that he was a pacifist. A lengthy legal dispute followed, of the kind only open to those who could afford a top-flight lawyer, and Wilson was eventually allowed to perform community service instead of fighting in Vietnam. His stance was anything but revolutionary, however. Asked about the morality of performing in South Africa under the auspices of the racist apartheid government, Wilson replied weakly that the Beach Boys were 'apolitical' – scant comfort to the country's beleaguered majority population.

With their visit to Czechoslovakia, the band became one of the first Western acts to perform behind the Iron Curtain since the crushing of the Prague Spring initiative. 'That was the epitome of the event transcending the music,' remembered vocalist Mike Love. 'The reception was probably the most unbelievable we ever got anywhere.' As Bruce Johnston recalled, 'The city was still occupied, so we didn't know what to expect. But to our amazement the kids were out in the streets, asking for our autographs. They wanted to know about America, the latest records, and rock'n'roll.' When the Beach Boys took part in the Bratislava Song Festival, they discovered that musical dissidence hadn't been entirely crushed. 'The local Czechoslovakian groups were singing protest songs,' Johnston reported. 'The Russians blanked these parts out of the televised part of the show.' The group's most provocative action was dedicating their latest single, 'Break Away', to ousted leader Alexander Dubček, who attended their show in Prague. This gesture was warmly received, but the Beach Boys' visit did nothing more to shake the social order than the Doors had achieved in Mexico.

Brazilian tropicalismo singers Caetano Veloso and Gilberto Gil had dreamed that their music, and its playful social satire, might undermine the authority of their country's military junta. That fantasy had been dissolved by their arrest in late December 1968. Even then, the musicians' naivety was remarkable: while thousands of Brazilian dissidents were being routinely tortured, Veloso still 'imagined they [would take] me to talk to some officer in São Paulo, who would treat us like average young guys who were interested only in amusing the public'. Veloso and Gil were fortunate: perhaps because they had begun to attract an international reputation, they were not handled with the same brutality meted out to other prisoners. But they were subjected to weeks of intensive interrogation, before being kept under house arrest. In high summer, Veloso and Gil were exiled from Brazil: they flew to Portugal, and then separated, Veloso camping out in London, Gil in Paris. Though they continued their careers, they were cut off from their native audience, who weren't able to hear their latest work.

Even in countries where voices of opposition could be raised without fear of reprisal, it was hard to calculate the value of a musical gesture. The best-selling record in Britain during July 1969 was 'Something in the Air', the debut single by Thunderclap Newman. The song, composed by Speedy Keen, took a languorous, ambiguous stance on political rebellion. 'We got to get together sooner or later,' Keen sang in a fragile tenor, 'because the revolution's here, and you know it's right'. In one verse, he advised his listeners to 'lock up the streets and houses', as if the upheaval might threaten property values; in the next, he was telling them to 'hand out the guns and ammo', because 'we're going to blast our way through here', as if they were the revolutionaries after all. Perhaps it didn't matter: the stoned elegance of the record spoke more clearly than words, and the revolution was merely the backdrop for a portrait of decadence and decay.

This ambivalent stance was shared by the Edgar Broughton Band, whose anarchistic approach to hard rock won them a cult reputation on the British underground in 1969. The Broughtons kindled their appeal by judicious use of the word 'revolution', and their PR agency issued posters featuring their photograph in the style of the Old West: 'Wanted: The Broughton Band, for plotting subversive acts involving treason, arson and corruption'. The precise nature of their treason was difficult to quantify, as they admitted that their lyrics were not intended to be subversive, though they did satirise US militarism in the extended canvas of 'American Boy Soldier'. Their rebelliousness often extended no further than talk. 'If we sell as many records as they would like us too, and if we sell as many as we want to,' noted guitarist Steve Broughton in June 1969, 'eventually we're going to turn people on to burning EMI [their record company] down.' The unthreatening nature of Edgar Broughton's political rhetoric was apparent when he described

EMI subsidiary Harvest Records as 'a product of the revolution . . . the revolution is always people and people buy a thing because it's their voice'. Pressed further, he conceded that for him, revolution was not a political process but an attitude of mind – hence the reference to a 'head revolution', in the tradition of John Lennon's plea for his hip listeners to 'free your mind instead'.

The Edgar Broughton Band did at least support political campaigns, from trade union strikes to squatters. When they handed over money they'd raised to the London Street Commune, who had taken over empty premises on Piccadilly in the name of the people, they were hailed as leaders, and appointed to the Commune's co-ordinating committee. Edgar appeared slightly embarrassed by the attention: 'I don't think I could possibly lead a revolution in the physical sense,' he conceded. 'It's not that I'm afraid of getting killed or anything like that, but the revolution must come from the people themselves.' Or, as he dreamed on another occasion: 'Where there is dissatisfaction and dissension, let the musical population in the street be the force of subversion.'

Their most effective contribution to the counter-culture – besides, perhaps, recording the hypnotic chant 'Out Demons Out' – was their championing of free concerts. Such events had become familiar on the San Francisco rock scene, usually acting as benefits for radical causes, from street clinics to Black Panther Party defence funds. But the Broughtons pioneered the free concert as an end in itself, undermining the rock industry by the simple step of removing money from the relationship that separated musicians from their audience. It was David Peel's street theatre writ large – and nowhere larger than in London's Hyde Park, where several free concerts were staged during the late 1960s and early 1970s. The first, a 1968 event featuring Mick Farren and the Deviants, was unpublicised and spontaneous, but it was followed soon afterwards by larger events starring Pink Floyd, Traffic, Fleetwood Mac and the Move. The impetus for the concert series came from management agency Blackhill Enterprises, who handled many of Britain's top underground acts – including, from early 1969, the Edgar Broughton Band. Their first Hyde Park appearance came in June 1969, when they joined the supporting cast for the only British concert by newly formed 'supergroup' Blind Faith. There was some irony in this: Blind Faith, featuring ex-members of Cream, Traffic and Family, had been heavily hyped by their record label, and the free show won them intensive publicity in the rock and mainstream press.

All of this, from Hyde Park to the Broughtons' local free shows, was just a curtain-raiser to the first of two major rock events in Britain that summer. On 5 July 1969, the Rolling Stones topped the bill in the park, two days after the sudden death of their recently sacked guitarist, Brian Jones. The Stones' appearance was pitched somewhere between a wake and a generational celebration – a symbol that the children of the rock age were claiming the past decade as their own. Clad in a white frock, unintelligibly drawling a Shelley poem as a tribute to his former colleague, Mick Jagger was nobody's idea of a revolutionary leader. He was routinely quizzed about radical issues when the Hyde Park show was first announced, laying down his views about the crisis of the Black Power movement ('It's very hard, really, because as soon as a leader comes along, he gets killed') and suggesting that 'they should just walk into South Africa and take over and forget about America'. 'They're trying to give the Negroes some pride in themselves,' added guitarist Keith Richards helpfully. 'That's the first stage. That's why they're coming on too strong with all this "kill, fight, kill" stage.'

Jagger was more eloquent when asked to reminisce about his brief incarnation as a demonstrator in Grosvenor Square: 'I enjoyed it! That kind of violence gives me a really nice buzz.' As he examined his motives more deeply, he uncovered the links between his exhilaration during the anti-Vietnam march, and his behaviour on stage: 'You can express violence in the same way that you are expressing something when you show off. It's that sort of buzz . . . It's the same feeling of exhibitionism or having a fling, everyone wants to get up and do something, and if you put something in common for people to kick against . . .' He trailed off, recalling what he was supposed to be promoting: 'That's why there's been no trouble at Hyde Park free concerts. There was nothing for anyone to kick against. No money changed hands, no barriers, so no trouble.' He sounded almost regretful. His comments pointed towards two contradictory positions: gatherings such as Hyde Park proved nothing, confronted nobody and advanced the revolution not a jot. But, at the same moment, by removing the profit motive from the entertainment equation, the Hyde Park shows also appeared to dissolve angst and antagonism at a stroke. It was a conclusion that he would test to the limit later in the year.

Meanwhile, the Stones filled Hyde Park with revellers, there was no hint of violence, and everyone departed with their morale boosted and equilibrium maintained. Several hundred thousand people, including all four Beatles, had gathered in one place, shared the sacrament, and moved on. But for anyone observing the scene closely, there were unsettling undercurrents. Was there not something patronising about the moment when the band were joined on stage by a group of African musicians? One anonymous reviewer thought so: '1969 is the year that the street fighting man meets black power, so a black drumming combo emerged from the wings, one in full jungle regalia, war painted and performing religiously to camera, like a hand-picked extra from *Sanders of the River.*' Was it meant to signify the Stones' primeval roots, or their empathy with Africa, or was it simply an exhibition of radical chic – a way of saying, look, we're down with the Negroes too? And if so, where did that leave Jagger's relationship with the African-American singer Marsha Hunt? The fact that, soon after Hyde Park, Jagger penned the Stones' anthem 'Brown Sugar', a lascivious celebration of sexual clichés associated with slavery, suggested that his view of blackness might not be entirely free of stereotypes.

But perhaps the Stones were merely reflecting their milieu, after all. The rock community was sufficiently self-aware by 1969 to avoid overt displays of racism. After all, most of the leading white bands were now prepared to perform alongside black musicians, feeling – as did the Beatles when they added R&B keyboardist Billy Preston for their January 1969 sessions – that these exotic creatures could add a freshness to their own increasingly stale sound. But sexual politics was still virgin territory for the rock aristocracy. An incident in the large 'press' enclosure in front of the Stones' stage in Hyde Park was typical. Besides the mainstream and underground media, the VIP pen held sundry rock stars and their consorts, and an indeterminate number of those who had talked or flirted their way into this prime viewing position. When the area became overcrowded, concert promoter Sam Cutler made a decision. 'There isn't room for everybody, so the chicks will have to leave,' he announced. Turning to the Hell's Angels motorcycle gang who were sullenly policing the ground in front of the stage, he snapped, 'Get rid of them.'

Pioneering feminist writer Germaine Greer was in that enclosure, though strangely she ignored this incident in her report. As *Oz* magazine's roving correspondent on the sexual revolution, Greer had enjoyed an ambivalent position towards male rock stars and their female followers. She was, after all, the author of a hyperbolic piece entitled 'A Groupie's Vision', in which she adopted the voice of 'the women who really understand what the bass guitar is saying when it thumps against their skin, a velvet-hard glans of soundwaves'. In Hyde Park, she was more concerned to witness 'the super- ficiality of the rock revolution', a lonely prophet in her vision that 'no, baby, the Stones are not one of you'. She asked some pertinent questions of the street fighting man and his disciples: 'Why did Mick Jagger not tell those quarter of a million people to take over the city? Why did they behave so well and pick up all their garbage? . . . The phenomenon had been contained. No one need be afraid of the Rolling Stones any more. They couldn't change a thing. They didn't want to change a thing.'

To confirm her conclusions, Mick Jagger had just given an interview to the London-based magazine *Student*. Was Jagger interested in politics? 'No.' Why not? 'Because I kind of thought about it for a long time and decided. I haven't got time to do that and understand other things. I mean, if you get really involved with politics, you get fucked up.' It was one of the more honest statements this inveterate obfuscator ever made. Yet it suited both the Stones and the underground – media and masses alike – to pretend that the band's leader was still a cultural revolutionary with the power to shake the walls of the city.

Other rock stars were less careful with their rhetoric than Jagger, espe- cially in company they considered hip, and therefore safe. Roger Daltrey, lead singer of the Who, was in Ann Arbor, Michigan, as the Stones prepared for their Hyde Park show. 'We're just not strong enough leaders,' he told the local underground rag. 'You need someone who's gonna make people jump. You need a Hitler figure to just say, "This is what it is". And Hitler was right for Germany at the time, they were really being shit on. He turned out mad at the end, but when he started, he was there, he just did marvellous things for the German people. You just need a Hitler figure, internationally, for kids.'[5]

If there was a rock star with the charisma to exert Hitlerian control over the underground audience, it was Bob Dylan – or, at least, the preternat- urally enigmatic Bob Dylan of 1965/66. For every A.J. Weberman, who detected the demise of Dylan's artistic and political credibility in the romantic clichés of the *Nashville Skyline* album, there were many who clung to the remnants of the myth. Hence the excitement aroused when Dylan announced that he would be performing at the second of the season's major rock events: the Isle of Wight festival in late August 1969. Rumours swirled through the under- ground that Dylan would be performing a three-hour set, accompanied by the Beatles and the Rolling Stones. Instead, fans were treated to a modest one-hour performance by a shy, somewhat awkward man in a white suit, who delivered no epiphanies and no message beyond, 'It's great to be here, sure is'. Rather than leading an apocalyptic raid on establishment culture, Dylan concluded his set with a new song, 'Minstrel Boy'. Its significance only became apparent when it was released on his *Self Portrait* album – an apt setting for a lyric that portrayed its maker as the minstrel boy, 'stuck on top of the hill', 'lonely still', 'heavy in toil' and in need of 'a coin . . . to save his soul'. It was a pithy speech of abdication.

With the Stones renouncing politics and Bob Dylan pursuing his own salvation, the Beatles were the last members of rock's ruling triumvirate whose cultural potency remained intact. John Lennon's crusade for world peace showed that he had not lost sight of his social responsibilities. But anyone expecting the Beatles' summer 1969 album, *Abbey Road*, to signal the mood of the times was disappointed. Exquisitely arranged though it was, there was nothing on the record that reflected the planet beyond the studio walls – nothing, that is, beyond Lennon's reheating of the clichés of 1967 ('because the world is round, it turns me on') and his transformation of Timothy Leary's campaign song into the self-referential mythopoeia of 'Come Together'. Writing in *Black Dwarf*, Lennon's one-time adversary, John Hoyland, examined the implications of the album's final message: 'in the end, the love you take is equal to the love you make'. He concluded it was a 'reactionary supposition' based on an unhealthy acceptance of the status quo.

As the record was released, only George Harrison offered a message, and his transcendental wisdom was deliberately unpolitical. 'It doesn't matter where you are or what you're doing,' he declared, because meditation would 'be able to conjure up that peace in the middle of Vietnam. You should be able to get in tune, or tune into that flow of peace.' He was asked about those who, like the protagonists of the group's song about Revolution, wanted to change the world. 'They can only make it good if they themselves have made it,' he replied mysteriously, 'and if each individual makes it himself, then automatically everything's alright. There is no problem if each individual doesn't have any problems . . . The problems are created more, sometimes, by people going around trying to fix up the government, or trying to do something.' The solution, he suggested, was to pray, to visualise a better world, and to recite the Hare Krishna Mantra – now available on the Beatles' Apple Records label, as seven inches of plastic enlightenment. Everything else was meaningless on the great wheel of karma: 'The Revolution can only be important if it is unimportant. The cycle's so big, each cycle upon another cycle. If you think of all those Iron Ages and Golden Ages and Stone Ages – they all eventually get back to where they started and go into another cycle, and we just happen to be in one of those cycles!'

So low had the Beatles' image sunk amongst the radical left that Abbie Hoffman and Fugs poet Tuli Kupferberg competed in front of an open microphone to ridicule Lennon and his wife, whom Hoffman renamed (without a hint of racism, of course) 'Oko Nono'. In any contest involving satirical invective, Hoffman was the inevitable victor. The Lennons' peace campaign, he pronounced, was 'an establishment form of pacifism'. He alleged that Lennon's Montreal bed-in was part of a CIA plot to distract the kids from the revolution. The proof, he claimed, was Lennon's notorious phone-call to the demonstrators in People's Park: 'Lennon wrote to the [US] State Department, or sent his messenger to the State Department, and said, "I will do a good service here, I will speak to the young people, I will tell them not to be violent, I will tell them not to shout 'kill the pigs'".' And he promised: 'I ain't gonna buy [Lennon's] records, I'm not interested. He doesn't say anything to me anymore.'

Neither, it appeared, did Lennon's peers: 'It's very awkward, that whole millionaire shit,' Hoffman complained. 'The music is becoming so irrelevant in this country, and their whole model, and their lifestyle. "The shock of rock'n'roll is a revolution." Columbia Record Company – that's their slogan now! People on the street don't believe that; it's shit.' He'd misheard the slogan, but his conclusion was firm – faith in the power of rock, and rock musicians, to lead any revolution was hopelessly misguided. Yet just two months earlier, Hoffman had described rock'n'roll as the frontline of the cultural revolution. What had changed his mind? Woodstock.

## DACHAU BLUES

What began with the Human Be-In, and flowered into ecstatic life at Monterey, was smothered in Chicago. After the debacle of the Yippies' Festival of Life, it was impossible to envisage a mass assembly of the counter-culture without cynicism and even fear. With each passing month, the festival concept lost its original connotations of celebration, and became a marketing tool. Soon every major city had its rock festival, at which increasingly large crowds endured increasingly appalling conditions while sitting hundreds of yards away from their heroes.

June 1969's Newport Pop Festival epitomised the new breed. It coincided with a concerted police campaign to stamp out the distribution of marijuana in the Los Angeles area. Instead, the audience amused itself with a cocktail of alcohol, amphetamines and an impure chemical hybrid known as Orange Acid. The result was incoherent violence, aimed at both the police and other fans. As reporter Ann Moses noted, 'Local government officials are preparing ordinances to guarantee there'll never be another gathering of the rock tribes. The few optimists who remained in rock were soon shaking their heads and repeating: "There'll never be another Monterey".'

Through spring and summer 1969, word spread about a gargantuan festival that would overshadow all of its rivals. It was scheduled for August, in the upstate New York town of Woodstock – a site chosen purely because Bob Dylan lived there. A small and previously peaceful community, heavily populated by artists, Woodstock politely declined the offer. It was only in July that Bethel, New York, farmer Max Yasgur agreed to rent his land to the festival promoters, a bunch of hippie capitalists with a utopian grasp of the sociological, musical and financial potential of what they were planning. To maximise their iconic power, they retained the Dylan-related name of Woodstock for their so-called Art & Music Fair. As the festival date neared, recording rights for the event were sold to Atlantic Records, whose boss, Ahmet Ertegun, secured the movie rights for his parent company, Warner Brothers. Even before the festival began, Woodstock had become a corporate symbol.

It was a summer of American idealism. On 20 July, US astronauts became the first to set foot upon the surface of the moon, fulfilling a decade-long national dream. It was an event, commentators suggested, which would change the course of history, and be remembered as the epochal moment of the century. Yet fewer than forty years later, the moon landing appears an irrelevant sidestep in mankind's progress. By contrast, the ephemeral hedonism of Woodstock has entered the memory of a generation as the pinnacle of a dream – a fantasy, perhaps, that men and women could share this planet in harmony.

'No one in this country in this century had ever seen a "society" so free of repression,' reflected underground journalist Andrew Kopkind after the dust had settled and the movie had premiered. 'Everyone swam nude in the lake, balling was easier than getting breakfast, and the "pigs" just smiled and passed out the oats. For people who had never glimpsed the intense communitarian closeness of a militant struggle – People's Park or Paris in the month of May or Cuba – Woodstock must always be their model of how good we will all feel after the revolution.' In this portrait of Woodstock, preserved by the three-hour documentary movie, the soundtrack albums, and the nostalgia industry that sparks fresh life into it at every anniversary, the festival was exactly what its promoters promised: three days of love, peace and music. Between 400,000 and 500,000 people filled Yasgur's land, shared their smoke and seed, and grooved to the music of acts whose names would forever be linked to the 'W' word – Crosby, Stills, Nash & Young, John Sebastian, Richie Havens, Santana, Sly & the Family Stone, and of course Jimi Hendrix, whose rambling, semi-experimental set climaxed in a rendition of the American national anthem that has assumed messianic importance.

Yet there were other Woodstocks, sharper, sourer and less easily assimilated into legend. The establishment, as represented by the po-faced leader writer of the *New York Times*, observed a sea of stoned humanity wallowing in mud, tutted at the disruption caused to the road network ('the New York State Thruway is closed, man'; one of many memorable soundbites from the movie) and concluded that the gathering was nothing less than an 'outrage'. The story was headlined: 'Nightmare in the Catskills'. The culprits were not just the promoters and the 'freakish-looking intruders' who attended the festival, but also their parents, *Times* readers among them, who 'must bear a share of the responsibility for this episode'. Woodstock was nothing less than a 'rebellion' against decent American morals, the paper snorted.

Morality was also the concern of many on the radical left, who viewed Woodstock as a means of defusing the revolutionary potential of both rock music and the counter-culture. French anarchist Jean Jacques Lebel, who became a specialist in the ethics of rock festivals, was filled with foreboding before the event. Woodstock, he warned, was not 'a mere million dollar operation. It plays a precise role in the anti-rebellion strategy of the Police State.' The organisers had been forced to construct 'a strong fence in open country to limit our playgrounds and contain us, they must sell us high-price tickets to their cultural penitentiary, and ram their merchandise down our throats'.

Lebel seemed to be suggesting a return to the folk tradition, whereby music existed for the people and was shared as a community resource. The

Woodstock fences were essential for a commercial enterprise, but they altered the atmosphere and ethos of the event. The promoters were eventually forced to declare the event 'a free festival' after non-paying participants pulled down the barricades. But, as critic Gary Herman noted later, 'The organisers' decision to let in the gate crashers was made in the knowledge that Warner Bros were turning the whole thing into a full-length feature film . . . Woodstock's initial loss of half-a-million dollars was recouped many times over by box-office returns and record sales.'

Herman's analysis, written after the last of the imitation Woodstocks, the Watkins Glen festival in 1973, stands as a pithy description of how idealism soured into cynicism: 'The organisers spent more on security – fences, guard-dogs and private police. Ticket prices went up, stages got higher and press enclosures got bigger. The performers who had once walked among the audience flew in by helicopter and less attention was paid to the audiences as human beings. At times it felt a bit like paying to get into Dachau.'

One man's Woodstock incorporated and epitomised all of these conflicting themes – celebrity and corporatism, the people and the elite, money and music, politics and pleasure, outrage and revolution. Perhaps inevitably, that man was Abbie Hoffman. There was a pause between the 1968 convention and the conspiracy trial, and Hoffman had been cruising on his fame and notoriety, a spectator as SDS split, the coalition of black and white dissolved, and People's Park was lost. He contented himself with speaking appearances at colleges, showing a short film inspired by events in Chicago.[6] Woodstock would return him to the centre of the stage – literally – and test his charisma and endurance to breaking point.

From the outset, Hoffman was at odds with the Woodstock philosophy. Nowhere in the advance publicity did the organisers propose anything more confrontational than love, peace and music. Those attending the festival might be against the war and against 'the man', but the event was always intended as an exhibition of a new lifestyle, not a political statement. Requested to provide a typically rousing manifesto in the festival programme, Hoffman responded with a grim essay entitled (in yet another allusion to Bob Dylan) 'The Hard Rain's Already Fallin''. Dylan's song had been inspired by the potential for imminent nuclear destruction during the Cuban missile crisis of 1962; Hoffman pricked the hippie bubble by highlighting the links between the repression of young American radicals (he and his fellow Chicago conspirators among them) and the recent drug busts of several major rock acts. 'Someday real soon', he warned, 'we're going to see posters in the post office that say "WANTED FOR CONSPIRACY TO INSPIRE RIOT"', and there smiling out at us will be pictures of our favorite rock groups. Unreal? Well, maybe you're not hip to what's been going down . . . The hard rain's already fallin' and it isn't just the politicos that are getting wet. Read the list: Jimi Hendrix, MC5, the Who (etc etc etc etc) – all have been busted recently. Busted because the authorities want to destroy our cultural revolution in the same way they want to destroy our political revolution.' In a reference to Columbia Records' crass marketing campaign, he continued: 'Maybe the man can't bust our music but he can sure as hell bust our musicians. If the government wanted to, it could bust rock groups on charges of conspiracy to incite riot.'

It was typical Hoffman rhetoric – incisive, simplistic, alarming – but it lacked any of his trademark humour. Yet his knife cut both ways. By exaggerating the political impact and importance of rock musicians, he not only pulled uninvolved fans into the mainstream of the movement, but also reinforced the artists' political responsibilities. It was with both these themes in mind that Hoffman made his dramatic entrance onto the festival stage.

'I was at a meeting at Abbie's house with Jerry Rubin before the festival,' recalls Barry Miles. 'They were already planning to "liberate" Woodstock, knock down the fences and throw it open to the people. I was with Allen Ginsberg, who was distressed about the violence that he was convinced was bound to ensue.' Hoffman's use of military rhetoric suggested that Ginsberg's fears were well founded. 'When culture becomes a nation it requires an army,' he explained. 'Our troops lay in that amorphous body of youth which, especially during the summer months, roamed the land in search of itself. A huge rock concert lasting a few days presented an opportunity to reach masses of young people in a setting where they felt part of something bigger.' Even Hoffman was not naive enough to believe that he could hope to compete with rock bands for the attention of the crowd, however. Joining forces with underground welfare activists from the Lower East Side, Wavy Gravy's Hog Farm, and the Diggers, he set about organising – at amphetamine speed – welfare provisions for a gathering many times larger than the promoters had ever imagined.

The precise details of these arrangements are, like most things attached to Hoffman's name, wrapped in mythology. In his self-serving, ebullient autobiography, *Soon To Be A Major Motion Picture*, Hoffman claimed sole credit for seizing some of the Woodstock resources and cash for the under-ground. His tale was that he had met the promoters weeks before the festival, and bargained for 200 free tickets, $10,000 to finance community groups to attend the event, and the right to approach the audience via stalls and leafleting. But Lower East Side activist Jeff Nightbyrd recalled that it was only on Max Yasgur's farm, as the audience were trickling onto the site, that he and Hoffman made their power-play. He recalled Abbie threatening to rerun the Chicago disruption in upstate New York, scaring the promoters into handing over around $65,000. 'Abbie was a big, powerful guy,' Barry Miles recalls. 'You wouldn't want to mess with him. Plus it was impossible to get a word in edgeways. He was always on speed or something, and he never stopped talking, so you couldn't argue with him.' Whatever the truth, the money went towards hiring a printing press so that Hoffman's team could issue broadsides and bulletins; bringing in emergency food and medical supplies; establishing a Vietnam-style field hospital; and securing blankets in which to wrap those who had suffered overdoses or sundry accidents during the festival. Hoffman also led a team that raided the truck holding the film crew's equipment. When he was challenged, he said, 'Let us have it, man. It's Warner Brothers' stuff.' He was gently persuaded that it was director Michael Wadleigh who would lose out financially if the gear was stolen.

The Woodstock movie encouraged the legend that the multitude fed itself on the 'pass it on' philosophy, like a living encapsulation of the hippie anthem, 'Get Together'. The truth was more sober: there were acute short-ages of drinking water and food, and the promoters had made only minimal provision for those suffering from bad trips or other misadventures. 'There's no morality here,' Hoffman told his friend, journalist Ellen Sander, during the festival. 'The helicopters bring in champagne for Janis Joplin's band, and people are sick in the field. I'm the conscience of this movement.'

His comments astutely pinpointed the divide between artists and audi-ence. With the honourable exception of Joan Baez, who maintained her long history of social activism by ferrying food from backstage to hungry members of the crowd, none of the musicians paid more than passing attention to the plight of their fans. Stephen Stills' stoned announcement came close to empathy: 'You people have got to be the strongest bunch of people I ever saw. Three days, man, three days.' But he soon retreated to the heli-copter waiting to convey him back to the comforts of the real world. As Hoffman saw it, life for the musicians equalled 'living at the Concord hotel

THERE'S A RIOT GOING ON 271

or the Holiday Inn in Liberty and buzzing in, stoned out of your head, in a helicopter. It meant being hustled under guard to a secluded pavilion to join the other aristocrats who run the ROCK EMPIRE. There one could dig the whole spaced-out scene and dine on California grapes and champagne, just forty yards below the Field Hospital where a thousand screaming freak-outs were happening and cats with barbed wire through their feet were moaning on the cots.'

Hoffman's dark vision of this supposed utopia was influenced by the cerebral feedback of one too many acid trips. 'It might have been the green tab,' he mused afterwards, 'the red one, the blue, the Darvon, four joints, no food, hash, no sleep for five days, witnessing the hundreds who had dragged their bodies through the hospital we had set up, the thousands waiting outside the gate to get treatment for bad trips, or the fact that I had tried to ball every woman I ever wanted in one day and they all said no. Whatever it was, I had a bummer. One of those rare acid trips when everything caves in.' Jarred out of sympathy with his surroundings, Hoffman railed at the hedonism and carelessness around him like Coleridge's Ancient Mariner, subjecting anyone who strayed into his path to a stream of agonised invective. Co-promoter Michael Lang, his head reeling with the possibility that he and his colleagues might be about to take a financial bath, was an early target. 'The difference between me and you is that you would run Bob Dylan for president and I would run John Sinclair,' Hoffman told him enigmatically. Then he was back on Ellen Sander's shoulder, boasting: 'I'm the only one here who cares about the people.' Sander wasn't about to let him down easy; she was enraptured by the giant love-in unveiling around her. 'Bullshit, Abbie,' she replied. 'There's real growth happening here. What you guys are into is destruction.' 'Right!' roared Hoffman, his eyes dancing with possibilities. 'I think these kids should go home and kill their parents. KILL the culture.' They both cracked up with laughter, and then Hoffman was gone, his sights set on another joust with Lang.

John Sinclair's name kept floating to the surface through Hoffman's paranoid, hallucinogenic haze. In mid-July, the WPP leader had learned that his revolutionary protégés, the MC5, were formally distancing themselves from his management company. Then on 21 July, Sinclair went on trial for his 1967 pot bust. Five days later, he was found guilty. As he was led out of court, he screamed at the judge: 'You've completely revealed yourselves, you've exposed yourselves even more. Power to the people! Off the pigs!

You will die!' The judge remembered Sinclair's conduct when he sentenced him to a prison term of nine and a half to ten years for possessing two marijuana cigarettes. The MC5 immediately offered to pay his defence expenses, before realising that they were in severe debt themselves.

Like most of his activist comrades, Abbie Hoffman was outraged by Sinclair's treatment. 'John is a mountain of a man,' he wrote in a communiqué. 'He can fuck twenty times a day and fight like a wild bear. He and his White Panther brothers and sisters from Ann Arbor, Michigan, are the most alive force in the whole Midwest.' Sinclair's home turf was a training ground for the revolution, he continued: 'In Ann Arbor, the kids are learning karate. In Ann Arbor, the women know how to handle shotguns. In Ann Arbor, they are prepared to build and defend the Nation by any means necessary. In Ann Arbor and in other places like that around the country they ain't into peace and music, they're into WAR and MUSIC. Right on!'

Hoffman was still fired with the same radical zeal at Woodstock. When he resumed his sparring with Mike Lang, the promoter promised vaguely that they'd do something for Sinclair – make an announcement, something, you can trust me – the following day. But Hoffman was too antsy to wait. 'How *can* I trust you?' he asked Lang. 'You're just a capitalist.'

At which point, history shatters like a glass dropped on concrete, and the shards are impossible to mend – although everyone present remembers the solitary fact that the glass was broken. Hoffman was a notorious rewriter of his own story; every time, events changed and motives shifted another ninety degrees. In the immediate aftermath of Woodstock, he recalled taking advantage of a clear run to the stage, and strolling out to the microphone in front of half a million dazed hippies to begin a speech about the injustice of Sinclair's imprisonment. Then, he said, the mike was switched off, and he sauntered back to Lang's side. 'What the fuck did you do that for?' the promoter supposedly said. 'I was just doing my thing,' Hoffman replied. After which Lang persuaded him to sit and listen to the next band: the Who.

The trouble is, nobody else remembers the story that way. Hoffman may have attempted to commandeer the stage before the Who began playing, but that detail isn't mentioned in any other account. His friend Jean Jacques Lebel told an entirely different tale: he and Abbie had been backstage talking to the Who and their management, not just to Mike Lang. As Lebel perceived the band's motives, 'They were in it to make money, man, they didn't give a shit about John Sinclair or anybody else. But Abbie's exuberant discourse made them feel guilty, and while they were tuning up nothing was happening anyway. And [Roger Daltrey] said, all right, you have exactly three minutes to read your political message about John Sinclair while we are tuning up. The idea was that Abbie would make this statement and I would say it in French and in Italian to make it very international. But the problem is that Abbie took too much acid.'

Nobody had ever accused the Who of being a political band. On the basis of the opinions quoted earlier in this chapter, Daltrey's world-view was a little naive. But then so was the idea of approaching him as the Who's in-house thinker. That role belonged to their songwriter and guitarist, Pete Townshend. He had recently penned all but two of the songs that comprised their epic rock opera, *Tommy*, and had struggled through dozens of inter-views intended to explicate his philosophy. Political revolution didn't feature in his conversation, which was dominated by problems of communication, and the inner peace he had gained from his study of the Indian guru, Meher Baba.

Not that inner peace was always apparent when Townshend took to the stage. Like Mick Jagger, he confessed to being overwhelmed by the power of his band's music, and the inherent violence of rock'n'roll. In front of an audience, the insecure intellectual was transformed into a rampaging rock god, caring little for anyone who happened to cross his path. On 16 May 1969, Townshend had clubbed a policeman off stage at the Fillmore East in New York. The cop was trying to warn the audience that the building next to the theatre was on fire – a casualty of the simmering war between its owner, Bill Graham, and the New York Motherfuckers. Even before the Who took the stage at Woodstock, Townshend was battling grumpily against an acid trip started by a spiked drink. A journalist who met him backstage described him as 'surly'. The editor of the Woodstock movie, Thelma Schoonmaker, recalled a collision between Townshend and the film's director and chief photographer, Michael Wadleigh: 'Sometimes Wadleigh would jump up on the stage and move around the performers, and it was on one of those occasions that Pete Townshend of the Who kicked him off the stage.' Filming assistant Anne Bell remembered that Townshend 'became annoyed and kicked Wadleigh's camera, causing the eyepiece to smash into his face. Luckily Mike was not hurt badly, but we were all shaken as we watched Townshend stomp and smash his guitar at the finale.' Another report suggests that Wadleigh was kicked squarely in the groin by the guitarist, though this appears to be an exaggeration. Schoonmaker decided that with a subject this volatile, the film crew should tread with caution: 'We told all the cameramen to stop filming, and then gradually, as the Who became engrossed in their performance, we started filming again.' Townshend's impatience with intruders was readily apparent to everyone. But Abbie Hoffman was scarcely in a physical or psychological condition to register anything beyond his own consciousness. And so the scene was set for a mythic encounter between rock and the revolution, as two celebrities clashed in front of the largest audience yet assembled for any musical event.

Despite Jean Jacques Lebel's claim that Hoffman was scheduled to speak while the Who prepared for their performance, recordings demonstrate that Abbie invaded the stage during their rendition of *Tommy*. They had just completed their current hit single, 'Pinball Wizard', and had paused before the next song. 'I'm on the side of the stage watching the show,' recalled Country Joe McDonald, 'and there was a pause and they're gonna go into another number and boom! There's Abbie talking very loudly into the microphone. He said, "How can you people sit out there having so much fun when John Sinclair's rotting in prison for possession of two joints?"' Hoffman recounted how 'I lunged forward, grabbed the mike and shouted out "FREE JOHN SIN…".' The recording doesn't lie: you can hear Abbie shout, 'I think this is a pile of shit while John Sinclair rots in prison,' before Townshend interjects: 'Fuck off!' There's a momentary pause, then Hoffman cries the word 'I', only for Townshend to shout him down: 'FUCK OFF MY STAGE!' Another pause – and then a sardonic cheer from the audience, anxious to hear the Who resume.

What evoked that approval from the crowd? Who biographer Dave Marsh recounted that Townshend had pushed Hoffman off the stage with a combination of boot and guitar. Hoffman's 1969 account was more dramatic: 'CRASH. Pete Townshend, lead guitarist, had clonked me over the head with his electric guitar, and I crumpled on the stage. There we were shaking fists at each other and yelling, him doing stuff like "Get the fuck outta here", and me doing the "You fascist pig" number. I leaped the chasm from the stage to the barricade wall, flying like some shaggy-dog Tarzan. I scrambled over the wall, leaped ten feet to the ground, and started to climb People Hill.'

Townshend supposedly said that attacking Hoffman was 'the most political thing I ever did'. But Danny Fields remembered Townshend coming off stage and asking him who the intruder had been, then expressing regret when he found out. 'When I asked him about it later, Pete said he hadn't recognised Abbie,' Barry Miles confirms. 'He thought Hoffman was just some lunatic who had wandered onto the stage.'

In later years, both participants reconsidered their behaviour. 'What he was arguing for was very valid,' Townshend commented on one occasion. What he had experienced as a momentary explosion of instinctive violence, which might have been aimed at anyone within the reach of a swinging guitar, had mutated in his mind into a socio-political drama with psychological overtones – irresistible, therefore, to a man with Townshend's capacity for self-examination.

Hoffman's capacity was more defensive: self-preservation. While Townshend's image as an uncontrollable guitar god was strengthened by the fracas, Hoffman had to endure the fate of passing into history – or at least rock history – as the idiot who was crowned by a guitar at Woodstock. Until his death, he repeatedly revised his account of the fiasco, sometimes claiming that it hadn't happened, sometimes boasting that his actions had been an outpouring of revolutionary spirit.

Pete Townshend's reflection on this encounter with the revolution would shape his writing for the next few years, as he teased and tormented himself with the concept of responsibility, and how it was shared between the artist and his audience. For Abbie Hoffman, too, the fall-out was enduring and provocative. Sullen and silent on the long drive back to Manhattan, he worked his way from embarrassment into an interpretation of the Woodstock debacle that saved his face and made a passionate political point. 'When I left Chicago, I felt we had won a great victory,' he wrote the following month. 'Leaving Woodstock I was not so sure of what exactly had happened. Figuring out who was the enemy was not only difficult but the mere posing of the question seemed out of place. Were we pilgrims or lemmings? Was this really the beginning of a new civilisation or the symptom of a dying one? Were we establishing a liberated zone or entering a detention camp?'

The weekend after Woodstock, Hoffman turned up at the door of Ellen Sander's New York apartment, high on the vision of a movie he intended to call *Woodstock Nation*. He was hazy about the scenario, though it would reflect his conviction that his meeting with Pete Townshend was a glorious triumph in the tradition of Chicago – a fiasco that had screwed up the established order and was therefore a revolutionary act. Sander recalled that he was more enraptured by the opportunity that screenings of the film would give for Yippie theatrics: 'The movie stops,' he fantasised, 'and somebody comes out and demonstrates how to make firebombs. At the end, people are going to rip out the seats, we're gonna tell them to tear the theatre down and go out and make revolution in the streets.'

Sander had experienced a different Woodstock to Hoffman's; horrified by his intervention during the Who's set, she had surrendered herself to the music and the immensity of the crowd, and felt heartened by the 'groovy' way in which police officers and hippies had co-operated. Appalled by Hoffman's perversion of what she saw as the true Woodstock ethic, she penned an open letter to her friend, which ran in underground newspapers across America. 'You're so enraptured with the vision of yourself as a latter-day Che,' she lectured him, 'that you'll make anything and anyone your enemy in order to continue this bullshit.' And she ended with a rousing dismissal of Hoffman's political analysis: 'Abbie, the age of politics is over. The revolution is finished. It served its purpose, and it's irrelevant now . . . Fuck your rhetoric, man. Get it on, dance, dance to the music, and stop trying to exploit it . . . Everyone else loved it at Woodstock. The only unhappy people there were the political crazies.'

By the time the article had appeared, Hoffman's manic exuberance was way beyond restraint. He'd run with his initial concept, abandoned the movie, and taken to the floor of his editor's office at Random House, scribbling a manuscript that was published – under the title of *Woodstock Nation*, naturally – just six weeks after the festival. It was billed as 'A Talk-Rock Album', and the contents included essays about John Sinclair, the aftermath of Chicago, Elvis Presley, and Che Guevara, alongside searching analysis of the festival itself. 'I emerged exhausted, broke and bleeding from the WOOD-STOCK NATION,' he wrote. 'It was an awesome experience but one that made me have a clearer picture of myself as a cultural revolutionary – not a cultural nationalist, for that would embrace a concept of hip capitalism which I reject – and not a political revolutionary either. Political revolution leads people into support for other revolutions rather than having them get involved in making their own. Cultural revolution requires people to change the way they live and act in the revolution rather than passing judgements on how the other folks are proceeding. The cultural view breeds outlaws, politics breeds organisers.'

Whether he realised it or not, Abbie Hoffman was abdicating from the role of revolutionary crown prince; his future pronouncements would take on the increasingly apocalyptic tone of an exiled prophet. As a means of shedding any lasting guilt from his actions at Woodstock, he set aside all of his earnings from *Woodstock Nation* for radical causes – some of it to cover the defence's expenses at the upcoming Chicago trial, the rest for similar legal funds in support of the Motherfuckers and John Sinclair. Yet Woodstock and its aftermath continued to exercise his imagination. When his book was republished in 1971, he added a poignant afterword, entitled 'The Head Withers as the Body Grows'. His perception of the festival had now slipped into almost unbearably sharp focus: 'Somewhere deep inside the bowels of the monster born in Bethel also lay the kernel for its destruction. Perhaps it was the egocentric greed of the Rock Empire itself. Maybe it was the strain of cannibalism inherited from our parents and exaggerated when cramped into railroad flats in the slums or on muddy slopes in front of gargantuan stages. The rapes, the bad acid burns, stealing from each other, they, too, were part of the Woodstock experience . . . Woodstock without any politics, without a commitment to self-defense of the Nation, is a shuck. A tin-pan alley rip-off. When they say, "Hey, man, politics is not where it's at", what they are really saying is, "Don't bug me, I wanna keep all my dough and the status quo".' It was a belated response to Ellen Sander: culture without revolution was no culture at all.

On a more prosaic level, Hoffman had ingested one vital lesson from his Woodstock experience. In a manual intended for those who wanted to undermine the culture of capitalism, he approached the tricky subject of what an activist should do at a rock concert. 'During intermission, or at the end of the performance,' he instructed his readers, 'fight your way to the stage. Lay out a short exciting rap on what's coming down. Focus on a call around one action. Sometimes it might be good to engage rock groups on dialogue about their commitment to the revolution. Interrupting their concert is frowned upon, since it is only spitting in the faces of the people you are trying to reach.' Plus, he might have added, there was a good chance you would find yourself face down on the grass, a guitar-shaped bruise sprouting on your head.

## GIRLS SAY YES, WOMEN SAY NO

Joan Baez might have shared Abbie Hoffman's concern for the audience at Woodstock, but her strict philosophy of non-violence was at odds with his carefree adventurism. 'It was wonderful,' Baez said of the festival, 'but it wasn't any fucking revolution. It was a three-day period during which people were decent to one another because they realised that if they weren't, they'd all go hungry.' Several months pregnant at the time, Baez was midway through an American concert tour that was being filmed for a documentary entitled *Carry It On*. Its focus was the anti-war campaign she was staging with her husband, activist David Harris.

The couple had met during a draft board demonstration in 1967, and for the next five years their personal and political lives were impossible to separate. On 15 July 1969, Harris was sent to prison for three years, on charges of evading the draft. 'There I was driving around in a black Jaguar,' she said of her life before she met Harris, 'and David showed me the alternative. It's not a matter of giving away all your money; that can be as phony as keeping it all. But there is something else you can do. It's a re-evaluation of lives. You must become so involved with another way of thinking that the philosophy permeates into every area of your life.'

Already imprisoned twice herself after anti-war protests, Baez decided to dedicate her career to stopping the Vietnam conflict. 'In the midst of all these things,' she wrote in her concert programme, 'how could I pretend to entertain you? Sing to you, yes. To prod you, to remind you, to bring you joy, or sadness, or anger.' She continued to refuse to pay the taxes that would be set aside for the war effort, and handed over most of her earnings to Harris's organisation, The Resistance. Some concerts included interactive demonstrations, where young men could make a public display of handing in their draft cards. 'I was not only anti-commercial,' she admitted later, 'I was impossible,' and her record sales suffered accordingly.

Despite her total immersion in the campaign, she experienced rhetorical sniper-fire from the radical left, who regarded her lack of commitment to violent revolution as a sign of bourgeois reticence. With her sisters, Pauline and Mimi, she also aroused displeasure from another section of the movement. The three women posed for what they considered to be a humorous anti-war poster, their faces appearing above the slogan: 'Girls say yes to boys who say no'. 'I thought it was clever,' Baez explained. 'The feminists hated it because it said "girls" and because the women shouldn't have to answer to anyone, especially men, not yes or no. They wanted the poster taken off the market. I honest to God didn't know what they were talking about. But I kept running back and forth to the kitchen, fixing them sandwiches and lemonade, while they nudged each other and looked in exasperation at the ceiling.' In her defence, she cited her husband and guru: 'David raved on about The Resistance and called women "chicks".'

As the feminist movement grew in strength and confidence, a fault-line slowly opened in the radical left. There was already a division between those who regarded black power as a valid revolutionary cause, and those who saw it as a distraction from the onward march of the global working class. Now the same pattern was repeated across the gender boundary. British feminist pioneer Sheila Rowbotham attended a festival of revolution at Essex University, and was shocked by the opposition she encountered: 'The festival was broken up continually by a group of students who regarded any structured discussion on women's liberation as a violation of their "freedom".' Her disquiet was mirrored in the USA. 'Inverse red-baiting has become popular on the left,' reported Margie Stamberg in March 1969, 'wherein those in women's liberation are considered bourgeois, with the only true reds being women who remain in "the movement".' Roz Baxandall, who had participated in the raid on the Miss America pageant in 1968, concluded that the counter-culture was rotten with sexual stereotypes: 'The free sexual revolution has only served to oppress women, and especially radical women. If she doesn't want to sleep with men, a woman is "hung up". If she does, she's known as someone's wife or girlfriend. And men still look down on women who have gone through lots of men in the movement. The reverse, of course, is not true.'

Radical men, said Germaine Greer, 'may be chauvinistic, and may reap female adulation and their reward for conspicuousness in the movement – we have all seen Tariq Ali marching with his blonde harem.' Rock critic Ellen Willis, a member of the New York feminist collective Redstockings, noted dolefully: 'All around me I see men who consider themselves dedicated revolutionaries, yet exploit their wives and girlfriends shamefully without ever noting a contradiction.' She penned an open letter on the subject of sexism, and sent it to the American radical newspaper *The Guardian*. In a perfect example of the movement's attitude to women's liberation, Willis's Letter to the Left wasn't published.

It was a measure of rock music's isolation from the counter-culture it claimed to represent that not a single hint of this debate registered in discussions with musicians, let alone in the music that they made. Instead, underground rock indulged its pathological fetish of regarding women as sexually voracious, endlessly and effortlessly available, a fitting reward for male superstardom – in other words, as groupies. These almost mythical creatures were everywhere in the rock press during 1969, trading stories of conquests in the pages of *Rolling Stone*, setting themselves up as role models for impressionable teens, even masquerading as male-controlled rock performers themselves, as in the case of the GTOs (alias Girls Together Outrageously), assembled by the notoriously sexist Frank Zappa. Then there were the Plastercasters, a high-profile groupie collective whose sole delight was immortalising erect male penises (or 'rigs') in plaster. To the extent that they were responsible for generating and then documenting the hard-ons they were casting, these women did control their own destiny. But their antics, which commanded weighty coverage in the underground press, still saw women being defined by the famous (and famously well-hung) men whose penises they had sampled.

Meanwhile, the gender roles described in song remained unchanged. As ever, the Rolling Stones led the way, thanks to the enduring sexism of their lyrics, which was epitomised by another lip-licking account of sexual exploit-ation, 'Stray Cat Blues'. One of the first and most blatant celebrations of the groupie scene, it found Mick Jagger stretching his acting powers to the limit as a lustful rock star, presented with a young admirer for his delectation. Fifteen years old when the Stones recorded the song in 1968, the 'stray cat' had become thirteen by the time the song hit the road in late 1969. 'Jailbait' was now a common subject for rock lyricists, and had been since Chuck Berry had concealed his desires under the pretext of documenting the social lives of schoolgirls. Folk-rock star Donovan scored a global hit single with 'Mellow Yellow' (featuring the lines 'I'm just mad about Fourteen, Fourteen's mad about me') and also recorded the 1969 groupie ode 'Superlungs (My Supergirl)', the heroine of which was 'only fourteen but she knows how to draw . . . She ain't quite grown up but her breathing's real good'.

Adolescent girls were now (apparently) legitimate and not at all obscure objects of desire for musicians almost old enough to be their fathers, and many underground newspapers openly printed images that would be the subject of 'child porn' investigations by the police if they were discovered in someone's possession today. Not that anyone in search of fuel for their fantasies had to hunt out a small-circulation periodical. Illicit sexual images were on sale in every record shop in Britain. The most notorious was offered by the 'supergroup' Blind Faith. Their 1969 album featured a frontal nude photograph of an 11-year-old girl, clutching a phallic object in the form of a glistening silver model of a futuristic spaceship. The craft is pointing towards her (just out of shot) genitalia, while the girl looks startled, as if she has been interrupted on the verge of a forbidden act.

The image aroused mild controversy in the British press, who reported that the girl in the photograph was Ginger Baker's daughter. In fact, she was unrelated to the band. Photographer Bob Seideman explained that he wanted a model who would illustrate 'the beginning of the transition from girl to woman . . . that temporal point, that singular flare of radiant innocence'. He thought he'd found his icon on a London tube train: 'She was wearing a school uniform, plaid skirt, blue blazer, white socks and ball point pen drawings on her hands. It was as though the air began to crackle with an electrostatic charge. She was buoyant and fresh as the morning air. I approached her and said that I would like her to pose for a record cover for Eric Clapton's new band. She said, "Do I have to take off my clothes?" My answer was yes. I gave her my card and begged her to call. I would have to ask her parents' consent if she agreed.'

Seideman was disappointed to discover that when he visited the girl's parents, his model 'had just passed the point of complete innocence and could not pose'. Fortunately her younger sister was ready to oblige: 'She was glorious sunshine, Botticelli's angel, the picture of innocence, a face which in a brief time could launch a thousand spaceships. We asked her what her fee should be for modelling; she said a young horse.' And so the deal was done: innocence was sold, male sexual fantasy fulfilled, the girl's image distributed to millions of homes around the world – except in the USA, where it was removed, not because the girl was under age but because she was exposing her breasts.[7]

Although a passion for under-age girls could apparently be incorporated into the symbolic language of rock, women's liberation was beyond the pale. So, too, was the latest radical movement that dared to speak its name in the summer of 1969: gay liberation. The first stirrings of what was then called the 'homophile' movement can be traced back to 1967, when local groups formed on the US West and East Coasts. That year, the phrase 'Gay Power' was first heard as a rallying call. In California, the Committee for Homosexual Freedom was founded in 1968.

What happened in New York's Greenwich Village solidified these far-flung groupings into a national, and soon a global, crusade. On 27 June 1969, city police raided a popular homosexual meeting place, the Stonewall Inn, on Christopher Street. They claimed that they were targeting unlicensed bars: it was apparently pure coincidence that their raids targeted bars frequented by gay men. There was a brief outbreak of violence, with bricks and even a parking meter thrown at the cops. Folk-singer Dave Van Ronk, a mainstay of the Greenwich Village folk scene, was alerted to the disturbance from his vantage point three doors down at the Lion's Head bar. When he intervened to protest against the police's brutal treatment of the young clientele, he was arrested and charged with attempted assault.

The Stonewall was neither the first nor last New York gay bar to suffer this harassment, but its status as an iconic rendezvous point stirred the city's young homosexual men into action. For the next two nights, they staged what became known as the Stonewall Riots, an exaggeratedly alarming name for a weekend-long street protest, which created an outraged community out of a myriad of isolated individuals. For the mainstream press, the police action was an occasion for cheap humour. 'Homo Nest Raided', ran the headline in the *New York Daily News*; 'Queen Bees Are Stinging Mad'. The underground press achieved a more measured and accurate tone, and their accounts documented some of the chants and songs that united the crowd that weekend: 'I'm a faggot and I'm proud of it'; 'I like boys'; and, of course, 'Gay Power'. There was even a Stonewall anthem: 'We are the Stonewall Girls/We wear our hair in curls/We have no underwear/We show our pubic hair'. It wasn't 'We Shall Overcome' or 'I'm Black and I'm Proud', but it did indicate a sense of unity that would soon be translated into action.

On 9 July, New York was treated to its first meeting under the 'Gay Power' banner. Three weeks later, the Gay Liberation Front was created. It soon began issuing its own paper, *Come Out!*[8] The Front prepared a manifesto: 'We are a revolutionary homosexual group of men and women formed with the realisation that complete sexual liberation for all people cannot come about unless existing social institutions are abolished,' it declared. 'Babylon has forced us to commit to one thing: revolution.' The conclusion could have been echoed by the women's movement: 'Any revolution that does not deal with the liberation of the total human being is incomplete.' The counter-culture was widening, and so was the united front against the repressive capitalist society. But feminism and gay power were also sowing the seeds for the moment, soon to come, when personal transformation would become more important than collective activism, and the movement would threaten to fragment into a million pieces, each living out its own psychodrama and pursuing its own form of liberation.

And fragments were all that gay liberation could muster as a soundtrack in 1969. Homosexuality was the Great Taboo, a carefully concealed element of rock culture. Musicians and fans were still routinely insulted as 'queers' when they ventured out in public with long hair, beads or anything that could be interpreted as feminine garb. Only one narrow world openly accepted homosexuality: Andy Warhol's Factory, the New York home of the Velvet Underground, whose leader Lou Reed had received electro-shock treatment as a teenager to repress his gay leanings. Several of Reed's songs, especially 'Sister Ray' ('still sucking on my ding-dong', indeed), reflected the same fervid sexuality as Warhol's underground movies, seasoned with the druggy sadism of William Burroughs' novel, *The Naked Lunch*. Beyond the Factory, there were countless musicians who would later claim some homosexual allegiance, from Elton John and David Bowie to camp 1950s rocker Little Richard. But none of them yet had the courage to profess his desires in public, even if their preferences were an open secret amongst their peers.

The most obvious presence of homosexuality in the music business came from the English school of gay show business managers and record company bosses. They included such leading names as Larry Parnes (mentor of a stable of pop heart-throbs, such as Billy Fury), Sir Joseph Lockwood (managing director of EMI, the company which signed the Beatles) and of course the Beatles' manager, Brian Epstein. The last of these managed to combine a tempestuous and increasingly dangerous private life with show business renown and financial success. His sexual preferences were an open secret amongst his colleagues and clients, but not widely known by the public until John Lennon's interview with *Rolling Stone* magazine in December 1970. As early as 1968, Beatles biographer Hunter Davies had slipped the adjective 'gay' into his account of Epstein's life; but this usage of the word was still unfamiliar to English ears, at least, and so the revelation passed unnoticed.

In retrospect, rock – especially British rock – was full of sexually ambiguous figures who might have acted as role models for those intending to fight for gay liberation. There was Ray Davies of the Kinks, extremely camp on stage and the composer of the mildly suggestive 1965 single 'See My Friend'; his younger brother Dave, whose autobiography exposed a vivid history of bisexuality throughout the latter stages of the decade; the Rolling Stones, who happily (indeed gaily) posed in drag for a photo session, and whose features seemed to grow more androgynous with every passing month; but not perhaps John Lennon, who beat up an old friend at Paul McCartney's 21st birthday party, after being accused of having a gay relationship with his manager.[9] There was speculation about the lyrical imagery on Bob Dylan's mid-1960s albums (all those sword-swallowers and complaints about his lover being so hard), especially given Dylan's close friendship with the joyously homosexual, straight-man-lusting poet Allen Ginsberg. But it was widely assumed that all pop stars were healthily – indeed, voraciously, like their groupie admirers – heterosexual. It would be three years before a pop performer with any degree of media prominence would proudly claim to be gay; and almost as long before the radical left was prepared to accept gay rights activists as fellow travellers towards the revolution. Before they could think of coming together, homosexuals still had to come to terms with living apart.

## GOING FISHING

David Crosby of the Byrds had described the ideal – ideal for men, that is – hippie relationship in his 1967 song 'Triad'. 'Why can't we go on as three?' he asked a pair of his female admirers. It was a hipper rephrasing of a California chorus from earlier in the decade: 'two girls for every boy'. The song was rejected on moral grounds by his band, who sacked him soon afterwards, but accepted by the more adventurous Jefferson Airplane. Not until 1968 did he re-emerge with a new project, and then it took almost a year to cut through the bureaucratic red tape so that he could record with Stephen Stills (the chronicler of the Sunset Strip riots, from the Buffalo Springfield) and Graham Nash (from the somewhat less political English group the Hollies). Their effervescent vocal harmonies and refreshing blend of acoustic and electric textures won them immediate acclaim. For live work, they recruited Stills' former colleague, Neil Young, as an equal partner, and the quartet's turbulent internal politics mirrored the idealistic uncertainty of the times.

Born outspoken, Crosby had enraged the Byrds by using their concerts as a vehicle for his opinions of psychedelic drugs (good) and the assassination of President Kennedy (an establishment cover-up). Now all four members of CSNY (as the quartet became known) were free to comment on the chaos swirling around them. Their lengthy concerts mixed personal confessions with rousing political anthems, establishing CSNY as arguably the most iconic rock band in late 1960s America. Enraged by injust-ice and government oppression, they railed against the Vietnam War, racism, police harassment and anything that might prevent them from flying their freak flags and getting high. Yet anyone approaching CSNY for political leadership was likely to be disappointed.

'I laugh at the SDS and I laugh at those fucking parlor-pink revolutionary kids going around saying, "I'm a revolutionary by trade",' Crosby scoffed. 'They haven't any idea what it is, man. They should go watch a newsreel of the last three days of Budapest and think it over. Asshole kids.' Stills, who had been raised as an army brat in Latin America, concurred: 'I remember getting into a fight with this little chick from the Weathermen in the middle of Chicago Airport, and she really annoyed me coming on with all that revo-lution business. I mean, I would like to take some of these people to Latin America and show them a real revolution.'

At the same time, Crosby was prone to making statements such as 'I do want to blow this political system'. But how? 'There is no answer that I know of to save us,' he said, exposing the same fatalism with which he would face his own crippling drug addiction a decade later. 'Somehow *Sgt Pepper* did not stop the Vietnam War. Somebody isn't listening. Now, I am doing my level best as a saboteur of values, as an aider of change, but when it comes down to blood and gore in the streets, I'm taking off and going fishing.' Stephen Stills had used exactly the same line in an earlier discus-sion about revolutionary apocalypse.

Escaping Armageddon by boat: that was the scenario of 'Wooden Ships', written by Crosby and Stills with Paul Kantner of Jefferson Airplane. It was a utopian song about avoiding responsibility for your fellow man: 'Horror grips us as we watch you die,' CSN sang, but meanwhile 'we are leaving, you don't need us'. Not that they were staying around to make sure. 'Guess I'll set a course and go,' CSN's recording of the song concluded. 'That was the prevailing philosophy of his circle,' says Crosby's friend and fellow song-writer, Jackson Browne. 'They all had boats and this ideal life – hippies with huge amounts of money, sailing off into an ethereal future that couldn't possibly exist, because there was nowhere they could go where they could escape what was happening in the rest of the world.'

Even more than Crosby and Stills, Kantner and the Airplane were given to grand statements of revolutionary rhetoric. During a May 1969 concert in Miami, technicians turned off the group's PA system when they exceeded the venue's strict curfew. Kantner reacted like any outlaw would, ripping into the offending workers and promising, 'Wait till we burn down your society.' For this righteous anger, he was arrested and charged with disturbing the peace – 'we should have been arrested as traitors a dozen times', he says today – though the case was subsequently dropped. 'Compare the Airplane's much-vaunted revolutionary spirit with the not-so-harsh realities,' noted radical critic Ed Leimbacker, 'trumped-up pot busts, Grace giving the power-to-the-people salute, Marty swearing sweetly on Dick Cavett [US talk show]. That, you see, is where it's at for the Airplane. Theatricality. Harmless words and grand gestures rather than truly radical action.' As Kantner admitted when the revolutionary fervour had burned out, 'We were all punks in high school and we were always rebelling against authority.'

Yet with 1969's *Volunteers* album, which included their arrangement of 'Wooden Ships', the Airplane set out to make a decisively revolutionary statement. Its heady blend of sloganeering and anthemic choruses certainly convinced the London underground magazine *Oz*, which declared: 'In the States they so nearly have a revolution. Everything there is so wired up it's ready to blow. The Jefferson Airplane is a body of people who have always been very involved in the American front, and now, for those of us who still doubt it, they have finally declared themselves Volunteers.'

The album was book-ended by two songs built around a bluegrass banjo lick that David Crosby had taught to Paul Kantner. 'We Can Be Together' – its title a restatement of the hippie anthem 'Get Together', which the Airplane had recorded three years earlier – surged towards a rousing chorus, which stole the name of the New York anarchist group, the Up Against The Wall Motherfuckers. Kantner's lyrics sent out a warning to the establishment: 'We are obscene lawless hideous dangerous dirty violent and young . . . All your private property is target for your enemy, and your enemy is we.' 'Volunteers', meanwhile, delivered the most simplistic of messages ('got a revolution') across a driving R&B rhythm that was far more intoxicating than any call to arms.

Many observers were cynical about the Airplane's revolutionary status. The jazz magazine *Down Beat* described 'We Can Be Together' as 'ludicrously smug, self-important and self-dramatising'. Worse still, it declared, was 'Volunteers': 'By now it should be obvious even to today's young, middle-class, radical millenarians that a revolution is not a pep rally or a street festival but a psychodrama. Successful revolutionaries and even reformers have generally had to work hard and have often had to make great sacrifices. People are dying in Vietnam and getting manhandled in the streets – and along comes [Marty] Balin with his revolution-is-fun song.' 'We didn't feel we had to shoot anybody,' Kantner responds today. 'Our weapons were intellectual. We just pulled all of America's dirty baggage out into the light, and allowed people to make their own healthy decisions. Our watchword was "Question authority". People had never really done that before.'

Ever since they'd tried to smuggle the word 'trips' onto their first record, the Airplane had been engaged in constant skirmishes with their record company. 'You should fuck with people who need to be fucked with,' Kantner says, 'it's a civic obligation.' By 1969, they'd secured sufficient leverage to force the label to accept the word 'motherfuckers' in a song – they even performed 'We Can Be Together' uncensored on an unwitting TV show – but their freedom didn't extend to the lyric sheet, where the offending line was rendered as 'up against the wall fred'. For Ed Leimbacker, this epitomised the Airplane's brand of 'ineffectual revolution'. It was a conclusion shared by certain members of the band. 'Jack Casady and I are pretty nonpolitical,' shrugged guitarist Jorma Kaukonen, who described Kantner as 'very politically naive'. Casady's judgement was no more supportive: 'I don't think there was tremendous deep thought about the situation. Paul waving his guitar over his head like Che Guevara, and pumping his guitar in the air in military fashion, was all OK theatre.' Only one song on the album offered more than chic rhetoric: Grace Slick's ecology ballad, 'Eskimo Blue Day', with its prophecy of global warming: 'Snow cuts loose from the frozen, until it joins with the African sea'.

Jefferson Airplane weren't the only rock band flirting with righteous revolutionary imagery. Hard rockers Steppenwolf, a group of Canadian emigrants best known for the biker anthem 'Born To Be Wild', delivered a concept album about the state of the American national psyche, entitled *Monster*. Its title suite traced the country's proud history, and charted its decline into paranoia and repression. The suite ended with a verse that was widely interpreted as a call for revolution: 'America, where are you? Don't you care about your sons and daughters? Don't you know we need you now? We can't fight alone against the Monster.' Few were drawn to the barricades by this image, however, and Steppenwolf's moment of political punditry soon passed.

In any case, the relevance of using multi-national corporations to sell revolution to the masses was moot. 'Pop music has become a financial staple of

US imperialism,' concluded one underground commentator. 'What's going down is money. Columbia Records nets billions from sales. On album jackets recording artists are called "revolutionaries", but CBS, which owns Columbia, has defence contracts to help murder revolutionaries. Rock stars wail out anger and scream revolt, and leave concerts in Cadillacs.' For the first time, radicals began to suspect that rock musicians might need liberation as much the minorities they claimed to be representing. 'How do we deal with the rock hip imperialists who are ripping us off?' came one anguished cry. 'We've got to get the message across to the artists, get them to be non-exploitative.'

The first move to save rock from itself came in Seattle. On 10 August 1969 police attacked audience members at a free rock concert. The incident triggered two days of rioting, much of it aimed at the purveyors of 'hip capitalism' – record stores, boutiques – and major corporations. Later that year, Seattle high school students boycotted a popular venue, the Eagles Auditorium, after promoter Boyd Grafmyre announced that any audience member suspected of smoking dope or provocative sexual behaviour ('making out') would be expelled and banned. The kids rejected the offer of assist-ance from the Weatherman collective, and instead formed the Eagles Liberation Front. Their manifesto encapsulated a sense of alienation that was shared by critics and fans: 'Rock expresses the ethos of our commu-nity, its force is filled by our struggle. But over the years, the established entertainment industry – promoters, agents, record companies, media and every name group – have gradually transformed our music into an increas-ingly expensive commodity. They have stolen our music. We are taking it back!' This was a new call: for the first time, 'every name group' was under suspicion of crimes against its audience. Boyd Grafmyre soon cut ticket prices at the Eagles, and (just like Bill Graham at the Fillmore) offered use of the auditorium free for community benefits. Buoyed by their success, the ELF vowed to fight on, and employ the same tactics against bands who charged excessive ticket prices. Although the ELF itself soon faded away, the debate about concert tickets lingered on – with unforeseeable results.

'I have very little faith in rock'n'roll entertainers as being anything in this society but bourgeois sell-out people,' declared San Francisco DJ Roland Young, who was fired from his post with KSAN after he repeated militant Black Panther rhetoric live on air. 'It's the ability the society has to incor-porate anything into it, and turn it into a commercial item.' Ed Leimbacker, shifting his sights from the *Volunteers* album for a moment, agreed: 'What's most in trouble [in 1969] is the so-long-supposed "revolutionary spirit" of rock – that schizophrenic dream of wishful thinking and self-hype. Take a closer look at the Establishment. See, it's made of rubber – it co-opts by expanding, by stretching a little bit further and absorbing all the freaky excesses and aberrations . . . Big Brother moves over just enough; and as soon as he gets a piece of the action, the Angry Young Man settles for a lip-service revolution full of sound and fury and signifying nothing.'

A so-called 'tribal rock opera' epitomised the problem. Set amongst a commune of draft-dodgers, its songs offering a Tin Pan Alley pastiche of psychedelic rock, *Hair* was ubiquitous in 1969. It was firmly ensconsed on Broadway and in London's West End, while productions were running in most of the capitalist world's major cities – though not in Mexico, where the government shut it down after one performance. The most surprising aspect of *Hair*'s appeal was that it transcended racial as well as generational boundaries. In August 1969, the month of Woodstock, the Los Angeles cast staged a short run of *Hair* in San Diego's Mountain View Park, for an African-American audience. The Black Panthers were primed to picket this bourgeois distraction, until they discovered that their followers loved it.[10] The cast's next stop was Chino Prison, where they converted Mexican-American convicts to the tribal rock crusade.

But the biggest triumph was yet to come. At an anti-war Moratorium demonstration in San Francisco, the local cast of *Hair* performed before a crowd of committed activists – exactly the audience that might have been expected to see through what Roland Young called 'one of the most decadent bourgeois trips that has ever gone down'. But *Hair*'s pop anthems received an ecstatic response. So too did Crosby, Stills, Nash & Young. David Crosby bellowed his disapproval of President Nixon's policies so loudly that he blew his voice for the band's evening show at Winterland Ballroom. Stephen Stills marked the occasion by reviving his Buffalo Springfield hit, 'For What It's Worth', using it as the launching pad for a diatribe about the state of the nation. As the song finished, Stills screamed into the microphone: 'Politics is bullshit! Richard Nixon is bullshit! Spiro Agnew is bullshit! Our music *isn't* bullshit!' It was an ambiguous (not to mention self-serving) message for an anti-war gathering, which was repeated by both Stills and Crosby over the next few months. Stills was sufficiently impressed by his own courage to suggest that he would undoubtedly have attracted government attention: 'If there's a list, I'm on it.' But when CSNY's manager,

David Geffen, was asked whether any official pressure was being applied to his clients because of their 'subversive' views, he replied: 'Absolutely none. David Crosby insists that he has, but I think it's more paranoia than anything. I mean, David has said some of the most outrageous things in concert about Nixon, but I don't think Nixon cares very much. He probably doesn't know who David Crosby is.'

## THE PIGS ARE VAMPING

We will witness student disorders in the fall which will surpass anything we have seen before. Student militancy will sweep major campuses and flow into the streets of our major cities as the competing factions of SDS strive to prove that each is more 'revolutionary' than the other, and as antiwar protest organisations seek to escalate the fervor of opposition to the Vietnam War. You will see it most likely by October 15, certainly by November 15.

(White House internal memo, 12 August 1969)

Presidential aide Tom Charles Huston hadn't chosen those dates accidentally: Moratorium demonstrations were scheduled to take place across the USA on both days. Some two million people – only 1 per cent of the American population, but still the largest number so far – took part in the October event. Film stars such as Shirley Maclaine and Woody Allen spoke against the war in Manhattan. A month later, half a million people gathered at the Washington Monument, to sing 'We Shall Overcome' and 'Give Peace a Chance', and listen to Arlo Guthrie, Peter, Paul & Mary and (inevitably) the New York cast of *Hair*. The November Moratorium coincided with a White House initiative known as National Unity Week, in which patriotic rallies were co-ordinated to overshadow the Moratorium – or so they vainly hoped. More than a million handbills proclaiming 'Support the President' were distributed to colleges, where most of them were burned by student activists.

It was in San Francisco that the most controversial Moratorium action took place. The rumpus was sparked by Black Panthers leader David Hilliard, effectively running the organisation during Huey Newton's prison sentence and Bobby Seale's embroilment in the Chicago Conspiracy Trial, which had begun on 24 September 1969. The Panthers were floating an adventurous form of international diplomacy, whereby they would negotiate with the

North Vietnamese government for the release of US prisoners of war. In return, Washington would agree to free Huey Newton and Bobby Seale from jail. Eldridge Cleaver travelled to North Korea in September for talks with Hanoi's representatives. He told reporters that 'it's time for revolution to explode', and said that any tactics were valid in the struggle – from bombing US Army bases to assassinating the president. 'We need words that will make the soldiers, sailors, marines and special forces of the US imperialists turn their guns against the commanding officers,' he declared. And he called for firing squads to be prepared for Presidents Nixon and Johnson, Army commanders and 'all warmongers and exploiters'. Moving into his stride, Cleaver continued: 'We need articles by journalists that will inflame the masses, that will spur on the revolutionary temptation to kidnap American ambassadors, hijack American airplanes, blow up American pipelines and buildings, and to shoot anyone who uses guns and other weapons in the blood-stained service of imperialism against the people.'

Safely removed from American jurisdiction, Cleaver was free to utter these threats. When David Hilliard took to the stage at the San Francisco Moratorium a few weeks later, the spirit of Eldridge Cleaver was burning through his veins. Speaking without notes, he launched into an epic tirade about white America's wickedness, and as his adrenalin level rose, so did his rhetoric. 'We say down with the American fascist society,' he cried. 'Later for Richard Milhouse Nixon, the motherfucker. Richard Nixon is an evil man. This is the fucker that unleashed the counter-insurgent teams upon the Black Panther Party. This is the man that sends his vicious murderer dogs out into the black community, and invades upon hungry kids and expects us to accept shit like that idly. Goddamn that fucking man! We will kill Richard Nixon. We will kill any motherfucker that stands in the way of our freedom.' Large portions of the crowd, reliving 1967's love-ins via the *Hair* recital and CSNY's brief performance, howled their disapproval. Two weeks later, Hilliard was arrested and charged with conspiracy to murder the President of the United States – though, like many Panther cases, it was eventually dropped before reaching court.

Hilliard's outburst at the Moratorium soon paled alongside events in Chicago. The times were now unravelling so quickly that several compelling stories ran simultaneously in the same city, and the Panthers had a role to play in them all. Meanwhile, they remained the target for harassment from Mayor Daley's cops. Every month there was another shoot-out, and each time accusations were traded through the pages of the straight and hip press, ricocheting back and forth at bullet speed.

The most notorious episode began when an informer within the Panthers' ranks told the FBI that the party was storing weapons, possibly illegal, in an apartment at 2337 West Monroe Street. The address was a crash-pad for many Chicago Panthers, including Fred Hampton, the unchallenged superstar of local black revolutionary politics, and William O'Neal, an undercover FBI agent. O'Neal had worked his way up to Chief of Security in the local BPP organisation, and had become Hampton's trusted bodyguard. In the small hours of 4 December 1969, agents from the tactical unit of the State Attorney's Office, supported by local police and FBI, raided Hampton's residence. When the first shots rang out, Hampton's friend Louis Truelock tried to wake him with the immortal lines: 'Chairman! Chairman! Wake up! The pigs are vamping!' But Hampton had apparently been drugged, and didn't stir. His partner, Deborah Johnson, recalled: 'I heard a voice from another part of the apartment saying, "He's barely alive", or "He'll barely make it". Then I heard more shots. A sister screamed from the front. Then the shooting stopped. I heard someone say: "He's as good as dead now".'

Nine minutes of almost constant gunfire resulted in the death of Hampton and his comrade Mark Clark; and serious injuries to four other Panthers. State's Attorney Edward Hanrahan made the official statement: 'The immediate violent criminal reaction of the occupants in shooting at announced police officers emphasises the extreme viciousness of the Black Panther Party. So does their refusal to cease firing at the police officers when urged to do so several times.' But examination of the crime scene suggested that only two out of the dozens of shots came from within the apartment; the rest originated from the police. Far from initiating the gunfire, Hampton and Clark had been shot down in cold blood; evidence suggested that Hampton had been unconscious when his fatal wounds were delivered. The press took up the case, and Hampton was added to the Panthers' growing list of martyrs.[11] At his funeral, the avowedly non-violent Rev. Ralph Abernathy, Dr Martin Luther King's successor as head of the Southern Christian Leadership Conference, asked: 'If they can do this to the Black Panthers today, who will they do it to tomorrow? If they succeed in repressing the Black Panthers, it won't be long before they crush any party in sight – maybe your party, maybe my party. I want to tell you this, Fred – you did not die in vain. Though my fight will be non-violent, it will be militant.

There will be no peace in this land.' And so it seemed: almost every day brought more bulletins of arrests and shoot-outs.

Hampton's murder aroused outrage across the movement, and amongst Panthers sympathisers outside the USA. But another, even more prominent member of the BPP had been attracting even wider news coverage. His treatment threatened to undermine the Nixon administration's reputation around the globe. It was merely a shocking sub-plot in a prolonged episode that brought the antagonism between straight and hip America into sharper relief than ever before, and connected the worlds of politics, radical theatre and music in a tragicomedy of bizarre proportions.

## THEATRE ON TRIAL

The place, once again, was Chicago: the United States District Court, Northern District of Illinois, Eastern Division. The plaintiff: the United States of America. The defendants: David T. Dellinger, Rennard C. Davis, Thomas E. Hayden, Abbott H. Hoffman, Jerry C. Rubin, Lee Weiner, John R. Froines and Bobby G. Seale. The presiding judge: Julius J. Hoffman (no relation). The charges: that between 12 April and 30 August 1968, the defendants entered into a conspiracy with other parties, named and unnamed, to travel across state lines with the intent of inciting a riot; encourage the use of incendiary devices; and obstruct police officers in their duties. The backdrop: the Democratic National Convention in Chicago. The small print of the charges – pages of 'Overt Acts' and 'Counts' – added up to a comprehensive summary of attempted urban revolution, aimed at eight men who had been carefully selected as representatives of the entire anti-war movement – radicals, academics, Yippies and Panthers alike.

Hoffman and Rubin represented the movement's surreal wing, a responsibility they carried happily into the trial. Having promised that they would shake the establishment, they regarded their inclusion as a badge of honour. Seale was indicted specifically for his speech in Lincoln Park, but also as a representative of the black liberation movement. David Dellinger, a veteran of peace protests from the 1940s onwards, was one of the leaders of the Mobe organisation. Rennie Davis, an activist with SDS since the early 1960s, had also supported Mobe. Tom Hayden took a similar route to Chicago, via SDS and Mobe, attracting national attention in late 1967 with his trip to North Vietnam to secure the release of American prisoners. Lee Weiner was a graduate student with a heritage of anti-war activism, whose chief role in

Chicago was as a marshal for the Mobe protests. The final defendant was another Mobe marshal, John Froines, a professor at Oregon University.

From the outset, there were obvious weaknesses in the government's conspiracy charges. Bobby Seale's involvement in Chicago had been limited to a stopover of no more than four hours – long enough to travel from the airport to Lincoln Park, and back to the airport. He had taken no part in planning the protests, and apart from being introduced at the microphone by Jerry Rubin, had not met any of his fellow defendants. Weiner and Froines, as marshals, had also not been party to any of the preparations for Chicago; they appeared to have been selected for trial purely because of their academic backgrounds, to illustrate the scope of the supposed conspiracy. The remaining five defendants – each of whom was a defiant opponent of America's war policy – fell into two distinct groups, whose tactics and actions were frequently at odds during the Convention week. Commentators observed that it wasn't just these eight men who were on trial, or even a generation of non-conformists; it was the very right to disagree openly with the American government.

Proceedings began on 24 September 1969; they finished nearly five months later, on 20 February 1970. There followed a lengthy appeals process, at the end of which all the guilty verdicts were overturned, and most observers, even those normally respectful of the American legal system, agreed that the entire episode had been a farce. Perhaps this was inevitable in any trial that featured a judge who ignored basic legal principles, displayed open contempt for the defence, and apparently believed that he had missed his calling as a stand-up comedian; and also the two most prominent members of the Yippies, who undermined attempts by their fellow defendants to turn the trial into a political debate, and undermined still further the idea that the legal process was anything other than a vaudeville routine.

Yet the slapstick had a dark undercurrent. While the other (white) defendants were happy for radical lawyers William Kunstler and Leonard Weinglass to speak on their behalf, Bobby Seale insisted that Charles Garry, the veteran of several cases involving the Panthers, should be his lawyer. None of the defence team objected, but there was a problem: Garry was hospitalised in California, and was unable to appear in court for several weeks. Judge Hoffman had the power to delay the trial, but refused to do so. In retaliation, Seale frequently interrupted proceedings to demand that he be allowed to conduct his own defence. Again and again, the jury was dismissed while

Bob Dylan, the unwilling poster boy of anti-war campaigners in the 1960s. His followers waited in vain for Dylan to declare his opposition to the conflict in Vietnam. (© *John Cohen*)

South Vietnamese women offer a carefully choreographed welcome to the US Secretary of State in 1964. First-hand experience of war was more traumatic, for civilians and combatants alike. (© *Larry Burrows/Time Life Pictures;* © *Keystone*)

Huey Newton, Minister of Defense for the Black Panther Party – one of a generation of activists who drew political inspiration from the surreal imagery of Dylan's 1965 album. (© *Stephen Shames/Polaris, courtesy of eyevine*)

A year before their commercial breakthrough, Latin-rock band Santana supplied a soundtrack to the Peace & Freedom Party's 1968 election campaign. (© *Andrew Sclanders Collection*)

Jazz saxophonist Archie Shepp, whose black nationalist rhetoric provoked violent opposition from the music industry. (© *Frank Driggs Collection*)

White folksingers such as Judy Collins and Phil Ochs were increasingly drawn into the anti-war and black power struggles.(© *Ralph Crane/Time Life Pictures;* © *Andrew Sclanders Collection*)

Eldridge Cleaver, rapist turned revolutionary. His righteous fervour and reckless daring led him into exile, and then expulsion from the Black Panther Party. (© *David Fenton*)

South African singer Miriam Makeba and her husband, activist Stokely Carmichael. Once the public face of the Black Power crusade, Carmichael was forced to take refuge in Guinea after falling out with his comrades in the Panthers. (©*STR/AFP*)

Feminism and Black Power combined forces at a 1969 Black Panther Party rally in New Haven. (© *David Fenton*)

Film director Jean-Luc Godard whispers the secret meaning of his essay in revolution and rock, *One Plus One*, to Mick Jagger. The finished movie baffled the Rolling Stones, leading Jagger to declare that Godard was 'an idiot'. (© *Larry Ellis/Express*)

Phil Ochs at a campaign benefit for Senator Eugene McCarthy in 1968. Attempting to work both inside and outside the system, Ochs was also supporting the Yippies' attempt to make the election an irrelevance. (© *Bob Gomel/Time Life Pictures*)

The assassination of Martin Luther King in 1968 provoked jazz-soul singer Nina Simone to abandon the peaceful campaign for civil rights and lend her support to the Black Panther Party. (© *Jack Robinson/Hulton Archive*)

At the height of student boycotts of US universities in summer 1970, Bob Dylan chose to accept an honorary degree from Princeton – alongside Coretta Scott King (widow of the murdered civil rights leader). (© *William E. Sauro/New York Times*)

Press conferences were a familiar weapon for the revolutionary left. Jerry Rubin fronted a rally for the Chicago Seven (with fellow defendants Lee Weiner, Abbie Hoffman & Rennie Davis at right of picture), while Black Panther Party leaders Bobby Seale and David Hilliard opted for the more modest setting of their Oakland HQ. (© *Silverman/New York Times*; © *David Fenton*)

Black power activist Michael X exchanges radical tokens with John Lennon and Yoko Ono, on the roof of the Black House in North London, February 1970. (© *Terry Disney/Express*)

The National Guard faces down protestors at Kent State University, 4 May 1970. Minutes later, there were "four dead in Ohio". The Weather Underground staged their own Days of Rage confrontation on the streets of Chicago, creating nothing but disillusionment and photo opportunities. (© *Howard Ruffner/Time Life Pictures;* © *David Fenton*)

Angela Davis, a Communist university professor who unwittingly became an icon of the Black Power movement. Her Afro hairstyle was soon a familiar image on student posters. (© *Hulton Archive*)

Yoko Ono, John Lennon and untutored percussionist Jerry Rubin perform at the Ann Arbor benefit concert designed to force the release of imprisoned White Panther Party founder John Sinclair, 10 December 1971. (© *David Fenton*)

Seale raged and Judge Hoffman waved his protests aside. Either the trial collapsed into complete chaos, or the confrontation had to be resolved.

A month into the proceedings, Seale once again interrupted testimony to question a witness in his role of his own defender. 'I am warning you,' the judge interrupted, 'that the court has the right to gag you. I don't want to do that. Under the law you may be gagged and chained to your chair.' 'Gagged?' Seale shouted back. 'I am being railroaded already.' The next morning, the court was full of armed marshals. When the chief prosecuting lawyer began to discuss Seale's conduct, the Black Panther leader finally flipped. Crashing his hands down on the desk, he ranted at the 'racist, fascist pig'. 'Let the record show that the tone of Mr Seale's voice was one shrieking and pounding on the table and shouting,' commanded the judge, as the marshals jostled to control Seale, and the defendant ended up on the floor. What followed was a tableau from the dark ages. Seale was locked onto a metal chair, with handcuffs, leg irons and a choking gag forced around his head and into his mouth. 'Give me your assurance that you will let me defend myself,' Seale mumbled through the cloth. 'I can't understand you, sir,' the judge responded callously. The jury were ushered back into the courtroom and watched in disbelief as the defendant squirmed and gasped for air. 'Your Honour, he is being choked to death, tortured,' cried out one of the defendants. 'You may as well kill him if you are going to gag him,' Abbie Hoffman called out. 'This isn't a court, this is a neon oven.' In his eyes, another Holocaust was on the horizon.

And so it continued. The following morning, Seale was again dragged, handcuffed and gagged with bandages tied tightly around his head, into his place in the courtroom. Even the prosection called for the judge to intervene. Aware that he was losing control, the judge took a radical decision: he declared that Seale was guilty of sixteen counts of contempt of court, and sentenced him to a total of four years of imprisonment. At the same time, he announced that Seale's actions had contributed to a mistrial, and that therefore the Black Panther leader should no longer be included in the conspiracy. He was dragged out of court by the marshals, screaming, 'I'm put in jail for four years for nothing?' while spectators booed, whistled and chanted 'Free Bobby! Free Bobby!'

Seale's treatment provided the perfect rallying call for opposition to the Chicago Conspiracy trial. It symbolised everything that the movement detested about the American administration: its almost instinctive violence, its disregard for natural justice, its innate racism, its brutality, its refusal to listen to the voice of reason. Photographers had been barred from the court-room, but artists captured the inhumanity of Seale's gags in vivid sketches that resembled images from the Spanish Inquisition.

Yet still some of the counter-culture's most prominent figures could not be stirred into making an open gesture of support for Seale. Graham Nash of CSNY recalls: 'Wavy Gravy, who was a friend of mine, called me and said that the Chicago defendants needed money. He wanted CSNY to play a benefit concert for them. David Crosby and I said we'd go immediately, because we thought what had happened to Bobby Seale was disgusting. You cannot tie a man down in court, and gag him, and call it a fair trial. But we couldn't persuade Neil Young or Stephen Stills to go.' His colleagues' apathy stirred Nash into writing a song entitled, simply, 'Chicago': 'When your brother's bound and gagged, and they've chained you to a chair, won't you please come to Chicago . . . or else join the other side.' Nash's chorus revealed his conviction that a band as powerful as CSNY wielded more than symbolic power: 'We can change the world, rearrange the world'. But having relieved his frustration, Nash returned to work with CSNY, prepared to overlook his colleagues' failings in the belief that their music would speak louder than their lack of action.

As the Chicago defence team offered their evidence, they called in favours from several of CSNY's peers, who were more willing to raise their heads above the parapet. They proposed to offer evidence from the leading members of the counter-culture, to prove that far from inciting the demonstrations, the defendants had merely been reflecting the views of a vast minority of American opinion.

On 11 December, William Kunstler called to the stand a key player in the Yippies' festival: Phil Ochs. 'The most fun we had in the courtroom was bringing in our singers,' Jerry Rubin admitted after the trial was over. 'The revolution is poetry – and our generation's poetry is our rock music. Could we get Julie [alias Judge Hoffman] to allow our singers to sing in the court-room – or would that be behaviour unbefitting to a courtroom?' He soon found his answer. Ochs was quizzed about his involvement with Rubin, the search for Pigasus, the pig's arrest, and his part in the demonstrations in Lincoln Park. 'Kunstler asked Ochs what he did next,' Rubin recalled. 'As Ochs began to answer we carried in Exhibit 549, Ochs's guitar, and handed it to him while Julie jumped 300 feet in the air.' Ochs told Kunstler that

Rubin had asked him to sing 'I Ain't Marching Anymore' in Lincoln Park. 'This is the guitar I played on,' he said, looking at the case in front of him. 'How can you tell?' quipped the judge. 'You haven't even looked at it.' There followed some gentle slapstick while the exhibit was formally identified. Kunstler then asked Ochs to sing the song. Defence lawyer Schultz objected: 'Let's get on with the trial.' The judge concurred. As Rubin saw it, 'The guitar – a deadly dangerous weapon – was removed from Ochs and not allowed into evidence. It is a sign of the power of music that it is barred from the courtroom. Who knows the possible effect on the hearts and souls of the jurors if they had been allowed to hear Phil sing "I Ain't Marching Anymore"? What better way to explain what's going on in the streets!' The judge told Ochs he could step down. As the singer moved away, Judge Hoffman slipped in a punchline: 'Don't forget your guitar.'

Arlo Guthrie appeared at the personal request of Abbie Hoffman. 'I really didn't want to go – I was scared,' he admitted after testifying. 'He said, "Come on", so I went. And I got there, I got briefed, and I got on the stand and I did "Alice's Restaurant". You're not allowed to sing, but Alice is mainly talking, so I got away with it. I got through most of the song.' The trial transcript shows that Guthrie's monologue went almost uninterrupted, but when he attempted to break into the chorus of the song, the inspiration for a contemporary Hollywood movie, the judge interjected: 'Oh, no, no. No, I am sorry. I don't want the theatre owner where this picture is shown to sue me. No singing. No singing. No singing, sir.' Guthrie was adamant that the conspiracy charge couldn't stick: 'The defence is trying to prove that the structure of the Yippie movement is non-violent, and that therefore these people did not go to Chicago for violence – that there was no conspiracy. The actual thing happened right there, so there couldn't possibly have been a conspiracy.'

Another performer to fall foul of Judge Hoffman's allergy to music was Judy Collins. Asked about her contribution to the March 1968 press conference at which the Yippie movement had been launched, Collins paused for a second, and then burst into the chorus of the peacenik folk anthem, 'Where Have All the Flowers Gone'. 'Just a minute, young lady,' interrupted the judge. 'He sent the guard over to shut me up,' Collins recalls. 'The man put his hand over my mouth. I think at that point I was in complete shock, that this could happen in a courtroom.' After William Kunstler queried his objection, Judge Hoffman barked: 'I forbid her from singing during the trial.

I will not permit singing in this courtroom.' So instead Collins recited the entire lyric of the song – 'That still seems a pretty appropriate thing to do,' she says today – before explaining why she, like Guthrie, had finally decided not to appear at the Yippies' festival. Throughout her testimony, the judge treated her like an endearingly errant teenager, with little of the hostility he had reserved for male witnesses. His condescending attitude became clear when she attempted to provide an extended answer to one of the prosecution's questions. 'Will you, young lady?' Judge Hoffman began; then, as Collins continued, he asked her: 'Do you hear very well? Do you want to move your hair back?'

The most farcical confrontation between the establishment and rock culture at the Chicago Conspiracy trial came on 20 January 1970, when the defence called their next witness: Country Joe McDonald. 'It was a strange experience to be on the witness stand,' he recalls today, 'because my father had also been on a witness stand back in 1954, in front of the California committee investigating Un-American Activities.' Sixteen years later, McDonald exposed his disrespect for the farcical nature of the trial from the start. 'Country Joe came into the courtroom moving his mouth as if chewing long and slow and deep on gum,' reported one observer. 'By the time he reached the witness stand and raised his right hand, everyone in the courtroom was watching the movement of his mouth.' The clerk of the court intervened: 'You will remove your gum, sir.' 'What gum?' McDonald drawled, like a hippie James Dean. 'The gum you are chewing on,' replied the flustered clerk. McDonald, his mouth still moving, stared the man down for a few seconds. 'I am afraid I don't have any gum,' he said.

This episode set the tone for a dialogue that could have been scripted by Groucho Marx. As Jerry Rubin saw it, 'Joe and [judge] Julie didn't hit off too well. Joe spoke in a slow, quiet, acid manner. He was really stoned. He took his time. If everyone had talked as slow as Joe, the trial might have lasted five and a half years.' McDonald introduced himself as 'a minister in the Universal Life Church' and 'a rock and roll star'. 'I assume that his Christian name is Country,' said the judge in the first of a series of droll asides. 'What is your real name?' McDonald replied: 'I am afraid I don't understand what real means.' 'He is known throughout the world as Country Joe,' William Kunstler chipped in politely. 'That is what you say,' the judge rejoined. 'I have never heard of him.' Kunstler tried again: 'Are you known throughout the world as Country Joe?' he asked the singer. The prosecution objected to this circular line of questioning, and the testimony at last moved beyond identity into the realms of memory. McDonald recalled his first meeting with Jerry Rubin, and was then asked to pick out Abbie Hoffman. 'He is that handsome fellow with the handsome jacket on,' Country Joe said. The judge scolded him: 'Do not characterise him as being handsome or in any other such manner.' 'I am sorry,' McDonald mumbled. 'I have never been in a trial before.'

And so it continued. Inevitably, the opportunity came for McDonald to break into song. As Jerry Rubin recalled, the incident had been carefully choreographed: 'We sat in a restaurant during lunch break, dreaming up the afternoon's fantasy. "Vietnam Rag" [aka "I-Feel-Like-I'm-Fixin'-To-Die Rag"] would be Joe's contribution to [Judge] Julie's heart attack and one afternoon's fun and entertainment. But this time we would have to escalate. Could Joe go into a trance and forget where he was? Could he pretend he was in the middle of a be-in, rock festival, dance hall, even in the midst of a shower? Then everybody – judge, marshals, prosecution – would try to shut Joe up, and he'd think it was part of the show. Joe is a stoned freak and a stoned freak can create his own environment. Bill [Kunstler], Abbie and I started laughing – just in anticipation.'

The moment came when McDonald was asked to recall his first meeting with Hoffman. He explained that he had told Abbie that he had the perfect song for the festival. To illustrate the point, he began to sing: 'And it's one, two, three, what are we fighting for? Don't ask me, I don't give a damn, next stop is Vietnam.' Rubin remembered: 'The courtroom was rent with madness. You would have thought that Joe had pulled out a M-16 [rifle]. They tried to stop him but Country Joe was in another universe.' A posse of marshals rushed to interrupt McDonald, shaking and jostling him, but silence was only achieved when Deputy Marshal John J. Gracious grabbed the singer's jaw and clamped it shut with his hand. 'The judge would like to speak to you,' Gracious growled. Hoffman sighed wearily, and said once again: 'No singing is permitted in the courtroom.' 'It *was* a strange place to try to sing a song,' McDonald notes sardonically today.

Under cross-examination, prosecution lawyer Richard Schultz tried to persuade McDonald to admit that he knew the Yippies were planning to promote 'public fornication' in Chicago's parks. He soon wished he hadn't bothered, as the singer embarked on a lengthy description of his role as a wordsmith. 'Certain words have certain connotations and multi-meanings to them,' Country Joe explained slowly, 'and in the world that I live in, in what is probably called the hippie underground, when we refer to fornication, we are not really referring to the actual sexual act of fornication at all times; we are referring to a spiritual togetherness that can be done without physical contact at all.' Schultz tried again: 'Did they tell you when they were negotiating with public officials that people during the Convention would fuck in the parks?' McDonald smiled for a second, remembering an incident the previous spring, when he had led an audience in Worcester, Massachusetts, through the Fish Cheer, spelling out the word 'FUCK'. 'I got arrested for saying that,' he told Schultz. Quizzed about the possibility that he might have been paid for appearing at the Yippie festival, McDonald drawled back: 'I never discuss money with my friends.' At which point Schultz abandoned the unequal struggle, and the gap between the straight and hip worlds widened another few inches.

After months of frequently shambolic testimony, and lengthy closing arguments, the judge sent the jury out to consider its verdict on 14 February 1970. He then proceeded to hand out sentences for contempt of court, not only to the defendants but to their attorneys as well. Each of the defendants was allowed a few minutes to respond to the charges, producing perhaps the most eloquent testimony heard during the entire trial. David Dellinger went first, speaking for the entire movement: 'You want us to be like good Germans, supporting the evils of our decade, and then when we refused to be good Germans and came to Chicago and demonstrated, now you want us to be like good Jews, going quietly and politely to the concentration camps while you and this court suppress freedom and the truth. And the fact is that I am not prepared to do that.' As Dellinger continued to speak, the judge attempted to force him to be quiet, before ordering a marshal to take him out. His teenage daughters rose in his defence, marshals leaped to quell their protest, and the entire courtroom was engulfed in chaos. While Jerry Rubin chanted 'Heil Hitler' at Judge Hoffman, lawyer William Kunstler broke down in tears, sobbing: 'My life has come to nothing. I am not anything anymore. You destroyed me and everybody else. Put me in jail now, for God's sake, and get me out of this place.'

Four days later, on 18 February 1970, the verdicts were finally announced. Lee Weiner and John Froines were found not guilty; each of the other defendants was found not guilty of the primary charge of conspiracy to incite a riot, but guilty of individual charges of the same offence. Before the judge passed sentence, on 20 February, he again allowed the guilty defendants to speak. 'I am going to jail because I am part of a historical movement,' Jerry Rubin told him. 'This is the happiest day of my life.' Judge Hoffman then sentenced each man to five years in prison. Outside the courthouse, the defendants' partners and children tore up and burned symbolic judge's robes, to denote the death of American justice. Two weeks later, the appeals court allowed the five men out on bail. More than three years of legal battles lay ahead, at the end of which all the convictions would be overturned. Judge Hoffman's tactics had backfired: the irrational way in which he handled the trial, especially his treatment of Bobby Seale, had sabotaged the government's case. Moreover, the five months of courtroom drama had focused the attention of the world on the great divide in American culture – feeding the widespread belief that the nation was on the verge of civil war between generations and ideologies.

## DEATH VALLEY

The murder of Fred Hampton and the blatant injustice of the Chicago Conspiracy trial suggested that America was now out of control, no more able to restrain its violent impulses at home than it was to tame the guerrillas of the Viet Cong. The nation was now held together by paranoia and hatred – of outsiders, dissidents, non-conformists, any strand of society that ran 'counter' to the American way. As the inverse reflection of mainstream culture, the movement was inevitably distorted by the national mood of aggression. If, as Abbie Hoffman believed, the peace and love ethos of Woodstock had translated into apathy, then the only alternative to the violence of the American government was equally extreme violence. But, as both the establishment and the counter-culture discovered during the darkening months of 1969, violence pollutes everyone it touches. As the Chicago trial grew ever more absurd, and the clampdown on black power suffocated the country's morality, so the movement began to mutate into an uncontrollable force, just as likely to wound its own supporters as it was to strike at the enemy.

The rapid implosion of the student anti-war movement illustrated the way in which every version of America was now tearing at its own entrails. The emergence of the Weatherman collective in June 1969 promised a future in which activists would become more militant and more incisive – but also more elitist, to the point where any pretence at representing a mass movement would be abandoned. As the hippie hordes made their way home from Woodstock in August 1969, Weatherman announced a National Action to demand the end of the Vietnam War. Three of the collective, Kathy Boudin, Bernardine Dohrn and Terry Robbins, issued a statement to explain their decision, under the (inevitably) Dylan-derived title of Bringing the War Back Home: Less Talk, More National Action. Their aim, they declared, was 'to build an anti-imperialist, working-class youth movement in the mother country; a movement that allies with and provides material aid to the people of Vietnam, of the black and brown colonies, and to all oppressed people of the world'. Hence the need to Bring the War Home – and where else was home in 1969 but Chicago? Weatherman's mass National Action was scheduled for 8–11 October, to coincide with the prosecution testimony in the Conspiracy trial. Like the Yippies' Festival of Life, the National Action was planned as a multi-faceted event. There would be a memorial rally for Che Guevara, on the second anniversary of his death; a 'Jailbreak' for school and college kids; a militant women's action; a 'youth-rock music festival'; an event designed to 'Stop the Trial'; and a march through the city centre. 'We must be prepared to defend ourselves in the event of any vicious attacks by the Chicago pigs,' Weatherman advised. They believed that the Action would put the convention protests of 1968 into the shade.

Across the remnants of SDS, the Weather agenda dominated discussion that summer. To maintain the links with the counter-culture, the collective's adherents continued to borrow imagery from rock music. A report from the Ohio branch of Weatherman was headed 'Who Do They Think Will Bury You', a line from Bob Dylan's song 'Sad-Eyed Lady of the Lowlands'. A collective from Detroit and Ann Arbor, who dubbed themselves the Motor City Nine in tribute to the MC5, borrowed a line from the Doors in their manifesto, 'Break on through to the Other Side'. Like anthropologists, they described how Detroit's thriving rock culture brought together 'thousands of freaks, bikers and greasers, digging the music and each other, and turning on to dope ... We go there and talk to them about the need to organise ourselves as a fighting force against the Man, taking side with the people of the world.'

Weather philosophy extended from the barricades to the bedroom. Group members were encouraged to share sexual contact in every possible combination, regardless of physical attraction. Self-criticism sessions were also staged, in which each member would be systematically attacked by his or her fellow activists, in order to ensure that nobody's ego would get in the way of the revolution. The collective offered their support to every possible liberation movement, sending delegations to Cuba and North Vietnam, backing feminist and gay rights groups, and treating the Black Panthers as the de facto leaders of the struggle against imperialism.

This all-encompassing approach, and the upcoming National Action, seemed to offer the dazed and fragmented American left a rallying point – an opportunity to rebuild the revolution, and apply it to every aspect of life. Weatherman intended that the Action should flow seamlessly into the Moratorium a week later, in which they intended to take a major role. By the end of the year, their revolutionary momentum would surely be unstoppable.

They weren't the only radical collective preparing for a future made in their own image. Deep in Death Valley, in the Californian desert, on a ranch 'borrowed' from an old man named Spahn, lived a hippie commune known as 'The Family'. During Woodstock weekend, the Spahn ranch was raided by California state police, who believed that the Family were involved in an auto theft ring – stealing Volkswagen cars and converting them into dune buggies. Finding the site deserted, the cops carried out a rudimentary search, and then left.

Their investigations might have been more intensive had they realised that a member of the commune, a young musician named Bobby Beausoleil, was in the custody of their colleagues in Los Angeles, charged with first-degree murder. Beausoleil – who had played in the original line-up of the folk-rock band Love – had brokered a drug deal with a motorcycle gang, the Straight Satans. When the bikers complained that the acid he had sold them was bad, Beausoleil assumed that he had been fleeced. Accompanied by two female cohorts from the Family, and briefly assisted by the commune's leader, he had questioned his source, Gary Hinman, at knifepoint. His victim was cut and stabbed for several hours, before being dispatched with a wound to the heart. Beausoleil's error was stealing Hinman's car, in which he was arrested on 6 August. He was scheduled for trial as the sole assassin.

By keeping silent about his comrades, Beausoleil was maintaining revolutionary solidarity. Although they maintained no links with political groups, the commune shared the belief of the Panthers and Weatherman that America was ripe for total cultural transformation. The impetus came from their leader, a 34-year-old lifelong criminal named Charles Manson. Since his early

teens, Manson had spent almost his entire life behind bars, in teenage institutions, reformatories and adult prisons. He was an inveterate thief, who
specialised in stealing cars, and also had convictions for various forms of
assault, including one instance of raping another young man.

Yet Manson had interests that were unusual in a career criminal. During
one of his brief periods of freedom in the late 1950s, he had joined the
infant Scientology movement. In prison, he studied radical forms of
psychology, and maintained a strong interest in the development of human
potential. In the days leading up to Beausoleil's arrest, for example, Manson
had been staying at the Esalen Institute in California, a prototype New Age
centre on the Big Sur coastline. His research gave him a defiant belief in
his own spiritual and psychological power, which was interpreted by those
he met as a dazzling form of charisma that verged on the supernatural. 'He
gave off a lot of magic,' recalled Family member Lynne Fromme. 'Everyone
was always happy around him. But he was a sort of changeling. He seemed
to change every time I saw him. He seemed ageless.' Endlessly shifting shape
but remaining the same, Manson had all the requirements of a cult leader.

For a man who had been imprisoned between 1960 and March 1967, he
also had an effortless command of recent developments in popular music.
An aficionado of country stars such as Hank Williams and Lefty Frizzell in
his youth, Manson had resented the influx of rock'n'roll stars, such as Elvis
Presley, who had swept his heroes aside in the mid-1950s. Emerging into
an utterly transformed California, however, Manson immediately adopted
the style and ethics of the psychedelic era. By the end of 1967, he had
assembled not only a coterie of devotees, but also an impressive collection
of original songs. 'The first time I heard him sing,' recalled his disciple
Sandra Good Pugh, 'it was like an angel. He wrote songs, made them up as
he went along. Some were beautiful, happy songs. Others would be sad and
moving.'

Though he was older than any of rock music's icons – older, indeed, than
Elvis Presley – Manson's fluent guitar playing and soulful voice won him
admirers among California's hip elite. The key connection came when Beach
Boys drummer Dennis Wilson picked up two Family girls hitchhiking outside
Los Angeles. The heart-throb of an internationally known rock band, Wilson
had little difficulty in seducing the two girls, and he was stimulated by the
prospect of meeting the other women in their commune. What he hadn't
bargained for was the intoxicating impact of their guru. When Wilson heard

Manson's music – flowing folk-rock, like Tim Buckley or Fred Neil, but with lyrics that reflected the cult leader's explorations of psychology – he believed he had discovered a major new talent. He brought his musical collaborator, Gregg Jakobson, out to the commune, and the two men considered signing Manson to the Beach Boys' record label, Brother.

By the end of 1968, the Family had moved to a winter retreat in Canoga Park, which Manson – an admirer of the Beatles' ability to capture the mood of the times – nicknamed Yellow Submarine. His interest in the group took on a darker complexion when he heard their November 1968 release, a double-album entitled simply *The Beatles*. It was the record that contained John Lennon's evocations of urban uprising, 'Revolution 1' and 'Revolution 9', alongside a cacophonous McCartney rock tune named 'Helter Skelter'. Manson replayed these tracks over and over, and claimed that he could detect a hidden message from the Beatles, intended for his ears alone. It was a sure sign of madness, but his Family were so infatuated by their belief in his genius that they accepted his interpretation. For several months, Manson had been making elliptical comments about the revolution – not an unusual trait in the counter-culture, except that Manson's vision was more obsessed with apocalypse than liberation or justice. 'I'm going to have to start the revolution,' he told one of his followers. Fired by the Beatles' personal messages, he began to sketch out a scenario whereby American civilisation would descend into racial war. Blacks, he believed, would soon be killing rich whites in their homes, and scrawling the word 'pigs' on the walls in their victims' blood. His role was to incite the war. But his motives remained obscure. Sometimes he seemed to share militant black contempt for white bourgeois culture; sometimes he appeared to despise the black man, and wanted to encourage the killing so that the police would retaliate against the African-American community; sometimes he imagined that black and white would destroy each other, and then he would emerge from Death Valley to take control of what was left of America. All the evidence, he said, was in the Beatles' songs, from the Piggies 'clutching forks and knives to eat their bacon', to the Blackbird 'waiting for the moment to arise', and of course the Revolution to come. Most compelling, because of its sonic aggression, was 'Helter Skelter'. Manson was unaware that the phrase referred to a British fairground attraction. To his ears, 'Helter Skelter' was the apocalypse, a trigger phrase for blood-letting and racial retribution. As he later testified, 'Helter Skelter means confusion. Confusion is coming down fast . . . I hear what it relates. It says, "Rise!". It says, "Kill!".' As Gregg Jakobson recalled, 'Manson believed that the Beatles were prophets and the songs contained portents of the doom of the white race.'

Through the early months of 1969, as Manson developed his fantasies, a procession of Los Angeles rock luminaries followed Dennis Wilson out to the Family's communal homes, attracted by tales of teen sex, and by the eerie undercurrents of Manson's music. Wilson and Jakobson were now trying to minimise their contact with the Family, but their friends, such as singer Neil Young and record producer Terry Melcher (the son of film star Doris Day), had no such inhibitions. Melcher first visited the Spahn ranch in mid-May, and returned frequently over subsequent weeks. In early June, however, he made a flip comment about Manson's music within the songwriter's earshot, and Manson erupted into a violent rage. He threatened Melcher with a slow and agonising death. The record producer, more accustomed to the gentler whims of the Beach Boys and the Byrds, fled the scene in terror. He was even more perturbed when Manson's threats reached into his Bel Air mansion in the hills above Los Angeles.

Melcher had already decided to rent the house out for the summer, to film director Roman Polanski and his actress wife, Sharon Tate. On the morning of 9 August 1969, he awoke to discover that while Polanski was away in Europe, Tate (then eight and a half months pregnant) and four friends had been savagely murdered in his house. They had been variously shot or stabbed, before three of the bodies were tied up with nooses. The solitary decoration on the wall – a poster for the 1967 Monterey International Pop Festival – stared down at them as a mocking reminder of more idealistic times. The following day, a bourgeois couple named Leno and Rosemary LaBianca were murdered in similar circumstances.

Like Melcher, Los Angeles' wealthiest inhabitants were seized by dread; security firms profited from the panic, as electric gates and barbed-wire fences sprouted in the Hollywood hills. Meanwhile, police struggled to solve the murders. As the cops delved into the private lives of the victims in the Tate murders, they discovered that several of them were heavy drug users. Could this be another case, like Bobby Beausoleil's attack on Gary Hinman, in which drug debts or disagreements would have inspired someone to kill? Four known dealers were targeted by police; bizarrely, two of them were ex-fiancés of the pop singer Mama Cass Elliott. But all of them had watertight alibis, and so the LA police continued to flounder. Meanwhile, California state police monitored the activities at the Spahn ranch. On 14 October 1969, there was a second raid, luridly reported in the local press: 'The last survivors of a band of nude and long-haired thieves who ranged over Death Valley in stolen dune buggies have been rounded up . . . Some of the women were completely nude and others wore only bikini bottoms, deputies said.' After a short period in custody, the 'nude and long-haired thieves' were released on bail, and returned to the Spahn ranch, where Charles Manson resumed the more serious business of plotting race war and revolution.

Meanwhile, another group followed their own blueprint for revolution. On 6 October, the leaders of the Weatherman collective reached Chicago for their National Action, which they were already describing as the Days of Rage. Activists prepared themselves for a street battle, wearing heavy boots (for stomping on 'pigs') and motorcycle helmets, and carrying clubs or iron bars. The Weather collective had envisaged a mass gathering of revolutionary stormtroopers, tens of thousands strong, to strike fear into the American heartland. But the National Action enticed fewer than a thousand participants, who were outnumbered by the watching police. There were speeches, and an appearance by three of the defendants in the conspiracy trial: Abbie Hoffman, Tom Hayden and John Froines. But words weren't enough to convey Weatherman's Rage. Upon a signal, the activists rampaged Chicago's plush Gold Coast district, smashing limousines and shop windows. During the resulting melee, dozens of people were injured, and around 10 per cent of the Weathermen were arrested. It was a dubious victory.

Lincoln Park was earmarked for a 'youth-rock music festival', under the evocative title of 'Wargasm'. But when a few hundred supporters arrived, they found no musicians or stage, only the watchful presence of Chicago police. The chief Weather activists were elsewhere, revising their tactics to accommodate the lack of revolutionary fervour. Everyone present was instructed to prepare for a grand confrontation with the fascist state on Saturday. 'Probably a lot of us will get shot,' said one of the collective. 'But for every one of us that goes down, there will be five to take his place.' That night, there were more planning meetings, which were interrupted early on Saturday morning by a police raid. The stunned activists put up little resistance, dispiriting many of those who had planned to take part in the climactic demonstration. If Weatherman could not fend off a few dozen policemen, how could they overthrow a police state?

That question was answered at midday on Saturday. At the moment when the demonstration was scheduled to begin, not a single Weatherman was to be seen in Haymarket Square. Gradually, activists began to trickle into the city centre, in sheepish tens and twenties. Eventually there were around 300 marching through the city, shepherded by police cars, mounted officers and scores of cops on foot. 'Is this it? Are these all?' said one incredulous policemen as the meagre demonstration passed. Suddenly the activists split into three groups, and for a second there was chaos, as the police reeled around, trying to determine which direction to follow. Hand-to-hand fighting followed. Struggling police and demonstrators careered through plate glass windows, or beat each other to the ground with clubs. Richard Elrod, a lawyer working for the city council, was photographed as he triumphantly grabbed hold of a demonstrator. Less than a minute later, he lay on the ground, paralysed from the neck down. The police alleged that he had been thrown head first against a concrete wall, but subsequent evidence proved that he had tripped and fallen into the wall while trying to make a citizen's arrest. It was the most serious incident of a week in which Weatherman had promised to strike a decisive blow against the system, but succeeded merely in demonstrating the sparseness of their support, and their ineffectiveness when faced with the forces of the state. As the fighting died down, there was one final statement of defiance. A Weather leader made an impromptu address to a small group of onlookers. 'We have shown the pigs that we can fight. We have shown the pigs that they have to overextend themselves on another front. We have taken the movement a qualitative step further. We are now going to split into groups of four or five and take to the subways and buses. We are going to take the lessons we have learned here in Chicago home with us as we go back. We are going to bring the war home!'

It was a proud but empty call. Weather activist Shin'ya Ono hastily wrote an 18,000-word defence of the Days of Rage, boasting that it had been a triumphant justification of the group's political strategy.[12] But numbers spoke louder than words. Even during the National Action, events organised by other SDS factions had drawn larger crowds than Weather operations. And a week later, the first of the Moratoriums proved that traditional SDS campaigning was far more popular with radical Americans than Weatherman's street fighting.

As the year staggered to a close, paranoia closed in with claustrophobic speed. The lunacy of the conspiracy trial convinced the movement that a fair trial was impossible in Nixon's America. The assassination of Fred Hampton proved that the government was prepared to confront its opponents with lethal force. It was a time for solidarity, for trusting your sister and brother, for believing that the movement's divisions could be healed.

That proved to be impossibly naive. The first crack appeared at the start of December 1969, when Los Angeles police revealed that they were charging members of Charles Manson's 'hate-filled cult band of hippies' with the Tate and LaBianca murders. Most of those who sympathised with the movement, from political activists to mellow hippies, stared into the eyes they saw on TV, and wondered what linked Manson's madness with their own imagination; what had perverted the late 1960s ideal of communal living, sexual freedom and musical expression to the extent that it could become a springboard for barbaric slaughter.

## FREEDOM TO DIE

On the same day that 'nude hippies' were arrested on the Spahn ranch in Death Valley, Mick Jagger held a business meeting in London with the Rolling Stones' newly appointed business adviser, Prince Rupert Loewenstein – a merchant banker born into the long-deposed Bavarian royal family. Like the Beatles, who had announced early in 1969 that they were in danger of going bankrupt, the Stones were facing a financial crisis. Their minimal earnings from the record contracts they had signed in 1963/64 were being wildly outstripped by their spending, and the group faced a crippling tax bill. Loewenstein was recommended to Jagger by a mutual friend, and the Stones asked him to investigate their business affairs. At their 14 October meeting, he told Jagger that to improve their tax status they should become residents of France for two financial years. Jagger realised that April 1970 would be too soon for the group to organise such a move, and so they fixed April 1971 as the deadline.

Three days after this meeting, the Stones flew to the United States, to prepare for a lengthy concert tour. Unknown to Decca, their record company in London, they were also planning to begin work on an album, which they would hold back until they were ready to launch their own label after the Decca deal expired in spring 1970. On 27 October, as Bobby Seale's feud with Judge Hoffman in Chicago neared its climax, the Stones held a press conference in New York. While the national media asked predictable questions about the group's image and sexual habits, the underground press focused on the unprecedentedly high ticket prices that the Stones were demanding. Jagger insisted that the issue was completely out of their control: 'We didn't say that unless we walk out of America with "x" amount of dollars we ain't gonna come. We're not really into that sort of economic scene. Either you're gonna sing and all that crap, or else you're gonna be a fucking economist.'[13]

Conscious that the controversy was rumbling across the country, Jagger did his best to maintain his radical image. At each show, the Stones performed their militant anthem, 'Street Fighting Man'. When they reached Chicago, Jagger didn't let the opportunity slip. 'This is for all of you and what you did to your city,' he announced. But the furore over ticket prices refused to die down. 'Those fuckers are making $2 million on the tour, and Mick Jagger practically spit in Abbie Hoffman's face when Abbie asked him for some bread for the Chicago 8,' one fan remarked in Berkeley. As the tour reached its final stand in New York, the Stones made a fateful decision. They had heard that the Grateful Dead were planning a free concert in San Francisco's Golden Gate Park on 6 December. At a Manhattan press conference, Jagger announced that the Stones would also be appearing at the show. It was news to the concert's promoter, Bill Graham, who was faced with explaining to the city's authorities why he had been keeping the Stones' participation a secret.

For a few days, the confusion seemed to settle. Besides the Stones and the Dead, the show would also feature the Band, Dr John, Fred Neil and Ali Akbar Khan; and it would be filmed by a crew under the direction of Haskell Wexler, whose most recent movie, *Medium Cool*, was a critically acclaimed drama-documentary set during the 1968 Democratic Convention. Proceeds from the film would be diverted to 'groups that do things free'. Yet the Stones continued to chip away at the radicalism of their gesture. Quizzed about his commitment to the revolution at the New York press conference, Jagger laughed and said: 'You can't ask a question like that at a thing like this.' According to radical DJ Roland Young, the Stones' true colours were being revealed: 'Mick Jagger was contacted and asked to make a public appeal for the Black Panthers' defence fund. He said not only would he not do that, but if any political speeches were made on the stage, they wouldn't play. And this is the group that put out "Street Fighting Man". See, it's a shuck and it's a sham.' The San Francisco Mime Troupe had intended to confront the Stones about their apathy; instead they were told that their presence at the free show would not be welcome.

As the concert date neared, permission to use Golden Gate Park was withdrawn: San Francisco's city council were concerned that the crowd would be unmanageably large. On 4 December, local news bulletins were divided between the arrests in the Tate/LaBianca murder case, the court appearance by Charles Manson, and the uncertainly surrounding the Stones' concert. Meanwhile, the group were down in Alabama, recording at Muscle Shoals studio, and that evening, the night Fred Hampton was murdered, they were told that a new site had been found for the show: Altamont Motor Speedway, some fifty miles north of San Francisco. As radical journalist Sol Stern and his friends discovered, 'Altamont was just a few miles from Santa Rita, the prison farm where several hundred people had been taken and brutalised by the Alameda County Sheriff's deputies during the People's Park fighting in Berkeley. "Far out", said one of the more imaginative Berkeley activists. "Why don't we turn the whole thing into a march on Santa Rita after the concert and demand that all the prisoners be freed". And for several minutes, some of us were captivated by the image of several hundred thousand marching rock enthusiasts approaching the prison, chanting "free the prisoners".'

It was never going to turn out that way. What happened next has passed into rock mythology as the antithesis of Woodstock; the end of the 1960s; the death-knell of hippie idealism. Around 500,000 people fought their way to the barren location, to discover inadequate sound and sightlines, no food, water or toilet facilities, unbearable desert heat, and little refreshment beyond cheap booze and downers. Security was left to the Hell's Angels motorcycle gang, who were hopelessly incapable of coping with a crowd so large and restless. Doom clouded the air from the beginning; the Hell's Angels responded to any annoyance, such as an audience member staring them out or daring to touch one of their bikes, with mindless violence.

Any hope of political awareness had vanished. Sol Stern reported: 'The first disastrous experience of the day came to the Berkeley radicals who tried to relate to the crowd in a political way. Some of them circulated with buckets collecting money for the Black Panthers' legal defence fund and met with indifference and even hostility from the solidly anti-political rock audience.'

After an opening set from the Flying Burrito Brothers that barely stirred the massive, sullen crowd, the first big-name band took to the stage. Jefferson Airplane prided themselves on speaking for revolutionary youth, but they were powerless in the face of so much darkness. As they performed their most radical anthem, 'We Can Be Together', fighting erupted, and the band were forced to stop playing. When singer Marty Balin leapt into the crowd to stop Hell's Angels from beating up a spectator, he too was clubbed to the ground and briefly left unconscious. That set the vibe for the day: for the first time, rock stars had to appear in front of spectators who were patently not in awe of their fame. Crosby, Stills, Nash & Young delivered an abridged, faltering set, clearly disturbed by the violence unfolding before them. 'Watching [David] Crosby's discomfort on the stage,' Sol Stern recalled, 'I remembered that the same group had played in Golden Gate Park at the November Vietnam Moratorium before a quarter of a million peace marchers. Crosby had taken an obvious slap at some of the political speakers who had preceded him – Black Panther David Hilliard, Dolores Huerta of the Delano grape strikers and Rennie Davis of the Chicago 8. The musician told the crowd, "We don't need any politicians, politics is bullshit". He implied that all we needed to get everything right was the music. But at Altamont his music failed him; it was unable to affect the violence that was engulfing his band, and he watched dumbfounded as the Angels kicked his fans in front of his stage.'

Sensing that the situation was beyond their control, the Grateful Dead refused to perform, and escaped back to the safety of the city. 'There was one thing beforehand that we all should have spotted,' recalled guitarist Jerry Garcia wryly. '[Emmett] Grogan wrote up on the blackboard up at the Grateful Dead office, just as the site had been changed from whatever the first one was, a little slogan which said something like "Charlie Manson Memorial Hippie Love Death Cult Festival". Something along those lines, something really funny, but ominous.' So there was a lengthy delay until the Rolling Stones were prepared to perform, heightening the tension and malevolence of the crowd. The Stones' reluctance was understandable; Jagger had been punched in the face backstage as he arrived at the venue. Among the masses, journalist Lester Bangs allowed himself a moment of elation: 'My God, THE STONES, there they are, and suddenly you're transfigured at the sight of Jagger bursting onstage in an incredible capelike orange-and-black robe.' But the Stones and their majesty soon became irrelevant, with fighting breaking out at their feet, and song after song interrupted, as Jagger called out dolefully to the crowd, 'Brothers, brothers, why are we fighting?' By now, brotherhood had long since fled the speedway. Instead, an 18-year-old black kid, Meredith Hunter, drew a gun and was stabbed to death by Angels. Or maybe he was stabbed first and drew later. It scarcely mattered.

His body was left bleeding in the dirt, a gaping wound in the side of his skull, while the Stones stumbled through 'Under My Thumb'. The world premiere of their sex'n'slavery drama, 'Brown Sugar', passed unnoticed; they hustled through the customary finale of revolutionary defiance, 'Street Fighting Man', in their desire to end their ordeal as quickly as possible. Then it was over, and Meredith Hunter's body still lay in the dust.

It took a while for the news to spread, but even without the murder or a clear sight of the Angels at their most demonic, anyone who was at Altamont knew that it hadn't been a festival. That didn't stop the leading pop paper, the *New Musical Express*, from rating it as 'the world's most fantastic pop concert ever'. Their starry-eyed reporter misread the main event: 'Mick came in for a bit of bother when a long-haired blond youth jumped on him with intent to kill, but the ever-present Hell's Angels were on hand to deal with the bother.' But the paper did provide a tantalising piece of information that was soon forgotten: 'Though the concert was free, proceeds from TV coverage and films will all go to an orphanage for Vietnamese babies.' In 1970, Altamont was the focus of a documentary film entitled *Gimme Shelter*, fully endorsed by the Stones. There was no more talk of Vietnamese babies. For a free concert, Altamont turned out to be very lucrative.

Unlike the *NME*, the West Coast underground paper, the *Berkeley Tribe*, realised what Altamont symbolised. 'Stones Concert Ends It', blared the headline on the front page; 'America Now Up For Grabs'. 'Bringing a lot of people together used to be cool,' mused George Paul Csicsery. 'But at Altamont ... the locust generation came to consume crumbs from the hands of an entertainment industry we helped to create. Our one-day micro-society was bound to the death-throes of capitalist greed. America at Altamont could only muster one common response. Everybody grooved on fear. One communal terror of fascist repression. America wallows in the hope that someone, somewhere, can set it straight. Clearly nobody is in control.' Over the page, his colleague Henry Dankowski erected a mirror for his readers: 'We're turning into a generation whose thing is to be an Audience, whose lifestyle is the mass get-together for "good vibes". "What do you do?" "I go to concerts."' The debate about how Altamont had happened, what it meant, what it signalled for the 1970s, raged for weeks. One writer interpreted Altamont as proof that 'Underground Music is Dead' and that 'we should dig the music and forget the imposed social relevance of the musicians'.

Another said that it represented 'rock as commodity': 'as long as the pre-occupation with material acquisitiveness dominates the rock scene, rock will be almost (not quite) as managed as news releases in Vietnam'. Only two things were certain. After their 1969 US tour, nobody would ever mistake the Rolling Stones for political radicals. That particular piece of mythology was now defunct. And in the wake of Manson and Altamont, it could no longer be assumed that the counter-culture was a storehouse of moral virtue. If hippies could kill and watch others being killed in the name of rock and the revolution, then maybe everything the movement accepted as true had to be rethought. The 1960s were over, and so was the assumption that good vibes and righteous rhetoric could change the world for the better. Activists prepared for 1970, and a push towards a revolution that would be built on violence rather than love.

# SECTION III

# CHAPTER 5: 1970

The seventies are exploding. Armed violence is in the air. In Madison, Wisconsin, an underground terrorist organisation goes on the offensive carrying out four actions in three days. In Champaign, Illinois, two cocktails are tossed into a pig station house, setting a pig on fire. In Seattle two kids are stopped on the street for a hippie check, attack the pig, rip off his piece, and blow his head off. It's happening.

('Revolution in the '70s', Weatherman statement, January 1970)

The mythology of history tells us that 1968 was the high-water mark of counter-culture rebellion. But the student protests of that spring and summer were merely a prelude to the events of 1970. After the Days of Rage and the murder of Fred Hampton, a stark choice faced those who wished to alter the shape of American society: they could either return violence with violence, or face being crushed by the state. Weatherman opted for violence, after which its transformation from a faction of the student movement into an urban terrorist group was inevitable. Yet the Nixon administration was about to present the militant wing of the counter-culture with the perfect provocation. What happened at Kent State might have triggered an outburst that would have left the events of 1968 in the shade. Instead, just at the moment when armed rebellion seemed inevitable, the movement stepped back from the brink. Radical chic took the place of revolution, as rock stars and activists became increasingly intoxicated by each other's cultural power.

## HYMNS OF REVOLUTION
None of the radical groups who wished to attract mass support had openly stepped over the line that divided aggression from self-defence. Individual

Black Panthers, exhausted by harassment from 'the pigs', had shot first and debated tactics afterwards. But this was never the stated policy of the party, as laid down by the imprisoned Huey Newton and Bobby Seale. Weatherman was different. By establishing the bombing of strategic targets as a means of inciting the revolution, it declared itself to be at war with American society. There was no room for manoeuvre; the collective will ruled.

The group's politics were uncompromising. In November 1969, when other radicals rushed to the support of General Electric workers who had called a national strike, Weatherman demonstrated *against* the working-class rebels, classing them as 'pigs' just like their bosses. Equally repellent, to Weatherman's eyes, were the Moratoriums and Mobe anti-war demonstrations. The disquiet aroused by David Hilliard's speech in San Francisco, and the 'politics is bullshit' outbursts by hippie musicians, merely confirmed their distrust of the counter-culture.

Yet Weatherman hadn't entirely abandoned hope of converting other radicals to its cause. 'We should be leading large numbers of young people on the campuses and in the streets in struggles that focus on fighting for power,' announced the group's newspaper on the day of the Altamont concert. 'The highest acts of armed struggle, of course, do the most damage to The Man. But lower-level actions, like violent street-actions, have a real effect on the ability of pig Amerika to function all over the globe. We have to create chaos and bring about the disintegration of pig order. The future of our struggle is the future of crime in the streets.' To set the agenda for the next decade, Weatherman organised a National War Council, held on 27–30 December 1969, in Flint, Michigan, close to the White Panther Party power base of Ann Arbor. The 400 delegates at the Giant Ballroom were greeted by portraits of the world's revolutionary leaders, from Mao Tse-tung to Eldridge Cleaver, and a montage portraying Fred Hampton. Hanging from the ceiling was a giant cardboard model of a machine gun, for cutting down the imperialist paper tigers Mao had warned them about.

To cement the potential alliance with the White Panthers, whose prime motivation was to secure the release of John Sinclair, Weatherman booked the party's rock band, the Up. But when it was time for them to perform, Weather leaders told the band that the political discussion had become so intense that it would be inappropriate to interrupt it with anything as bourgeois as rock music. The Up departed, taking the White Panthers with them. Instead of experiencing the Up, Weather delegates were encouraged to make their own music with the aid of the *Weatherman Songbook*. The collective had composed radical new lyrics for some of the most familiar tunes in rock and pop history, and the results were surreal and utterly crass. When 1950s teen idol Bobby Darin penned the jaunty 'Dream Lover', for example, he can hardly have imagined it being transformed into a political anthem, with scant regard for the original rhythm. 'Because we need a party, to lead the fight, we need a Red Party, so we can learn to struggle right', ran the new chorus. Stranger still, songs from Leonard Bernstein and Stephen Sondheim's Broadway musical, *West Side Story*, were also redesigned in revolutionary garb. 'The most beautiful sound I ever heard' was no longer 'Maria', but the North Korean dictator, Kim Il Sung, leader of the most eccentric of all the globe's totalitarian Marxist regimes. The revised imagery was jarring, to say the least: 'I've just met a Marxist Leninist named Kim Il Sung, and suddenly his line seems so correct and so fine . . . Kim Il Sung, say it soft and there's rice fields flowing, say it loud and there's people's war growing.'

Seven years before the punk band the Clash seized on the phrase, Weather revised 'White Christmas' as 'White Riot'. Irving Berlin's familiar melody was stretched to encompass the new lyrics: 'I'm dreaming of a mass movement, that has the highest consciousness . . . May you learn to struggle and fight, or the World will off you cuz you're white'.

The Beatles' 'Yellow Submarine', that endlessly banal, endlessly malleable ditty, had already endured several political translations, though few as unconvincing as 'We all live in a Weather Machine'. The masses were now expected to sing: 'And our friends are all in jail, many more of them are out on bail. We demand a jury trial, cuz we know it drives them wild'. Another Beatles song borrowed for revolutionary purposes was the John Lennon composition originally intended for Timothy Leary, 'Come Together'. The chorus now read: 'Trash together, right now: off the pig'.

The two most juvenile entries in the *Songbook* might have won the William McGonagall award for poetic ineptitude. It was inevitable that Weatherman would borrow a tune from Bob Dylan, though ironic that they should choose his defiantly apolitical, non-specific 'Lay Lady Lay'. Chicago attorney Richard Elrod had been paralysed during the Days of Rage. Now he was treated as a figure of fun: 'Stay Elrod stay, stay in your iron lung. Stay Elrod stay, play with your toes a while.' Revolutionary consciousness and human sympathy were clearly incompatible. For crimes against musicality, however, nothing matched Weatherman's revision of the Supremes' soul hit 'Stop! In the Name of Love': 'Stop your imperialist plunder, we're gonna smash the state. Revolution has come, revolution has won.'

The *Weatherman Songbook* provided the musical distraction at the National War Council. There were also 'spontaneous' outbursts of chanting among the participants: 'Woman Power!', 'Red Army Power!', 'Power to the People!', 'Off the Pig!' and even 'Charlie Manson Power!' Indeed, the cult leader was enthusiastically claimed as a revolutionary comrade by Bernardine Dohrn. She described the accused murderer as 'a bad motherfucker', and rhapsodised over the Family's conduct after the Tate/LaBianca killings: 'Dig it, first they killed those pigs,' she exclaimed, 'then they ate dinner in the same room with them, then they even shoved a fork into a victim's stomach! Wild!' The room erupted into applause. On a wallchart in the conference room, Weatherman included the murdered actress, Sharon Tate, in a list of those deserving revolutionary vengeance, because she was 'a pig'.

Yet Dohrn's address, regarded by many participants as the highlight of the War Council, was far from a self-congratulatory piece of radical chic. 'We've made a lot of mistakes,' she admitted, blaming Weather's tactical errors on their collective 'white guilt trip'. Then she enumerated the issues on which the group had 'fucked up': 'We didn't fight around Bobby Seale when he was shackled at the Conspiracy trial. We should have torn the courtroom apart. We didn't smash them when Mobe peace creeps hissed David Hilliard on Moratorium Day in San Francisco. We didn't burn Chicago down when Fred [Hampton] was killed ... We've been wimpy on armed struggle ... We're about being a fighting force alongside the blacks, but a lot of us are still honkies and we're still scared of fighting. We have to get into armed struggle.'

While the delegates discussed the finer points of how and when to use revolutionary violence, the Weather leaders left one subject unspoken: the fact that many of them were out on bail after being arrested during the Days of Rage. With court dates and possible prison sentences awaiting them, Weatherman needed something more than a shift of political stance in order to survive. 'Some Weathermen said they did not expect to hold a public meeting of this sort ever again,' one observer noted. It was a clear sign that the organisation was about to undergo its own revolution.

## HEROIN IN THE GHETTO

From the safety of Algiers, Eldridge Cleaver maintained a running commentary on the progress of the American revolution. Although much of the radical left condemned Weatherman's naive aggression after the Days of Rage, Cleaver described this criticism as 'reactionary, invalid and valuable only to the enemy'. The pigs were bound to lose, he argued, because 'there are more of us than there are of them ... There are enough people in Babylon to kick pig ass from the Atlantic to the Pacific and back again.' For Cleaver, Weatherman occupied a role of almost mythic significance in the liberation struggle: 'In times of revolution, just wars, and wars of liberation, I love the angels of destruction and disorder as opposed to the devils of conservatism and law-and-order.'

Isolated from his Panther brothers, and increasingly at odds with the party leadership, Cleaver saw himself as a revolutionary leader in exile, his Algiers HQ the authentic American Embassy in Africa. He instructed his 'Black Brothers in Vietnam' that they should 'come to the aid of your people. Either quit the army now, or start destroying it from the inside. You need to start killing the racist pigs who are over there with you, giving you orders.' He told a visiting CBS-TV film crew that the time had come for President Richard Nixon and FBI chief J. Edgar Hoover to be killed. Meanwhile his small band of comrades – around 30 in all, including fellow Panther members, hijackers and bank robbers – were engaged in selling stolen cars that had been brought in from Europe, and forging US passports and other official documents. He ruled this community at gunpoint, each confrontation hardening his paranoia and ruthlessness.

Back in the mother country, the Black Panther Party was trying to distance itself from its associations with violence and criminality. As journalist Tom Wolfe described in a devastating (if impeccably snobbish) essay, Manhattan socialites were now competing to host fundraising events for the Panthers in their Upper West Side apartments. Conductor and composer Leonard Bernstein – whose work had recently been butchered by Weatherman – hosted one such 'party', which Wolfe attended and assiduously documented. Yet the gathering had a serious purpose: to raise funds for the defence of the 'New York 21', Panther members and sympathisers[1] who had been arrested in spring 1969 on charges of plotting to bomb a bewildering array of public buildings in the city. Besides the fundraisers, the Panthers also staged benefit concerts and rallies on the West and East Coasts; one such event, in Berkeley on 6 February 1970, starred Latin-rock band Santana, who had previously campaigned for the Peace & Freedom Party, the Panthers' allies in the 1968 elections.

Meanwhile, the daily harassment of the Panthers continued. An assault on the Philadelphia office of the party in January was typical: claiming that they had been shot at, police blew out the windows, poured petrol through the front door, and then ignited it. The entire stock of *Black Panther* newspaper back issues went up in flames in a San Francisco warehouse in February 1970. The blaze was ruled 'accidental' by police investigators, but after months of government interference with the paper's distribution, activists were unconvinced.

The government's paranoia about the party was illustrated by its treatment of actress Jean Seberg. The American-born star of Jean-Luc Godard's first feature, *À Bout de souffle*, Seberg was married to French novelist Romaine Gary. She had recently appeared in such mainstream movies as *Paint Your Wagon* and *Airport*, and became a passionate supporter of the black power crusade. From June 1969, the FBI closely monitored her activities, bugging her phone and opening her mail. Agents reported that she was linked romantically to Republic of New Afrika activist Hakim Abdullah Jamal, and later to a leading member of the Panthers, Raymond Hewitt. The Bureau judged her to be 'a sex pervert', and when she became pregnant, they alerted friendly journalists to the 'fact' that the baby's father was black. The stress aroused by a *Newsweek* story to this effect caused Seberg to suffer a miscarriage in August 1970. She sued the magazine for damages, won the case, and presented her winnings to the Panthers. But the combination of government harassment and grief at the loss of her child sent her spiralling into depression. She made regular suicide attempts on the anniversary of her loss, and eventually succeeded in killing herself in 1979 – the same year, ironically, in which the Bureau admitted that they had planted the *Newsweek* story. A typical FBI memo from 1970 illustrated Seberg's plight: it noted that she 'has been a financial supporter of the Black Panther Party and should be neutralised' – a chilling but accurate description of her fate.

Nationally and locally, the Panthers were under constant pressure, so it was inevitable that the party's unity would slowly crack. The Milwaukee branch was the first to disband, in January 1970, when local leaders decided that they could not operate under siege conditions. Some activists slipped sullenly back into the shadows, with no relief from their resentment but the drugs now flooding America's ghettos; others abandoned the Panthers' semi-legal route towards freedom, and formed small terrorist cells. But when the Panthers in Des Moines, Iowa, opted to pursue a more militant war of liberation, they were quickly expelled from the party, adding to the procession of 'traitors' and 'fifth columnists' exposed in the *Black Panther* newspaper.

From Algeria, Eldridge Cleaver issued ever more frantic pleas for the Panthers and their white sympathisers to strike a violent blow against the establishment. With Huey Newton and Bobby Seale in prison, David Hilliard was left to carry the weight of leadership, while still awaiting trial for his threat to kill the president. 'The concept of the Party as a liberation army overthrowing the American government is not realistic,' he recalled. 'The police dominate what we do, how we're seen. We wanted to create a party that would let us – and the black community – determine our own destinies. But now the state – FBI, police, Red Squads – is deciding our fate.'

The clearest insight into the Panthers' predicament came from Stokely Carmichael, their one-time comrade who had fled both the party and the country for Guinea. During a brief return to America in spring 1970, Carmichael once again deplored the pact between the Black Panthers and the Peace & Freedom Party. 'Today, we see twenty-eight members of the Black Panther Party dead,' he declared in a speech in Atlanta. 'There is not one dead member of the Peace & Freedom Party – not one! We see the Chicago Seven after their fiasco in Chicago allowed to smoke pot on TV and go scot free, yet Bobby Seale is sitting in jail.' He had been outraged by the behaviour of Jerry Rubin and Abbie Hoffman during the Chicago trial: 'Many people are carried away today thinking that the hippies and the Yippies and the white mother-country radicals are revolutionary,' he complained. 'They are not. What they are engaged in at Chicago was what Lenin called "infantile disorder".' Carmichael was not the first member of the revolutionary movement to warn against the dangers of drugs; since the mid-1960s, the more puritan elements of the left had dismissed psyche-delic chemicals as a distraction from the serious business of political activism. In the same tradition, Weatherman had attempted to banish drugs from the National War Council, although the collective's leaders were happy to inhale and trip out in more relaxed situations. In the counter-culture, unre-stricted use of drugs was effectively a common language, a central pillar of the hippie manifesto, alongside free love, free music and the freedom to dream.

Yet utopian dreaming had little to do with the heroin now pouring into America's ghettos. Dulling the pain of urban deprivation, quelling the desire for militant political action, trapping its users in a cycle of poverty and violence, heroin ravaged the nation's poorest communities like a plague. So rapid was its progress that many commentators have argued that the influx of heroin must have been approved, if not actually aided, by some office of the government, perhaps as an adjunct to the COINTELPRO campaign. In 1970, however, Stokely Carmichael was swimming against the tide. 'Many say that I am counter-revolutionary because I am speaking out against drugs in the community,' he admitted. 'Unfortunately they know nothing about the history of revolution.' He detailed a list of radical heroes who had fought against the lure of opium. 'Fighting against drugs is revolutionary,' he explained, 'because drugs are a trick of the oppressor. The reason why drug use has reached the proportion it has today in our community is that the political consciousness of our people is rising, and in order to dull the political consciousness of our people, the oppressor always sends more drugs into the community.' Heroin use, he concluded, was a form of 'genocide': 'you're killing our youth,' he told the pushers, 'and if you kill our youth, you kill our army'. Like an Old Testament prophet, Carmichael's pleas went unheard.

Heroin wasn't Stokely Carmichael's only point of departure from the black mainstream. His preoccupation, politically, culturally and emotionally, was his new home: Africa. 'It is the richest continent in the world,' he declared. 'It seems to me that any clear black ideology that talks about revolution, understanding the necessity of a land base, must be pointed towards Africa, especially since we've decided that we're an African people and Africa belongs to all African peoples. It is our homeland!' But the Black Panthers weren't fighting for freedom to leave America: they wanted freedom and self-determination *within* their adopted homeland. When Carmichael declared that white repression would eventually force all American blacks to seek refuge in 'Mother Africa' Huey Newton interpreted this as an admission of imminent defeat.

The increasingly repressive regime of president Sekou Toure in Carmichael's adopted home of Guinea fuelled Newton's misgivings. Twelve years after winning independence, Guinea was a land where all dissent was outlawed, and citizens were encouraged to inform on their neighbours. Historian Guy Arnold described how Toure '"discovered" a number of plots against himself during the [1960s] and used these to eliminate his opponents while also blaming France, the Ivory Coast and Senegal for fomenting discontent. By the end of the 1960s his dictatorship had reached its zenith but he had driven 500,000 of his people into exile and lost the confidence of the rest.' Ironically, 1970 found Toure under genuine physical threat, when around 350 soldiers who had fled the country launched an invasion under Portuguese command. The attempted coup merely hardened Toure's resolve to maintain strict control over his country, which resulted in mass arrests and executions.

In a nation where all the media were owned and operated by the government, entertainment and artistic expression were tightly monitored. Guinea boasted just one record company, Syliphone, which shared its logo with the ruling PDG party. Much of its output consisted of blatant propaganda for Toure and his beliefs, ranging from records of his speeches to anthems hymning his achievements. But aficionados of African music regard Syliphone's output of the late 1960s and early 1970s as equal to that of any country on the continent. Artists such as Bembeya Jazz (and their vocalist Demba Camaron) and Balla et Ses Balladines are still revered today, with Bembeya's blend of Cuban-sounding dance music and melancholy African melodies suggesting a subtext of pessimism beneath the official spirit of triumphalism.

That spirit was in short supply amongst the people of West Africa in early 1970; this was no fantasy land for militant black Americans. The region had been scarred for years by the ethnic divisions in Nigeria, culminating in the declaration of independence by Biafra and the resultant civil war. With the Biafran people being slowly starved into extermination, the rebel state had no alternative but to surrender to the Nigerian forces in mid-January. In other countries, under other leadership, this might have been the occasion for reprisals on a genocidal scale; but instead, the victorious General Gowan began the slow process of reunifying his homeland. Perhaps as many as two million people had died as a result of the conflict, however, and its repercussions were felt around the world.

In March 1970, Nigerian bandleader Fela Kuti, who had sympathised with the Biafran rebels, was forced to return home from exile in California. He left behind Sandra Smith, the woman he credited with introducing him to the concepts of black power and black pride. She joined him in Nigeria some six months later, allowing Kuti to show off this Black Panther member as a trophy. But Kuti found his fellow Nigerians slow to respond to the revolution he had experienced, both musically and philosophically. When he began and ended his performances in Lagos with the clenched fist salute that symbolised black power, audiences did not understand the significance of his gesture. Neither did they relate to his political agenda of 'blackism', which seemed irrelevant in a nation already under black rule. What did communicate was his music, which took the vibrant dance rhythms of West Africa and added the eclectic, drug-tinged funk of Sly & the Family Stone, the jazz-rock of Miles Davis' contemporary bands, and the street anger of the proto-rap outfit the Last Poets. Over the next few years, Kuti carried his Nigerian listeners on his own journey from African-American soul to a distinctively local form of musical militancy, which would set him at odds with his country's rulers for the rest of his life.

## X = BLACK POWER

The crusade for black power and the Nigerian civil war reverberated in unexpected places. In the old colonial capital of London, John Lennon watched with pride as TV reports showed US anti-war demonstrators singing his anthem 'Give Peace a Chance'. It was some justification for the vilification that had greeted his marriage to Yoko Ono and their own peace campaign. The pressure had taken its toll; both husband and wife were still struggling to beat the heroin addiction that had afflicted them sporadically for almost a year, and Ono had just suffered her second miscarriage. Yet Lennon continued to offer himself up for ridicule. The London premiere of a film documenting his penis in various stages of erection had done little (on any level) to boost his reputation. Even his musical projects seemed designed to court controversy: the week after the October Moratorium, he released a new single, 'Cold Turkey', inspired by his attempts to quit heroin. The song had already been rejected by the other members of the Beatles, from whom Lennon had become irrevocably estranged. The four men would never work together again.

None of his recent activities, however, attracted the opposition that greeted the peace event he announced on 25 November 1969. In summer 1965, to the horror of many previous recipients, the four Beatles had each been recommended for MBE (Member of the British Empire) awards by Harold Wilson's government. Lennon had given his award to his aunt, who displayed it on top of her television set, but now he sent a Beatles aide to retrieve it. Aunt Mimi was one of millions of citizens outraged to discover that he had broken with protocol by returning his medal to the Queen. Lennon sent handwritten notes to the British monarch and Prime Minster, and also to the Secretary of the Central Chancery, the office that administered the awards. They read: 'I am returning this MBE in protest against Britain's involvement in the Nigeria–Biafra thing, against our support of America in Vietnam and against Cold Turkey slipping down the charts. With love, John Lennon.'

His critics didn't know whether to be more appalled by the gesture, by the flippant tone with which he had addressed Her Majesty, or by the effrontery with which he had chosen to promote his single. 'I included the reference to the record as a gimmick or a twist to take the seriousness out of it,' he explained as the news broke. 'All anti-war movements make the same mistake. They get too serious and they get battered to pieces. The seriousness and uptight antics of the left and right wing approach doesn't work. To throw something camp or irrelevant into the situation makes it more valid.' Yet this apolitical stance won little sympathy from the same radicals who had rejected his earlier bed-ins as publicity stunts. Britain's role in 'the Nigeria–Biafra thing' had been obvious for more than a year by the time Lennon offered his disapproval, while more politically aware musicians had been lending their names to protests against the war since 1964.

A week after he had returned his MBE, Lennon was filmed sparring with an American reporter. His adversary was not a showbiz columnist or radical hippie, but Gloria Emerson, the high-brow, high-bred London correspondent of the *New York Times* – a formidable intellect, who had spent time in war zones around the world, and was about to begin a lengthy spell in Vietnam. Lennon and Emerson had been born worlds apart, and the Beatle's working-class consciousness was soon riled by the journalist's assumption of social and moral superiority. Goaded by Emerson's accusation that his MBE event had been a publicity stunt, Lennon snapped: 'If I'm gonna get on the front page, I might as well get on the front page with the word "Peace".' 'But you've made yourself ridiculous,' Emerson countered. 'To some people,' Lennon conceded, 'but I don't care – if it saves lives.' Emerson was flabbergasted: 'You don't think you've . . . oh, my dear boy, you're living in a never-never land. You don't think you've saved a single *life*.'

Thirty years later, Emerson reflected: 'If he had really wanted to stop the war in Vietnam, all he had to do was tell the US Army he wanted to go there to entertain the troops. Many entertainers did. And it would have thrown the Army into the most extraordinary panic. I think he could have stopped the war if he had gone.' It's an intriguing image – Lennon leading an audience of war-hardened American troops in a chorus of 'all we are saying is give peace a chance'.

Lennon was clearly uneasy and a little defensive about his choice of tactics. 'We're not going to Vietnam to die for it or going to Biafra to die for it,' he told another interviewer that week. '[But] we've considered everything – not dying, but going to the places.' He added prophetically: 'People prefer a dead saint to a living annoyance like John and Yoko. But we don't intend to be dead saints for people's conveniences.' He remained adamant that whatever movement still existed, he was not going to act as its vanguard: 'I believe that leaders and father figures are the mistake of all the generations before us. Everybody is a leader. People thought that the Beatles were leaders, but they weren't.' Cultural critic Karl Dallas wasn't convinced: he believed that the Lennons' fatal flaw was 'the thought that being John and Yoko gave them some sort of special power to achieve what Mr and Mrs John Nameless couldn't do; the failure to realise that being John and Yoko was precisely what disqualified them from the start . . . If you must go, prowl around the edge of the demos unrecognised and try your best to understand – because, being Mick [Jagger] or John or Bobbie [Dylan] or Joanie [Baez], what actually else can you do without fucking up the whole scene?' Yet Lennon remained convinced that 'the problem with the revolutionaries is that they get so serious, so involved, that they're now playing the politicians' and the establishment's game'. The argument wound round and back upon itself, and Lennon sat enmeshed in the coils, like a snake confused about whether the tail twitching in front of its head is its own or its enemy's.

'I can see his point in using advertising and big business methods to try and win peace,' commented British folk-rock musician Roy Harper, who was himself grappling with the repercussions of his own much less onerous fame. 'If John could get rid of his Rolls-Royce and his great big houses and come and live in the ghettos, and then start organising things, I'm sure he could get a lot more done.' What Harper didn't realise was that a representative of the ghettos had already decided to visit Lennon, dragging him away from peace towards the lure of revolutionary political action.

On several occasions in early December 1969, the receptionist at the Beatles' Apple headquarters announced an unexpected visitor for John Lennon: Michael Abdul Malik, formerly known as Michael X. Since his dalliance with the Rolling Stones in 1967 and his outspoken attacks on white power, Malik had served a prison term for contravening the Race Relations

Act. He emerged on parole in July 1968, as Lennon was working on 'Revolution' with the Beatles. He fell into the company of a London-based radical group called the Black Eagles, who self-consciously modelled themselves on the Black Panther Party. As the most notorious member of Britain's black power movement, he rapidly assumed the position of Minister of Defence. But his status would soon be overshadowed by his good fortune.

Malik befriended Nigel Samuel, the heir to a substantial London property empire, and godson of Labour politician and lawyer Lord Goodman. The youthful Samuel was clearly embarrassed by his wealth. When he met Malik, he was already channelling funds into a culture venue, the Arts Lab, and the influential underground newspaper, the *International Times* (*IT*). 'He felt he was getting his own back against racism in the Labour Party,' says his friend Barry Miles. 'He was also schizophrenic, which we didn't realise until later. Half the things he said didn't make any sense, but those were the days when R.D. Laing was telling us that schizophrenics were saner than any of us, so it didn't seem to matter.'

Bewitched by Malik's charisma, Samuel agreed to underwrite the British quest for black power. Besides financing the movement's activities, Samuel purchased a substantial property in Holloway Road, North London. The building – soon dubbed 'The Black House' as an echo of Eldridge Cleaver's headquarters in San Francisco – was originally intended to double as a community centre and an Afro-Caribbean supermarket. But it became a power base for Malik, where he could 'play the roles of Black Power leader, tycoon, religious head and reformed crook'.

At various times, Malik proclaimed himself the British leader of the Black Panther Party or its more radical American cousin, the Black Liberation Army. His media statements were often exaggerated, but journalists were swayed by the comparative opulence of the Black House into believing that Malik had a mighty organisation at his command. He greeted visitors from behind a vast oak desk, a portrait of Malcolm X on the wall behind him as proof of his lineage. 'I was afraid of Michael X,' admitted *IT* co-founder John Hopkins. 'He was an opportunist and there's nothing wrong with that. But I'm sure he was winding up the white liberal underground. His view of what was happening was probably a lot different from our view of what was happening.'

Amongst the black community, Malik found support from intellectuals and activists alike, as well as the criminals with whom he had mingled in

Notting Hill years earlier. He promised not only a radical uprising against white racism, but also a degree of community aid that the Black Panthers might have envied, had it materialised: free food programmes, assistance with legal aid, the formation of arts centres for Afro-Caribbeans. 'We plan to sweep our angry youth from the street corners into creativity,' boasted a Black House manifesto, 'into centres to listen unmolested to our own music which is so different in content and flow.' But it was not black music that provided the most lucrative source of funding for Malik's empire. He had burned many of his bridges to the white underground in 1967; during the Reading speech that had provoked his arrest, he had declared: 'The white liberal is a dangerous person. When he comes to help, he comes to destroy you.' But now he exploited Nigel Samuel's links to the hippie community, encouraging his patron (living in the Black House himself) to solicit dona-tions from leading pop managers, and suggesting that the two men should promote a rock festival.

'Michael was a persuasive guy,' explains Barry Miles. 'He became what-ever people wanted him to be. And he was absolutely charming. So he was incredibly manipulative, and very clever at making you feel relaxed, as if you were his closest friend. I was at a party with him once in this gorgeous fucking London house, surrounded by all kinds of important people – William Burroughs, Stephen Spender, businessmen, everyone. At one point in the evening he came over to me, opened up his jacket, showed me a bundle of cheques, and said "Another white liberal bites the dust!" He would spin these rich people his yarn, and in those voluptuous surroundings, how could they not write him a cheque? John Lennon was bound to be impressed by him. It was inevitable.'

Lennon's sympathy towards those protesting against the establishment encouraged Malik to believe that he might have found a bottomless source of revenue. So he launched a concerted campaign to prick the singer's conscience. His rhetoric was well-chosen: as a child of Liverpool, a city that had grown wealthy from the slave trade, Lennon was susceptible to calls for the redress of ancient wrongs. Malik told him it was right that a beneficiary of slavery should help to finance the liberation of the slaves' descendants. 'You have stolen the rhythms of the black people you knew in Liverpool,' he accused the superstar. 'You might have done it consciously or uncon-sciously. Anyway, now you owe us a debt.'

Despite his theoretical wealth, Lennon did not have instant access to the

Beatles' riches. The hiring of Allen Klein as their manager and Apple managing director earlier in 1969 had halted the quartet's spending sprees. Aware that funding a black revolution might not be a priority for Klein, Lennon agreed to back Malik with money from another company, Lennon Productions, which was owned solely by himself and Yoko Ono. To balance the books and calm the accountants, he offered Malik around £10,000 as an advance against the royalties for a book that would be entitled *A Black Experience*. There is no sign that either party ever expected the volume to be completed. According to the Black House treasurer, Terry X (aka Terry Radix), Lennon also laid his hands on a substantial sum in cash, which Terry and Malik collected in a brown paper bag from Yoko at Apple's office in Savile Row. After paying overdue wages to his Black House staff, Malik appears to have pocketed the remainder for his personal use.

It was a brief period of utopian optimism for Lennon, who left London in mid-December for Canada, where he announced plans for a Toronto Peace Festival the following summer. 'John totally believed that love could save us,' recalled Canadian Ritchie Yorke, who spent time with Lennon during this trip. 'He thought that if one person really stood up, things could be changed. I've never seen anyone so committed to a cause, regardless of the cost.'

After two weeks of peace frenzy in Canada, the Lennons flew to Denmark, where they relaxed for ten days with Yoko Ono's ex-husband, Tony Cox. At Cox's farm, Lennon suggested that he and Yoko should crop their hair in a symbolic gesture of cleansing and rebirth. At the height of Beatlemania in 1964, thousands of the group's fans had bought tiny pieces of the bed linen in which they had slept. How much more valuable, then, would Lennon's hair be? The locks were carefully scooped into a bag, and returned with the couple to England.

Michael Abdul Malik had been carefully waiting for news of the Lennons' reappearance, and he was among their first visitors at Apple in late January 1970. His earlier success at fundraising had prompted him to widen his net. He had already approached Mick Jagger and Marianne Faithfull, both of whom politely declined to help him. Now, in an excess of self-belief, he contacted Welsh pop idol Tom Jones, whose management immediately turned him away. Malik was more fortunate when he targeted black luminaries in the States. Comedian Dick Gregory and entertainer Sammy Davis Jr, both supporters of civil rights and black liberation, provided funds; while deposed heavyweight boxing champion Muhammad Ali offered him not only several thousand dollars, but also a pair of shorts stained with the blood of a recent opponent.

When Lennon was informed of these gifts, he recognised a potential public relations coup. He told Malik that he and Yoko Ono would visit the Black House a week later. Then he instructed his press agent, Derek Taylor, to alert the national papers to another Lennon event. Taylor and his Apple assistant, Richard DiLello, duly accompanied the Lennons to the Black House on 4 February 1970. Malik, standing side by side with his longtime associate, beat novelist Colin MacInnes, 'gave Richard and me the surliest welcome we'd had as associates of the famous', Taylor recalled. Lennon then commanded the Beatles' PR man to hand over money for a signed copy of Malik's ghostwritten autobiography, *From Michael De Freitas to Michael X*. Anxious not to embarrass his boss, Taylor complied.

The party climbed up to the Black House roof, where they waited for journalists to arrive. Twelve months earlier, Lennon and the Beatles had performed on the roof of their Apple HQ in central London, attracting enormous interest from press and public alike. After a solid year of bed-ins and other antics, however, news editors were growing weary of the Lennons, and only a handful of reporters and photographers attended. The ceremony went ahead, nonetheless. Lennon produced the bag of hair that he and Yoko had collected in Denmark, and held the contents triumphantly above his head. Malik posed rather coyly alongside them, holding Ali's boxing shorts. Then the two men exchanged their tokens. Malik's voice faltered as he told the press that he would have preferred to 'keep and cherish' the couple's hair, but that he intended to auction it. He hoped to raise funds for his organisation which, he claimed, required £120,000 to maintain its community presence. Lennon replied that he would be selling the shorts for the same cause, and predicted that his hair would probably fetch £119,000. 'Maybe some American will buy it,' he joked.

As Derek Taylor recalled, 'The press pictures were not pretty; the angry head of Malik and the shorn, scrubby, impudent scalps of John and Yoko, a long way from fabness by now. Little appeared in the evening newspapers and nothing in the papers next morning. We had blown it. Over-exposure. At last. They were to blame; I was to blame; we were all to blame.' Nor was any money raised for the Black House. After auctioneers Sotheby's and Christie's refused to handle the sale of the hair, Malik planned to divide it into thousands of minute portions, each artistically presented in a gift box. But nobody at the Black House had the patience to carry out such a scheme, and the Lennons' offering soon lay forgotten on an office shelf.

Three days after this abortive PR exercise, the Lennons accompanied Malik onto the popular BBC TV programme *The Simon Dee Show*. It was Malik's only exposure to the mainstream, and it won him few converts. Not that Lennon was abashed. 'We're going to do a poster with him, a John and Yoko poster,' he explained in mid-February. 'It will have "Black and White is beautiful" on it, and try to hustle a bit of bread for him. But mainly PR is the thing, showing that black is beautiful.' He continued to have faith in Malik's innate pacifism: 'As Michael said to us, he's in a fortunate position to be able to think in terms of non-violence, but he finds it difficult to explain to his brothers who are pushed up against the wall and killed by police cars that non-violence is where it's at.' The Black House community were, he claimed, matching up to their original manifesto: 'They're doing it in the ghetto, they're building the restaurant, they're giving away the excess food, they're trying to show people that they can do it in the most extreme circumstances.' It was moving testimony, although physical evidence of the Black House's social programmes was difficult to locate. Any doubts were apparently dispelled by Malik's character: 'He's a beautiful cat,' the singer insisted.

The media's passing interest in the relationship between Beatle and black power dissipated in the wake of Lennon's next public action. On 11 February 1970, he paid a total of £1,344 to cover the fines imposed on 96 British anti-apartheid activists. They had been found guilty of public order offences after a demonstration protesting against the appearance in the UK of the South African national rugby team. The campaign was supported by Members of Parliament, churchmen and journalists, and the Lennons' intervention prompted none of the media criticism that had been aimed at the earlier peace crusades. It seemed as if the maverick musician had been assimilated back into the mainstream of political debate.

Despite his association with Britain's premier champion of black liber- ation, however, Lennon said little to persuade other radicals that he was ready to become their mascot. 'Marching was alright for your parents,' he noted. 'We got more pay for the workers in the 1800s by marching, but I don't think it'll work this time, just marching up and down.' Mass action was clearly passé. What mattered now, Lennon reckoned, was to infiltrate the mainstream: 'We have to learn the language, we have to get out and talk to our parents and the establishment, because they obviously can't talk to us. It's up to us to take the initiative, not say, "Daddy, you old cunt", and then run away.'

Jerry Rubin and Abbie Hoffman would have been startled to hear Lennon doubting the extent of his, and their, power: 'What the underground has got to remember is they're still a minority, and they're not representative of the youth, any more than I am. And that's what we've got to realise, that we haven't got youth sewn up, by any means. We haven't even converted our own contemporaries, we're not even communicating fully with *them*.' It was a telling admission: if there was a Woodstock nation, then it might extend no further than the 500,000 who had attended the Woodstock festival. Drawing more from *The Wizard of Oz* than *The Communist Manifesto*, Lennon laid out his strategy for change: 'All we have to do is withdraw our energy from government, withdraw our yes and say no. It's as simple as that.'

Beyond his naive positivism, however, Lennon was ideally placed to report on the mindset of his peers, translating his own experience into the mood of the times. 'I think that a lot of people are in what they term as the Post-Drug Depression period,' he explained, 'where there's no hope and they're all hooked on various whatevers. I know a lot of people are knocking Dylan because he's singing songs about love, saying that he's not committed, no more war songs. He's singing about love now, and that's more committed than anything. We're been through the Post-Drug Depression and I think Dylan obviously has. Now we've resurrected hope in ourselves, and we're hoping to spread it around a bit.' But clearly he was hoping to inspire himself more than anyone: 'I wanted to start year one of the 1970s with a cleaned-out system and manifest it to myself in the mirror, to remind myself that we have reorganised on a physical level.' It was an early display of a central philosophy of culture in the 1970s: self-help and self-healing as a means of saving people and beyond them the planet.

As if to provide a role model for the era to come, the Lennons soon flew to Los Angeles, to begin several months of intensive Primal Scream therapy with the psychologist Dr Arthur Janov. There was no politics in the Primal Scream: all of life's ills, the fundamental neuroses that hampered every individual, could be traced back to an initial moment of agony experienced by a child unable to satisfy its desires. If patients excavated decades of buried emotions, they could unleash the primal scream that would reconnect them with their own pain. The late 1960s counter-culture had spawned a tradition of radical psychotherapy, in the work of revolutionary thinkers such as R.D. Laing and David Cooper. But their subversion of traditional psychiatric techniques refused to isolate the personal from the political. In Janov's worldview, which Lennon adopted as his own during 1970, all that mattered was the individual child and its longing for mother, food and warmth. Everything else – war, poverty, injustice – could be wished away, with a prayer or a scream.

## BALL OF CONFUSION

Such isolation was not available to young black America. With their revolutionary culture under assault from every angle, black radicals were quick to claim artists of every hue as their spokesmen, and just as primed to punish any sign of apostasy. James Brown's ambiguous relationship with political activism had already aroused comment, much of it critical, for several years. When he wasn't rhapsodising over the wonder of America, his music fulfilled every implication of his 1968 hit, 'I'm Black and I'm Proud'. But Brown the man was less reliable as an ally than Brown the musician. The Black Panther newspaper exposed him as a 'capitalist pig', who not only worked for the man but used the man's methods. Conscious of the need to retain the support of young African-Americans, Brown shrugged off his association with President Richard Nixon, who had courted him in an effort to secure more than a fragment of the black vote: 'Me and Nixon don't get along. He asked me to go along to Memphis in the campaign. I didn't want to be his bullet-proof vest.' Brown also rejected any distinction between radical blacks and 'respectable Negroes'. 'There is no such thing as a black militant,' he declared. 'When a person's tired of being treated like a puppet, that's when he's labelled a militant. Give him his rights and you'll have no trouble with him.'

It was a lesson he was slow to learn himself: in March 1970, Brown's entire band, the creators of the funk sound that had revolutionised R&B, laid down an ultimatum. Either they were treated with the respect enjoyed by other top touring bands, or they were quitting. Brown called their bluff, and assembled a line-up of unknown youngsters, with whom he cut the toughest, slickest music of his entire career – 'Get Up I Feel Like Being a Sex Machine', 'Soul Power' and the activist anthem 'Get Up, Get Into It, Get Involved'. During 1970, he released an album entitled *Revolution of the*

*Mind*, although it was funk that he kept reinventing. Only one thing stayed the same, despite his militant swagger: his knack for exploitation. By March 1971, Brown's new band, led by teenage bass maestro William 'Bootsy' Collins, had also walked out, infuriated by their low wages and their leader's tyrannical behaviour. The mind was the one part of James Brown that the revolution could never reach.

Elsewhere, militancy was leaving its mark in unexpected ways. Berry Gordy's Motown corporation in Detroit, black-owned and almost entirely black-staffed, had steered a course towards acceptance by white America throughout the 1960s. Acts such as the Supremes and the Temptations were groomed for plush supper-clubs, cabarets and uptown hotels. Motown encouraged its artists to remember the financial rewards of targeting the pop audience as well as the soul brothers and sisters. For every slice of downhome grit, there was an album of Broadway standards and Beatles covers to swallow.

Even in this conservative and relentlessly commercial milieu, however, there was room for change. Songwriters Barrett Strong (best known for his early 1960s hit 'Money') and Norman Whitfield decided to carry Motown into the heart of contemporary black America. During 1969 and 1970, the acts they handled – the Temptations, Edwin Starr, the Undisputed Truth – displayed hotter funk grooves than anything Motown had produced in the past. But the real revolution was in the words. Whitfield and Strong abandoned teen romance in favour of inner-city realism. The Temptations were now exhibiting their peerless vocal interplay on songs that tackled drug addiction in the ghetto ('Cloud Nine'), the turmoil of Vietnam-era America ('Ball of Confusion') and even the shift towards all things African ('Ungena Za Ulimwengu'). Most shocking of all, however, was a series of songs that cut to the heart of the black power debates. 'War' and 'Stop the War Now' (both recorded by the Temptations, but turned into hit singles by Edwin Starr) brought the anti-war movement into sharp focus on Top 40 radio. Meanwhile, 'Message to a Black Man' offered an unprecedented (for Motown) statement of racial pride and determination: 'My skin is black, but that's no reason to hold me back . . . because of my colour, I struggle to be free . . . no matter how hard you try, you can't stop me now'. As the song throbbed to a menacing climax, Dennis Edwards echoed James Brown's proclamation: 'I'm black and I'm proud'. Motown artists who had previously maintained a safe distance from political involvement, such as Martha Reeves & the Vandellas and the Four Tops, were now performing songs that commented directly on the war and the peace movement.

Motown's shift from pop to political analysis heightened the pressure on other black artists who coveted the mainstream. Sly & the Family Stone had triumphed at Woodstock, and by 1970 their blend of psychedelic rock, funk, soul and Top 40 pop had established them as one of the most popular recording acts in America. Their musical melange was echoed by their line-up, which combined black and white, male and female, under the leadership of Sylvester Stewart (alias Sly Stone). For black nationalist critics such as Amiri Baraka, the band's multi-racial approach was a sign of 'weakness'; the black members of the Family Stone were simply 'imitating imitations of ourselves'. Only black men were entitled to stake a claim to the revolution, Baraka argued: 'We are the real warriors, and we must plan the real war.' Stewart's songs rejected this race-based response to the outside world; as he wrote in 'Everyday People', his manifesto was 'different strokes for different folks'. By 1970, however, his personal life was beginning to mirror the plight of the ghettos, as cocaine addiction sent him spiralling out of control. His name became synonymous with 'no-shows', and when he failed to appear at a giant free concert in Grant Park, Chicago (home of 1968's convention protests), a riot ensued. 'Sly is a political group,' complained the park's head of security. 'He appeals to the hardcore black ghetto group, and that's a dangerous thing, right there.' But the riot actually owed more to the alcohol consumed during the delay, and then the anger sparked by Stewart's absence, than by any display of black militancy.

The political ambivalence of Sly & the Family Stone's music was also apparent in the work of the man still revered as the most influential and adventurous rock musician of all time, Jimi Hendrix. He was, according to Abbie Hoffman, 'the only rock performer I know of who gave bread to anything most of us would call "radical".' Hendrix's FBI files reveal that that the guitarist intended to perform a benefit concert for Hoffman and the other defendants in the conspiracy trial. The concert never took place, but Hoffman confirmed that 'he laid some bread on us for the trial', and also financed 'a marijuana mail-out' to the defendants.

Hendrix had made his reputation in England, working with two white British musicians. Despite the fact that blues, R&B and soul underpinned most of his work, he was marketed and recognised as a rock musician — and a 'wild man', untamed, as if fresh from the jungle. Hence the lack of

interest sparked by his eventual return to black America. As author Greg
Tate argued, 'All boundary crossers face the inherent problem of coming
back. In Hendrix's case, his timing could not have been worse. Here, after
all, was a Black artist who stepped way on the other side of America's
racial/musical/political divide at a time when lines were being drawn in the
sand.'

His achievement – or curse – was to be colour-blind, and to encourage
colour blindness amongst those around him. In the England of 1967, where
most people routinely referred to blacks as 'niggers' or 'coons', Hendrix
managed to transcend the country's inherent racial prejudice by becoming
a rock guitar hero, and therefore an honorary white.[2] In return, Hendrix
threw himself into the exclusively white milieu of the rock aristocracy,
accepted as a race-free brother by the likes of the Beatles, the Rolling Stones
and Cream. Only when it came to sex, and the timeless clichés about the
virility and physique of black men, did his race become relevant to his appeal,
and then the stereotype seemed to work in his favour, boosting his mystique
and exotic appeal.

In America, where the divide between black and white was immediate
and unavoidable, Hendrix's racial choices appeared more significant. When
his original band, the Jimi Hendrix Experience, broke up early in 1969, he
returned home to New York. As he resumed contact with his pre-fame
friends, his racial identity became impossible to ignore. Back in England,
Hendrix could insist: 'Music is stronger than politics. I feel sorry for the
minorities, but I don't feel part of one.' In New York, he was regularly
quizzed about his support, or otherwise, for the Black Panther Party. 'On
at least two reported occasions,' alleges Greg Tate, 'he was accosted backstage by members of the Panthers out to hit him up for cold cash money.'
Maybe it was coincidence, a purely musical decision, and maybe not; but
when Hendrix formed a new band, Gypsy Sun & Rainbows, with whom he
performed at Woodstock, every one of the musicians was black.

Two weeks after Woodstock, Hendrix made a symbolic gesture to Harlem,
appearing at a street festival organised by the United Block Association.
Appearing on a flatbed truck on the corner of 139th Street and Lenox
Avenue, he performed to the first entirely black audience he had seen since
his days on the R&B circuit in the mid-1960s. Before the show, he was
approached by a militant black nationalist, who told him: 'Brother, it's time
for you to come home.' Hendrix replied ambiguously: 'You got to do what

you have to do and I have to do what I have to do.' He had already taken to introducing his guitar extravaganza, 'Voodoo Child (Slight Return)', as 'the Black Panthers' national anthem'. At this show, however, it became 'the Harlem national anthem'. Hoping that his appearance signalled a new political awareness, the Black Panther Party claimed prematurely that Hendrix would soon be performing a benefit on their behalf. 'They asked me to do a concert,' he confirmed in his final interview a year later, 'which was not a problem except I felt like it put me in a box. I was honoured and all that, but there are a lot of political implications, so I left it all to [his manager] Mike Jeffrey.' 'So you ducked it?' the interviewer asked. 'No,' Hendrix said hurriedly, eager to dispel any suggestion of an insult to the Panthers.

It wasn't only black militants who were pressuring him. His name was included in publicity surrounding the 15 November 1969 Moratorium in Washington, DC. As with the Panthers, nobody had asked his permission first, and once again he didn't appear. But when promoter Sid Bernstein suggested that he should take part in the Vietnam Moratorium Committee's Winter Carnival for Peace, at Madison Square Garden on 28 January 1970, Hendrix agreed. The Carnival was a multi-racial, multi-genre affair, featuring white jazz-rockers Blood, Sweat & Tears, black folkie Richie Havens, white soul band the Rascals and black balladeer Harry Belafonte, among many others. There was even a telegram of support from the Rolling Stones, who were keen to alleviate the damage caused to their reputation by the Altamont fiasco. The mild-mannered Belafonte provided the evening's most caustic rhetoric: 'There can never be peace as long as there's racism,' he declared. Looking out at the audience, and the anti-war movement beyond them, he noted: 'You do not find many blacks – not because the blacks are not committed to peace but because most of them are trying to get the same foot off their necks.' It wasn't racism that was weighing Hendrix down that night, however, but drugs. Having ingested a near-lethal cocktail of chemicals – he claimed that his drinks had been spiked – he was forced to abandon the show after a couple of chaotic songs. With that performance, his second all-black outfit, the Band of Gypsys, ended their brief career. But their funk-based music left its mark on Hendrix, who continued to experiment with the genre for the rest of his career, often to the bemusement of his white rock audience.

The Winter Carnival did nothing to relieve Hendrix's political dilemma. By now, the underground press had picked up on the issue. 'I heard about that too,' he joked with one interviewer who asked him whether he was lining up alongside the Panthers. 'Tell me all about it.' But was it true? Hendrix sighed, and whispered: 'No, man. Listen. Everybody has wars within themselves. We form different things and it comes out to be war against people and so forth and so on.' It was his standard interview technique; blur the subject with vague talk and repetition. This time, the questioner wouldn't let him off so easily. How did he feel about the Panthers? 'I naturally feel part of what they're doing,' Hendrix conceded. Then he paused, and added: 'In certain respects. Everybody has their own way of doing things.' Again, he drifted off into obscurity: 'They get justified as they justify others,' he mumbled, 'in their attempts to get personal freedom.' One more time, his inquisitor cut back to the point. Did Hendrix support the Panthers? 'Yeah,' he said firmly – and then wavered: 'But not the aggression or the violence or whatever you want to call it. I'm not for guerrilla warfare.' Neither were the Panthers, at least officially; their line was self-defence. But Hendrix had clearly bought the media portrayal of the Panthers, just as he had swallowed the peacenik philosophy of the hippies who had accepted him as their own. As he noted on another occasion, 'Everybody has their own propaganda.'

In November 1969, Hendrix was recording in New York with Buddy Miles, watched by his friend Alan Douglas. During a break, they were visited by Alafia Pudim, who was signed to Douglas's record label as a member of the Last Poets. Pudim launched into a lengthy 'toast', a rhythmic monologue delivered with swagger and street smarts. Buddy Miles told him to recite it again, while he laid down a backbeat. Not to be left out, Hendrix picked up a bass guitar, and over the next thirteen minutes, the three men recorded a track that was released after Jimi's death under the title of 'Doriella Du Fontaine'.

Unknown at the time of this session, the Last Poets burst onto the American black music scene in spring 1970 with a self-titled debut album that sounded unlike anything else on the soul charts. It was sparse and startling: three street poets declaiming messages of ghetto realism and revolution, supported by chattering hand-drums. Each voice resounded like a preacher, rhythmic and compelling, forcing his audience to stop in their tracks. The message was urgent: Wake Up, Niggers!

'I started writing in order to have an explosion, to channel off the frustration, the oppression, the implosion,' Pudim explained after the album was released. 'We're just a minor valve in the ghetto.' The group took their name from lines written by exiled South African activist Willie Kgositsile: 'When the moment hatches in time's womb, there will be no art talk,' he wrote. 'Therefore we are the last poets of the world.' The Last Poets' role was truth-telling – expressing the views of the people, but also communicating reality *to* the people. That was how they had begun, in East Harlem's Mount Morris Park (renamed Marcus Garvey Park after the black nationalist pioneer in 1973), reading poetry on 19 May 1969, which would have been Malcolm X's 44th birthday. Out of a huddle of would-be poets and communicators, three young men coalesced under the name of the East Wind Associates, after a Harlem poetry workshop.

A few weeks later, Alan Douglas switched on public broadcast TV, and saw the trio laying down their intimidating street poetry. Intrigued, he rang the station, spoke to the poets, and arranged to meet them the next day on a Harlem street corner. When he arrived, they told him to stand several yards away, and then launched into their entire repertoire like messengers from the future. By Douglas's account, he whisked them immediately into a recording studio, where they cut their first album in less than three hours. But Pudim remembers things differently. He says that the East Wind Associates whom Douglas saw were Abiodun Oyewole, Felipe Luciano and Gylan Kain. Only Oyewole agreed to sign a recording contract, the other two men feeling that commercial gain would pervert the message of their music, so Oyewole recruited two other poets from the East Wind workshop, Pudim and Omar Bin Hassan (an admirer of LeRoi Jones/Amiri Baraka).

What the three men shared was an intuition that black America might be undermining its own potential. 'Niggers Are Scared of Revolution,' Bin Hassan declared: 'Niggers tell you they're ready to be liberated, but when you say, let's go take our liberation, niggers reply, I was just playing.' The same fear underpinned 'When the Revolution Comes', a vision of black utopia; Oyewole knew that instead of planning for revolution, 'niggers will party, and bullshit, and party, and bullshit, and party . . .' and the Poets' voices trailed sarcastically to a standstill as a measure of their contempt. On Gashman, Oyewole blamed beautiful black women for sapping men's revolutionary spirit as they drained their juices. So this was no easy ride into radical chic (or, indeed, feminism). Yet the conviction of its message exuded a pride in the blackness of black experience that was intensely attractive to its audience. Despite minimal airplay, *The Last Poets* became the best-selling R&B album in the country by May 1970.

The record was beaten into the shops by the debut album from another street collective, the Watts Prophets. *The Black Voices: On the Streets in Watts* was inspired by the same impulse, to document ghetto life in poetry. Sexuality occupied a larger place in the Prophets' landscape than in the Poets', but they had no time for any man who acted like a 'cream puff' instead of a 'tough'; as the song said, 'I'll stop calling you niggers when you start acting like a black man'. This was an altogether less complex vision of the world, in which the Prophets could proclaim: 'Things gonna get greater later, when black men declare war and become the oppressor, and learn the value of murder in the first degree'. That was a movie fantasy; in the same situation, the Last Poets would have reminded those black men to watch their backs, and remember the names of their enemies.

For Gil Scott-Heron, whose own poetry and-percussion debut, *A New Black Poet: Small Talk at 125th and Lenox*, was also released in 1970, those enemies included the 'pale-faced motherfuckers' of SDS. 'The new word to have is revolution', he complained on 'Comment #1', accusing white radicals of distracting their black counterparts with their dilettantism. The question of the hour, Scott-Heron declared, was 'Who will survive in America?' The most enduring performance on the album was 'The Revolution Will Not Be Televised', a sardonic commentary on white America's inability to process any reality that had not been interpreted and distorted by the mass media.

These voices from the streets – the Poets, the Prophets, Scott-Heron – stood out from the R&B mainstream not just for their verbal propulsion and skeletal music, but for their unrelenting clarity of vision. 'There's a thing with a whole lot of black music today, soul music,' opined radical DJ Roland Young. 'It's not really revolutionary, it's reformist or at the most it's cultural revolutionary – the theme's basically black, the ghetto.' It wasn't enough to describe the plight of black America, Young said; the point was to change it. 'Black music can end up being negative if it doesn't express a way out of the oppression,' he concluded. For genuinely revolutionary music, Young believed, blacks should turn to avant-garde jazz – 'the lifestyle of the musicians as well as the art form itself, the music of Archie Shepp and Cecil Taylor and John Coltrane'. Coltrane was three years dead, of course; the once militant Shepp had been exiled to France, unable to secure a US record deal; while Taylor had effectively been banished from the jazz mainstream since 1966 by critics and producers unable to comprehend the mind-stretching nature of his music. It was a long way from revolution in motion.

Theorist, jazz critic and activist Amiri Baraka was certainly convinced that the music had lost its ability to bite. Writing about Ornette Coleman, the standard bearer of free jazz since 1959, and Albert Ayler, the screeching siren of the tenor saxophone, Baraka complained about the musicians' 'world weariness and corny self consciousness (which is white life hangaround total – i.e. what you get for being wit dem) . . . Ornette and Albert now describe bullshit, so *are* bullshit.' By the end of 1970, Ayler's body would be found in New York's East River; it remains uncertain whether he was the victim of suicidal despair or murder. Coleman, meanwhile, had settled into the role of grand vizier of jazz, still expanding his repertoire and scope, but no longer the hub of a revolution. One jazz musician in 1970 was prepared to lend his name and work to the cause of transforming the world; ironically, he was white. Bass player Charlie Haden had provided the heartbeat for Coleman's pioneering quartet between 1959 and 1961. He had since worked with a variety of adventurous musicians, among them harpist Alice Coltrane, widow of the legendary saxophonist. In 1969, he assembled a band that he dubbed the Liberation Music Orchestra. 'I just wanted to voice my concerns about what was going on in Vietnam,' he recalled. '[The United States] shouldn't have been involved. They should have allowed Vietnam to settle its own problems.' Haden dedicated his life and art to opposing both the Vietnam War and racism in America. 'From now on,' he proclaimed, 'every album, every concert, every note, every breath will be devoted to ending racism, poverty and exploitation in America. I want to make people aware of the fact that black children are dying of malnutrition, starvation and lead poisoning here, while there are a few men who control the wealth and economy with more money than they could ever spend in 500 lifetimes, making their money from the war in Vietnam and from exploitation in this and other countries.' For the first Liberation Music Orchestra album, he revived political anthems from the Spanish Civil War of the late 1930s, and penned new material in the same tradition with pianist Carla Bley. Among his compositions was 'Song for Che', also recorded by Ornette Coleman.

Haden's *Liberation Music Orchestra* album was ecstatically received by critics, but its record label, Impulse!, were clearly concerned about both its title and its contents. Initially, they neglected to advertise the record; when they were challenged, they first claimed that they couldn't afford to promote it, and then admitted that they were wary of offending their stockholders. After their neglect was publicised, the company was shamed into purchasing ads. The record eventually won awards in both France and Japan as the best jazz album of 1970.

Because he was white, Haden was not invited to appear at June 1970's Revolutionary Black Music Festival, promoted by the Black Panther Party at the Electric Factory in Philadelphia. The event was masterminded by Cal Massey, the cruelly overlooked composer of 'The Black Liberation Suite', who died just two years later. It featured such talents as Freddie Hubbard, McCoy Tyner, Jackie McLean and Betty Carter, none of them previously known for their militancy, alongside the Panthers' own songstress, Elaine Brown. What was most noticeable, however, was that 'Revolutionary Black Music' was represented entirely by jazz; radicals working in the soul and R&B vein, from James Brown to the Last Poets, were conspicuous by their absence. An event featuring those two artists, alongside the likes of the Temptations, Nina Simone and maybe even Jimi Hendrix, would have raised both the proceeds and the profile of the cause considerably. But, with the exception of Simone, none of those performers might have felt comfortable in 1970 about appearing under the Panthers' banner.

## HIP CAPITALISTS

After the gradual ebbing of revolutionary optimism through 1969, many rock performers with weighty underground credentials edged away from radical political commitment. Arlo Guthrie, fresh from his cameo appearance at the Chicago Conspiracy Trial, was now convinced that political engagement was worthless. 'The reason that people are dropping out, man,' he told an interviewer in his characteristic drawl, 'is not because of political pressure, but because of alienation, and I don't see that another political movement is going to help it. I think the problem is personal.' Within a matter of weeks, he was ready to denounce radicalism completely: 'I'm not interested in whether there are parts of the press that want me to be political,' he explained. 'It just doesn't interest me. I'm interested that when my kid grows up, he knows what a chestnut tree is.' Guthrie expected his child to live, like the tree, in a world divorced from petty social concerns, such as environmentalism or racism.

Country Joe McDonald, his fellow Chicago veteran – another singer who played the trial having avoided the convention – aroused some disquiet amongst his activist supporters when his *C.J. Fish* album appeared in the spring of 1970. It included the song 'Hey Bobby', a cry of political betrayal aimed at his long-time hero, Bob Dylan, inspired by 'Dylan's abdication of responsibility to his movement-oriented audience'. Yet exactly the same charge was being thrown at McDonald, as 'Hey Bobby' was the record's sole political statement.

In any case, Dylan rejected the burden of responsibility. 'People shouldn't look to me for answers,' he told his biographer, Anthony Scaduto, in 1970. 'I wasn't going to fall for being any kind of leader. And because I wanted out, [magazines] all started to rap me. But who could live up to that kind of thing? I wasn't into politics. I didn't want any part of that. But the times are tough. Everybody wants a leader.' It was as close as Dylan came to understanding his youthful disciples: 'I don't know what's going down on campuses, what's in their heads. I have no contact with them, and I'm sorry they think I can give them any answers. Because I can't. I got enough to keep me busy without looking for other people's problems.' Was he interested in radical politics at all? 'It's all bullshit,' he replied. 'It's petty.' What about his responsibility to his audience? 'There's no attempt there to reach anybody but me.'

In spring 1970, however, that wasn't strictly true. After his remarkable output in 1967, when he composed the songs known as *The Basement Tapes* and the contents of his *John Wesley Harding* album, Dylan had been suffering – or had elected to suffer – from writer's block. Aside from the attractive but surface-thin *Nashville Skyline* album, and occasional collaborations with country performers, Dylan had effectively been silent for more than two years. Now he began to assemble an album deliberately designed to fox and tease his admirers. Strictly for his own pleasure, which was enhanced by the thought of how confused his fans would be, he prepared a collection of cover versions, old folk songs, patchy live recordings and desultory new material, and packaged it for the world's delight under the provocative title of *Self Portrait*. Aficionados scoured the record for political or artistic significance, missing the point that it was the absence of such qualities (the beauty of Dylan's singing aside) that was the point. As an example of hip easy listening, *Self Portrait* was something of a masterpiece. But its primary aim was to deconstruct Dylan's image as a leader of men and masses. Even the country standards that he covered seemed to reinforce the message: 'Take Me as I Am (or Let Me Go)', for example.

Although Dylan's output continued to puzzle many observers, his music, new and old, did serve to boost a fledgling industry that was heralded (in two headlines for the same article in the magazine *Rolling Stone*) as both 'The New Capitalism' and 'The Rock and Roll Liberation Front?' The business in question was bootlegging: the illegal manufacture, distribution and sale of records containing material that had not been authorised for release. It began in 1969 with *The Great White Wonder*, a compilation of Bob Dylan recordings that the artist was not intending to make available to the public. Sold openly, at first, in hip record stores, and later by mail order or under the counter, bootlegs did little to dent the rapidly expanding profits of the major record companies. But their very existence, undercutting both the legal system and the artistic rights of the performers, became a sizeable irritant. The bootleggers claimed that they were merely servicing the public by supplying them with music they were desperate to hear, which was partly true; but they also benefited from the proceeds, paying neither the artists nor their record and publishing companies for the privilege.

Soon bootleggers were stealing from each other, copyright being an irrelevance in an un-policed market. There was disquiet in the underground press that these 'hip capitalists' were exploiting the very people they were claiming to serve. From Madison, Wisconsin, came the first sign that bootlegging might acquire moral and political dimensions. 'Some of us who feel that freak-rock belongs to the people from whence it came have liberated Dylan and Beatles tapes and returned the music to the people,' announced a necessarily anonymous source. This collective pledged to make available some of the most eagerly sought-after 'underground' recordings – Dylan's appearance at the Isle of Wight festival, and the Beatles' postponed *Get Back* album – at budget price. 'The albums sell for $3.00,' the source continued, 'and every penny except for the cost of manufacture will be returned to the community. The bail fund [for local dope busts] especially will benefit. This album is a step toward reclaiming the people's music from filthy capitalist record companies.' This initiative never extended beyond the Wisconsin area, despite vague promises from other manufacturers that they would be donating some of their future profits to the artists, and some to the Black Panthers and the anti-war movement.

By summer 1970, this idealism was forgotten in the rush to obtain the latest illicit 'releases', by an increasing array of performers. Despite regular complaints from punters that they had been 'burned' by poor-quality pressings, bootlegging continued to enjoy outlaw approval from the rock media and fans alike. There were even 'booklegs' offering unedited texts of Bob Dylan's unpublished mid-1960s 'novel', *Tarantula*. One edition claimed cheekily: 'Author's royalties from the sale of this book are being donated to the Caladan Free School [named for a fictional planet created by science-fiction author Frank Herbert]. Publisher's profits will contribute to the furtherance of Woodstock Nation.' Impossible to verify, promises of this kind heightened the sense that bootleggers were part of the liberation movement, not quick-buck capitalists.

Instinct, and Tom Wolfe's phrase, 'radical chic', allowed the counter-culture to distinguish between the Columbia Record Corporation's boast that 'The Revolutionaries are on CBS', and the bootleg industry's declaration that they were ripping off 'the man' for 'the people'. Columbia's Dylan releases stank of profit and compromise; Dylan bootlegs seemed to remove the barriers between artist and listener, despite (or perhaps because of) the fact that their contents had been exposed against the artist's will. The same process of empathy and identification was at work when the movement weighed the credentials and sincerity of would-be revolutionaries, enabling many to claim Charles Manson and his Family as allies, for example, or to denounce John Lennon as a traitor.

All of these antennae broke down when feminism entered the equation. Suddenly, acclaimed counter-culture leaders could find themselves on the wrong side of the barricades, without having moved an inch. During an interview with an underground newspaper, while his wife Robin cooked his supper, Country Joe McDonald, the Brandoesque, gum-chewing hero of the Chicago conspiracy hearings, struggled to contend with a new set of political morals. He'd recently recorded the soundtrack for the Swedish porn movie *Quiet Days in Clichy*, loosely based on the work of novelist Henry Miller. His theme song portrayed the chief female character: 'spoiling the coffee, burning the eggs, all of her brains are between her legs'. When he performed this song at college concerts, he was invariably greeted with boos and catcalls from women. 'I'm not really sure what I think about it,' he reflected wryly. 'I don't like people shouting "Off the Pig" at *me!*' The experience left its mark, and McDonald began his first tentative study of the principles of feminism.

## WITCH SIDE ARE YOU ON?

It was a journey few of his fellow (male) luminaries were prepared to take. Abbie Hoffman was widely quoted as saying: 'The only alliance I would make with the women's liberation movement is in bed.' He was speaking for most of the male movement, few of whom had progressed beyond the gender stereotypes of the late 1960s. In late January, a group of New York feminists could finally take no more. Exasperated by 'their' underground press still being awash with casual sexism[3] and gratuitous nude pin-ups, they focused their attention on the offices of *RAT (Subterranean News)*. This paper, which concentrated on rock, underground events and the revolution, noticed a heavy increase in sales when it featured a front-cover portrait of a nude woman labelled 'Slum Goddess', and had repeated the trick on several subsequent occasions.

During a daring raid, members of WITCH (Women's International Conspiracy From Hell) seized the offices, and then the contents, of *RAT*. WITCH had already enlivened the feminist debate with their appearance at Wall Street to put a hex on the financial centre of New York, and their intervention in a bridal fair at Madison Square Garden. Less publicised was the curse they had placed upon the participants in the Chicago Conspiracy Trial, tarring both the establishment and the rebel defendants with the same brush of sexism. WITCH founder Robin Morgan had taken part in the formation of the Yippies, but quickly lost faith in Hoffman and Jerry Rubin's egotism and sexual stereotyping.

Morgan's group also aligned themselves with the organisation SCUM (Society for Cutting Up Men), founded by Valerie Solanas – best known for shooting artist Andy Warhol on the same day that Robert Kennedy was assassinated. SCUM's manifesto laid down a peculiarly uncompromising brand of feminism: 'Life in this society being, at best, an utter bore and no aspect of society being at all relevant to women, there remains to civic-minded, responsible, thrill-seeking females only to overthrow the government, eliminate the money system, institute complete automation and destroy the male sex.' It was rhetoric worthy of Jonathan Swift's 'Modest Proposal', but Solanas was entirely serious, albeit more than slightly disturbed. 'SCUM will coolly, furtively, stalk its prey and quietly move in for the kill,' she announced. 'The few remaining men can exist out their puny days dropped out on drugs or strutting around in drag or passively watching the high-powered female in action, fulfilling themselves as spectators, vicarious livers or breeding in the cow pasture with the toadies, or they can go off to the nearest neighbourhood suicide centre where they will be quietly, quickly and painlessly gassed to death.'

Solanas's manifesto was the most extreme document issued in the name of the American Revolution – not just because of its author's questionable sanity, but also because it was an outburst of pure rage, not a rational blueprint for action. By aligning themselves with Solanas and SCUM, WITCH were standing up for a woman's right to express her craziness and fury. Solanas acted as a totem of female power, a hint that women could match any violence and madness offered by men.

Little of the feminist writing in the liberated *RAT* displayed the extremism of Solanas's work. Yet the manifesto that opened the first feminist *RAT* bore a distinctively SCUM-like tone: 'Death to the bureaucrats, death to the sexists, death to those who care more about egos than they do about change. ALL POWER TO THE REVOLUTION.' An anonymous Weatherwoman contributed a torrent of predictable rhetoric: 'The time has to be seized if we are to bring this motherfucker down and women must play a large part in it. The fight against chauvinism must go on at the same time we fight the pig, or the struggle is just a tea party. Women must pick up the gun and kill the pig.'

None of which would change the world, or do more than comfort the converted. Robin Morgan's contribution to revolutionary feminism was different. In a passionate piece entitled 'Goodbye to All That', she set out to demolish the movement's male chauvinism. She cautioned her female readers to beware 'the liberal co-optive masks on the face of sexist hate and fear, worn by real nice guys we all know and like, right? We have met the enemy and he's our friend. And dangerous.' The culprits were 'the friends, brothers, lovers in the counterfeit male-dominated Left. The good guys who think they know what "Women's Lib", as so they chummily call it, is all about – and who then proceed to degrade and destroy women by almost everything they say and do.'

Then she began to name names, a pantheon of hip radicals. Weatherman ('the Weather Vain') was pilloried for its 'image and theory of free sexuality but practice of sex on demand for males'. Tuli Kupferberg and the Fugs 'always knew they hated the women they loved'. Abbie Hoffman had conformed to Hollywood stereotype, as the man 'who ditches the first wife and kids, good enough for the old days but awkward once you're making it'. John Sinclair was 'the new counterfeit Christ', a bastion of sexism. The Sexual Revolution was simply 'reinstating oppression by another name'. At Woodstock, 'a woman could be declared uptight or a poor sport if she didn't want to be raped'. The entire counter-culture was a sham, the movement a farce, the revolution was a recipe for sexism.

Another *RAT* contributor, Arlene Brown, extended Morgan's argument. In a piece provocatively entitled 'Has Anyone Reading this Article Met a Woman Bass Player?', she contended that musicians 'thrive on a male ego, subservient "chick" relationship, which the whole hippie rock culture re-inforces'. In her most revealing insight, Brown listed the acceptable images for women in the rock world: 'a mod, "pretty", long-haired, mini/maxi-skirted, or bell-bottomed, passive, sweet chick, nice enough to be at the side of any strong, manly rock musician or business man. Or . . . a bra-less, long-skirted, sweet mother earth, commune hippie chick. Both of these are distortions. And accepted roles. Just as the aggressive, dominant, creative genius is the role that men play, and what women LOOK UP to. And that's not *my* revolution!' The faces of those stifled figures of gender conformity could be seen in thousands of magazines, on album covers, backstage at gigs, at demonstrations, throughout the immutable chauvinism that was the counter-culture.

What were the escape routes from this fate? Grace Slick of Jefferson Airplane still retained her independence, but offered ambiguous support for her sisters. 'Women's liberation is one thing,' she noted, 'but going around and imitating men is a little sad.' Maybe she had in mind her friend Janis Joplin, who continued her slide towards destruction by attempting to out-drink and out-drug her male cohorts; she eventually died of a heroin overdose in October 1970. 'In a world of men,' wrote feminist Susan Hiwatt, 'Janis sang our stories. When she died, one of the few ties that I still had with rock snapped. It can't be that women are a people without culture.' The culture was there, but it was disguised to survive. Joni Mitchell hid her sublime talent behind an image that crossed Brown's 'passive sweet chick' and 'sweet mother earth', and was defined in the rock media by her superstar lovers. Meanwhile, Joan Baez evaded sexual categorisation by emphasising her political activism rather than her music.

There was an alternative, but it took a maverick with imagination to conjure it up. Enter Naomi Weisstein, a feminist and rock'n'roll fan in Chicago. 'I was lying on the sofa listening to the radio,' she recalled, 'a rare bit of free time in those early hectic days of the women's movement. First, Mick Jagger crowed that his once feisty girlfriend was now "under my thumb". Then Janis Joplin moaned with thrilled resignation that love was like "a ball and chain". Then the Band, a self-consciously left-wing group, sang: "Jemima surrender, I'm gonna give it to you". I somersaulted off the sofa, leapt up into the air, and came down howling at the radio: "Every 14-year-old girl in this city listens to rock! How criminal to make the subjugation and suffering of women so sexy! We'll organise our own rock band!" The task would be to change the politics while retaining rock's impact.' So she founded a group with the self-explanatory title of the Chicago Women's Liberation Rock Band.

In her zeal to 'change our consciousness, to refuse to continue our frenzied worship of men', Weisstein and her bandmates cut away the trappings of rock stardom, which separated artists from audience. 'We were extremely interactive with our audiences,' she explained, 'rapping with them and asking them which songs they liked, and keeping the sound level at a reasonable roar.' But lest this sound like a watering-down of rock's confrontational theatricality, the Chicago Women's Liberation Rock Band offered militancy in songs (their repertoire included 'Papa Don't Lay that Shit on Me' and 'Don't Fuck Around With Love') and action. Weisstein described a key moment in their live shows: 'Assuming the sneering voice of your average low-life male sexist, I began: "A women's liberation rock band. Farrrr out! Farrrrr fucking out. Hey, I'd like to see you chicks in your gold lame short shorts and feathers on your tits." I went on to imitate Mick Jagger singing "Under My Thumb": "There is a squirrelly dog, who once had her way . . ." Then I asked the audience: "And do you know what he says then? He says, 'It's alright'. Pause. 'It's alright? It's alright? Well, it's not alright, Mick Jagger, and IT'S NEVER GOING TO BE ALRIGHT AGAIN!"'

Exhilarating though Weisstein's stagecraft was, it didn't have a chance of mass acceptance. When the Chicago Women's Liberation Rock Band were finally offered a recording deal, by the tiny independent label Rounder Records, they had to share an album with a similar band from New Haven, as if they were exotic African tribes being documented for reasons of anthropology rather than music. In 1970, African tribal music would have been a more commercial proposition than women's liberation, the revolution that still had no voice to sing.

## INSIDE AN EXPLOSION

I don't think anybody said it better than Tolstoy. The difference between establishment violence and revolutionary violence is the difference between dog shit and cat shit.

(Joan Baez, 1970)

There are now few hopeful projects on the left, and the only likely alternative lifestyles seem to be Weatherman adventurism and the Yippie freakout.

(*New York Review of Books*, 1970)

'How does it feel to be inside an explosion?' asked a poem widely reprinted in the underground press during the summer of 1970. It was an increasingly relevant question. US officials estimated that between January 1969 and April 1970, there had been more than 4,000 incidents involving explosives and firebombs reported across the nation, and more than 35,000 bombing threats. *Scanlan's* magazine carried out its own research, suggesting that the government's figures under-estimated the scale of attacks. This was not, *Scanlan's* concluded, 'the work of some isolated terrorist nuts, but part of an overall guerrilla war which has been waged in hot pursuit of American institutions for at least three years'.

Forty people were believed to have died in these attacks, most of which could not be attributed to any recognised group (although the public tended to blame all of them on the Black Panther Party). Judge John Murtagh, best known for his handling of one of the obscenity cases that broke the spirit of the comedian Lenny Bruce, nearly joined that number. In February 1970, shortly after he was named as the presiding judge for the trial of the New York Panther 21, his home was firebombed, though he survived uninjured.

The identity of the bombers became clear a month later. On the morning of 6 March 1970, a vast explosion destroyed a townhouse on West 11th Street in Greenwich Village. The building was the home of the Wilkersons, who were away at the time. They had left the house in care of their daughter, Cathy, who unbeknown to them was a member of the Weatherman collective. Cathy and her friend, Kathy Boudin, stumbled out of the ruins, severely shocked and with most of their clothes blown off by the blast. The wife of actor

Dustin Hoffman, who lived next door, rushed to their aid and gave them something to wear. But within minutes, the two young women had vanished.

When the police and fire brigade arrived, they found the body of a young man, Ted Gold, who had been killed as the building collapsed around him. (It had been Gold, an aficionado of Bob Dylan's music, who had suggested that Weatherman name themselves after one of his songs.) Searching through the rubble, police also discovered a large cache of dynamite, which had survived the blast intact, and other items of bomb-making equipment. Only weeks later did police realise that two other activists, Terry Robbins and Diana Oughton, had been blown to pieces in the explosion, while they were manufacturing bombs intended for terrorist attacks.

As news spread through the Weatherman network, activists faced a stark choice: abandon the armed struggle, or go underground. So began the transformation of a student splinter group into a terrorist organisation, in its new non-sexist identity of the Weather Underground. The media salivated over the events that had led Diana Oughton from a small-town middle-class background to the most notorious revolutionary group in the land. Oughton was feted as a martyr in the counter-culture, 'Diana' becoming as recognisable as 'Che', 'Mao' and 'Huey'. In 1971, she was the subject of two songs recorded by Paul Kantner and Grace Slick of the Jefferson Airplane. 'Huntress of the moon and a lady of the earth, Weather Woman Diana,' the pair sang, canonising Oughton as a mythical hero of the age – sitting in their radical pantheon alongside Charles Manson, an album of whose songs was released on the same day as the townhouse explosion. 'Diana was a Roman goddess, so the song was as much about the spirit of women who take control as it was about Diana Oughton,' Kantner claims today. 'Oughton fell in with guys who were so stupid that they blew themselves up. Now, I didn't mind people blowing things up as a political statement, as long as they didn't hurt anyone. In fact, Abbie Hoffman gave me a piece of the Minneapolis courthouse as a souvenir of one of their bombings. I made him sign it! Capitalists hold property in higher regard than people, so blowing things up was a heavy statement as far as the establishment was concerned.'

Kantner and Slick's 1970 summit meeting with Abbie Hoffman and his second wife, Anita, was documented in the underground press with the same gravity as the Vietnam peace talks. Kantner told Hoffman that he admired Charles Manson. 'Do you identify with Manson because he has long hair?' Hoffman asked him. 'No,' Kantner replied, 'it's because he's getting fucked over because of the long hair. He's just getting burned by the same people that are burning us all. I'm not really interested in what he is or even if he's guilty or not.' Kantner noted that 'all these weird little colleges we play in have helmeted crazies, really good old revolutionary crazies'. 'Do you have a model for the revolution?' Hoffman wondered. 'No, I just expect it to happen,' Kantner said. 'The government's doing it by itself. There's not very much you have to do other than point it out.' Her mind attuned to the spirit of the age, Slick added: 'It's like watching a very slow bomb explode.'

Despite the Airplane's revolutionary rhetoric, Kantner remained dubious about the benefits of political action. 'Instead of protesting about the war with twenty people,' he admitted, 'I'd rather take those same twenty people out into the woods and get them high.' Slick favoured a more direct method of subversion. In April 1970, she was invited to the White House along with other alumni of Finch College, from which President Nixon's daughter Tricia had recently graduated. She asked Abbie Hoffman to be her escort, not realising that the invitation was for her alone. 'He was the only man standing in line up in front of the White House to get in,' she recalled, 'so they were looking at him funny.' Her plan was to introduce herself to the President: 'I had in my pocket 600 mikes of acid. I'm picturing myself being introduced to Richard Nixon . . . and then the acid in the pocket goes into the cup. I had it all planned, but then they didn't let us in!' Nixon was not even at the White House that afternoon, so he was in no danger of being spiked by Hoffman. But both he and the Airplane regarded such japes as worthwhile. 'Abbie was one of the funniest guys I've ever known,' Kantner recalls. 'He was a stand-up comedian, really, not a politician. He made me laugh, so inevitably I was converted to his cause.'

The joke was lost on the Nixon administration. Vice-President Spiro Agnew had Hoffman and the Weather Underground in his sights. At a dinner in St Louis, he commented: 'As for these deserters, malcontents, radicals, incendiaries, the civil and uncivil disobedients among our youth, the Revolutionary Action Movement, Yippies, hippies, yahoos, Black Panthers, lions and tigers alike – I would swap the whole damn zoo for a single platoon of the kind of young Americans I saw in Vietnam.'[4]

It was Vietnam, and Nixon's ambiguous strategy in South-East Asia, that aroused the fury of Agnew's 'lions and tigers' in spring 1970, provoking one of the most notorious incidents of the era, and inciting the Weather Underground to launch a concerted bombing campaign on the American mainland. Although the long-running Paris peace negotiations seemed to have stalled, National Security Advisor Dr Henry Kissinger had been authorised by the President to carry out secret talks with representatives of the North Vietnamese government – who threatened to pull out if they were publicised. Meanwhile, Nixon championed his policy of 'Vietnamisation', which – he claimed in April 1970 – would result in 150,000 US soldiers returning home during the next year as the South Vietnamese regained control of their own armed struggle.

Events undermined Nixon's strategy. Under the politically neutral leadership of Prince Sihanouk, the neighbouring state of Cambodia had been offering a safe haven to Viet Cong fighters. In March 1970, Sihanouk was deposed, and Nixon decided to strike against the North Vietnamese army and Viet Cong troops stationed on Cambodian soil. On 30 April 1970, he claimed that North Vietnam had attacked Cambodia, and that the new government had requested military aid. In response, he ordered US troops to attack across a 100-mile front. Although the 'invasion' of Cambodia did result in the deaths of several thousand North Vietnamese troops, many historians believe that its long-term military significance was minimal. In fact, it may have had an adverse effect, driving the surviving Viet Cong and Vietnamese army forces deeper into Cambodia, thereby destabilising the country. The US troops were withdrawn, in any case, by the end of June, emphasising the haphazard nature of the operation.

Nixon had clearly not anticipated that activists would regard the invasion as an act of naked aggression. When the US Army was forced to concede that they had also resumed the bombing of North Vietnam, there was outrage across the nation's colleges and universities. The full spectrum of protests, legal and otherwise, erupted – sit-ins, fire-bombings of army offices, marches, boycotts. And then there was Kent State.

## FOUR DEAD IN OHIO

The campus of Kent State University in Kent, Ohio, was merely one of hundreds of educational establishments hit by what *Time* magazine called 'a nationwide student strike'. Protests began on 1 May, when more than 1,000 students (by no means a majority) gathered to denounce Nixon's policies, chanting the Weather Underground's slogan, 'Bring the war home'. There was an outbreak of violence at a nearby bar that night, but this was attributed to alcohol-fuelled bikers, not students. Regardless, Kent's mayor declared a state of emergency in the town, and in what many observers regarded as the first of several over-reactions, requested the presence of the National Guard. The first platoon to arrive on campus discovered that the ROTC building was on fire – ostensibly the subject of student arson, though no culprits were ever caught, and some investigators have alleged that the blaze was ignited by agents provocateurs. Policemen and firemen were subjected to a barrage of rocks, and the National Guard commander called for re-inforcements. Governor Jim Rhodes told National Guard officers that they were facing 'the worst type of people that we harbour in America. I think that we're up against the strongest, well-trained, militant, revolutionary group that has ever assembled in America.' Rumours spread amongst police and soldiers that groups of Black Panthers or Weather Underground activists were freshly arrived at Kent State. The stage was set for tragedy.

What happened at Kent on 4 May 1970 brought the war home – not the Vietnam War, but the war between generations, ideologies and lifestyles. It was entirely avoidable, certainly misguided, probably an accidental misuse of power rather than a planned act of military aggression. But the confrontation that erupted just after noon seemed to provide an archetypal demonstration of state brutality and trampled innocence.

A protest against the National Guard, and against every aspect of the Nixon administration, was scheduled to begin at midday. The officers of the university claimed that they had the authority to cancel the gathering, and distributed leaflets to that effect. But 2,000 students still flocked to the Commons, a hilly area in the centre of the campus. The initial speeches were interrupted by the National Guard, who shouted an order to disperse. When the students refused to move, the Guard launched canisters of tear gas in their direction, and the situation dissolved into chaos. Some of the students tied handkerchiefs or sweaters around their faces to avoid the gas, and lobbed the smoking canisters back at the National Guard. Others picked up rocks and other missiles and pelted the Guardsmen. Officers later claimed that they had also come under attack from petrol bombs and even gunfire, though this was never confirmed.

Startled by this unexpected retaliation, the Guardsmen retreated up a small hill from which most of the campus was visible. As they reached the summit, they turned almost as one, as if by military order, and more than twenty of them opened fire. The gunfire telescoped time – some said it lasted a matter of seconds, others claimed it extended for as long as a minute – and when it ceased, bodies were strewn across the campus. Four students lay dead: two of them had been involved in the protests, two had merely been walking to their next class. A dozen more were wounded, some critically. The casualties were scattered across a large area, suggesting that the Guardsmen had fired indiscriminately.

There were inquiries, a succession of them, over the next decade, after which the injured students and the families of those who'd been killed agreed to an out-of-court settlement. In return, the National Guardsmen who fired the fatal shots issued a 'statement of regret', though they denied that this equated to an apology. They consistently claimed that they'd been fired upon first; that they had been in fear for their lives; and that they had acted spontaneously, rather than being ordered to shoot. Lawyers for the victims, meanwhile, alleged that the shootings were both planned and unprovoked, and that a senior officer had commanded the Guardsmen to fire at students whom they knew to be unarmed. The event is still the subject of controversy today, nearly forty years on – another focus for conspiracy theories, alongside the unsolvable murders of King and the Kennedys.

In the immediate aftermath of the killings, the American public was sharply divided, with age and race the most reliable guides to opinion. The majority of white adults believed that the students had brought the tragedy upon themselves; black Americans, and young whites, were equally convinced that the authorities were to blame. Perhaps the most telling fact is this: ten days after the Kent State shootings, two students were shot dead in similar circumstances at Jackson State University. This time, the public response was muted. Both of the Jackson State casualties were black.

Between those two tragedies, there was a hastily arranged Mobe demonstration. It should have been a mass rally of dissidence and disobedience; instead, scarred by factionalism, it was no more than 'a picnic in the park', according to one commentator. Neither was the Nixon administration shaken by singer Bobby Darin's 'Phone for Peace' campaign, whereby those opposed to the Vietnam conflict tried to overwhelm the White House switchboard. The anti-war movement slipped back into depression. 'We had faltered when history demanded decisive action,' wrote Chicago trial veteran David Dellinger. 'Instead of being exhilarated by the ability of the people to stand up to the government, they were disheartened to think that the war continued, even though somewhat abated, and that protest action was petering out as divisiveness and the summer doldrums took over. An unwarranted and unnecessary sense of powerlessness gripped the movement, contributing to the growing crisis of self-confidence.'

But Kent State acted as a rallying-point for the wider counter-culture beyond the movement. After several years of maintaining an apolitical stance, for example, *Rolling Stone* magazine's resolve finally cracked when it saw its readers being gunned down in cold blood. For once, the paper's 'Random Notes' news column was led by a story more urgent than the latest infighting amongst the Beatles or CSNY. 'It comes clear that the Nixon Presidency is going to be the most dangerous – the most disastrous – in the Nation's history,' it squawked belatedly. 'Either Nixon must be forced into resignation or he must be impeached.' The brief commentary ended with an air of helplessness: 'Do something.'

Street musician David Peel dubbed his second album, released in the wake of Kent State, *American Revolution*. 'That was how it felt,' he says today. 'It was like a civil war had broken out – the counter-culture fighting the culture. Black Panthers were being shot, students being gunned down – the body count kept getting higher.' Campuses became the focus of the counter-culture's protests. Students abandoned their educational programmes to concentrate on community activism. Strikes disrupted previously moderate colleges. 'Prior to the Kent State tragedy,' wrote rock commentator Ritchie Yorke, 'the majority of youth could remain sympathetic to the alternative cause but they didn't need to be activists. Now, observers say that most kids have made personal decisions. You either do something about changing the bull-like rush of the Establishment, or you become part of the Establishment. No longer is there any middle ground.'

What was missing from these student uprisings was a sense of purpose. With little or no leadership being provided by the luminaries of the 1968 Chicago convention – there was silence from the Yippies and most of the remnants of SDS – all that remained was chaotic, formless dissidence. Veteran peacenik Joan Baez, who had just formed an organisation entitled War Tax Resistance with Pete Seeger and Allen Ginsberg, attempted to fill the gap. The day after Kent State, she visited Stanford University, the alma mater of her imprisoned husband, David Harris, to channel protests into peace demonstrations. Even at this moment of crisis, Baez's non-violent principles were unshakeable: 'I'm all for closing down the universities. I don't think what many of them teach is relevant anyway. But I can't see [the point of] tearing down the buildings. I say, let's use them, let's create something different inside them.' Many of her fellow artists felt that they could speak most effectively through their music. The Grateful Dead performed a free show for striking students at the Massachusetts Institute of Technology on 6 May; Country Joe & the Fish added several benefits to their schedule.

Their San Francisco contemporaries, Jefferson Airplane, had scheduled a free concert in New York's Central Park in the aftermath of Kent State. Students from New Haven, Connecticut, contacted the band to suggest that they should cancel the show, and instead support *their* protests. Some band members, apparently including Grace Slick and Marty Balin, wanted to back the students, but the rest believed that the New York concert should go ahead. And so it did, with Slick berating the Central Park crowd for not being in New Haven themselves.

Slick's ambiguous political stance was spotlighted from several angles during this period. Ian Underwood, keyboardist with Frank Zappa's band, recalled the Airplane at a New York student demonstration, 'inciting the kids to near enough riot. Then, about fifty guys from a construction site came down and started kicking the shit out of these kids. Right away, Grace Slick started yelling for the kids to cool off and quit being so stupid with all this violence nonsense.'

In a more radical moment, Slick noted that universities were clamping down on concerts that might incite revolutionary fervour: 'At first they let it go because they thought it was just music, but now they are frightened because they think the music will cause kids to do things they don't want them to do – run wild in the streets and riot.' Other reports suggested in the weeks after Kent State that students were choosing to demonstrate rather than attend concerts. 'The shootings', reported Ritchie Yorke, 'have had a tremendous effect on the entire music industry. Pop has been taking something of a back seat to politics. The ranks of regular concert-goers have been drastically thinned, and it's difficult to judge how long it will be before the situation returns to the norm, if ever.' Promoter Bill Graham welcomed the new trend: 'I think that Kent and Jackson woke up a lot of youth. They were really the first war casualties on our homeland since the 19th century. And there were a lot of do-nothing people who now want to do something. If I'm going to lose a patron because he wants to do something else instead of freaking out to rock'n'roll every weekend, then as far as I'm concerned, fine.'

Not every section of the rock community shared Graham's enthusiasm. Members of the British band, Jethro Tull, who were touring US colleges in the aftermath of Kent State, complained that their audiences were tense and distracted, rather than hedonistic. 'The kids are so depressed', reported Ian

Anderson, 'that they don't feel like enjoying themselves. Although we're English, we sympathise with these kids, but one would hope that by getting in there and playing our music we can cheer them up a bit.' Their manager, Terry Ellis, lamented the fact that at several university shows, students had insisted on using their stage as a forum for political comment. Ellis clearly felt that this was inappropriate: 'There are plenty of Pete Seegers, Peter, Paul & Marys, and Joan Baezs in the world to remind them of the realities they face every day. Jethro would like to entertain these kids, give them a bit of relief and help them forget them just for a while. We feel that's the purpose of entertainment.'

His view was not widely shared in May 1970. 'There will almost certainly be a trend towards very politically oriented pop acts in the very near future,' Ritchie Yorke suggested. The clearest example of what he described as 'entertainment for the revolutionary troops' was directly inspired by Kent State. Two weeks after the shootings, David Crosby thrust the 15 May copy of *Life* magazine – bearing a graphic picture of one of the murdered students – into the face of his bandmate Neil Young, and told him that they had to do something. Young's response to the tragedy was 'Ohio' – a passionate rock anthem hinged around the chant, 'Four dead in Ohio'. 'Tin soldiers and Nixon's coming,' the song began, referring both to the National Guardsmen and their ultimate commander, 'we're finally on our own'. And that was how it felt for the counter-culture after Kent State: abandoned by their country.

Crosby, Stills, Nash & Young recorded 'Ohio' two days after the song was written, and it was on the radio by late May – though not on AM pop stations, where programme directors were unwilling to air a song that openly criticised the President. Via word of mouth and late-night airplay on FM rock stations, it forced its way into the US Top 40, the most immediate and arguably the most potent musical protest of the Nixon era. The song was not universally popular: Kent State student Gerald Casale recalled that 'we just thought rich hippies were making money off of something horrible and political that they didn't get'. But the symbolic significance of one of America's most popular bands reacting so vocally to a political event was huge.[5] 'I think there will be more bloodshed,' Graham Nash noted. 'Something has to happen. I just don't know what is going to happen.' Neil Young was widely quoted as saying that 'he was afraid to perform throughout the country. He was afraid of concert riots, and possible violence.'

Visions of the National Guard invading CSNY's concert halls stemmed from the same all-encompassing paranoia that inspired David Crosby's 'freak flag' anthem 'Almost Cut My Hair', released on the band's *Déjà Vu* album a few weeks before the Ohio shootings. Widely derided in retrospect, Crosby's song did capture the sense of alienation shared by a generation dreading the sight of a police car in their mirrors. 'I'm not giving in an inch to fear,' Crosby sang defiantly. But as in his earlier song 'Wooden Ships', he already had an escape route planned, in 'that sunny Southern weather' – presumably out of reach of the racist 'Southern Man' that Neil Young had just portrayed in song.

The Beach Boys, whose only history of dissent was Carl Wilson's refusal to accept the draft, made an uncharacteristic foray into political commentary on a song entitled 'Student Demonstration Time'. Penned by future Republican voter and apostle of Transcendental Meditation, singer Mike Love, it offered a concise, if rather crass, summary of what had happened at Kent: 'They said the students scared the Guard, though the troops were battledressed. Four martyrs earned a new degree: the Bachelor of Bullets'. Love's lyrics also namechecked other confrontations, from Berkeley Free Speech and People's Park to Jackson State. But his conclusions were anything but militant: 'I know we're all fed up with useless wars and racial strife, but next time there's a riot, well, you best stay out of sight'. The song ended with the whole band chanting, 'Stay away when there's a riot going on', like crew-cut student advisors on the CIA payroll.

Many believed that the situation had already passed the point of no return. 'It is not just students or anti-war activists involved in this,' declared Jefferson Airplane manager Bill Thompson. 'It's the whole long-haired culture, which is a threat to Nixon and Agnew and those kind. The music is a large part of this revolution we talk about, and the repression comes down on the bands too. We're fighting it just by continuing to play.' Thompson's vision chimed surreally with Vice-President Agnew, whose response to Kent State was to pity those students who believed that 'radicals are the architects of a brave, new, compassionate world, spiced with rock music, acid and pot'.

## BLOOD, SWEAT & BULLSHIT

As Ritchie Yorke had reported and predicted, revolution had become part of the common currency of rock in 1970. 'You may argue with the term "revolution",' noted musician Robert Lamm several decades later, 'but for those of us who were sweaty kids in our late teens or early 20s, that sure was a sexy word.' Lamm was the most political member of the jazz-rock band Chicago. Their second album was released shortly before Kent State, under the self-explanatory title of *Chicago II*.[6] At Lamm's insistence, it featured a pledge of allegiance: 'With this album, we dedicate ourselves, our futures and our energies to the people of the revolution . . . and the revolution in all its forms.' Their debut album had featured a suite inspired by events in their hometown during the Democratic Convention; now they concocted an anti-war collage entitled 'It Better End Soon'. But as its fourth movement made clear, there were limits to their radicalism: 'We gotta do it right, within the system. Gonna take over, but within this system.' It was something short of a declaration of war.

The album remained on the American sales chart for more than two and a half years, which testified to its musical impact and to the appeal of radical chic. Chicago could not be entirely accused of opportunism; they made information about voter registration available at their concerts, so that their fans could be heard 'within this system'. Yet as Lamm's colleague Walter Pankow explained later, the majority of the band had never intended to man the barricades. Their stance, he said, 'was misinterpreted by a lot of the nutcases. The SDS and the Chicago Seven and all kinds of people were approaching us on the basis of rioting, of "Hey, let's tear the system down". All of a sudden we were being enlisted to become politically involved to the hilt. I'm sure that had a lot to do with our longevity and people taking us seriously; however, it got to the point where it almost became a burden, in light of the fact that it started to infringe on the musical goals.' As Pankow describes it, 'We decided to entertain people . . . we put our politics on the shelf.' In retrospect, the misgivings of the underground press seem percipient. 'The biggest revolution of all will be in Chicago's bank account,' wrote one disgruntled reviewer: 'I am unable to understand how a group of talented writers and musicians, having been exposed first hand to the bloodiest travesty of man's supposed humanity to his own kith and kin and the resultant tour de farce of American justice that was Chicago 1968–70, could dare to produce such a spiritually weak album and dedicate it to "the revolution".' As another writer asked, 'If Chicago really wants to make a social statement, why doesn't the group schedule a press conference and publicly denounce their hometown by changing their name?'

Chicago's closest musical counterparts, Blood, Sweat & Tears, chose the period of student uprising after Kent State to set out on a tour of Eastern Europe, under the auspices of the US State Department – or, as Abbie Hoffman insisted, the CIA. He wasn't joking: the tour was promoted by the United States Information Agency (USIA), which had been formed in 1953 by senior officers of the CIA. Steve Katz was the band member least happy about representing America abroad, but even he arrived home 'disenchanted with Communism after discovering that nobody can own a store except the state'. He might have been more confused had he realised that Czechoslovakia's leading psychedelic band, the Plastic People of the Universe, had recently had their government licence withdrawn, because they'd been performing socially unacceptable material by Western acts such as the Velvet Underground and the Fugs. They were forced to return their state-owned instruments, and denied access to rehearsal space.

Naivety was a persistent problem for Blood, Sweat & Tears; the previous year, they had been dumbfounded by the idea that their record company (CBS) was allied to an arms manufacturer. They seem to have believed that their trip would be accepted as having no political significance, and also that they would be free to act as they liked whilst they were in Eastern Europe. The latter idea was dispelled after their first concert in the Romanian capital, Bucharest, where officials were so appalled by their rhetoric and music that they sent a lengthy list of instructions to the American Embassy. The band, they insisted, must dress more conservatively at their next show in the city, play at reduced volume, and accentuate the jazz rather than rock elements of their music. To ensure that these instructions were obeyed, dozens of secret policemen infiltrated the audience. Blood, Sweat & Tears carried on regardless, and when they threw a tambourine into the crowd – also strictly forbidden – a small riot ensued, and the police called a halt to the show. Blood, Sweat & Tears were informed that their presence in Romania was no longer welcome.

A few weeks later, Blood, Sweat & Tears were booked to appear at Madison Square Garden in New York. The Yippies, in a rare public event during the latter part of 1970 – Jerry Rubin was in jail, writing his book *We Are Everywhere*, and Abbie Hoffman was resting after the Chicago trial – staged their own press conference, to announce that they would be picketing the concert, in disgust at the band's co-operation with the CIA, 'whose sole purpose is to spread bullshit lies about what goes on here and instigate the overthrow of governments that serve people'. They entitled their protest Blood, Sweat &

Bullshit, dumping twenty pounds of manure outside the entrance to the venue. The Yippies called on their supporters to boycott BS&T, and also to avoid stores that stocked their records. As for the band, the Yippies called on them to cut their hair like the CIA 'straight pigs' they were working for. The boycott had little visible effect: the band's third album topped the US charts, and they continued to enjoy commercial success for several years to come, despite a sharp decline in the quality of their music.

*Blood, Sweat & Tears 3* (even their album titles mirrored Chicago's) was released by Columbia Records two weeks after the same label issued Bob Dylan's deliberately obfuscating *Self Portrait*. The Yippies didn't need to mount a media campaign to denounce Dylan's apostasy from the revolution; the media beat them to it. The British underground newspaper the *International Times* concluded that 'Dylan's no longer a leftist – he's as far right as you can get – at least on the evidence of this album. He's complacent, uncaring, and seemingly dedicated to a solid conservative way of life . . . He can still feel for the rebels, but his own writing is now set firmly on the establishment side.' 'What is this shit?' was the legendary opening to Greil Marcus's *Rolling Stone* review. But Marcus made an intriguing political point: 'One's reminded that art doesn't come – perhaps that it can't be heard – in times of crisis and destruction; art comes in the period of decadence that precedes a revolution, or after the deluge. It's prelude to revolution; it's not contemporary with it, save in terms of memory.' In which case *Self Portrait* was an irrelevance, and Weatherman – drawing on the electrifying Dylan of 1965–66 – were dragging Dylan into a revolution he'd foretold years earlier.

As a prelude to *Self Portrait*, Bob Dylan travelled to Princeton on 9 June 1970 to receive an honorary doctorate in music. It was five weeks since Kent State had emptied the nation's schools, colleges and universities in protest against the war, the government, and the educational system that fed them. Now Dylan was prepared to accept an honour from one of the most prestigious institutions in the country. One underground newspaper queried why Dylan was kowtowing to a university run by men who 'have taken time off from their war contracts'. His aide, Ben Saltzman, who accompanied Dylan, his wife Sara and David Crosby to the ceremony, reassured the counterculture that the singer was not siding with the establishment. Saltzman claimed that Dylan 'had decided to accept the degree as a gesture to the student movement and to what has been happening on campuses across the country'.

But that was Saltzman speaking, not Dylan. The truth was probably more banal: that Dylan had agreed to pick up his degree because it had been offered to him. As David Crosby recalled, 'Bob didn't want to go. I said, "C'mon Bob, it's an honour!" Sara and I both worked on him for a long time. Finally he agreed.' They shared one of Crosby's legendarily powerful joints in the car and, Crosby said, 'I noticed Dylan getting really quite paranoid behind it. When we arrived at Princeton, they took us to a little room and Bob was asked to wear a cap and gown. He refused outright. They said, "We won't give you the degree if you don't wear this." Dylan said, "Fine. I didn't ask for it in the first place." Finally we convinced him to wear the cap and gown.' This doesn't sound like a man making any kind of political gesture, for or against the students or the war; it was the response of a natural non-conformist, with an adolescent attitude to authority, who (in the words of the song he composed about his Princeton experience, 'Day of the Locust') 'sure was glad to get out of there alive'.

Maybe Dylan had feared a demonstration from the Yippies or the Weather Underground, or some other group who'd taken his surreal songwriting of the mid-1960s as a manifesto. As Vice-President Spiro Agnew had just reminded the nation, 'There is a group of students committed to radical change through violent means.' Just a few hours after Dylan accepted his honorary doctorate, several explosions rocked the headquarters of the New York City Police. That night, the Weatherman collective issued a communiqué claiming credit for the bombing, which had injured several people and caused nearly a million dollars' worth of damage. 'Nixon invades Cambodia,' they explained, 'and hundreds of schools are shut down by strikes. Every time the pigs think they've stopped us, we come back a little stronger and a lot smarter. They guard their buildings and we walk right past their guards.' They listed the sins of the 'pigs' – Fred Hampton, Kent State and the rest – and warned that 'the time is now. Political power grows out of a gun, a Molotov, a riot, a commune . . . and from the soul of the people.'

While Dylan manufactured a cloud of artistic confusion to hide from the public, Weatherman – the organisation which had borrowed his imagery as their own – had hidden themselves among the public, withdrawing from surveillance by the police and the FBI, adopting false identities, preparing for a lifetime of guerrilla warfare within the belly of the state. Two weeks earlier, Bernardine Dohrn had delivered 'A Declaration of a State of War': 'Our job is to lead white kids to armed revolution . . . Kids know that the lines are drawn; revolution is touching all of our lives. Tens of thousands have learned that protest and marches don't do it. Revolutionary violence is the only way.'

To replace the masses and their rallies and marches, Weatherman had to create a new homeland. Gone was the disparagement of white radicals that had come out of the National War Council in December. Back then, the White Panthers' rock band, the Up, had been dismissed as an irrelevance. Now, Weatherman was prepared to make peace with the counter-culture, and build 'a culture of life and music'. As Dohrn explained, 'We fight in many ways. Dope is one of our weapons ... Freaks are revolutionaries and revolutionaries are freaks. If you want to find us, this is where we are. In every tribe, commune, dormitory, farmhouse, barracks and townhouse where kids are making love, smoking dope and loading guns.'

There was no longer a revolutionary elite, Weatherman had decided. There was only the mass of 'revolutionaries' and 'freaks', a youth army who shared a culture and a cultural enemy. It was the glorious optimism of 1968 rewritten for a fresh decade. Weatherman had laid down the foundations of a new world by blowing up the symbols of the old one. Everything else was up to the people. But were the people listening?

## DO NOTHING

> So Nixon kills four straight-looking kids in the centre of AmeriKa, in a small town filled with his silent majority. Friends in England ask: 'What can we do?' The answer is simple: do nothing. There is nothing you can do. There is no support you can give, unless you are ready to go across the ocean armed.
>
> (Mal Doror article in the *International Times*, June 1970)

On 18 June 1970, Britain faced its first General Election since March 1966. After four years of economic depression, the Labour government offered itself to the people under the slogan, 'Now that Britain's Strong, Let's Make it Great to Live In'. Besides the financial stability and increased wealth that all political parties routinely promise, Labour pledged to maintain its isolation of the racist regimes in the former British Commonwealth countries of South Africa and Rhodesia. The opposition Conservative Party campaigned on its traditional territory – lower taxes, private ownership of the public services, and an end to immigration. Within the narrow realm of traditional

British politics, there were vast differences between the two platforms. But for anyone intoxicated by the talk of American revolution, there was little room for expression – a handful of self-proclaimed Socialists were standing for election, a single Anti-War Radical candidate, and around fifty members of the Soviet-backed Communist Party of Great Britain.

Whereas the 1968 US election had transfixed the nation, mainstream and movement alike, the British poll aroused only minimal passion in the underground. The rock newspaper *Melody Maker* printed a symposium, 'Pop and the Election', in which musicians and personalities stated their preferences. The stars divided fairly equally between idealistic socialists with nobody to vote for, self-confessed capitalists, and hippies who claimed no interest in politics. Robert Wyatt, drummer, vocalist and composer with Soft Machine, explained that he came from a 'staunch Socialist family', and 'would always vote for the nearest thing to a Communist Party, although once they get into power all systems are pretty bad'. He then revealed that he was working for the third party in the poll, the middle-of-the-road Liberals. Robin Gibb of the Bee Gees said he would vote Conservative, out of self-interest. Disc jockey John Peel and Led Zeppelin vocalist Robert Plant pleaded apathy, as did guitarist Eric Clapton. 'I don't see that it matters which government is elected,' he explained, 'because the country is really run by the youth. Youth is the prophet of the age and they have taken over. As Steve Stills once said, "A good rock band can outdraw the President of the United States".' But who held the most power?

The election campaign coincided with a changing of the guard on the British rock scene. The public had belatedly discovered that the Beatles had split: Paul McCartney isolated himself in Scotland, while John Lennon continued his psychotherapy in California. In the wake of Altamont, the Rolling Stones maintained a low profile. The music papers were dominated by a new breed of hard rock bands – Led Zeppelin, Deep Purple, Black Sabbath, Uriah Heep and many more – who made no claim to be speaking for their generation, and were therefore more in touch with their male, teenage followers than their politically aware elders.

Attempts to reproduce the revolutionary fervour of America seemed to be doomed to failure. As the Chicago Conspiracy Trial neared its climax, for instance, there was a benefit concert for the defendants at the customary psychedelic meeting place of the Roundhouse in North London. 'It was hardly "Up against the wall motherfuckers",' one observer noted, 'and more like "All you need is love". It must have been embarrassing for the hard-core left-wingers who turned up with the scent of blood in their nostrils and their fists ritualistically clenched. The dancing, punch-filled freaks . . . were not out to kill the pigs and wreak violent revolution.'

Even diehard revolutionaries appeared to have lost enthusiasm for the struggle. The collective who produced the radical newspaper *Black Dwarf*, scene of the debate between John Lennon and John Hoyland in 1968, fell apart in February 1970. Tariq Ali and four other comrades left to form a new magazine, *Red Mole*. 'Tariq and his comrades came out in favour of a Trotskyist party in South Africa,' Hoyland recalls, 'and they denounced the African National Congress, Nelson Mandela's party. That fuelled a revolt on the paper.' 'Perhaps one day the journalists will disappear up their own arses,' the *International Times* noted cynically, 'and the people will have a revolution all by themselves.' The *Red Mole* faction were members of the Trotskyist party, the International Marxist Group, one of several left-wing organisations – others included the International Socialists and the Socialist Labour League – who claimed to have recognised the conditions for imminent revolution. They eschewed the parliamentary route to power, which was perhaps just as well: when the Conservatives toppled Labour in the June election, Socialist/Marxist candidates polled just 0.14 per cent of the vote – and around 80 per cent of those went to Communist Party supporters.[7]

Conservatism extended from young voters to their rock idols. In 1968, Lennon and Jagger had confronted the revolution head-on. Now even those self-confessed revolutionaries the Edgar Broughton Band were edging away from the fray. Broughton denied that they were 'a revolutionary group', preferring to describe them as 'a revolutionary force', by which he meant a long-haired band who could upset taxi drivers. 'We get attacked by both sides, the freaks and the left, the Marxists, who say we are not doing anything,' he said. 'But we are not the revolution.' The sense of betrayal could be traced through the underground press. 'Watch out! Broughton is a fake!!' exclaimed one outraged ex-fan. 'It's high time you wised up to Chairman Edgar. For fuck sake, EXPOSE him!' The band's manager, Peter Jenner, was forced to rise to their defence: 'I think that Edgar's much more involved in the revolution now than he was, in the sense that the Stones are. I mean, the Stones all drive around in their fucking Jaguars, or whatever they've got. No one suggests that Jagger is anything but loaded . . . but the thing with Jagger is what he stands for, the way he acts, has done more for the situation than any number of young long-haired stoned freaks rushing around talking about revolution.' In fact, Jenner argued, the Broughton Band had discovered that the real fakes were the radicals, not the musicians: 'They've been burned too often by these bloody revolutionaries. They've appeared at too many benefits that have been a wank in all senses.'

The world of benefit concerts was one that Mick Farren and his late 1960s band, the (Social) Deviants, knew only too well. Their first album, *Ptooff!*, was financed by Nigel Samuel, the same man who was funding Michael X's Black House. 'I'd always been throwing shitfits over what I saw as concessions to the corporate capitalist music industry,' Farren recalled, 'and demanding to know why the cream of the underground bands were being sold off to EMI and Decca. Surely if we could get our shit together to distribute underground newspapers, psychedelic posters and comics, why the hell couldn't we do the same with bigger-ticket items like records?' *Ptooff!* wasn't just manufactured independently; it was distributed through 'head shops' and radical booksellers, in a unique attempt to escape the straitjacket that large companies imposed on the music industry.

Many observers greeted this gesture as the launch of a crusade against capitalism. The Deviants were now expected to donate their services free of charge to anyone who asked, as long as the request had some vague link to the underground or the movement. 'We were also assumed to be packing the entire counter-culture into the truck,' Farren noted, 'and taking it round the country like some revolutionary revival show.' Unable to follow Pink Floyd or the Grateful Dead's path from cult acclaim to commercial acceptance, the Deviants were typecast as, in Farren's phrase, 'the killer-clowns of the revolution'.

After two more albums and a disastrous tour of America, Farren was informed by his fellow Deviants that his principled bohemianism was preventing the band from achieving stardom. Bitter experience and political acumen combined to produce a clear-sighted vision of what lay ahead: '1970 will be a year in which escapism will be peddled to the kids in the underground in the guise of revolution.' Certainly the British rock audience preferred Edgar Broughton's orthodoxy to the almost psychopathically uncommercial approach of Farren's next album, *Mona – The Carnivorous Circus*.

'Escapism' rarely came in a more attractive package than that offered by the Rolling Stones. They toured Europe in the summer of 1970, and Mick

Jagger was still ready to spout radical rhetoric. 'I want to earn money on our new records,' he told a Danish newspaper, 'not for the sake of the money but to invest it in other things, such as the Black Panther breakfast programme for ghetto children. We have already set aside some bread for them, in fact.' And he repeated his disgust that major record companies were almost inevitably involved with the manufacture of arms. 'I want the money to fight this with,' he declared. It was a stance echoed by his sidekick, Keith Richards. 'We found out that all of the bread we made for Decca was going into making little black boxes that go into American Air Force bombers to bomb fucking North Vietnam,' he complained. 'They took the bread we made for them and put it into the radar section of their business. When we found that out, it blew our minds. Goddamn, you've helped to kill God knows how many thousands of people without even knowing it. I'd rather the Mafia than Decca.'

A journalist for the *International Times* took the Stones at their word. '[Jagger] can form his own company with the bread gained from record sales over the last few years,' he instructed, 'and then make a positive action – bringing out cheap records – against the strictly regulated price system within the industry! After eight years of making fortunes for themselves, and even larger fortunes for the Decca/London Group, the Rolling Stones' contract with Decca has expired, and by not renewing it, the Stones have put themselves into the position of having Workers' Control over their own product.' It was a vision of financial utopia – the Deviants' disavowal of capitalist writ large. But the writer recognised that the Stones might follow the Beatles by forming an 'independent' label under the umbrella of a multinational corporation. 'If the Stones go the same way,' he concluded, 'they prove themselves to be the complete antithesis of their music, and Jagger will be as big a shit-kicker as any middle-aged head of any middle-aged company, who sees rock music purely in terms of more material comfort for himself and his fellow honkies.'

In public, Jagger maintained his stance as a man of the people. 'We are not making any money out of this,' he claimed as the 1970 tour began. 'It has only been arranged as a friendly gesture for our European fans.' Yet the scene at the Stones' concert in Paris highlighted their politically ambiguous position. Outside the Olympia theatre, fans mingled with demonstrators calling for the establishment of a Palestinian homeland and the expulsion of Israel from the territory it had invaded in the Six Days War of 1967.

From the crowds came chants of 'power to the people' and a reprise of the most idealistic slogans from May 1968. 'Entrance cost up to one week's salary for a young worker here,' noted French anarchist Jean Jacques Lebel. Inside, the Stones mingled with the city's social elite – aristocrats, actors, entrepreneurs, artists, and Nicaraguan model Bianca Perez Morena de Macias, with whom Jagger began a relationship that night. What none of the demonstrators, or the Stones' radical supporters around the world, knew was that the band was already planning two years of tax exile, and was negotiating with all of the major global record corporations (excluding Decca), in search of the most lucrative deal possible for the rights to handle the Stones' 'independent' label. Donations to the Black Panther Party did not feature in the negotiations.

## ISLE OF PHUN

In the summer of 1970 Mick Farren threw himself into a grandiose, doomed project: a rock festival organised by the people, for the people. The result was Phun City, staged in late July in the unlikely surroundings of Ecclesdon Common, near Worthing on the sleepy Sussex coast. The posters promised performances from many name bands, plus 'Vast & Wondrous Amounts of Food, Drink & Shitting'. The only missing element was money, which was eventually supplied by Radio Caroline owner Ronan O'Rahilly. He stipulated that it should be a free festival, and so everyone involved was destined to end up in debt. As Mick Farren noted afterwards, 'We lost six grand, but the people got it on.'

A month later, the people – more than 250,000 of them – gathered at what was supposed to be the British Woodstock. It was the third and, for nearly three decades, last Isle of Wight festival. It starred many of the stars of the Woodstock movie; it marked the final official appearance of Jimi Hendrix on a British stage; it was documented on film and several albums; it remains the biggest UK rock festival of all time. It has passed into legend as a golden moment of hippie bliss, the high-water mark of the British counter-culture. But the last gathering of the tribes was also the moment when the fragile coalition between the rock underground and its political counterpart was fractured beyond repair.

In his role as unofficial conscience of British rock, Mick Farren inevitably played a key role in the fracas. Fresh from his money-burning experience at Phun City, he did some back-of-an-envelope calculations and predicted that the promoters, Ricky Farr and the Foulks brothers (alias Fiery Creations), could not possibly break even unless they erected 'the most horrendous security measures, and I couldn't come up with an image of any possible site that didn't look like a prison camp. As it turned out, even my imaginings were completely outstripped by reality.' Farren watched in horror as iron fences were built, while security men patrolled the border with off-duty police dogs. There was no festival village, no funfair or pleasure garden, no link to the utopian gatherings of 1967 except for the music. But there was a hill, overlooking the site, over which the guards and their Alsatians had no control. This, Farren and his associates decided, would be the home of the festival dissidents.

As admirers of the imprisoned White Panther leader, John Sinclair, Farren and friends decided to appoint themselves the British arm of the White Panther Party. They haunted Fiery Creations like the ghosts at Ebenezer Scrooge's bedside, issuing a succession of increasingly militant bulletins about the festival and its morals. A week before the event, a leaflet bearing the brand of the White Panthers' Ministry of Information circulated around hip London. 'The Isle of Wight Festival is an obvious example of capitalist interests seeking to exploit the energy of the People's music,' it began. The leaflet pinpointed the weaknesses in the festival security, and promised that the Panthers would be 'running a free festival on land adjoining the official site'. It ended with the stock revolutionary slogan of the age: 'Power to the People'.

Alerted to the strategic significance of the hill, fans began arriving there several days before the festival began. Over the next few days, French anarchists and Hell's Angels staged lightning attacks on Fiery Creations' iron fences. By the time the music began, the perimeter had become a battleground, and few of those inside could be unaware of the ideological struggle that was underway. By Saturday, Farren had widened the war to encompass the artists. 'Performers are on that stage because, and only because, of the people,' his latest bulletin insisted. 'But their projection is always towards a front-stall elite. In other words, their audience is basically a bunch of rich honkies. It is true that for a festival run on these lines, groups expect large amounts of money before they appear, but the kids must realise that all profit from the freaks is being put back into the honky community.' The gulf between the promoters and the Panthers was now as broad as that between capitalists and the people, Farren argued.

Late Saturday night, there was a summit meeting on the hill (now named Desolation Row, after Bob Dylan's 1965 song). The Panthers, Jean Jacques Lebel's French anarchists, the Hell's Angels, even the radical youth section of the parliamentary Liberal party, the Young Liberals, agreed that they should launch a symbolic assault on the security fence. The Angels and the anarchists volunteered as shock troops, and they moved on their target at ten o'clock on Sunday morning, when the bulk of festival-goers were still asleep. They breached the fence in several places, and the promoters finally realised that their fight was lost. Early that afternoon, the Foulks brothers announced that the Isle of Wight was now a free festival. Like the piercing of the fence, this concession was more symbolic than real. But for many who were there, it altered the ambience of the festival. 'Sure, we'd heard some good music,' observed Rod Allen, who documented the festival, 'but for those prices, that's the least we expected. When the turnstiles (and some of the fence) came down, the vibes changed instantly. Suddenly, we felt that the music was there because the performers wanted us to hear it – and for no other reason.' Ironically, the artists were the only section of the festival community unaffected by the decision. But the promoters were horrified. Farren remembered Rikki Farr taking the microphone that afternoon, and howling at the crowd: 'You bastards, you ruined everything. I'll see you in hell before you come onto my island again!'

Farren had no regrets. He was more troubled by the hierarchical society on the festival site. As White Panther Party spokesman, he had already called for supporters 'to bring community pressure to bear on those of our brothers who, through greed or obsession for status, exploit people'. At the Isle of Wight he saw 'a VIP enclosure surrounded by fences and protected by guards; and kids walking into the medical tent in a state of collapse because they hadn't eaten for two days.' It was a scene 'that was practically as vicious as Tsarist Russia'. Jean Jacques Lebel reckoned that the audience were as complicit as the promoters: 'Only vegetables can spend three days and nights without food, packed like cattle into a filthy arena surrounded by walls and private guards and police dogs and not even protest, just because music is being played.' But the chief culprits, both men agreed, were the performers.

'The Isle of Wight was just the ultimate paradox,' Farren argued. 'You had someone like Jim Morrison saying theoretically, if not in actual words, "tear down the walls, break down the capitalist barriers", and the whole thing being set up to maintain his elite position in society.' Lebel castigated the stars, who 'spend so much time in chauffeured limousines and ritzy houses and press conferences and first-class flights and living like millionaires and sometimes becoming millionaires, that they are completely out of touch with what actually goes on at festivals apart from their own stage performances.' One of the highest paid performers at the Isle of Wight was Joni Mitchell. 'It was a hostile audience to begin with,' she remembered. 'A handful of French rabble-rousers had stirred the people up to feel that we, the performers, had sold out because we had arrived in fancy cars – Neil [Young] and I had rented an old red Rolls.'

Her choice of transport proved to be the least of Mitchell's problems. Armed only with acoustic guitar and piano, she faced a crowd who were already restless because of the long pause between performers. As she recalled, 'In the second number, a guy in about the fifth row, flipped out on acid, comes squirting up and lets out a banshee wail, guttural, demented, devils at his heels. It's as if a whale came out of the water, the waves, the energy from him spreads to the back so fast.' Within minutes, a hippie scrambled onto the stage and began to add arrhythmic percussion to her utopian song about the Woodstock festival. The invader was no stranger, but someone Mitchell had known when she'd lived in a commune amidst the caves of Matala, under the nose of the Greek military regime. As the song ended, the hippie reached over and took Mitchell's microphone. 'I have an announcement that I've been asked to make,' he told the crowd. 'Desolation Row is this festival, ladies and gentleman.'

Was this the voice of the hill, the anti-festival, launching a commando raid on the 'honky community'? Or simply an acid trip searching for self-expression? Backstage, the hippie – known to Joni as Yogi Joe – could only supply an enigmatic answer. 'I believe this is my festival,' he declared. 'If I had been allowed to go on stage, we might have discovered that I was one of the most coherent people around here.' He also claimed that promoter Rikki Farr had appointed him 'the head of the official committee to paint the fences invisible . . . because it was embarrassing him'.

Regardless of his motives, the crowd felt he was one of their own. As Farr's security tried to pull Yogi Joe off the stage, they began to boo. Mitchell had already started her next song, but as the catcalls rose, she stopped, stared tearfully into the face of the storm, and made a rambling call for 'some respect'. It worked: as she described the scene portentously nearly twenty years later, 'the beast lay down'. She won widespread praise for her courage.

But Jean Jacques Lebel felt he had witnessed the star system in action: 'I saw a coloured Asian man, obviously on a heavy acid trip, climb on stage and try to speak while Joni was tuning up. He was very brutally kicked about by stagehands. And Joni said: "Don't behave like tourists. It's hard to play music up here for all these people. Give us some respect." Didn't that man deserve some respect too, Joni? Or is respect due only to "stars"?'

With the talent being abused by the audience, and the very concept of commercial performance coming under attack, Rod Allen predicted that the Isle of Wight would signal 'the end of the rip-off form in festivals'. Allen envisaged a future of free concerts, with 'the bills . . . paid by giant advertisers as part of their new social-conscience kick, putting money back into the community'. The inaugural Glastonbury festival, held over a weekend in September 1970, certainly provided an alternative model for promoters: admission cost a third of what Fiery Creations had charged at Worthy Farm, and included free milk from the owners' cows; fewer than 2,000 people attended; and the event was designed as a celebration of the underground spirit, not a means of exploiting it. Yet Glastonbury couldn't boast any stars to match those at the Isle of Wight – the Who, the Doors, Joni Mitchell, Leonard Cohen, and Jimi Hendrix, who bade farewell to the British stage with a sporadically brilliant performance racked by self-doubt. It was as if Hendrix was mirroring the confusion haunting the festival and the British counter-culture. Less than three weeks later, Hendrix's body was found in a London apartment, after an apparently accidental drug overdose. The fire of the 1960s underground had been extinguished, and the embers were now ashes, scattered in the wind.

## POLITICAL PRISONERS

In February 1970, acid guru Timothy Leary was jailed in Orange County, California for possession of two marijuana cigarettes. Like John Sinclair in Michigan, he received a sentence of ten years' imprisonment, to be served in the minimum security California Men's Colony West prison. On 12 September, six days before Jimi Hendrix drew his final breath, Leary undertook a daring escape bid, climbing into a tree and onto a roof, edging hand by hand along a telephone cable, and then dropping to earth beyond the prison wall. Within a few minutes, a car arrived to whisk Leary to a safe house in Oakland. It was there that he discovered who had helped plan his escape, and provided his transport to freedom: the Weather Underground.

The organisation had been approached by a group of elite drug dealers named the Brotherhood of Eternal Love, and promised substantial funds if they could pluck Leary from the clutches of the law. Ever since, there have been suspicions about the Brotherhood's motives; some have alleged that the dealers were controlled by the CIA, and that Leary was allowed to escape so that his movements could be tracked. Indeed, there are conspiracy theorists who believe that Leary himself was a CIA agent. If that was true, then he was perfectly placed to act as an informer: within a month, he had been smuggled out of the country, and sent to the Algerian headquarters of Eldridge Cleaver's exiled Black Panthers. Cleaver certainly had his doubts about his guest; he ordered Leary and his wife to be held under house arrest, suspecting that they were reporting on his activities to the American government.

In advance of his escape, Leary penned a letter to his comrades in the underground – perhaps the most over-excited manifesto to come out of the American radical left. It was released by the Weather Underground alongside their own communiqué, which proudly took the credit for his release and described Leary as 'a political prisoner' whose work had brought closer a utopian society built on the values of peace and love. 'Letter from Timothy Leary' was different. It declared the commencement of World War Three, 'waged by short-haired robots whose deliberate aim is to destroy the complex web of free wild life by the imposition of mechanical order'. The previously pacifist LSD scientist was now calling for his readers to 'defend life by all and every means possible against the genocidal machine'. The American government was, Leary declared, 'an instrument of total lethal evil'. The movement should 'arm yourself and shoot to live . . . To shoot a genocidal robot policeman in the defense of life is a sacred act.' And so it continued, piling hyperbole upon extravagant boast, until the peroration: 'Listen, the hour is late. Total war is upon us. Fight to live or you'll die. Freedom is life. Freedom will live.' There was a final, defiant postscript: 'WARNING: I am armed and should be considered dangerous to anyone who threatens my life or my freedom.'

The CIA's finest minds could hardly have composed a more convincing demonstration of revolutionary fervour, with just enough of Leary's old rhetoric – 'create organic art, music . . . blow the mechanical mind with Holy Acid . . . dose them' – to ring true. There was no hint that Leary would soon turn informer, to help the US government prove that the Weather Underground had aided his escape. But if the CIA had masterminded Leary's release, did that mean that they were also, accidentally or deliberately, financing the terrorist attacks of the Weather Underground? And where did the Brotherhood of Eternal Love fit into this intelligence/dissidence nexus? Wheel upon paranoid wheel, the entire scenario tripped out the synapses as expertly as Dr Leary's chemical concoctions.

Yet paranoia was rarely far from the surface of radical America in 1970. *Stage Fright*, the new album by Bob Dylan's former backing musicians The Band, captured the mood with a contemporary resonance missing from their earlier work. 'Police signs and flashing lights,' sang Richard Manuel on 'Just Another Whistle Stop', 'I wonder who went down tonight?' Another song, 'The Rumor', rekindled the mistrust of the McCarthy era, nearly two decades earlier. 'It's a-coming, a brand new day', promised the chorus, before a solo vocalist punctured the illusion, moaning 'no, no, no' like a man racked with disillusionment.

The impending trial of Charles Manson hung over the counter-culture like a curse, a grim fulfilment of the old proverb about being careful what you wished for. Manson and his Family had desired liberation and chaos, not necessarily in that order, and now faced imprisonment as a reward for their chaos. Huey Newton was released from prison on 5 August 1970, pending a retrial on legal niceties, but he emerged into a Black Panther Party riven by internal (FBI-inspired) feuds, and exhausted by a succession of trumped-up charges. 'Free Huey!' had been the battle cry for nearly three years, but what did his freedom achieve? Newton proved to be less inspirational as a free man than he had been as a prisoner; his speaking voice was thin and dull, a grave disappointment alongside the trademark rabble-rousing of the imprisoned Bobby Seale and the exiled Eldridge Cleaver. More pertinently, Newton appeared powerless to prevent the virtual civil war that was erupting within the Panthers' ranks, as tactical divisions emerged between those who followed the Newton/Seale line, and those entranced by the more militant rhetoric of Cleaver. All too often, these disputes tumbled into violence; the FBI watched with glee as the party veered towards self-destruction. Only much later did it become apparent that the Bureau had fuelled the split, sending an abusive and accusatory letter to Cleaver in Algiers over the faked signatures of the party's leaders in Oakland.

There were other pressures on Newton, not least the temptation of women, drugs and fame. Newton was swamped by interview requests, not just from underground newspapers but from national news magazines. He was even offered a makeover by a public relations firm in Hollywood. 'Too many so-called leaders of the movement have been made into celebrities, and their revolutionary fervour destroyed by mass media,' he wrote in his 1973 autobiography. It was an accusation that his detractors would soon begin to level at Newton himself.

Other myths were in the making. Two days after Newton gained his freedom, there was a shoot-out at a courtroom in San Rafael, California, and three young black men were killed. This was the latest chapter in a violent saga that had begun in February 1970, when three long-term prisoners in Soledad jail, George Jackson, John Cluchette and Fleeta Drumgo, were charged with murdering a guard. He had been thrown over a prison balcony, in apparent retaliation for the killing of three black convicts in the same jail.

The three accused men were pictured in the *Los Angeles Times*: 'Their faces were serene and strong, but their waists were draped in chains. Chains bound their arms to their sides and chains shackled their legs. "They are trying to impress upon us that we have not yet escaped from bondage", I thought.' The voice belongs to Angela Davis, a lecturer at the University of California, who woke up one morning to find herself denounced in the *San Francisco Herald-Examiner* as a Maoist and a gunrunning member of the Black Panther Party. Both accusations amused Davis, who was a staunch member of the Communist Party, and who had criticised the Panthers for refusing to follow the orthodox Marxist–Leninist route to revolution. When she first became aware of the men who would become famous as the Soledad Brothers, she was embroiled in a legal battle to retain her job.

She soon sublimated her own problems beneath the struggle to secure justice for the three Brothers. As she researched the story, she discovered that George Jackson was a habitual criminal, who had been behind bars since his early teens. He had been sentenced to a lengthy prison term in the early 1960s for his part in a $70 robbery; though he admitted his previous offences, he claimed that this time he was an innocent bystander. 'A determination began to swell in me', Davis recalled, 'to do everything within the limits of the possible to save George from the gas chamber.' She began to correspond with Jackson, after which 'a personal intimacy began to develop between us'. This intensified when she visited the prison and was intoxicated by the Soledad Brothers' bruised beauty: 'Chained and shackled, they were standing tall and they were beautiful. George looked even more vibrant than I had imagined.'

Angela Davis became a close confidante of the Jackson family, in particular George's 16-year-old brother Jonathan. 'He reminded me of my youngest brother,' she recalled. On 7 August 1970, Jonathan Jackson arrived at the San Rafael courthouse with several guns hidden under his coat. When prisoners Ruchell Magee, William Christmas and James McLain arrived in the court, Jackson pulled out a gun, aimed it at the judge, and threw the other firearms to the convicts. 'We are the revolutionaries!' Jackson called out. 'All right, gentlemen, I'm taking over now.' Each of the men took a hostage, and dragged them at gunpoint towards a waiting van. But before they could escape police opened fire on the van, killing Jackson, Christmas, McLain – and the judge.

The teenager had been planning to demand the freedom of the Soledad Brothers, in return for letting the hostages live. When police examined his guns, they discovered that one of them was registered to Angela Davis. An arrest warrant was immediately issued in her name, on charges of murder, kidnapping and conspiracy. Fearing that she was about to be railroaded and possibly killed, she took the fateful decision to run. 'Turning myself in to Ronald Reagan and his accomplices would have been equivalent to placing my head voluntarily on the executioner's block,' she explained. For the next ten weeks, she disguised herself and kept moving, but she was eventually tracked down in a New York hotel on 13 October 1970. Her claim of total innocence and her previous record of harassment at the hands of the authorities in California won the sympathy of everyone who had ever supported the Black Panthers – particularly when it was revealed that the prosecution would push for a death sentence if she were convicted. Davis had no doubts why she had been arrested: 'The reactionary pig forces of this country have chosen to persecute me because I am a Communist revolutionary, participating together with millions of oppressed people throughout the world, designed to overthrow all of the conditions that stand in the way of our freedom.' Lawyer Leo Branton, who was also working for Jimi Hendrix's family to untangle the legal morass surrounding his estate, agreed to represent Davis. Soul singer Aretha Franklin quickly offered to cover Davis' bail money, explaining that it was 'not because I believe in Communism, but because she is a black woman and she wants freedom for black people'. Her gesture was courageous in a culture where five Black Panther members in New Jersey could be arrested for the crime of 'singing a revolutionary song'.

There were clear ideological differences between Davis and the Black Panthers, but from prison George Jackson succeeded in bridging them. He was appointed an honorary field marshal in the party, while Huey Newton welcomed Davis into the collective struggle for black power. With Newton available for interviews, Davis' adventures filling the front pages, and Jackson's collection of prison letters, *Soledad Brother*, winning sympathetic reviews in the mainstream press, the profile of the black liberation movement had rarely been higher. Yet, as Newton admitted later, the Black Panther Party was 'in a shambles'. He laid down the standard excuses – harassment from the government, shoot-outs, feuds with rival groups. Most damning, however, was his belief that the party 'had lost sight of its initial purpose and become caught up in irrelevant causes. Estranged from Black people who could not relate to it, the Black Panther Party had defected from the community.' From the vantage point of 1973, he singled out a culprit: Eldridge Cleaver. But for the moment, the two men, separated by the Atlantic Ocean, maintained an uneasy truce. Cleaver continued to spout unrealistic rhetoric, telling the *New York Times* that 'the revolutionary prospects inside the United States are very bright' and that 'it would give me great satisfaction if Richard Nixon should be killed'.

The strains within the Newton/Cleaver coalition were exemplified by the farce that was the Revolutionary People's Constitutional Convention in Washington, DC. It was intended as a three-day conference on the future of the revolution, across a weekend in late November 1970, combining black and white radicals. 'They wanted the Black Panthers to write a new Constitution, overthrow the government by force, and implement it,' Newton said of his white comrades. But events in Washington illustrated that far from overthrowing the Nixon administration, the Panthers could not even organise a conference. Nobody had thought to confirm the booking with the managers of the hall, and delegates arrived on Friday night to discover that there was no venue and no programme. Newton did succeed in organising an impromptu concert and rally in a church the following night, but even then the star speaker, Cleaver's wife Kathleen, failed to appear. The party blamed a conspiracy by 'the fascist ruling class' for the debacle, but the blame clearly lay closer to home. Newton tried to turn the chaos to his advantage, claiming that 'when [the revolution] did not come about in Washington, we got critical letters claiming we were no longer the vanguard of the movement. I paid no attention. In fact, we were glad to be rid of the [white] radicals because all they did was talk.'

Though Newton was suspicious of white radicals, he still solicited support from leading white members of the counter-culture. On a plane trip from California to New York in September 1970, he made friends with the San Francisco acid-country-rock band the Grateful Dead. 'We had a nice long rap,' guitarist Jerry Garcia explained. 'We liked the cat and were pretty impressed with him. We thought that if there was ever anything we could do for him, we'd try to do it.' Newton filed the band's numbers away for future reference; so did the FBI, whose informers were able to monitor the mid-flight conversation for their bosses.

A less obvious convert to the Panthers' cause was the mellow singer-songwriter James Taylor. 'My father was a socialist,' he says today, 'and my politics have always been in that tradition.' In autumn 1970, his album *Sweet Baby James* seemed to signal the influx of a generation of introspective performers, for whom politics was a disturbing distraction from the everyday problems of love and the soul. But Taylor was a keen observer of the movement, despite noting that 'I can't preach against capitalism and make as much bread as I do – it's incompatible'. He explained how hard it was for the radical left to relate to the masses when they were subject to extreme pressure from the government. 'The Black Panthers are being pushed,' he said that October. 'The formation of the Black Panther Party was justified by the conditions prevalent at that time. In certain situations there certainly IS a need for violence. There's just a danger of trying to apply it to all situations, irrespective of need.' But unlike the Dead, who had told Newton that they would play benefit concerts for the Panthers, Taylor believed that his political beliefs needed to be kept separate from his music. 'Too many people use rock music to attract an audience, and then preach,' he commented, 'which is false advertising, I think. I don't really dig it all that much.'

While Taylor was concerned that politics might damage the sensitivity of his music, his view was not universally shared. The same week when his comments appeared in print also brought the first live appearance by a band called the Lumpen (after the *lumpenproletariat*, a term coined by Karl Marx to describe the lowest stratum of society). All four members belonged to the San Francisco chapter of the Black Panthers, and they sang together informally while collating copies of the party newspaper. At the suggestion of the Panthers' cartoonist and Minister of Culture, Emory Douglas, they formed 'a revolutionary culture cadre'. Lumpen vocalist Michael Torrence explained, 'Elaine Brown had already recorded an album of revolutionary songs . . . and this quartet singing in a R&B or Soul form could be a useful political tool.' Douglas christened the group 'for the brothers on the block, the disenfranchised angry underclass in the ghetto'.

One of the group, Bill Calhoun, wrote two songs that the Lumpen recorded as a single, 'No More' and 'Bobby [Seale] Must Be Set Free'. After they performed at local community centres and Panther rallies, they were taken under the wing of the party's national Ministry of Culture in Oakland. 'It was determined that as representatives of the Black Panther Party and to capture the imagination of the people,' Torrence remembered, 'the Lumpen had to perform at a high level – the "product" had to be good. We recruited progressive musicians from the community and they became the Lumpen's band – the Freedom Messengers Revolutionary Musicians.' The group now resembled the Temptations, whose songs they reworked into political anthems such as 'There's Bullets in the Air for Freedom' and 'Old Pig Nixon'. Their interpretations of popular material were less extreme than those in the *Weatherman Songbook*. Indeed, it could be argued that when they altered the words of, say, the Impressions' 'People Get Ready', they were only fleshing out the political message that songwriter Curtis Mayfield had originally implied. When they composed their own material, they could speak without restraint, in songs such as 'Revolution is the Only Solution', 'We Can't Wait Another Day' and 'Set Sister Erika Free' (referring to Erika Huggins, Bobby Seale's co-defendant in his murder trial).

By late November 1970, the party felt confident enough of the Lumpen's abilities to publicise their single in the *Black Panther* newspaper. As the paper crowed, 'The Lumpen sing about what needs to be done, how to do it, and then go forth and put it into practice, using their creative talents.' They spent November on the road, and were one of the attractions promised to the delegates at the Washington convention. A live show at Merritt College was recorded and shopped around to the major record companies. By the end of the year, they were back in California, headlining at events such as the Revolutionary Christmas Party in West Berkeley, and a Panthers R&B show at the Blue Gardenia in Oakland, where they performed under a banner that read: 'Death to the Fascist Pigs'. Despite their local fame, the Lumpen weren't removed from their duties as party members. 'We did all the political and day-to-day work that was required of every rank and file comrade,' Michael Torrence

explained. 'The music was simply another facet of service to the Party and
the revolution. Furthermore, since we were an educational cadre, rigorous
study was necessary to be able to translate the ideology of the Black Panther
Party into song.' Like the Women's Liberation Rock Bands in Chicago and
New Haven, the Lumpen were pioneering a propaganda-based rock style that
would soon be adopted by one of the most famous musicians in the world.

## NO MORE JIVING

Weatherman is the heaviest white scene in the history of the AmeriKan
revolution. The Weathermen have come to the end of language, the
end of dialogue ('no more jiving') and are taking care of business.
                         (Mal Doror article in the *International Times*, June 1970)

At 3.40am on 24 August 1970, a police dispatcher in Madison, Wisconsin,
received a 911 call. 'OK, pigs,' announced a young male voice, 'now listen
and listen good. There's a bomb in the Army Math Research Center, the
University, set to go off in five minutes. Clear the building. Get everyone
out. Warn the hospital. This is no bullshit, man.' Three minutes later, another
911 call confirmed that the warning had indeed been 'no bullshit'. A camper
van loaded with 2,000 pounds of ammonium nitrate soaked in aeroplane
fuel had exploded outside the Research Center. Despite the early hour, the
building was not empty: a handful of security staff were on duty, and also
some physicists. Four men were injured in the blast, and a 33-year-old research
student was killed. Until the Oklahoma City bomb in 1995, this was the
biggest terrorist explosion ever carried out on American soil.

The local underground newspaper, *Kaleidoscope*, was soon contacted by a
group who called themselves variously the New Year's Gang (after a previous
attack on 1 January 1970) or the Vanguard of the Revolution. They demanded
the release of three imprisoned members of the Black Panther Party; the
abolition of the ROTC recruiting organisation on the Madison campus; and
the relaxing of the discriminatory 'women's hours' rule at the University of
Wisconsin, whereby female students had to obey a stricter curfew than their
male counterparts. If these demands were not met, the New Year's Gang
declared, then they would unleash 'revolutionary measures of an intensity
never before seen in this country'.

It was rhetoric worthy of the Weather Underground, who continued to bomb government targets across America without inflicting any fatalities. Their targets included an army base in Presidio, California; the Marin County courthouse where Jonathan Jackson had died (this in protest at the arrest of Angela Davis); and official buildings in Chicago, New York and Massachusetts. Despite Governor Knowles' suspicion that the Madison bomb had either been planted by the Weather Underground or the Black Panthers, the New Year's Gang proved to be an independent group of four students and graduates, led by Karl Armstrong. He was arrested two years later, and sentenced to a lengthy prison term. He expressed no regrets about the bombing, but claimed that he had not intended to cause any injury or loss of life. Both his younger brother and another teenage student were caught later, but the fourth member of the Gang, one Leo Burt, completely vanished. This has added to speculation that he may have been an undercover agent of the FBI. In the late 1970s, investigators suggested that the Bureau knew in advance about the attack. Armstrong himself later claimed that he had been allowed to carry out the bombing to discredit the anti-war movement.

As terrorist bombings increased, previously unknown groupings entered the fray, such as the women-only Proud Eagle Tribe, who carried out an attack on Harvard University in October 1970. Abbie Hoffman was initially ecstatic about the sheer theatricality of it all. Two years after Chicago, he took stock of how the movement had fared since then: 'The Lower East Side was OD'ed on heroin. People's Park was born by *us* and crushed by *them*! Woodstock Nation was born and diluted by the celluloid world of hip capitalism. The Black Panthers have emerged as the most revolutionary force in the land. The Weathermen have unleashed the rage inside each Yippie, and Yippies have turned on the Weathermen to digging culture. A new breed of stoned revolutionaries sneak around the country blowing pot and blowing up pig-sties!' But within a few weeks, he was warning that 'Now we are in heavy times. The post-Altamont blues have set in. Scag [heroin] has come to town. People stab each other. Rock is dead. Folks say The Revolution is over.' This reflected the growing feeling that the current situation could not hold. The demonstrations after Kent State, which had seemed to mark a renaissance in popular protest, had become dulled memories. For all the positivism expressed by the Weather Underground, only the most blinkered radical could imagine that there were revolutionary masses awaiting the signal for seditious action.

Even if there had been crowds gathering in city squares, the vanguard forces were hardly in a position to lead them. 'Next week families and tribes will attack the enemy around the country,' boasted Weather leaders Bernardine Dohrn, Jeff Jones and Bill Ayers in an 8 October 1970 communiqué, announcing what they called their 'Fall Offensive'. But all three were deep in hiding, unable to surface in case they were arrested. They still talked loudly: 'If Nixon invades Cuba, bombs North Vietnam, intervenes in the Middle East,' they declared, 'we must all move fast. Figure out strategic weak points of the enemy. Look to the Arabs. With the underground and mass movement responding together, we could shut down every international airport in Amerika within 24 hours . . . we are bringing a pitiful helpless giant to its knees.' This was pure fantasy; they might as well have been planning to liberate the Moon from the Apollo astronauts. For all their talk of 'an international conspiracy', they were alienated from each other, from their radical soul mates, and from the masses they intended to lead.

It was from this position of isolation that they emerged that December with one of the most humane documents ever produced in the name of revolution. It bore the (inevitably) Dylan-inspired name 'New Morning – Changing Weather', and was signed by Bernardine Dohrn. Dated 6 December, it arrived four days later, by special delivery of the US Mail, at the New York office of the Liberation News Service. From there it was disseminated to radical newspapers and magazines across the country. Perhaps the appetite for a lengthy statement of political principles was smaller than the Weather Underground imagined. But anyone who persevered through this lengthy document was rewarded with candid self-criticism, lucid analysis and poignant admissions of failure, rather than the standard revolutionary rhetoric of gun-toting and pig-rustling.

The key moment in Weather's development was what Dohrn called 'the townhouse explosion' that claimed the lives of Ted Gold, Terry Robbins and Diana Oughton in March. It was their cell in New York that had driven the organisation's strategy 'from firebombing to anti-personnel bombs'. Many members of the collective had resisted the shift towards 'the large scale, almost random bombing offensive that was planned', but they had agreed to follow the majority. This, so Dohrn now believed, was 'the military error' – 'the tendency to consider only bombings or picking up the gun as revolutionary'. It had arisen from the psychological pressure that surrounded a small group of activists who were adrift in enemy territory. After the deaths in March, Dohrn admitted, 'We became aware that a group of outlaws who are isolated from the youth communities do not have a sense of what is going on, cannot develop strategies that grow to include large numbers of people, have become "us" and "them".'

As fugitives on the run from America, the Weather Underground collective 'could not go near the Movement'. Weather's removal from the frontline of the struggle had made them reconsider every aspect of their philosophy, from their gender roles (equal and open) to their use of drugs (hallucinogenic – good; addictive – bad). Indeed, Dohrn's account adopted the semi-religious tone last heard in 1966–67 from hippies who wanted to withdraw from the city and get back to the garden: 'People have been experimenting with everything about their lives, fierce against the ways of the white man. They have learned how to survive together in the poisoned cities and how to live on the road and the land. They've moved to the country and found new ways to bring up free wild children. People have purified themselves with organic food, fought for sexual liberation, grown long hair. People have reached out to each other and learned that grass and organic consciousness-expanding drugs are weapons of the revolution.' It was a dramatic transformation: a year earlier, Dohrn had stood before the National War Council with a fork in her hand, to celebrate the Manson Family's butchering of bourgeois 'pigs'. Now she might have been laying down a manifesto for a commune in the California fields.

Rather than assaulting the military-industrial complex, Dohrn concluded, the Weather Underground's role was to inform America about the world's female revolutionary heroes, from the Viet Cong to the Palestinian Liberation Organisation, the Irish Republican Army to the Black Panther Party. There was no longer one blood-soaked path to revolution: like Chairman Mao launching his Cultural Revolution in 1966, Dohrn wanted a hundred flowers to bloom and decorate the many roads to freedom. 'We are in many different regions of the country,' she declared, 'and are building different kinds of leaders and organisations. It's not coming together into one organisation, or paper structure of factions or coalitions. It's a New Nation that will grow out of the struggles of the next year.'

This was inspirational rhetoric, a beacon to a generation ground down by disunity, false hopes and deflated dreams. There was only one problem: there was no highway to connect the creators of this New Nation with the millions who could bring it into life. Dohrn was asking the masses to trust in Weather's ability to turn fantasy into reality, without providing any guidance as to how isolated groups of converts could join together. Without the stale rigmarole of meetings, manifestos and doctrines, all that remained were a million unique visions of the future, destined never to coincide. The archetypal revolutionary cadre, the proud leaders of a nationwide struggle, had accidentally invented the new philosophy of the 1970s – where the personal became political, until the politics dissolved and the personal became all that existed. From bringing the war home with a bomb in every city square, to the obsessional self-regard of analysis, psychobabble and personal growth: it was a change in the weather, indeed.

## DYLAN'S CURRENT BAG

The Weather Underground's statement was released exactly a month after Bob Dylan's *New Morning* album. That record followed hard on the heels of the critically maligned *Self Portrait*, and was widely interpreted as a response to the controversy it had aroused (although every song on *New Morning* was recorded before *Self Portrait* was issued). *New Morning* was anticipated as a definitive statement that might reveal whether the movement could once again rely on Dylan as a mentor, guide and prophet.

The album's homely, placid charm remains undimmed after more than three decades, but in retrospect it sounds defiantly like a personal statement, not a rallying point for a generation. Its political message was that there was no overt message, not even in 'Day of the Locust', clearly inspired by Dylan's recent trip to Princeton. There was no war raging between the lines of his songs, no conflict to report beyond the walls of his home and the pull in his soul between the country and the city. Yet, as one reviewer of the album admitted, 'Dylan belongs in a very personal way to everyone who digs his music. He existed in our heads, we absorbed him and his music wholesale.'

In that climate, *New Morning* was greeted as a sermon from the mount. The most celebrated and overstated review of the album came from Ralph Gleason in the pages of *Rolling Stone*, just as the same magazine had exhibited the deepest sense of betrayal after *Self Portrait*. 'We've Got Dylan Back Again' was the headline over Gleason's triumphant piece. For him, the record provided a sense of community missing from American culture: 'I had the fantasy that all the other car radios were tuned to KSAN and the Dylan album was blowing their minds that very minute and I looked at the drivers as they went past me and they had smiles on their faces . . . This album is a sign. You believe that? I think I do.' Gleason conceded that 'the crazies' would dismiss the album as 'more pap for the people. It is avoidance. It is meaningless.' But its celebration of family, love and life rendered its lack of significance irrelevant, Gleason believed. Yet the critic couldn't help himself making demands on the artist. 'He's coming out again. Come on, Bob! We need you. That's the truth, man, we really do. Come out, Bob, come out! And he will . . .' There was much more in the same toe-curling style.

Why was Gleason so desperate for Dylan to ride into town like the cavalry? Because the nation needed a saviour. Gleason's portrait of America was etched with fashionable paranoia: 'Here we are. Tim Leary armed and dangerous in Algiers. Nixon armed and dangerous in the White House. Bombs bursting in Rochester and guns firing at random in Cairo. The Kent State massacre being blamed on the massacred, Jackson's dead accused of violence and the poison spreading all around, as no man can trust his brother and the country an armed camp . . . As we go into this dark night we will need what light, what sustenance we can get and that is just what he has given us. The brightest light and the strongest sustenance of all – hope. This is a hopeful album and my God how we need it.' For years, Gleason had been deriding fashionable radicalism in the pages of *Rolling Stone*, but finally he and the Weather Underground, the least likely of shipmates, had drifted into the same becalmed sea.

Not everyone in the movement was so ready to accept Dylan's 'new morning'. Country Joe McDonald had already lectured Dylan about his social responsibilities in his song 'Hey Bobby': 'Where you been? We missed you out on the streets. I hear you've got yourself another scene, it's called a retreat'. A bucolic album celebrating life with the family did nothing to calm McDonald's disquiet: 'Now he's like a ghost of his former self, and it drives me up the wall. I don't know where the real Bob Dylan went, but I don't believe this one . . . I don't know what happened to him, but something did – and he disappeared.'

One man thought he knew exactly what had happened to Bob Dylan: A.J. Weberman. The founder of the Dylan Liberation Front had kept up a relentless commentary – or 'interpretation', as he put it – of Dylan's work in the underground press. Central to his thesis was his belief that Dylan had abandoned his role as the conscience of a generation because of his 'current bag' – an addiction to heroin that, so Weberman claimed, was obvious to anyone who studied his work. While the rock press, over- and underground, struggled to come to terms with *Self Portrait*, Weberman honed in on his fixation: 'First of all there's Dylan's painting (on the cover) which bears no resemblance to Bob. It still says something . . . notice how one of the eyes is closed & the other one is open just enough to reveal a small pupil. This is symbolic of Dylan's current bag. Then there's the photo of Bob looking up at the sky. When I dug this I said, "Fuck, Dylan's still into the same bag he's been into since 1967" since he's still "turning his head up high to that dark & lonely sky".'

In a record that other critics found devoid of political significance – beyond, that is, its absence of politics – Weberman claimed to have unearthed telling clues. In Dylan's rewriting of the traditional folk tune 'Little Sadie', he found autobiographical significance, which 'concerns the rationale behind Dylan's current apoliticism'. If traditional words could be interpreted as if they were Dylan's own, so could those by other songwriters. When Dylan recorded Paul Simon's song 'The Boxer', Weberman analysed it as if Simon had been writing from inside Dylan's head. Under this scrutiny, Simon's line, 'I have squandered my resistance', was easy to translate as 'I have given up fighting American fascism'.

For several years, Dylan and his family had lived in Woodstock. Even though the Woodstock festival was held elsewhere, its name alerted the world at large to Dylan's presence in the town, and the procession of fans, admirers, stalkers and curiosity seekers coming to his door became intolerable. 'Roadmaps to our homestead must have been posted in all fifty states for gangs of dropouts and druggies,' Dylan noted in his mock-autobiographical *Chronicles Vol. 1*. In autumn 1969, he moved his family back to Greenwich Village, the scene of his ascent to fame.

Biographers have speculated that Dylan chose the unlikely hiding-place of New York as a means of reconnecting with his muse; Dylan himself claimed that it was 'in hopes to demolish my identity'. Whatever the reason, Greenwich Village brought Dylan within easy stalking range of his Liberation Front. His new home was only a few hundred yards from that of A.J. Weberman, who now had the perfect opportunity to combine his two sciences: Dylanology and garbology. On the night of 17 September 1970, as Jimi Hendrix lay dying 3,000 miles away in London, Weberman crept to Dylan's 19th-century townhouse on MacDougal Street, and confiscated his garbage bags. These were examined at the Liberation Front's headquarters, in search of evidence of Dylan's 'current bag'. Weberman found little to confirm or deny his theories about Dylan's heroin addiction, although the diapers and other pungent household waste convinced him that 'Dylan is a good father – he really loves his children'.

Weberman didn't just visit Dylan in secret. One Sunday, he made a more conventional trip to the singer's front door. Dylan spoke to him briefly: as Weberman described the encounter, 'To make a long story short, D told me "not to come round THE house anymore", capitalist private property bullshit & also symbolic since "house" is "mind" in D's symbology. So what he said was "Take me as I am or Let me Go" – STOP BEING A DYLANOLOGIST.'

But the relentless pursuit could not be halted that easily. Besides Dylan's private detritus, Weberman was also ready to interpret his villain-hero's public work. The title of *New Morning* was enough to raise the Dylanologist's hopes that the singer 'has finally got out of his current bag'. He felt betrayed to see the cover portrait, with Dylan's eyes 'revealing' that the singer was still cursed by heroin. Turning to the songs, Weberman conjectured that 'Went to See the Gypsy' – recorded in June 1970, several months before Dylan met him – was written about the encounter on MacDougal Street: Dylan goes on to deride & scorn my efforts to get him to see "the gypsy" – the people of the 3rd world who are often drafted to commit genocide in S.E. Asia . . . Despite D's cynicism I still say ALL POWER TO THE PEOPLE!'

By the end of 1970, Weberman was teaching a weekly class in Dylanology at the Alternate University, and customarily ending his bulletins with a rousing cry of 'All Power to the Dylanologists – Free Bob Dylan from Himself'. The Liberation Front insisted that, 'Bob is now part of the power structure and is a reactionary force in rock. This is a result of his having many millions of $ . . . Another factor is Dylan's c.b. [current bag], which makes him susceptible to arrest and also generally kills political response.' Weberman's conclusion was that 'Dylan must be dealt with'. If his Greenwich Village organisation was still restricted to a handful of acolytes, exasperation with Dylan was becoming widespread amongst those who still believed in revolution. 'All great art today is revolutionary,' proclaimed Jerry Rubin. 'Controlling all our own art is our way to liberation and creating communities. What if Dylan's profits went to financing revolution rather than Columbia Records?' In the *International Times*, Ray Gosling reinforced the point: 'Bob Dylan has made a fortune for the Columbia Corporation, and that is wrong.'

This knee-jerk opposition to Dylan's 'reactionary' methods and art would have been inflamed still further had it been widely known that the singer had become intrigued by the militant Zionist organisation, the Jewish Defense League. Formed in 1968, the JDL was run by Rabbi Meir Kahane, whose closest previous connection with the world of music was tutoring the young Arlo Guthrie for his bar mitzvah in the 1950s. Around 1965, Kahane went undercover as an agent for the FBI to infiltrate the John Birch Society, the racist, anti-Semitic group that had been the target of a satirical talking blues song by Bob Dylan in 1962. Emerging in 1968, Kahane founded the JDL – whose motto was 'Never Again' – to protect the Jewish diaspora around the world from the curse of anti-Semitism. He concentrated particularly on the plight of Soviet Jews, and the JDL was linked with terrorist attacks on several Soviet-owned buildings within the USA. Within the counter-culture, however, Kahane and his group were regarded as fascists and racists, whose 'extreme' views of Jewish doctrine threatened anyone who did not agree with their views. Hence the horror that the likes of Jerry Rubin would have felt had they realised that Dylan was not merely talking to Kahane, but also promising to finance the JDL's activities.

Kahane was far from the only political voice in Dylan's immediate milieu, however. Since the early 1960s, he had been close to film-maker and cine-matographer Howard Alk. Alk's most prominent film credit of the 1960s was as editor of the popular counter-culture movie *You Are What You Eat*. Alk shot some of the sequences for the documentary about Dylan's 1965 UK tour, *Dont Look Back*, and then collaborated with the singer on constructing the somewhat less orthodox chronicle of the 1966 excursion, *Eat the Document*. Alk's next project, and his first work as a director, reflected his radical passion. *American Revolution 2* focused on the protests at the Chicago convention in 1968, and included interviews with a number of activists, including members of the Black Panthers. 'One of the things we're trying to do is let you see that these men are revolutionists – political revolutionists,' he explained later. 'But they're not terrorists, they're not irre-sponsible madmen.'

As a convinced believer in the revolutionary potential of the United States, Alk was outraged by the death of Fred Hampton, and soon began to assemble documentary footage of the Black Panthers leader and his associates. The result was *The Murder of Fred Hampton*, which was premiered in 1971. The film was funded by Dylan's 1960s manager, Albert Grossman, who said of Hampton: 'That man's got to be heard.' Alk was still working on his film when he was asked by Dylan to review their work on *Eat the Document*. It is difficult to imagine a man as exercised by radical zeal as Alk not taking the opportunity to bend Dylan's ear about the cause of Fred Hampton and the Black Panthers.

## THE DREAM IS OVER

There were now inescapable parallels between Bob Dylan and John Lennon, who had made a cameo appearance in *Eat the Document*. Both men were regarded as heroes of the counter-culture, but had disappointed their most militant admirers. In October 1970, the former Beatle recorded his first solo album, *John Lennon/Plastic Ono Band*. It was heavily inspired by his Primal Scream therapy with Dr Arthur Janov. Some songs reflected the process of unearthing and unleashing the original childhood agony that, according to Janov's theory, seeded the growth of neurosis. Others, such as 'Mother' and 'My Mummy's Dead', presented with breathtaking candour the traumas that had fuelled Lennon's own psychological problems: the break-up of his parents' marriage, his abandonment by his mother and father, and the subsequent death of his mother shortly after they had reconnected in his teens. Yet there was also a sharp political edge to the record. This ranged from the social protest of 'Working Class Hero' ('keep you doped with religion and sex and TV, and you think you're so clever and classless and free, but you're still fucking peasants as far as I can see') to the denunciation of organised religion heard in 'God' and 'I Found Out'. Lennon was still some distance from aligning himself with any political group – 'I just believe in me, Yoko and me', he sang on 'God' – but stripping away decades of defence mechanisms had clearly reawakened his awareness of the class system. 'I think ["Working Class Hero"] is for people like me who are working class, who are supposed to be processed into the middle classes, or into the machinery,' he explained. 'It's a song for the revolution.'

A more personal problem inspired the opening lines of 'I Found Out', as Lennon lambasted 'the freaks on the phone [who] won't leave me alone'. One of them was Michael Abdul Malik, the former Michael X. Not content with Lennon's initial donations of money and hair to his Black House community centre in London, Malik nagged the singer for more cash in late 1970, to stave off the building's physical collapse. The Lennons discovered that the root of the problem was vandalism, carried out by some of the youths for whom the centre had been intended. Yoko Ono took a predictably conceptual stance to Malik's demands, suggesting that he should provide the adolescents with hammers, nails, and blank sheets of wood. Malik duly installed the equipment, but the kids merely used the hammers to cause more destruction. When he complained to the Lennons, Yoko sent him a metal sheet into which a nail had been banged, and a glass hammer. Decades later, this artefact would have electrified an auction-room devoted to Beatles memorabilia, but Michael Abdul Malik's needs were more immediate.

As Lennon's former PR man, Derek Taylor, observed, 'There had been stories of humiliation and torture at the Black House, but I in those times wouldn't believe anything bad of a "radical".' Similar tales had reached the ears of the Metropolitan Police, and Malik was summonsed to appear in court in February 1971, to answer charges of intimidating several former associates. On 2 February, while Lennon was mixing the tapes of his next single, Malik fled the country, returning to his native Trinidad.

There he used his reputation and charisma to rent a substantial suburban property outside Port of Spain, which became his second 'Black House'. He talked of founding a 'people's store' and an 'urban village', as if the utopia he'd planned for Camden Town in London could be made flesh in the Caribbean. From his new home in Christina Gardens, he bombarded the Lennons with letters and phone calls, demanding – as ever – money. He boasted of his intention to found an institution called the First University of the Alternative, and invited the Lennons to discuss it with him in person.

In April 1971, their quest for custody of Yoko's estranged daughter, Kyoko Cox, led the Lennons to the Virgin Islands. Their search proved fruitless, so the couple made the 500-mile hop to Port of Spain, where they spent two days with Malik and his wife Desiree. Malik milked their visit to the full, swaggering around Port of Spain's plushest nightclubs with the Lennons in tow, to boost his own celebrity status. When Lennon purchased a piano for his host's daughter to play, Malik invited the local press to photograph it. Subsequently, Desiree was a guest of the Lennons in London, when her husband shipped her off on a fund-raising mission. He used a familiar ploy, the book proposal: this time, it was Desiree who was the potential author of a memoir entitled *My Life With Michael X*. But the Lennons refused to lavish money on a second non-existent book, and when Desiree left the country, they considered that their involvement with Malik and his black power crusade was at an end.

Malik wasn't the only radical demanding some of Lennon's attention in late 1970. On 27 October, defence lawyers acting for Charles Manson announced their intention to call Lennon as a key witness. Ten days earlier, record producer Gregg Jakobson had delivered some compelling testimony about his involvement with Manson and his Family. During his evidence, he had explained Manson's fixation with the Beatles' 1968 *White Album*, which had led the cult leader to interpret the group's songs, Weberman style, as containing 'portents of the doom of the white race'. The particular recordings he mentioned included Paul McCartney's 'Blackbird', George Harrison's 'Piggies', Lennon's 'Sexy Sadie' and the avant-garde sound collage 'Revolution 9'. [8] But the most significant song in Manson's eyes was 'Helter Skelter', which he regarded as an unmistakeable instruction from the Beatles. Lennon refused the invitation: it was Paul McCartney who had written and sung 'Helter Skelter', he explained, and therefore his own testimony would be worthless. It was another graphic illustration of the social responsibility placed upon the fragile shoulders of rock stars. Bob Dylan would no doubt have sympathised with his plight.

'I'm sick of all these aggressive hippies, or whatever they are – the Now Generation – sort of being very uptight with me,' Lennon admitted in December. 'Just either on the street or anywhere, on the phone or demanding my attention, as if I owe them something. I'm not their fucking parents. They frighten me. There's a lot of uptight maniacs going round wearing fucking peace symbols.'

As he had sung on 'God', and repeated when he engaged in a lengthy interview session with *Rolling Stone* editor Jann Wenner, 'The dream is over'. Because the same song also included the shocking – for the times – line, 'I don't believe in Beatles', most listeners assumed that he was referring to the end of their specific 'dream'. But, Lennon clarified to Wenner, 'I'm talking about the generation thing. The dream's over, and I have personally got to get down to so-called reality.' It was as if Primal Scream therapy had demolished not only his emotional barriers, but also the naive trappings of his peace campaign. 'The same people are in control, the same people are running everything, it's exactly the same!' he exploded to Wenner. 'They *hyped* the kids.' He wasn't yet prepared to admit that he might have been partially responsible.

If everything he'd trusted for the last decade – rock'n'roll, the 1960s dream, his peace campaign – added up to nothing, where could Lennon find relief? Floundering in pain, Lennon needed another form of salvation. His lengthy disavowals in the song 'God' – 'I don't believe in Jesus, I don't believe in Buddha', and on through all the icons of spirituality and religion – and

his gradual lack of faith in the Beatles left him open to a more radical solution. 'When you talk about destruction, don't you know that you can count
me out, in,' he had sung in 1968, before deciding that 'out' was the way to
go. Now he was on the verge of confounding those who saw him as an
enemy of the movement. After two years of indecision, he was finally ready
to experiment with action. His engagement with radical politics promised
to tip the balance of power back towards the revolution, just when it seemed
as if that dream, as Lennon had declared, was over.

# CHAPTER 6: 1971

## BARD ON THE RUN

> When the pop star turned out not to be the revolutionary the politicos thought he was, they turned on him, cursed him and in the name of his failure announced rock dead.
>
> (Ralph J. Gleason, 'We Made It, We Survived', January 1971)

On 13 January 1971, Bette Shertzer, financial co-ordinator for the Committee To Defend The Panthers, wrote to Bob Dylan to acknowledge his donation. The Committee was raising funds for the legal defence of the New York Panther 21. In 1970, the average daily wage of an American man was $40 – and that was exactly what Dylan contributed to the Black Panther Party. It was an ambivalent gesture from a man rumoured to be a multi-millionaire, scarcely generous by any reckoning, and too small to have been inspired by political guilt. It might have been a sardonic brush-off, as if Dylan was saying: 'You want money? Here it is. Now leave me alone.'

The previous autumn, Dylan received a letter from Gerald Lefcourt, the radical lawyer who had represented many counter-culture luminaries in court. Lefcourt was writing on behalf of the Panthers' Chief of Staff, David Hilliard, to ask if Dylan would consider staging a benefit concert for the party. The $40 cheque was Dylan's only known response.

During the research for his 1971 biography of Dylan, New York journalist Anthony Scaduto uncovered a rumour that the singer had subsequently agreed to meet Hilliard and Huey Newton. 'Dylan was still enthused about Israel,' Scaduto reported, 'and as soon as they sat down Dylan began to lecture them on the Panthers' anti-Zionist pronouncements. Within moments

Hilliard leaped up, angry, and headed for the door shouting: "Let's get out of here! We can't talk to this Zionist pig!" Newton said to "cool it" and Hilliard returned to the discussion. It lasted for another hour or more, but was a stand-off. "I can't help you as long as the Panthers are against Israel", Dylan is said to have told them.' Scaduto relayed this rumour to Dylan, who responded with characteristic vagueness: 'What meeting? Why don't you talk to Huey about it?' But Newton was out of the country and Hilliard in jail by this point. To this day, it remains uncertain whether the meeting between Dylan and the Panthers ever took place.

In 1973, Newton published his autobiography, *Revolutionary Suicide*, without mentioning Dylan once. Likewise David Hilliard, in his 1993 memoir, *This Side of Glory*. Newton's omission is more surprising, given his well-documented passion for Dylan's work; soon after his release from prison in 1970, he was photographed in his apartment, standing stripped to the waist like a matinee idol, and surrounded – like Dylan on the front of his album *Bringing It All Back Home* – by cultural artefacts. The San Francisco telephone directory lay beneath a tower of books about black power. Copies of the *Black Panther* newspaper were piled on the floor. An album by jazz guitarist Wes Montgomery lay discarded at his feet. The camera caught Newton as he pulled another record out of its sleeve: Bob Dylan, inevitably. Huey had clearly not outgrown his obsession with 'Ballad of a Thin Man'.

If Newton had really encountered Dylan, he would surely have chronicled the occasion in his book. It's easy to imagine Dylan's friend Howard Alk encouraging him to go ahead, and Dylan feeling unable to resist challenging the Panthers' pro-Palestinian rhetoric. The Greenwich Village gossip is certainly believable – but also irrelevant. What's most telling about this meeting, whether or not it happened, is that the tale of Dylan's fall-out with Hilliard was being widely used against him as further evidence of his betrayal of the radical left.

If Dylan's donation to the Panthers' defence committee was also intended to throw the relentless A.J. Weberman off the scent, it didn't work. Out of curiosity or simply erratic judgement, Dylan found himself embroiled in a relationship, of sorts, with Weberman during January 1971. After their brief initial conversation in Dylan's lobby, Weberman took his Dylanology students on a field trip to MacDougal Street. In front of Dylan's house, they chanted Liberation Front slogans: 'Hey, hey, hey, Bob Dylan, time to give away your million', and 'Hey, hey, Bobby D, the revolution is in need of thee'. Then reality intervened. 'There's someone across the street who looks just like Dylan!' a woman exclaimed, as Weberman proudly pointed out where he'd found the singer's garbage. 'I looked up and saw Bob standing directly across the street from me,' Weberman reported afterwards. 'He was dressed in denim, wearing rimless glasses & it looked like smoke was coming out of his head. I just stood there. David Peel came over and pushed me forward. It was like High Noon.'

The two men confronted each other at arm's length. 'Al, why'd you bring all these people around my house for?' Dylan snapped. 'It's a demonstration against you and all you've come to represent in rock music,' Weberman replied defiantly. Dylan attempted to steer his pursuer towards his front door, to continue the discussion in private, but Weberman pulled the singer's hand off his arm, crying out: 'Cool it, man, that fucking hurts.' Instead, the two men started to walk down the street, leaving the Dylanology students gaping in disbelief. The conversation soon cut to the bone. 'Hey, Bob,' A.J. asked, 'what do you do with all your money?' 'It all goes to kibbutzim in Israel and Far Rockaway,' Dylan retorted, satirising the latest rumours on the street about his involvement with the Jewish Defense League. Weberman brought up the Panthers, and Dylan explained his disapproval of their stance on Israel and Palestine. But Dylan wasn't there to discuss politics. 'You know, Al,' he said, 'a lot of people have been asking me about your theories. They're going around saying that you're telling people I'm a junkie.' Weberman stood as tall as he could, and replied defiantly: 'Are you?' Dylan rolled up his sleeves and held his arms in front of Weberman's face. 'Clean,' he said, 'no track marks.' Weberman wasn't satisfied with physical evidence: the songs spoke louder to him than Dylan's skin.

No sooner had Weberman arrived home than the phone rang: it was Dylan. 'I was gonna offer you this job as a chauffeur,' he said teasingly. The next day he called back, and invited Weberman over. A.J. harangued Dylan at length about his lack of political commitment. 'I don't follow politics,' Dylan replied. His inquisitor was outraged: 'You've got to live up to your responsibility as a culture hero. You're DYLAN, man!' 'I'm not Dylan, you're Dylan,' the singer retorted.

Back home, Weberman typed up his recollection of the encounter. 'Talking to Dylan was like talking to a ghost,' he concluded. 'The old Dylan, full of ideas and stories, was gone, replaced with a shell.' Then he phoned Dylan's office, to tell them that he would be sending his account to the Liberation

News Service. Dylan complained that their conversation had been private, not an interview, but agreed to look through a proof. Another call ensued, during which the two men teased each other, Weberman with a radical fist, Dylan with a blade of subtle steel, obviously relishing the absurdity of it all.

That month, the *New York Post* printed a brief item in its business section, noting that several celebrities had each invested $250,000 in a real estate business at 1500 Broadway, which intended to build a skyscraper office block between 43th and 44th Streets in Manhattan. The piece named the celebrities as TV hosts Johnny Carson and Dick Cavett, comedian Woody Allen, and 'poet-guitarist Bob Dylan'. Meanwhile, Weberman had learned from another source that Dylan had bought shares ($20,000 worth, he estimated) in Ling-Temco-Vought, a multi-lateral business corporation that was involved in building planes and missiles for the US Air Force. 'If Dylan thinks he's gonna get away with shit like this, that slimey motherfucker is fuckin crazy,' Weberman exploded.

On 8 February 1971, Weberman picketed the world premiere of Dylan's 1966 tour movie, *Eat the Document*. The screening was a charity benefit, with proceeds going to the families of Pike County miners in America's richest coal state, Kentucky. He handed leaflets to the audience, dismissing Dylan's gesture as 'a drop in the bucket' that 'means shit'. 'Dylan has AT LEAST 5 million dollars', the leaflet claimed. 'Rock culture will always be nowhere if cats like Dylan are in its forefront,' Weberman complained, ending his rant with a familiar phrase: 'POWER TO THE PEOPLE'.

## POWER TO THE PEOPLE

Two days later, in his luxury mansion in Ascot, Berkshire, John Lennon recorded a single built around the same phrase. It opened with a rousing street choir chanting the chorus over the sound of marching feet, like a revolutionary rally in the studio. Under producer Phil Spector's direction, Lennon's heavily echoed vocal bounced through the speakers as if he was shouting down a megaphone. Soaked in radical chic, the lyrics revised Lennon's message from 1968: 'You say you want a revolution,' the first verse began, 'we better get it on right away'. Peace was now taking second place to violent dissent. Lennon also offered his first hint of feminism. The days of 'I'd rather see you dead little girl than to be with another man' were behind him. Now he was confronting his fellow radicals with their sexism:

'I got to ask you comrades and brothers, how do you treat your own woman at home? She's got to be herself, so she can free herself.' No other rock star had come so close to preaching a feminist message.

What had provoked this sudden outburst of radical zeal? 'Power to the People' was written by a jet-lagged Lennon on the evening of 21 January 1971. That morning, he and his wife had flown home from Japan. Waiting for them in Ascot were Tariq Ali and Robin Blackburn, two prominent members of the International Marxist Group, who were also co-editors of the fortnightly newspaper *Red Mole*. 'Tariq Ali had kept coming round wanting money for the *Red Mole*, or some magazine or other,' Lennon recalled just before his death. 'I used to give anybody money kind of out of guilt, because I was thinking, well, I'm working class and I am not one of them, but I am rich, so therefore I have to. Anytime anybody said something like that, I would fork out.'

Ali and Blackburn spent several hours with the Lennons, quizzing them for a lengthy interview that provided *Red Mole* with its best-selling issue. Faced by committed Marxist intellectuals rather than underground rock journalists, Lennon's political beliefs were given a more rigorous examination than in the past. 'The IMG were always contemptuous of the underground,' former *International Times* editor Barry Miles reflects. 'They thought we were a bunch of hedonist drug addicts. And they were probably right! Politically, I always felt they had no influence at all beyond their own very narrow milieu. So it was a coup for them to be interviewing Lennon.'

The interview began with Lennon admitting that he'd grown up hating authority figures 'as a natural enemy'. He claimed that he'd always taken a political stance in his career: 'I've never not been political, though religion overshadowed it in my acid days.' Speaking out against Vietnam in 1965/66 and making his notorious 'bigger than Jesus' comments were political statements, he claimed, though he conceded that, 'in the hurricane Beatle world, I got farther away from reality for a time'.

As the conversation progressed, Lennon tried to ingratiate himself with the activists, while Ali and Blackburn treated him more gently than they might have done a less famous figure. It took Yoko Ono to break through the numbing air of mutual respect. 'I want to incite people to loosen their oppression by giving them something to work with, to build on,' she commented. 'They shouldn't be frightened of creating themselves.' Conventional Marxist–Leninist logic suddenly dissolved, as the couple fired each other's imaginations. 'It seems that all revolutions end up with a personality cult,' Lennon concluded pertinently. 'Even the Chinese seem to need a father figure. I expect this happens in Cuba, too, with Che and Fidel.' He reflected for a second, and then sent a curve-ball into the arena: 'In Western-style Communism, we would have to create an almost imaginary workers' image of themselves.' 'That's a pretty cool idea,' Blackburn admitted. 'The Working Class becomes its own hero.' It was a startling rewind through a century of Marxism back to Marx himself, who had originally envisaged a dictatorship of the proletariat, not a dictatorship of the dictator.

Even after singing on his last album that 'a working class hero is something to be', Lennon refused to idealise the British proletariat. They had been repelled by 'our openness about sex', especially their nude album cover for *Two Virgins*, he explained. 'Also, when Yoko and I got married, we got terrible racialist letters – you know, warning me that she would slit my throat.' Shocking though that experience had been, it had hardened his political attitude: 'The more real we become, the more abuse we take, so it does radicalise us in a way, like being put in a corner.'

Gradually the formal interview softened into a discussion about tactics and objectives, with all four participants searching for a solution that could harness their collective energies. What happens when those in power resist the pressure for change? Lennon wondered aloud. Blackburn replied with a radical cliché that could have come from any street-corner broadside: 'Popular violence against their oppressors is always justified. It cannot be avoided.' Ono wasn't satisfied: 'All I'm saying is that perhaps we can make a revolution without violence.' Lennon took the classical Marxist line: 'But you can't take power without a struggle . . .' – 'That's the crucial thing,' Ali interjected, effectively a bystander as the couple invented their political philosophy – '. . . because, when it comes to the nitty-gritty,' Lennon continued, 'they won't let the people have any power. They'll give all the rights to perform and to dance for them, but no real power.' Then Yoko swept the rhetoric aside with a line that reunited the personal and the political: 'The thing is, even after the revolution, if people don't have any trust in themselves, they'll get new problems.' Lennon immediately translated her wisdom into politico-speak: 'If we took over Britain, then we'd have the job of cleaning up the bourgeoisie and keeping people in a revolutionary state of mind.'

As the interview wound down, Tariq Ali asked Lennon one final set-piece question: 'How do you think we can destroy the capitalist system here in Britain, John?' Lennon returned to the theme of his song 'Working Class Hero': 'I think only by making the workers aware of the really unhappy position they are in, breaking the dream they are surrounded by.' Once again, he was saying that the dream was over, but it needed a political Janov to shock the people into noticing the fact. In fact, he seemed to suggest, the Janov technique – uncovering the pain of reality by stripping away people's defences and distractions – could be translated into political action: 'The idea is not to comfort people, not to make them feel better, but to make them feel worse, to constantly put before them the degradations and humiliations they go through to get what they call a living wage.' No revolution without humiliation: it would be a brave liberation movement which adopted that as its battle cry.

After Ali and Blackburn had left, Lennon sat down and wrote a song. 'I spent an afternoon talking,' he explained, 'and we got to the point where my part in the revolution was songwriting. And that night I just came out with "Power to the People".' By 'the people', he explained, he did not mean merely the proletariat, as Marxist theorists such as Ali and Blackburn preferred to think. 'The people aren't a section. The people means everyone. I think everyone should own everything equally. The socialism I talk about is British socialism . . . we'd have a nice socialism here.' (It was a strange reprise of Paul McCartney's hope, three years earlier, for 'a kind of Western communism'.) Russia wasn't a communist country, he added, a sentiment the Trotskyists would have agreed with: 'It's a fascist state.'

Later, after his militant zeal had ebbed away, Lennon grew increasingly cynical about his motives for 'hanging out with the Cambridge Graduate School of Revolutionaries'. As he wrote: 'They made us feel so guilty about not hating everyone who wasn't poor that I even wrote and recorded the rather embarrassing "Power to the People", ten years too late.' He added a punch line: 'We kept the royalties, of course.' He forgot to mention that he had helped fund the production of *Red Mole*, as he had earlier with the *International Times* and would again in the future.

'Power to the People' burned with righteous passion, not opportunism. But some listeners weren't convinced that it did Lennon creative justice. Reviewers regretted its 'melodic simplicity' and commented that by turning the Black Panthers' slogan into a banal ditty, he had produced 'an unintentional put-down of Panther rhetoric'. Songwriter Paul Simon was more scathing. 'It's a poor record, a condescending record,' he commented. 'Like all of these cliché phrases, they're dangerous. What does that mean – power to the people? And who is he saying it to? Is he saying it to people who have any idea what it means?' Years before Lennon reached the same conclusion, Simon questioned his sincerity: 'He strikes me as being very interested in being seen or heard. Then I have to think, "What is he doing? What is the purpose of it? Is his purpose to get publicity for himself? Is his purpose to advance a certain political thought?" I don't know what his motivations are. Many things he's done, I think, have been pointless. Some have been in bad taste.' Simon was prepared to admit that 'he's generally a well-intentioned guy', while maintaining that Lennon had betrayed his craft as a songwriter. But 'Power to the People' did leap out of the radio like a 1950s rock'n'roll gem, which was at least half of the point. It was a sizeable hit around the world, sharing Top 20 chart space in the USA with an unexpectedly impassioned song by the normally mellow soul group the Chi-Lites: '(For God's Sake) Give More Power to the People'. Suddenly pop radio was alive with radical rhetoric.

## MAY DAY FOR THE MOVEMENT

Was this pure coincidence, a confluence of emotions, or a sign of genuine uprising? Were Lennon and the Chi-Lites raising the political temperature, towards the fever-pitch demanded by Weberman and the Weather Underground? The January 1971 assembly of the grandly titled National Coalition Against War, Racism & Repression – held in the city of windy revolution itself, Chicago – intended that it should be so. This was a last defiant gathering of the civil rights movement, the Yippies, the Mobe, SDS, the Panthers, every organisation that still dared to operate in open air. But this National Coalition was short on unity. Its only common ground was that it intended to challenge the Nixon administration on May Day 1971. The rest was disagreement – about the use of violence, the tactics of street protests, the eternal dilemma of harmonising the leaders and the led. Two of the survivors of Chicago 1968, Rennie Davis and Dave Dellinger, envisaged a flamboyant campaign of civil disobedience that would, in their words, 'stop the government'. Their goal was 'to create the spectre of social chaos, while maintaining the support or at least toleration of the broad masses of American people'. Even so, Davis warned, 'our tactics may divide us from certain constituencies'. The conference ended with half a dozen different plans for demonstrations in the same space at the same time. Each week brought fresh proposals, and to avoid shattering the fragile unity of the movement, every one of them was accepted. Soon May Day had extended to more than two weeks, a cacophony of protest that would surely either hasten the long-promised revolution, or else defuse radical energies for a generation to come.

Rennie Davis promised that this time there would be no 'movement generals' to pass down directives from on high. He was clearly attempting to prevent another conspiracy trial. But the question of leadership now haunted the figureheads of 1968. Three years after conjuring up ecstatic plans for Chicago, Yippie leaders Jerry Rubin and Abbie Hoffman had become the clown princes of the counter-culture. 'They were corrupted by power,' reflects Barry Miles. 'They took away a lot of the press and media attention from the real issues.' Rubin's image as a prankster was set in stone when he guested on David Frost's TV talk show in London. He arrived with a motley crew of Yippies, who squirted Frost with water, swore in front of the cameras, and acted like everyone's stereotype of boorish hippie radicals. While Rubin was thrilled by the disturbance he had created on live TV, his travelling companion Phil Ochs was less impressed – 'mortified', so his brother Michael remembers. Was this all the revolution amounted to, mocking a 'pig' for the amusement of armchair radicals?

'As far as Phil was concerned,' Michael Ochs explains, 'protest had to be beautiful. So he hated what Jerry Rubin did on the Frost show – he thought it was pointless. But at the same time, he would do almost anything for a free plane ticket. He was stimuli-driven, and always hungry for new experience, so if someone asked him to go somewhere and try something new, he'd always say yes. That's how he ended up in Sweden, where he played benefits to encourage US Army deserters. In retrospect, that might have counted as treason. But he got away with it. Ultimately, though, his music was always more important to him than his politics. He was aware that his musical celebrity made him vulnerable to being used, though I don't think anyone ever actually took advantage of him. He was a willing participant.'

It was a moment to remember Jerry Rubin's own dictum: 'Being a celebrity is a powerful weapon.' As Rubin realised, no one is more intoxicated by celebrity than the celebrity himself: 'To keep my sanity, I must remember the difference between myself and my image. Image is a powerful political weapon.' As Barry Miles recalls, 'He had the headband, he was sweating from all the drugs, he had a few days' growth of beard, he saw himself as this crazed revolutionary.' But there was a danger that by packaging himself as the terror of the establishment, Rubin might become a cartoon villain. 'If ever [I become] a non- or counter-revolutionary image, I'll change my name,' he promised. Changing his image was clearly out of the question.

Abbie Hoffman was anxious to avoid this fate. Like Rubin, he had played up to his public image. Rubin sabotaged David Frost; Hoffman flipped his finger at the establishment on Merv Griffin's show. He wore a shirt made out of the Stars and Stripes, a vision so upsetting that CBS blanked it out. Hoffman kept the gags coming, handing Griffin's co-host a joint and producing a copy of Chairman Mao's *Little Red Book* out of his jacket pocket. It was all very shocking, but its only effect was to reinforce Hoffman's legend. His wife Anita claimed that there was even talk of marketing Abbie like a children's puppet: 'I remember seeing a prototype of an Abbie doll which had massive curly black hair and a flag shirt.' As Hoffman admitted, 'When you operate in that kind of milieu, you've got to have some way of pinching yourself to make sure you're still a moralist or a revolutionary or a threat to society.'

By February 1971, however, Hoffman's celebrity was beginning to pall. So was the underground's assumption that Hoffman was an inexhaustible fountain of humour, energy and cash. He'd donated his book advances to radical causes, and had to stay on the lecture circuit, reprising his old routines, to make ends meet. Inevitably, he couldn't always satisfy the voracious demands of his public. 'If people relate to me as a public image,' he admitted, 'I do act aloof. What else should I do, spend my life signing autographs? If I refuse to be in some revolutionary dilettante's movie, I'm aloof; if I agree, I'm a media freak. You're damned right I'm aloof.'

The actual process of making a revolution, whatever that might require – changing hearts and minds, arming the *lumpenproletariat*, firebombing ROTC buildings – no longer featured in Rubin and Hoffman's lives. Hoffman continued to have faith in the latent power of student protest, which he saw as the embodiment of his cherished Woodstock Nation. But he was appalled by 'the egocentric greed of the Rock Empire', youth culture's inexorable slide into heroin addiction, the gradual dissolution of any political action within the underground. 'A revolution in consciousness is an empty high without a revolution in the distribution of power,' he noted. But gaining power had never seemed further away.

Inside his Michigan prison cell, White Panther Party leader John Sinclair could do little but fret over the prospects for revolution. Outside jail, the campaign to free him from his ten-year sentence for marijuana possession was slowly gaining momentum, as celebrities such as Jane Fonda and Allen Ginsberg joined the cause, and Detroit's most radical bands, the Up and Brat (but no longer the estranged MC5), played regular fundraising concerts. Sinclair viewed himself as a political prisoner, but his version of politics was anything but orthodox. In the wake of the long summer of student dissent after Kent State, he complained that 'Most of the things that people are doing now on campuses are not political ... The stuff going on now – trashing buildings, demonstrations and protests – is reactionary.' The students were just reacting spontaneously to 'the pig power structure', he believed. 'Well, you don't have a spontaneous revolution,' he lectured like an aggrieved parent. 'We have to learn the same lesson that black people learned: that the point is to seize control of your own community and make it operate in the best interests of the people of that community.' And he was still convinced that the most effective way of reaching and uniting the community was via rock'n'roll – and not just any rock'n'roll, either: 'Most pop music is still low-energy music! Low-energy culture prepares people to fit into the consumer (passive) system ... A high-energy culture prepares people for revolution! ... I want to say, and insist, that the music that you listen to shapes your life! Rock & Roll & Dope & Fucking in the Streets!'

But even Sinclair realised that rhetoric and role-playing would not change the world. Once upon a time he had been convinced that a 'Guitar Army', adrenalin-charged with the addictive fervour of rock, could sweep across the horizon like Chairman Mao's cultural revolutionaries and send bourgeois culture and pig power scurrying into oblivion. Now he could sense the hollowness behind rock'n'roll's image-mongering. 'Pop is an ugly fucking scene based on greed and exploitation on all levels,' he told his global congregation that spring. 'The people who are producing the music, the raw labour force, aren't yet aware of what's happening to them. They're swept up in the phony glamour and amphetamine excitement of the whole S*T*A*R scene and don't realise that they're being bled and sucked dry and used against their own people at the same time, which is the ugliest part of the whole picture.' He clung to the belief that rock stars were being led astray by 'the pigs who run the music industry', and that if their eyes were cleared of porcine illusion, they could stir up 'the youth and black masses and [lead] them in striking down the rule of the "owners", moving the people to change themselves from consumers into life-actors'.

This hope chimed with the propaganda issued by a British urban terrorist group that dubbed itself the Angry Brigade. Their sporadic series of attacks during 1970 and 1971 targeted politicians, embassies and corporate buildings. Though there were no fatalities (indeed, only one person was injured by their explosions), the Brigade were treated by police as a major threat to the establishment and the public. Speculation about their identities continued until the members of a London anarchist collective were arrested and charged in August 1971. The group's violence, so they claimed, was rooted in its disgust with 'the system' and 'the shoddy, alienating culture pushed out by TV, films and magazines'. On 1 May 1971, the Brigade planted a bomb in the fashionable West London boutique Biba. Justifying the attack in a communiqué, the anarchists twisted a line from Bob Dylan's song 'It's Alright Ma', to satirise the commercial fever of the age: 'If you're not busy being born, you're busy buying'. Boutiques, they declared, were 'modern slavehouses', which had to be torn down. 'You can't reform profit-capitalism and inhumanity,' they continued. 'Just kick it until it breaks. Revolution.'

Where the Angry Brigade differed from John Sinclair was that they didn't put their faith in role models and rock icons. What Sinclair clearly hadn't considered was the possibility that the agents of cultural liberation, and the 'pigs', might be one and the same – eyes wide open, unashamed, in their embrace of the 'Death Culture' of consumerism. Fresh from their lip-licking celebration of slavery and sexual violence, 'Brown Sugar', the Rolling Stones released the first album via their own record company in May 1971. *Sticky Fingers* demonstrated that, in sonic terms, the Stones packed as propulsive a punch as ever. But in every other way, it stank of the 'Death Culture', from its fashionably decadent drug imagery ('Dead Flowers', 'Sister Morphine') through its Andy Warhol artwork (well-packed jeans, complete with real zip for added excitement) to its small print – which revealed that the Stones' 'independent' record label was merely a subsidiary of the multinational Kinney corporation. Radicalism, political commitment, anything other than a camp pleasure in their own celebrity, was entirely absent.

The innate conservatism of *Sticky Fingers* could be disguised by the visceral pleasure of its music, which effortlessly extended the scope of their previous work. But no rhythmic diversion could disguise the Stones' choice of lifestyle. April 1971 was when the band went into tax exile. This was not their only display of fiscal prudence; to coincide with their relocation to France, the Stones' business advisor, Prince Rupert Loewenstein, began to invest their money in offshore tax shelters, ensuring that no government, capitalist or socialist, would ever be able to claim it in the name of the people. Mick Farren was the first of many underground critics to draw the inevitable conclusions: 'Their move to France, and what looks like full-time membership of insulated Riviera jetset surroundings, seems a symptom of the resignation and withdrawal that characterises the new album . . . They were talking about their own record company, of a co-operative, of supplying funds to groups like the Black Panthers. Today's reality is the Kinney group, French chateaux and tax evasion.' Yesterday's street fighting men, Farren noted, were now on the verge of 'becoming millionaires with nasty habits'.

He didn't have to wait long for the transformation to become complete. On 12 May 1971, Mick Jagger and model Bianca Perez Morena de Macias were married in St Anne's Chapel, St Tropez. It was the social event of the season, attended by rock aristocrats and socialites, actors and minor British royals. The popular press salivated over the details: the gold rings from a Paris jeweller, the yacht, the champagne, the limousines, the bride's perilously low-cut dress, the photographs taken by the Queen's cousin, Lord Lichfield. 'Was the whole ceremony a Yippie hoax?' asked *Oz* editor Richard Neville, before deciding: 'That day in St Tropez marked the end of any further pretence of Jagger as the figurehead of a radical lifestyle.'

## REACTIONARY SUICIDE

The crisis of leadership extended into the black power movement, where the rival factions of the Black Panther Party led by Huey Newton in Oakland and Eldridge Cleaver in Algiers jockeyed for position. Besides the pressure from Cleaver's International Section, Newton was being challenged closer to home. From the outside, the policy differences might have seemed minimal, but they were in danger of provoking murderous confrontation.

The split widened when the New York Panther 21 – whose trial began on 8 February 1971 – came out in support of Cleaver. 'Violence is the only legitimate form of revolutionary action,' they declared. They were scolded by none other than the Weather Underground (the newly renamed Weatherman organisation), who in their post-New Morning phase of development were keen to follow less confrontational routes towards revolution. The Panther 21 replied with an open letter in the New York underground press, proclaiming:

'We desperately need more revolutionists who are completely willing and ready at all times to kill.' Meanwhile, Newton was trying to persuade his party to widen its horizon, all the way from Vietnam to social issues, while pushing for a political rather than military resolution of the black liberation struggle. He regarded the Panther 21's letter as a gross breach of discipline, and announced that the miscreants were henceforth expelled from the party.

It was the trigger for three months of civil warfare, which effectively sank the Black Panther Party as a revolutionary force. On 26 February, Newton appeared on a TV talk show with a satellite link to Algiers, so that Cleaver could also be heard. The intention was to demonstrate that the Panthers were a unified international force. Instead, Cleaver openly criticised the Minister of Defense for the recent expulsions of the 21. Once the show was over, Newton raced out to a pay phone, to place a furious call to Cleaver. When his former ally refused to back down or apologise for his 'counter-revolutionary' behaviour, Newton told him that he, and the entire International Section, were no longer welcome in the party. Unknown to Newton, Cleaver was taping the call, and a recording was aired a few days later on TV. 'The Minister of Information had set me up,' Newton recalled. 'He was committing reactionary suicide, and trying to take me down with him . . . Eldridge's defection was now out in the open.'

So was the fatal split within the party. Many East Coast members resigned in protest at Newton's decision. The New York chapter of the Panthers went further and declared that they were throwing Newton and his cohort David Hilliard out of the party. Eldridge Cleaver followed suit. Casualties began to occur on both sides. The most notorious incident took place on 17 April, when the Cleaver faction kidnapped Samuel Napier, the long-time head of circulation for the Black Panther newspaper. He had travelled to New York to repair the damage and boost his paper's failing circulation. Instead, his body was found in the basement of the Panthers' office in Queens; six bullets had been fired into his head and body.

In the middle of this madness, on 5 March (the day after Cleaver announced that he had expelled Newton), the Panthers staged an Intercommunal Day of Solidarity with all political prisoners, at the Oakland Coliseum in California. The event had been arranged as a show of support for Angela Davis, Bobby Seale and Ericka Huggins, and of course the Panther 21, although all mention of their trial was hurriedly dropped from the agenda. Kathleen Cleaver had been scheduled to speak, but again she failed to appear. So the onus was passed onto Newton, who began with what sounded strangely like a plug for John Lennon's new single: 'If it weren't for the power of the people, I wouldn't be here tonight.' It proved to be the most rousing moment of his speech: his comrade Elaine Brown remembered how he 'stuttered through an arcane statement. The adoring audience of thousands had barely been able to applaud it, much less appreciate it.'

The audience was also treated to three radically different sets of music. Top of the bill were the unlikely figures of the Grateful Dead – white, steeped in folk and bluegrass as much as soul and R&B, with a predilection for expansive instrumental jams that could conjure up the sound of space. Even with an abridged set built around the mid-60s R&B hit 'Turn On Your Lovelight', they made little impact on the predominantly black crowd. Bassist Phil Lesh recalled a moment when the band slipped into a slow, soft piece of improvisation, which was greeted with a hearty bellow of 'FREE BOBBY SEALE' from the stalls, followed by prolonged cheering. 'We have some loose semi-association with the Black Panthers because we met Huey and got along well with him,' Jerry Garcia explained after the performance. 'We don't deal with things on the basis of content, the idea of a philosophy or any of that shit – mostly it's personalities. [The show] did what it was supposed to do – it made them some bread.' He added that the Dead admired some of the Panthers' social policies, notably their free breakfast programme for neighbourhood kids. 'But it's not our concern what they're doing or why they're doing it,' he said. Then his real feelings came through in a torrent: 'I'm convinced, more than ever, that politics is bullshit, always was bullshit and will be bullshit. It'll continue to be an empty, futile bullshit trip as long as people are willing to go for it. It doesn't get things done. It has no real relationship to the world in which we exist.'

The curious mismatch of the Dead and the Panthers was illustrated by the way the band's appearance was promoted. When the Intercommunal Day was first announced, the posters from the Panthers' Ministry of Information listed the Lumpen as the prime attraction alongside Newton, with the Grateful Dead's name buried in the small print alongside 'revolutionary jazz ensemble' the Vanguard. Somebody obviously noticed that the Dead were a hugely successful rock band, whose latest album (*American Beauty*) was high in the US national charts, and the poster billing was reversed. Even during the event, there was a clash of ideology between the hippies and the advocates of black power. The Dead were used to relaxed security backstage; the Panthers policed the event as if they were guarding a presidential candidate from assassination.

There were no such problems for the Lumpen, whose righteous set of political soul was ecstatically received. The Panthers' band were attracting a keen following for their music as well as their philosophy, even if Huey Newton believed that their 'primary purpose was not entertainment but political education'. His comment mirrored the most difficult issue facing the band: the competing demands of politics and music. They had recorded a live concert in the hope of securing an album deal, but major labels were terrified of their violent rhetoric. Elaine Brown could pursue a commercial career because her music was reflective rather than confrontational. But the Lumpen's blend of cutting-edge black music and outspoken lyrics was too hot for the business to handle. Within a few weeks, the group split up, as individual members became dispirited by their lack of acceptance. The Panthers' party newspaper took this as a signal not to waste any further space on culture, as weekly advertisements for records by the Lumpen and Brown, and various badges and posters, vanished from its pages at the same moment.

There were sound political reasons for this change of focus. Besides the ongoing skirmishes between the Newton and Cleaver factions, the black power movement was gripped by the legal battles taking place across the nation. The first in a series of startling verdicts came on 24 May 1971, when Bobby Seale and Ericka Huggins' murder trial ended with charges being dismissed after the jury failed to reach a verdict. The judge ruled that it would be impossible for the pair to receive a fair retrial, so Huggins was set free. Seale was held for another four days, until bail was arranged while he appealed his contempt of court sentence from the Chicago Conspiracy Trial.

For the first time since 1967, both Seale and Newton – the two original founders of the Oakland Panthers – were on the street together. It should have been a time for rejoicing and rebuilding momentum, but Seale was distressed to discover that Newton was now a heavy cocaine user. This left him unreliable and over-excitable, and also paranoid – seeing plots in every conversation around him. Meanwhile, Newton faced his own retrial for the 1967 murder charge. He called it 'a stale rerun of a familiar and flawed drama', and the prosecution case wasn't helped when a star witness admitted that he was scared of everyone in the courtroom. 'I don't know what the truth is myself,' he confessed. Eleven members of the jury still found against

Newton, but because there was one hold-out, the judge ruled another mistrial. A third trial followed in October 1971, and this time several witnesses changed their stories. The jury was deadlocked, and after three attempts, Newton was free. A fourth trial was cancelled and all charges against the Panthers' leader were dismissed.

So too was the case against the Panther 21, all of whom – even those who had fled the country – were acquitted of every charge against them. Each of these legal marathons had robbed the defendants of precious time and energy. Even if the government had not succeeded in jailing these prominent Panthers, the cases had stalled the party's momentum at a time when they seemed to pose a real threat to the stability of the American government. Through it all, the Panthers sabotaged their own progress with schisms and shoot-outs, which continued to rumble into the summer of 1971.

Such was the global notoriety of the Black Panther Party that even the whiff of association could trigger repercussions. In the company of Sun Ra, Marzette Watts and Archie Shepp, horn player Clifford Thornton contributed to many of the most ambitious free jazz albums of the 1960s. In December 1966, he had joined Watts for the sessions that produced the long-delayed (until 1971) album *Marzette & Company* – half of which was filled by a track dubbed 'Backdrop for Urban Revolution'. The following year, in the aftermath of John Coltrane's funeral, Thornton led another memorable session, which spawned his own album, *Freedom & Unity*. By the time it was released in 1969, the lead track had been titled 'Free Huey' in tribute to Newton. Thornton was a frequent visitor to France, joining Shepp for several recording sessions. In October 1970, he was one of several American artists to perform at a jazz event sponsored by the Paris Committee for Solidarity with the Black Panther Party. A month later, he recorded a live album in the same city, issued in 1971 as *The Panther & The Lash*. It included a joyous sequel to 'Free Huey' entitled 'Huey Is Free', plus a composition by his collaborator, percussionist François Tusques, which echoed the Panthers' battle cry: *'Tout Le Pouvoir au peuple'*.

Throughout this period, Thornton had experienced no problems in entering and leaving France. But on 17 February 1971, he flew to Paris for six scheduled concerts. He passed through the customs check, and was walking towards the taxi rank when he was stopped by security guards and instructed to return to the immigration office. There he was told that he was required to leave France by the next available flight. When he queried the decision, he was shown a letter from the Minister for the Interior, ruling that he was no longer welcome on French soil, as he was suspected of being a member of the Black Panther Party. The golden era of American free jazz in Paris was over, by government command. Fortunately François Tusques remained, leading his Intercommunal Free Dance Music Orchestra through a 1971 album that included a piece dedicated to Bobby Seale's co-defendant, Ericka Huggins.

A similar incident affected Charlie Haden, the leader of the Liberation Music Orchestra. In 1971 his Orchestra played at the International Jazz Festival at Cascais, in Portugal. Haden introduced 'Song for Che' by dedicating the performance to 'the black people's liberation movements of Mozambique, Guinea and Angola'. Behind him, band members Dewey Redman and Ed Blackwell raised the clenched fist salute that symbolised black power. This affront to Portuguese colonial rule in Africa could not be allowed to pass unrewarded by the country's one-party government, the Estado Novo, which was attempting to quell unrest from students and workers. When Haden arrived at Lisbon airport the next day, he was arrested by secret police and held under laws that banned public displays of political dissent. Ironically, it was the local US cultural attaché who secured Haden's release, a rare case of the American administration aiding the cause of the African liberation movement.

Haden and Thornton were far from being the only prominent jazz musicians who had nailed their flag to the allied causes of black power and the anti-war movement. Composer/arranger Ilhan Mimaroglu amassed a chorus, orchestra, narrators, tape collages and the quintet fronted by tenor saxman Freddie Hubbard, to produce the experimental album *Sing Me a Song of Songmy*. Its vivid blend of electronic sound, elegiac saxophone, and poetry by Che Guevara and the Vietnamese writer Nha-Khe captured both the horror of war and the turmoil of a society in the process of disintegration. Cannonball Adderley issued *The Price You Got to Pay to Be Free*, the title track of which featured his 15-year-old nephew lambasting the Nixon administration. Rahsaan Roland Kirk formed the Jazz & People's Movement, a loose assembly of musicians dedicated to ending racist selection policies in TV orchestras. In the company of Lee Morgan and several dozen demonstrators, Kirk succeeded in disrupting talk shows hosted by both Merv Griffin and Johnny Carson. Leroy Jenkins, Norris Jones (aka Sirone) and Frank Clayton formed the Revolutionary Ensemble, whose influences spanned from avant-garde jazz to chamber music, and whose early music was inspired by their disgust for American involvement in Vietnam. Legendary trumpeter Miles Davis, whose stew of free jazz, funk and rock influences had shocked and thrilled the jazz community, had maintained a strict distance from overt political commitment. He declared that 'I am not a Black Panther or nothing like that', but then explained: 'I don't need to be, I was raised to think like they do.' The ferocious intensity of his music told its own story.

This politically inspired creative surge was mirrored across black American culture. Even as the Panthers fragmented, artists in many genres and fields responded to their struggle for self-respect, political independence and self-defence. In soul music, artists such as Curtis Mayfield and Marvin Gaye began to explore the limits of freedom for themselves and the black community. Gaye had paid little mind to politics in the past, but his collaborator, Four Tops singer Renaldo 'Obie' Benson, dragged him into the real world. Watching the turmoil on American streets and in Vietnam, Benson 'started wondering what the fuck was going on. What is happening here?' He channelled his misgivings into a song called 'What's Going On', imagining that it might be suitable for Joan Baez. When Benson played it to Gaye, the singer agreed to record the song if he could take a share of the royalties. 'What's Going On' became a hit single and the title track of a landmark soul album that ranged across the entire spectrum of contemporary black experience, from the church to the ghetto.

Gaye still clung to the hope of salvation from God, rather than the gun. So did Curtis Mayfield, the R&B poet of the civil rights movement. As the leader of harmony soul group the Impressions, Mayfield had charted the progress of the black liberation movement's peaceful wing, via songs such as 'People Get Ready', 'It's All Right', 'Choice of Colors' and 'This Is My Country'. By 1969, black militants were protesting about his lack of political urgency; it didn't help that he was prone to making patriotic statements such as: 'America, with all your hang-ups, we're proud of you.' Convinced that violence would only lead the black nation into self-destruction, Mayfield insisted that they should 'get together' and 'unite behind our leaders'. He didn't include the Black Panthers in the latter category: 'they aren't a national organisation,' he insisted, 'they don't have the muscle'. But with each passing year, a more frantic edge of despair entered Mayfield's work, and the message implicit in rousing anthems such as 'Move On Up' carried more weight than the evasive lyrics.

Evasive wasn't an adjective that could be applied to the two groups operating under the name of the Last Poets at the start of 1971. After the
commercial success of the album that Alafia Pudim, Omar Ben Hassen and
Abiodun Oyewole had released the previous year, a rival trio of versifiers
emerged, under the name of the Original Last Poets. It included the two
men who had refused the invitation from producer Alan Douglas to record
alongside Oyewole – Gylan Kain and Felipe Luciano – and their fellow street
poet, David Nelson. They were featured in *Right On!*, a documentary film
made by Herbert Danska, which chronicled their environment and its influence on their work. A soundtrack album was released in February 1971,
confusing those who were waiting for a second release by the 'real' Last
Poets. This duly followed a month later, under the name of *This Is Madness*.
To add to the chaos, Abiodun Oyewole was serving a prison term for robbing
an office of the racist Ku Klux Klan. By now, the Last Poets were under
close surveillance by FBI officers as part of the COINTELPRO campaign
that had caused such problems for the Black Panther Party. It was no surprise
that Omar Ben Hassen soon joined Oyewole in prison, after a drugs bust
for which he proclaimed his innocence.

In this climate, it was a brave black man who could take on the cultural
establishment – and win. That man was Melvin Van Peebles, an actor, screen-
writer, musician, producer and director. He had worked within the Hollywood
system to deliver the mildly subversive comedy *Watermelon Man* in 1970. The
obstacles he confronted along the way convinced him that his next feature
had to be created outside the major film corporations. Moreover, it would
be designed specifically for a black audience, with none of the concessions
– sentimentality, polite liberalism – that Hollywood demanded when race
was under the spotlight. 'I made the picture because I was tired of taking
the Man's crap,' Van Peebles explained twenty-five years later. 'The biggest
obstacle to the Black revolution in America is our conditioned susceptibility
to the white man's program. The fact is that the white man has colonised
our minds.'

In Van Peebles' wry account, the concept of his film came to him in the
Mojave Desert in February 1970. As he told it, he pulled off the road,
reached into his pants, and let his imagination run riot as he masturbated
himself to a joyous climax. Just over a year later, on 31 March 1971, *Sweet
Sweetback's Baadasssss Song* premiered at the Grand Circus Theatre in Detroit.
After breaking the Grand Circus's box office record, it did equally strong

business across America, exhibiting in local ghetto cinemas and porn theatres that weren't on Hollywood's distribution map.

With *Sweet Sweetback's Baadasssss Song*, Van Peebles created a chaotic, unvarnished portrait of the urban black experience, rich in violence, confrontation with the police, and erotic exhilaration. Sweetback, portrayed by Van Peebles himself, was a sexually prolific, street-wise, tough-talking action hero, under constant threat from white harassment, whether that came from police or roaming bikers. The film's sexual politics were anything but progressive – Sweetback only had to drop his trousers for women to begin rolling in ecstatic anticipation.[1] But the experimental feel of the film, all quick cuts and cameraeye framing, matched the unprecedented black viewpoint. There was only a passing reference to black politics in the film, when Sweetback rescued an activist in an unnamed street organisation from the clutches of 'the pigs'. But every aspect of *Sweet Sweetback*, from its distribution to the defiant survival of its hero, exuded the same heady militancy as a demonstration by the Panthers or a speech by Eldridge Cleaver. So did the film's soundtrack album, with its gospel chanting reaching back to the days of slavery, and Last Poetsstyle raps delivered over churning instrumental tracks. Huey Newton declared the movie a revolutionary black masterpiece, and said it was required viewing for party members.

With cultural serendipity, *Sweet Sweetback's Baadasssss Song* was released just as the black power movement spawned a new organisation that might have been fashioned after Van Peebles' hero. As the Panthers descended into civil war, many militants feared that it was losing its power to fight. In April 1971, a number of these activists went undercover, in imitation of the Weather Underground, and declared themselves the Black Liberation Army (BLA). Unlike the Weather organisation, the BLA operated as a loose confederation of cells, without any central leadership. It was able to make periodic strikes at the establishment, shooting policemen or staging robberies to pay for food or weapons. Despite its aggressive appearance, the formation of the BLA was actually a signal that black power, as a mass movement, was losing its momentum. Isolated urban terrorists could not realistically hope to lead a revolution. And *Sweet Sweetback* was only a film, not a road map to revolutionary utopia.

## LOOKING REAL PRETTY

Post-revolutionary utopia fuelled *Blows Against the Empire*, the late 1970 'space opera' created by Jefferson Airplane mainstay Paul Kantner. His earlier song

'Wooden Ships' had imagined the aftermath of a nuclear holocaust, as hippie survivors boarded sailboats to escape the chaos of a dying civilisation. *Blows Against the Empire* extended the landscape into outer space, as the Kantner commune distanced itself from the madness of Nixon's America. Kantner and Grace Slick were about to have their first child, China (pictured on the cover of their next album, *Sunfighter*, the record which included their hymns to Diana Oughton). On *Blows Against the Empire*, they fantasised about keeping their baby out of the clutches of 'Uncle Samuel'. 'I don't want his chances of freedom, ever to be that slim,' they sang, 'let's not tell them about him!' The glee in their voices heightened the unreality of it all. By the time their starship had carried them through galaxies way 'past Andromeda', Kantner and Slick had cast themselves adrift from their generation and their culture. Though the album's music expertly conveyed both the depths of their political disquiet and the dream-like expanse of space, *Blows Against the Empire* was anything but the 'revolutionary call to arms' that one critic claimed to hear. Today, Kantner recoils at any suggestion that the album was elitist: 'Who said there was only one starship? There could be a whole fleet of them.' Likewise he dismisses the criticism that its theme was escape: 'You've got that wrong. It's about natural evolution for our species, as the few explore the universe on behalf of the many. It's about refusing to be hemmed in by this world, and accepting the possibility of making a new start in idealistic circumstances.' But for listeners left on the ground, idealism was a poor substitute for action.

The limits of Jefferson Airplane's revolutionary potential were demonstrated in 1971 when they formed their Grunt Records label. Like the Beatles with Apple and the Rolling Stones with Kinney, this was a boutique operation, controlled by the same corporation who had been censoring their work since 1966. As their friend Jerry Garcia put it, 'they're still working for RCA'. 'This can be one of the biggest things in the record industry,' boasted Airplane manager Bill Thompson. 'If we're successful, other companies will have to give artists more freedom. The artist has been fucked too long.' Thompson added that every Grunt artist would receive exactly the same deal, and that the label would run as a co-operative, with profits shared between the workers. Airplane's creative freedom was still endangered by RCA, who scolded Grace Slick when she penned 'Son of Jesus', which they perceived to be blasphemous. It soon became apparent, too, that there was an exception to the co-operative arrangement – the Airplane themselves, who were contractually ensured 51 per cent of the company's profits, and also allowed unlimited studio time at company expense, unlike the acts they signed. Though this deal made sound financial sense – the Airplane were easily the most commercial act in the stable – it was hardly an ideological triumph.

Political pressure surfaced in other areas of the Airplane's career. There was disquiet in the East Coast underground press, who felt that the band balanced out their free concerts on the West Coast by charging excessive prices in New York, Boston and Washington. The left was also distressed when the Airplane debuted 'Crazy Miranda'. Written by Grace Slick, the song painted a picture of a woman searching for love, who 'lives on propaganda, she believes anything she reads. It could be one side or the other, *Free Press* or *Time Life* covers.' The idea that the underground press and the mainstream media were equally manipulative offended many activists. So did Slick's explanation of what had inspired the song, which was taken as an affront to feminist solidarity: 'In Boston, some chick came in, and she weighed about 200 pounds and she hadn't washed her hair and she had on dirty pants and a dirty shirt and a cap all slung down to one side and she looked like a mess.' Slick segued straight into talking about 'women's lib', as if she had swallowed the media caricature of feminists as grotesques.

Stereotypes still defined how women were seen. When singer Vincent Furnier adopted the stage name of Alice Cooper, he won publicity for his horror movie theatrics. But his attitude towards feminism was far more shocking than anything in his cartoon world. 'Women should be used as sex objects,' he proclaimed in late spring 1971. 'I think that's what they're best at. I don't think it's any insult, because that's what their main purpose in life is.' He completed his sexual politics lecture by describing feminists as 'horny dykes'.

The emergence of the 'all-chick' rock band Fanny at the end of 1970 sparked another bout of sexism. Discussion of their music was buried beneath the novelty of four women playing dynamic rock'n'roll. Keyboardist Nicky Barclay summarised the band's standard riposte to their press coverage: 'The sole purpose of this group is to make good fucking music. That's all. The fact that we are all girls is just that, a fact. We may be a novelty as far as some people are concerned, but shit, so were the Beatles.' But her protests had little impact. 'I wish they'd play topless,' one male reviewer drooled. 'What little yummies,' wrote another. Even *Rolling Stone* succumbed to this temptation. 'These Four Girls Have Got Class', was the amazed headline over a profile by Michael Sherman. He classified the band members by their appearance, rather than their musical ability: 'the zoftig little shag-cut redhead', 'slim and pretty', 'not as [much] pretty as striking' and, sadly, 'the drummer'. The same page carried a feature about singer Rita Coolidge who was, of course, 'looking real pretty'. No male journalist would have considered judging Joe Cocker or Black Sabbath by their looks.

One rock star made a conscious effort to buck the trend. Having come under fire from feminists himself, Country Joe McDonald underwent a conversion experience during a visit to Chile. Salvador Allende's socialist Popular Unity government had recently been elected on a platform of nationalising businesses run by American corporations and breaking away from US control of the economy. Film directors Saul Landau, Raoul Ruiz and Nina Serrano requested McDonald's presence as a representative of the American left, to watch Chile's fight to escape US influence. He appeared in their movie *Que Hacer*, a semi-fictional, semi-documentary study of a country in the midst of its own revolution. In Chile, he stayed in a commune for the first time. 'It blew my mind,' he admitted. 'In my own family we're going through this thing now, a women's lib thing, breaking down some of the stereotyped roles. In Chile I saw a kind of lifestyle which is where people just do whatever they want to do and they trust each other.' Watching as traditional gender roles were abandoned, and all household duties from childcare to cooking were shared, McDonald witnessed feminist theory turning into practice. 'Now I have a real strong urge to start a family, a large family, perhaps twenty-five or thirty people,' he explained. It was the hippie dream of 1966–67 reborn, with a new sense of political awareness. This grounding in practical feminism would soon have a major impact on McDonald's work as a songwriter and performer.

In Ann Arbor, Michigan, the members of the White Panther Party were still attempting to live out McDonald's dream. With John Sinclair sidelined in prison, the WPP had lost key activists to drugs busts, and suffered the media fall-out from the MC5's decision to abandon their cause. One of Sinclair's closest cohorts in the party, Pun Plamondon, had been busted with John's wife, Leni Sinclair, on their journey back from the Woodstock festival. Plamondon had chosen to leave the country rather than face a certain prison sentence. He took his place on the FBI's 'Ten Most Wanted' list – the first white radical to gain this distinction, much to the White Panthers' delight.

But in July 1970, Plamondon returned to the USA with the aid of two other Panthers, Skip Taube and Jack Forrest. He intended to hide out in the woods, but the three men were stopped by police when they dumped empty beer cans beside the road. Once Plamondon's fugitive status was discovered, all three were thrown into prison. When John Sinclair heard the news, he reacted furiously to this breach of party discipline, denouncing the culprits as 'crazed individualists who were living in a fantasy world of their own'. Once he'd calmed down, and studied his political textbooks, he emerged with the shocking news that 'we had not been "revolutionaries" at all but merely rebels acting more out of our frustration and anger than anything else'.

In the ensuing confusion, Sinclair suggested that the WPP should change their name to the Woodstock People's Party. As the Woodstock festival began to be exploited by corporations as a marketing tool, it seemed unwise for a group of would-be revolutionaries to tie themselves to the same brand. It was Plamondon who solved the dilemma, by offering the WPP another possible identity: the Rainbow People's Party. Vague, optimistic, expansive – it was the perfect name for a self-professed Marxist–Leninist group who were intending to present themselves as a 'communal, classless, anti-imperialist, anti-racist and anti-sexist . . . culture of liberation'. In practical terms, the new party's energies were devoted to the same causes as before: freeing John Sinclair and their other jailed brothers, maintaining a communal lifestyle and, of course, furthering the global revolution, insofar as that was possible for a bunch of Ann Arbor hippies.

Though the last of these aims was over-optimistic, the Rainbow People's Party did make slow progress towards fulfilling the others. The Grande Ballroom in Detroit hosted a long series of benefit gigs titled 'Free John Now!'; Sinclair's protégés the Up recorded a single with that title; there was even an underground newspaper devoted to news of Sinclair and his fellow prisoners of war. Hopes were raised when the Michigan State Legislature revised the penalties for drug offences; the maximum sentence for marijuana possession would now be 90 days. As Sinclair had already served nearly two years of a ten-year sentence, activists speculated that the Detroit courts would soon decide that he had suffered enough.

Not that Sinclair was wasting his time behind bars. After more examination of his textbooks, and much soul-searching, the previously macho White Panthers leader declared that he had been guilty of persistent sexism. 'Free Our Sisters/Free Our Selves!' he announced in a June 1971 bulletin. 'Sexism is really insidious,' he explained, 'because it's so deeply ingrained in our beings that it's unconscious. Even when we think we're free of it, we're still fouled up and don't realise it.' He admitted that while he had paid lip service to the ideal of equality with his wife, he had still assumed that she would take full responsibility for taking care of the children, the home and the food. Now he had seen the light, and urgently wanted his freedom, so that he could put his new ideals into practice.

Four thousand miles away, John Lennon was achieving his own enlightenment. 'I found myself being a chauvinist pig with [Yoko],' he admitted. 'Then I started thinking, "Well, if I said that to Paul, or asked Paul to do that, or George, or Ringo, they'd tell me to fuck off". And then you start to realise: you just sort of have this attitude to women, which is just insane! It's like an attitude to blacks! It's just beyond belief, the way we're brought up to think of women.' Daily life with Yoko Ono offered a reality check: 'She's a red hot liberationist and was quick to show me where I was going wrong.' Like Sinclair, Lennon saw that his deficiencies were mirrored in the wider movement: 'I'm always interested to know how people who claim to be radical treat women. How can you talk about power to the people unless you realise the people is both sexes?' Ono completed the lesson: 'You can't love someone unless you are in an equal position with them. If you have a slave around the house, how can you expect to make a revolution outside it?' Then she added a human touch: 'The problem for women is that if we try to be free, then we naturally become lonely, because so many women are willing to become slaves, and men usually prefer that. So you always have to take the chance: "Am I going to lose my man?" It's very sad.' Almost alone amongst feminist theorists in 1971, Ono was convinced that, for women, the benefits of sexual liberation had to be balanced alongside emotional needs and physical reality.

## GOD SAVE US

Sexism and sexual liberation were uneasy bedfellows in the underground press. Many papers continued to sprinkle nude photographs of young women across their pages as decoration and enticement. Among them was Richard Neville's *Oz* magazine. Yet it was not photos that brought issue 28 of *Oz*, published in May 1970, to trial at the Old Bailey in London, but words and cartoons. *Oz* 28 was affectionately known as 'Schoolkids' *Oz*', because most of its contents had been written and 'edited' by a panel of teenagers. The issue became notorious for a cartoon – drawn by a 14-year-old boy – in which Rupert Bear fucked his grandmother with an impressively large penis.

This issue brought three editors and publishers of *Oz*, Neville, Felix Dennis and Jim Anderson, to the dock of Court No. 2 at the Old Bailey on 23 June 1971. The prosecution charged that the trio had 'conspired with certain other young persons to produce a magazine' intended to 'corrupt the morals of young children and other young persons', by trying to 'arouse and implant in the minds of these young people lustful and perverted desires'. Moreover, the magazine was 'an obscene publication', which – to make matters much worse, in the eyes of the law – had been sent around Britain in 'a postal packet'. The London underground press had been busted several times before, but never with such force or malice. The British counter-culture believed that its way of life was now on trial. The case also aroused outrage among the liberal left – writers, philosophers, broadcasters, even politicians – who believed that they were witnessing an attack on fundamental civil liberties.

As a symbol that the British underground was united on this issue, a benefit concert was staged in March 1971 on the site of one of London's now defunct psychedelic clubs, Middle Earth. The ironically named Oz Police Ball starred a strange mixture of acts: 1950s rock'n'roll icon Gene Vincent, folk miserabilist Roy Harper, rock comedian Viv Stanshall, disc jockey John Peel and, in keeping with *Oz*'s sexual politics, a stripper (female, of course). The *International Times* predicted: 'The forthcoming *Oz* obscenity trial at the Old Bailey may well prove to be the straw that breaks the camel's back – and sparks off insurrection among hippies and revolutionaries all over the country. In effect our whole country will be on trial with *Oz*.'

It was a call that *Oz* and *International Times* subscriber John Lennon could not ignore. Having created a Top 10 hit out of the radical slogan of 'Power to the People', Lennon was eager to act out his ideals in public. When a New York-based radio station, WPAX, prepared programmes for broadcast to the North Vietnamese population, he and Yoko Ono immediately contributed an exclusive thirty-minute tape. He donated his white piano to a fundraising exhibition for *Oz*'s defence, titled Ozjets D'Art, at the Clytie Jessop gallery in London. Then in late April 1971, he wrote a song called 'God Save Oz', a catchpenny protest tune, vague enough for any purpose ('Oh, god save us from the war/Oh, god save us from the street') but with just enough *Oz* references to fit the bill. Nearly a month later, as a prelude to recording a new album, he cut the track as a potential single. Along the way, he amended the song's title to 'God Save Us', perhaps in the hope of boosting sales outside the UK. But he wasn't convinced that the record was worthy of his name, so he took the artistically wise but commercially disastrous step of replacing his voice with that of an unknown session singer, Bill Elliott. 'God Save Us' was intended for release before the *Oz* trial began, but it didn't emerge in Britain until late in the proceedings. Radio play was minimal, and so were the royalties that eventually trickled into the magazine's defence fund. Not that Lennon didn't try: Apple Records took out advertisements in every sympathetic journal in an attempt to increase sales. 'Every major country has a screw in its side,' the copy read; 'in England, it's *Oz*. *Oz* is on trial for its life. John and Yoko have written and helped produce this record – the proceeds of which are going to *Oz* to help to pay their legal fees. The entire British underground is in trouble, it needs our help.' But the adverts cost much more than the record ever earned.

Despite his political disagreements with the revolutionary left, Lennon retained a basic sympathy with the aims of the movement. 'I always take care of the underground, whatever I'm doing,' he boasted that summer. 'I lend them money or invest in them or whatever, because I think they're important. I get asked every two days for at least £5,000, and I usually give it. So I'm going to try to set up a foundation that can be small, a John and Yoko one, and we might take a dollar a head or anything that's donated at concerts.'

If Lennon had really wished to aid the counter-culture, he could have donated a percentage of his earnings from his next album. The basic tracks for the *Imagine* LP were completed by the end of May. Lennon had already cut a murky but atmospheric anti-war song, 'I Don't Want To Be A Soldier' – a song so vague that it stood no chance of becoming a street anthem. At the May sessions, he recorded a more rousing 'protest' tune, 'Gimme Some Truth', although its target was nothing more specific than hypocrisy, with only a passing reference to 'Tricky Dicky' [Nixon]. The only other target for Lennon's wrath on the album was Paul McCartney, who was maligned for his personality and music, but not (yet) for his political stance.

What's still most striking about the album is its lack of direct political comment. It was as if Lennon had two personalities – the agitated activist, and the mature artist. The title song, which only gained its reputation as a musical landmark in later years, illustrated the point perfectly. It was an extension of the 'wish-poem' concept pieces in Yoko Ono's book

*Grapefruit*. Lennon's fantasy included 'no religion', a concept he'd already denounced on his previous album, and 'no possessions', a theory that he knew he would never be able to practise. What was missing was any call for political change beyond universal world peace. On his last single, he had sung: 'You say you want a revolution, you better get it on right away'. Three months later, his message to the planet was that they should imagine 'nothing to kill or die for . . . all the people, living life in peace'. The coda completed the picture. 'You may say I'm a dreamer,' Lennon sang, 'but I'm not the only one. I hope some day you'll join us, and the world will live as one.' It was a return to his utopianism of 1969: if people imagined a solution to their problems, then their dreams would come true. It was a complete reversal of his earlier discussions about the class struggle with Tariq Ali and Robin Blackburn. But a week after recording *Imagine*, the Lennons flew to New York, where they were introduced to two men who would transform their political philosophy: Jerry Rubin and Abbie Hoffman.

## PEOPLE'S PEACE

On 22 January 1971, President Richard Nixon delivered his State of the Union address in Washington. The next session of Congress, he declared, could look forward to ending the war in Vietnam. He said that peace talks were making progress, and that his policy of Vietnamisation – passing the military burden from the USA to the government of South Vietnam – was bearing fruit. Indeed, within three months, he was able to announce that a further 100,000 American troops were being withdrawn from the battlefield.

It was a time for official optimism. In a stunning demonstration of how deeply the establishment had been affected by the rhetoric of the counter-culture, Nixon declared that his government was 'opening the way to a New American Revolution – a peaceful revolution in which power was turned back to the people – in which government at all levels was refreshed and renewed and made truly responsive. This can be a revolution as profound, as far-reaching, as exciting as that first revolution almost two hundred years ago – and it can mean that just five years from now America will enter its third century as a young nation new in spirit, with all the vigour and the freshness with which it began its first century.' It was a utopian vision for a nation already anticipating its bicentennial celebrations of 1976.

Nixon's New American Revolution shared nothing but extravagant rhetoric with the revolution that was still the declared aim of the movement.

Anti-war activists displayed little faith in Nixon's ability or intention to end the conflict in Vietnam on anything like acceptable terms. Ironies abounded. Although Nixon heralded the imminent return of US troops, the American Forces Network banned soldiers from hearing Freda Payne's hit soul record 'Bring the Boys Home', on the grounds that it might provide aid and comfort to the enemy. Veterans returned to take part in the Winter Soldier Investigation in Detroit, an inquiry into US war crimes supported by benefit concerts given by Phil Ochs, and David Crosby & Graham Nash. While official peace talks stalled in Paris, American and Vietnamese students negotiated their own People's Peace Treaty – celebrated by a conference in Ann Arbor, and a concert starring a predictable line-up of radicals, from Phil Ochs and David Peel to Jerry Rubin and Jane Fonda. Of all the celebrities who campaigned against the war, few gave themselves more totally than Fonda; and few suffered more harassment. On a speaking tour to raise money for Vietnam Veterans Against the War, she had been arrested in Cleveland for drug smuggling and disturbing the peace (the latter charge was brought when she protested her innocence). The case had to be dropped when Fonda proved that the offending 'drugs' were merely vitamin pills. Though this incident illustrated that she was already under strict government surveillance, she refused to be cowed. In March 1971, she flew to Paris for personal talks with the North Vietnamese foreign minister, Nguyen Thi Binh. She used the occasion to criticise President Nixon's policies and the conduct of US soldiers, and was accused of treason by some commentators.

Fonda's pronouncements were unimpeachable, from a revolutionary perspective; she hymned the Black Panther Party, for example, and claimed that she and her generation were 'children of the revolution, born to be rebels. It runs in our blood.' But talk was cheap for an Oscar-winning movie actress. More convincing was her decision, alongside fellow film star Donald Sutherland and activist Fred Gardner, to launch a radical theatre troupe called FTA. In military slang, the initials customarily meant 'Fuck the Army', but Fonda and her cohorts swore that they stood for 'Free the Army'. FTA toured America and territories overseas, performing for audiences of troops in venues close to army bases. The first show was in Fort Bragg in April 1971, followed a month later by two deluxe concerts on the Monterey festival site. These featured various radical singers and actors, including folkie Len Chandler (a veteran of the early 1960s protest scene), rock bands Big Brother and Cat Mother, and pop singer Johnny Rivers. Nina Simone also joined

Fonda's troupe, while Country Joe McDonald attended maybe half a dozen shows over the course of as many months. 'I was a bit cautious about the whole thing from the start,' he recalls, 'because I didn't really know many of the organisers.' Afterwards, he complained that, behind the scenes, the star actors were making fun of the soldiers' working-class backgrounds. 'The movement has been duped by Fonda and Sutherland,' he declared. 'I'm not going to be any part of their ego trip.' Today he admits that there were additional reasons for quitting FTA: 'I really did not want to go with them to the Philippines and Japan. I was tired of being on the road, and just didn't want to travel anywhere.'

Nixon's government was predictably appalled by FTA's activities, and some of the president's staff set out to denigrate Fonda's public image. But they were quite happy to solicit their own celebrity support. Presidential counsel Charles Colson advised Nixon that former Democratic Party supporter Frank Sinatra might be ripe for Republican plucking: 'He is thoroughly disenchanted with liberals, as evidenced by his support of Reagan and his current friendship with the Vice President. Most of our Hollywood friends believe that Sinatra is the most influential celebrity in the country, because if he goes, so go many other prominent figures, particularly new stars.'

The same logic influenced A.J. Weberman's relentless pursuit of Bob Dylan: the hope that the target of the Dylan Liberation Front might abandon his policy of political apathy, and suddenly offer himself to the revolution as an active figurehead. Weberman wasn't the only person disappointed by Dylan's current stance: Rabbi Meir Kahane of the Jewish Defense League complained that, for all Dylan's interest in his organisation, the donations he had been promised had not yet arrived. Weberman had an explanation for this: Dylan had donated $5000, A.J. claimed in May 1971, under the name of his deceased father, Abraham Zimmerman. This was sufficient for Weberman to allege 'DYLAN SUPPORTS RACIST & COUNTER-REVOLUTIONARY ORGANISATIONS'. Weberman had a message for anyone who sympathised with the Dylan Liberation Front: 'Don't buy any more Dylan records & try to return the ones you don't dig, like NASHVILLE SKYLINE, SELF PORTRAIT, etc.'

A boycott of Dylan's work would only take effect slowly. Weberman had a more immediate plan: a celebration of Dylan's 30th birthday on Sunday 23 May 1971. This was no ordinary party; it was a Million Dollar Bash Block Party (named after a song from Dylan's 1967 *Basement Tapes*), to be held outside the singer's home. Weberman promised that the DLF would 'present Dylan with some very special birthday gifts', while entertainment would be supplied by David Peel & the Lower East Side.

Around 400 people – a mix of Dylan obsessives and the mildly curious – duly gathered on MacDougal Street. Weberman arrived carrying a birthday cake, tastefully decorated with hypodermic needles. He handed out photocopies of a letter to Johnny Cash that he had retrieved from Dylan's trash, and badges that read 'Free Bob Dylan!' He was interrupted by a small boy, who told him: 'Bob Dylan isn't here. He's in Israel.' The boy was right: Dylan was in Jerusalem, where the following day he was photographed in front of the Wailing Wall. In *Chronicles*, Dylan pretends that his trip to Israel was merely an attempt to throw his radical pursuers off the scent. But his comments to local journalists suggested that he was considering the idea of bringing his family to live in Israel – not just to avoid Weberman and the DLF, but also for religious reasons. The only consolation for Weberman was that two weeks after the birthday party, John Lennon was pictured on the cover of the *New York Post*. On his lapel was a small badge he'd been given by Abbie Hoffman, which read: 'Free Bob Dylan!'

## A BRAND-NAME FOR REVOLT

When he met John Lennon in June 1971, Abbie Hoffman was once again a celebrity, after almost a year of abstinence from publicity. As in 1968, his fame was based on his political activities – what he'd done, and more importantly, what the government feared he might do. 'Hoffman's a Jew,' Nixon announced definitively during a secretly taped meeting in the White House, as if that explained why he was such a thorn in the government's side. What antagonised the President was the belief that Hoffman had been one of the prime movers in the events of April and May 1971, when the anti-war movement enjoyed one last, joyous communion in the streets of America's major cities. It was as if the disunity and depression of 1969 and 1970 had vanished, as if it was early 1968 again, and the counter-culture believed that it could alter the course of American history. It was a moment built for Abbie Hoffman.

The Yippie founder had nothing to do with planning the 'May Day' demonstrations, although he did help to drum up support. The protests were intended to be multi-faceted, to heighten the sense that it was an entire people who were appalled by Nixon's policies, not just a predictable crowd outside the Capitol Building in Washington. 'May Day' eventually stretched out over eighteen days, beginning with a mid-April demonstration – outside the Capitol Building, of course – featuring more than 350,000 people. The Beach Boys consolidated their newly militant image by performing, at an event that began with a tape of Jimi Hendrix's incendiary rendition of the 'Star Spangled Banner'. Meanwhile members of Vietnam Veterans Against the War began several days of street-theatre actions, which aroused more sympathetic press coverage than the protests arranged by the radical left. Similar events occurred across the rest of the month, with San Francisco seeing its largest ever anti-war assembly.

Everything built towards another march to the Pentagon, nearly four years after the events reported by Norman Mailer in *Armies of the Night*. On 3 May, Washington saw its most populous and chaotic demonstration of the entire Vietnam conflict. Police were primed for violent revolutionary action in the spirit of the Weather Underground, and responded accordingly. Seven thousand demonstrators were arrested, Hoffman's nose was broken by a police truncheon, and around 1,000 prisoners of the police were marshalled into RFK football stadium, surrounded by barbed wire. It was a sudden vision of how a police state might feel. Hoffman and fellow Chicago veteran Rennie Davis were arrested on exactly the same conspiracy charges they had faced three years earlier. But this time the government knew better than to allow them the global publicity of a trial, and the charges were quietly dropped a few months later.

The Washington demo created the illusion that the movement was reborn, stronger and more militant than ever. But events outside the capital were more sparsely attended. An anti-war concert at the 20,000-seater Hollywood Bowl in California attracted no more than 4,500 people, perhaps because the bill – which featured movement staples Country Joe McDonald and Joan Baez alongside the Joy of Cooking, the Association and Don Everly of the Everly Brothers – lacked genuine star names, and a righteous cause was no longer enough. For Everly, however, the show offered a rare chance to salve his conscience. 'We played Saigon once,' he recalled years later, 'a benefit for the Tan Son Nhut orphanage. That night we sat on the roof of this house and watched them napalming stuff outside the city. We played a lot of hospitals in the Philippines too, full of Vietnam casualties. That's when it began to dawn on me that something was dreadfully wrong with that war. I became very political in my mind, totally anti-Nixon, but there didn't seem to be much I could do about it. We were working nine, ten months of the year; we were really out of touch with what was going on in the world.'

Everly wasn't the only one who had lost touch. The May Day demonstrations concentrated the mind of radical America on ending US involvement in Vietnam. Yet much closer to home, other issues demanded attention, and were virtually ignored by everyone in the movement. Across the Texas border in Mexico, for example, protestors were being greeted not with truncheons, but with guns. After the Tlatelolco student massacre of October 1968, the Mexican government had cracked down hard on obvious signs of dissent. In the face of this harassment, many students and other would-be rebels preferred to imitate America's hippies rather than its political activists. The line between the two camps was often impossible to recognise, however, especially when Mexico's most progressive rock musicians began to experiment with satire and non-conformism.

Since his death in 1919, Emiliano Zapata Salazar had passed into Mexican legend for his revolutionary exploits against the authorities. He was Mexico's Che Guevara, a totem of freedom and courage, struck down in his prime by government treachery. After Tlatelolco, student leaders in Mexico City used Zapata's image as a banner of liberation. In 1970, a psychedelic rock band formed under the name La Revolucion de Emiliano Zapata. Their first, self-titled album carried Zapata's familiar portrait; the second featured a collage of radical slogans and images, including such iconic figures as Chilean president Salvador Allende, union activist Cesar Chavez and Che Guevara. The band poked fun at Mexico's conservative moral code with such songs as 'Nasty Sex', while their live shows won official disapproval, especially when they performed their deliberately confrontational 'I'm a Revolutionary'.

A single rock band could do nothing more than voice its dissatisfaction with the country's ruling elite. In any case, Mexico evaded any easy division into underground (anti-war, pro-rock, anti-American, pro-American culture) and establishment. The country's counter-culture, a movement known as La Onda Chicana, aroused disapproval from both the government and from the Marxist left. Rock music, especially sung in English, was regarded by both sides as an alien invasion, an unwelcome American influence that endangered Mexico's own culture. It mattered little whether the English-language words were preaching armed revolution or placid acceptance of the status quo; in the eyes of the old left and the right, this influence over Mexican youth had to be resisted.

The complications of the revolt against authority were revealed by the events of 10 June 1971. In a surreal repeat of Tlatelolco, student protestors gathered in Mexico City to march in defence of their freedom to think, dress and act as they wished. A column of government vehicles approached the marchers, carrying hundreds of identically dressed young men in blue jeans, many of them wearing their hair longer than the demonstrators. They launched themselves at the students like a paramilitary army, attacking them with clubs and handguns. For a few minutes, chaos ensued, as gunfire ricocheted wildly through the streets; and then the young men withdrew. Police officers watched the assault without intervening. As at Tlatelolco, students were left to carry away the bodies of their comrades. Around fifty people are believed to have died, hundreds were injured, and an unknown number 'disappeared', never to be seen again. Although the government claimed to have no knowledge of the paramilitaries, who went under the name of Los Jalcones (the Falcons), activists believed that they had been trained by official police and army forces, and were operating with the regime's full approval.

The Mexico City massacre eradicated the protest march as a tool of dissent; no students would dare to risk another Jalcones attack. But opposition to the government-approved culture was still expressed in the pages of *Piedra Rodante*. As its name suggested, this magazine began as a Mexican edition of *Rolling Stone*, but the editors distanced themselves from their US sponsors, claiming that the Americans had treated them as colonials and children. *Piedra Rodante* became a vital tool in publicising the Mexican equivalent of Woodstock: a rock festival at Avandaro.

Avandaro attracted around 200,000 people on 11 September 1971, a remarkable show of youthful defiance in the wake of the June massacre. But the event was sponsored by McCann-Erickson Stampton, the US affiliate that handled the distribution of Coca-Cola in Mexico. Banners lined the route to the festival site, reading: '*Paz y amor* [Peace and love]. Coca-Cola.' Moreover, almost every act who performed at Avandaro sang in English, and the American flag was draped over the stage, and waved by many in the crowd. Which America were they celebrating – the nation of Nixon or the Doors? Woodstock or Vietnam? Many left-wing observers were appalled by the lack of political awareness among the crowd. One student leader complained that the government was eager to promote mass distractions of this kind, 'looking to drown out the just and valid voices of rebellion and dissatisfaction among youth, hoping that with a few pesos spent on drugs, the repression of 1968, the massacre of Tlatelolco, the assassins of 10 June, all of the injustices committed against the people, will be erased'. But the right-wing press attacked the 'orgy' of sex and drugs that they claimed to have seen at Avandaro, and alleged that the festival had sowed the seeds of revolutionary upheaval to come.

The day-long concert was broadcast live on Mexico radio – until a member of the band Peace & Love called out, '*Chinga su madre quien no canta*' ('Fuck your mother if you don't sing'), during the provocatively entitled 'Marihuana Boogie'. The organisers had taken trouble to ensure that political activists weren't allowed to speak to the crowd, but Alejandro Lora, the 18-year-old lead singer of the band Three Souls In My Mind, did his best to subvert the rule. 'You've heard lots at this festival about peace and love,' he told the vast audience, 'and that's cool, but it's not rock'n'roll. To show that we care about what happened on 10 June, we're going to play a song by the Stones, called "Street Fighting Man".' Three Souls In My Mind were arguably the most politically oriented band on the Avandaro bill, but even so, Lora was realistic about the gulf between radical rhetoric and political action. When people heard the band's music, he explained later, 'they feel like a guerrilla, but they're not going to take up arms or beat up the president. Yet they feel like they've participated in a political meeting by listening to the Three Souls. It's a psychological escape, which I think the government should recognise as such.' With his courageous political anger, and his acceptance that any revolutionary fervour felt by his audience was a passing illusion, Alejandro Lora grasped better than most the naivety of imagining that rock music was always a radical force.

Like Woodstock, Avandaro became a brand-name for officially sanc-tioned revolt – claimed by fans as a symbol of freedom, and by activists as proof that corporatism would always conquer freedom. Bands who had never dared to utter a word against the establishment sold records by invoking 'the spirit of September 11'. Meanwhile, the Mexican government regarded Avandaro as a code-name for some devilish form of subversion. Songs that mentioned the festival – starting with 'Avandaro', by the band Rosario – were banned from airplay on Mexican radio. Record companies were encour-aged to withdraw their sponsorship from local rock bands, and concentrate on foreign imports, or traditional folk tunes. Mexican fans were now free to hear such would-be revolutionaries as Jefferson Airplane, but not their much milder local equivalents. Live concerts were gradually squeezed out of existence by ever more stringent government regulations. Even *Piedra Rodante*, the voice of the Mexican counter-culture, soon perished. Those bands that survived were driven underground, forced to perform in secret or in private, and faced with the choice of singing bland material in Spanish, or not being allowed to record. Just months after Avandaro had united Mexican youth, rock had effectively been robbed of its cultural power. Only Three Souls In My Mind continued to mine political and social themes in their work. Far from launching a revolution, rock had been used to suppress dissidence. After 1971, there was still music in Mexico, but the culture that provided it with its symbolic power, to shock and shake the system, was gone.

## VILLAGE PEOPLE

On Tuesday 1 June 1971, John Lennon and Yoko Ono flew to New York City, having completed their *Oz* single a few hours before their departure. On Wednesday afternoon, the Apple Records office in Manhattan was contacted by Jerry Rubin, asking the Lennons to call him. Two hours later he rang the office again, was briefly put on hold, and then found himself speaking to Ono. She arranged a rendezvous with the Yippie leader in Washington Square Park the following Saturday afternoon.

Meanwhile the Lennons toured bohemian New York. On Friday evening, they were browsing in a Village clothing store called Limbo, with their friend, radical DJ Howard Smith. 'That wasn't the kind of store which would close down for famous people to shop behind closed doors,' recalls street musician David Peel. 'The owner insisted that stars had to mingle with everyone else. So John and Yoko were just there like regular shoppers. A friend of mine told me they were there, so I rushed over and said, "Hi, I'm David Peel from Elektra Records".' Smith, who was on speaking terms with the entire cultural population of Greenwich Village, made the initial introductions. 'He wanted to show John and Yoko the Village scene,' Peel explains, 'and I was one of the icons of that scene.' When Smith told them that Peel performed every Sunday afternoon in Washington Square Park, the Lennons agreed to come down that weekend and watch him play.

In the early hours of Saturday morning, they took part in a free-form improvisation game on Smith's overnight show on WPLJ. The Lennons slept for a few hours, and then dragged themselves out of bed for their appointment with Jerry Rubin. The Yippie had encountered his share of celebrities in recent years, but the prospect of meeting Lennon still thrilled him. In the aftermath of May Day, he had felt 'depressed and confused' by the movement's lack of progress and momentum. 'Then a friend sat me down and played [Lennon's songs] "Working Class Hero" and "Hold On John", which could be "Hold on Jerry" or "Hold on Anybody",' he explained. 'I realised that on a mini scale, I had many of the same problems, and had been going through much of the same suffering as John Lennon . . . Music had never been made on such a personal level before. This man was talking about himself in a universal way.'

Rubin insisted on bringing his sidekick Abbie Hoffman along to Washington Square, together with Hoffman's wife Anita. 'We see them walking towards us,' he recalled like an excited schoolboy. '[Lennon's] wearing American flag sneakers and she's dressed all in black.' Lennon's shoes alone would have made an instant connection with Hoffman, after his adventures with a Stars and Stripes shirt the previous year. 'We run up to meet them,' Rubin gushed as he looked back on the meeting. 'It's love at first sight. Great vibes. The greatest. We dug his sense of humour, we were knocked out by her sincerity, there was never a moment of anyone trying to project any kind of image. At one time we're all talking in the back of their car and John says, "I want to go to China", but then he stops and he wonders if the Chinese know about the Beatles song 'Revolution'. So he says, "That's all right, I'll just tell them Paul wrote it".'

The five ended up in the Hoffmans' apartment, swapping war stories and registering how the Lennons and the Yippies had each used the media to further their political ends. 'Yoko told me and Abbie that they considered us to be great artists,' Rubin recalled. 'So Abbie said, "That's funny, we always thought of you as great politicians."' Hoffman presumably kept quiet about the time he had accused the Lennons of being pawns of the US State Department.

The following afternoon, they were back in Washington Square Park with their new friends. 'I couldn't believe it,' David Peel says. 'I really didn't think they would come. But there they were. I already knew Abbie Hoffman from the days of the Yippie demonstration at Grand Central Station, and he introduced me to Jerry. Then I sang for John and Yoko. I sang them "Have a Marijuana" and a new song I'd written called "The Pope Smokes Dope". John loved them, and so we all walked off round the East Village, singing "have a mari-mari-marijuana", over and over again, while I played guitar.'

That night, Peel wrote a song about the experience, called 'The Ballad of New York City – John Lennon/Yoko Ono'. 'New York City is your friend,' the chorus announced, while Peel also encapsulated the couple's first week in the Village: 'You played and jammed at Fillmore East, you shopped and sang on New York streets. You also met the underground. Welcome to a freaky town! You also came for other reasons, New York wants it to be freedom.' It wasn't exactly poetry – Peel clearly didn't own a rhyming dictionary – but it convinced Lennon that he had chanced upon an authentic source of street art. 'John said, "Are you making a record?",' Peel recalls. 'I said, "No, I'm on my own label, RLF Records". He said, "Would you like to be on Apple?" By the end of the week, we were in the studio together.'

For the next month, the Lennons, Rubin, Hoffman and Peel hung out as friends, the Americans guiding the visitors through the hotspots of New York bohemia. In subsequent years, Lennon was almost callously dismissive of his new milieu, describing Rubin and Hoffman as 'the Mork and Mindy of the Sixties' and 'two classic, fun-loving hustlers'. He explained that 'I'm pretty movable as an artist, you know. They greeted me off the plane, and the next minute I'm *involved*, you know.' But no plans were laid or conspiracy hatched during these initial weeks of fraternisation. The Lennons and the Yippies concentrated on each other as people, rather than symbols. As Rubin recalled, 'All five of us were amazed at how we had been into the same kinds of things all these years.' When the Lennons flew out of New York on the night of 13 July, they had already decided to leave England and move to America.

They arrived in London as their *Oz* record was released, credited to the unknown Bill Elliott & the Elastic Oz Band. The Lennons had work to do – promoting the paperback edition of Ono's book, *Grapefruit*; finalising the imminent release of Lennon's *Imagine* album; and completing their film of the same name. But they still found time to involve themselves in radical causes. On 28 July, the three *Oz* editors were found not guilty of conspiracy, but guilty of publishing obscene material and sending it via the postal system. A week later, the three defendants were sentenced to prison terms of fifteen, twelve and nine months. The news was greeted with a spontaneous riot outside the Old Bailey. Among the banners held by the demonstrators was one that borrowed a phrase from Bob Dylan: 'Your sons and your daughters are beyond your command'. The Lennons and Ringo Starr lent their names to a petition calling for the sentences to be overturned. On 11 August, there was an *Oz* protest march through the streets of London, following a rally at Marble Arch. The Lennons took their place at the front of the column. Lennon grabbed a loudhailer and sang the chorus of 'Power to the People' over and over again. Photographers captured his image, as he held a placard prepared by the Trotskyist magazine *Red Mole*. It read: 'FOR: The IRA. AGAINST: British Imperialism'. A row of marching soldiers revealed the identity of the enemy.

## A LOCAL AFFAIR

Two days earlier, the British Army had launched Operation Demetrius in Northern Ireland. At dawn, soldiers swooped on hundreds of homes in the province's Catholic community, searching for members and sympathisers of the Irish Republican Army (IRA). Three hundred and forty-two Republican supporters were arrested, and more than 200 were held in prison camps. Many of them alleged that they were beaten and tortured by soldiers when they were taken into captivity. This policy was called internment, and was intended by the British and Northern Ireland governments to remove present and potential terrorists from the streets. In the eyes of the Republican move-ment, which had been campaigning for an independent, unified Ireland for longer than a century, the internees were being held 'Without Charge or Trial in Concentration Camps'.

'I was in Ireland when it happened,' recalls Tom McGuinness, former bassist with Manfred Mann, who in 1971 was a member of successful pop band McGuinness Flint. 'It was a huge blow. Everyone in the Irish Republic was really shocked. I equated it with what had been happening in South Africa, when people were being jailed for their views, without trial. I was sad, but most of all I was angry.' Like Lennon, McGuinness came from Irish stock. 'My father was in the original IRA,' he explains, 'so I was raised to be very aware of the Irish Republican tradition. I knew that Northern Ireland was an English colony.'

August 1971 was not the first time that internment had been used to restrain militant Republicanism. The tragedy of Ireland is that history not only repeats itself, but itself becomes a battleground. Both the Loyalists (aka the Unionists, the Protestants who wish to maintain the union of Great Britain and Northern Ireland) and the Republicans (the Catholics seeking a single Irish state) base their crusades around triumphs and tragedies from the long distant past. When the sorry series of events that became known euphemistically as 'The Troubles' began in 1968–69, new landmarks were soon added to the calendar of remembrance.

Thomas Wolfe Tone, who led the rebellion of United Irishmen in 1798, made a memorable pronouncement of the Republican principle: 'To subvert the tyranny of our execrable government, to break the connection with England, the never failing source of all our political evils, and to assert the independence of my country'. Those goals inspired the Easter Rising of 1916, during which the IRA declared that Ireland was now an independent republic. Their leaders paid for their daring with their lives. In 1921, Britain accepted the foundation of the Irish Free State, initially as a dominion of the British Empire. The six counties of Ulster, with a predominantly Protestant population, remained part of the United Kingdom, and Ireland entered a new state: partition.

For the next forty years, the IRA attempted to eject British influence from Northern Ireland. In 1963, however, the IRA's Dublin leadership adopted a strikingly different goal: socialist revolution in the Marxist tradition. They now called on working-class Protestants and Catholics to unite against the forces of imperialism. More immediately, they expected both sides of the divide to campaign for civil rights, ending the pernicious discrimination against the Catholic minority that was the bedrock of life in Northern Ireland. Long-term Republicans were shocked by this shift of direction, and the IRA's influence waned.

In February 1967, the Northern Ireland Civil Rights Association (NICRA) was formed, demanding an end to electoral and social injustice. A series of marches and rallies led towards the events of October 1968 – when the province's government banned a NICRA march in Derry, there was a confrontation between protestors and the (Protestant) police force, the RUC, and two days of rioting ensued on the Bogside (the inner-city Catholic enclave of the city). Within days, militant students formed a new organisation, People's Democracy (PD), with a more overtly socialist agenda. After limited concessions from the government, PD began a civil rights march from Belfast to Derry on New Year's Day 1969. It was modelled on the African-American march from Selma to Montgomery in 1965, and like its predecessor, it was the target of violence from political opponents and police alike.

Events spiralled, and in August 1969, the British government introduced troops to the streets of Northern Ireland, to protect the Catholic minority from Loyalist aggression. To the horror of IRA traditionalists, the British soldiers were initially welcomed by many Catholics as saviours. By the end of 1969, the IRA had split into two equally strong but starkly divided factions. The 'Officials' aimed to achieve a socialist republic via the ballot box; the 'Provisionals' wanted no truck with the electoral process, maintaining the IRA's original aim of expelling the British without bothering with Marxist theories of revolution.

The birth of the Provisionals attracted little interest beyond hardcore Republican circles, until summer 1970, when they launched their first military actions. This coincided with an aggressive British Army search of Catholic homes in Belfast, on 3 July 1970, sparking gun battles in which five people were killed. Members of the Catholic community now began to reconsider their opinion of the British soldiers in their midst. As violence grew, Protestant militants formed their own paramilitary organisations. The stage was set for a protracted conflict that threatened to mutate into civil war.

In the rest of Britain, public opinion regarded the Irish crisis as a local affair, incomprehensible to anyone in England. It was only in December 1970, for example, that the underground newspaper *Friends* noticed The Troubles for the first time, describing Ireland as 'Britain's Vietnam'. Gradually, though, the deteriorating situation became impossible to ignore. In March 1971, the day after a gun battle between Official and Provisional IRA cadres in Belfast, a group of teenage soldiers, off duty in a Belfast pub, were lured into the street and shot by Provisional gunmen. This established the image of the IRA as callous criminals in the eyes of most British citizens, few of whom understood the background to the fighting, let alone the complexities of the Official/Provisional split. With bombings and sectarian shootings a regular feature on the streets of Belfast, Edward Heath's government in London felt that it had to intern those it believed to be causing the violence. Ironically, many of those held in the initial raids were middle-aged or older, and had taken no part in recent IRA activities. As historians of the Provisional IRA noted, the organisation 'had been handed an endlessly productive mine of propaganda. Internment succeeded in uniting the IRA's fiercest enemies inside the Catholic community behind them, and lent some credence to their claims to legitimacy.'

Internment finally awakened John Lennon to the urgency of the situation. Despite his proud Irish roots, he hadn't responded when he was quizzed about the province during his *Red Mole* interview. Now – perhaps having read one British left-wing paper's promise that Ireland offered 'the most advanced revolutionary situation in Europe' – he used the *Oz* protest march to highlight the cause of the IRA. He also began to educate himself in the history of Ireland, and to find comparisons between UK involvement there, and the American intervention in Vietnam.

While the situation in Northern Ireland reached boiling point, a strike in Scotland attracted weighty coverage in the media. The Conservative government of Edward Heath announced that they were intending to lay off three-quarters of the workers at Upper Clyde Shipyards in Glasgow. Those who kept their jobs faced a savage pay cut. Outraged by the destruction of a traditional trade in an area already enduring mass unemployment, the workers occupied the shipyard and withdrew their labour. Young strikers sang Lennon's 'Power to the People' on the picket lines; their older counterparts opted for traditional union ballads. Their trade union launched a fighting fund, and John Lennon and Yoko Ono immediately sent them a cheque for £1,000. The money was accompanied by a bunch of red roses. When a photographer asked the burly shipbuilders to pose with the flowers, the answer was curt: 'Fuck off'. A Glaswegian himself, former Cream bassist Jack Bruce played a benefit gig for the strikers. Journalist Bob Houston used the comparison between the two gestures to illustrate how poorly the Lennons understood the men whom they were supporting: 'Jack Bruce, son of a militant trade unionist and a former member of the Young Communist League choir in Glasgow, would have known better than to send red roses.' Bruce added to the implied criticism of Lennon's working-class credentials: 'The only people who have the kind of money that's needed are the Stones and the Beatles,' he declared. 'The Beatles had a go with Apple, but they didn't attack the structure. They tried to make the same system work better for themselves, and that's not the answer. Apple was a tremendous opportunity, really fucked up because they didn't have the right roots, I suppose. The Beatles always seemed so middle class in outlook and attitude.'

The apparently unchanging British class system spread its tentacles around the debate about rock and its capacity to change society. While Lennon and Bruce squabbled over their proletarian roots (virtually non-existent in Lennon's case), Mick Jagger was completing his dizzying ride up and down the social ladder, from middle-class suburbia to faux cockney earthiness and back to the aristocratic elite (while retaining his London taxi-driver drawl as a trademark of sincerity). Could the revolution be kickstarted by bourgeois white males? Could a middle-class art student – Pete Townshend of the Who, for example – change the world?

Ever since he had manhandled or nudged Abbie Hoffman off the stage at Woodstock, Townshend had been racked by self-doubt about his role as an artist. It wasn't Hoffman's plight that nagged at his soul, although he conceded that the Chicago defendants had been through the mill. It wasn't even anything so easily described as political guilt; he had, after all, described his 'collision' with Hoffman as 'the most political thing I ever did'.[2] But with a guitar in his hand, Townshend first felt omnipotent, and then began to worry that he might be misusing that power or, worse still, not using it at all.

'I believe rock can do anything,' the Who's guitarist declared in 1970. 'It's the ultimate vehicle for everything. It's the ultimate vehicle for saying anything, for building anything, for killing and creating. It's the absolute ultimate vehicle for self-destruction.' He would test all sides of that equation to their limit over the next few years, ploughing his creativity and his band's reputation into ever more portentous projects that might solve the mystery of what rock meant. Townshend's mind was under siege from a mass of competing impulses – the band's daredevil hedonism, his own intake of drink and drugs, his spiritual debt to his guru, Meher Baba, his generation's political yearnings, and his music. All of these factors came together to form the epic film, theatrical production, double-album and life-changing self-examination that would have been *Lifehouse*. Thirty years later, he was still teasing at the edges of this conceptual behemoth, trying to analyse exactly what he had been trying to prove. In 1971, the project collapsed into confusion, from which the Who were able to salvage one of rock's finest albums, *Who's Next* – much to Townshend's dissatisfaction, as he believed that he had sacrificed some of the key ingredients of his masterwork in the interests of commercial success.

In 1970, John Lennon had written a song entitled 'Instant Karma!', an attempt to demythologise his own fame. ('John Lennon keeps reminding people that he is no longer a star', *Rolling Stone* magazine noted in July 1971.) It sounded like a political rallying-cry, but with no goal beyond self-expression and self-awareness. 'Why on earth are you there', Lennon sang to his captive audience, 'when you're everywhere, come and get your share'. And again: 'Who on earth do you think you are? A superstar? Well, right you are.' Pete Townshend was now asking himself the same questions.

'The aim is change,' he wrote in one of his perceptive columns for the *Melody Maker* in the early months of 1971. 'The idea is to make the first superstar, the first real star who can stand and say that he deserves the name. That star would be us all.' Hence *Lifehouse*, which he envisaged as a suite of songs (and much more) that would be developed in concert, changing as they reflected the input of the audience, until the artificial chasm between performer and listener would be removed and their roles would become interchangeable. It was an attempt to identify with his audience, to become his audience, to let his audience become him, to achieve a liberation of creativity, openness, awareness and spirituality, to make everything one and one everything, one transcendent note that could change the world. It was the most impossibly utopian of all rock's grand visions, and it was doomed to fail.

The Who premiered Townshend's new material at the Young Vic Theatre in London, which he had chosen as the venue for his interactive experiment. He was affronted to be greeted by someone in the crowd shouting, 'Capitalist pigs! Bastards! Get off the stage!' It set the tone for a troubled few months, in which Townshend lost sight of his initial inspiration, the movie concept crumbled into dust, and the Who's fans failed to live up to their hero's expectations. 'Rock can't be held responsible for what it says or does, but the audience can,' Townshend had proclaimed in typically grandiose style that year. But the Who's audience preferred not to influence the music, as biographer Dave Marsh reported: 'The crowd inside was content to sit and soak as long as the Who played, a pattern that was maintained throughout, not just on this tour but for the rest of the decade as well. So the Who toured in continuing comfort, and their audience (like all rock audiences at this time) became increasingly irrelevant, except as a means of footing the bills. The bonds between band and fan were severed now; in a world without true connections, only shallow symbols remained.'

Among those 'shallow symbols' were *Who's Next*, and two 1971 singles, 'Won't Get Fooled Again' and 'Let's See Action'. The dynamism of the band's music transformed almost everything they played into a potential anthem, and *Who's Next* was full of material that sounded like a call to arms. Yet Townshend's self-doubt had become so inextricably entwined with his songwriting that even the most blatantly rousing material resisted easy interpretation. There was a defiant cry of 'it's only teenage wasteland' in the album's opening cut, 'Baba O'Riley', but the setting was so vague – England after the apocalypse? Woodstock? – that the phrase seemed to signify more than it meant.

Bursting onto the radio like a natural successor to 'Street Fighting Man', 'Won't Get Fooled Again' virtually begged for clenched fists to be thrown into the air. 'Meet the new boss,' Roger Daltrey cried at the end of the song, 'same as the old boss', and anyone who had to bow their knee to an authority figure nodded their head in recognition. Elsewhere, Townshend appeared to be echoing John Lennon's complaint that the stylistic changes of the 1960s had done nothing to alter the power structure. 'The parting on the left is now the parting on the right,' Daltrey sang, 'and the beards have all grown longer overnight.' So the song was widely interpreted as a call for revolution, as a generation refused to be fooled again by the empty promises of capitalism. Unless, of course, it was the promise of revolution that had betrayed its believers, and Townshend was swearing that he would never lose his head again to empty political idealism. In this light, the narrator was looking back at the revolution of the street fighting men, when 'the shotgun sings the song', and realising that utopia was no nearer than it had been under the 'old boss'.

The Who's mass audience accepted 'Won't Get Fooled Again' as a thrilling, visceral performance, reacting to the music rather than the words. But a bunch of radicals, led by Mick Farren, challenged Townshend about his philosophy during a party at drummer Keith Moon's house. Farren and several associates followed through with an open letter to the Who leader, expressing the 'feelings of puzzlement and worry that we feel when playing the new single. Whereas the music is still strong, kicking-out, aggressive music, the lyric is seemingly defensive and negative, even potentially damaging to the consciousness of kids who still strongly identify with the Who as an extension of their lifestyles. In fact it's calculated to bring down anybody seeking radical change, in what we know you agree is a depressingly corrupt society. Why?'

In typically passionate style, Townshend rejected Farren's heroes-and-villains view of the world. 'I suppose if I wasn't cunt enough to be a Rock star I would be round there with you,' he wrote. 'A lot of my people are. The fact is, and it's not really surprising to you, I'm not with you. Neither in your neighbourhood nor frame of mind.' He claimed that the Who's role was not to provide false hope, but to reflect the negativity felt by 'the kids' about 'the fight for power which is being waged in their name, but not on their terms, not using their ethics'. It was a clear slap in the face to anyone who claimed to represent the youth revolution. Townshend explained that 'Won't Get Fooled Again' was 'partly personal' – inspired, it emerged later, by his uneasy dealings with a commune near his West London home – but mostly a scream against those who were telling the Who, and the kids, how to feel and what to do. 'I know the song is negative,' he concluded. But he was outraged by the suggestion that the Who might in some way be exploiting their audience by making a living from music. 'We're the only fucking Rock band, apart from the Grateful Dead, that know what is happening in the audience at a gig,' he exploded. 'We play hard, often, long. We think, we work, we worry, we give money away, we re-invest money in our music, in the road circus, we write, we record, we might even get a little negative at times, but we ain't fucking well trying to escape from nowhere . . . We know what we have to do.'

The guitarist advised Farren and his comrades to consult the Who's forthcoming single for further information. Then, he promised, they would be able to 'read our frustration at not being able to truly push Rock through as the alternative society it deserves to be. Listen to the band play as the shotguns sing.' Three months later, the Who released 'Let's See Action', with a rousing chorus as compulsive as Lennon's 'Power to the People'. 'Let's see action,' it ran, 'let's see people, let's see freedom up in the air . . . Let's be free, let's see who cares'. Surely this was the shot to start the revolution? Again, the small print suggested otherwise. The subject of the battle cry was not 'the people' who might rise up against oppression, but Townshend's guru, his 'avatar', who could transport him to a realm where 'time and life can meet'. For all its radical fervour, 'Let's See Action' preached acceptance of the spiritual journey ahead. 'I'll get to where I'm gonna end up,' Townshend sang fatalistically, 'and that's all right with me.' Or, as John Lennon had once promised on 'Revolution', 'Don't you know it's gonna be all right'. In each song, the writer only had his own salvation in mind. To reinforce the point, 'Let's See Action' ended with a chant of 'Nothing is, everything is, nothing is, everything . . .' – circular, endless, offering no escape from Townshend's logic.

The Who's leader was hypersensitive to the slightest criticism from the public, and to any charge that he might be abusing his fame. In the pages of *Melody Maker*, he kept up a lengthy correspondence with disillusioned fans. One of them, Tim Thorp, deplored the 'incredible fees' that the Who and their peers charged for concert appearances, and the rock community's lack of concern for social issues. 'The answer is simple,' Thorp declared. 'They are not the hero figures which we make them – they are capitalists hiding behind a mask of freedom and anti-materialism. [But] the answers to other questions are not so simple. Why do young people allow their ideals to be rubbed into the ground by the people they are idolising? Why do people tolerate such exorbitant prices? Why not a boycott of gigs and records? Is our desire for music stronger than our ideals?' It was a rehearsal for the blast of cynicism that would fuel the punk movement.

Townshend's response was thoughtful rather than impulsive. He chewed again at the boundaries that separated audience and artist – 'the feeling we get when watching, say, Dylan: that maybe we expect too much from him and this elevation confuses him, setting up a wall between us and him'. He conceded that 'most Rock musicians' "power" is used to perpetrate their own status', but explained that it was naive to imagine that musicians, even within a band such as the Who, shared the same ideals and goals, and could therefore work as a united political force. But he vowed that the band's idealism was still alive, despite the distractions imposed by working 'within a corrupt and apathetic democracy'. When his sincerity was questioned, however, his patience snapped: 'All right! The game's up! I admit it. Not only do we charge too much for entry to our performances, but we all made it in the first place by sleeping with record company executives. Of course my ideals aren't really what I PRETEND they are. I'm merely indulging in honest to God lying. Why tell the truth anyway? People don't listen . . . Fuck off the lot of you!' The exchange marked the end of Townshend's attempt to demythologise stardom; like *Lifehouse*, his willingness to lay himself bare for his audience dissolved into an angry haze. Yet his desire to explain his music, as well as perform it, never left him, and his subsequent career was blotted with equally futile efforts to justify his existence and fame, to a rock culture that had long since lost the passion to care.

## ROCK LIBERATION

Any rock fans disgusted by their heroes' selfish disregard for the outside world had one giant gesture to cheer them in 1971: the Concerts for Bangladesh. On 1 August, George Harrison led a superstar cast in two performances at Madison Square Garden. They were intended to raise funds for the starving, flood-stricken people of Bangladesh. The catastrophe had received little publicity in the West, and even less financial aid. Harrison's attention was drawn to the crisis by his friend, the sitarist Ravi Shankar. The maestro had merely requested Harrison's help in organising a small benefit concert, but Harrison agreed to capitalise on his fame by playing his first ever solo shows, and persuading his friends to join him. A Beatles reunion was stalled by trivial disagreements with John Lennon and Paul McCartney, but Harrison achieved an even more impressive coup: persuading Bob Dylan out of his reclusive semi-retirement and back onto an American stage for the first time in more than three years.

Dylan had released just one record since his *New Morning* album a year earlier: a single, entitled 'Watching the River Flow'. The song did little to ease the pressure from A.J. Weberman and the Dylan Liberation Front, as Dylan complained about 'people disagreeing everywhere you look, makes you just wanna stop and read a book'. During rehearsals for the Bangladesh concerts, Harrison asked his friend if he would perform some of his vintage material. 'Are you gonna play "I Want To Hold Your Hand?",' Dylan snapped back. But when he finally took to the stage, he had magically transformed into the politically charged folk-singer of the early 1960s, dressed in blue denim, clutching an acoustic guitar and prepared to sing the protest anthems that had encouraged a generation to question its elders.

His appearance convinced Weberman that the singer had rediscovered his social conscience. In return, the Dylan Liberation Front agreed to abandon its campaign. Instead, Weberman and David Peel announced the formation of the Rock Liberation Front (RLF). The organisation was based at Weberman's apartment on East 5th Street in the Village. Along with its soon-forgotten sister organisation, the Rock Culture Movement, the RLF was formed 'in order to establish a relationship of understanding and participation in the World of Rock', Weberman proclaimed. 'It's a world of fun, peace, and happiness. This privilege should not be extended to only the Rock professionals, but should be part of everybody's life. Our Rock Culture has been getting ripped off too long! There's got to be a stop to this . . . RIGHT NOW! We are all going to help together and help each other.'

There followed a 22-point manifesto, which ended with the delightfully democratic: 'Finally – any suggestions that you come up with – let us know!' The RLF promised to institute 'free rock seminars', publish a regular newsletter, 'have free international rock music people's hostels throughout the world', form an 'International Arts & Culture Center' and 'celebrate our own rock holidays'. More pertinent was the RLF's intention to 'have demonstrations against rip-off people in the world of rock'. They demanded more free concerts from top acts; reduced ticket prices for those gigs that weren't free; and 'a real people's music company, controlled by the people'. 'When we made those demands of the industry, they were futuristic,' Peel explains. 'I was looking for a dream of how music could be – for, by and to the people.'[3]

The RLF's power was minimal. As Weberman admits, 'The Rock Liberation Front was basically me and David Peel, and anyone else who was around at the time.' But they voiced the growing belief that rock had sacrificed its principles and was now part of the problem rather than the solution. John Sinclair's frequent missives from his Detroit prison were devoted to precisely this point. As his comrade Ken Kelley of the White Panther Party noted, 'Led Zeppelin now charge $75,000 a gig. That's just absurd. Who the fuck needs $75,000 for an hour's performance? No one's asking Led Zeppelin to come out and join us at the barricades. [But] we are asking them to stop coming over charging these high prices ... They're ripping off the people.'

That was exactly the situation that the Rock Liberation Front intended to redress. To launch the RLF into the public eye, Weberman and Peel gathered together around 100 friends, and journeyed uptown to the plush townhouse that housed the law practice run by Paul McCartney's father-in-law and legal advisor, Lee Eastman. 'We figured McCartney could use some liberating,' Weberman explains. 'It was around the time he had released that album [*Ram*] that was really inane and said nothing about what was happening on the street. He was supposed to be a representative of youth culture, but he was just a businessman. We reckoned he could use a wake-up call.' The RLF staged a mock funeral right there on Park Avenue to emphasise the death of the ex-Beatle's ideals, with a black Cadillac hearse and a coffin bearing his picture. McCartney wasn't at the Eastman office during the brief demonstration, but he proudly rang Lennon when it was over. 'I hope they're not after me,' Lennon commented a couple of weeks later. 'I think it's funny as shit. Paul said to me on the phone: "Well, I'm the rebel now, and I'm enjoying it". He thinks *that's* [being] a rebel.'

In early September 1971, Lennon had left Britain for the last time. He and Yoko Ono installed themselves in the well-appointed St Regis Hotel in midtown Manhattan, and sent word down to the Village that they were in town. Among their first visitors was David Peel, who explained that he was involved in the Rock Liberation Front. Lennon had already been appointed a Lifetime Deputy Minister of Culture in the Dylan Liberation Front; now he became an enthusiastic supporter of the RLF as well. Within a matter of days, he was spouting RLF rhetoric to interviewers from mainstream magazines: 'Why should [audiences] pay? I've got everything I need. I've got all the fucking bread I need.' Soon he was telling the *New Yorker*: 'I don't want that big house we built for ourselves in England. I don't want the bother of owning all these big houses and big cars, even though our company, Apple, pays for it all. All structures and buildings and everything I own will be dissolved and got rid of. I'll cash in my chips and anything that's left I'll make the best use of. [Yoko]'s been working on me to get rid of the possessions complex, which is something that happens to people who were poor, like myself.' He was the working-class hero again, ready to live out the fantasy of his own song: 'Imagine no possessions, I wonder if you can'.

A month after the Lennons' arrival in New York, Jerry Rubin returned from a lengthy visit to Chile, where he had been sampling the socialism of Salvador Allende's government. He soon found himself at the chic Manhattan restaurant Serendipity, in the company of John and Yoko. 'They tell me that they've made a decision,' he recalled. 'They say, "Jerry, we're too young to retire, we'll retire when we're 80. We don't want to live in Ascot, we want to do things." Yoko says that they want to be part of the movement for change in America. John says he wants to put together a new band, he wants to play, and he wants to give all the money back to the people. I was so ecstatic, I embarrassed them. This was the most important conversation I could ever remember being involved in. I told them I wanted to work with them.'

To ensure that he couldn't renege on his decision, Lennon announced it in public. 'I want to do something political, and radicalise people, and all that jazz, and this would be the best way,' he declared. 'So now I feel like taking a really far-out show on the road, a mobile, political, rock'n'roll show. I mean political, because everything I do is political. I would take people with me who could speak to the kids, who could speak to them in the foyer, catch them on the way out. Panthers, Weathermen. They can hand all the gear out. I don't want to create a riot or a fight in each town, but I just really want to paint it red.' He declared that he was 'a revolutionary artist', and announced that he had appointed Jerry Rubin as his political advisor. 'It was only meant half seriously,' Rubin explained. 'My part was to be helping to set things up and helping to determine where the money should go.'

Rubin clearly saw Lennon as his new partner-in-pranks, a Yippie by nature if not by name. The ex-Beatle could take the place of Abbie Hoffman, whose slow descent into depression had gathered speed over the summer. Like Rubin, Hoffman had been disillusioned by the hollow aftermath of May Day. Rather than a resurgence of revolutionary activity, the vast anti-war demonstrations seemed to have led to nothing. In summer 1971, tentative plans were announced for the launch of a political party to be called, blandly, the Coalition. It would fight the 1972 presidential election, taking the place of the Peace & Freedom Party. But the Coalition would stop a long way short of entering pacts with the Black Panthers, as the PFP had done four years earlier. Its chosen candidate for President was consumer activist Ralph Nader; the civil rights campaigner Revd Jesse Jackson ran as his Vice-President.

Meanwhile, the movement laid down plans for another round of peace protests in October 1971. At the centre of these was a Moratorium, scheduled for 13 October. But there was no central organisation to provide the impetus for the event, as the prime movers behind May Day, such as Rennie Davis and Abbie Hoffman, were trapped in legal battles. Although John Lennon watched gleefully as protestors chanted 'Power to the People' as well as 'Give Peace a Chance', only a small fraction of the numbers who had answered the May Day call attended the Moratorium in Washington.

By then, Abbie Hoffman had already penned an open letter to the counter-culture, headed: 'I Quit the Movement'. In exhausted, almost bewildered tones, he documented how he had been exploited by those who saw him as an inexhaustible fund of cash and energy. 'There was this terrific May Day call from Washington,' he revealed, 'asking me to solicit money and objects of art from John Lennon and Yoko Ono for those busted in the demonstrations. I asked if I was included in the bail fund (again, I'm facing the heaviest charges of anyone, remember). They answered, "Oh, you're different, you're not in May Day".'

His celebrity was now being exploited in other ways. In the summer of 1971, he spent several days at underground radio station ZBS in Berkeley. 'We hired a band called the Joint Chiefs of Staff,' recalled ZBS DJ Meatball Fulton. 'We recorded Abbie singing songs that were anything but political – "Cool Water", "Ave Maria", etc. There was a tank of nitrous oxide in the studio, the stuff they fill balloons with, and Abbie and the band would take a hit of that and just burst into giggles. It made your voice sound like a chipmunk.' Out of these recordings, tapes of ZBS phone-ins in which callers insulted Hoffman and he responded in kind, and some traditional jazz instrumentals, the ZBS collective concocted a record that was credited to Hoffman and called *Wake Up, America!* Hoffman heard the results, and immediately asked for the project to be stopped. But ZBS decided that it deserved to be released, and outvoted him. It was the ultimate Yippie prank, played on the man who had invented the genre. To his credit, Hoffman eventually agreed to drop his opposition to this virtually unlistenable album, provided he was allowed to contribute a disclaimer, pasted to the back cover of every copy. Ironically the ZBS collective later agreed with Abbie that the record should have been withdrawn.

*Wake Up, America!* was simply one example of the chaos that surrounded Abbie Hoffman, and he had finally had enough. 'This is a sort of retirement letter, I suppose,' he wrote in his 'Quit' piece. 'Not that I'm going off to the country or anything. Let's just call it a parting of the ways. No more calls for me to do benefits or come to demonstrations or do bail fund hustles. Divorce is never an easy matter. After a few years perhaps we can be friends.' The Hoffman family travelled to the Virgin Islands, where they sat out the rest of the year. Meanwhile, Jerry Rubin gained the kudos of leading the world's most prominent rock star into what remained of the revolutionary vanguard.

## BORN IN A PRISON

The black power movement could ill afford such luxuries as retirement in the Caribbean. During the summer of 1971, several of its key figures were removed from the fray. In June, US leader Ron Karenga and three of his followers – including his second wife – were given lengthy prison sentences in Los Angeles. They were convicted of the assault and false imprisonment of two young women. Karenga claimed that the victims had been plotting to poison him. 'Vietnamese torture is nothing compared to what I know,' he told them, and then proved the point with whips, hoses and heated irons. The conviction effectively signed the death warrant of US as a coherent organisation.

On 18 August 1971, ten days after Huey Newton's second murder trial ended in disarray, the FBI and the Jackson Police Department mounted a pre-dawn raid on a remote Mississippi ranch. In the eyes of its owners, the twenty-acre property was sovereign soil: the seat of government for the Republic of New Afrika. Formed three years earlier with the support of exiled revolutionary Robert F. Williams, the RNA aimed to reclaim the Deep South as New Afrika, a homeland for the descendants of American slaves, which would remove them from the tyranny of white rule. The Deep South was the RNA's 'Promised Land', a nation that would offer 'clean air, a modern free home of your own, and a life without crime or want, a life where black people [could] really live as brothers and sisters'.

The RNA's founders were two close friends of Malcolm X; one of them, Brother Imari Abubakari Obadele, was appointed the Republic's President. The organisation's birth coincided with the first wave of national paranoia about the activities of black power groups, so the RNA was closely monitored by the intelligence agencies. Early suspicion centred on the group's first national convention, staged at New Bethel Church in Detroit – where the minister was the Reverend C.L. Franklin, the father of soul singer Aretha Franklin. He protested to the authorities when the church was besieged by local police and all those attending the convention were arrested. Subsequent RNA gatherings attracted equally unwelcome attention. By building an official 'government' site in Jackson, the RNA was seeking to create a territory that could exist beyond the reach of the US authorities.

In the weeks preceding the August 1971 raid, individual members of the RNA, including Brother Imari, were arrested on minor charges relating to weapons and theft. The RNA regarded this as blatant police harassment, so when Jackson's cops allegedly promised the President that they would be back in force, the RNA prepared themselves for an onslaught. The invaders arrived with guns, tear gas grenades and even a tank, but the only casualties in the short battle that followed were the police, one of whom was shot dead. Eleven members of the Republic were arrested and charged with murder, treason and other offences. Among them was the President, even though he was not present during the raid. Eight of the eleven were subsequently sentenced to life imprisonment, including Brother Imari, convicted of conspiracy to commit murder.

In late August, the three 'Soledad Brothers' – George Jackson, John Cluchette and Fleeta Drumgo – were scheduled to go on trial for supposedly murdering a prison guard eighteen months earlier. During that period, Jackson had become a national celebrity, as the author of *Soledad Brother*. The eloquence of his writing won him an audience far beyond the usual ranks of sympathisers. Alongside those of Newton, Eldridge Cleaver, Bobby Seale and Malcolm X, his name became a byword for revolutionary defiance. Celebrities adopted his cause as their own, from Isaac Hayes, who played a benefit concert for the Brothers 'because they were political prisoners', to former Animals leader Eric Burdon, who had written a song entitled 'Soledad'. Hayes' interest in the case reflected his enduring concern about America's racial divide; Burdon's, however, was a case of political tourism – literally. 'I drove down the freeway [past Soledad prison],' he explained. 'There were blue skies and I was feeling good – maybe I was high. Then I saw all that barbed wire and walls. I knew nothing about Angela Davis or the Soledad Brothers, but that doesn't matter. I just stopped at the nearest café and wrote the way it hit me, the way I felt.' The blues-based 'Soledad' reflected his horror that 'anyone can be driving down the freeway, listening to their stereo tapes, smoking dope and be[ing] free when, on the other side of the wire, there are guys who are being beaten up and treated like animals for doing the same thing'.

As the fame of Jackson and his book spread, the Soledad Brothers became not just a symbol of black injustice but also a living example of the inhumane treatment meted out in America's harshest prisons. During the late 1960s, Jackson had formed the Black Guerrilla Family, a prison-based movement devoted to Marxist–Leninist revolution and reform of the prison system. On the morning of 21 August 1971, Jackson discussed his crusade with Liberation News Service reporter Karen Wald. 'We're all familiar with the function of the prison as an institution serving the needs of the totalitarian state,' he told her. 'We've got to destroy that function . . . it's one of the strongest institutions supporting the totalitarian state. They put us in these concentration camps here, the same as they put people in tiger cages or "strategic hamlets" in Vietnam. The idea is to isolate, eliminate, liquidate the dynamic sections of the overall movement, the protagonists of the movement. What we've got to do is prove this won't work. We've got to organise our resistance once we're inside, give them no peace, turn the prison into just another front of the struggle, tear it down from the inside.' As the prison guards signalled that Wald's time was up, Jackson had time for a final statement: 'I'd like to say Power To The People! And I'd like to say that . . . we must use, as Malcolm X puts it, any means necessary to take power. I'd like to say that we really have no alternatives in the matter, and that it's ridiculous or worse to think that we do. That's what I'd like to say.'

After Wald left San Quentin, Jackson met one of his attorneys, a young white man named Stephen Bingham. Later that day, Jackson was gunned down in the prison yard, and pronounced dead at the scene. Everything that happened between those two events is open to question. The prison authorities stated that Bingham had smuggled both a wig and a gun into San Quentin, and surreptitiously passed them to Jackson. Once his lawyer had left, Jackson hid the gun under a wig, then overpowered a guard, and released other prisoners from their cells. During the break-out, several white guards and inmates were herded into a cell, where their throats were cut. Only one of the inmates survived. The alarm was raised, and armed warders from other parts of San Quentin surrounded Jackson and his comrades. The official story maintained that Jackson then made a break for the prison wall. After refusing to stop, he was shot down. As soon as his death was announced, Bingham went into hiding, which the government claimed was proof that he had been involved in Jackson's attempted escape. Far from being a political leader, the authorities maintained, the brutality of Jackson's rebellion demonstrated that he was merely a callous criminal, prepared to take life to save his own.

Almost every aspect of this account was challenged in the years to come. Bingham eventually resurfaced in 1984, and two years later he was charged with having aided Jackson's escape. The jury found him not guilty, plunging a dagger into the heart of the official story. Meanwhile, the circumstances of Jackson's death remained obscure. Some people were prepared to believe that the Soledad Brother had masterminded an escape attempt, but that he was shot in cold blood as he tried to surrender; or perhaps that he effectively sacrificed his life to prevent his comrades from being killed. Others alleged that Bingham had, after all, delivered Jackson a gun – maybe deliberately, maybe accidentally; maybe the gun was actually a fake, intended to be switched for a real weapon after Jackson was shot; maybe he was encouraged to escape, so that he could legitimately be cut down; maybe . . . The story changed with every narrator.

The black power movement had no doubts. Jackson was a martyr, whose death was another grievous insult to the African-American community. Seven thousand mourners gathered for his funeral at St Augustine's Episcopal Church in Oakland. 'Inside the church the walls were ringed with Black Panthers carrying shotguns,' Huey Newton recalled. 'George had said that he wanted no flowers at his funeral, only shotguns.' The coffin arrived to cries of 'Power to the people' from the crowd, while Nina Simone's recording of the anguished civil rights anthem 'I Wish I Could Know How It Felt To Be Free' filled the church. Elaine Brown sang a self-penned song giving thanks for Jackson's life. The eulogy was given by Newton, who described Jackson as 'my hero . . . He showed the love, the strength, the revolutionary fervour characteristic of any soldier for the people . . . He left a standard for the liberation armies of the world. He showed us how to act.'

Three months before Jackson's death, the inmates of the Attica State Correctional Facility in upstate New York had issued a manifesto deploring the degrading conditions they were being forced to endure. As more and more activists were plucked from the streets and thrown into jail, so the level of political consciousness rose. 'From 1967 through 1970 there was this uprising throughout America's prisons,' explained Attica State inmate Herbert X. Blyden. 'What we found in Attica in 1971 was the influx of prisoners from other outlying New York institutions confined in Attica. There was the Young Lords, the Panthers, the Five Percenters [and] the Weathermen.' Jackson's death sent the temperature amongst these militants soaring. On the morning of 22 August, hundreds of Attica State prisoners tied their black shoelaces around their arms as a mark of respect, and refused breakfast as a symbolic fast in Jackson's memory.

As August ended, anger inside Attica grew to fever pitch. New York's Commissioner of Correctional Services, Russell Oswald, promised reforms, but not immediately. Prisoners dismissed his response as 'a lot of words'; and so the stage was set for confrontation. There was nothing unusual about the decision to move two prisoners into solitary confinement on 8 September, but it launched a series of events that culminated in a riot. The next morning, several hundred prisoners seized control of D-Yard, holding many guards as hostages, and issued what became known as 'The Five Demands'. 'WE are MEN!' they declared. 'We are not beasts and do not intend to be beaten or driven as such. The entire prison populace has set forth to change forever the ruthless brutalisation and disregard for the lives of the prisoners here and throughout the United States.'

For four days, the standoff continued. New York's Governor, Nelson Rockefeller, refused demands to attend the scene. But many observers believed that the authorities could not have attempted to retake the prison and free the hostages without Rockefeller's approval. On 13 September, a canister of CS gas was dropped into D-Yard from a helicopter, and marksmen began firing on the prisoners. When the firing ceased, and state troopers and prison staff regained control of the yard, 39 men – 29 prisoners, 10 hostages – lay dead. In total, 43 people lost their lives during the disturbances. Governor Rockefeller described the handling of the riot as 'reasonably restrained'.

## THE HOSTAGE

It was John Lennon's 31st birthday: 9 October 1971. That morning, he and Yoko Ono had attended the opening of their art exhibition at the Everson Art Museum in Syracuse, two hours' drive from the Attica State Correctional Facility. When the exhibit closed for the day, the party began. The Lennons' hotel suite was filled with celebrities and friends – among them Ringo Starr, record producer Phil Spector, Allen Ginsberg, and Jerry Rubin. While Lennon's ubiquitous tape recorder and film crew documented the event for posterity, the guests held a spontaneous jam session.

Amidst the musical chaos, Lennon toyed with a new composition. 'It was conceived on my birthday,' he confirmed later, 'we ad libbed it, then we finished it off.' In its semi-complete state, the song sounded banal; it gained little in stature when Lennon and Ono completed the lyrics in subsequent weeks. But it *was* a revolutionary protest song, hot off the political press, with a timely title: 'Attica State'. Four years later, Lennon was asked how his involvement with Rubin and Abbie Hoffman had affected his work. 'It almost ruined it, in a way,' he replied. 'It became journalism and not poetry . . . I was making an effort to reflect what was going on. Well, it doesn't work like that. It doesn't work as pop music or what I want to do. It just doesn't make sense.'

Nothing confirmed that judgement more clearly than 'Attica State'. Set to the most skeletal of tunes, the song was an exercise in fake passion, as the second-hand rhetoric swamped any hint of sincerity.[4] 'Attica State, Attica State, we're all mates with Attica State', the Lennons chanted patronisingly. Having established a mood, they added a ragbag of radical cliché and pure nonsense. 'Rockfeller pulled the trigger, that is what the people feel', the song continued, confusing 'the people' with themselves and Jerry Rubin. When Lennon sang that 'fear and hatred clouds our judgement', he might have been referring to his own work.[5]

'Helping the movement through culture' was one of the aims of A.J. Weberman's Rock Liberation Front, and Lennon's song fitted the bill. Bob Dylan remained distressingly silent on matters of contemporary culture, but A.J. had kept to his promise not to hassle the singer. In late summer 1971, however, Weberman was persuaded to root through Dylan's garbage can one more time. This was not an official DLF raid, but a photo opportunity: a journalist – 'beautiful' and 'busty', A.J. recalled excitedly – and photographer from Associated Press were researching a story about his exploits, so he agreed to exhibit his technique. As he recalled, 'The camera clicked just as I heard someone scream, "Get the hell out of my garbage! You filthy animal! I can't throw anything away without you pawing through it!" It was Sara Dylan.' The singer's wife continued to shout at the hapless garbologist, uttering threats of violence if he didn't leave the Dylan family alone. 'I urged the photographer to get a picture quick,' Weberman remembered. '"She's a nut", I said. But the reporter and photographer were halfway down the block.'

Guilt-stricken, Weberman tried to leave an apology with Dylan's secretary. 'That afternoon I was walking down Elizabeth Street,' he continued, 'with my head bowed down to my shoes trying to figure out where I was really at, when I heard a bicycle stop a few feet in back of me. I thought nothing of it. Then, seemingly out of nowhere, an arm clasped around my neck. I wrenched it loose, turned around, and saw it was Bob Dylan.' The singer began to punch the Dylanologist, but Weberman was too surprised to respond in kind. 'Instead I tried to calm Dylan down and block his punches,' he explained. 'But he was having too much fun to stop. He threw me down on the ground and he began to knock my head against the pavement. Finally some local freaks pulled Dylan off. Dylan ripped the DLF button from my shirt, got on his bicycle and rode off into the sunset.' Weberman caught his breath, then reached for an empty bottle in the street, and chased after his idol. 'I sneaked up behind him and was ready to let him have it with the bottle, Brooklyn style, but couldn't do it,' he admitted. 'Dylan was right. I shouldn't have messed with his junk.' As he walked shame-faced down the street, a tramp walked up to him and asked with the voice of experience: 'Did he get much money?' 'That was *Bob Dylan*,' Weberman said to the flabbergasted bum.

Within two or three weeks, John Lennon and Yoko Ono moved to an apartment on Bank Street in the West Village, about a quarter of a mile from Dylan's garbage. While Dylan maintained his distance, Lennon gathered the Chicago Conspiracy Trial defendants around himself as a radical cloak. A procession of movement superstars made their way to his new home – Jerry Rubin and David Peel, of course, although Lennon refused

Peel's entreaties to invite Weberman into the fold, as Lennon thought A.J. sounded insane; Bobby Seale and Huey Newton from the Panthers; Dave Dellinger and Rennie Davis from the anti-war brigade; and Irish film-maker John Reilly.

As one of the Global Village collective, Reilly had become a familiar figure in the New York underground. Global Village was founded in September 1969, and pioneered the use of video technology in documentaries. Reilly had worked with Vietnam Veterans Against the War and the Gay Activist Alliance, and established video workshops in prisons. But it was his links with the National Association for Irish Freedom that led him to the Lennons. This New York-based group connected the US Communist Party with the Irish Republican movement, helping to raise awareness of the struggle for a united Ireland, and to solicit cash from American sympathisers.

The Lennons contacted Reilly with a proposal for a film that would examine the situation in Northern Ireland from a Republican perspective. Their company, Joko Productions, would finance the documentary, while Reilly would enjoy creative control. Lennon realised the power of his celebrity for publicity purposes, so he wrote a song entitled 'The Luck of the Irish',[6] and invited Reilly to film him and Yoko as they performed it in their apartment. 'Luck of the Irish' was divided between political verses sung by Lennon, and more poetic (and sentimental) visions of Auld Ireland delivered by Ono. Unlike 'Attica State', the song did have a vague connection to Lennon's own life, if only as an Englishman of Irish descent. But its ideology was as one-sided as his analysis of the prison massacre, as he decried 'a thousand years of torture and hunger' in a land that was 'raped by the British brigands'. '[They] blame it all on the kids, the church and the IRA,' he declared of his fellow countrymen, 'while the bastards commit genocide.' Back in London, the counter-culture echoed his concern, marching en masse in a protest against internment. 'There was a spirit among everybody that I haven't felt since the Vietnam marches in 1968,' one participant insisted. 'It can't have pleased the pig Heath to hear 30,000 people chanting, "Victory to the IRA".'

Fired by his first experiments with political songwriting, John Lennon proceeded to add feminism to his list of causes. In early 1969, he and Yoko Ono had been interviewed by the British women's magazine *Nova*. The front cover highlighted a memorable quote from Ono: 'woman is the nigger of the world'. It was inspired, she explained later, by her early experience of sexism with Lennon and the other Beatles. Lennon was so struck by the phrase that he attempted to build a song around it. His initial efforts came to nothing, but after writing 'Attica State' and 'Luck of the Irish', he tried again. 'It was the first women's liberation song as far as I was concerned,' he recalled shortly before his death. Though its lyrics sounded like a collage of headlines from feminist magazines, the song had a sense of emotional involvement lacking in his other protest material. Lennon had personal experience to draw upon, and it showed. Several lines sounded like a confession of his attitude towards his first wife: 'We make her bear and raise our children, then we leave her flat for being a fat old mother hen. We tell her home is the only place she should be, then we say she's too unworldly to be our friend.'

Each new song – and there were several more in various states of creation, from the simple chorus 'Free the People' to another exploration of feminism, 'Man is Half of Woman' – was proudly unveiled to Lennon's radical friends. He also slipped friendly DJs advance tapes of 'Luck of the Irish' and 'Attica State', bypassing the usual bureaucracy of the music business. 'People always talk about my music as if it's some new craze I'm into,' he complained. 'Really it's been a natural evolution from "All You Need Is Love" to "Give Peace a Chance" to "Power to the People" to "Attica State". It's the same evolution that a lot of people have been through.' One of them was Jerry Rubin, who was increasingly excited by Lennon's transformation into a movement superstar. 'One day I come over to their apartment,' he recalled. 'They're on the bed doing an interview for French TV. They invite me to come on the bed and be interviewed with them. One of the reporters asks me, "Hey, Jerry, when's your next single coming out?", and John says, "Right, you should be a member of the band. If you're gonna work with us you should play music with us."' A rock'n'roll fanatic since his teens, Rubin revelled in his proximity to stardom. 'Immediately the three of us began fantasising,' he noted in his memoir. 'We would launch a musical, political caravan, tour the United States, raise money to feed the poor and free prisoners from jail. The shows would combine music and fun with political consciousness raising, and all the money would go to the people!'

Rubin was entrusted with making the fantasy come true. In return, he left another mark on Lennon's creative process. Lennon was familiar with the name of John Sinclair from the White Panther leader's frequent missives to underground magazines. Rubin added flesh to the bone, explaining Sinclair's revolutionary significance and the injustice of his imprisonment, and passing Lennon a copy of a poem by former Fugs member Ed Sanders, called 'The Entrapment of John Sinclair'. Lennon immediately began working on a song to highlight the issue. He had become a radical music machine: insert a cause, and a protest tune would spew out.

## SYMBOLS OF SINCERITY

> I don't want to die and leave a few sad songs and a hump in the ground as my only monument. I want to leave a world that is liberated from trash, pollution, racism, bigotry, parochialism, a thousand different brands of untruth and licentious usorious economics.
>
> (George Jackson, April 1970)

Early November 1971 found folk-singer Joan Baez on stage in New York. Besides her customary protest material, her performance included a new song. It was called 'To Bobby', and it was addressed to an old friend who had chosen to abandon the peace movement. The chorus was a call to the heart: 'Do you hear the voices in the night, Bobby? They're crying for you. See the children in the morning light, Bobby, they're dying.'

The song was addressed to her former lover, one-time protégé and long-time inspiration, Bob Dylan. When he was informed about the song, Dylan reacted dismissively. What Baez didn't know was that Dylan had just recorded his first overt protest song since 1963. In late October, a friend – perhaps Black Panthers sympathiser Howard Alk? – had given Dylan a copy of George Jackson's first collection of prison letters, *Soledad Brother*. Dylan devoured the book, and then apparently poured out his feelings in a five-verse ballad. The song, simply entitled 'George Jackson', was scheduled for rush-release as a single in late November.

'George Jackson' was greeted with fanfares by those who had lamented Dylan's 'betrayal' of the movement. 'Dylan's coming around,' A.J. Weberman crowed. 'I feel great. When I started harassing Dylan through the media, I didn't think my chances of affecting his head were too good. But the objective of the Dylan Liberation Front has been reached. I don't think Bob would have changed without the Dylan Liberation Front's pressure.' In the *Village Voice*, Robert Christgau expressed delight that 'Dylan responded with real human sympathy to a hideous assassination'.[7] Dylan biographer Anthony Scaduto was initially sceptical, wondering whether the song had been written to cool the flames of criticism, but concluded that it 'works, as music, and as an effective verbalisation of the anguish so many felt over the killing'. Even Mick Farren, who sounded as if he would rather have branded Dylan a hypocrite, conceded that 'I may be naive, but I really feel that Dylan has put out this single because Jackson's murder is something that, even in his seclusion, he cannot ignore'.

On the surface, 'George Jackson' was a heartfelt cry of pain from a man who always claimed to be motivated by injustice, rather than politics. It opened with the time-honoured blues formula, 'I woke up this morning', before describing how Dylan found 'tears in my bed' because 'they killed a man I really loved'. The depth of his compassion was undermined, however, by the fact that Dylan had only become aware of Jackson a matter of hours before writing the song. Subsequent verses veered from straight factual reportage ('they sent him off to prison for a seventy-dollar robbery') to creative interpretation ('Authorities, they hated him, because he was just too real'). In the next verse, the guards were 'frightened of his power', which rang true, and 'scared of his love', which didn't. All the love in Jackson's prose was reserved for his friends: for his enemies, he promised nothing but violent retribution.

But it was the final verse of Dylan's song that was the most enigmatic. It began with a statement that few in the movement would have questioned: 'Sometimes I think this whole world is one big prison yard'. But the following lines subverted the easy radicalism of the song: 'Some of us are prisoners, the rest of us are guards'. Absent was Jackson's belief that there was a moral difference between the oppressors and the oppressed; in Dylan's world, they were both 'us', both trapped in the prison yard. He had employed the same ambiguity nearly a decade earlier, in 'Only a Pawn in their Game', undercutting the moral simplicities of the folk protest movement. Now he was mythologising a hero of the movement while subverting the hero's philosophy.

Dylan's motives soon came under harsh scrutiny from the underground press. The managing director of Dylan's record label was asked whether the singer was contributing any of his profits to the Soledad Brothers' defence fund. 'There has been no discussion of this so far,' he replied. (There's an entirely believable story that a journalist asked the same question of a CBS publicity assistant, who replied: 'Are the Soledad Brothers on our label?') Meanwhile, George Jackson's mother let it be known that while she appreciated her son being the subject of Dylan's song, she would have been much happier if she had received some of the royalties, as she was living below the poverty line. 'Is George going to be turned into comfortable myth?' asked a writer on the British paper *Ink*. 'Betrayed through brave, liberal pop songs and posters?' Within weeks of his death, Jackson's face was indeed available as a poster, in a range that also included sundry nude models, Mick Jagger, Che Guevara and, of course, Bob Dylan. Young women were taking pictures of Angela Davis to their hairdresser and demanding an Afro of their own. Revolutionary symbols littered the counter-culture. But could they be translated into action?

John Lennon thought they could. 'We're just in the inception of revolution,' he told a journalist in the final weeks of 1971. With Jerry Rubin, he had sketched out an expansive plan for transporting the revolution around the world. The enterprise would be called the John & Yoko Mobile Political Plastic Ono Band Fun Show. The musical portion would be provided by the Lennons and several of their closest friends: Eric Clapton, Klaus Voormann, Jim Keltner and Nicky Hopkins, with Phil Spector as their director. Local 'street bands' would be added to the bill in each city; Lennon suggested the MC5 in Detroit, for example, or the Pink Fairies in London. Travelling with the Lennons would be a troupe of activists, ready to carry the spirit of revolution onto the streets and into the arenas.

In November 1971, the Republican Party of Richard Nixon announced that they would be staging their National Convention in San Diego during August 1972. Few observers doubted that Nixon would win the nomination, and then the presidency. But like Chicago in 1968, San Diego became a beacon of revolutionary optimism. Among those who were determined to follow the light was Allen Ginsberg. November 1971 found him in the studio with Bob Dylan, improvising hypnotic musical performances that teetered between chaotic rock and the avant-garde. Besides the magnificent 'September on Jessore Road', a travelogue of death and political despair inspired by the Vietnam War, and a playful song about gay liberation, they concocted a blues tune entitled 'Going to San Diego' which called for its listeners to 'sing a peaceful song' at the Convention, and for Nixon's party to 'announce the end of the war'.

The Ginsberg/Dylan sessions were financed by John Lennon, via his stake in the Beatles' company, Apple Records. When Lennon heard 'Going to San Diego' and 'George Jackson', he began to imagine a scenario in which he and Dylan would act as co-headliners on a tour that could determine the result of the 1972 election and send radical flames flickering across America. Jerry Rubin raised a potential problem. Lennon had been vocal in his support of A.J. Weberman's Rock Liberation Front: 'Join the RLF before it gets you,' he had told his former colleague Paul McCartney in a recent open letter. But Weberman was *persona non grata* with Dylan. In fact, Dylan had visited Rubin earlier in the year, pleading with him to stop the Dylanologist from persecuting him. Rubin had been forced to tell Dylan that he had no power over Weberman. But now a crisis was at hand. Why not, Rubin suggested, write an open letter to Weberman, demanding that he leave Dylan alone?

Rubin and Weberman were acquaintances rather than friends, but Rubin had been happy to lend his name to the RLF's campaigns. Lennon and Ono had never met Weberman, though they admired the spirit of his demonstrations. The other participant was David Peel, Weberman's chief supporter through the history of the DLF and RLF. Peel was about to record an album for Apple with the Lennons producing, so he was presumably unwilling to upset his superstar sponsor. 'Peel's an opportunist,' Weberman says curtly today. It was the street singer's name that appeared first on the statement issued in the name of the Rock Liberation Front at the end of November 1971. Although the RLF was essentially Weberman's plaything, the four radicals had taken it upon themselves to seize the name for their own devices, as if they were Huey Newton banishing a Maoist maverick from the Black Panthers. Before 'George Jackson', Dylan had been a 'pig' trading on fading glories. Now he was a saint of the movement, whose name might inspire the revolution. The open letter bears reprinting in full:

We ask A.J. Weberman to publicly apologise to Bob Dylan for leading a public campaign of lies and malicious slander against Dylan in the past year. It is about time someone came to Dylan's defence when A.J. published articles and went on radio calling Dylan a junkie – which he never was – attacked Dylan for 'deserting the movement' – when he was there before the movement and helped create it – and publicised Dylan's address and phone – exposing Bob and his wife and children to public embarrassment and abuse.

Dylan is more than a myth – he is a human being, like you and me. He has feelings and sensitivities like you and me. Who is there among us who has not had his consciousness shaped by the words and music of Bob Dylan? Yet who raised his or her voice or uttered a word to defend Dylan when A.J. Weberman began his personal campaign of slander against Dylan – in the true tradition of the sensationalistic press willing to print anything against someone famous – even demonstrations at Dylan's home – for god's sake – can't Dylan have some privacy! Can't he have some peace of mind in his own home to think and write and make music and be with his family?

Weberman took advantage of Dylan's fame. If Bob Dylan attacked A.J. Weberman, who would listen or publish it? If A.J. Weberman has some 'inside gossip' or 'the real truth' about Bob Dylan, everyone is all ears because everyone wants to talk about Bob Dylan. Stories spread from person to person in an ever-widening circle of exaggeration and bullshit. No one cares to find out the truth about Bob Dylan, the person. They are too busy amusing themselves by telling outlandish stories about Bob Dylan – the myth – whom they have never met.

Weberman tried to make a name for himself by attacking Dylan and proclaiming himself a Dylanologist or something like that. No one else named Weberman an expert on Dylan. Weberman calls himself an expert, and all of a sudden the press is all over him trying to get information or gossip about Dylan. Now whenever someone writes about Bob Dylan, they also interview A.J. because he is a self-proclaimed authority on Dylan's music. A.J. claims everything Dylan writes is either about Weberman or heroin. What bullshit!

'Weberman is to Dylan as Manson is to the Beatles – and Weberman uses what he interprets [in] Dylan's music to try and kill Dylan and build his own fame. Now A.J. Weberman takes credit for Dylan's 'George Jackson' song. More egocentric bullshit. Dylan wrote it in spite of Weberman and in spite of 'the movement'. Dylan wrote it because he felt it.

A.J. Weberman's campaign – and the movement's complicity with it – is in the current fad of everyone in the revolution attacking each other and spreading false rumours about each other. It's time we defended and loved each other – and saved our anger for the true enemy, whose ignorance and greed destroys our planet.

The Rock Liberation Front: David Peel, Jerry Rubin, Yoko Ono, John Lennon.

The hypocrisy and contradictions in this statement were manifold: Lennon had proudly worn one of Weberman's 'Free Bob Dylan!' badges as a statement of support for the Dylan Liberation Front; just because Dylan was 'there before the movement' didn't mean that he couldn't have 'deserted' it since; Lennon had been a keen supporter of the underground newspapers responsible for publicising Weberman's 'sensationalistic' stories; and Weberman had been one of the first to welcome Dylan's apparent 'return' to the movement with 'George Jackson'.

In the spirit of Stalin's Russia, Lennon and his friends persuaded Weberman to confess to his sins and apologise to Dylan and to the movement. The same underground newspapers that ran the open letter from the 'RLF' also printed Weberman's cowed response:

Dear People,
    Please accept my apologies for past untrue statements and also the harassment of Bob Dylan and his family. From now on I'll leave them alone. If any nasty articles come out about him, I'm sorry. I wrote them long ago and I'm doing my best to have them killed.
    Sincerely,
    A.J. Weberman, Minister of Defence, Rock Liberation Front.

It was a public humiliation for Weberman, delivered by one of the few artists he considered worthy of his 'interpretation'. 'I didn't write that apology,' he claimed later. 'John Lennon wrote it and I signed it, hoping for the best. I guess one of the reasons I did it was cos of the "George Jackson" single – I thought that Dylan might really be getting back into it – but as it turned out Dylan kept all the bread from that single and just did it to get me off his back.' Weberman described the RLF letter about him as 'bullshit'. 'Jerry Rubin encouraged me to attack Dylan,' he recalled. 'He came over to my pad and told me that the DLF was right on, and that Dylan was definitely a pig – and I looked up to him at the time. David Peel played at the [Dylan] birthday party, supplied the sound equipment, etc., and John Lennon wore a DLF badge on the front cover of the *New York Post*, said Dylan took junk in a *Rolling Stone* interview[8] and wrote "I Don't Believe in Zimmerman". Not a word of this was mentioned in their attack on me. It was like entrapment – they egged me on, gave me the equipment, then busted me for it.'

As far as Jerry Rubin was concerned, Weberman was expendable, his contribution to the movement outweighed by the potential power of Dylan's support. 'I thought that when Dylan saw he was free of A.J., he'd be so appreciative that he would agree to tour the country with John and Yoko,' Rubin explained later, 'raising money for political causes and rallying people to go to San Diego. We'd make musical history as well as political history. The whole thing was going to revive the 1960s. That was my plan.' It was a scheme that soon filtered into the ears of the FBI, who were monitoring the activities of any organisation planning to campaign against Nixon's re-election. The New York branch of the recently formed People's Coalition for Peace and Justice (PCPJ) was watched with keen interest by FBI agents and informers. One of the latter told the authorities about the cunning plan being hatched by the underground: 'PCPJ is presently planning to hold a peace concert at an unknown location in New Hampshire during the New Hampshire Presidential Primary. Plans presently are to have John Lennon and Bob Dylan take part in the concert. A peace concert has also been planned for the Boston area after the New Hampshire concert.'

There was one flaw in the plan: Bob Dylan had no intention of taking part. 'Lennon was trying to get Dylan into the tour,' remembered Yippie activist Stew Albert. 'We couldn't ever get a commitment from Dylan. But Lennon said he was sure that if the tour started getting big headlines, Dylan would jump into it.' What Dylan needed, Lennon reckoned, was to smell the heady scent of revolution coming out of the East Village. So he invited Dylan down to the studio where he was producing David Peel's album, *The Pope Smokes Dope*. In honour of the occasion, Peel unveiled a new song en-titled 'The Ballad of Bob Dylan'. It was a tribute to Dylan as an icon of the protest movement: 'Who is coming back again, fighting with his songs . . . Who will help us with the answers when he sings his songs, Who is controversial when he sings against the wrong? Who is not afraid?' The solu-tion to each question was, as Peel sang, 'Bob Dylan, Robert Zimmerman'. Rather than responding to the call to arms, Dylan told Peel that he didn't want him to use his real name, and then flounced out of the session between two bodyguards from the Jewish Defense League. 'But the song worked,' Peel contends today. 'It was supposed to get him feeling vulnerable, get him back in touch with the people. And it did. It made him blink.'

Not for the first time, Allen Ginsberg was deputed to convince Dylan to take the plunge. Once again, Dylan politely declined. After guesting at a New Year's Eve concert by the Band, the singer slipped out of New York to spend the winter at a retreat in Arizona, far away from radicals and rock stars. His escape marked the end of any fantasy that he might participate in a rock'n'revolution campaign against President Nixon.

John Lennon showed no signs of sharing Dylan's fear of over-exposure, as he continued to amass causes and commitments at a feverish pace. He supervised David Peel & the Lower East Side as they cut street anthems such as 'Everybody's Smoking Marijuana', 'The Hippies from New York City' and 'I'm Gonna Start Another Riot'. Lennon was also preparing material for an album of his own. At the start of December 1971, he wrote 'John Sinclair', a bluesy steel-guitar stomp that compressed the story of the White Panther/Rainbow People's Party leader's imprisonment into three short verses. He played the song to Jerry Rubin, who phoned Sinclair's wife Leni with the news. She contacted Yoko Ono, and after a brief conversation the Lennons were added to the bill of an ambitious benefit concert set for the 15,000-seat Crisler Arena in Ann Arbor the following week.

## FREE JOHN NOW!

The Michigan justice system was slowly coming to terms with its change of sentencing policy for cases of marijuana possession. Sinclair's lawyers were convinced that he would soon be freed, but the Michigan State Supreme Court was determined to delay their decision as long as they legally could. Although both sides knew the outcome was inevitable, the court refused to allow Sinclair to be released on bail while the law worked its laborious way. 'The authorities don't want to see John back on the streets,' one observer noted, 'because they are afraid of the brilliant organising he has done in the alternate culture of Detroit.'

The injustice suffered by Sinclair was universally acknowledged, but that wouldn't persuade the Michigan public to attend a concert at which the star attractions were David Peel, the White Panthers' rock band the Up, local heroes SKT, jazz activists Archie Shepp and Roswell Rudd, and cult rock attractions the Joy of Cooking and Commander Cody & His Lost Planet Airmen. There were speakers, too – Bobby Seale, Allen Ginsberg, Jerry Rubin, Ed Sanders, Rennie Davis, Leni Sinclair – but most of them had appeared at a hundred rallies and demonstrations in recent years.

Then Leni Sinclair announced that the Lennons would be taking part, and the remaining tickets sold in a matter of hours. John and Yoko asked Phil Ochs to attend, and Stevie Wonder was also persuaded to show up. Many spectators expected a superstar jam session in the tradition of George Harrison's Bangladesh benefits. To prepare for the event, the White Panthers issued a fundraising single which coupled the Up's protest tune, 'Free John Now', with a chant by Allen Ginsberg, 'Prayer for John Sinclair'. The Lennons agreed to pay for the entire concert to be filmed, with the intention of issuing a movie via their own production company, all earnings from which would fund Sinclair's street politics.

On 8 December 1971, two days before the concert, the Michigan State Legislature confirmed that marijuana possession would henceforth count as a misdemeanour, not a crime. The maximum sentence would be one year, except in cases where it was obvious that the defendant was holding the drug for his or her own use, in which case a 90-day maximum would follow. Leni Sinclair greeted the news as a triumph for the White Panthers. 'We can't help but take some credit for ourselves, because we started working for the lessening of marijuana penalties back in 1966,' she told reporters. 'It's not a perfect bill, by any means, but it is a great step forward.' There was a glaring omission in the new law, however: it did not apply retrospectively. The State Legislature was therefore under no obligation to free its existing prisoners, such as Sinclair. As the Freedom Rally began early in the evening of 10 December, his fate was still hanging in the wind.

Allen Ginsberg opened proceedings with a newly revised version of his 'Prayer for John Sinclair'. 'To Ann Arbor for the first time,' he intoned, 'comes Yoko Ono and John Lennon, who prays for revolution himself, every time he turns into a human elf, here to set John Sinclair free, to deliver Ann Arbor a political eternity.' What ensued was an eternity, indeed, which stretched deep into the early hours. The Up performed rock'n'roll standards such as Elvis Presley's 'Jailhouse Rock' and Chuck Berry's 'Nadine', rewritten by John Sinclair with new political lyrics. ('Nadine' became 'Bernardine, Sister is that You?', in honour of the underground Weatherwoman, Ms Dohrn.) Phil Ochs won a standing ovation by transforming his early 1960s protest tune 'Here's to the State of Mississippi' into 'Here's to the State of Richard Nixon'. 'Here's to the land you've torn out the heart of,' the chorus ran, 'Richard Nixon, find yourself another country to be part of.' Stevie Wonder delivered a set of dynamic funk and soul, which garnered the most prolonged applause of the night. 'Stevie was really upset about this kind of injustice,' his friend Gypsie Jones explained afterwards. 'He felt that it was ridiculously crazy to give Sinclair that much time for just one marijuana cigarette. He said it was such an irrelevant thing to do – especially when on the other hand someone who killed thousands of people in Vietnam is set free. Stevie hates injustice.'

A phone hook-up to Jackson State Prison allowed the audience to hear

John Sinclair, his voice breaking with emotion as he spoke to his wife. Jerry Rubin described the evening as 'the first act of the Rock Liberation Front', neatly erasing A.J. Weberman's earlier demonstrations from history. His lengthy speech previewed the Lennons' set, promising songs about Sinclair, the IRA and Attica State. Every time the word 'revolution' was spoken, the crowd howled their approval. Rubin wasn't only concerned with the cause of the day: for him, the revolution stretched out ahead towards California. 'A lot of events like this one will take place between now and San Diego,' he announced. 'We want a million of you to turn up at the Republican National Convention to humiliate and defeat Richard Nixon!' Another tumultuous roar surged from the audience.

Four hours later, when the Lennons had still not appeared on stage, the atmosphere was altogether less triumphal. There was a full hour's delay between the end of Stevie Wonder's set and the anticipated arrival of the headliners. When the lights eventually dimmed, the audience was outraged to discover that the next act was not John Lennon, but David Peel. His pot-smoking anthem, 'Have a Marijuana', might have been hand-rolled for the occasion, but the crowd failed to appreciate the significance, preferring to boo Peel and hurl insults at his band. But Peel wasn't a veteran of Washington State Park for nothing, and relished the confrontation. 'They hated us,' he says today with pride. 'People couldn't stand me. I said, "Look, I'm not here to entertain you, I'm here to bring you a message. If you want entertainment, watch TV!" I made sure I took my time to get my message across.'

Eventually Peel gave the audience what they wanted, and left the stage. A few seconds later, to the audience's horror, he was back – this time accompanied by John Lennon, Yoko Ono, Jerry Rubin and a guitarist. Rubin proudly stood behind some hand drums, as Lennon counted the impromptu band in. What followed was a set that teetered between chaos and competence. 'Attica State' was ruined by Ono's inability to stay in tempo. 'Luck of the Irish' was only mildly more dignified. Then Ono sang her feminist rallying-cry, 'Sisters O Sisters', to lukewarm response. Finally, Lennon spoke to the crowd. 'We came here not only to help John and to spotlight what's going on,' he announced, 'but also to show and say to all of you that apathy isn't it, and that we can still do something. OK, so flower power didn't work. So what? We start again.' He led the band through a rousing rendition of the song he'd written for John Sinclair, then signalled his farewell to the exhausted, slightly disappointed audience. There had been no superstar jam after all, unless Jerry Rubin and David Peel counted, and for most people they didn't. There was no Beatles reunion; not even some rock'n'roll to reward the crowd for their endurance. It was as if Lennon was warning them that if there was going to be a revolution, everything would be up for grabs, even their own expectations of how a superstar should perform.

A little over forty-eight hours after Lennon left the stage, with $26,000 having been added to the coffers of the Defence Committee, the Michigan Supreme Court overruled its own judgement that John Sinclair should not be granted bail. He heard the decision via a radio in his cell, the media having been notified before his lawyers. After twenty-eight months, Sinclair was free. 'The seven justices drafted their own escape route,' the Liberation News Service declared. 'They didn't want to see the size of the next revolution-and-rock rally.' Instead, they resigned themselves to seeing the movement greet Sinclair's freedom as a stunning victory over the forces of oppression. In particular, the Lennons were heralded as the heroes of the hour. 'They took this two-year effort over the top,' Sinclair recalled, 'playing a huge role in getting me out of prison.'

Later that week, Lennon, Ono, Peel and Rubin reprised their triumph on network television, via an appearance on *The David Frost Show*. Some activists watched cynically as Jerry Rubin acted out the role of rock star on national TV. Was this all that his revolution amounted to – the fulfilment of a teenage fantasy? The next night, the Lennons took to the stage of the legendary Harlem R&B venue, the Apollo Theater, to raise money for the families bereaved in the Attica State massacre. Roused from his retirement by the news about John Sinclair, Abbie Hoffman had flown back to New York, and one night before Christmas, he and Rubin visited the Lennons at their Bank Street apartment. The four of them took a knife, and each made a small incision in their thumbs, letting their blood trickle onto the cover of *Be Here Now*, a spiritual guide by the hippie guru Ram Dass. As their trails of blood mingled, American, English, Japanese all coagulating into one, they swore an oath of allegiance. As Lennon had promised, they were ready to start again. The dawn of revolution had come at last.

# CHAPTER 7: 1972

## A POLITICAL WOODSTOCK

> This year is the year for everyone to come back and start again, to come together again, in new ways, to build our culture without male chauvinism, bad drugs and crazy freakouts. We should try to build our culture once more, only this time with more self-awareness and self-control. We need more public events, even a huge political Woodstock at the Republican National Convention next August in San Diego. 1-2-3-4, many more Ann Arbors! And it is only the beginning . . .
>
> (Jerry Rubin, January 1972)

Emboldened by the release of John Sinclair, the movement saw 1972 as a new dawn. In fact, it was the final hurrah – but nobody had told John Lennon and A.J. Weberman, who soon discovered that they were the last men standing on the revolutionary left. Briefly, however, the future seemed to burn red with the heat of rebellion. It was as if the world had been swept back four years, to the Yippies' plans for a revolution in Chicago, an end to the war, the latent power of the counter-culture focused on overthrowing repression and installing a utopian regime dedicated to every imaginable form of liberation. Even the backdrop was similar, as the Nixon administration celebrated Christmas by intensifying its bombing of North Vietnam. Ahead lay the promise of Lennon and Jerry Rubin's radical circus, shepherding the movement towards a climactic show of force in San Diego.

White House staff grew increasingly paranoid about the prospect that the planned coronation of the incumbent President might mutate into a second Chicago. 'Anti-war demonstrators would love to destroy our Convention,'

Nixon's Chief of Staff, Bob Haldeman, told counsel John Dean, 'but we're not going to let it happen.' He deputed Dean to investigate the movement's plans for interrupting the convention. A subscription to the underground press was all that he needed.

Everything seemed to coalesce around the figure of John Lennon. Jerry Rubin noted in January 1972: 'For the past five months in New York City people have been feeling that the worst is over and that people are creating again and coming together again and something new is in the air. Somehow the arrival of John and Yoko in New York has had a mystical and practical effect that is bringing people together again.' Although he already knew that Bob Dylan would not be joining the cavalry charge, Rubin wasn't prepared to abandon such a potent icon. Dylan, he insisted, had 'signalled an omen of the return to activism when he appeared unannounced at the Bangladesh concert in Madison Square Garden. It's great,' he concluded, 'everyone is almost going back to the early 1960s and starting out all over again.'

As Lennon recalled cynically in the late 1970s, 'It was fun meeting all the famous underground heroes (no heroines): Bobby Seale and his merry men; Huey Newton in his very expensive-looking military clothes; Rennie Davis and his "You pay for it and I'll organise it"; John Sinclair and his faithful Ann Arbor Brigade; and dear old Allen Ginsberg, who if he wasn't lying on the floor "ohming", was embarrassing the fuck out of everyone he could corner by chanting something he called poetry very loudly in their ears (and out the other).' He too realised that he had occupied a totemic position in the movement: 'It seemed that without John and Yoko's drawing power, there wasn't going to be a revolution. The Left and Right were both labouring under that illusion.'

Disavowing his political activities entirely by the end of his life, Lennon claimed that he and Yoko Ono had always 'thought the whole idea stunk, and was not only dangerous but stupid'. Ono herself insists that 'I made John and myself isolated from the rest, as our friends were trying to lash out, wanting to bomb the White House, something violent like that. I insisted that we should keep doing things in a peaceful way, because violence breeds violence.' But while Ono may have retained her peacenik sensibility throughout, Lennon seemed besotted by his new comrades. When the couple were offered the opportunity to co-host Mike Douglas's afternoon TV talk show, he rattled with excitement as he prepared a fantasy guest list. Amongst the radical faces he planned to fling in the faces of middle America were

Seale and Newton, Rubin and Hoffman, the Sinclairs, Irish republican socialist MP Bernadette Devlin, the mothers of the students shot at Kent State, the sisters of fugitive Weatherwoman Bernardine Dohrn and jailed activist Angela Davis, and no doubt David Peel & the Lower East Side for musical diversion. The producers eventually whittled down the list, but when the programmes were filmed in mid-January, they did offer Seale and Rubin the chance to preach to a 'straight' audience. 'None of them knew how to talk to the people,' Lennon complained later, 'never mind lead them!' Rubin was also allowed to play percussion when Lennon jammed with one of his musical idols, Chuck Berry. Rubin described this as 'the culmination of every musical fantasy I've ever had', reinforcing the doubts of those who wondered whether the Yippie's affection for Lennon had more to do with hero-worship than revolutionary passion.

A week before the Mike Douglas shows, the Lennons played host to a series of summit meetings in Bank Street. Present were John and Leni Sinclair, David Peel, Allen Ginsberg, Ed Sanders, Jerry Rubin, and his fellow Yippie Stew Albert. The Sinclairs were beginning to doubt Lennon's commitment to the anti-Nixon tour, and wanted to hear it from John and Yoko themselves. After the first of their meetings, Sinclair declared: 'We're serious about our program. We're serious about John and Yoko. Now I'm ready to build a motherfucker socialist music empire in this country, where the music and the people are co-terminal, where they have the same beginning and the same end.' The Lennons admitted that if Rubin hadn't pulled them into the Sinclair Freedom Rally, they might never have taken the plunge of going out on the road. 'Now we have the taste of playing again,' Lennon told Sinclair, 'and we can't wait to do more. We want to go around from town to town doing a concert every other night for a month, at least. It will be the regular scene, without the capitalism. We'll pay for the halls, and the people will pay to get in, but we'll leave our share of the money in the town where it can do most good.' Sinclair asked him whether he was aware how much opposition he was about to arouse. Lennon replied that his manager, Allen Klein, would be able to handle any problems, but Sinclair was clearly concerned that Klein might be just the kind of capitalist businessman they were trying to overthrow. In the end, they agreed to rely on optimism. 'This is going to be a motherfucker to organise,' Sinclair conceded, 'but if it works we'll be developing strong relationships with youth cadres all over America.' Rubin butted in excitedly: 'It'll work. It's gonna *happen*.'

Yet fault lines were already developing within the new alliance. Freshly released from prison, Sinclair wanted action, not rhetoric, and he was concerned that his prime allies, Rubin and Lennon, were too enchanted with each other to make any political progress. Meanwhile, Lennon was coming under gentle pressure from Klein, who was concerned that his client might be damaging his commercial potential. The singer was also struggling with Sinclair's urge to take charge of the campaign. In retrospect, Lennon considered that 'the biggest mistake Yoko and I made in that period was allowing ourselves to become influenced by the male-macho "serious revolutionaries", and their insane ideas about killing people to save them from capitalism and/or communism.'

Yet their enthusiasm convinced the American government that something significant was happening. The bizarre behaviour of the Nixon administration over the next year can only be explained by a culture of paranoia within the White House. After years of public derision, Nixon had grown accustomed to feeling surrounded by enemies. Meanwhile, his government had witnessed an outbreak of urban terrorism unprecedented in recent American history, and four years of global protests about its foreign policy. It seemed oblivious to the fact that its opponents were in disarray – that the Democratic Party was fatally split over its foreign policy, and that the movement had become almost totally detached from the masses it claimed to represent. In retrospect, it's clear that Lennon, Rubin, Sinclair and the rest could have been allowed to organise and plot to their heart's content, without ever threatening Nixon's re-election campaign. But the White House and the FBI preferred to see conspiracy on a grand scale, and boosted each other's suspicions on a daily basis.

So Lennon was added to the list of dangerous radicals who required constant surveillance by FBI agents. As a British citizen with a conviction for drug possession, he was vulnerable to the whims of the US Immigration Service, who had allowed him into the country on a series of temporary visas. Government departments began to collaborate on a plan to smother the ex-Beatle's radical energy. If Lennon were deported, the FBI believed, the plot against the Republican Convention would dissolve. In later years, Lennon blamed Jerry Rubin for exaggerating the extent of their proposals on TV. But Lennon was just as culpable, and wielded much more power as a celebrity. Naive enthusiasm and official paranoia were set on a collision course, which was bound to end in the immigration courts. Ironically, in another classic piece of White House miscalculation, the struggle to throw

Lennon out of the country generated more publicity for his political sympathies than he could have mustered himself, and added to the impression that the Nixon administration was losing its senses.

Some hint of the FBI's thoroughness is provided by the documents released under the Freedom of Information Act, after years of lobbying by academic Jon Wiener. For example, an agent in the New York office noted that Jerry Rubin, described as 'Extremist' and 'Key Activist', had appeared at a press conference on 11 January 1972. Rubin, the agent pointed out, had cut his hair since the photographs in the Bureau's files had been taken. In case his boss was in any doubt, he scrawled the message, 'ALL EXTREMISTS SHOULD BE CONSIDERED DANGEROUS' across the foot of his memo.

That belief was shared by many in the Nixon White House. On 27 January, the Attorney General, John Mitchell, met Nixon's counsel, John Dean, and Gordon Liddy, the counsel for the newly formed Committee to Re-Elect the President (CREEP). Liddy unveiled a sheaf of proposed undercover operations, collectively known as Gemstone, to counter opposition to Nixon. Several of them anticipated the Watergate scandal, as Liddy suggested illegal surveillance of Democratic presidential contenders, infiltration of the Democratic Party's campaigns, and the payment of agents provocateurs to disrupt their rallies and meetings. But the most outlandish plan, which Liddy dubbed Operation Diamond, was aimed at safeguarding the Republican National Convention. To prevent 500,000 protestors arriving in San Diego, among them armed urban guerrillas, Liddy said that the White House should sanction the detention of prominent anti-Nixon campaigners. These dissidents could be flown to Mexico, where they could be interned until Nixon's re-election had been secured. Mitchell was mildly sceptical that such a plan was feasible, and refused to allocate any CREEP money to Operation Diamond. But nobody at the meeting appears to have been shocked by the illegality of Liddy's idea.

On the evidence that was being furnished to the FBI in early 1972, John Lennon and Jerry Rubin would undoubtedly have featured on Liddy's list of targets. The Bureau's undercover informers noted that Yippie veteran Stew Albert and Chicago trial defendant Rennie Davis had founded a group called the Allamuchy Tribe. From a New Jersey farmhouse, they were planning a series of demonstrations that would lead up to the San Diego convention. The FBI noted that Lennon had supplied a cheque for $75,000 to fund Albert and Davis's work. 'The alleged purpose of the group', one informant explained, 'would be to spearhead tours throughout the major states holding primary elections in 1972, presenting New Left movement messages, and attempting to encourage large numbers of individuals to demonstrate at the Republican National Convention in San Diego.'

The Allamuchy Tribe never existed as such; it was an informal name for the activists, perhaps invented by an FBI informer. But by late January, the Tribe leaders had moved to Greenwich Village, where they used Lennon's money to rent a warehouse space on Hudson Street, close to the Lennons' Bank Street apartment. There they planned to operate the Election Year Strategy Information Center, or EYSIC. But the warehouse was derelict, and so EYSIC was relocated to the office occupied by the Global Village film company, which was working on Lennon's Irish documentary. The FBI now believed that Lennon was in close collaboration with 'May Day', the activists behind the 1971 anti-war demonstrations. There is no evidence to suggest that the ex-Beatle was involved in the minutiae of political planning. But the likes of Rubin, Davis and Albert had such wide contacts that they could be described in a dozen threatening ways, to make it sound as if a vast conspiracy of dissidents was at work.

Four days after he had heard Gordon Liddy's plans for dealing with dissidents, John Dean sent his Chief of Staff, Bob Haldeman, a lengthy memo detailing 'Potential Disruption at the Republican National Convention'. He reeled off a list of opposition groups planning action in San Diego: the People's Coalition for Peace & Justice, the Yippies, the Worker-Student Alliance of SDS, the New American Movement and the San Diego Convention Coalition. Jerry Rubin and other Chicago veterans were mentioned as possible troublemakers. But Dean's tally did not include John Lennon, EYSIC or the Allamuchy Tribe.

In January 1972, Lennon and Rubin decided that the Rock Liberation Front required a less specific name if it was to campaign against the Nixon presidency. Lennon suggested that the group should call itself 'Yes'. The CIA told FBI boss J. Edgar Hoover that Yes – an acronym for 'Youth Election Strategy', supposedly – was 'an international news service which will include the use of video tapes, films and special articles'. That was actually a description of the work being carried out, quite legally, by Global Village. 'Also to be included in the project,' the CIA continued, 'will be a caravan of entertainers, which will follow US election primaries and raise funds for local radical groups along the way.'

The CIA memo also pinpointed the issue that would soon supplant Nixon's re-election as the key distraction in Lennon's life. 'Project organisers are seeking to avoid publicity at present,' it stated, 'in order not to jeopardise the stay of John Lennon, who is in the United States on a one-month visa.' The memo was inaccurate: Lennon had actually been granted a six-month visa to remain in the USA back in August. But it was due to expire on 29 February.

Lennon's immigration status had first been raised with the White House on 4 February, when Strom Thurmond, the Republican Senator for South Carolina, wrote to presidential assistant William Timmons. Yet another of the multifarious government bodies who were monitoring its opponents had composed a page-long summary of the threat posed by Lennon to the administration. In his covering note, Thurmond added: 'This appears to me to be an important matter, and I think it would be well for it to be considered at the highest level. As I can see, many headaches might be avoided if appropriate action be taken in time.'

The White House promptly referred the matter to the Immigration and Naturalisation Service (INS). They reported that Lennon's lawyers had recently applied for the singer to be given an extended visa, as he wished to become a US citizen. After consulting with the White House, the INS took the executive decision to turn down Lennon's request, and give him notice to quit the country. Unfortunately, there was a bureaucratic glitch, and his existing visa was renewed on 1 March. Only on 6 March was the mistake realised, and his lawyers were then informed that he must leave the USA by 15 March. The lines had been drawn for an enervating battle that would last for more than three years.

Through February and March, the FBI's informants continued to report on Lennon's activities and connections. 'Project Yes' seemed to widen in scope with each bulletin. Lennon, Rubin and friends were now treated as the hub of the People's Coalition for Peace and Justice, which was described by the FBI as involving 'over 100 organisations which are using massive civil disobedience to combat racism, poverty, repression and war'. Lennon would supposedly be performing several concerts before the San Diego convention, 'backed up by lesser rock group talents'. At these, the FBI insisted, the singer would 'urge the audience to (a) register to vote; (b) work for the legalisation of marijuana; and (c) get to San Diego for the GOP [Republican Party] Convention'. None of these activities, it should be noted, contravened American law.

As surveillance on Lennon and his friends was stepped up, however, so an element of conflict became evident. One FBI informant noted that Lennon and Ono 'seem uninterested' and 'are passé' about US politics. Another noted that Lennon, Rubin, Davis and Albert were all 'heavy users of narcotics', but that Rubin and Davis had been quarrelling with Lennon about 'his excessive use of narcotics'. One report concluded that 'John Lennon appears to be radically orientated, however he does not give the impression he is a true revolutionist since he is constantly under the influence of narcotics'.

The FBI didn't quantify these statements, making it uncertain whether Lennon was consuming copious amounts of marijuana, or something more insidious. But in late January, Lennon and Ono did travel to the US Virgin Islands 'for their health'. Later that year, they made a similar trip to California so that Lennon could be weaned off his addiction to methadone. As Lennon had been using heroin sporadically since late 1968, it is entirely possible that he had become hooked on the drug – or its substitute, methadone – and that the problem was arousing anxiety amongst his radical comrades. If Lennon had been arrested in possession of illegal drugs, he could have been deported immediately, circumventing the lengthy immigration appeals process. Under the circumstances, it seems strange that the White House was not able to secure an arrest – a minor example, perhaps, of the systematic incompetence that would allow the Watergate scandal to mutate over the next two years.

By mid-March 1972, Lennon's importance as a catalyst for disruption of the San Diego convention – let alone a revolutionary assault on the US government – seemed to have subsided. One FBI agent described the EYSIC organisation as 'dying on the vine'. Another source noted that 'many former leaders of the PCPJ and YIP have been discredited in the eyes of "rank and file" activists of these organisations as they feel that former leaders such as JERRY RUBIN have "become self-made superstars" and are only interested in obtaining fame and publicity for themselves'. Instead, the responsibility for organising the San Diego protests had fallen upon John Sinclair – and John Lennon, who the FBI had already decided was distracted by other matters.

## A JAUNDICED EYE

At the start of the year, poet and Fugs member Tuli Kupferberg had cast a jaundiced eye over the movement and its future. Everywhere he looked, he saw stasis and decay – underground papers going bust or losing their nerve, kids abandoning dope and losing themselves in booze, the anti-war movement sapped by Nixon's apparent moves towards peace, mysticism replacing activism as the defining impulse of the counter-culture. 'There is a quietness around the movement,' he said. 'Is it the quiet after the storm or before the storm? No one knows.' But he predicted that President Nixon would win the 1972 election. 'He will even end the war if that is necessary (end it for Americans, anyway),' he said perceptively. He dismissed the revival of the Yippies' four-year-old Chicago scenario ('somehow one cannot get it up for that any more'), but concluded that there was no other alternative, as 'The Democrats are in disarray and no viable third party seems to be around'.

From the belly of the beast, the Weather Underground had surfaced every few months during 1971 to set off a bomb, without arousing any great outrage or applause. The Black Panther Party had exhausted itself in its prolonged legal battles. Huey Newton and Bobby Seale were free, at last, but Newton's increasingly erratic, cocaine-fuelled behaviour was making political activity almost impossible to co-ordinate. Meanwhile, Eldridge Cleaver continued to issue ultra-militant statements from Algeria, but he was struggling to retain control of his International Section, and refugees from his camp complained that he was using dictatorial tactics to hold on to his power. Over just a few months, the membership of the Panthers in the USA had virtually dissolved; one estimate suggested that there were fewer than 200 activists by spring 1972.

In Oakland, the Panthers were still strong enough to stage a Black Community Survival Conference in March 1972. Bobby Seale made his usual fiery impact as a speaker, while the Persuasions – an a cappella group from New York who were heavily involved in community affairs – also appeared. But this was a rare moment of local coherence for the Panthers. Nationally, their financial situation had grown so parlous that Huey Newton decided to set up business as a concert promoter, under the name of Oakland & The World Entertainment, convinced that his reputation alone would make him a force to be reckoned with. His first concert was at the Oakland Auditorium, scene of past Panthers rallies. His Panthers comrade Elaine Brown was booked as the opening act, to preview the material that she was recording for her second album. Topping the bill were Ike & Tina Turner.

Like many black R&B performers who had been systematically cheated,

Ike Turner's attitude to promoters ranged from suspicious to contemptuous. When the Panthers presented him with a cheque to cover the final instalment of their fee, he announced that unless he was paid in cash, there would be no show. Bobby Seale attempted to use his charisma to calm the situation, but Turner slammed the dressing-room door in his face. Then Newton entered the fray, with an entourage of Panther bodyguards. 'Motherfucker,' he shouted at Turner, 'you have one minute to start the show. If you're not on stage in one minute, we're going to break up all your instruments and kick your motherfucking ass. Is that clear?' Ike & Tina duly took the stage. But after their first song, Ike told the audience that he had been threatened by the Panthers, had still not been paid in full, and was not prepared to play any more. As the audience began to boo, a fistfight broke out between the Turners' musicians and the Panthers' security staff. Ike Turner was knocked unconscious, Tina Turner fled for safety in tears, and even Elaine Brown punched out a member of the Turners' female vocal trio, the Ikettes. The Turners filed official complaints with the police, claiming assault by Newton and Brown, but no charges were ever pursued. The Ike & Tina debacle marked the end of Newton's ambitions as a promoter, and the Black Panther Party slipped further into financial chaos and tactical confusion.

It was now much easier to rouse public sympathy for an individual case than a revolutionary party. While the Panthers' influence on black America slowly ebbed away, Angela Davis – due for trial on her murder charges in spring 1972 – had become a cause célèbre around the globe. Celebrities from across the show business spectrum offered their services in her defence, from Aretha Franklin to Sammy Davis Jr – who, a White House memo noted in March 1972, had raised some $38,000 towards her legal costs with a benefit concert in Los Angeles. It was not just Angela Davis' political stance and protestation of innocence that attracted support: her trademark Afro hair had become a symbol of black pride in the media, all the more effective for being attached to a photogenic young woman. The Hungarian rock group Locomotive GT had already dedicated an album to Davis; now John Lennon and Mick Jagger added their names to the cause.

'Sweet Black Angel', recorded early in 1972 by the Rolling Stones, was a landmark in itself: the band's first recognisable protest song. But Jagger's opening lines revealed that it was Davis the icon whom he admired, not the Communist or black power activist: 'Got a sweet black angel, got a pin-up girl. Got a sweet black angel, up upon my wall'. Jagger was notorious for affecting a Southern US accent; now he attempted to mimic the cadences of a black slave from a Hollywood drama, patronising Davis and her race with every line: 'Now de judge he's gonna judge her, for all dat he's worth, Well de gal in danger, de gal in chains...' His final line compounded the stereotypes, as he begged his listeners to 'free de sweet black slave'.

'Angela', recorded by Lennon and Ono in March 1972, was equally misguided. If their song about Attica State had relied on threadbare radical rhetoric, their paean to Ms Davis illustrated the perils of placing political necessity before creative inspiration. No amount of radical passion could make poetry out of lines such as 'Sister, our love and hopes forever keep on moving oh so slowly in the world', or 'Sister, there's a million different races but we all share the same future in the world'. And for banality and irrelevance, there was little in Lennon's catalogue to match this: 'They gave you coffee, they gave you tea, they gave you everything but equality.' It was more like an advertisement for the prison's catering services than an anthem for the black power movement.

## IRELAND AND THE ANGLO PIGS

The Lennons' tribute to Angela Davis was earmarked for their next album, planned as a musical newspaper – a collection of topical songs and radical anthems, hot off the street. All of their recent exercises in political song-writing – 'John Sinclair', 'Woman is the Nigger of the World', 'Attica State' – would feature on the record, alongside other freshly written material. Yoko Ono penned 'We're All Water', which marked the US President's pioneering visit to Communist China in February 1972 by suggesting, 'There may not be much difference between Chairman Mao and Richard Nixon, if we strip them naked'. Lennon contributed 'New York City', a Chuck Berry-styled rocker that chronicled the couple's first six months as residents of Manhattan, with references to Jerry Rubin and David Peel, and a defiant message to the Immigration Service: 'If the man wants to shove us out, we're going to jump and shout, the Statue of Liberty says "come"!'

None of this was unduly controversial, except to those who questioned Lennon's abilities as a political songwriter. But two songs were more perilous expressions of radical chic. He had already written 'The Luck of the Irish' for John Reilly's film. Now events inspired a second, even more outspoken commentary on the Irish situation. On 30 January 1972, there was Bloody Sunday. More than thirty years later, the precise events of that afternoon in

Derry are still the subject of inquiries and accusations. They followed in the wake of a heightened bombing campaign by the Provisional IRA, which had begun in Belfast the previous September, and crossed to London by late October, when an explosion forced the closure of the Post Office Tower. Even the mainstream Irish newspapers were now comparing the IRA to the Viet Cong liberation forces in South Vietnam.

The unchallenged facts about Bloody Sunday are that thirteen people were shot dead by members of the Parachute Regiment of the British Army. The tragedy followed a civil rights march that had descended into a stone-throwing confrontation with troops. Both sides blamed the other for initiating the gunfire, but the casualty list was decidedly one-sided. The next day, the *Irish Press* newspaper commented: 'If there was an able-bodied man with Republican sympathies within the Derry area who was not in the IRA before yesterday's butchery, there will be none tonight.'

Like Neil Young with Kent State two years earlier, Lennon felt the news like a slap in the face. He immediately documented the shootings in a song entitled 'Sunday Bloody Sunday'. The first verse was in the classic finger-pointing tradition of the protest song movement: 'The cries of thirteen martyrs filled the free Derry air . . . Not a soldier boy was bleeding when they nailed the coffin lids!' Thereafter, Lennon threw himself into the Irish conflict as a participant, referring to 'this sweet emerald isle' as if he had never left Ireland's shores, and 'our marches', like a veteran civil rights campaigner. He assailed 'you Anglo pigs and Scotties sent to colonise the north', compared the prisons in which Republicans were held to 'concentration camps', distanced himself from 'the bloody English hands', and lapsed only once into New York revolution-speak, when he declared: 'Internment is no answer, it's those mothers' turn to burn'.

Lennon then proceeded to dictate policy to those on every side of the conflict. Republicans were encouraged to 'put the English back to sea' and 'keep Falls Road free forever from the bloody English hands'. The Protestant majority in the six counties of Ulster were told to 'Repatriate to Britain, all of you who call it home'. Finally, there was a message to the British government: 'Leave Ireland to the Irish, not for London or for Rome'.

On the Saturday after Bloody Sunday, Lennon, Ono, Jerry Rubin and Stew Albert joined several thousand demonstrators outside a symbol of British authority – well, the BOAC airline office on Fifth Avenue in Manhattan – to protest against the shootings. 'We were all there to show our sympathy for the thirteen people who were mercilessly shot down by the British imperialists,' he explained. 'The purpose of the meeting was to show solidarity with the people who are going to march tomorrow in Northern Ireland. Representatives of the IRA spoke, including some secret leaders who had flown in especially for the meeting, considering it important to try to awaken the American Irish who are rather middle-class.' Lennon spoke briefly to the crowd to stress his own Irish ancestry – strictly working-class, of course – before performing 'The Luck of the Irish' with Ono. The following day, there was an anti-internment meeting at the Irish Institute, a few blocks away on 48th Street. Many different groups of Republican sympathisers were represented, including the National Association for Irish Freedom (the organisation with which John Reilly had been working), the Irish Republican Clubs, the American Committee for Ulster Justice, and the Northern Aid Committee. An FBI informer was also present, inevitably, and reported significantly that when someone attempted to sway the meeting towards funding the IRA's armed struggle, he was howled down. Lennon was not present, but when the discussion turned to a protest march planned for early March, it was revealed that the ex-Beatle had agreed to provide musical entertainment for the demonstrators. In the event, this march never took place.

Since November, Lennon had been trumpeting 'The Luck of the Irish' as his next single release. A hastily recorded Christmas record appeared instead in December 1971, but not in Britain. The song was credited to both Lennon and Ono, which Lennon's music publishers believed was a deliberate attempt to deny them 50 per cent of the royalties. They took out an injunction to prevent the UK release. The dispute simmered into the New Year, forcing Lennon to abandon his plans to issue 'The Luck of the Irish' as an instant response to the Bloody Sunday killings.

Instead, the honour of being the first rock star to commemorate the shootings fell to his former bandmate, Paul McCartney. The two men had been involved in a public battle of words about the Beatles' business affairs in the closing months of 1971, with Lennon denouncing his former songwriting partner as a hapless and hopeless conservative. McCartney's response to Bloody Sunday was undoubtedly heartfelt; he recorded his protest record just two days later. But it is hard to imagine that he did not take some pleasure in beating Lennon to the Republican punch, while also answering the criticisms of the Rock Liberation Front the previous summer.

The news that McCartney's new band, Wings, would be rush-releasing a single entitled 'Give Ireland Back to the Irish' was greeted with some amazement. McCartney sounded as if he could scarcely believe it himself: 'I always used to think, God, John's crackers, doing all these political songs.' The song itself was less incendiary than Lennon's contributions to the debate, and even more banal. Beyond the implications of the title, which opposed British government policy, the lyrics favoured peaceful persuasion rather than violent confrontation. It was difficult to imagine the self-consciously radical Lennon singing lines like these: 'Great Britain, you are tremendous, and nobody knows like me. But really, what are you doing, in the land across the sea?' McCartney's most adroit move was to personalise the song, to force the listener to imagine how the conflict must feel: 'Tell me how would you like it, if on your way to work, you were stopped by Irish soldiers? Would you lie down, do nothing? Give in? Or go berserk?'

The single was in the shops within four weeks of the shootings, with an instrumental version on the flipside in case DJs were afraid to air the lyrics. 'Give Ireland Back to the Irish' was immediately 'BANNED EVERY-WHERE', as McCartney's adverts proudly declared. No radio or TV station in the UK would play the song, and the government-owned General Post Office, who operated the telephone system, refused to allow McCartney the chance to promote the song on a special phone line. A representative of the BBC summed up the general reaction of British broadcasters: 'We have decided not to play this record because we feel the lyrics adopt a definite standpoint on the Northern Ireland situation, and are therefore clearly politically controversial.' McCartney responded with sarcasm, and then anger: 'I think the BBC should be highly praised for guarding our youth against the contaminating effect of my opinion. Up 'em!' EMI Records, the global corporation who distributed Lennon and McCartney's records, was clearly unwilling to upset one of its most commercially lucrative artists, but still wanted to distance itself from the sentiments he had expressed. 'The song is not anti-British,' a company spokesman insisted. 'There is no incitement to violence. The lyrics represent a comment from Paul McCartney on the present situation in Ireland. As an international record company, EMI does not hold any political views and is issuing the record in the usual way. The comments made by Paul McCartney are not necessarily those of the other three Beatles or that of Apple.' The final line must have brought a wry smile to John Lennon's face.

McCartney and Lennon weren't the only 1960s pop stars to comment on the Irish situation in February 1972. McGuinness Flint issued 'Let the People Go', capturing Tom McGuinness's outrage at the policy of internment. 'The band didn't really exist at that point,' he explains, 'but we used that name because it was known to the public. Manfred Mann and Mike Hugg, who owned Maximum Sound studio, donated their facilities free of charge.' He had assumed that the song's outspoken message might affect airplay in the UK, but had not anticipated a total ban. As a result, 'Let the People Go' failed to chart, despite the fact that the band had scored two Top 5 hits within the previous 18 months. McCartney's record was more successful, achieving Top 30 status in the UK and US. But his plan to defeat BBC censorship failed: when their pop station listed the week's Top 20 hits, the announcer referred demurely to 'a record by Wings', its title being too offensive to mention.

There was a crucial difference between McCartney's song and those by Lennon and McGuinness Flint, however. McGuinness Flint announced that they would be donating all their royalties from 'Let the People Go' to the families of those who were suffering internment. 'We played concerts for them in Dublin and London,' McGuinness confirms today. 'The record got a lot of airplay in Ireland, and it was used in a documentary called *The Men Behind the Wire*.' Lennon had already pledged that when 'The Luck of the Irish' was released, all his earnings would be given to 'the civil rights movement', a description broad and vague enough to calm the media. McCartney, however, made no such pledge: if any of the royalties from 'Give Ireland Back to the Irish' found their way to charities or political organisations, he kept that information secret. Politics was not McCartney's strongest suit, and after 'Give Ireland Back to the Irish', he wisely absented himself from frontline debate. As a sarcastic comment on the furore, he based his next single on the nursery rhyme 'Mary Had a Little Lamb'.

Lennon's appreciation of Irish politics was a little deeper than McCartney's. To explain the thinking behind their recent protest songs, he issued a press statement entitled (inevitably) 'The Luck of the Irish'. The Lennons had been attacked in some quarters for ignoring the victims of violence. Now, for the first time, they were prepared to concede that the agents of imperialism might be human as well: 'Of course we sympathise with soldiers who are killed or wounded, anywhere, as we feel for the American soldiers forced to fight in Vietnam, but our deepest sympathies must surely go to the victims of British and Amerikan Imperialism.' The Amerikan 'k' showed that Yippie rhetoric was still alive. 'Blaming the problems of Northern Ireland on the IRA is like blaming Vietnam's problems on the NLF,' Lennon's statement continued. 'Some British politicians say the policy of the IRA is to goad the security forces into going "berserk", firing blindly, etc. How "berserk" do they think the Catholic minority feel – especially with everybody knowing how unjustly they've been treated?' This was as close as Lennon ever came to justifying IRA tactics, as a reasonable response to injustice. He begged the United Nations to intervene in 'this tragic affair', to prevent a situation where 'the working class gets massacred'. Tellingly, he ended his credo by prodding the guilt of those with Irish ancestry: 'We also ask for the American Irish to wake up to their responsibility in the same way the Jewish people respond to the problems of Israel.' Implicit in this final sentence was a demand that American citizens should fund any organisation that sought to represent the Republican cause. Nowhere in the statement was there any distinction between those groups who were committed to the ballot box, and those who preferred to rely on the bullet.

With his usual confused passion, Lennon was now torn between John Sinclair and Jerry Rubin's plans for San Diego, and his desire to affect the political situation in Northern Ireland. By late February 1972, he and Yoko Ono were assuring the Northern Ireland Civil Rights Association that they were intending to focus all their efforts on the Irish question. After they had completed their album, they planned to stage an all-star benefit concert at Madison Square Garden – clearly hoping to match the impact of George Harrison's 1971 performances for Bangladesh. All profits from this concert, which would also be filmed and recorded, would be directed towards the Civil Rights Association. The next stage of their plan involved a concert tour of Ireland itself, again for fundraising purposes. 'When the two do eventually arrive in Ireland,' a source commented, 'it looks as though they'll be helping out for some time, since friends over there are currently engaged in finding them not only a base for operations but also somewhere to live.'

Within two months, then, Lennon and Ono had pledged to take part in two major concert tours, on opposite sides of the Atlantic, with the aim of swaying the US Presidential election and speeding up the reunification of Ireland. Even allowing for a rock star's customary arrogance, this was an ambitious schedule, and there is little sign that Lennon had considered how these two aims could be satisfied. By early March, the question had become irrelevant. For the first time, the Lennons realised that they might not be able to flit backwards and forwards across the ocean at will. Indeed, it became apparent that if they left the United States, they might be unable to return. This prospect not only threatened their political activities, but also limited their chances of seeking out Yoko's daughter, Kyoko – one of the prime reasons for their relocation to the USA. Lennon faced a choice: fighting the US government and reneging on his commitments to Ireland, or else giving up all hope of finding Kyoko. But then fate seemed to offer a third way.

It sprang from the most unlikely of sources. After his betrayal by his Rock Liberation Front allies in November, A.J. Weberman had been sunk in gloom. For several weeks, he trudged around the wintry streets of Greenwich Village, selling dope. Then he had a phone call from underground journalist Tom Forcade: Lennon's manager, Allen Klein, was staging a press conference at his Manhattan office to discuss his handling of the live album from George Harrison's recent charity concerts. The previous week, *New York Magazine* had alleged that Klein was secretly diverting more than a dollar from the sale of each package into his own company, ABKCO, while pretending that all the proceeds were being given to the Bangladesh relief effort.

It was an occasion built for the Rock Liberation Front. Weberman took the RLF's Minister of Art, his wife Ann Duncan, and the Minister of Information, Frank Rose, plus two photographers, to the conference. As Klein began to justify himself, the RLF contingent waited for their moment. Then record producer Phil Spector, who was producing John Lennon's current sessions, entered the room, equally ready for a confrontation. He and Duncan began screaming at each other, and Spector raised his fists to punch her out. One of his bodyguards had to intervene. Weberman and Spector swapped insults – 'Go back to the 50s, Spector'; 'Stay in the garbage can'. Then Klein was shown an RLF flyer that Weberman had handed out that morning, promising a demonstration outside the ABKCO building later in the week. 'I think it's time to show Mr Weberman out,' Klein drawled, as two more bodyguards moved in. Negotiations went downhill from there. Spector grabbed Duncan again; Weberman slapped him away. 'The next time I hit you, you capitalist scumbag,' Weberman told the producer, 'it'll be a punch in the nose, and you'll never be able to snort coke again!' Eventually Weberman was manhandled into the ABKCO lift, triumphant – the RLF was back in business.

Spector was in the studio with Lennon when Weberman led a picket of

ABKCO several days later. Around 20 RLF supporters marched up and down outside 1700 Broadway, carrying signs proclaiming that Klein and Spector were capitalist pigs. A.J. led them in chanting, 'Klein come clean, where's the buck fourteen?' and 'You'll wonder where the money went, when Klein runs a charity event'. When mainstream media journalists arrived to cover the demonstration, Weberman told them he was aping the Black Panthers' free breakfast programme by launching a Free Food for Starving Music Execs Programme. 'We figured that if Klein was so desperate for money that he had to take it out of the hands of starving kids, he must be a hungry motherfucker,' Weberman recalls, still excited by the memory of the demonstration nearly 35 years on. 'Then, a few days later, I got a phone call from Yoko.'

In one of the abrupt shifts of allegiance that marked his entire career, John Lennon had suddenly decided that he didn't trust his trusted manager. Using the logic that his enemy's enemy must be a friend, he decided to contact Weberman, whom he had manoeuvred out of the RLF just three months earlier. 'We went over for tea to Bank Street,' Weberman recalls. 'John and Yoko were there, stark naked. We started hanging out together. I used to interpret his songs, the way I had with Dylan, tell him what he was really saying, and he loved it. I used to interpret McCartney's songs too, because I figured Lennon wrote many of them himself. Lennon used to tell me all the time how much he hated McCartney, how he wanted to punch him out.'

It was at the Bank Street apartment that Weberman claims he met a drug dealer with connections to the IRA: 'There was this guy who was totally wacked, man. He was smuggling Lebanese hash into the US, and selling it wrapped in white cheesecloth. With the money he got for the hash, he'd go into gun stores and purchase weapons, and then ship the weapons back to Ireland. Lennon introduced me to this guy, who was a total fucking revolutionary from the Irish Republican Army. I said to Lennon, "Man, you're pretty well connected back in England. Now I'm gonna hook you up here in the United States."'

The dealer's connection with Lennon was drugs, not the IRA, though the ex-Beatle must have been entranced by the glamour of a direct link to the organisation that was taking on the British government. Weberman introduced him to a group that has long been rumoured to have acted as a fundraising body for the IRA during the late 1960s and early 1970s. 'I hooked him up with Noraid,' he says. 'I told him, "These guys are just a front for the IRA, it's as simple as that, man."' Noraid – the Irish Northern Aid Committee – is still in operation today, its mission 'to support by peaceful means a free and independent 32-county Ireland'. It also campaigns on behalf of political prisoners, and aids the families of those victimised in the struggle for a united Ireland. Its operations in the USA during this period offered an invaluable source of cash to the Republican movement. Despite decades of denials, its opponents insist that Noraid's cash was often diverted towards the armed struggle, rather than its victims. Now that cash was about to be topped up by the receipts from Lennon's song 'The Luck of the Irish'.

In the wake of the Bloody Sunday debacle, and then the British government's decision to establish direct rule of Northern Ireland, the Northern Ireland Civil Rights Association rapidly lost prestige. Many of its supporters switched their allegiance to the Provisional IRA. Although 'The Luck of the Irish' did not prove to be one of Lennon's most lucrative songs, the loss of this income must still have made a significant dent in NICRA's finances. 'Lennon gave Noraid this huge contribution,' Weberman says proudly, 'and they had a big party to celebrate. They invited me – at last I was a hero! Everyone was saying, "Hey, this is Weberman, he turned Lennon on to us". I said, "Look, he would have found you anyway. I just speeded things up."'

In 2000, former British MI5 employee David Shayler claimed that he had seen secret government documents relating to Lennon's links with the IRA. In particular, he alleged that Lennon had contributed £175,000 to IRA funds.[1] In reply, Yoko Ono stated: 'My husband did not give money to the IRA. My husband gave money . . . when it was asked, by people who were in need . . . I sent money to Ireland (among other countries) but the cash was always intended for children, orphans and women in need. Even in the 1960s I did not believe violence was a way of getting things.'

Shayler and Ono's comments are not as contradictory as they sound. High amongst Noraid's priorities was helping the families of (Catholic) victims of the Troubles in Ireland. Lennon and Ono could have passed such a substantial sum to Noraid, in the hope or belief that it would be directed towards 'children, orphans and women in need'. Likewise, the British security services could easily have found evidence of such a donation, and interpreted it as proof that Lennon was knowingly funding the IRA. The missing link in this chain – still highly controversial, 35 years on – is what exactly happened to the money given to Noraid.

What is known is that Lennon had a meeting around this time with Gerry O'Hare, who was then a prominent member of the Provisional IRA. 'There were Irish Americans in New York who kept him briefed on the situation,' O'Hare explains. 'I was over there on a speaking tour, and a guy said to me, "Would you like to meet John Lennon?" I said, "Are you spoofing?" But two days later I went up to his apartment. He didn't have much time because he was doing something else, but he gave me ten minutes.' O'Hare asked whether Lennon would be prepared to do a fundraising concert for the Republican movement. 'He offered to do one in Dublin,' O'Hare confirms. 'He said he was serious about it, but I got the impression that if he did one in Dublin, he also wanted to do one in Belfast too, for the Protestant community. But he said he had a problem, that if he left America he might not be able to get back in. He kept saying that he wanted to get "back home", and that until that happened, the concert would have to be put on hold. And then, of course, it faded from our priorities. But he knew who I was, and where I was coming from. He gave me the impression he was genuine. He was a powerful person to have on your side.' Like his promise to play a civil rights benefit in New York, however, Lennon's offer to the IRA went unfulfilled.

In the entire history of rock and the revolution, however, no event would have proved more controversial than Lennon performing a benefit concert for the Provisional IRA. After Bloody Sunday, the IRA's campaign widened its scope and intensity. On 22 February, an explosion at the HQ of the Parachute Regiment in the southern England town of Aldershot killed five female catering workers, a chaplain and a gardener. (That bomb was planted by the Officials, not the Provisionals, but the distinction was moot as far as the British public was concerned.) Further outrage was stoked by a restaurant bombing in Belfast ten days later, in which two sisters – shopping for a wedding dress – had their legs blown off. By late March, the British government had dissolved the parliament of Northern Ireland, and had imposed direct rule of the province from London. This had been a short-term IRA aim, in the accurate belief that it would heighten Catholic resentment of the British. But as the IRA's attacks became more indiscriminate, the organisation began to shed much of the sympathy it had attracted over the previous year. If Lennon had staged his benefit, he would have faced extreme vilification from press and public alike in Britain, where even the underground newspapers were now recanting their earlier backing for the IRA.

By March 1972, however unlikely it might seem, A.J. Weberman had replaced Rubin as Lennon's guide through revolutionary New York. The RLF founder introduced the ex-Beatle to his friends and allies, notably Tom Forcade – an ex-air force pilot and one-time member of the Weather Underground. Born Kenneth Gary Goodson, he had worked as an intelligence agent during his flying days. Then he witnessed an unprovoked assault by a group of Arizona policemen on a bunch of hippies. He left the air force, and founded UPS, the Underground Press Syndicate, a news agency for the counter-culture.

Forcade carried that spirit into Greenwich Village, where he fell in with the RLF and the remnants of the Yippies. There, with the assistance of Weberman and several cronies, he formed an organisation called the Zippies, designed to rekindle the original spirit of the Yippies. In the intense milieu of Greenwich Village, where every switch of allegiance felt like the shifting of tectonic plates, the emergence of the Zippies concentrated minds and fractured old friendships. The major casualty was Jerry Rubin. Although everyone on the New York underground was eager to join John Lennon's gang, Rubin's groupie-like behaviour had been more blatant than most. His intimates perceived that he was more interested in being seen on TV than in organising revolutionary action. There were other complaints: Rubin's cleanliness wasn't all it might have been (comrades moaned that he didn't know the meaning of the word 'deodorant'); he had used Yippie money for his own private adventures; and he took credit for other Yippies' ideas. Forcade, Weberman and the Zippies were also afraid that Rubin might be alienating Lennon from the revolution. The mistrust could just as easily be returned, as Barry Miles recalls: 'Allen Ginsberg always thought that the Zippies were some kind of counter-intelligence force, in the pay of the FBI. He felt that they were just crazed guys from the Lower East Side, who purposely disrupted peaceful demonstrations in order to devalue them in the eyes of the public.'

Despite his own friendship with Ginsberg, Lennon shared none of these qualms. Via his underground connections, Weberman secured Lennon a phone connection that couldn't be bugged by the government. By his account, Lennon was a volatile character: 'If I ever said anything bad against Dylan, he wanted to punch me out. He would leap out of bed with no clothes on, and throw himself at me. Yoko had to restrain him from punching me on several occasions. I was afraid of him, physically intimidated. He was bigger than me, stronger than me, and he had experience of beating guys up from

Liverpool.' Lennon's continued struggle with heroin scarred his life on Bank Street, shortening his temper, distracting him from work, and making him an unreliable ally. But in public, on his frequent talk show appearances, when he'd spout radical rhetoric and play his latest protest songs, he sounded like an unshakeable revolutionary. It was this carefully erected myth that the US government accepted as truth, and set out to demolish.

## HEAR ME ROAR

John is a feminist. Anybody is, who is aware of women's struggle and what they have to go through in the male society. It's harder for men to become feminist, of course . . . but I think that part is the most interesting, because in the end we have to really come together and work together. Without men's co-operation, it's not going to work.

(Yoko Ono, 1980)

Lennon, after going out of his way to sympathise with the feminist movement in 'Power to the People', scarcely allows Yoko to complete a sentence on national television.

(critic John Mendelsohn, 1972)

In summer 1972, investigative TV reporter Geraldo Rivera took a film crew to San Francisco to document John Lennon and Yoko Ono's visit to the city. Lennon was receiving treatment for methadone addiction, although they didn't mention that on film. But they did perform an impromptu rendition of Lennon's feminist anthem, 'Woman is the Nigger of the World', with Ono mimicking sexist innuendo ('show us your tits') between Lennon's lines. Recorded for their 1972 album, *Some Time in New York City*, the song inspired one of the most passionate performances of Lennon's career, echoed by stirring saxophone and guitar solos. The sincerity of his feminist principles could not be doubted, even if he did not always live up to them.[2]

'Woman is the Nigger of the World' attracted predictable opposition, from broadcasters and from many in the African-American community. Radical comedian Dick Gregory assembled a collection of black celebrities to demonstrate their support for Lennon's use of the forbidden 'n' word. TV host Dick Cavett was forced to issue a warning before Lennon could perform the song. In his defence, Lennon read out a statement by black

California politician Ron Dellums: 'If you define "nigger" as someone whose lifestyle is defined by others, whose opportunities are defined by others, whose role in society is defined by others, the good news is you don't have to be black to be a nigger in this society. Most of the people in America are niggers.' For a second, Lennon must have imagined that he had written the ultimate revolutionary anthem. But unlike 'Power to the People', 'Woman is the Nigger of the World' failed to capture the public imagination, and the single reached no higher than No. 57 on the US charts. Its appeal was severely restricted by lack of airplay. One programme director at a New York radio station commented: 'We're just not ready for it. I think it will offend people. I tried it out on a couple of girls in the office, and they thought it was offensive.' He had not considered the possibility that they might find being addressed as 'girls' equally offensive.

'It was long before Helen Reddy's "I Am Woman",' Lennon noted later. 'So it was the first women's liberation song, as far as I'm concerned.' In fact, Reddy's song was both written and released a year before Lennon's, although it did not become a national hit until autumn 1972. Reddy had formed a feminist women's group with rock critic Lillian Roxon, in 1971. 'I started writing', she explained, 'because I had a couple of things to say that no one else was saying. It's particularly difficult for women to know how to write and what to say. We're all filtered through the male vision of the world and it's only been very recently that women have tried to find out how they react to things.' She was an unlikely revolutionary: her breakthrough hit was a song from the God-rock musical *Jesus Christ Superstar*, and her image was always mainstream rather than radical. But her defiant pride in her gender struck a new note in popular music. 'I am woman, hear me roar,' her song began, before she declared: 'I've been down there on the floor, and no one's ever gonna keep me down again . . . You can bend but never break me, cause it only serves to make me more determined to achieve my final goal.'

Arranged as a Broadway showstopper rather than a political anthem, 'I Am Woman' insinuated its way into the global consciousness as the theme song to a highly clichéd movie account of feminism, *Stand Up and Be Counted* (written and directed by men). As the song hit the charts, Reddy made a memorable appearance at a National Organisation of Women meeting in Los Angeles. Delegates read out the lyrics to many of the era's most popular records, and analysed their sexual politics. Rod Stewart & the Faces' 'Stay With Me', a portrayal of a teenage boy's encounter with a prostitute, aroused particular scorn. 'We played a great many Top 20 songs and all of us were shocked by the lyrical content,' Reddy recalled. 'We were all listening with high school girls, talking about the effect of those lyrics. It was an extraordinary experience.' She was quoted as finding it 'incredible that so many rock musicians, committed to ending racial discrimination, continue to write songs that put down women' and added: 'Many rock stars who speak on equality are with women in their personal lives who they treat very badly.' She had a tart message for male radicals: 'You can't scream "Right On" with one fist, and "Down Bitch" with the other.'

The success of 'I Am Woman' reflected the extent to which women's liberation had entered popular culture. It was often mocked and frequently misunderstood, but it was a revolution in progress. Laws were being rewritten to reduce discrimination; attitudes in the workplace were slowly changing; women were staking their claim to independent thought and action. Meanwhile, radical women's groups were springing up across America and Europe, with specialist media to match – as evidenced by the launch of magazines such as *Ms* in the USA and *Spare Rib* in the UK. They were the most visible of a network of papers and journals that stretched from *Socialist Woman* and *Red Rag* to *Ain't I a Woman* and (reclaiming a Bob Dylan line) *It Ain't Me Babe*.

Feminism was just as prone to internal conflict as any other section of the movement. Activists argued furiously over the correct political line on every issue from abortion to heterosexual relationships. The divisions could surface everywhere, and the Chicago Women's Liberation Rock Band was not immune. According to keyboardist Naomi Weisstein, 'The band lasted three years and broke up in an agony of hatred and hidden agendas.' She blamed the movement's insistence that every member was equal, and there should be no leaders – a principle easier to pledge than obey. In 1972, the band performed in front of a hostile, predominantly male audience at Bucknell University in Pennsylvania. As Weisstein recalled, 'Huge fraternity boys were screaming and baring their canines in the middle of the floor like turf-threatened gorillas. I offered to calm the audience with a stand-up comedy introduction. Concerned about my leadership role, the band refused to let me do this. Instead, another band member, inexperienced in such situations, made a stumbling presentation, which further enraged the audience. At this point I – gulp – improvised a new monologue, producing (eventually) giggles, then guffaws. Afterwards the band was furious at me for my success in reversing the audience's mood.' A few months later, when Weisstein took a brief leave of absence from the band, they split up. 'It is an irony', she commented, 'that the revolutionary vision of utopia that had made our performance so powerful was the same ingredient that had destroyed us.'

If sisterhood was sometimes hard to maintain, then exposure to male musicians was usually sufficient to renew feminist solidarity. As one women's liberation leaflet asked sarcastically of its readers, 'Are you the teenybopper, bitch, cheater, foxy lady or "honey"-type portrayed in rock music?' If the casual sexism of rock lyrics wasn't provocative enough, then the stars themselves could be relied upon to compensate. Most of them paid lip service to the emergence of women as a benefit to society, while maintaining the exploitation of teenage groupies that had long been considered an occupational reward.

After six months in the New York underground, John Lennon realised that so-called radical men were no more honourable. He later claimed to have scolded his comrades about the gender imbalance: 'Where's the women socialists? Where's the women left-wingers? Where's the women in on the meeting about how they're going to overthrow the government?' His complaint wasn't entirely accurate: in theory, women such as Abbie Hoffman's wife Anita and John Sinclair's wife Leni were regarded as fully fledged members of the revolutionary elite. But, as Joan Baez was discovering, that kind of equality wouldn't necessarily reach as far as the home. When her activist husband David Harris was released from prison, she was disappointed to discover that he refused to help her with housework, on the grounds that it was too boring. Baez apparently told him that she didn't like doing it either, but somebody had to. A few months later, the couple separated, and later divorced.[3]

The exception to this parade of celebrity chauvinism was Country Joe McDonald. Baptised in gender equality in his Chilean commune, he attempted to live out his feminist principles. During 1972, he made the conscious decision to swap roles with his partner, feminist academic and writer Robin Mencken. 'I assumed taking care of our child, getting her to school, cooking and shopping,' he explained. 'Once you endure that situation, both the good and bad of it, you know how oppressive it can be on a day-to-day basis. Any man who won't take care of children or refuses to wash dishes or when faced with cooking doesn't know how to begin, is an infant, a spoiled child. It's up to the women to say, "Take care of yourself", because most people won't volunteer if someone is already taking care of them.'

His early 1972 album *Incredible! Live!* documented his contemporary stage act, with its self-conscious radical chic and tributes to Chairman Mao and Angela Davis. Its appearance freed him to begin work on a darker selection of material, released a year later on his *Paris Sessions* record. Initially his intention was to compose 'love songs . . . with a revolutionary depth. I'm trying to say something other than "I love you and I need you", for people who have been through that and are trying to establish a meaningful relationship.' Gradually, his range widened, as he explored the constricting image of gender roles in television ('Fantasy') and film ('Movieola'). 'Coulene Anne' exposed male violence, while 'Revolutionary Housewife Blues' and 'Sexist Pig' satirised men's presumption of power. 'He's a fool who thinks his tool is the revolution', he sang on the latter, neatly skewering those radicals who exploited their fame for sexual favours. 'I think I'm the only person who's really writing feminist material now,' he boasted.

McDonald's commitment didn't end with words and music. He became the first male rock star to recruit female musicians, not in traditional roles – adding some decorative flute or cello, perhaps – but as equal members of the group. 'It was a political statement,' he explains. 'It worked out really fine. It was the easiest band to work with that I ever had, and I think that was because of the mix of male and female players. Of course, there was a bit of sexual experimentation within the group, which also made road travel more pleasant!'

A key figure in McDonald's All-Star Band was former United States of America vocalist Dorothy Moscowitz. 'There were several men in the band as well, and Joe was equally mischievous (or capricious, depending on your point of view) with all of us,' she recalls. 'When drummer Anna Rizzo had to leave while we were touring in Georgia, Joe called a local agent, specifying he wanted a female drummer. When our saxophonist Tucki Bailey left us in Los Angeles, Joe found a woman violinist to join us. Having women working back-up was very unusual in the early 70s. I don't think the reason was necessarily misogyny, just cultural habit. Language reflected that. For instance, if a woman played assertively, she was known as "ballsy", but if a male musician played sensitively, he was known as "sensitive" or "trippy", never "ovarian", god forbid!'

McDonald discovered that his audiences preferred to hear him reprise his anti-Vietnam anthems rather than explore uncomfortable gender issues. 'Occasionally couples would get into big arguments over ["Sexist Pig"],' he recalled gleefully. 'The raunchy language was bold for its day,' Moskowitz adds, 'but I always thought that Joe's exploration of sexual inequality was quite apt.' But a significant portion of McDonald's fan-base rejected the dry funk of *Paris Sessions*, which sold substantially fewer copies than his earlier records, not least because his label, Vanguard Records, 'literally didn't know what [the album] was about'. The irony was that in 1972 it was easier for a middle-of-the-road pop singer to deliver a feminist message than a radical folk and rock musician with a long history of activism.

As Moskowitz notes, McDonald's non-sexist band aroused bemusement on the road. 'I think the occasion we all remember', she says, 'is the Fête de l'Humanité, a Communist Party affair of lavish proportions held on the outskirts of Paris. I went to check the piano, but was shooed away by some self-important French sound tech: "You cannot touch. Zees eez for zee piano player." I said, "I am the piano player". "No, no, no, eez for Country Joe's piano player." "Um, I AM the piano player." "No, no." We went at it, back and forth, several times, until Joe finally intervened. At that same gig, our saxophonist was heckled and booed by several men in the audience. My guess is that they were offended by the fact that she was pretty, blonde and youthful, yet able to play a growling – or should that be "ballsy"? – solo.'

Not that being male in Paris was enough to guarantee a warm reception. On an earlier, solo tour of France, one of McDonald's shows was interrupted by leftists, eager to 'save' the musician from the corporatism of the music business by invading the stage and claiming it for the people. 'I was sat on stage by myself playing one of the guitars I had with me,' McDonald recalls, 'and then all these guys came up. One of them picked up the other guitar, and I was afraid they would steal it. They seemed quite friendly to me, but they were getting in the way of my act and making me nervous. Of course, it didn't help that they didn't speak English and I didn't speak French.' It was a classic confrontation between activists and a radical musician, each unable to comprehend the other's language.

A similar gulf of understanding still separated the struggle for gay liberation from the counter-culture and what remained of the movement. Some revolutionary activists despised the idea of homosexuality so much that they suggested gay liberation was a CIA plot, designed to harm the reputation of more wholesome liberation movements. The Gay Liberation Front gathered members on both sides of the Atlantic, staged rallies and revelled in their identity. But support from prominent members of the revolutionary left was minimal.

Few rock stars were prepared to make a public pledge of support for the GLF, although Pink Floyd headed a benefit concert in April 1971. David Bowie followed suit in October. Three months later, he told *Melody Maker*, 'I'm gay, and I always have been.' He had worn a 'man's dress' on the cover of his 1970 album, *The Man Who Sold the World*; and had been affecting an increasingly camp demeanour in recent months. But anyone in the GLF who anticipated that Bowie would now throw himself wholeheartedly into their campaign was destined to be disappointed. After his 'gay' announcement, he played no further benefit gigs. Instead, he distanced himself from the GLF, and then backed away from his own statement of sexual preference. 'I'm gay' was fine as a publicity move, it seemed, but not as a manifesto.

## GOING TO THE CANDIDATES' DEBATE

We have to stop the killing of Vietnamese people. If voting for McGovern will stop that, then we should vote for McGovern . . . but I don't think it's going to do enough.

(Jane Fonda, April 1972)

Young voters are going to take the power, and we're gonna use it.

(John Sinclair, January 1972)

A few weeks out of prison, John Sinclair was back in the vanguard of the struggle. But now he was prepared to try a more orthodox approach to changing the system than violent revolution. In the April 1972 city council elections in his hometown of Ann Arbor, Sinclair placed the might of the Rainbow People's Party behind the campaign of the Human Rights Party. They stood for an end to the Vietnam War, racism and sexism; control of local police by the community; and the legalisation of marijuana. It might not have been the revolution he'd expected to inherit from Chairman Mao, but it was serious reform, and Sinclair was convinced that his intervention could transform democracy from a farce into a celebration. 'There are more than 30,000 students and maybe 10,000 freaks in the city,' he declared, 'and we're gonna elect us some city officials who are gonna be responsive to the people's needs. We're gonna bring rock'n'roll politics to this town, man, and we're gonna change things and make them work.' Two of their candidates were elected to the council.

The same dream of 'rock'n'roll politics' was mooted during the 1972

Presidential race. While Richard Nixon sailed virtually unopposed towards nomination as the Republican candidate, the Democrats stumbled from one crisis to the next. The reputation of Edward Kennedy, younger brother of JFK and Robert F. Kennedy, had been tarnished by his involvement in a 1969 scandal, which ended in the death of a young female companion. That left Edmund Muskie as the frontrunner, but he fell victim to a combination of Republican dirty tricks and human frailty.

Senator George McGovern then emerged as the unlikely candidate. He ran on an anti-war ticket, gathering a passionate following among young activists. Actors Warren Beatty and Shirley Maclaine organised a succession of fundraising concerts, which starred performers ranging from Barbra Streisand and Simon & Garfunkel to Chicago and Country Joe McDonald. Indeed, Chicago's 1972 US tour was virtually a McGovern roadshow, with every concert offering voter registration booths and Democratic propaganda. The British paper *Melody Maker* noted cynically: '"George is hip", said a member of Columbia Records' New York office. He must be: Chicago have so many stickers and banners on stage declaring his excellence that you can hardly see the band.' Support for the candidate ranged across the counter-culture. Former Country Joe & the Fish bassist Bruce Barthol was now working in street theatre, writing songs for a company who combined members of the San Francisco Mime Troupe and the East Bay Sharks. 'We wrote a street opera for McGovern,' he recalls. 'It was called *US: Like It or Lump It*. We were convinced he was going to win.'

The McGovern rallies coincided with a significant sharpening of the conflict in Vietnam. In May, Nixon launched Operation Linebacker, which involved the heaviest shelling yet of civilians in the North Vietnamese capital of Hanoi. There was outrage amongst anti-war activists, yet this failed to produce anything more than a meagre turnout for the traditional May protests. It was as if the whole country was waiting for the election to decide the issue, and until then Nixon could be allowed a free hand. 'I wish people of this country really knew what they're doing in Vietnam right now,' complained actor and activist Jane Fonda, who had been demonised by the mainstream media after an earlier visit to North Vietnam.[4] 'If they did [know], I think they'd rise up. I really don't believe there is a human being in this country who would not change overnight if he knew what Nixon was doing to the people of Indochina.' But even she seemed to feel that there was nothing to do but wait for McGovern to take power.

Not that Nixon was ready to give up office easily. A protest on the steps of the Capitol Building on 3 May 1972 epitomised the way in which the White House was now treating dissent. When special White House counsel Charles Colson saw a flyer for the demonstration, he sent it to fellow staff member Jeb Magruder. 'I am sure our friends who would like to send more SAMs [surface-to-air missiles] to North Vietnam to shoot down US pilots will be present,' he wrote. Then he suggested some typical Watergate-era theatrics: 'Now that we have a little warning, let's orchestrate this one perfectly. I think without any doubt we can get a couple of Viet Cong flags, several posters and perhaps one or two scalps. Would you put your troops into this and let me know how it is set up in advance so that we can perhaps turn the publicity our way for a change.'

'It turned out to be an interesting event,' recalls Judy Collins. 'Jane Fonda was there, Donald Sutherland, and Daniel Ellsberg, the Pentagon Papers guy. He was shouted down by a group of roughnecks. I didn't realise who they were, but it was obvious from the start that they didn't belong, that they were "shills", who were there to cause trouble. It was only much later that I discovered they were the same guys who were connected with the Watergate break-in.' The 'troops' mustered by Colson were none other than the Cuban 'Plumbers' who were caught inside the Watergate Hotel a few weeks later.

George McGovern won the California state primary on 6 June, which virtually ensured that he would be nominated as the Democratic candidate a month later. The same day, President Nixon sent his senior staff a memo, in which he insisted: 'The fact that Abby [sic] Hoffman, Jerry Rubin, Angela Davis, among others, support McGovern should be widely publicised and used at every point . . . Nailing him to his left-wing supporters and forcing him either to repudiate them or to accept their support is essential.' Nixon speechwriter Pat Buchanan chimed in: 'McGovern has said that the May Day [anti-war] demonstrators would not be on the streets but "having dinner at the White House" if he were elected . . . We have an idea for a commercial – juxtaposing [Nixon] and McGovern on the May Day demonstrators and indicating a vote for McGovern is a vote to have Rubin and Hoffman ("Guess Who's Coming to Dinner") at the White House.'

This was not merely a dirty tricks manoeuvre (although it was that as well). Rubin and Hoffman, the agents provocateurs of 1968, whose antics had helped to fasten the final nails in the Democrats' coffin, were now planning to campaign for the Democratic Party's choice. Rubin rationalised his choice by claiming McGovern as 'a left-wing candidate' who was 'contributing to the defeat of the traditional Democratic Party and Republican Party'. That, of course, was precisely what would doom his campaign. Rubin and Hoffman, though, were entranced by their candidate's promise that every American soldier would have left Vietnam within three months of his election.

Just before McGovern won the California primary, the Republicans switched the location for their National Convention from San Diego to Miami Beach – the same venue where the Democrats were due to meet a month later. The official reason was a financial dispute with authorities in San Diego, but as Jeb Magruder admitted later, Miami was chosen because it offered tighter security against the 'massive demonstrations' they were expecting. 'The hotel that would be our convention headquarters seemed vulnerable,' Magruder recalled, 'because it was located on an island just offshore that was easily reached from the mainland. We had a vision of an armada of thousands of wild-eyed hippies swimming across the inlet and overrunning our defences.' The switch simplified the job of organising protests against the two major parties. The Yippies printed flyers showing Abbie Hoffman in a short dress, alongside a slogan that parodied a contemporary airline advert: 'High! I'm Abbie. Fly me to Miami.' Alongside the crucial convention dates, the flyer promised 'Ten Days to Change the World'. Tom Hayden had once called for the movement to stage 'two hundred, three hundred Chicagos'. Now two Chicagos were scheduled, a month apart, and what happened might alter the course of American history and stop the war – or so the Yippies believed.

## VOICE OF SANITY

Once the Black Panther Party had supplied the revolutionary zeal that fired and inspired the rest of the movement. Now, like John Sinclair, Abbie Hoffman and Jerry Rubin, they were prepared to concede that democracy might achieve more than insurrection. As the Yippies prepared to subvert and take part in the election at the same time, two of the most prominent Panther leaders announced that they would be standing for public office. Bobby Seale had become a voice of sanity in the party in comparison to the increasingly erratic Huey Newton. Now he declared that he intended to run as Mayor of Oakland. Meanwhile, Elaine Brown – having completed her second album, for Motown's Black Forum label – was attempting to win a place on the Oakland city council. The two activists began the lengthy process of introducing themselves to the electorate as champions of the poor and oppressed, while distancing themselves from the Panthers' more aggressive activities.

Even two years earlier, the Panthers would have expected – and been asked – to take their place in the vanguard of any demonstrations against the nation's potential leaders. Now their influence had shrunk so dramatically that they were virtually irrelevant, except as a bogeyman to frighten conservatives. Yet several of their campaigns had eventually reached a successful conclusion. The Soledad Brothers – or at least the two survivors of the trio, George Jackson now being six months in the grave – were declared innocent of the charge of murdering a prison guard. Then, on 4 June 1972, Angela Davis was found innocent on charges relating to the Jonathan Jackson shoot-out in 1970. 'Who got free today?' drawled Mick Jagger on stage that night in Seattle. 'Angela Davis got free today. Fucking great.' Later that month, Madison Square Garden hosted 'An Evening with Angela Davis', intended as a gesture of thanks to her supporters, and a means of paying her legal bills. The freed academic spoke from a bullet-proof glass cage, while musicians such as the Voices of East Harlem, Jimmy Witherspoon, Jerry Butler and Pete Seeger performed.

A few days before that concert, John Lennon and Yoko Ono's political album, *Some Time in New York City*, was finally released. Given the harassment he was now enduring over his immigration status, Lennon might have begun to wish he had never started the project in the first place. Amongst its ten new songs were 'Angela' and 'John Sinclair', both somewhat irrelevant now that their subjects had been freed. The album was packaged as a parody of the *New York Times*, with the lyrics printed as news stories, and graphics and photographs illustrating the Lennons' views on feminism, the situation in Ireland and black power. The heads of Richard Nixon and Chairman Mao were pasted onto nude dancing bodies, to illustrate a key line from Ono's song, 'We're All Water'. This illustration was widely censored in the USA – not for political reasons but to protect record-buyers from the sight of naked flesh. Inside, the album was held in a paper bag that reprinted a British Army recruitment advert. Over the top was stamped the phrase: 'FIT TO DIE'. This image was omitted when the album was belatedly released in Britain several months later.

Two postcards that were also included in the package summed up the Lennons' political situation that summer. The first showed the Statue of

Liberty wearing the glove of black power, a minor masterpiece of radical chic. The second requested fans to write to the US government, demanding that Lennon should not be expelled from the USA. *Some Time in New York City* is by far the most overtly (and self-consciously) 'revolutionary' record ever issued by a major rock artist, and it appeared at the moment when Lennon was under intense scrutiny from several sections of the US government. He had been given a series of ultimata by the Immigration Service, but each of these edicts had been successfully appealed by his legal team. Lennon's attorney, Leon Wildes, complained that 'his client felt he was being deported due to his outspoken remarks concerning US policy in South-East Asia'. Lennon was now being followed by unmarked cars and equally anonymous agents. On the advice of his attorney, he went on TV to tell the nation: 'They think we're going to San Diego, or Miami, or wherever it is. We've never said we're going, there'll be no big jam with Dylan, because there's too much going on.'

Under these circumstances, it is uncertain whether Lennon was pleased or horrified to find himself the subject of the only article ever published by the *Black Panther* newspaper in support of a white radical. Titled 'Ex-Beatle Told to Love It or Leave It', it summarised the pressure that Lennon was enduring from the Nixon government, and listed his radical gestures of recent months – his friendship with Bobby Seale, and his songs about Angela Davis and Attica State. The paper clearly did not employ a team of researchers: Lennon was described as being 'no stranger to oppression and poverty, having been born of working-class parents in one of the most miserable sections of London, England, the ghetto of Liverpool'. That might have made him laugh, but he would have been less amused to be identified as the composer of 'Give Ireland Back to the Irish'. Clearly, to the Panthers, these English ghetto kids all looked the same.

Ironically, the Panthers' newspaper ignored the efforts of jazzman Archie Shepp to keep the plight of the widows and families of the Attica State casualties in the spotlight. While Lennon's song about the prison shoot-out was about to enjoy massive publicity, Shepp's finely crafted *Attica Blues* album received little notice, even after he played a concert at the institution on 4 July 1972. The record included recitations by radical lawyer William Kunstler, the veteran of the Chicago conspiracy fiasco and numerous Black Panther trials. 'I saw [the record] as a prime way to get funds into the Attica Defence Committee,' he explained. 'With a record like *Attica Blues* we can participate over a long period of time, not only with our royalties but [with] the actual work [that] will go on. We have so many people involved in the movement who can lend their voice – Angela Davis, Bobby Seale and so on – and they can all sell records.' But who was prepared to take that kind of commercial and political risk? *Attica Blues* did not inspire a raft of imitations, and soon Shepp was forced to abandon such controversial material.

For the moment, at least, John Lennon did not face similar pressure – partly because he was a director of his own record company, partly because his name still guaranteed a certain level of commercial acceptance. But his transformation into a political animal was about to be put to the test of public opinion. Although Lennon later regretted that his political engagement had come close to 'ruining' his work as a songwriter, by 1980 he was still sufficiently proud of the material on *Some Time in New York City* to compare it to Bertolt Brecht, and call it 'pretty interesting theatre'. The first preview of the record to be published in Britain – by Roy Hollingsworth in *Melody Maker* – dubbed it 'The People's Album', and gushed: 'When in future we start talking of protest songs, then we'll have to start with these. They contain the strongest, most heartfelt, sincere comments I think we've ever heard on record. It will certainly go down as the heaviest record ever made . . . It is the full fist of revolt. And it hurts.'

This was a lonely voice. Stephen Holden's review in *Rolling Stone*, with its parade of unflattering epiphets, set the prevailing tone. Wilfred Mellers in the *New Statesman* referred to Lennon's 'infantilism'. In *Cream*, Charles Shaar Murray called the album 'irritating, embarrassing and, finally, just plain unpleasant', and commented: 'I find it astonishing that the John Lennon who used to be able to see through pretentious phonies, hip pseuds, and radical chic should fall into those very same traps.'

Some of this criticism was undoubtedly justified; some was provoked by embarrassment that Lennon was still repeating the same, increasingly unfashionable refrain. But by the time that *Some Time in New York City* was released, he had effectively distanced himself from most of those who had inspired his political activism. He had told Rubin and Hoffman that he was unwilling to join them in Miami Beach. 'Jerry couldn't keep his damn mouth shut, as usual,' he bitched in 1980. 'He was already onto the press, blabbing off . . . That was enough to get Immigration on us.' Now, again on the advice of his attorney, he cancelled plans for a feature-length documentary of the John

Sinclair rally, proceeds from which were supposed to be earmarked for causes of Sinclair's choosing. Lennon and Ono summoned Sinclair to their apartment for a meeting, but didn't get out of bed, much to his disgust. 'You'd have to see them in their fucking bed,' he recalled years later. 'It was just like you were the peasant and they were the royalty. It was humiliating. I've been beaten and probed in my orifices [in prison], but this was *really* humiliating.' Lennon's memory of the incident was equally cynical: 'We always insisted on keeping physical and legal control over any film footage which included us in it. John Sinclair threatened to sue us, even after we helped get him out of prison!' In one of his final interviews, he damned all his radical friends: 'They're all lunatics.'

What the press and the FBI did not know was that, contrary to appearances, Lennon and Ono had not abandoned their involvement with those who were attempting to disrupt proceedings in Miami. That summer, the Zippies staged a playful assault on the Republican Party. 'We knew the Republicans were bugging everyone, so we bugged them, literally,' A.J. Weberman recalls gleefully. 'Yoko Ono had done that film, *Fly*, so she knew where we could get hold of some flies. Then we let 500 of them loose in the Republican headquarters!' In early June, the Zippies published a thin newspaper entitled *Beach Blanket Struggle*. Inside the paper was a full-page advertisement for the Apple Records release *The Pope Smokes Dope* by David Peel & the Lower East Side. On the surface, it was a logical piece of promotion, as Peel was a Zippie sympathiser himself. What wasn't obvious was that Apple Records – in the person of one of its four directors, John Lennon – had paid $50,000 for the advertisement, approximately one hundred times more than the commercial value of the ad. 'I told him we were going to have a riot in Miami,' Weberman explains, 'and that we needed money to get buses and bring in the demonstrators. So basically he was helping to finance the riots. John gave us a couple of thousand of dollars in cash, and the rest came from this ad. He had some idea what was going to happen – he knew that there was a chance that it would turn out not to be a peaceful event, but he still gave us the money. So you can't tell me that he didn't believe in violence. He helped to pay for it.' The ruse of using an Apple ad to disguise the donation threw the government off the scent. Had they realised what Lennon was up to, they would surely have used the evidence to have him deported immediately. Instead, Lennon remained in the USA to fight – subtly – another day.

## REVOLUTION BLUES

American politics congealed and decayed as convention season approached. On 15 May, Governor George Wallace of Alabama was shot and paralysed in an assassination attempt. Having run as a strong independent candidate in 1968, he was attempting this time to secure the Democratic nomination, despite his long history of having pandered to the most racist elements of Southern society. The sympathy vote won him several state primaries in subsequent weeks, until George McGovern's triumph in California put paid to Wallace's dream for another four years.[5]

McGovern's Sisyphean task was to satisfy those Democrats who admired him as a left-wing anti-war campaigner, without offending those who supported Wallace. His campaign stumbled when he appointed Thomas Eagleton as his running mate – and Eagleton chose to conceal his slightly troubled psychiatric history. After details of his electric shock treatment for nervous exhaustion became public, McGovern pledged his colleague '1000%' support, and then abruptly dropped him from the ticket.

Meanwhile, President Nixon veered between euphoria, as he watched the Democratic Party steer itself into a blind alley, and panic, as the situation in Vietnam showed no sign of easing. To follow his groundbreaking trip to China in February, Nixon visited Moscow in May. Meanwhile, elements of his White House staff continued to pursue ever more risky intelligence operations, climaxing on the weekend in mid-June 1972 when 'the Plumbers' – the Cuban exiles who were being used for the administration's secret breaking-and-entering and bugging activities – were arrested inside the Democratic Party's offices in Washington's Watergate Hotel. There were no immediate links between the burglars and the White House, so the Democratic Convention took place in early July without any reference to Nixon's shenanigans.

Fundraising concerts for the McGovern campaign continued to be staged on both the West and East Coasts. Neil Young's contribution to the cause was to write and (with Graham Nash) release a single entitled 'War Song'. 'There's a man [who] says he can put an end to war,' ran the chorus, highlighting (but not naming) McGovern. Young's lyric referred topically but rather irrelevantly to the shooting of Wallace, but concentrated its fire on Nixon: 'In the morning when you wake up, you've got planes flying in the sky. Flying bombs made to break up all the lies in your eyes.' A later verse alluded to America's increasingly violent conduct of the war: 'Burn that jungle down and kill those Vietnamese', Young sang. Unlike Young, Paul

Simon appeared at the McGovern concerts, but he insisted that his music and political beliefs were entirely separate. 'I don't see what one thing has to do with another,' he stated at the end of May. 'The fact of the matter is that popular music is one of the industries of this country. It's all completely tied up with capitalism. It's stupid to separate it.'

Joan Baez had never suffered any qualms about mingling her art and her principles; her conscience demanded nothing less. A few days after the Watergate burglary in Washington, Baez was in the same city herself, leading a demonstration called Ring Around Congress. She had devised the anti-war protest with Cora Weiss, head of the Liaison Committee that sought to maintain human links between the peoples of America and North Vietnam. Weiss recalled that 'the demonstration was the target of the heaviest government interference of any demonstration that was ever held, anywhere'. But the most vocal opposition came from the local black community, who complained that their taxes were paying for policing this almost exclusively white demonstration. What was intended as a display of international solidarity degenerated into a racial confrontation. Having campaigned for her release, Baez attempted to contact Angela Davis, in the hope that she might mediate in the dispute. Instead, she was told that Ms Davis was 'ours, not yours'. Baez concluded that Ring Around Congress was 'the most difficult, demoralising, battering, discouraging task I have ever taken on in my life'. That same month, the remnants of the Black Panther Party staged their own Anti-War African Liberation Voter Registration Survival Conference in Oakland. This time there was no Grateful Dead to confuse the party's supporters, merely R&B music in ancient and modern styles from Sisters Love and John Lee Hooker. The middle-aged bluesman became the only 'celebrity' ever interviewed by the *Black Panther* newspaper, and responded in kind, blaming 'the white man' for the influx of drugs into the ghetto. If, as it seemed, the movement was splitting along racial lines, the only beneficiary was the Nixon administration that both sides claimed to despise.

Interviewed as a celebrity by *Rolling Stone* magazine, the now almost irrelevant Huey Newton showed off his colour-blind musical taste by playing his guest an album by Joan Baez. Newton also treated the interviewer to *Shaft*, Isaac Hayes' album of music from a recent hit movie. Like *Sweet Sweetback's Baadasssss Song*, which Newton had promoted in the *Black Panther* paper, *Shaft* was a black-led thriller aimed squarely at the African-American audience. Unlike Melvin Van Peebles' film, however, *Shaft* was produced by a Hollywood corporation, MGM. Its clichéd portrayal of the black urban experience – most of its characters were gangsters, pimps or whores – titillated a mass audience, but was criticised by many commentators. This critical divide widened when *Shaft* inspired dozens of imitations – not just several increasingly tired sequels, but an entire genre that soon became known as 'blaxploitation' movies.

There was a strict formula to these films, from the soundtrack (wah-wah guitar and chattering percussion to the fore) to the cartoon-like violence and sexual stereotypes. Their tone varied from street-tough (the fist-in-the-face realism of *Superfly* and *Across 110th Street*) to hysterical (*Blacula* and *Blackenstein*). By 1972, such stellar names as Curtis Mayfield (*Superfly*), James Brown (*Black Caesar*) and Marvin Gaye (*Trouble Man*) had been recruited to score blaxploitation films. Of these, only Mayfield's soundtrack transcended its origins, neatly subverting the hoodlum ethos of the film with a suite of songs exposing the power that drug dealers held over the ghetto. Yet it was *Superfly* that attracted the wrath of Huey Newton, who declared that the film was 'part of a conspiracy'. The initial New York screening was picketed by members of the civil rights organisation NAACP, who like Newton deplored the fact that black people were being caricatured for the purpose of entertainment. This was not the first blaxploitation protest: a few weeks earlier, the Black Panthers had staged a demonstration on the set of *The Mack* in Oakland, after the producers exploited African-American extras by paying them lower wages than their white counterparts.

Blaxploitation was not the only example of mainstream black culture to feel the wrath of the Panthers. The *Black Panther* paper prepared for the Presidential election in November by accusing R&B icon James Brown of having 'souled out' by supporting Richard Nixon's candidacy. The Panthers were heartened by Stevie Wonder, who celebrated his independence from the production factory at his record label, Motown, by releasing the stunning album *Talking Book*. It included 'Big Brother', an overt attack on the Nixon administration and the white establishment beyond. At a time when most leading black artists were distancing themselves from militant organisations, Wonder continued to pledge his support to the Panthers' community operations, playing benefit concerts or donating to the party's food and sickle cell anaemia programmes.

Social awareness dominated American soul music during 1972, as everyone from the O'Jays and Roberta Flack to Funkadelic and James Brown began to explore issues raised by the turbulence of recent years. But there was no longer a political vehicle to carry this passion forward. The Democratic Party did its best to channel the anger and cynicism of black America, but much energy was being diverted towards the increasingly powerful Nation of Islam, separatist in philosophy and action. Like the Weather Underground, the newly formed Black Liberation Army numbered a few dozen militants, nothing more, and only represented a threat to those who were unfortunate enough to be in the vicinity of one of their sporadic bomb explosions. Despair, cocaine and heroin conquered the ghettos, and a monologue from James Brown (such as his 1972 hit single 'King Heroin') wasn't enough to turn things around. Even the self-conscious poets of the ghetto streets, the Last Poets, disintegrated in an excess of greed and mutual recrimination that year. The title of what seemed likely to be their final album, *Chastisement*, told its own story. So did the No. 1 hit single by the O'Jays, 'Back Stabbers', which echoed the suspicion and paranoia that now swept the African-American community as coke and smack took their toll.

No record captured that deadening sense of desperation with more fidelity than Sly & the Family Stone's *There's a Riot Goin' On*. From its Stars-and-Stripes cover design to its entirely silent title track, the album reeked of exhaustion and boredom – with America, with the revolution, with activism, with optimism, with the hope of redemption. Sly Stone himself was lost in a haze of cocaine and angel dust. Yet enough of his instinct and insight remained to sketch out the bleakness of black America's future. If there was a riot going on, it was in Stone's house, where drugs took precedence over music and over life. 'Dying young is hard to take,' he sang on the final track, 'Thank You for Talking to Me Africa', 'but selling out is harder'. It was the perfect soundtrack for a liberation movement that could see its integrity and enthusiasm ebbing away.

## WELCOME TO MIAMI BEACH

The Yippies and Zippies treated McGovern's coronation at the Democratic Convention in Miami as a dry run for the more spectacular Republican fire-works to come. They joined gay rights activists, feminists, black militants, Vietnam veterans and other protestors outside the convention hall, or camped out in Flamingo Park. There the Yippies staged a Senior Citizens Rally, and the Zippies joked that the likes of Rubin and Hoffman were already senior citizens themselves. The Zippies responded with a Smoke-In – marijuana, not tobacco, of course – at the Bay Shore Golf Club. But these demonstrations were half-hearted affairs, defused by the hope that the Democrats had, for once, selected a candidate who represented the Yippies and Zippies as well as the American heartland. To illustrate that he understood young people, McGovern quoted Woody Guthrie's folk tune 'This Land is Your Land' in his acceptance speech, and also referred to the Byrds' folk-rock hit 'Turn! Turn! Turn!' It seemed as if a generational shift had taken place in the political mainstream.

The Republican Party came to Miami Beach in late August, and the movement tried to mass its courage and self-belief for one last radical push that might shake the establishment to its foundations. The omens were unfavourable. John Lennon and Yoko Ono opted out of attending the demonstrations they were helping to finance. Instead, they were in New York, rehearsing for two upcoming concerts at Madison Square Gardens – not to fund the Irish civil rights movement, as they'd originally pledged, but to raise money for children in care homes. The beneficiaries might have been selected to prove how unthreatening the couple were to the American administration. Meanwhile, the Jefferson Airplane pulled out of a free concert that they had scheduled for the weekend before the convention, just as so many bands had deserted the flag on the eve of Chicago four years earlier. If the Airplane came, so would several other major acts. But, as Norman Mailer reported, the Airplane 'did not wish to come. Grace Slick was supposed to have said that demonstrations are of no use after the Eagleton affair because McGovern is sure to lose. There are some who had thought that the point was to embarrass Nixon and protest the war regardless of who won the election, but in any case a lesson has been taught which will not be learned. It is that one should not try to found a revolution on musicians; because the delicate instrument of their body can all too easily be damaged, they are all prone to desert.'

What remained to be seen was whether it was possible to found a revolution on self-confessed revolutionaries. Maybe 1,000 or 2,000 people who would have welcomed that description made the trip to Miami, and a large proportion of them were undercover agents of the FBI, the Florida police, and other organisations who had a vested interest in protecting Nixon and his government. In 1968, Jerry Rubin and Abbie Hoffman had been consummate outsiders. In 1972, they held official press credentials, as they were researching a book entitled *Vote!*

The Zippies were outraged by what they saw as a Yippie sell-out. Rubin and Hoffman claimed that half of their advance would be going into financing the renaissance of the Yippies as a political party, but chief Zippie Tom Forcade alleged that it actually went into a bank account credited to 'YIP Inc', which was controlled by the two men. 'The Yippies held no demonstrations of their own,' Forcade complained, 'and the only thing they did was to rent an elephant to march in a parade and rent some floodlights for a Hollywood Spectacular effect . . . Not only did they steal from the people's energy, but they denounced us as cops and *agents provocateurs* 'cos we stood up to the pigs.' This Zippie defiance comprised an attack on some of the buses that were bringing Republicans to the convention hall; and then a desperate, doomed march towards the same venue, which was brought to a rapid halt by police clubs and tear gas. They were rewarded by a raid on the evening after President Nixon had delivered his acceptance speech. 'The cops raided the Zippie house,' Weberman recalled. 'They held guns on us while they beat the shit out of us. Then they said we had five minutes to get out of town, or they would blow our heads off. When we got to our cars, we found the pigs had slashed our tyres in retaliation for us having slashed theirs.'

That was the closest that Miami came to experiencing a revolution: a ragged band of trouble-makers being treated like teenage hoodlums. For Richard Neville, the Republican Convention proved only that the movement was 'in a state of shambles'. Tom Forcade accused the Yippies of having 'kissed the government's ass' and declared that Miami illustrated that Rubin, Hoffman and their friends were just as porcine as the 'pigs'. Chicago trial defendant Tom Hayden concluded that 'it was very difficult to be in Miami and not understand that whatever fantasies one might have had about significant change in the United States were just that'. Richard Neville agreed: 'Flamingo Park, on the final Wednesday, conjured up an image of what it must have been like on the eve of the final battle of the Confederate Army.' It was a damning comparison: it suggested that the movement would not only lose the war, but also the verdict of history.

## WHERE ARE YOU NOW, MY SON?

America's biggest selling album in 1972 was the fifth release by Chicago, the band who two years earlier had dedicated their lives and music to 'the revolution'. They were slowly easing themselves into a lucrative career as purveyors of elegant 'adult contemporary' music, in place of the strident jazz-rock with which they had made their name. But *Chicago V* was still recognisably the work of artists who continued to fret about the progress of their country, their generation, and the revolt that they had hoped both to lead and to document. Almost every song on the album was tinged with a sense of retrospective loss or defiant, if sometimes foolhardy, optimism. On 'Alma Mater', they sang, 'we must set brand new goals, we must not lose control', like Soviet bureaucrats assembling the next five-year plan. A voice in 'Saturday in the Park' proclaimed, 'Listen, children, all is not lost'. Another voice, which the narrator of 'State of the Union' found impossible to ignore, still demanded: 'Tear the system down'. 'Dialogue' was devoted to a strangely alienated conversation between two students, one an activist, the other blissfully unconcerned about political concerns. It ended with a chorus that sounded like self-hypnosis, proclaiming: 'We can make it happen, we can change the world now'.

Yet as Richard Nixon strolled towards his inevitable re-election, the landmine of Watergate still carefully concealed, it was difficult to imagine that anything had changed since his assumption of power four years earlier. If the war was ending – and on 26 October, Nixon's Secretary of State, Henry Kissinger, declared firmly that 'peace is at hand' – then it owed more to diplomacy than to any uprising of the people, young or old. There was a growing distaste for the Vietnam conflict, a national instinct that the United States might be better served by preserving its own borders rather than crossing those in South-East Asia.

Kissinger's proclamation was the result of several months of secret negotiations with the North Vietnamese government. They continued past the election in early November, but by mid-December it was apparent that they had reached an impasse. On 16 December, law professor and former Army Brigadier General Telford Taylor led a small group of concerned American citizens on a human rights mission to North Vietnam. Besides maintaining relations between the people of the two countries, the purpose of the mission was to deliver mail to US prisoners of war. The delegation, dubbed the Committee for Solidarity, included Barry Romo, one of the leaders of Vietnam Veterans Against the War and a Maoist activist; Michael Allen, the Dean of the Divinity School at Yale; and Joan Baez.

Two days later, the American government launched Operation Linebacker II. In an attempt to convince the South Vietnamese government that it would continue to defend its interests, the US staged eleven nights of intensive B-52 bombing raids on the cities of Hanoi and Haiphong. Baez and her party experienced at first hand the ferocity of American firepower. To document the terror she was living through, she taped the sounds of the bombing. Portions of this unnerving recording formed the backdrop to the side-long title track of her next album, 'Where Are You Now, My Son?' – which she described ironically as 'a record company's nightmare'. 'I have always ended up choosing the leper causes,' she says wryly, 'and I don't mind being treated like a leper in the process.' Though his voice wasn't heard on the recording, Henry Kissinger's 'peace is at hand' message resounded through every inch of tape, a testament to another dark month in the broken promised land.

Four years of hope and defiance had ended a month earlier, on election day, 7 November 1972. McGovern had promised peace; Nixon had announced that, under his command, peace was already in the nation's grasp. America chose to believe the incumbent president, afraid of switching leaders at this moment of peril, afraid of McGovern's ultra-liberal stance on the wars at home and abroad, afraid of the company he had kept or might keep, afraid of change that might come out of left field and whirl the country into unpredictable territory. The statistics told the story with relentless accuracy. Nixon attracted 47.1 million votes, or 60.7 per cent of the popular vote. McGovern won only 29 million (37.5 per cent). Translated into the electoral college that officially decides Presidential contests, these scores ensured that Nixon carried every state apart from Massachusetts (and Washington, DC, treated as a separate entity for electoral purposes). The college re-elected Nixon, by 520 votes to 17. It was the most devastating landslide in US history.

There was no consolation for the left in the small print, either. A staunch conservative with a history of supporting racist groups was the leading 'third' candidate, polling 1.4 million votes. Linda Jenness of the Socialist Workers Party managed 88,000 votes. Benjamin Spock, representing the People's Party, the authentic voice of the movement, could not even top this score, attracting just 78,759 supporters. Just 0.1 per cent of the electorate stood up to be counted as supporters of the left. On that showing, the movement was ready to be buried, alive or nearly dead.

That evening, as the votes were counted and the TV networks offered exit polls predicting the outcome, an election night party was held – symbolically enough – in the SoHo apartment of Jerry Rubin. Results began to flash onto the screen around 7.00pm. Within two hours, Nixon's re-election was official; McGovern had yet to win a single state. 'It was far more depressing than expected,' recounted British radical journalist Jonathan Green, who attended the party. 'People who had struggled for years to see the end of Nixon, of Johnson before him, of the war, of racism, of every inequality in the States, had only four more years of the same to look forward to.'

Later on, as the crowd thinned out, John Lennon and Yoko Ono arrived with several members of their band. They had spent the day at the Record Plant East studio, where they were working on a collection of Ono's feminist songs – a groundbreaking project that represented the fullest musical statement yet of women's liberation, in all its facets, from ecstasy to despair. They had broken off the sessions to watch the election results, and Lennon had attempted to drown his sorrow in tequila. A few months earlier, he had begun to suspect that Jerry Rubin was a CIA agent, who had shopped him to the US government as a radical threat, and provoked the immigration battle that was now the backdrop of his daily life. Rubin's friends had convinced him that the Yippie founder was on the level. But it was Rubin who had sucked the Lennons into the revolutionary fray, who had convinced them that they only had to enter the struggle to tip the balance in the direction of righteousness. Now here they were, the hucksters who had seduced Lennon – Rubin, Abbie Hoffman, Allen Ginsberg – sprawled helplessly on the floor, weeping for their lost dreams.

Lennon was more angry than sad. He felt as if he'd been duped. He crashed through the door, bottle in hand, bellowing 'Up the revolution' as a sarcastic commentary on his comrades' failure. When he spied Rubin and Hoffman, he launched into a tirade about 'pigs' and 'middle-class Jews', those charlatans who had sapped his energy and tipped him into a desperate struggle with the American government. He couldn't even write any more, his creativity ground down by the unrelenting legal process. Meanwhile he had to spend his days helping his wife record *her* songs, with *his* band, for *his* record label, songs that exposed him and his sex as the bastards he'd always feared he might be. As he had predicted two years earlier, the dream was over.

Radical theatre director Judith Malina, who had just published a book about the decay of the movement entitled *The Enormous Despair*, attempted to calm him down. 'I want to cut you with a knife,' he screamed into her face. She recalled him ranting almost incoherently, pouring out his frustration and sense of betrayal like a public exhibition of Primal Scream therapy. 'I'm going to join the Weathermen,' he bellowed at one point. 'I'm going to shoot a policeman.'

Lennon's almost deranged anger broke up the party. Rubin's guests slipped away quietly, embarrassed to be around this icon who was meant to be the midwife of the revolution, but had mutated into its decomposing corpse. While Ono watched silently, Lennon began hitting on Rubin's room-mate (and Hoffman's sometime lover), Carol Realini. Then he led her into the next room. When she told him she was uncomfortable at the idea that his wife was just outside the door, Lennon told her that he no longer wanted to be married. Swayed by his celebrity and – now that they were alone and he had exhausted his anger – his charm, she let him continue. The last guests at the party attempted to raise their voices to hide the unmistakeable sounds of a man and a woman having sex. Then Lennon re-emerged, motioned silently to Ono, and the couple left. The next day they resumed their musical exploration of feminism. 'What a bastard the world is,' Ono wrote in her most searing analysis of male–female relations. That morning, meanwhile, Rubin, Hoffman and all the last stragglers of the movement woke up to a new America, which looked identical to the old one. There was just one difference – all their fantasies, all their hope, all their glory, were gone.

# EPILOGUE

I've come to believe that all of our radical activity in the late 1960s might actually have prolonged the Vietnam War.

(Allen Ginsberg)

It was, according to Tom Hayden, 'a shambles'. Hayden – veteran of SDS and the Chicago Conspiracy trial, and about to become the husband of fellow radical Jane Fonda – was speaking a few weeks before Nixon's crushing re-election. But his comments suggested that the result was already inevitable. How was it possible, he wondered aloud, that the 'nationwide student movement, [the] anti-war movement, [the] youth culture where people could express themselves as human beings without it being a crime' – how was it possible that this apparently vast reservoir of radical passion should have drained away to nothing?

As he scratched around for answers, he slowly unpicked the thread of the counter-culture. What had killed the movement, he suggested, wasn't political repression or FBI harassment, or even (in the classic Marxist equation) a mismatch of economics and social conditions. The culprit was none other than the counter-culture itself, 'the sense that the kind of things that were supposed to be naturally ours were getting out of our control'. He singled out 'the absorption of Yippie-type theatrics into the media': the leaders of the movement had allowed themselves to become distracted by the possibility of stardom and ego gratification. Worse still, however, was 'the feeling that people had been ripped off on a widespread basis by the absorption of rock music into the commercial culture'. As soon as 'The Revolutionaries Are On Columbia Records', they are no longer revolutionaries. When 'The Man Can't Bust Our Music', the music is already busted, in every sense of the word.

The irony was that Hayden himself was already a media star. His words reflected the comfort of a man who could expect to attract attention and command lucrative earnings for the rest of his life. Members of the black power movement had been living under rather more extreme pressure, fearing for their lives rather than fretting about the sincerity of John Lennon or Mick Jagger. Yet the music and the movement had been so intertwined that it was easy to believe they were supporting each other. Hayden and his comrades were chilled by the realisation that rock and the revolution might actually have been diverting and sapping each other's energy.

Over the next few years, many of the veterans of this inconclusive struggle recanted their radical pasts, and swapped their revolutionary idealism for self-obsession. Others refused to betray their political zeal, and had to face new enemies: derision, depression, the awareness that history had passed them by. Either path could lead to self-destruction, as the drugs that had seemed to represent liberation took their toll on bodies and psyches alike. Meanwhile, the world continued to turn, and to change, often in unexpected ways. Heroes revealed their feet of dust; villains fulfilled the dreams of their enemies. Nobody's preconceptions survived unchallenged.

In the late evening of 23 January 1973, Neil Young was approaching the climax of a performance in New York. Between songs, a roadie scurried onto the stage, and handed him a sheet of paper. Young took a glance, and then strode to the microphone. 'Peace has come,' he announced. The 20,000-strong audience howled its approval.

A few minutes earlier, President Richard Nixon had commandeered America's television and radio networks for a historic announcement: 'We today have concluded an agreement to end the war and bring peace with honour in Vietnam and South-East Asia.' The deal would take effect in four days' time, he promised. All American prisoners of war would be released; all American troops would be returning home. The sovereignty of South Vietnam, and its people's right to determine their own future, were guaranteed. 'Let us be proud', Nixon concluded, 'that America did not settle for a peace that would have betrayed our allies, that would have abandoned our prisoners of war, or that would have ended the war for us but would have continued the war for the fifty million people of Indochina.'

His opponent in the 1972 election, George McGovern, had pledged to bring home the troops within three months. Now Nixon had achieved the same feat. There was symbolism, perhaps, in the fact that his announcement came the day after the death of former President Lyndon Johnson, whose career and health had been ravaged by the war. And there was irony in the fact that Neil Young's fans, like everyone who had signed up for the movement, had to cheer Nixon as he delivered the peace that had appeared to be beyond anyone's reach.

The USA duly removed its troops from Vietnam by 29 March 1973. The veterans returned home to find that they were an embarrassing reminder of a disastrous foreign policy. 'They were sold the biggest fucking lie in the world,' contends singer Eric Burdon, who has played many benefit concerts for Vietnam vets. 'It took twenty years for the truth to come out about exactly how bad their deal was. If Americans don't examine the war as closely as we in Europe examine World War Two, then they'll keep falling into deeper and deeper shit.'

By the time the troops returned, it was clear that 'peace' was a flexible concept. The American government had secretly pledged financial and military support to the South Vietnamese regime, to ensure that the North Vietnamese did not use the ceasefire as the trigger for a new assault. But the weakening Nixon administration could not live up to that promise. Although the war was officially over, the conflict continued, as North Vietnam's army and the Viet Cong guerrillas gradually increased their pressure on the South. In March 1975, the two forces seized several major towns in South Vietnam, and began an inexorable push towards Saigon. The South's government begged the US President for immediate aid, but Congress refused to release the necessary funds. In late April, the South Vietnamese leader resigned. On 30 April, North Vietnamese troops raised their flag in Saigon. It was immediately renamed Ho Chi Minh City, in honour of the late guerrilla leader who had launched their movement of national liberation several decades earlier.

As the invaders reached Saigon, helicopters hovered over the US Embassy. They dropped rope ladders down to the roof, and the last remaining American personnel scrabbled to safety, minutes before the North Vietnamese entered the compound. The chaotic, humiliating scenes were broadcast around the world. Yet the chaos in South-East Asia was only just beginning. While Vietnam commanded media attention, a tragedy of unimaginable proportions was unfolding across the border in Cambodia. American troops had left the country on 12 April 1975; five days later, the capital,

Phnom Penh, was seized by a self-confessed revolutionary army: the Khmer Rouge. Under the leadership of Pol Pot, the Khmer Rouge imposed Year Zero – a policy of genocide masquerading as a Marxist dictatorship of the working class. Millions died in the so-called killing fields, until the unified republic of Vietnam overthrew Pol Pot's regime on Christmas Day 1978. Vietnam then had to fight off an invasion by troops from another Communist dictatorship, China. Western dissidents who had welcomed the demise of US colonial power in South-East Asia were left to consider whether the ideals of liberation and self-determination could ever withstand such horrors.

As the mass murders of Cambodia demonstrated, there were consequences to every political action that were unforeseen, and sometimes unbearable. On 11 September 1973, the democratically elected socialist government of Chile was overthrown by a military coup. The rebel generals were aided and encouraged by the tacit support of the American government, after the CIA had helped to destabilise the vulnerable regime of President Salvador Allende. He was shot dead – ostensibly by his own hand, though many dispute this version of events – during the uprising. Thousands of his supporters were arrested, tortured and, in many cases, killed. The *coup d'etat* remains a gaping scar on the history of modern geopolitics.

The same Western governments who had opposed the North Vietnamese lined up behind the Chilean junta headed by General Pinochet. Yet this time protests in these countries were muted. 'I think a lot of it had to do with exhaustion,' suggests Judy Collins. 'We were so convinced of the righteousness of the anti-war movement in Vietnam, that we had nothing left to give.' Collins recorded 'The Prayer of a Labourer', an anthem written by Victor Jara, the folk-singer and activist who was savagely murdered in the aftermath of the coup. 'I knew his wife, Joan, and she brought me the song. It connected me to the struggle for human rights in Chile,' she recalls. Phil Ochs had befriended both Allende and Jara. In spring 1974, he organised a benefit concert in New York for the Friends of Chile. 'Everyone was excited,' remembers his friend Arthur Gorson, 'because Phil was back with a cause, and was feeling passionate again.' Ochs even managed to persuade his rival and friend, Bob Dylan, to make a drunken appearance at the concert. But two years later Ochs committed suicide, his morale shattered by personal, artistic and political despair. 'Our father was a manic depressive,' recalls his brother Michael, and the darkening times forced Phil into this grim family tradition.

Phil Ochs' hate-figure, Richard Nixon, experienced his own Calvary of the soul in the wake of his 1972 election victory. Within weeks, it became apparent that White House staff had been involved in the bugging and burglary of the Democratic Party's headquarters in the Watergate Hotel. As the truth slowly surfaced, Nixon was forced to sacrifice one key staff member after another, until finally there was no one left to blame but himself. Exposed to the American people as a chronic liar, Nixon became the first President of the United States to resign his office, on 9 August 1974. The previous evening, he announced his decision in a televised address. Immediately after the speech, Neil Young and his bandmates in CSNY took to the stage of Roosevelt Stadium in New Jersey, and revealed the news to the crowd. As with peace in Vietnam, both musicians and audience regarded Nixon's departure as a victory. Yet within a month, Nixon had been pardoned for any crimes he might have committed by his successor, Gerald Ford, and justice was left undone. It scarcely seemed to matter that a few days later, Ford also issued a blanket pardon to all those who had evaded the Vietnam draft.

When he signed the document that removed Nixon from the threat of prosecution, Gerald Ford effectively sealed the death warrant for his own presidency. In 1976, he lost the election to the Democratic governor of Georgia, Jimmy Carter. The new President was 52 years old when he assumed office, but he appealed blatantly to the youth vote by dropping quotations from Bob Dylan's songs into his campaign speeches. On the verge of the election, he told *Playboy* magazine that he had actually met Dylan in 1974. '[Dylan] said he didn't have any inclination to change the world, that he wasn't crusading,' Carter revealed.

That was hardly news; Dylan had explained as much during the January 1974 concerts that comprised his first full-scale American tour for eight years. There was no need for protest songs or political activism, he told a *Newsweek* reporter, because 'everybody's thinking the same thing'. Ticket demand for the tour broke all previous records, and his performances were greeted as a triumphant rebirth of 1960s optimism at a moment of national peril.

Yet one man was unmoved by the hype. As the tour opened in Chicago, A.J. Weberman stood outside the stadium and handed out leaflets that carried a familiar message: 'Free Bob Dylan?' Weberman's rhetoric hadn't changed: 'Why pay high ticket price$', he asked, 'when Dylan is worth million$?' He pronounced that 'the Dylan you'll see is an imposter', as 'the real Dylan was killed by cynicism' – and then he reeled off his accusations about drug abuse, shares in arms manufacturers, hypocrisy and Zionism, the same litany of complaints that he'd been offering to the underground since the dawn of the 1970s.

So powerful was the media furore surrounding the tour, however, that Weberman found himself newsworthy for the first time in years. Interviewers quizzed Dylan about his involvement with the Jewish Defense League and told him that he was being described as 'an ultra-Zionist'. 'I'm not sure what a Zionist really is,' Dylan responded. 'I don't know how these things get started, really. It's just gossip.' But his friend and fellow performer Mimi Farina (sister of Joan Baez) felt sufficiently concerned about the stories to pen an open letter to Dylan in the *San Francisco Chronicle,* expressing her fears that he was helping to finance the Israeli military. 'The money you earn is the money we are willing to give you,' she declared. 'If it is going to support the taking of more lives, we should know that before we buy our tickets.' The story was forgotten by almost everyone except Weberman after the tour ended.

In 1975, Dylan released his first 'protest' song since 'George Jackson' in 1971. 'Hurricane' was a cinematic tale of injustice, inspired by the apparently unjust imprisonment of black boxer Ruben 'Hurricane' Carter. Dylan's compelling performance seemed to denote a long-awaited rebirth of social and political awareness in his work. Not that the record was universally popular. 'Every four years Dylan writes a "new" protest song,' complained critic Lester Bangs, 'and it's always about a martyred nigger.' His cynicism was echoed by acid guru Timothy Leary, who denounced what he saw as 'the Outlaw Exploitation Game... more fun and easier than Texas oil-drilling. Just wait until the next martyr is discovered and watch it gush. Who's next? Here comes Hurricane Carter and another cheap shot at the charts.'

But Leary was hardly an unimpeachable witness. He had been recaptured by US federal agents in 1973, and agreed to identify the members of the Weather Underground who had helped him escape from prison three years earlier. He was sent back to jail himself for a further three years, and emerged to find himself a pariah amongst radicals. His exposé of Dylan was published in the conservative magazine *The National Review*. So outraged were his former friends by his apparent shift of alignment that they formed an organ-isation called PILL: People Investigating Leary's Lies.

'How the hell did we get here so quick, from the ideologies of the 1960s to this? The parents of today's young black Americans were talking about going back to Africa to resettle, as a radical statement. Now the sons and daughters of those people are going back to Africa, and to other parts of the world, in Marine Corps uniforms, in tanks and huge aircraft, to settle political deals. People talk about the hallucination of the 1960s. But *that's* hallucination as far as I'm concerned.' (Eric Burdon)

Leary's journey from prophet of LSD enlightenment to government informer paled alongside that of the man who had given him sanctuary in Algeria, Eldridge Cleaver. Increasingly at odds with the Algerian government, Cleaver moved his family and the remnants of his political organisation to Paris at the start of 1973. 'I was to spend three years there,' he explained later, 'and my inner restlessness and spiritual emptiness were to reach awful proportions'. By 1974, he had opened tentative channels with the US govern-ment, to determine whether he might be allowed to return home. The following year, he experienced a nervous break-down, during which his former radical heroes paraded before his eyes. At the end of the line was Jesus Christ. 'That was the last straw,' he recalled. 'I just crumbled and started crying. I fell to my knees, grabbing hold of the banister; and in the midst of this shaking and crying, the Lord's Prayer and the 23rd Psalm came into my mind.' The convicted rapist and proud revolutionary was now ready to be acknowledged as a born-again Christian.

On 18 November 1975, Cleaver flew home to New York, where he was ar-rested and escorted to San Diego. His former comrades assumed that he too was prepared to become an informer; the Revolutionary Student Brigade described him as 'a traitor to the struggle of black people, and the struggles of all people for liberation'. He remained a prisoner until 1980, when he used his freedom to launch a missionary campaign known as the Eldridge Cleaver Crusades. Over the next decade, he toyed with the Moonies and the Mormons, while retaining his links to evangelical Christianity. He even attempted to run for the US Senate as a can-didate for the same Republican Party that had once been his sworn enemy.

Meanwhile, the Black Panther Party had disintegrated. 'Most of them seem to have been killed,' author Michael J. Arlen wrote in 1973, 'or are dead anyway, or in jail, or disappeared; receded or engulfed, maybe, into some other dimmer mainstream. And, one remembers, there were never so very many of them to begin with.' Huey Newton was still ostensibly running the party until summer 1974. By then, his drug-fuelled paranoia had alienated him from his former allies. When he was charged with beating a 17-year-old prostitute to death, he fled to Cuba, ironically following Cleaver's escape route from the USA. He returned to stand trial in 1977; once again, hung juries and talk of witness intimidation ensured that all charges against him were dismissed. But Newton was now trapped in the twilight world of cocaine, which had claimed so many of his brothers. He was jailed for illegal possession of a firearm in 1987; then twice again the following year for drugs offences. In August 1989, he was shot dead on his home turf of West Oakland, after a dispute over a drug deal.

As the Panthers shed their idealism, those members who had switched allegiance to the Black Liberation Army were picked off, one by one, succumbing to arrest or the bullet. So too were the leaders of the Weather Underground: some were captured after moments of carelessness during their years in hiding, while others turned themselves in, to relieve the pressure of living in constant fear. Other revolutionary icons suffered similar fates. Neither of the two prime Yippies, Jerry Rubin and Abbie Hoffman, survived beyond middle age. Hoffman was arrested for drug dealing in 1973, and then went underground himself – though in keeping with his irrepressible energy, his new identity reinvented him as an environmental lobbyist. He committed suicide in 1989, unable to live with the extremes of his manic depression. But at least his idealism remained intact. After the fiasco of 1972, Jerry Rubin abandoned politics, preferring to follow the paths of self-help and spiritual enlightenment. They led him towards careers as a stockbroker and entrepreneur, exploiting the revolutionary chic that he had helped to create. In their twilight years, Hoffman and Rubin staged nostalgic debates for money, offering a glimpse of the Yippie exhilaration of old. But the two men scarcely communicated off stage, as neither was able to comprehend the other's beliefs or lifestyle. Rubin was knocked down and killed while jaywalking in 1994.

The Panthers were reborn in 1989, although none of the survivors of

Huey Newton's cabinet recognised the legitimacy of the New Black Panther Party. They prefer to concentrate on the most positive aspects of the old party's legacy: its declaration of black pride and defiance, its social programmes, its determination to speak and act against oppression. The Panthers' detractors remember only the catalogue of violence. But at least the party is still remembered in the 21st century. The Yippies endure only as a fading memory and a museum – the latter superintended by their old comrade-turned-goad, A.J. Weberman.

The Dylanologist continues to 'interpret' Dylan's work, searching for clues to confirm his conviction that the singer's 'current bag' is HIV/AIDS. He also believes that Dylan has consistently alluded to the two men's unusual 'relationship' in his songs. Dylan, meanwhile, maintains a safe distance from his one-time stalker, and continues to plead ignorance of politics in any form. Nonetheless, Weberman claims that Dylan's 2006 album *Modern Times* is full of allegorical commentary on the Israel/Palestine dispute.

According to Weberman, John Lennon continued to support the activities of the Zippies beyond the 1972 election. 'John paid for the postage costs of the *Yipster Times* newspaper,' he says. It is a matter of record that Lennon was also financing the British newspaper *International Times* in 1973. But his battle with the Immigration Service, which continued until 1976, sapped his desire to indulge in more urgent radical gestures. Instead, on April Fools' Day 1973, Lennon and Yoko Ono staged a press conference in New York, at which they proclaimed themselves ambassadors for the newly imagined state of Nutopia. 'Its flag was the white flag of surrender,' Ono explained a decade later, 'a surrender to peace.'

Thereafter, the couple edged away from political commitment. 'It's not that I'm above politics,' Lennon explained in one of his final interviews, 'it's that politics isn't what I do.' To prove the point, he rewrote his own past, claiming: 'I dabbled in so-called politics in the late 1960s and 1970s more out of guilt than anything. Guilt for being rich and guilt thinking that perhaps love and peace isn't enough and you have to go and get shot or something, or get punched in the face, to prove I'm one of the people. I was doing it against my instincts.'

Lennon was murdered in 1980, and to this day some people choose to belief that he was the subject of a government assassination plot, because he was too dangerous a radical to be allowed to stay alive. That hardly chimes with a man who, in the weeks before his death, was reprising the wish-fulfilment philosophy of his 1969 peace campaign: if people had a problem, all they needed to do was imagine a solution, and it would come to pass.

If there was any vestige of radicalism in his household, it came from his wife. Her 1973 album *Approximately Infinite Universe* – the record on which the couple had been working before the ill-fated election night party – was a landmark in feminist music. 'I don't think the feminist movement were particularly happy with me,' she says in retrospect. 'I don't think that they knew how to deal with me. I was a wife – the wife of a Beatle! – and the initial feminist movement was mostly white middle-class career women, who were very naive about the rest of the female species. To them I was just Mrs Lennon. So songs like "I Want My Man to Rest Tonight" didn't go down very well. The notion of trying to communicate and reach out to men was considered humiliating.' It is perhaps not a coincidence that after Ono recorded a second feminist record, *Feeling the Space*, she and Lennon separated for eighteen months.

One of their final public actions as a couple was to issue a statement in support of their old friend Michael Abdul Malik. Soon after the Lennons had visited him in Trinidad, two of his associates were murdered. He was convicted of the crime, and sentenced to death by hanging. Lennon and Ono urged the British public to rise up against the inhumanity of the death sentence: 'Every time we turn our backs on someone who needs help, we take a step backward in time. Please help save a life.' Lennon offered the piano on which he had written several Beatles songs, so that it could be auctioned to raise funds for Michael's appeal.

Among their fellow members of the International Committee to Save Michael X was Judy Collins. She rejects the idea that Malik was a murderer, a charlatan or, as his first biographers claimed, a 'false messiah'. 'I have a very different sense of him,' she reveals. 'I got to know him, and I saw him as a man with real qualities and values, who had a definite mission, to improve the situation of his people.' But the International Committee split after its British representatives insultingly referred to Yoko Ono as 'John Lennon's Jap wife'. Despite high-ranking legal representation, Michael X was hanged on 16 May 1975. 'I remember that night very well,' Collins says. 'I guess I'm undauntingly naive. I always thought that if everyone knew the facts, then the right decision would be made. But it wasn't.'

Violence, naivety and despair: Michael X's execution seemed to close the book on the revolution that rock stars and radicals alike had been awaiting for the previous decade. When a small urban terrorist group called the Symbionese Liberation Army (SLA) carried out several murders, and kidnapped heiress Patricia Hearst, there was no revolutionary vanguard to claim them as sisters and brothers. In a foretaste of the celebrity-obsessed culture of decades to come, even the remnants of the underground press devoted more attention to Hearst's decision to join her captors' struggle than to their political motives. When the SLA revealed that their party anthem was the Crusaders' jazz-funk instrumental 'Way Back Home', the group hastily distanced themselves from the connection. There were no Lennons or Jaggers eager to send the SLA pianos or royalty cheques.

'You've always got to have good tunes if you're marching. But the tunes don't make the march. Basically, rock and roll isn't protest, and never was. It's not political. It promotes interfamilial tension – or it used to. Now it can't even do that, because fathers don't ever get outraged with the music. So rock and roll's gone, that's all gone.' (Mick Jagger, 1980)

In 1975, former student leader Tom Hayden wistfully recalled the revolution that never was. 'The original theory of Weatherman was that we were in a situation of virtual fascism, because of Nixon's policies,' he declared. 'And therefore the only recourse, in their view, was resistance against this closed system. That's proven, I think, to be a fear that did not unfold. The democratic process came through. We're not living in a police state.' A decade after the movement first raised the flag of revolution, Hayden was content to trust in democracy, and the power *of* – rather than *to* – the people. He could not have realised that he had just lived through a golden era of democracy, when the people had the power to fight their government, and imagine that they might affect its actions at home and around the world; and when musicians were prepared to endanger their careers, and sometimes even their lives, in the cause of political freedom. But that dream, like so many, was over.

# ACKNOWLEDGEMENTS

Many of the most prominent figures in this narrative are no longer here to tell their tale. Old age is inevitable, but murder, suicide and misadventures with drugs have also taken their toll. Of those who remain, many now prefer not to acknowledge their role, active or passive, in this saga; a few have become professional historians of their own lives, who demand payment in advance for their memories.

Some of the veterans of this tumultuous era, however, have not only survived with their minds and ideals intact, but are less reticent about their role in history. Over the last two decades, and particularly during my lengthy period of research for this project, I have been fortunate enough to interview many of the participants in, and observers of, the events in this book. Whether or not they are quoted directly in the text, their reminiscences, analysis and enthusiasm have proved invaluable. Many thanks, therefore, to the following: Joan Baez, Tony Barrow, Bruce Barthol, Steve Blauner, Jackson Browne, Eric Burdon, Joseph Byrd, John Cale, Judy Collins, David Crosby, Dave Davies, Ray Davies, the late Ahmet Ertegun, Mick Farren, John Fogerty, Steve Gebhardt, the late Allen Ginsberg, Arthur Gorson, Richie Havens, Judy Henske, John Hoyland, Peter Jenner, Bruce Johnston, Paul Kantner, Al Kooper, Greil Marcus, Country Joe McDonald, Roger McGuinn, Tom McGuinness, John Mellencamp, Barry Miles, Joni Mitchell, Dorothy Moskowitz, Graham Nash, Bob Neuwirth, Michael Ochs, Andrew Loog Oldham, Yoko Ono, May Pang, Tom Paxton, David Peel, the late John Phillips, Robbie Robertson, Smokey Robinson, Leon Russell, Anthony Scaduto, Clive Selwood, Bill Siddons, Larry Sloman, Stephen Stills, the late Derek Taylor, James Taylor, Don Was, A.J. Weberman, Bob Whitaker and Bill Wyman. In addition, Johnny Rogan very kindly interviewed Gerry O'Hare on my behalf.

The revolution, surreal and sometimes illusory, was conducted as much in the media as in the streets. What happened was often less important than what was reported and disseminated to the public at large. So it was obvious from the start of this project that contemporary sources would provide a priceless insight into the body, mind and soul of the counter-culture.

Besides my own collection of books and periodicals relating to rock and the movement, built up over the last 35 years, I have relied upon the vast resources of the British Library, the University of London Library, the New York Public Library and what remains of the British public library service (who needs books when you can borrow jigsaws and computer games?).

But my deepest debt is owed to Andrew Sclanders of Beat Books (www.beatbooks.com), specialist dealer in rare publications relating to the 60s counter-culture and much else besides. He generously opened the doors of his archive to me, allowing me access to a huge amount of printed material that would otherwise have been beyond my reach. His wide-ranging expertise in this area was also extremely useful.

Others who have contributed directly to my research, and to whom I therefore owe many thanks, include Kieron Tyler, Johnny Rogan, Andy Muir, Sean Body, Mark Paytress, Louise Cripps, Stuart Batsford, Jeremy Collingwood, Chris Charlesworth, Daryl Easlea, Clinton Heylin and my colleagues at Christie's, including Carey Wallace, Sarah Hodgson, Helen Hall and Katherine Williams. Apologies to anyone I've forgotten.

For political or counter-cultural education, inspiration and encouragement, past and present, I am indebted to Toby Lumsden, Andrew Dean, Debbie Cassell, Julie Skelton, Rick Tucker, Caroline Ross, Jim Version, Tom Ovans, Lou Ann Bardash, Caroline Shaw and Sarah Smith.

My agent, Rupert Heath, worked hard to thrash a decent book proposal out of me, and secured me a very welcome deal. Andy Miller was the editor brave enough to take the project on, and his continued enthusiasm has kept my spirits up during the darkest hours. At Canongate, I would also like to thank Jamie Byng, Dan Franklin, Una McGovern, Helen Bleck and Jenny Vass. For once, I haven't forgotten to mention the other members of the Doggett family: my mother Pat, brother Paul, sister-in-law RoseAnne, niece Anna and nephew Alick.

Finally, this book could not have been written without the constant love and endless support of my remarkable wife, Rachel Baylis; and the welcome distraction and enthusiasm for life provided by my wonderful daughters, Catrin Mascall and Becca Mascall. Along with Minky and Fred, I love you all very much.

# NOTES

## PROLOGUE

1 The speech was issued on an album by the most successful black-owned record label of the 1960s, Motown.

2 *Freedom Now* was mysteriously omitted when the rest of the Candid Records catalogue was reissued in the early 1970s.

3 Farrakhan also wrote and recorded the Nation's anthem, 'A White Man's Heaven is a Black Man's Hell'.

4 Manhood was central to Cleaver's self-image: he was in prison for rape. 'I started out by practicing on black girls in the ghetto . . .' he wrote later, 'and when I considered myself smooth enough, I crossed the tracks and sought out white prey . . . Rape was an insurrectionary act. It delighted me that I was defying and trampling upon the white man's law, upon his system of values, and that I was defiling his women.'

## CHAPTER 1: 1966

1 The phrase was borrowed within a few months by a San Francisco rock band fronted by Grace Slick.

2 Not that it could be assumed that the Newport audience would share Ochs' political stance. Abbie Hoffman recalled attending the festival in 1965: 'Len Chandler, a black folk singer, did an antiwar song, and everyone around me joined in. When the song was over, he gave a three-sentence

rap about how he opposed Johnson's war. People booed. The same people who sang along booed him for saying what the words of his song implied. Strange, eh?'

## CHAPTER 2: 1967

1 Barry Miles' recollection is that the Beatles were able to transport the cash to Greece and convert it into local currency. 'Then they came back, brought all the money back with them, and made this huge profit,' he recalls. 'It was classic Beatles. All they'd done was go on holiday and take lots of acid, and they'd made what anyone else would have regarded as a fortune.'

2 Collins was in the process of assembling a fundraising album for the protest group Women Strike For Peace. *Save The Children: Songs from the Hearts of Women* was released in May 1967, with contributions from performers such as Joan Baez and Buffy Sainte-Marie. 'This record was born out of a great frustration,' Collins wrote in her liner notes. 'What can we do as women to save the children, to stop the slaughter? We refuse to accept war with breakfast and atrocities with the evening meal. We ask with this record that you do all within your power to END ALL WARS.'

3 Vanguard drew again on Madison Avenue's finest minds to sell the 1968 Fish album, *Together*: 'Country Joe & the Fish are you. The things that you are: questioning, idealistic, involved; concerned with the love, the confusion and the excitement of the life you live today.'

## CHAPTER 3: 1968

1 Ockene died of leukaemia in 1969, in his mid-30s. Friends contend that his death was the result of a CIA/FBI dirty tricks campaign.

2 This could almost have been a song from an Elvis movie, its title no more ridiculous than 'There's No Room to Rumba in a Sports Car', 'Yoga Is as Yoga Does' or 'Song of the Shrimp'.

3 Perhaps appropriately, the group was founded by Patrick Vian, son of the surrealist writer Boris Vian; even more appropriately, the group soon divided into two factions, one socialist, the other overtly Trotskyist.

Showing a deep sense of irony, the Trotskyist band named itself
Komintern, after the Communist grouping of Soviet Bloc countries.

4 The song had to be rewritten during the sessions to reflect the death of
a second Kennedy brother.

5 They also seized control of a future goldmine, as Miles notes today: 'The
way the tax dodge worked, it was important for the Beatles to set up as
many companies as they possibly could. Then they registered the names
in every country in the world where you can register trademarks. Decades
later, Apple and the Beatles made a vast amount of money out of their
lawsuits against Apple Computers.'

6 'I was wrong to assume that Dylan was a political songwriter,' McDonald
concedes today. 'That was an impression I picked up from the press, and
from songs like "Blowin' in the Wind" and "The Lonesome Death of
Hattie Carroll". I should have realised that, like me, Dylan has always
written a lot of different types of songs.'

7 Fresh from the Chicago debacle, several prominent members of the
Yippies, among them Abbie Hoffman, Ed Sanders and Paul Krassner,
planned to travel to the German/Czech border in mid-September 1968,
'to confront the Russian pigs'. The intention was to speak at a rally-cum-
rock festival in Elsen, West Germany, before leading an estimated 5,000
demonstrators on a long march to free Prague from the Soviet troops.
'Pigs are pigs everywhere,' Hoffman explained. This wildly over-
optimistic plan was stalled when he was arrested on an internal US flight
a few days before the departure date. After briefly considering the idea
of leaving America for good, Hoffman decided to stay at home, and the
Yippie invasion of Czechoslovakia was abandoned.

8 Proving that irony can be a dangerous weapon, the British popular press
seized on their mid-1980s discovery of a rehearsal tape of 'No Pakistanis'
to claim that McCartney was secretly a racist.

9 The programme was abruptly cancelled at the start of its third season,
in 1969, after the brothers objected to the CBS network's attempts to
censor its political content.

10 Two months later, the Beatles enacted a very similar scenario in London, as the climax of their film *Let It Be*.

## CHAPTER 4: 1969

1 The group were soon forced to shorten their name to Chicago after pressure from the genuine Transit Authority, which controlled the city's transport network.

2 Nevertheless, the provocative impact of the *Two Virgins* artwork should not be underestimated. As just one example, authorities at the University of Hartford in Connecticut closed down the student newspaper when it reprinted the offending photographs.

3 In a display of populism, the record was promoted under the banner, 'YOU are the Plastic Ono Band'.

4 The Latin rock band Los Lobos, formed in the mid-1970s, adopted their name in tribute to this organisation.

5 Daltrey also used this occasion to comment on racial tension in Britain: 'England is full up,' he commented. 'They have to stop people from moving in.' He wasn't alone in this opinion. In 1970, diehard R&B fan Rod Stewart – still a year away from global fame – came out in support of the racist philosophy of right-wing Conservative politician Enoch Powell. 'I think Enoch is the man,' he told the *International Times*. 'I'm all for him. This country is overcrowded. The immigrants should be sent home. That's it.' Fortunately for him, these comments were never reprinted in the mainstream press.

6 Its soundtrack, prepared by Ed Sanders, included a song specially written by Phil Ochs.

7 This was far from the last rock album to exploit a pre-teen girl as a sexual object; *Virgin Killer*, a 1977 album by the German hard rock band the Scorpions, was merely the most extreme example. Even a casual glance through the pages of the music press during the mid to late 70s could elicit countless instances of 'jailbait' as a form of rock marketing.

The careers of the Runaways and Britney Spears were arguably built on this premise, for example.

8 The British equivalent, launched alongside the UK GLF in 1970, was named *Come Together*, after John Lennon's song for the Beatles.

9 In a 1971 open letter, Lennon playfully told McCartney, 'I know you're camp!' and was then disappointed when the line wasn't published by the British rock paper *Melody Maker*, in case it was libellous.

10 Unsurprisingly, Amiri Baraka had no truck with this decadence: '*Hair* is the most vicious, counter-revolutionary play going. It promotes a kind of integrationist, dope-above-hope, psychedelic Pantherism . . . Finally all it shows is a nefarious way of getting sucked back into a American ideology that is dying.'

11 White singer-songwriter Ronee Blakely, rather than a black performer, composed the most eloquent musical tribute, simply named 'Fred Hampton'.

12 His essay, published in the radical journal *Leviathan*, reversed the Bob Dylan lyric from which they had borrowed their name: it was entitled 'You Do Need a Weatherman to Know Which Way the Wind Blows'.

13 Jagger abandoned his studies at the London School of Economics around 1962 to pursue a musical career.

## CHAPTER 5: 1970

1 The defendants included Afeni Shakur, who became pregnant during the trial. Her son, the future hip-hop star Tupac Shakur, was born just after the verdicts were delivered in May 1971.

2 Many rock fans uninterested in black music worshipped Hendrix without noticing the colour of his skin.

3 As one example from a thousand, the *Los Angeles Free Press* reported on a May 1970 peace concert at the University of Southern California. The

event was something of a fiasco; headliner Joe Cocker was too ill to perform, and Phil Ochs couldn't find his way in through the crowds. But that was no excuse for R.E. Masson's review, which concentrated on 'braless Candy Givens' from the band Zephyr, and her 'aroused nipples'.

4 In 1971, Agnew – or perhaps one of Agnew's children – heard Eugene McDaniels' mildly anti-establishment soul/jazz/rock crossover, *Headless Heroes of the Apocalypse*. He complained to the senior executives of Atlantic Records, who swiftly withdrew the album from sale.

5 The song also deflected criticism about the price of CSNY's concert tickets. Students organised a boycott of one show in St Paul – which was cancelled after Stephen Stills broke his leg in a car accident.

6 For the next fifteen years, all their albums carried the same band logo and a numerical variant on this title – *Chicago III*, *Chicago IV* and the rest. This had the effect of making the band seem like a multi-national corporation rather than, as they were briefly, a politically aware rock outfit.

7 Perhaps the most telling statistic concerned the youth vote. The voting age had recently been cut from 21 to 18, and pundits speculated that this might boost left-wing candidates. Instead, the majority of under-21-year-old voters opted for the right-wing Conservative Party. The revolutionary left chose to ignore these omens.

8 Three firebombings in New York City earlier in the year had been claimed by a group calling itself Revolutionary Force 9, in dubious honour of this track.

## CHAPTER 6: 1971

1 The New York underground paper *Women's Liberation* reprinted the *Sweet Sweetback* film poster, and defaced it with the messages 'Fuck this shit' and 'Fuck this racist bullshit'.

2 The Black Panther Party certainly believed it was a political act. In 1970, members of the Panthers distributed leaflets to the audience outside several Who gigs, accusing the band of having assaulted a brother and

made money in the process. 'The irony is that we are behind them as a whole,' Townshend noted.

3 A more practical version of the RLF was formed in Britain by Mike Evans and Mike Hart. The Music Liberation Front, or MLF, was intended to campaign against 'clampdowns on people's rights to play music when and how they like'. The MLF promoted concerts on a co-operative basis, and briefly attracted the interest of Pete Townshend, who offered to play benefit gigs for the cause. The offer wasn't fulfilled.

4 One line in the song, 'Free the prisoners and jail the judges', was lifted directly from a chapter heading in Jerry Rubin's revolutionary manual, *Do It!*

5 Folk-singer Tom Paxton composed a more intelligent and poignant account of events at Attica State, entitled 'The Hostage'. 'It's riveting, because it gives you the human picture from both sides,' says Judy Collins, who also recorded the song. 'It's not a surface picture, it's not an easy picture, and it's not naive.' Unlike Lennon's song? 'Exactly.' Paxton is more forgiving of Lennon's political efforts: 'John Lennon couldn't write a bad song. He was going through a very interesting journey back then. He had a way of making politics personal.'

6 He borrowed the phrase from the front cover of a recent issue of the London underground newspaper *Ink*. The debt was repaid when he sent the paper a set of the lyrics several months before the song was released on record. Ironically, the Lennons' performance was not included in Reilly's final cut of the movie, which was premiered in October 1973 at the Mercer Arts Center in New York, under the revised title of *The Irish Tapes*. Joko Productions had been wound up several months earlier, resulting in the withdrawal of the Lennons' financial support.

7 Showing a remarkable lack of political acumen, the British pop paper *Disc & Music Echo* referred to Jackson as 'a Negro convict who had committed suicide'.

8 Lennon's precise quote from the *Rolling Stone* interview was: 'I just remember before that we were both in shades and both on fucking junk.'

A reference to Allen Ginsberg immediately afterwards suggests that he was referring to meetings during Dylan's UK tours in 1965 or 1966, rather than in 1969, as an initial reading might suggest.

## CHAPTER 7: 1972

1 Shayler said that the documents also proved that Lennon had been secretly funding the Trotskyist group the Workers Revolutionary Party during the early 1970s. WRP activists from that period have denied this, saying that they would have welcomed such a donation, but had no contact with Lennon.

2 Lennon could rarely be accused of sidelining his wife in his work. Almost every new single coupled one of his songs with one of hers. Even when he performed a TV duet with Chuck Berry, he allowed Ono to add some squalling vocal interjections. Berry was less welcoming, rolling his eyes spectacularly as Ono punctuated his rock'n'roll anthems with cackles and screams.

3 Sexism didn't tell the full story. 'One of the last fights that David and I had before we split up was because he felt used by me,' Baez admits. 'And it was absolutely true. For all my insecurities that I was somebody's left-over dumb Mexican, I had taken on the behaviour of a queen, because I had been treated like that as a star. It wasn't conscious on my part, but I had really swallowed him up and, in a sense, used him for whatever my unknown purpose was. He was too young, and I was too nuts. He felt used, and so did I. Excellent recipe for divorce.'

4 'I was approached by Jane Fonda to go to Vietnam with her, and I turned it down,' admits Roger McGuinn of the Byrds. 'I didn't want to stick my neck out. She called me a coward and stomped off – and she was right!'

5 The shooting occurred at an outdoor campaign rally in Maryland, as Wallace's supporters were being serenaded by country singer Billy Grammer – best known for 'Gotta Travel On', a song Bob Dylan recorded on his 1970 album *Self Portrait*.

# SOURCES

## FOREWORD

'What can one say when confronted': Stephen Holden, *Rolling Stone*, 20 July
  1972

## PROLOGUE

'What are your opinions': recording of press conference

'Vietnam was not a burning issue': author interview

'For years, on the Beatles' tours': Sheff, *The Last Interview*, p.187

'Brian asked the Beatles': author interview

'Paul would do that': author interview

'What happens if you identify': quoted in Badman, *Beatles Off the Record*,
  p.259

'a civil war . . .': underground press advertisement

'Being a celebrity': *We Are Everywhere*, p.172

'the biggest teach-in': *Do It*, p.37

'If I'd been Phil Ochs' father': author interview

'Hard animal rock energy': *Do It*, p.18

'Rock'n'roll marked the beginning': *Do It*, p.19

'Speeding thru space': 'Beginning of a Poem of These States', *Collected Poems*,
  p.369–72

'utilised the literary and artistic': thefugs.com/history

'our concept that there was': ibid.

'and wherever spontaneous concerts': Fugs promotional leaflet, 1965

'People are ready to die': quoted in John Wilcock, 'Who The Fugs Think
  They Are', *The Best of the Realist* (ed. Krassner), p.180

'Total Assault on the Culture': ibid.

'a man who's laughing': ibid.

'I heard protest songs': author interview

'The right-wing was always': author interview

'embody an example': *Deliberate Prose*, pp.9–13

'The Hell's Angels called': *Do It*, p.45

'now obsessed with the Vietnam War': Schumacher, *Dharma Lion*, p.455

'Dylan was coming that night': *Spontaneous Mind*, p.435

'A love song can be political': recording of press conference, Hamburg, May 1984

'Dylan told me one time': author interview

'I don't really understand': interview with Marc Rowland, New York, 23 September 1978

'How many protest singers': recording of press conference

'Jerry had sent a message': *Deliberate Prose*, p.18

'I AM A LIVING CREATURE': McClure, *Star*, Grove Press, p.90

'This is worse than Mississippi': *Time*, 24 July 1964

'100 skilled revolutionaries': ibid.

'the noise of Congo drums': ibid.

'It was time for the blacks': *Soul On Ice*, p.201

'It is the jazz issuing': ibid., p.203

'a call for black revolutionaries': *New York Times*, undated cutting, 1965

'Most jazz critics have been white': *Black Music*, p.11

'I think that perhaps the most creative': *Conversations with Amiri Baraka*, p.15

'The only difference is that': recording of concert

'The music is finally most musicians' strongest': *Black Music*, p.209

'Politically, I see jazz': Skip Laszlo, 'Behind the Beat of a Different Drummer', *The Wire* No. 1, 1982, p.23

'When I say "nationalize"': C.A. Parks, 'Self-Determination and the Black Aesthetic', *Black World* 23, 1973, pp.69–70

'Even though Radio is "black"': *Raise Race Rays Raze*, pp.12–13

'a music that will reflect': *Black Music*, p.129

'to present free concerts': Baskerville, *The Impact of Black Nationalist Ideology*, p.125

'An art that would reach the people': *The Autobiography of LeRoi Jones*, p.298

'Sun Ra became our resident': ibid.

'Would any record company': *The Jazz Revolution of the 1960s*, p.246

'The only bad incident': *The Autobiography of LeRoi Jones*, p.307

'The hope is that young blacks': reprinted in *Home: Social Essays* (1966)

'Soon things began to get wild': quoted in Watts, *Amiri Baraka*, pp.135–36

'While these whites were in Mississippi': ibid., p.500

'Despite my many experiences with whites': in Goldman, *The Death & Life of Malcolm X*, p.33

'His style, fearlessness': *Soul On Ice*, p.75

'the chickens have come home': quoted in Goldman, op. cit., p.118

'I'm for the freedom': ibid., p.222

'I'll probably be shot to death': ibid., p.263

'I call it "Malcolm Forever"': liner notes to *Fire Music* LP

'Do I really want to be integrated': Baldwin, *The Fire Next Time*

'I am about 28 years': *Down Beat*, 16 December 1965

'anti-war; it is opposed to Vietnam': 'Point Of Contact', *Down Beat Music 66*, p.19–31

'I am an anti-fascist artist': *Down Beat*, 16 December 1965

'Don't you wonder just what': ibid.

'I said, "All right, man"': ibid.

'We shall have our manhood': *Soul On Ice*, p.59

'I am angry at the insurgents': ibid., p.144

'How I'd just love to be in Berkeley': ibid., p.19

'The rock cats can no longer': recording of radio broadcast

'the horrible jungle of death': ibid.

'We are now in the Year of Fire': ibid.

'I got frustrated with those cats': *Seize the Time*, p.24

'to go to the black community': ibid., p.27

'It took us three days': ibid., p.29

'They claimed to function as an underground': *Revolutionary Suicide*, p.71

## CHAPTER 1: 1966

'We have paraded, we have picketed': quoted in Wells, *The War Within*, p.93

'Negroes are defined by two forces': *Stokely Speaks*, p.32

'The link between America's undercover support': *Soul On Ice*, p.115

'Throw your Beatle and rock'n'roll records': Noebel, *Communism, Hypnotism & the Beatles*

'obviously aimed at instilling fear': Noebel, *Rhythm, Riots & Revolution*

'There was a decision on the part': in Hampton/Fayer, *Voices of Freedom*, p.288

'The disagreement over whites': ibid.

'We're passing now into a time of death': reprinted in *The Movement Towards a New America* (Goodman ed.), pp.13ff

'Any external or social action': from *The Politics of Ecstasy*

'the telephones of which he knows': 'How Does A Beatle Live', in *The Lennon Companion* (Thomson/Gutman eds.), pp.74–75

'There's something else I'm going to do': ibid.

'It makes Western three-or-four-beat': quoted in John Robertson, 'The Beatles Anthology', *The Journal* No. 1, p.36

'We are all old men': ibid.

'After getting high or tripping': *Tomorrow Never Knows*, pp.79–80

'At a rally for a radical candidate': well.com/~cjfish/begin

'There was no fantasy of rock stardom': author interview

'the absurdity of the US Defense': author interview

'representing ROTC units': author interview

'I'd scheduled one of Nam': author interview

'Fluxus – which was about the synthesis': author interview

'Not one cogent thing is said': Walter Kerr, *New York Times*, 11 November 1966

'an irregular chain of improvisation': Harold Clurman, *The Nation*, 28 November 1966

'almost all our language has been taxed': *Collected Poems*, pp.394–411

'As US language chief': quoted in Schumacher, *Dharma Lion*, p.463

'That was a typical gesture': author interview

'a fucking heavy duty capitalist': Holzman/Daws, *Follow the Music*

'I want to be the first left-wing star': quoted in liner notes to *Elektra Classics* 2-CD, 2001

'Do you really believe in what your songs': liner notes to *I Ain't Marching Anymore* LP

'There's nothing noble about what': Eliot, *Death of a Rebel*, p.93

'Phil wasn't motivated by money': author interview

'In Vietnam, a 19-year-old Viet Cong': liner notes to *I Ain't Marching Anymore* LP

'I wouldn't be surprised to see': 'The Year of the Topical Song', Newport Folk Festival programme

'The Vietcong are right': quoted in Noebel, *Rhythm, Riots & Revolution*

'The stuff you're writing is bullshit': *Bob Dylan* (1972 edn.), p.176

'I am not going to volunteer': quoted in Baez, *And A Voice To Sing With*, pp.120–21

'bashed on regardless': ibid., p.118

'It was a thing of beauty': author interview

'It definitely caused us problems': author interview

'I began thinking about HUAC': *Do It*, p.59ff

'I wanted to write something': author interview

'The opening shots were fired': *IT*, 12 December 1966

'In the memoirs of the period': *The Feminist Challenge*, p.52

'*IT* started out being interested': author interview

'You have to start a national': quoted in Friedan, *It Changed My Life: Writings on the Women's Movement*, 1976, p.80

'John [Lennon] and Paul [McCartney]': quoted in Glenn A. Baker, *The Beatles Down Under*

'They had become supremely indifferent': ibid.

'The only position for women in SNCC': much quoted, but impossible to locate an original source; hence possibly apochryphal

'SNCC proposes that it is now time': *Stokely Speaks*, p.40

'I'm not going to beg': film of speech, 1966

'would destroy the unity': *Power on the Left*, p.206

'These rebellions were violent uprisings': *Stokely Speaks*, p.103

'The inner city in most major urban': ibid., p.43

'We are not going to wait for white people': ibid., p.49

'The nature of the panther': quoted in Boyd, *Black Panther for Beginners*, p.7

'George Wallace was then head': *Voices of Freedom*, p.269

'A man needs a black panther': *Stokely Speaks*, pp.20–21

'We were at the stage of testing': *Revolutionary Suicide*, p.114

'Wherever brothers gathered': ibid., p.115

'nothing less than a revolution': Norman Mailer, *Advertisements for Myself*

'engaged in the deepest, most fundamental': *Soul On Ice*, p.110

'The embryonic spirit of kamikaze': ibid.

'It was as if singing black music': quoted in Elsner, *Stevie Wonder*, p.66

'something that is actual in the world': *Black Music*, pp.206–207

'group of Myddle-class white boys': ibid., p.205

'The Beatles . . . injecting Negritude': *Soul On Ice*, p.202, p.204

'a generalising in passionate': ibid., p.206

'superficial advance': ibid., p.207

'Hey, Bobby Dylan': quoted by Cleaver, *Soul On Ice*

'There is a class of whites': *Revolutionary Notes*, pp.74–75

'I could hear the melody': *Seize the Time*, p.183

'Huey says that whites looked at blacks': ibid., p.185

'Dylan was trying to get a political': *Rolling Stone*, 4 March 1971, p.31

'This song Bobby Dylan was singing': *Seize the Time*, p.186

'a people and an energy': *Black Music*, p.185

'James Brown's screams, etc': ibid., p.210

'more "radical", Blacker': ibid.

'Only thing gonna stop us today': recording of speech, 1968

'The next thing comes the marines': ibid.

'The polarisation is much more acute': *IT*, 16 January 1967

'We're all dropping jellied gasoline': *Sing Out*, December 1967/January 1968, p.44

'a yellow papier-mâché submarine': *Time*, 21 April 1967

'The Beatles can sing': *Raise Race Rays Raze*, p.35

'"We all live in a yellow submarine", with all their': *Black Music*, p.205

'The Yellow Submarine may suggest': 'Beatles, Plane Again', *P.O. Frisco*, 2 September 1966, p.6

## CHAPTER 2: 1967

'thousands of them': in Wolfe, *The Electric Kool-Aid Acid Test*

'Materialism and empire': press release to *Berkeley Barb*

'20,000 blown minds together': *IT*, 13 February 1967

'kept busting into our meetings': quoted in McNally, *A Long Strange Trip*, p.177

'Let's make it fun, not misery': ibid.

'The crowd reacted mildly': Wilcock, *IT*, 13 February 1967

'The words didn't matter': McNally, *A Long Strange Trip*, p.179

'Turn on to the scene': quoted by Wilcock, *IT*, 13 February 1967

'There was a difference between Berkeley': author interview

'There was great potential here': quoted by Wilcock, *IT*, 13 February 1967

'The dichotomy over political action': ibid.

'You suddenly experience the soul': quoted in John Robertson, 'The Beatles Anthology', *The Journal* No. 1, p.36

'What could we do?': quoted in Badman, *Beatles Off the Record*, p.259

'it is impossible to avoid': *Time*, 6 January 1967

'When they are not patrolling': *Time*, 3 February 1967

'I spun around in my seat': quoted in Boyd, *Black Panthers for Beginners*, 1995, p.19

'I see now that Eldridge': *Revolutionary Suicide*, p.133

'A few weeks after this': ibid., p.132

'keeping the enemy off balance': ibid., p.122n

'good for nothing but running': ibid.

'The purpose of a Black Cultural': RAM manifesto

'The fact of music was the black poet's': *The Autobiography of LeRoi Jones*, p.337

'A lot of black people are schizophrenic': 'An Interview With LeRoi Jones' by Robert Allen, Smith/Jones (eds.), *Conversations With Amiri Baraka*, p.15

'Swahili is a pan-African language': quoted in Brown, *Fighting for US*, p.10

'There must be a cultural revolution': in *The Black Power Revolt*, p.168

'All art must reflect the Black Revolution': 'Black Art', in *New Black Voices* (Chapman ed.), pp.477ff

'We say the blues are invalid': ibid.

'The Rolling Stones come on': *Black Music*, p.124

'Jazz, no matter the intellectual basis': ibid.

'short, stocky, bald': *The Autobiography of LeRoi Jones*, p.350

'wants a music that will reflect': *Black Music*, p.129

'I think so, I think they look all over': quoted in Kofsky, *The Jazz Revolution of the 1960s*, pp.438–39

'In the halls of his government': *Raise Race Rays Raze*, p.80

'We don't know what they mean': *Time*, 3 February 1967

'I looked out the window': author interview

'They're sitting there with their diamonds': *The Rolling Stone Interviews Vol. 2*, p.256

'If the patient is not strapped': *Time*, 5 May 1967

'disturb public order, promote subversive': *Time*, 7 July 1967

'The idea was [to] get an island': Miles, *Many Years From Now*, p.378

'They didn't care about the military': *The Beatles*, p.246

'Danger! Dictatorship!': leaflet distributed via underground press

'I'm not worried about the political situation': Davies, *The Beatles*, p.315

'I was horrified by their stance': author interview

'We're kind of hitting out': *New Musical Express*, 21 January 1967

'I rather admire the Chinese': *New Musical Express*, 4 February 1967

'I hope there is a civil war': ibid.

'an almost blind acceptance': *New Musical Express*, 4 February 1967, p.14

'Teenagers the world over': quoted in Paytress, *The Rolling Stones: Off the Record*, p.120

'No matter how many raids': *IT*, 13 March 1967

'It wasn't what I thought': quoted in John Robertson, 'Beatles Anthology', *The Journal* No.1, p.37

'brings fulfilment to the life': Maharishi Mahesh Yogi, *On the Bhagavad-Gita*, p.19

'I am concerned with the suffering': *IT*, 15 December 1967, p.11, p.13

'His Holiness doesn't understand': quoted in William Kloman, 'The Maharishi Meets the Press', *The Rolling Stone Rock'n'Roll Reader*, pp.20ff

'literally started yelling at him': 'The Maharishi and Me', *IT*, 16 February 1968, p.3

'Allen knew a lot of people': author interview

'He, the Maharishi, hadn't covered': 'The Maharishi And Me', p.3

'this is action over and above': *Time*, 10 March 1967

'We have argued and demonstrated': quoted in Wells, *The War Within*, p.126

'I have no doubt that the Communist': ibid., p.135

'On the speaker's platform': *Do It*, p.66

'We were pissed off': *Do It*, p.66

'Man, I learned one thing': 'How Not To Blow It', *Berkeley Barb*, 21–27 April, 1967

'Be happy, be free': Monterey festival poster

'the mutants of the psychedelic': *Oracle* Vol. 1 No. 4

'are not just dropping out': quoted in Bromell, *Tomorrow Never Knows*, p.99

'As of this date, we 8,000 Democrats': quoted in *Time*, 30 June 1967

'the revolution that began with James Dean': 'Pop in the Police State', *IT*, 2 June 1967, p.14

'The real revolutionary proletariat': *Stokely Speaks*, pp.88–89

'What you need is to get': quoted in Humphry/Tindall, *False Messiah*, p.34

'If ever you see a white man': ibid. p.64

'The party that calls itself': 'Michael X & The Flower Children', *Oz* 7, pp.13ff

'the mobile butcher shop': in *The Black Power Revolts*, p.119

'I do not want to be part': *Stokely Speaks*, p.55

'When I decide to kill': ibid., p.70

'Let us save our national honour': recording of speech

'Black people must now move': quoted in Heath, *Off the Pigs*, p.13

'During this period we were having': *Soul On Fire*, p.119

'neutralise ... destroy any attempts': FBI Memorandum

'The Black Liberation movement': *The Autobiography of LeRoi Jones*, p.375

'I felt the clubs, the guns': ibid., p.370

'I watched it happen': author interview

'Berry told us to shut the studio': author interview

'It was racial, but they kinda tried': quoted by Steve Waksman, *American Quarterly*, 2001

'"Light My Fire" rises through the radio': reprinted in *Underground Digest* No. 1, pp.92–94

'Do what your leaders tell you': *Raise Race Rays Raze*, pp.84–85

'"We're A Winner" is more revolutionary': 'An Interview with LeRoi Jones', *Conversations with Amiri Baraka*, p.24

'To sing lies about America': *Raise Race Rays Raze*, p.131

'As we headed into the city': 'Riots I Have Known & Loved', makemyday.free.fr/wk1

'the band that will prepare us': 'Fire Music', *Oracle* Vol. 1 No. 6, p.6

'We felt that we could be the vanguard': makemyday.free.fr/wk1

'a total cooperative tribal living': *Guitar Army*, p.341

'During the Detroit Uprising': ibid., p.342

'We moved to the beatnik neighbourhood': makemyday.free.fr/wk1

'We will force you to support us': 'When the Mode of the Music Changes, the Walls of the City Shake', *IT*, 27 February 1967, pp.8–9

'It summarised for me all the doubts': quoted in Tamarkin, *Got A Revolution*, p.130

'Today, a revolution can be accomplished': reprinted in Eisen (ed.), *The Age of Rock*

'I've always been attracted to ideas': quoted in Goodman (ed.), *The Movement*, p.374

'There can be no revolution': *Distant Drummer* Vol. 1 No. 1, p.9

'the home of Marxist minstrels': in *Christian Crusade* journal, 1967

'Either out of ignorance': *Time*, 20 January 1967

'She should remember that protest': ibid.

'I was considered a hippie': author interview

'Peace was always controversial': author interview

'In many ways those performances': author interview

'The Americans are fighting': quoted in Tate, *Midnight Lightning*, pp.20–21

'There's no source out there': in *Revolution for the Hell of It*

'Fuck Lyndon Johnson!': Schumacher, *There But For Fortune*, p.169

'The audience was caught off guard': author interview

'I am going to try and talk': 'Resistance Grows on Day of Terror', *Berkeley Barb*, 20–26 October 1967, p.3

'Something is disastrously wrong': 'Joanie Goes To Jail Again', *Rolling Stone*, 23 November 1967, p.7

'hard-eyed revolutionaries': *Time*, 27 October, 1967

'When the tear gas was let off': author interview

'right in the front, taking pictures': *Rolling Stone*, 26 October 1968, p.24

'It was the first time in the history': *Do It*, p.120

'It's not that we can't do anything': 'Hurray! It's Over', *Berkeley Barb*, 3–9 November 1967, p.6

'Does protesting the war': quoted in Schumacher, op. cit., p.171

'Suppose one day 5,000 trucks': *Do It*, p.138

'He needed a companion': author interview

'Lots of people believed it was real': author interview

'The dudes on the block': *Revolutionary Suicide*, p.76

'Huey showed that you also have to have': *Conversation with Eldridge Cleaver*, p.101

'found guilty, because I lacked a jury': *Revolutionary Suicide*, p.88

'There were some shots': ibid., p.176

'Our political awareness': quoted in *Dear Sisters*, p.51

## CHAPTER 3: 1968

'There has never been a year': *1968*, p.xv

'the year that rocked the world': subtitle of Kurlansky's book

'Rubin said that it was inspirational': Clavir/Spitzer (eds.), *The Conspiracy Trial*, p.397

'said that it would be a good idea': ibid., p.349

'I said we should have a better name': ibid., p.448

'It was his idea that the presence': ibid., pp.492–93

'a convening of all people': ibid., p.398

'I helped design the party': ibid., p.288

'Phil loved the idea': author interview

'It would be rather difficult': ibid., p.426

'it was a good idea to do something': ibid., p.442

'if there were no permits': ibid.

'He said that politics had become': ibid., p.295

'present different ideas of what is wrong': ibid.

'YIPPIES MEET NATIONAL DEATH PARTY': press statement published
 throughout underground media

'Chicago in August will harbor': 'Rossman Raps Rubin', *Berkeley Barb*,
 22–28 March 1968, p.3

'Dellinger was older than the other guys': author interview

'to see a celebration of life': *The Conspiracy Trial*, p.461

'My background made me': author interview

'I hated having to play': author interview

'I was always very leery': author interview

'The music will be free': press statement, 1 March 1968

'Invitations are now going out': ibid.

'Hoffman asked me if I could contact': *The Conspiracy Trial*, p.295

'We talked about it to Abbie': author interview

'Kids asked each other': *Do It*, p.165

'I shall not seek, and will not accept': recording of TV broadcast

'A self-appointed coterie': *Rolling Stone*, 11 May 1968, p.1

'I can't think of a revolutionary': *Time*, 17 May 1968

'That song is my personal favourite': author interview

'We both saw rock as an opportunity': author interview

'You need to recall': author interview

'I joined the band': author interview

'I take issue with the thought': author interview

'They always struck me': author interview

'an amazing Fender Telecaster': author interview

'They were constantly relating to me': *The Conspiracy Trial*, pp.442–443

'I turned up for a draft physical': author interview

'I was born a feminist': author interview

'Many of us feel': transcript of speech

'Stokely warned that whites': *Revolutionary Suicide*, p.195

'were brought into the free speech movement': ibid.

'I dig Stokely': *Conversation with Eldridge Cleaver*, p.103

'I went to a junior high school': *Soul On Fire*, p.26

'was personally thanked': *The NME Book Of Rock*, *c*.1973

'I tried to convince the mayor': *The Politics of Soul*, WGBH documentary

'if the show was cancelled': ibid.

'Twenty-four hours ago': ibid.

'We got down to Newark': quoted by Hank Bordowitz, 'Burning Down The House', jimihendrix.com/magazine

'ruthlessly attacks not only imperialism': Franklin Rosemont, 'The Invisible Axe of Jimi Hendrix', *Chicago Seed*, 3–24 November 1967

'the audience had no racial identity': 'Soul Together', *Rolling Stone*, 10 August 1968, p.18

'It had a tremendous impact': Bowman, *Soulsville USA*, p.146

'it affected me for a whole year': ibid., p.144

'My husband persuaded me': to Mary Ellison, *Record Collector*

'That there is a holocaust coming': *Ramparts*, May 1968

'We were walking on eggshells': *Soul On Fire*, pp.22–23

'I pled not guilty': *Target Zero*, p.308

'It was a sickening sight': quoted in Boyd, *Black Panthers for Beginners*, pp.38–39

'I didn't even know him': *Rolling Stone*, 26 October 1968, p.24

'That could have been my son': Van Peebles, *Panther*, p.81

'We were the hip new thing': author interview

'That was the only political benefit': author interview

'The footage of this was incredible': quoted by Rose, *Living in America*, p.65

'I was never into black power': ibid., pp.55–56

'When the militant Black Power offshoot': *New Musical Express*, 9 November 1968, p.6

'a Black Power artist': *New Musical Express*, undated cutting, *c*.1970

'We know the Negro deejay': King Records advertisement

'No communication can ever come': recording of performance

'Politics was never my forte': Veloso, *Tropical Truth*, p.198

'I was a tropicalista': ibid., p.201

'I took part in demos and rallies': *Musician*, October 1990, p.52

'There was all this violence': 1995 interview, quoted by songfacts.com

'This country's so weird': *IT*, May 1968

'It was nothing like as violent': author interview

'He definitely felt that he ought': author interview

'Demonstration in Grosvenor Square': *IT*, May 1968

'That's our way out': ibid.

'I can imagine America': ibid.

'Right, he said we should do something': Cott, *He Dreams What Is Going On Inside His Head*, pp.53–70

'I have no idea, really': ibid., pp.86ff

'There can only be a short time left': 'The Perfumed Garden', *IT*, 19 January 1968, p.10

'I must not lose you': ibid.

'in the grip of a total and manic delusion': 'The Perfumed Garden', *IT*, 5 April 1968, p.11

'We could have said': ibid.

'a kind of Western communism': recording of press conference

'to see if we can create things': ibid.

'The concept as outlined by Paul': 'Apple', *Oz* 14, p.25

'I wanted to say what I thought': Wenner, *Lennon Remembers*, pp.110–112

'I wasn't sure': ibid.

'I thought I was painting in sound': quoted in Miles, *Many Years From Now*, p.483

'To really understand Dylan': 'Dylanese', *Graffiti* Vol. 1 No. 8, pp.4ff

'Dylan's new album': 'Fried Fish Conference', *Other Scenes*, May 1968, p.19

'How can he be apathetic': 'Fried Fish Conference', ibid.

'Abbie was a clown': author interview

'urge revolution in America': FBI memorandum

'the lady across the street does': this and subsequent quotes from *Sing Out* interview, reprinted in McGregor, *Bob Dylan: A Retrospective*, pp.265ff

'lashing out at the approaching armed tractor': Schumacher, *There But For Fortune*, p.183

'a pretty confused album': *L.A. Free Press*, 7 February 1969, p.2

'They asked me if I would come': Clavir/Spizter (eds.), *The Conspiracy Trial*, p.427

'I would never have gone': author interview

'they veil their talent with a slew of insults': *Billboard*, 9 March 1968, p.18

'Right now, we are selling peace': *Jazz & Pop*, November 1968, pp.36ff

'We're in a revolution right now': ibid.

'A lot of people are going to get hurt': ibid.

'Success is a motherfucker': author interview

'If we had gone to the Yippies' festival': author interview

'Johnson and his delegates': Yippie flyer

'This will be an organising job': *New Left News*, undated cutting, *c.* August 1968

'I felt Abbie was trying to exclude me': in Sloman, *Steal This Dream*, p.135

'The opening sentence was something': *The Conspiracy Trial*, p.289

'I've got bad news for you, boys': Stew Albert in Sloman, op. cit., p.133

'They were not even speaking': author interview

'drunk motorcyclists': ibid., pp.442–443

'To the experienced few': 'Riots I Have Known & Loved', makemyday.free.fr/wk1

'The amphetamine was in the air': *L.A. Free Press*, 7 February 1969, p.5

'tangible fear': 'Riots I Have Known & Loved', makemyday.free.fr/wk1

'I could see a number of people': *The Conspiracy Trial*, p.359

'the first phalanx of motorcycle cops': 'Riots I Have Known & Loved', makemyday.free.fr/wk1

'There were moments with Yippie': *L.A. Free Press*, 7 February 1969, p.5

'The thing I'm proudest of': ibid.

'Phil was genuinely hurt': Schumacher, *There But For Fortune*, p.200

'It was like the soul of the country': *Oz* 23, p.37

'He was very depressed after Chicago': author interview

'the ugliness of power': 'Everybody's Chicago Blues', *Rolling Stone*, 28 September 1968, pp.1, 10

'Chicago was the truth': *Rolling Stone*, 26 October 1968, p.24

'Of course it's subversive': 'Street Fighting Man', *New Musical Express*, 14 September 1968, p.3

'Che Guevara's band': *IT*, 4 October 1968, p.15

'Maybe you were not in San Francisco': *New Musical Express*, 23 November 1968, p.16

'Time magazine came out': Cott, *He Dreams What Is Going On In His Head*, pp.53–70

'To say the Beatles are guilty': *Rolling Stone*, 21 December 1968

'It is puritanical to expect': quoted in Riley, *Tell Me Why*, p.257

'clear unmistakeable call': *Berkeley Barb*, 30 November 1968

'indifference to politics': *Sovietskaya Kultura*, 3 December 1968; quoted in *IT* 46, p.3

'Many people hope that their courage': *The Listener*, 3 October 1968

'the seed of the new cultural revolution': *Black Dwarf*, 13 October 1968 'we [can] understand why it wasn't released': *Black Dwarf*, 27 October 1968, p.1

'We took "Street Fighting Man"': author interview

'It was called "Thang Loi!"': author interview

'I adored the Beatles': author interview

'a repressive, vicious': *Black Dwarf*, 27 October 1968

'I squirm when I read some': author interview

'I don't worry about what you': *Black Dwarf*, 10 January 1969, p.4

'was never intended to be as big': ibid.

'You smash it': ibid.

'In "Revolution", you say that people': ibid.

'The feeling I've got from songs': ibid.

'The generation being canonised': Harvey Perr review, *L.A. Free Press*, 19 July 1968, p.36

'Revolution means what is going on': *New Musical Express*, 19 April 1969, p.2

'The Black Panthers made these kids': unidentified cutting

'Black America promptly refused it': soulgeneration.co.uk

'The whole power structure': quoted in Newton, *Revolutionary Suicide*, p.201

'I just shot two dudes': Newton trial testimony

'Some of the leadership wanted': *Soul On Fire*, p.102

'His own paranoia': ibid., p.101

'I finally got to Huey': ibid.

'would be the equivalent': ibid., pp.126–127

'I was surrounded with escape plans': ibid., p.130

'I had won': ibid., p.132

'When a Black man is in bed': in *Destroy This Temple*, MacGibbon & Kee, London, 1971, pp.57–59

'DWARF DESIGNER': *Black Dwarf*, 10 January 1969, p.9

'one left man coming up to me': in Wandor (ed.), *Once A Feminist*, p.17

'WITCH is an all-woman Everything': WITCH manifesto, distributed to underground press

'It wasn't political': Tamarkin, *Got A Revolution*, p.176

'I think we're more conservative': *Kaleidoscope* interview, reprinted in *IT*, 1 August, 1969

'That, you see, is where it's at': *Ramparts* review, reprinted in *Conversations with the New Reality*, pp.106ff

'Eldridge Cleaver Welcome Here': 'Rock For Sale', reprinted op. cit., p.117

'The Jefferson Airplane is the only rock group': quoted in *Rolling Stone*, 7 December 1968, p.8

'The Yippie people like toy guns': *Rolling Stone*, 14 June 1969, pp.26ff

'I was very disappointed': ibid.

'I don't think Godard understands': *IT*, 4 July 1969, pp.14–15

'They said, "There will be 8,000 people"': *The Wire*, December 1986/January 1987, pp.49ff

'Nothing happened': *IT*, 1 January 1969, p.4

'it was in the interests of the white regimes': *Africa: A Modern History*, p.204

'This was surely the moment': Melly, *Revolt Into Style*, pp.118ff

'follow the lead of the revolutionary workers': anti-war poster

'Pop [music] acts out revolt': Melly, ibid.

'It seemed like the end of everything': author interview

'What we were doing was certainly': *Tropical Truth*, p.216

'Neither Gil nor I had imagined': ibid.

'The days of being a "rebel"': quoted in Zolov, *Refried Elvis*, p.125

'I was at the International Youth Camp': author interview

'We knew almost nothing': author interview

## CHAPTER 4: 1969

'We're just not strong enough leaders': *Ann Arbor Argus*, 10–25 July 1969, p.23

'Fuck off!': recording of performance

'The ad had really missed the mark': Davis, *Clive*, pp.123–124

'filth, slanderous and libellous': this and subsequent quotes from 'Sabotaging the Dissident Press' by Angus Mackenzie, in *Unamerican Activities* (Janowitz/Peters eds.), pp.165–166

'Goddamn your culture': Vache (ed), *Black Mask*, p.7

'The worst fear is the fear': ibid., p.114

'in America, to truly live': quoted in 'New York Trauma' by Monica Sjoo-Trickey, *IT*, 18 October 1968, p.5

'What's real to us': *Black Mask*, pp.116–117

'Everywhere we turn': ibid.

'The Fillmore's interests': ibid., p.133

'Nobody wanted to liberate': quoted in *Rolling Stone*, 7 December 1968, p.4

'Tonight the people return': *Black Mask*, p.132

'messed them up a bit': ibid., p.138

'They projected themselves': ibid.

'In 1965 when we began': Bill Graham press release, 1971

'Before I left in 1968': author interview

'Total Assault on the Culture!': reprinted in *Guitar Army*, pp.67ff

'We mean John Coltrane': ibid., p.68

'for having a noisy band!': ibid., p 93ff

'the men pounding on the table': Holzman/Daws, *Follow The Music*, pp.259–260

'I'd never met anyone like Sinclair': ibid.

'I was intrigued by how the MC5': ibid., p.260

'I said to the MC5': ibid., p.262

'Elektra is not the tool': ibid.

'I suggested they find another label': ibid.

'What's obscene are city streets': *Newsweek*, 19 May 1969

'to put the "cultural revolution"': *Guitar Army*, p.344

'We *breathe* revolution': ibid., p.104

'You wanted to be bigger than the Beatles': quoted in *IT*, 7 October 1971, pp.8–9, 17

'I could dig John living in the commune': 'Shattered Dream' by Ben Fong-Torres, *Rolling Stone*, 8 June 1972, pp.23ff

'rock and roll in a lot of ways': quoted in *IT*, 7 October 1971, pp.8–9, 17

'On "Tell All The People"': David Prockter, *Dark Star* 22, 1979, p.22

'He was obscene': reported in *Rolling Stone*, 5 April 1969

'We had seen the Living Theater': ibid.

'I sang about American Revolution': author interview

'We always believed in doing it': author interview

'One day this guy came up': author interview

'I'd met Abbie Hoffman': author interview

'I only interpret the best': *Rolling Stone*, 4 March 1971, p.37

'I felt betrayed': author interview

'I started talking about politics': *Dylan in Woodstock*, p.62

'It was sometimes hard to tell': ibid., p.96

'I can only relate to Chicago': *Revolution for the Hell of It*, p.114

'There were never any Yippies': ibid., p.121

'my trip to hell and back': *L.A. Free Press*, 7 February 1969, p.5

'I had an office': author interview

'Phil was definitely under surveillance': author interview

'It's like the soul of the country': *Oz* 23, p.37

'It's like you don't have the heart': ibid.

'Awful. The whole thing is depressing': quoted in Thompson, *The Great Shark Hunt*, p.189

'The anti-war parade': ibid., pp.189–190

'Many of those now calling me afraid': *Stokely Speaks*, pp.184–185

'six months in a wretched': *Soul On Fire*, p.132

'There is certainly the possibility': Boyd, *Black Panthers for Beginners*, p.55

'When you're twenty': author interview

'Everybody knows the revolution's coming': *Ann Arbor Argus*, 24 January–7 February 1969

'The establishment, especially in America': *Rolling Stone*, 1 March 1969

'Zappa didn't speak in terms': *IT*, 13 June 1969, p.9

'The Beatles are part of the establishment': *IT*, 28 March 1969, pp.13–14

'EMI (who have the *real* control)': *Ink*, 23 September 1971, p.2

'it's a funny world when two people': *New Musical Express*, 12 April 1969, p.4

'I'm as violent as the next man': *IT*, 27 February 1970, pp.11, 19, 20

'mainly at people with violent inclinations': ibid.

'Our job is to write': in Wenner, *Lennon Remembers*, p.93

'People's Park amounted': *The Sixties*, p.355

'Listen, there's no cause': recording of broadcast

'create a soulful socialism': *The Sixties*, p.359

'firming up his newfound status': *Any Old Way You Choose It*, p.99

'The Progressive Labor Party': markriebling.com/leary

'We must be a revolutionary movement': manifesto included in Jacobs, *Weatherman*, pp.51ff

'It has been almost a year': SDS flyer

'an American Liberation Front': quoted in Heath, *Off the Pigs*, p.82

'which will include the revolutionary forces': *Conversation with Eldridge Cleaver*, p.54

'we have to fight a revolutionary struggle': ibid.

'the more I think about my future': ibid., p.38

'I'm a fat mouth and a fool': ibid., pp.128–129

'Fela was singing in Yoruba': quoted in Jay Babcock, 'Fela: King of the Invisible Art', *Mean*, 1999

'Sandra gave me the education': ibid.

'It was incredible': to *New York Times*, 1987

'I remember him telling me': Babcock, op. cit.

'you've just got to dig sly': Giovanni, *Black Feeling Black Talk*, pp.75–76

'i wanted to write a poem': ibid., pp.88–89

'David cried': *A Taste Of Power*, p.185

'it was a strange song': ibid., p.186

'is far less controversial': *Down Beat*, 28 May 1970, p.18

'Revolutionary Record': advertisement, *Black Panther*, 22 November 1969, p.17

'It was a small supper-club': author interview

'apolitical': quoted in *Rolling Stone*, 6 July 1968, p.8

'That was the epitome': in *The Beach Boys: An American Band* film

'The city was still occupied': ibid.

'The local Czechoslovakian groups': ibid.

'imagined they [would take] me': *Tropical Truth*, p.216

'If we sell as many records': *Zigzag*, August 1969, pp.4ff

'a product of the revolution': ibid.

'I don't think I could possibly': Steve Williams, 'Music for the Hell of It', *IT*, 10 October 1969, p.21

'Where there is dissatisfaction': *IT*, 14 January 1970, p.5

'It's very hard, really': *IT*, 4 July 1969, pp.14–15

'I enjoyed it!': ibid.

'1969 is the year': *IT*, 1 August 1969, p.10

'the women who really understand': 'A Groupie's Vision', *Oz*, February 1969

'the superficiality of the rock revolution': 'Mozic & the Revolution', *Oz*, October 1969

'Was Jagger interested in politics? "No".': *Student,* issue 2/2, p.31

'We're just not strong enough leaders': *Ann Arbor Argus*, 10–25 July 1969, p.23

'It doesn't matter where you are': *IT*, 29 August 1969, p.3

'The Revolution can only be important': ibid.

'an establishment form of pacifism': *International Free Press*, 1 November 1969, pp.6–7

'Local government officials': *New Musical Express*, 5 July 1969, p.12

'No one in this country': 'Coming of Age in Aquarius', in *Conversations with the New Reality*, pp.39ff

'Nightmare in the Catskills': *New York Times*, 18 August 1969, p.34

'a mere million dollar operation': 'Containing Hip', *RAT Subterranean News*, 12–26 August 1969, pp.15, 26

'The organisers' decision to let in': 'When the Kissing Had to Stop', *Let It Rock*, June 1974, pp.26ff

'Someday real soon': in *Woodstock Nation*, pp.75ff

'I was at a meeting at Abbie's house': author interview

'When culture becomes a nation': ibid.

'Abbie was a big, powerful guy': author interview

'Let us have it, man': in Bell (ed.), *Woodstock*, p.82

'There's no morality here': Ellen Sander, 'It's The Sound', *L.A. Free Press*, 5 September 1969, pp.31, 41, 47

'You people have got to be': recording of performance

'living at the Concord hotel': *Woodstock Nation*, pp.4–5

'It might have been the green tab': ibid.

'The difference between me and you': original quote unsourced, but Hoffman paraphrases his remark in *Woodstock Nation*, p.141

'I'm the only one here': Sander, op. cit.

'John is a mountain of a man': *Woodstock Nation*, pp.62–63

'How *can* I trust you?': ibid., p.143

'They were in it to make money': in Sloman, *Steal This Dream*, p.178

'Sometimes Wadleigh would jump': in Bell (ed.), *Woodstock*, p.152

'became annoyed and kicked': ibid., p.116

'We told all the cameramen': ibid., p.152

'I'm on the side of the stage': in Sloman, op. cit., p.178

'I lunged forward': *Woodstock Nation*, p.143

'CRASH. Pete Townshend': ibid.

'the most political thing': quoted in Marsh, *Before I Get Old*, p.350

'When I asked him': author interview

'What he was arguing for': quoted in *New York Daily News*, 30 July 1999

'When I left Chicago': *Woodstock Nation*, p.91

'The movie stops': Sander, op. cit.

'You're so enraptured': ibid.

'I emerged exhausted': *Woodstock Nation*, p.7

'Somewhere deep inside the bowels': ibid., p.157

'During intermission': in *Steal This Book!*, 1971

'It was wonderful': *Rolling Stone*, 14 April 1983, p.19

'There I was driving around': *Melody Maker*, 6 June 1970, p.7

'In the midst of all these things': quoted in Baez, *And A Voice To Sing With*, p.168

'I was not only anti-commercial': ibid.

'I thought it was clever': ibid., pp.152–153

'The festival was broken up': in Wandor (ed.), *Once A Feminist*, p.18

'Inverse red-baiting': 'Marry Or Die', in Goodman (ed.), *The Movement*, pp.48–49

'The free sexual revolution': quoted ibid.

'may be chauvinistic': *Oz*, February 1970

'All around me I see men': 'Letter To The Left', in *Dear Sisters*, p.51

'the beginning of the transition': angelfire.com/wi/blindfaith/vvcov69

'We are a revolutionary homosexual': GLF manifesto

'I know you're camp!': manuscript of Lennon letter

'I laugh at the SDS': reprinted in *The Rolling Stone Interviews Vol. 1*, pp.395ff

'I remember getting into a fight': *Hit Parader*, August 1971

'That was the prevailing philosophy': author interview

'we should have been arrested': author interview

'Compare the Airplane's': in *Conversations with the New Reality*, pp.106ff

'We were all punks': *Dark Star* 17, October 1978, p.18

'In the States they so nearly': Paul Bandey's review, *Oz* 27, p.35

'ludicrously smug': Harvey Pezar's review, *Down Beat*, 1 October 1970, p.20

'By now it should be obvious': ibid.

'We didn't feel we had to shoot': author interview

'You should fuck with people': author interview

'ineffectual revolution': *Conversations with the New Reality*, pp.106ff

'Jack Casady and I': *Dark Star* 6, December 1976, p.7

'Pop music has become': Bonny Cohen, in *Old Mole*, 1 August 1969

'How do we deal with the rock hip': KBUR-FM radio broadcast, quoting Mark Kramer

'Rock expresses the ethos': quoted by Jeff Berchenko in *Great Speckled Bird*, 9 February 1970

'I have very little faith': *Leviathan* interview, reprinted in Goodman (ed.), *The Movement*, pp.420ff

'What's most in trouble': *Conversations with the New Reality*, p.104

'one of the most decadent bourgeois': *Leviathan* interview, op. cit.

'If there's a list, I'm on it': 'Stills & Young' by Richard Williams, *Melody Maker*, 10 January 1970, p.5

'Absolutely none': *New Musical Express*, 29 July 1972

'We will witness student disorders': *From The President*, p 39

'We need words': in Heath, *Off the Pigs*, p.163

'We say down with the American': ibid., pp.164–165

'I heard a voice from another part': Arlen, *An American Verdict*, pp.140–141

'The immediate violent criminal': ibid., p.20

'If they can do this to the Black Panthers': Wilkins & Clark (eds.), *Search & Destroy*, p.5

'I am warning you': Clavir/Spitzer (eds.), *The Conspiracy Trial*, p.153

'racist, fascist pig': ibid., pp.154ff

'Give me your assurance': ibid., p.163

'Your Honour, he is being choked': ibid., p.169

'I'm put in jail': ibid., p.189

'Wavy Gravy, who was a friend': author interview

'The most fun we had': *Do It*, p.196

'Kunstler asked Ochs': ibid.

'This is the guitar I played': *The Conspiracy Trial*, p.291

'The guitar – a deadly dangerous': *Do It*, p.196

'Don't forget your guitar': *The Conspiracy Trial*, p.291

'I really didn't want to go': *IT*, 27 February 1970, pp.14–15

'Oh, no, no. No, I am sorry': *The Conspiracy Trial*, p.427

'The defence is trying to prove': *IT*, 27 February 1970, pp.14–15

'Just a minute, young lady': *The Conspiracy Trial*, p.460

'He sent the guard over': author interview

'I forbid her from singing': *The Conspiracy Trial*, p.460

'That still seems a pretty': author interview

'Will you, young lady': *The Conspiracy Trial*, p.462

'It was a strange experience': author interview

'Country Joe came into the courtroom': Schultz, *The Chicago Conspiracy Trial*, p.229

'You will remove your gum': *The Conspiracy Trial*, p.441

'Joe and [judge] Julie': Do It, pp.196, 198

'a minister in the Universal Life Church': *The Conspiracy Trial*, p.441

'We sat in a restaurant': *Do It*, pp.196, 198

'The judge would like to speak': *The Conspiracy Trial*, p.442

'It *was* a strange place': author interview

'Certain words have certain connotations': *The Conspiracy Trial*, p.443

'You want us to be like good Germans': ibid., p.580

'My life has come to nothing': ibid., p.581

'I am going to jail': ibid., p.599

'to build an anti-imperialist': in Jacobs, *Weatherman*, p.175

'We must be prepared to defend': ibid., p.178

'thousands of freaks': ibid., p.156

'He gave off a lot of magic': *Time*, 12 December 1969

'The first time I heard him': *San Jose Mercury News*, 3 December 1969

'I'm going to have to start': Manson trial transcript

'Manson believed that the Beatles': reported in *IT*, 5 November 1970, p.5

'The last survivors of a band': *San Francisco Chronicle*, 15 October 1969

'Probably a lot of us will get shot': reported in Jacobs, *Weatherman*, p.216

'We have shown the pigs': ibid., p.225

'We didn't say that': recording of press conference

'Those fuckers are making': reported by Sol Stern, 'Altamont: Pearl Harbor
    to the Woodstock Nation', in *Conversations with the New Reality*,
    pp.45ff

'You can't ask a question': recording of press conference

'Mick Jagger was contacted': reprinted in Goodman (ed.), *The Movement*,
    p.420ff

'Altamont was just a few miles': Stern, op. cit.

'The first disastrous experience': ibid.

'Watching [David] Crosby's discomfort': ibid.

'There was one thing': *Garcia: A Signpost To New Space*, p.115

'My God, THE STONES': 'Altamont', *IT*, 28 January 1970, p.11

'the world's most fantastic': *New Musical Express*, 13 December 1969, p.12

'Bringing a lot of people': *Berkeley Tribe*, 12–19 December 1969, p.1

'We're turning into a generation': ibid., p.4

'Underground Music is Dead': Arthur A. Pitt in *IT*, 28 January 1970,
    p.13

'rock as commodity': 'Greg', in 'Abbey Road: Beatles as Aging Children', in
    *The Movement* (Goodman ed.), pp.374ff

## CHAPTER 5: 1970

'The seventies are exploding': 'Revolution in the 70's', in Jacobs, *Weatherman*, pp.448ff

'We should be leading large numbers': 'National War Council', ibid., p.339

'Because we need a party': the complete *Weatherman Songbook* can be found in *Weatherman*, pp.351ff

'Dig it, first they killed': quoted ibid., p.347

'Some Weathermen said they did not expect': ibid., p.349

'reactionary, invalid': ibid., p.293

'Black Brothers in Vietnam': quoted in Heath, *Off the Pigs*, p.257

'a sex pervert': the relevant documents are available on the FBI's Freedom of Information website

'The concept of the Party': *This Side of Glory*, p.284

'Today, we see twenty-eight members': *Stokely Speaks*, p.195

'Many say that I am counter-revolutionary': ibid., p.209

'It is the richest continent': ibid., pp.202–203

'"discovered" a number of plots': Arnold, *Africa: A Modern History*, p.224

'I included the reference': *New Musical Express*, 29 November 1969, p.3

'If I'm gonna get on the front page': footage in film, *Imagine: John Lennon*

'If he had really wanted to stop': interview with *Feed* magazine, *c*.2000

'We're not going to Vietnam': *Melody Maker*, 13 November 1969, p.19

'the thought that being John and Yoko': Dallas, *Singers of an Empty Day*, p.118

'the problem with the revolutionaries': *New Musical Express*, 20 December 1969, p.3

'I can see his point in using advertising': *IT*, 28 January 1970, p.16

'He felt he was getting his own back': author interview

'play the roles of Black Power leader': Humphry/Tindall, *False Messiah*, p.75

'We plan to sweep our angry youth': quoted ibid., p.77

'The white liberal': quoted ibid., p.64

'Michael was a persuasive guy': author interview

'You have stolen the rhythms': quoted ibid., p.90

'John totally believed that love': *Rolling Stone*, 22 January 1981, pp.50–51

'gave Richard and me the surliest welcome': Taylor, *Fifty Years Adrift*

'The press pictures were not pretty': ibid.

'We're going to do a poster': *IT*, 27 February 1970, pp.11, 19, 20

'Marching was alright': ibid.

'What the underground has got': ibid.

'I think that a lot of people': ibid.

'Me and Nixon don't get along': quoted in Ray Brack, 'The Man Vs 'Negroes'',
 *Rolling Stone*, 30 January 1970, p.11

'There is no such thing as a black militant': in Alan Smith, 'James Brown –
 Outrageous Extrovert', *New Musical Express*, 24 October 1970, p.11

'We are the real warriors': *Raise Race Rays Raze*, p.109

'Sly is a political group': quoted in *Rolling Stone*, 3 September 1970, pp.11–12

'the only rock performer I know': *Woodstock Nation*, pp.158ff

'All boundary crossers': *Midnight Lightning*, p.12

'Music is stronger than politics': quoted ibid., p.47

'On at least two reported occasions': ibid.

'Brother, it's time for you': ibid., p.20

'They asked me to do a concert': *New Musical Express* interview, 11 September
 1970

'I heard about that too': John Burks interview, *Rolling Stone*, 19 March 1970,
 pp.36ff

'I started writing in order': Jonathan Cott, 'The Last Poets & Apocalypse',
 *Rolling Stone*, 3 September 1970, p.20

'There's a thing with a whole lot': quoted in Goodman, *The Movement*, pp.420ff

'world weariness and corny': *Raise Race Rays Raze*, p.120

'I just wanted to voice my concerns': jazzweekly.com/interviews/chaden

'The reason that people are dropping': *IT*, 27 February 1970, pp.14–15

'I'm not interested in whether': *Friends*, 25 March 1970, pp.13–15

'Dylan's abdication': Norma M. Whittaker, 'Country Joe at Home', *Other
 Scenes*, August 1970

'People shouldn't look to me': quoted in *Bob Dylan* (1996 edition), p.269

'Some of us who feel': *Kaleidoscope*, 18 March 1970

'Author's royalties from the sale of this book': bootleg edition of *Tarantula*,
 'Wimp Press, Hibbing'

'The only alliance I would make': quoted in Gillian G. Gaar, *She's A Rebel*,
 p.117

'SCUM will coolly, furtively': *SCUM Manifesto*, pp.79, 80, 82–83

'Death to the bureaucrats': *RAT Subterranean News*, 6–23 February 1970,
 p.2

'the liberal co-optive masks': 'Goodbye To All That', in *Dear Sisters*, pp.53ff

'thrive on a male ego': reprinted in *IT*, 27 August 1970, p.13

'Women's liberation is one thing': *Beetle* (Toronto), November 1974, pp.41ff

'In a world of men': 'Cock Rock', in Eisen (ed.), *Twenty-Minute Fandangos and Forever Changes*, pp.146–147

'I was lying on the sofa': 'Days of Celebration and Resistance', in *Dear Sisters*, pp.306–307

'I don't think anybody said it better': quoted in 'There's Something Happening Here', *Earth Island* issue 1, p.3

'There are now few helpful projects': John H. Schaar/Sheldon S. Wolin, 'Where Are We Now', *New York Review of Books*, 7 May 1970, p.3

'How does it feel to be': in Jacobs, *Weatherman*, pp.504ff

'the work of some isolated terrorist nuts': *Scanlan's* magazine, undated cutting

'Diana was a Roman goddess': author interview

'Do you identify with Manson': *East Village Other* interview, reprinted in *Zigzag*, September 1970, pp.5ff

'Instead of protesting about the war': ibid.

'He was the only man standing': *Dark Star*, June 1981, p.36

'Abbie was one of the funniest guys': author interview

'As for these deserters': quoted in *Friends* issue 4, p.7

'a nationwide student strike': *Time*, 18 May 1970

'the worst type of people': recording of press conference

'We had faltered when history': quoted in Wells, *The War Within*, p.449

'It comes clear that the Nixon Presidency': 'Random Notes', *Rolling Stone*, 28 May 1970, p.4

'That was how it felt': author interview

'Prior to the Kent State tragedy': Ritchie Yorke, 'Disc Biz Hit by Trends', *New Musical Express*, 4 July 1970, p.16

'I'm all for closing down': Jacoba Atlas, 'Baez on Struggle Mountain', *Melody Maker*, 6 June 1970, p.7

'inciting the kids to near enough riot': undated issued of *KLAP*, c. late 1970, p.5

'At first they let it go': 'The Functioning Anarchy of Jefferson Airplane', *New Musical Express*, 27 June 1970, pp.4, 16

'The shootings have had': Yorke, op. cit.

'I think that Kent and Jackson': quoted in John Morthland, 'Kent Aftermath: Teen Turmoil Poison at B.O.', *Rolling Stone*, 25 June 1970, pp.1, 8, 9

'The kids are so depressed': Jacoba Atlas, 'Campus Strikes Hit Tull', *Melody Maker*, 6 June 1970, p.4

'There are plenty of Pete Seegers': ibid.

'There will almost certainly be': Yorke, op. cit.

'we just thought rich hippies': quoted in McDonough, *Shakey*, p.346

'I think there will be more bloodshed': quoted in Zimmer (ed.), *The CSNY Reader*, p.76

'he was afraid to perform': *Melody Maker*, 6 June 1970, p.4

'It is not just students': in Morthland, op. cit.

'radicals are the architects': quoted in Tamarkin, *Got A Revolution*, p.219

'You may argue with the term': in William Ruhlmann's liner notes to Chicago CD box set

'With this album, we dedicate': *Chicago* LP liner notes

'was misinterpreted by a lot': Ruhlmann, op. cit.

'The biggest revolution of all': Mark, in *International Times*, 9 April 1970, p.13

'If Chicago really wants': Don Buday, in *Los Angeles Free Press*, 30 April 1971

'disenchanted with Communism': quoted by David Felton, *Rolling Stone*, 3 September 1970, p.10

'whose sole purpose is to spread': 'Blood Sweat & Bullshit', *IT*, 22 October 1970, p.9

'Dylan's no longer a leftist': Steve, *IT*, 3 July 1970, p.5

'have taken time off from': quoted by Scaduto, op. cit, p.267

'had decided to accept the degree': quoted in *Rolling Stone*, 9 July 1970, p.7

'Bob didn't want to go': in Heylin, *Behind The Shades*, p.321

'There is a group of students': quoted in Tamarkin, *Got A Revolution*, p.219

'Nixon invades Cambodia': in Jacobs, *Weatherman*, p.515

'Our job is to lead': Raskin (ed.), *The Weather Eye*, p.16

'So Nixon kills four': Mal Doror, 'Kerosene News', *IT*, 5 June 1970, p.6

'Pop and the Election': *Melody Maker*, 6 June 1970, pp.16–17

'It was hardly': *Friends*, 20 February 1970, p.4

'Tariq and his comrades': author interview

'Perhaps one day the journalists': *IT*, 12 March 1970, p.2

'a revolutionary group': Nick Logan, 'Revolution & the Broughtons', *New Musical Express*, 8 August 1970, p.4

'Watch out!': *IT*, 3 December 1970, p.7

'I think that Edgar's much more': *IT*, 20 November 1970, p.11

'I'd always been throwing shitfits': *Give the Anarchist a Cigarette*, p.155

'We were also assumed': ibid., p.164

'1970 will be a year': *IT*, 14 January 1970, p.5

'I want to earn money': quoted in *IT*, 10 September 1970, p.1

'We found out that all of the bread': *The Rolling Stone Interviews Vol. 2*, p.292

'[Jagger] can form his own company': *IT*, 27 August 1970, pp, 5, 14

'We are not making any money': quoted in Paytress, *The Rolling Stones: Off The Record*, p.19

'Entrance cost up to one week's salary': *IT*, 5 November 1970, pp.9, 22

'We lost six grand': quoted in Allen, *Isle of Wight 1970*, p.5

'the most horrendous security measures': *Give the Anarchist a Cigarette*, p.284

'The Isle of Wight Festival': White Panther Party leaflet

'Performers are on that stage': White Panther Party communiqué

'Sure, we'd heard some good music': Allen, op. cit, p.5

'You bastards, you ruined': *IT*, 10 September 1970, pp.7ff

'to bring community pressure': White Panther Party leaflet

'a VIP enclosure': *IT*, 10 September 1970, pp.7ff

'Only vegetables can spend': *IT*, 5 November 1970, pp.9, 22

'The Isle of Wight was just': *Melody Maker*, 3 July 1971, pp.24–25, 42

'spend so much time': *IT*, 5 November 1970, pp.9, 22

'It was a hostile audience': *Q*, May 1988

'I believe this is my festival': film of festival

'the beast lay down': *Q*, May 1988

'I saw a coloured Asian man': *IT*, 6 May 1971, p.10

'the end of the rip-off form': Allen op. cit., p.5

'a political prisoner': Jacobs, *Weatherman*, p.516

'waged by short-haired robots': reprinted in *IT* issue 89, pp.2, 15

'Too many so-called leaders': *Revolutionary Suicide*, p.292

'They are trying to impress': Davis, *An Autobiography*, p.250

'He reminded me': ibid., p.265

'Turning myself into Ronald Reagan': Heath, *Off the Pigs*, pp.254–255

'The reactionary pig forces': ibid.

'not because I believe': quoted in *New York Times*, 27 June 1971

'in a shambles': *Revolutionary Suicide*, p.329

'They wanted the Black Panthers': *Revolutionary Suicide*, p.298

'the fascist ruling class': Heath, *Off the Pigs*, p.188

'when [the revolution] did not come': *Revolutionary Suicide*, p.298

'We had a nice long rap': 'Fuck, No, We're Just Musicians', *Organ*, June 1971, pp.14ff

'My father was a socialist': author interview

'I can't preach against capitalism': *IT*, 5 November 1970, p.15

'a revolutionary culture cadre': Michael Torrence memoir at itsabouttimebpp.com

'Elaine Brown had already recorded': ibid.

'The Lumpen sing about': Monk Teba, 'A Message to Black Entertainers', *Black Panther*, 14 December 1970, p.5

'We did all the political': Torrence, op. cit.

'Weatherman is the heaviest': Mal Doror, 'Kerosene News', *IT*, 5 June 1970, p.6

'The Lower East Side was OD'ed': 'We are All Outlaws in the Eyes of Amerika', *IT*, 13 August 1970, pp.7, 14

'Now we are in heavy times': *Woodstock Nation*, pp.161–162

'Next week families and tribes': *The Weather Eye*, pp.22ff

'the townhouse explosion': ibid., p.17; the entire *New Morning – Changing Weather* manifesto is ibid., pp.26–34

'Dylan belongs in a very personal way': John Coleman, *Friends*, 13 November 1970

'We've Got Dylan Back Again': *Rolling Stone*, 26 November 1970

'Now he's like a ghost': quoted in *Rolling Stone*, 27 May 1971

'First of all there's Dylan's painting': reprinted in *IT*, 3 July 1970

'concerns the rationale': ibid.

'Roadmaps to our homestead': Dylan, *Chronicles*, p.116

'in hopes to demolish': ibid., p.118

'Dylan is a good father': *IT*, 31 December 1970, pp.7, 15

'To make a long story short': 'Weberman Strikes Again', *IT*, 5 November 1970, pp.12, 14

'has finally got out': ibid.

'Bob is now part of': *IT*, 31 December 1970, pp.7, 15

'All great art today': *We Are Everywhere*, pp.110–113

'Bob Dylan has made a fortune': *IT*, 9 April 1970

'One of the things we're trying': quoted by Clinton Heylin, 'A Profile of Howard Alk', *The Telegraph* issue 18, 1984

'I think ["Working Class Hero"]': Wenner, *Lennon Remembers*, p.93

'There had been stories': Taylor, *Fifty Years Adrift*

'I'm sick of all these aggressive': Wenner, op. cit., p.70

'I'm talking about the generation': ibid., p.11

## CHAPTER 6: 1971

'When the pop star turned out': *Rolling Stone*, 4 February 1971, p.19

'Dylan was still enthused about Israel': *Bob Dylan*, p.281

'If Dylan thinks he's gonna get': reprinted in *IT*, 16 June 1971

'a drop in the bucket': Weberman leaflet

'Tariq Ali had kept coming round': Peebles (ed.), *The Lennon Tapes*, p.42

'The IMG were always contemptuous': author interview

'as a natural enemy': this and subsequent quotes from the *Red Mole* interview reprinted in Thomson/Gutman (eds.), *The Lennon Companion*, pp.165ff

'I spent an afternoon talking': *Melody Maker*, 2 October 1971, pp.24–25

'hanging out with the Cambridge': 'The Ballad of John & Yoko', *Skywriting by Word of Mouth*, pp.25–26

'It's a poor record': in Luftig (ed.), *The Paul Simon Companion,* p.100

'stop the government': quoted in Wells, *The War Within*, p.471

'They were corrupted by power': author interview

'mortified': author interview

'As far as Phil was concerned': author interview

'Being a celebrity': *We Are Everywhere*, p.172

'He had the headband': author interview

'If ever [I become]': Rubin, op. cit., p.173

'I remember seeing a prototype': Sloman, *Steal This Dream*, p.225

'When you operate in that kind': ibid.

'If people relate to me': 'Tales of Hoffman' [dated 8/2/71], *Oz* 34, p.10

'the egocentric greed': *Woodstock Nation*, p.157

'A revolution in consciousness': in *Steal This Book!*

'Most of the things that people': reprinted in *IT*, 13 August 1970, pp.5, 12

'Most pop music is still low-energy': ibid.

'Pop is an ugly fucking scene': *IT*, 25 March 1971, pp.16–17

'the shoddy, alienating culture': Angry Brigade communiqué #6

'modern slavehouses': Angry Brigade commuiqué #7

'Their move to France': 'Millionaires with Dirty Habits', *Ink*, 1 May 1971, p.15

'Was the whole ceremony': 'Sympathy for the Holy Ghost', *Ink*, 29 May 1971, pp.1, 5

'Violence is the only legitimate': reprinted in *East Village Other*

'We desperately need more': ibid.

'The Minister of Information': *Revolutionary Suicide*, p.302

'If it weren't for the power of the people': *Black Panther*, 13 March 1971, p.8

'stuttered through an arcane': *A Taste of Power*, p.282

'We have some loose semi-association': *Creem* interview, reprinted in *IT*, 22 April 1971, pp.8–10, 15

'primary purpose was not entertainment': *Black Panther*, 13 March 1971, p.8

'a stale rerun of a familiar': *Revolutionary Suicide*, p.313

'I am not a Black Panther': quoted in Paul Tingen, *Miles Beyond*

'started wondering what the fuck': in Edmonds, *What's Going On*, pp.95–96

'get together': 'The Impressions', *Rolling Stone*, 16 January 1970, pp.44ff

'I made the picture': *Sweet Sweetback's*, p.vii

'revolutionary call to arms': Hugh Nolan in *IT*, 25 February 1971, p.21

'Who said there was only one': author interview

'This can be one of the biggest': quoted in Nick Ralph, 'Grunt Records', *Dark Star* 15, p.30

'In Boston, some chick came in': *Beetle* (Toronto), November 1974, pp.41ff

'Women should be used': quoted in *Zigzag* 22, *c.* August 1971, p.13

'The sole purpose of this group': *Rolling Stone*, 24 June 1971, p.13

'I wish they'd play topless': quoted in *Cream*, January 1972, pp.21ff

'These Four Girls Have Got Class': *Rolling Stone*, op. cit.

'It blew my mind': 'Fixin' To Live Rag', *Organ*, May 1971

'crazed individualists': *Guitar Army*, p.350

'communal, classless': Rainbow People's Party manifesto

'Free Our Sisters/Free Our Selves': *Guitar Army*, p.295ff

'I found myself being a chauvinist': McCabe/Schonfeld, *John Lennon: For The Record*, p.57

'She's a red hot liberationist': in *Red Mole* interview

'I'm always interested to know': ibid.

'The forthcoming *Oz* obscenity': *IT*, 8 April 1971, p.5

'I always take care of the underground': McCabe/Schonfeld, op. cit., p.39

'opening the way to a New American': recording of speech

'I was a bit cautious': author interview

'The movement has been duped': in Bill Davidson, *Jane Fonda: An Intimate Biography*, p.168

'I really did not want to go': author interview

'He is thoroughly disenchanted': *From The President*, p.225

'DYLAN SUPPORTS RACIST': *Ink*, 16 June 1971

'present Dylan with some very special': Dylan Liberation Front leaflet

'We played Saigon once': *The Rolling Stone Interviews: The 80s*, p.148

'looking to drown out the just': in Zolov, *Refried Elvis*, p.214

'That wasn't the kind of store': author interview

'depressed and confused': Stu Werbin, 'John & Jerry & David & John & Leni & Yoko', *Rolling Stone*, 17 February 1972, pp.1, 6, 8, 10, 12

'I couldn't believe it': author interview

'John said, "Are you making a record?"': author interview

'the Mork and Mindy of the Sixties': *Skywriting by Word of Mouth*, p.25

'I'm pretty movable as an artist': in Cott/Doudna (eds.), *The Ballad of John & Yoko*, pp.152–153

'All five of us were amazed at how': Werbin, op. cit.

'I was in Ireland': author interview

'had been handed an endlessly productive': Bishop/Mallie, *The Provisional IRA*, p.189

'Jack Bruce, son of a militant': 'Sauchiehall Street Apache Stomp', *Cream*, September 1971, p.28

'the most political thing': quoted in Marsh, *Before I Get Old*, p.350

'I believe rock can do anything': quoted in Marsh, op. cit., p.361

'The aim is change': quoted in Marsh, op. cit., p.372

'Rock can't be held responsible': quoted ibid., p.368

'I suppose if I wasn't cunt enough': *IT*, 9 September 1971, pp.8, 19

'incredible fees': *Melody Maker*, 25 September 1971, p.15

'the feeling we get when watching': 'Creators or Capitalists?', *Melody Maker*, 16 October 1971, p.13

'All right! The game's up!': 'Townshend Hits Back', *Melody Maker*, 6 November 1971, p.56

'in order to establish': Rock Liberation Front manifesto

'When we made those demands': author interview

'clampdowns on people's rights': small ad in *Frendz*, 2 September 1971, p.14

'The Rock Liberation Front': author interview

'Led Zeppelin now charge': *Earth Island* No. 1 (1970), pp.7ff

'We figured McCartney': author interview

'I hope they're not after me': McCabe/Schonfeld, op. cit., p.75

'Why should [audiences] pay?': ibid., p.36

'They tell me they've made': Stu Werbin, 'John & Jerry & David & John & Leni & Yoko', *Rolling Stone*, 17 February 1972, pp.1, 6, 8, 10, 12

'I want to do something political': McCabe/Schonfeld, op. cit., p.36

'It was only meant half seriously': Werbin, op. cit.

'There was this terrific May Day': 'I Quit the Movement', *Los Angeles Free Press*, 1 October 1971, pp.7, 11

'We hired a band called': whirlitzer.org/zounds

'This is a sort of retirement': 'I Quit the Movement'

'Vietnamese torture is nothing': quoted in contemporary reports of the trial

'clean air, a modern free home': Republic of New Afrika manifesto

'because they were political prisoners': *Rolling Stone*, 17 February 1972, p.16

'I drove down the freeway': 'Eric Unburdened', *Melody Maker*, 7 August 1971, p.19

'We're all familiar with the function': brown.edu/Departments/African_American_Studies/wayland_fac_seminar/interview/george_jackson.html

'Inside the church the walls': *Revolutionary Suicide*, p.309

'my hero . . . He showed the love': ibid., p.310

'From 1967 through 1970': Hampton/Fayer (eds.), *Voices of Freedom*, p.544

'a lot of words': quoted in Wicker, *A Time to Die*, p.9

'It was conceived on my birthday': recording of Lennon performance

'It almost ruined it': in Cott/Doudna (eds.), *The Ballad of John & Yoko*, pp.152–153

'The camera clicked just as I heard': memoir on Weberman's Dylanology website, *c.*1998

'There was a spirit among everybody': '30,000 Marchers Can't Be Wrong', *Frendz*, 25 November 1971, p.7

'It was the first women's liberation': in Peebles (ed.), *The Lennon Tapes*, pp.48–50

'People always talk about my music': Werbin, op. cit.

'One day I come over': ibid.

'I don't want to die and leave': *Soledad Brother*, p.235

'Dylan's coming around': Liberation News Service interview

'Dylan responded with real': *Village Voice*, December 1971

'I may be naive': ibid.

'Is George going to be turned': *Ink*, 17 December 1971, p.7

'We're just in the inception': recording of TV broadcast

'Join the RLF before it gets you': Lennon manuscript

'Peel's an opportunist': author interview

'We ask A.J. Weberman': printed in *Village Voice*, 2 December 1971

'Dear People, Please accept my apologies': ibid.

'I didn't write that apology': *IT*, 19 June 1972, p.4

'I thought that when Dylan saw': Wiener, *Come Together*, p.196

'PCPJ is presently planning': reprinted in Wiener, *Gimme Some Truth*, p.127

'Lennon was trying to get Dylan': Wiener, *Come Together*, p.196

'But the song worked': author interview

'The authorities don't want to see John': *IT*, 4 November 1971, p.4

'We can't help but take some credit': *Ink*, 7 January 1972, p.6

'To Ann Arbor for the first time': recording of performance

'Stevie was really upset': Elsner, *Stevie Wonder*, p.110

'the first act of the Rock Liberation Front': recording of performance

'They hated us': author interview

'We came here not only to help John': recording of performance

'The seven justices drafted': *Ink*, 7 January 1972, p.4


**CHAPTER 7: 1972**

'This year is the year': 'Let's Start Again', *Ink*, 21 January 1972, p.8

'Anti-war demonstrators': in Wells, *The War Within*, p.534

'For the past five months': 'Let's Start Again'

'It was fun meeting all the famous': *Skywriting by Word of Mouth*, pp.25–26

'thought the whole idea stunk': ibid.

'I made John and myself': author interview

'None of them knew how to talk': *Skywriting by Word of Mouth*, pp.27–28

'the culmination of every musical fantasy': *Growing (Up) At 37*, p.12

'We're serious about our program': Stu Werbin, 'John & Jerry & David & John & Leni & Yoko', *Rolling Stone*, 17 February 1972, pp.1, 6, 8, 10, 12

'the biggest mistake Yoko and I made': *Skywriting by Word of Mouth*, p.31

'ALL EXTREMISTS': in Wiener, *Gimme Some Truth*, p.129

'The alleged purpose of the group': ibid., p.147

'Potential Disruption': *From the President*, pp.360–362

'an international news service': Wiener, op. cit., p.157

'This appears to me to be': ibid., p.3

'over 100 organisations which are using': ibid., p.145

'seem uninterested': ibid., p.179

'heavy users of narcotics': ibid., p.213

'John Lennon appears to be radically orientated': ibid., p.215

'dying on the vine': ibid., p.217

'many former leaders': ibid., p.225

'There is a quietness': 'Fuck America', *Ink*, 21 January 1972, p.8

'Motherfucker, you have one minute': Brown, *A Taste of Power*, p.339

'If there was an able-bodied man': *Irish Press*, 31 January 1972

'We were all there to show our sympathy': Lennon recording

'I always used to think': *Rolling Stone*, 31 January 1974, p.22

'We have decided not to play this record': quoted in *Rolling Stone*, 30 March 1972, p.13

'The band didn't really exist': author interview

'We played concerts for them': author interview

'the civil rights movement': Lennon letter, *IT*, 6 April 1972, p.4

'Of course we sympathise': ibid.

'When the two do eventually arrive': *IT*, 9 March 1972, pp.38, 49–50

'Go back to the 50s, Spector': 'Weberman Beats Up Phil Spector', *IT*, 18 May 1972, pp.12–13

'We figured that if Klein': author interview

'We went over for tea': author interview

'There was this guy': author interview

'I hooked him up with Noraid': author interview

'Lennon gave Noraid': author interview

'My husband did not give money': quoted in Giuliano, *Lennon in America*, pp.44–45

'There were Irish Americans': Johnny Rogan interview

'Allen Ginsberg always thought': author interview

'If I ever said anything bad': author interview

'John is a feminist': Peebles (ed.), *The Lennon Tapes*, pp.55–56

'Lennon, after going out of his way': *Rolling Stone*, 20 January 1972

'It was long before Helen': Peebles, op. cit., pp.48–50

'I started writing': Jacoba Atlas, 'She Am Woman!', *Melody Maker*, 23 December 1972, p.35

'We played a great many Top 20': ibid.

'Huge fraternity boys': 'Days of Celebration and Resistance', in *Dear Sisters*, pp.306–307

'Are you the teenybopper': *IT*, 27 August 1970, p.13

'Where's the women socialists?': Peebles, op. cit., pp.56ff

'I assumed taking care of our child': *Rolling Stone*, 7 June 1973, p.10

'love songs . . . with a revolutionary': *Melody Maker*, 20 May 1972, p 31

'I think I'm the only person': *Zigzag* 37, pp.33ff

'It was a political statement': author interview

'There were several men': author interview

'Occasionally couples would get': *Dark Star*, December 1977, p.23

'I think the occasion we all remember': author interview

'I was sat on stage by myself': author interview

'I'm gay, and I always have been': *Melody Maker*, 22 January 1972

'We have to stop the killing': *Rolling Stone*, 25 May 1972, pp.28–30

'Young voters are going to take': Rainbow People's Party manifesto

'There are more than 30,000 students': ibid.

'George is hip': *Melody Maker*, 10 June 1972, p.10

'We wrote a street opera': author interview

'I wish people of this country': *Rolling Stone*, op. cit.

'I am sure our friends': *From The President*, pp.435–436

'It turned out to be an interesting event': author interview

'The fact that Abby Hoffman': *From The President*, pp.462–463

'McGovern has said that': ibid., p.471

'a left-wing candidate': *IT*, 19 June 1972, pp.17–18

'The hotel that would be our convention': quoted in Wells, *The War Within*, p.549

'his client felt he was being deported': Wiener, *Gimme Some Truth*, p.227

'Ex-Beatle Told to Love It or Leave It': *Black Panther*, 20 May 1972, p.5

'I saw [the record] as a prime way': Valerie Wilmer, 'Attica Blues', *Melody Maker*, 19 August 1972, p.16

'The People's Album': Roy Hollingsworth's review, *Melody Maker*, 10 June 1972, p.9

'infantilism': *New Statesman*, 27 October 1972

'irritating, embarrassing': *Cream*, November 1972, pp.13ff

'Jerry couldn't keep his damn mouth': Sheff, *Last Interview*, p.116

'You'd have to see them': Goldman, *The Lives of John Lennon*, p.450

'We always insisted on keeping physical': *Skywriting by Word of Mouth*, p.28

'We knew the Republicans were bugging': author interview

'I told him we were going to have': author interview

'I don't see what one thing': in Luftig (ed.), *The Paul Simon Companion*, pp.99–100

'the demonstration was the target': Wells, *The War Within*, p.550

'the most difficult, demoralising': *And A Voice to Sing With*, pp.184–192 'part of a conspiracy': quoted in *Rolling Stone*, 23 November 1972, p.6

'souled out': *Black Panther*, 4 November 1972, p.4

'did not wish to come': *St. George & the Godfather*, p.167

'The Yippies held no demonstrations': 'Enemies of the People', *IT*, 26 August 1973, pp.7–8

'in a state of shambles': 'Right On! Mr President', *IT*, 18 September 1972, pp.8–9

'kissed the government's ass': 'Enemies of the People'

'it was very difficult to be in Miami': *Rolling Stone*, 9 November 1972

'I have always ended up': author interview

'It was far more depressing': 'Re-election Phrolics', *IT*, 2 December 1972, p.6

'I want to cut you with a knife': Goldman, *The Lives of John Lennon*, p.451

## EPILOGUE

'I've come to believe': author interview

'a shambles': *Rolling Stone*, 9 November 1972, p.29–30

'They were sold the biggest fucking lie': author interview

'I think a lot of it had to do': author interview

'Everyone was excited': author interview

'[Dylan] said he didn't have any inclination': *Playboy*, November 1976

'everybody's thinking the same thing': *Newsweek*, 10 January 1974

'Why pay high ticket price$': Weberman leaflet

'I'm not sure what a Zionist is': *Knockin' On Dylan's Door*, p.46

'The money you earn is the money': *San Francisco Chronicle*, 1 January 1974

'Every four years Dylan': *Village Voice*, 7 March 1976

'the Outlaw Exploitation Game': *The National Review*, 16 April 1976

'How the hell did we get here': author interview

'I was to spend three years there': *Soul On Fire*, p.163

'I just crumbled': ibid., p.191

'a traitor to the struggle of black people': quoted in Van Peebles, *Panther*, p.126

'Most of them seem to have been killed': *An American Verdict*, p.98

'John paid for the postage': author interview

'Its flag was the white flag': 'Surrender to Peace', in *Give Peace A Chance*, p.29

'It's not that I'm above politics': Sheff, *The Last Interview*, p.95–96

'I don't think the feminist movement': author interview
'Every time we turn our backs': Humphry/Tindall, *False Messiah*, p.207
'I have a very different sense': author interview
'You've always got to have good tunes': *Rolling Stone*, 21 August 1980, p.41

## NOTES

'I started out by practicing': ibid., p.14
'Len Chandler, a black folk singer': *Soon to be a Major Motion Picture*, p.79
'Then they came back': author interview
'This record was born out of': liner notes to *Save the Children* LP
'The way the tax dodge worked': author interview
'I was wrong to assume that Dylan': author interview
'England is full up': *Ann Arbor Argus*, 10–25 July 1969, p.23
'I think Enoch is the man': 'Rod The Mod', *IT*, 17 December 1970, p.17
'*Hair* is the most vicious': *New York Times* interview, reprinted in
    *Conversations with Amiri Baraka*, p.92
'braless Candy Givens': *Los Angeles Free Press*, 29 May 1970, p.33
'The irony is that we are behind them': *Melody Maker*, 13 February 1971
'It's riveting, because it gives you': author interview
'John Lennon couldn't write': author interview
'a Negro convict': quoted in *IT*, 30 December 1971
'One of the last fights': author interview
'I was approached by Jane': author interview

# BIBLIOGRAPHY

Ali, Tariq: *1968 & After: Inside the Revolution* (Blond & Briggs, London, 1978)

Allen, Rod: *Isle of Wight 1970: The Last Great Festival* (Clipper Press, London, 1970)

Allyn, David: *Make Love Not War: The Sexual Revolution: An Unfettered History* (Little, Brown & Co., New York, 2000)

Anderson, David L.: *The Columbia Guide to the Vietnam War* (Columbia University Press, New York, 2002)

Arlen, Michael J.: *An American Verdict* (Doubleday, New York, 1975)

Arnold, Guy: *Africa: A Modern History* (Atlantic Books, New York, 2005)

Badman, Keith: *The Beatles: After the Break-Up 1970–2000* (Omnibus Press, London, 1999)

Badman, Keith: *The Beatles Off the Record* (Omnibus Press, London, 2000)

Badman, Keith: *The Beatles: The Dream is Over: Off the Record 2* (Omnibus Press, London, 2001)

Baez, Joan: *And a Voice to Sing With: A Memoir* (Summit Books, New York, 1987)

Bangs, Lester: *Psychotic Reactions and Carburetor Dung* (Heinemann, London, 1988)

Baraka, Amiri: *Raise Race Rays Raze: Essays Since 1965* (Random House, New York, 1971)

Baraka, Amiri: *Conversations With Amiri Baraka* (University Press of Mississippi, Jackson, 1994)

Baraka, Amiri: *The Autobiography of LeRoi Jones* (Lawrence Hill, Chicago, 1997)

Barbour, Floyd B. (ed.): *The Black Power Revolt* (Expanding Horizons Books, Boston, 1968)

Baskerville, John D.: *The Impact of Black Nationalist Ideology on American Jazz Music of the 1960s & 1970s* (Edwin Mellen Press, Lewiston, 2003)

Bauldie, John: *Bob Dylan & Desire* (Wanted Man, Bury, 1984)

Bauldie, John & Gray, Michael (eds.): *All Across the Telegraph: A Bob Dylan Handbook* (Futura, London, 1988)

Baxandall, Rosalyn & Gordon, Linda (eds.): *Dear Sisters: Dispatches from the Women's Liberation Movement* (Basic Books, New York, 2000)

Bell, Dale (ed.): *Woodstock* (Michael Wiese Productions, Studio City, 1999)

Berke, Joseph (ed.): *Counter Culture* (Peter Owen, London, 1969)

Berman, Paul: *A Tale of Two Utopias: The Political Journey of the Generation of 1968* (W.W. Norton, New York, 1996)

Bew, Paul & Gillespie, Gordon: *Northern Ireland: A Chronology of the Troubles 1968–1999* (Gill & Macmillan, Dublin, 1999)

Bishop, Patrick & Mallie, Eamonn: *The Provisional IRA* (Corgi, London, 1988)

Bouchier, David: *The Feminist Challenge* (Macmillan, London, 1983)

Bowman, Rob: *Soulsville USA: The Story of Stax Records* (Books With Attitude, London, 1997)

Bradley, Patricia: *Mass Media & the Shaping of American Feminism, 1963–1975* (University Press of Mississippi, Jackson, 2003)

Bromell, Nick: *Tomorrow Never Knows: Rock and Psychedelics in the 1960s* (University of Chicago Press, Chicago, 2000)

Broom, Alexander & Breines, Wini (eds.): *Taking it to the Streets: A Sixties Reader* (Oxford University Press, Oxford, 1995)

Brown, Elaine: *A Taste of Power* (Pantheon Books, New York, 1992)

Brown, H. Rap: *Die Nigger Die!* (Lawrence Hill, Chicago, [1969] 2002)

Brown, Scot: *Fighting For US: Maulana Karenga, the US Organisation, and Black Cultural Nationalism* (New York University Press, New York, 2003)

Carmichael, Stokely: *Stokely Speaks: Black Power Back to Pan-Africanism* (Random House, New York, 1971)

Carmichael, Stokely & Thelwell, Ekwueme Michael: *Ready For Revolution: The Life & Struggles of Stokely Carmichael* (Scribners, New York, 2003)

Chapman, Abraham (ed.): *New Black Voices* (Mentor, New York, 1972)

Childs, Marti Smiley & March, Jeff: *Echoes of the Sixties* (Billboard Books, New York, 1999)

Christgau, Robert: *Any Old Way You Choose It* (Penguin, Baltimore, 1973; revised edn. Cooper Square Press, New York, 2000)

Christgau, Robert: *Christgau's Guide: Rock Albums of the 70s* (Vermilion, London, 1982)

Clavir, Judy & Spitzer, John (eds.): *The Conspiracy Trial* (Jonathan Cape, London, 1971)

Cleaver, Eldridge: *Soul On Ice* (Dell, New York, 1968)

Cleaver, Eldridge: *Post-Prison Writings & Speeches* (Jonathan Cape, London, 1969)

Cleaver, Eldridge: *Soul On Fire* (Hodder & Stoughton, London, 1979)

Cleaver, Eldridge: *Target Zero* (Palgrave Macmillan, New York, 2006)

Collier, Peter & Horowitz, David: *Destructive Generation: Second Thoughts About the 60s* (Free Press, New York, 1996)

Cook, Richard & Morton, Brian: *The Penguin Guide to Jazz on CD, LP & Cassette* (Penguin, London, 1994 edition)

Coote, Anna & Campbell, Beatrix: *Sweet Freedom: The Struggle for Women's Liberation* (Picador, London, 1982)

Cott, Jonathan: *He Dreams What Is Going On Inside His Head* (Straight Arrow, San Francisco, 1973)

Cott, Jonathan & Doudna, Christine (eds.): *The Ballad of John & Yoko* (Michael Joseph, London, 1982)

Cott, Jonathan: *Back to a Shadow in the Night: Music Writings and Interviews 1968–2001* (Hal Leonard, Milwaukee, 2002)

Dallas, Karl: *Singers of an Empty Day: Last Sacraments of the Superstars* (Kahn & Averill, London, 1971)

Darlington, Andrew: *I Was Elvis Presley's Bastard Love-Child & Other Stories of Rock'n'Roll Excess* (Critical Vision, Manchester, 2001)

Davidson, Bill: *Jane Fonda: An Intimate Biography* (Signet, New York, 1991)

Davies, Hunter: *The Beatles: The Authorised Biography* (Heinemann, London, 1968)

Davis, Angela: *An Autobiography* (Hutchinson, London, 1975)

Davis, Clive: *Clive* (Ballantine, New York, 1976)

Davis, James Kirkpatrick: *Assault on the Left: The FBI & the Sixties Antiwar Movement* (Praeger, Westport, 1997)

Denisoff, R. Serge: *Great Day Coming: Folk Music & the American Left* (University of Illinois Press, Urbana, 1971)

Dickstein, Morris: *Gates of Eden: American Culture in the Sixties* (Penguin, New York, 1989)

Doggett, Peter: *Are You Ready for the Country* (Penguin, London, 2000)

Doggett, Peter: *The Art and Music of John Lennon* (Omnibus Press, London, 2005)

Downing, David: *Future Rock* (Panther, St Albans, 1976)

Draper, Robert: *The Rolling Stone Story* (Mainstream Publishing, Edinburgh, 1990)

Dunn, Christopher: *Brutality Garden: Tropicalia & the Emergence of a Brazilian Counterculture* (University of North Carolina Press, Chapel Hill, 2001)

Dylan, Bob: *Tarantula* (pirate edition, attributed to Wimp Press, Hibbing, *c.*1970)

Dylan, Bob: *Chronicles Volume One* (Simon & Schuster, London, 2004)

Editors of *Ramparts* (eds.): *Conversations with the New Reality* (Canfield Colophon Books, San Francisco, 1971)

Editors of *Rolling Stone*: *The Rolling Stone Record Review* (Pocket Books, New York, 1971)

Editors of *Rolling Stone*: *The Rolling Stone Interviews Vol. 1* (Warner Paperback Library, New York, 1971)

Editors of *Rolling Stone*: *The Age of Paranoia: How the Sixties Ended* (Pocket Books, New York, 1972)

Editors of *Rolling Stone*: *The Rolling Stone Interviews Vol. 2* (Warner Paperback Library, New York, 1973)

Editors of *Rolling Stone*: *The Rolling Stone Record Review Vol. II* (Pocket Books, New York, 1974)

Editors of *Rolling Stone*: *Knockin' on Dylan's Door* (Michael Dempsey, London, [1974] 1975)

Edmonds, Ben: *What's Going On?* (Mojo Books, Edinburgh, 2001)

Eisen, Jonathan (ed.): *The Age of Rock 2: Sights & Sounds of the American Cultural Revolution* (Vintage Books, New York, 1970)

Eisen, Jonathan (ed.): *Altamont: Death of Innocence in the Woodstock Nation* (Avon Books, New York, 1970)

Eisen, Jonathan (ed.): *Twenty-Minute Fandangos and Forever Changes: A Rock Bazaar* (Vintage, New York, 1971)

Eliot, Marc: *Death of a Rebel* (Anchor Press, New York, 1979)

Elsner, Constanze: *Stevie Wonder* (Everest Books, London, 1977)

Epstein, Jacob: *The Great Conspiracy Trial* (Random House, New York, 1970)

Evans, Mike (ed.): *The Beatles Literary Anthology* (Plexus, London, 2004)

Farber, David: *Chicago 68* (University of Chicago Press, Chicago, 1988)

Farren, Mick: *Give the Anarchist a Cigarette* (Jonathan Cape, London, 2001)

Ferlinghetti, Lawrence: *Who Are We Now?* (New Directions, New York, 1976)

Fong-Torres, Ben (ed.): *The Rolling Stone Rock'n'Roll Reader* (Bantam Books, New York, 1974)

Friedan, Betty: *It Changed My Life: Writings on the Women's Movement* (Random House, New York, 1976)

Gaar, Gillian: *She's A Rebel: The History of Women in Rock'n'Roll* (Blandford Press, Poole, 1993)

Gaddis, John Lewis: *The Cold War* (Allen Lane, London, 2005)

Garcia, Jerry, Reich, Charles & Wenner, Jann: *Garcia: A Signpost to New Space* (Straight Arrow, San Francisco, 1972)

George, Nelson: *The Death of Rhythm & Blues* (Omnibus Press, London, 1988)

George, Nelson: *Hip Hop America* (Penguin, New York, 1998)

Ginsberg, Allen: *First Blues* (Full Court Press, New York, 1975)

Ginsberg, Allen: *Collected Poems 1947–1985* (Penguin, London, 1995)

Ginsberg, Allen: *Deliberate Prose: Selected Essays 1952–1995* (Penguin, New York, 2000)

Ginsberg, Allen: *Spontaneous Mind: Selected Interviews 1958–1996* (Penguin, London, 2001)

Giovanni, Nikki: *Black Feeling Black Talk/Black Judgement* (Morrow Quill, New York, [1968] 1979)

Gitlin, Todd: *The Sixties: Years of Hope, Days of Rage* (Bantam, New York, 1987)

Giuliano, Geoffrey: *Lennon in America* (Robson Books, London, 2000)

Goldman, Albert: *The Lives of John Lennon* (Bantam Press, London, 1988)

Goldman, Peter: *The Death & Life of Malcolm X* (University of Illinois Press, Urbana, 1979)

Goodman, Mitchell (ed.): *The Movement Towards a New America* (Pilgrim Press, Philadelphia, 1970)

Green, Jonathon: *Days in the Life: Voices from the English Underground 1961–1971* (Heinemann, London, 1988)

Green, Jonathon: *All Dressed Up: The Sixties & the Counterculture* (Jonathan Cape, London, 1998)

Greer, Germaine: *The Female Eunuch* (Paladin, London, 1971)

Greer, Germaine: *The Madwoman's Underwear* (Picador, London, 1986)

Guillory, Monique & Green, Richard C.: Soul: *Black Power, Politics & Pleasure* (New York University Press, New York, 1998)

Guy, Jasmine: *Afeni Shakur: Evolution of a Revolutionary* (Atria Books, New York, 2005)

Hampton, Henry & Fayer, Steve: *Voices of Freedom* (Bantam, New York, 1990)

Heath, G. Louis: *Off the Pigs! The History and Literature of the Black Panther Party* (Scarecrow Press, Metuchen, 1976)

Hersey, John: *The Algiers Motel Incident* (Bantam, New York, 1968)

Heylin, Clinton: *The Great White Wonders: A History of Rock Bootlegs* (Viking, London, 1994)

Heylin, Clinton: *A Life in Stolen Moments: Bob Dylan Day by Day: 1941–1995* (privately published, 1996)

Heylin, Clinton: *Bob Dylan: Behind the Shades: The Biography – Take Two* (Viking, London, 2000)

Hilliard, David & Cole, Lewis: *This Side of Glory* (Little, Brown & Co., Boston, 1993)

Hoffman, Abbie (as 'Free'): *Revolution for the Hell of It* (Dial Press, New York, 1968)

Hoffman, Abbie: *Woodstock Nation* (Random House, New York, 1969; revised edn., Pocket Books, New York, 1971)

Hoffman, Abbie: *Steal This Book* (Pirate Editions, New York, 1971)

Hoffman, Abbie: *Soon To Be a Major Motion Picture* (Perigree, New York, 1980)

Hoffman, Jack & Simon, Daniel: *Run Run Run: The Lives of Abbie Hoffman* (Tarcher Putnam, New York, 1996)

Holzman, Jac & Daws, Gavan: *Follow the Music* (FirstMedia, Santa Monica, 2000)

Howard, Clark: *American Saturday* (Richard Marek, New York, 1981)

Humphry, Derek & Tindall, David: *False Messiah: The Story of Malcolm X* (Hart-Davis MacGibbon, London, 1977)

Jackson, George: *Soledad Brother: The Prison Letters of George Jackson* (Penguin, Harmondsworth, 1971)

Jackson, George L.: *Blood In My Eye* (Bantam, New York, 1972)

Jacobs, Harold: *Weatherman* (Ramparts Press, San Francisco, 1970)

Jacobs, Ron: *The Way the Wind Blew: A History of the Weather Underground* (Verso, London, 1997)

Janowitz, Anne & Peters, Nancy J. (eds.): *Unamerican Activities: Pen American Center Report: The Campaign Against the Underground Press* (City Lights Books, San Francisco, 1981)

Jezer, Marty: *Abbie Hoffman: American Rebel* (Rutgers University Press, New Brunswick, 1993)

Jones, LeRoi: *Black Music* (Morrow, New York, 1967)

Jouffa, Francois: *Les Annees 60* (Michel Lafon, Paris, 1993)

Kempton, Murray: *The Briar Patch* (E.P. Dutton, New York, 1973)

Kent, Jeff: *The Last Poet: The Story of Eric Burdon* (Witan Books, Stoke-on-Trent, 1989)

Kofsky, Frank: *John Coltrane & the Jazz Revolution of the 1960s* (Pathfinder, New York, 1998)

Koven, Mikel J.: *Blaxploitation Films* (Pocket Essentials, Harpenden, 2001)

Krassner, Paul (ed.): *The Best of The Realist* (Running Press, New York, 1984)

Krassner, Paul: *Confessions of a Raving Unconfined Nut: Misadventures in the Counter-Culture* (Simon & Schuster, New York, 1993)

Krassner, Paul: *The Winner of the Slow Bicycle Race* (Seven Stories Press, New York, 1996)

Kurlansky, Mark: *1968: The Year That Rocked the World* (Vintage, London, 2005)

Landy, Elliott: *Dylan in Woodstock* (Genesis Publications, 2000)

Leary, Timothy: *Confessions of a Hope Fiend* (Bantam, New York, 1973)

Lennon, John: *Skywriting by Word of Mouth* (Pan, London, 1986)

Lester, Julius: *Look Out, Whitey! Black Power's Gon' Get Your Mama!* (Grove Press, New York, 1969)

Lester, Julius: *Revolutionary Notes* (Grove Press, New York, 1969)

Lewis, Roger: *Outlaws of America* (Pelican, Harmondsworth, 1972)

Lewisohn, Mark: *The Complete Beatles Chronicle* (Pyramid Books, New York, 1992)

Lockwood, Lee: *Conversation with Eldridge Cleaver* (Jonathan Cape, London, 1971)

Luftig, Stacy (ed.): *The Paul Simon Companion* (Schirmer Books, New York, 1997)

Luftig, Stacy (ed.): *The Joni Mitchell Companion* (Schirmer Books, New York, 2000)

MacCabe, Colin: *Godard: A Portrait of the Artist at 70* (Bloomsbury, London, 2003)

Maclear, Michael: *Vietnam: The Ten Thousand Day War* (Thomas Methuen, London, 1981)

Maharishi Mahesh Yogi (trans.): *On The Bhagavad-Gita: A New Translation & Commentary Chapters 1–6* (Penguin, Harmondsworth, 1969)

Mailer, Norman: *The Armies of the Night* (New American Library, New York, 1968)

Mailer, Norman: *Miami & the Siege of Chicago* (Weidenfeld & Nicolson, London, 1968)

Mailer, Norman: *St. George & The Godfather* (Arbor House, New York, 1972)

Mairowitz, David Zane: *The Radical Soap Opera* (Wildwood House, London, 1974)

Marine, Gene: *The Black Panthers* (Signet, New York, 1969)

Marks, J.: *Mick Jagger* (Abacus, London, 1974)

Marquesee, Mike: *Chimes of Freedom: The Politics of Bob Dylan's Art* (The New Press, London, 2003)

Marsh, Dave: *Before I Get Old: The Story of the Who* (Plexus, London, 1983)

McCabe, Peter & Schonfeld, Robert D.: *John Lennon: For the Record* (Bantam, New York, 1984)

McDonough, Jimmy: *Shakey* (Jonathan Cape, London, 2002)

McGregor, Craig (ed.): *Bob Dylan: A Retrospective* (Morrow, New York, 1972)

McNally, Dennis: *A Long Strange Trip* (Bantam, London, 2002)

Melly, George: *Revolt Into Style: The Pop Arts in Britain* (Penguin, Harmondsworth, 1972)

Michener, James A.: *Kent State: What Happened & Why* (Random House, New York, 1971)

Miles, Barry: *Paul McCartney: Many Years From Now* (Secker & Warburg, 1998)

Miles, Barry: *Ginsberg: A Biography* (revised edition Virgin, London, 2000)

Mitchell, Juliet: *Woman's Estate* (Pelican, Harmondsworth, 1971)

Naipaul, Shiva: *Black & White* (Abacus, London, 1981)

Neises, Charles P. (ed.): *The Beatles Reader* (Pierian Press, Ann Arbor, 1984)

Neville, Richard: *Playpower* (Paladin, London, 1971)

Neville, Richard: *Hippie Hippie Shake* (Bloomsbury, London, 1995)

Newton, Huey P.: *Revolutionary Suicide* (Wildwood House, London, 1974)

Noebel, David: *Communism, Hypnotism & the Beatles* (Christian Crusade Publications, Tulsa, 1965)

Noebel, David: *Rhythm, Riots & Revolution* (Christian Crusade Publications, Tulsa, 1966)

Norman, Philip: *The Stones* (Penguin, London, 1993)

Nuttall, Jeff: *Bomb Culture* (Paladin, London, 1970)

Oliver, John A.: *Eldridge Cleaver Reborn* (Logos, Plainfield, 1977)

Oudes, Bruce (ed.): *From the President: Richard Nixon's Secret Files* (Harper & Row, New York, 1989)

Palmer, Tony: *Born Under a Bad Sign* (William Kimber, London, 1970)

Palmer, Tony: *The Trials of Oz* (Blond & Briggs, London, 1971)

Paytress, Mark: *The Rolling Stones: Off the Record* (Omnibus Press, London, 2003)

Pearson, Hugh: *The Shadow of the Panther* (Perseus Publishing, Cambridge, 1996)

Peck, Abe: *Uncovering the Sixties: The Life & Times of the Underground Press* (Pantheon, New York, 1985)

Peebles, Andy (ed.): *The Lennon Tapes* (BBC Books, London, 1981)

Percival, Dave (ed.): *The Dust of Rumour* (privately published, 1985)

Perry, Charles: *The Haight-Ashbury: A History* (Random House, New York, 1984)

Philbin, Marianne (ed.): *Give Peace a Chance* (Chicago Review Press, Chicago, 1983)

Pickering, Stephen: *Praxis: One* (No Limit, Berkeley, 1971)

Quartim, Joao: *Dictatorship & Armed Struggle in Brazil* (New Left Books, London, 1971)

Raskin, Jonah (ed.): *The Weather Eye: Communiqués from the Weather Underground* (Union Square Press, San Francisco, 1974)

Rhodes, Lisa L.: *Electric Ladyland: Women & Rock Culture* (University of Pennsylvania Press, Philadelphia, 2005)

Riley, Tim: *Tell Me Why: A Beatles Commentary* (The Bodley Head, London, 1988)

Rogan, Johnny: *Neil Young: Zero to Sixty* (Omnibus Press, London, 2000)

Rose, Cynthia: *Living In America: The Soul Saga of James Brown* (Serpent's Tail, London, 1990)

Rowbotham, Sheila: *Woman's Consciousness, Man's World* (Pelican, Harmondsworth, 1973)

Rubin, Jerry: *Do It!* (Simon & Schuster, New York, 1970)

Rubin, Jerry: *We Are Everywhere* (Harper Colophon Books, New York, 1971)

Rubin, Jerry: *Growing (Up) At 37* (M. Evans & Co., New York, 1976)

Ryback, Timothy W.: *Rock Around the Bloc: A History of Rock Music in Eastern Europe and the Soviet Union* (Oxford University Press, Oxford, 1990)

Saul, Scott: *Freedom Is, Freedom Ain't: Jazz & the Making of the Sixties* (Harvard University Press, Cambridge, 2003)

Scaduto, Anthony: *Bob Dylan* (Abacus, London, 1972; revised edn. Helter Skelter, London, 1996)

Schultz, John: *The Chicago Conspiracy Trial* (Da Capo, New York, 1993)

Schumacher, Michael: *Dharma Lion: A Critical Biography of Allen Ginsberg* (St Martin's Press, New York, 1992)

Schumacher, Michael: *There But For Fortune: The Life of Phil Ochs* (Hyperion, New York, 1996)

Seale, Bobby: *Seize the Time: The Story of the Black Panther Party* (Hutchinson, London, 1970)

Seale, Bobby: *A Lonely Rage* (Bantam, New York, 1979)

Selvin, Joel: *Summer of Love* (Plume, New York, 1995)

Selvin, Joel: *Sly & the Family Stone: An Oral History* (Avon Music, New York, 1998)

Sheff, David: *Last Interview: All We Are Saying – John Lennon & Yoko Ono* (Sidgwick & Jackson, London, 2000)

Sinclair, John: *Guitar Army: Street Writings/Prison Writings* (Douglas, New York, 1972)

Slick, Grace: *Somebody to Love: A Rock-and-Roll Memoir* (Warner Books, New York, 1998)

Sloman, Larry: *Steal This Dream: Abbie Hoffman & the Countercultural Revolution in America* (Doubleday, New York, 1998)

Solanas, Valerie: *S.C.U.M. Manifesto* (Olympia Press, New York, 1968)

Sounes, Howard: *Down the Highway: The Life of Bob Dylan* (Doubleday, London, 2001)

Stapleton, Chris & May, Chris: *African All Stars* (Quartet, London, 1987)

Stephens, Chris & Stout, Katharine: *Art & the 60s: This Was Tomorrow* (Tate Publishing, London, 2004)

Tamarkin, Jeff: *Got A Revolution!* (Helter Skelter, London, 2003)

Tate, Greg: *Midnight Lightning: Jimi Hendrix and the Black Experience* (Lawrence Hill, Chicago, 2003)

Thompson, Hunter S.: *The Great Shark Hunt* (Picador, London, 1980)

Thomson, Elizabeth & Gutman, David (eds.): *The Lennon Companion* (Macmillan, London, 1987)

Tingen, Paul: *Miles Beyond: The Electric Explorations of Miles Davis 1967–1991* (Billboard Books, New York, 2001)

Unger, Irwin: *The Movement: A History of the American New Left 1959–1972* (Dodd, Mead & Co., New York, 1974)

Vache, Jacques (ed.): *Black Mask & Up Against the Wall Motherfucker* (Unpopular Press/Sabotage Editions, London, 1993)

Van Deburg, William L.: *New Day in Babylon: The Black Power Movement & American Culture 1965–1975* (University of Chicago Press, Chicago, 1992)

Van Peebles, Melvin, Taylor, Ula Y. & Lewis, J. Tarika: *Panther: A Pictorial History of the Black Panthers* (Newmarket Press, New York, 1995)

Van Peebles, Melvin: *Sweet Sweetback's Baadasssss Song* (Payback Press, Edinburgh, 1996)

Varon, Jeremy: *Bringing the War Home: The Weather Underground, The Red Army Faction & Revolutionary Violence in the Sixties and Seventies* (University of California Press, Berkeley, 2004)

Veloso, Caetano: *Tropical Truth; A Story of Music & Revolution in Brazil* (Bloomsbury, London, 2003)

Victor, Christian & Regoli, Julien: *Vingt Ans de rock Français* (Editions Albin Michel, Paris, 1978)

Wandor, Michelene (ed.): *Once A Feminist* (Virago, London, 1990)

Ward, Brian: *Just My Soul Responding: Rhythm & Blues, Black Consciousness & Race Relations* (UCL Press, London, 1998)

Watson, Ben: *Frank Zappa: The Negative Dialectics of Poodle Play* (Quartet, London, 1995)

Watts, Jerry Gafio: *Amiri Baraka: The Politics & Art of a Black Intellectual* (New York University Press, New York, 2001)

Way, John B. (ed.): *Hungry as a Raccoon* (privately published, 1993)

Weberman, A.J.: *Dylan to English Dictionary* (privately published, 2005)

Wells, Tom: *The War Within: America's Battle Over Vietnam* (University of California Press, Berkeley, 1994)

Wenner, Jann S.: *Lennon Remembers* (Verso, London, 2000)

Wicker, Tom: *A Time To Die* (Ballantine, New York, 1976)

Wiener, Jon: *Come Together: John Lennon & His Time* (Random House, New York, 1984)

Wiener, Jon: *Gimme Some Truth: The John Lennon FBI Files* (University of California Press, Berkeley, 1999)

Wolfe, Tom: *Radical Chic & Mau-Mauing The Flak Catchers* (Bantam, New York, 1971)

Zimmer, Dave: *Crosby, Stills & Nash: The Authorized Biography* (Omnibus Press, London, 1984)

Zimmer, Dave (ed.): *4 Way Street: The Crosby, Stills, Nash & Young Reader* (Da Capo, New York, 2004)

Zimroth, Peter L.: *Perversions of Justice: The Prosecution & Acquittal of the Panther 21* (Viking, New York, 1974)

Zollo, Paul: *Songwriters on Songwriting* (Da Capo, New York, 1997)

Zolov, Eric: *Refried Elvis: The Rise of the Mexican Counterculture* (University of California Press, Berkeley, 1999)

Among the periodicals consulted were *Ann Arbor Argus, The Beetle, Berkeley Barb, Berkeley Tribe, Billboard, Black Dwarf, The Black Panther, Black World, Chicago Seed, Collage, Countdown, Crawdaddy, Cream, Creem, Dark Star, Disc & Music Echo, Distant Drummer, Down Beat, Earth Island, East Village Other, FAPTO, Free John Now!, Freek Press, Frendz, Friends, Fusion, Goldmine, Graffiti, Great Speckled Bird, The Guardian, Hit Parader, Ink, Les Inrocks, International Free Press, International Times* (IT), *Jazz & Pop, Kaleidoscope, Let It Rock, Leviathan, Life, Los Angeles Free Press, Mad Magazine, Melody Maker, Mojo, Musician, The Nation, National Catholic Reporter, National Review, New Musical Express* (NME), *New Statesman, New York Review of Books, New York Times, The Observer, Old Mole, Open City, Oracle, The Organ, Other Scenes, Oz, Playboy, P.O. Frisco, Q, Ramparts, RAT Subterranean News, The Realist, Record Collector, Record Mirror, Red Mole, Rolling Stone, The Royal's World Countdown, San Francisco Express Times, Sing Out!, Song Hits Magazine, Spare Rib, Steps, Student, The Telegraph, Time, Time Out, Underground Digest, Vanity Fair, Village Voice, The Wire, Women's Liberation* and *Zigzag.*

# INDEX